MUSIC EDUCATION IN CANADA

MUSIC EDUCATION IN CANADA

A Historical Account

J. Paul Green and
Nancy F. Vogan

University of Toronto Press
Toronto Buffalo London

© University of Toronto Press 1991
Toronto Buffalo London
Printed in Canada

ISBN 0-8020-5891-4

Printed on acid-free paper

Canadian Cataloguing in Publication Data

Green, J. Paul (James Paul), 1929–
    Music education in Canada : a historical account

    Includes bibliographical references.
    ISBN 0-8020-5891-4

    1. Music – Instruction and study – Canada – History.
    2. School music – Canada – History.   I. Vogan,
    Nancy F. (Nancy Fraser), 1945–   .   II. Title.

MT3.C2G73 1991   780'.7'0971   C90-095659-3

This book has been published with the help of a grant from the Canadian
Federation for the Humanities, using funds provided by the Social Sciences
and Humanities Research Council of Canada.

Contents

vi Contents

PART III NEW DIRECTIONS

Acknowledgments

The authors wish to thank all those who have helped in so many ways. The completion of this manuscript would have been impossible without the cooperation of our colleagues in music education, as well as numerous people in other fields. Throughout the preparation period of almost ten years we were sustained by the generous response of musicians, educators, administrators, historians, librarians, archivists, and others who gave freely of their time – in interviews imposed upon busy schedules, correspondence, and other forms of counsel and direction. We wish to acknowledge support from the University of Western Ontario and Mount Allison University as well as financial assistance from the Social Sciences and Humanities Research Council of Canada.

We are indebted to Helmut Kallmann for his pioneer work in the history of music in Canada, to Campbell Trowsdale for his exhaustive study of public school music in Ontario, to Dale McIntosh for his historical accounts of music in British Columbia, and to Paul Woodford for his research into music education in Newfoundland. Others whose written materials have provided insight into special areas of our history include Diana Brault, June Countryman, Earl Davey, Alan Smith, and the late Phyllis Blakeley. We are also grateful to student research assistants at Mount Allison University and graduate students at the University of Western Ontario. Mabel Laine in her own congenial and encouraging way offered advice and shared the resources of EMC. And we recall with fond memories the late George Proctor, who was a motivating influence and personal inspiration for both of us.

We recognize the tremendous contribution of Sarah Green for word-processing and formatting the manuscript; indeed, she was consulted frequently and, not surprisingly, by the project's end had edited and rewritten various passages of the text. In a similar manner, Wayne Vogan read each version of the manuscript as it developed and contributed immeasurably through his editorial suggestions. Rebecca Green also read several chapters, enhancing the final result through her constructive criticism. More than once, David Lenson solved technical problems through his computer wizardry.

To Ron Schoeffel, Senior Editor of the University of Toronto Press, we owe much gratitude for his encouragement and his confidence in the project, and we appreciate the editorial expertise of Anne Forte and Theresa Griffin.

Finally, we acknowledge the patience and love of our immediate families – Sarah, Rebecca, Gretchen, and Amy Green and Wayne, Margaret, and the late Harry Vogan.

Abbreviations

AR	Annual Report of the Department of Education
BCMEA	British Columbia Music Educators' Association
BCSITA	BC Schools Instrumental Teachers' Association
CAIS	Creative Artists in the Schools
CAMMAC	Canadian Amateur Musicians/Musiciens amateurs du Canada
CAPAC	Composers, Authors, and Publishers Association of Canada Limited
CAUSM	Canadian Association of University Schools of Music
CBA	Canadian Bandmasters' Association
CBAM	Canadian Bureau for the Advancement of Music
CBC	Canadian Broadcasting Corporation
CFMTA	Canadian Federation of Music Teachers' Associations
CGEP	Collèges d'enseignement général et professionel
CMCentre	Canadian Music Centre
CMEA	Canadian Music Educators' Association
CMQ	Conservatoire de musique du Québec
CNE	Canadian National Exhibition
CNR	Canadian National Railways
CPR	Canadian Pacific Railway
CUMS	Canadian University Music Society
EMC	Encyclopedia of Music in Canada

FAMEQ	Fédération des associations de musiciens éducateurs du Québec
ISME	International Society for Music Education
JMC	Jeunesses musicales du Canada
MELAB	Music Education Laboratory
MENC	Music Educators' National Conference
MMEA	Manitoba Music Educators' Association
MTNA	Music Teachers' National Association
NBMEA	New Brunswick Music Educators' Association
NBTA	New Brunswick Teachers' Association
NFB	National Film Board of Canada
NSMEA	Nova Scotia Music Educators' Association
NYO	National Youth Orchestra of Canada
OCE	Ontario College of Education
OEA	Ontario Educational Association
OMEA	Ontario Music Educators' Association
OSB	Ontario School for the Blind
QMEA	Quebec Music Educators' Association
RCCO	Royal Canadian College of Organists
RCMT	Royal Conservatory of Music of Toronto (TCM 1886–1947)
SA	Salvation Army
SMEA	Saskatchewan Music Educators' Association
TCM	Toronto Conservatory of Music (RCMT 1947–)
TSO	Toronto Symphony Orchestra (renamed TS 1967–)
UBC	University of British Columbia
UNESCO	United Nations Educational, Scientific and Cultural Organization
UWO	University of Western Ontario
WBM	Western Board of Music

Prologue

The primary purpose of this study was to furnish a historical account of music education in Canada. Initially, the research focused on how music instruction evolved in Canadian society and made its way into the public schools. It seemed appropriate, however, to widen the original scope of the work; indeed, to get a clear understanding of this facet of Canadian life, it became necessary to examine the embryonic forms of musical activities which emerged in the home, in the church, and in the community, for these existed long before music was offered in the public schools. And even after music was introduced into the schools, other institutional structures and organizations were created to expand the range of opportunities, many of which were not available within the context of public education. It would be remiss, therefore, to present a historical view that did not recognize the role and contribution of private teachers, church organists, choir leaders, and other community musicians. Nor can the traditions of religious and ethnic groups be excluded, for they too have had a profound influence on music education. In short, this evolution of school music is portrayed within a cultural milieu which comprises many aspects of musical activity in an emerging network of national and provincial institutions, community programs, and agencies of government support.

Since Confederation, education has been administered as a provincial jurisdiction. A federal-provincial division of powers can be problematic for the shaping of an integrated work which encompasses all systems of education. Yet there is a need for a perspective which is truly national, offering something more than a succession of provincial histories. Accordingly, an effort was made to recognize local and regional differences while at the same time viewing music education as a national movement. Parts I and II of this book are structured on a geographical basis, but Part III, which reveals an increasingly complex pattern of growth after the Second World War, has been organized thematically. Because Newfoundland was not part of Canada until 1949, a separate chapter devoted to the origins and traditions of this relatively new province is included in Part II. In Part III, the particulars of music education in Newfoundland have been merged with those of the other provinces. There has been no attempt to give a detailed chronology of events beyond 1967, when Canada celebrated its first hundred years as a nation. What has been presented in bringing this history to a conclusion is a general description of the principles, programs, and trends characterizing Canadian music education in the past two decades.

The research for this project has yielded a large body of historical facts, dates, and statistical data; in cited passages the original language has been retained in order for the flavour of the times to be preserved. Much of this encyclopaedic detail has been embodied in the text so that the information will be available for future generations. There are, conversely, other places where this history has been allowed to lapse into vignettes of colourful individuals or detailed descriptions of their pursuits. This has been done intentionally, for the truth is that music education has survived bureaucracies, apathies, and other adversities, primarily because of outstanding musicians and teachers devoted to a common cause. This history can only be enhanced by occasional glimpses of a personal nature.

1 Metlakatla Brass Band, Port Simpson, British Columbia, c 1880

2 Mount Allison Conservatory Orchestra, Sackville, New Brunswick, 1895

3 A.T. Cringan

4 Gilbert and Sullivan's *Pirates of Penzance*, directed by S.N. Earle, Charlottetown, 1910

5 British Columbia Musical Festival Concert in Vancouver, 1928

6 Mount Cashel Orphanage Band, Arthur Bulley, bandmaster, St John's, Newfoundland, c 1926

7 String class from a convent school in St John's, Newfoundland, c 1930

8 The Edmonton Schoolboys' Band, Vernon Newlove, conductor

9 Saturday morning broadcast from CKY studio, Winnipeg, 1930s

10 The Edmonton Schoolboys' Band on parade

11 Departure of the Kamloops Junior Symphony Orchestra for the 1939 competitive festival in Vancouver

12 The Canadian Legion Junior Symphony Orchestra of Kamloops,
Archie McMurdo, conductor

13 Irene McQuillan on CBC 'Airway to Song,' Halifax, 1943

14 Children listening to broadcast, St Joseph's School, Halifax

15 Sir Ernest MacMillan signs autographs for admirers

16 A MacMillan Fine Arts Club rally in Stanley Park, Vancouver, c 1939

17 Loading music equipment

18 A 'music meet' in rural Saskatchewan

19 A classroom visit by Rj Staples, provincial director of music for
Saskatchewan, 1950s

20 Barrie Collegiate Band, W.A. Fisher, conductor

21 North Toronto Collegiate Orchestra, Jack Dow, conductor

22 The Leslie Bell Singers at the CNE bandshell, Toronto

23 Chorale Notre-Dame-d'Acadie, Moncton, Sœur Marie-Lucienne, director

24 Summer school session for teachers in the Maritimes, Mount Allison
University

25 Zoltán Kodály receiving an honorary degree from the University of
Toronto, 1966

26 Shinichi Suzuki at the thirteenth ISME conference, held in London, Ontario, 1978

27 Carl Orff

28 The National Youth Orchestra in Massey Hall, Toronto, Victor Feldbrill and
Wilfrid Pelletier, conductors, December 1960

29 Faculty of Music Singers, University of Western Ontario, Deral Johnson,
conductor

30 R. Murray Schafer with a class at l'Université de Montréal

PART I

EMERGING PATTERNS

1

Quebec

If the history of music education in Canada has been fundamentally shaped by the social milieu, one of the best illustrations of this interaction is that of church and community. Nowhere was this so evident as in Quebec, where from the earliest days of colonization Roman Catholic institutions played a dominant role in the cultural life of the people, assuming sweeping authority and control in the realm of education. Roger Magnuson identifies a long-lasting consequence: 'Formal education came to New France in the seventeenth century with the arrival of Catholic missionaries from the mother country, who worked to instruct the Indians in the mysteries of the faith and to provide a measure of learning to the colonists. Although the "ancien régime" achieved only modest results in learning, it left in its wake a tradition of clerical participation in education that persisted almost to the present.'[1] Clerical participation in education included work in music, for, as Willy Amtmann notes, 'music was part of a remarkable general education in the monastic colleges of France and most of the priests who arrived at Quebec had undergone a musical training which aided them in the pursuance of their task.'[2] A small group of Récollet priests came in the summer of 1615, but it was the arrival of the Jesuits in 1626 that marked the real beginnings of educational developments in the country. When Père Paul Le Jeune arrived in 1632 as Superior of the Jesuit mission he began to teach the native children liturgical chants. Three years later a Jesuit college and seminary opened in a 'small building within the confines of Quebec to house the seminary for Huron boys and the college for young Frenchmen.'[3] Instruction in the elements of Gregorian chant and musical notation was given to the young students and also to the future priests.

Not all instruction was given by members of religious orders. Martin Boutet, who arrived in the colony in 1645 with his wife and two daughters, was soon entrusted with the training of choir boys at the parish church and later at the Jesuit college, the first example of a choir school in Canada. Boutet, who has been described as a 'fosterer of Church music, and eminent teacher of navigation,' was 'an experienced musician, a capable player of the viol, and a competent singer.'[4] Amtmann suggests that he may also have given instruction in organ, but there is very little reference to instrumental music in the early documents.

Education for young women, including instruction in music, became available with the arrival of the Ursulines in 1639. One of the Ursulines, Marie de St-Joseph, played the viol; she taught some of the young Indian and French girls to play this instrument and thus became one of the first teachers of instrumental as well as vocal music. By the end of the eighteenth century the prospectus of the Young Ladies' Academy at the Ursuline Convent in Quebec City indicated that tuition was offered in 'Music on the Organ, Harp, Piano-Forte, Guitar and Accordion,' and 'Vocal Music.'[5] The Ursulines were the first of many female religious orders to teach music. In fact, they established a pattern which has prompted writers to declare that in Quebec, music education 'has been largely the preserve of the Roman Catholic female religious orders, which have established schools and academies where children (in later years boys as well as girls) can be enrolled for a general education and, in some instances, specifically for music training.'[6]

Following the conflict of 1759 Quebec became a British colony with an English-speaking Protestant minority and a French-speaking Catholic majority. There were conflicting views between these groups on many issues, including education. Magnuson describes the incompatibility of their views and its result:

While both cultures were convinced of the need for schools, they differed sharply as to their character and organization. British authorities envisaged a centralized school system common to both peoples. The French, for their part, were suspicious of any educational arrangement that did not take into account their religion and language. As a result, educational progress lagged in what was Lower Canada, and it was not until the 1840s that the ground-work for a public school system was firmly laid. The schools established were divided along religious lines in deference to the bi-religious personality of the lower province: Catholic schools for the French and Protestant schools for the English.[7]

The educational system thus established in Quebec remained in effect almost unchanged until major educational reform was brought about in the 1960s with the implementation of the Parent Commission Report. Hence, education for Protestant and Catholic children in Quebec developed along entirely different paths, reflecting the diversity of their respective religious traditions.

MUSIC IN ROMAN CATHOLIC EDUCATION

In addition to the Ursulines, other female orders who came to Quebec established convent schools shortly after their arrival. Those most active in the field of music included les Sœurs de la Congrégation de Notre-Dame, founded in Montreal in 1658, who began to offer piano instruction in 1834; les Sœurs des Saints Noms de Jésus et Marie, founded in Montreal in 1844, who began piano instruction the following year; les Sœurs de Ste-Croix who arrived in Canada in 1847 and gave piano lessons at their boarding schools beginning in 1848; and les Sœurs de Ste-Anne, a new order established in Quebec in 1850. This last order operated a boarding school in Lachine which placed much emphasis on music, and which became the model for many others within the order.

The music training offered by these religious orders, usually in piano and singing, was sometimes given by lay instructors; it was available primarily at convents in Montreal and Quebec. After 1850, however, music teaching became more common at convents in other parts of the province as well, particularly at the approximately sixty houses run by les Sœurs de Ste-Anne. The type of instruction was expanded in the second half of the nineteenth century; by 1897 the convent at Lachine had an orchestra consisting of four pianos, six violins, four guitars, three mandolins, and a harp.[8]

Music was introduced into the public elementary schools of the Montreal Catholic School Commission in 1873, the same year that the first official school curriculum guide was published. In the course of study issued in 1886, singing was suggested as an activity for the morning opening exercises; solfège was also included. Accounts indicate, however, that only thirty minutes per week was allotted to music and that after the fourth grade no time allotment was given. (This same allotment of thirty minutes was still listed in the 1960s.) Among the texts approved for these schools were *Le Chansonnier des écoles* by A.J. Boucher and *Petit traité de solfège* by Charles Labelle.

The Catholic school system did not include public high schools. After completing elementary school, students who wished to further their education entered convent schools (for girls) or classical colleges or seminaries (for boys), where instruction in vocal and instrumental music was often available for an additional fee. In classical colleges and seminaries, particular importance was placed on music for the liturgy, as one of the primary goals of these institutions was the training of young men for the priesthood. However, instrumental instruction was included in some of the seminaries and classical colleges. When a Scottish regiment with a German band director by the name of Adam Schott arrived in Quebec City in 1833, the students of the Jesuit seminary asked authorities to obtain Schott's services as an instructor. Their interest ultimately led to the formation of the St Cecilia Society.[9] In 1892 the Montreal Catholic School Commission appointed the noted Montreal musician Guillaume Couture as director of solfège, with a mandate to introduce music instruction into several of the elementary schools. Couture received very little support from school authorities, and his appointment lasted for only three years. No replacement for this position was named until 1937, when Claude Champagne was appointed to the post.

It seems that little attention was given to music in the Catholic schools following Couture's short tenure. There was no special remuneration for those giving instruction in music, and in 1914 George Parmalee, English Secretary of the Department of Public Instruction, wrote that music was 'optional in the Roman Catholic schools.' However, there were certain schools in which music received more attention, for Parmalee went on to say that in 'schools under the control of the Roman Catholic Commissioners of Montreal special teachers are employed who have produced good results.' These teachers 'used the staff notation entirely, in preference to the Tonic Sol-fa system.' In speaking of rural elementary systems, he stated that teachers chose 'generally to neglect the subject or to teach it by rote.'[10] Almost all the schools under the jurisdiction of the Catholic School Commission served French-speaking students, so providing instruction for the minority of English-speaking Catholics continued to be a problem.

MUSIC IN PROTESTANT EDUCATION

Music instruction for English-speaking Protestants was available in the Montreal area as early as 1789, when Charles Watts from England established a music school in the city. Ladies' schools often advertised that tuition in 'Music, Drawing, French and Fancy Needlework' was offered, and many musicians gave private instruction in their own studios. In addition, there were choral societies and church choirs as well as some activity in instrumental music such as regimental bands. It was felt by members of the Protestant community, however, that more music education should be provided for their children. The first formal action was taken in Montreal. In 1851 the commissioners of the Protestant School Board of Montreal 'resolved to employ a music master for an hour and a half every Saturday to instruct the children in singing.'[11] Very little is recorded about this appointment, but a newspaper account of the closing exercises of the High School of Montreal read as follows: 'The prizes having been distributed by Dr Leach, after a suitable address to the scholars, Mr Follenus, the Music Teacher, called out his different classes, and forming them into one choir, presided at a seraphine, while a Duett from the opera of La Norma was most tastefully sung, and well acted by two boys, Palmer and Follenus. The whole choir then gave in excellent style the war song from the same opera, "On to the field."'[12] A John Follenus was listed as professor of music in the Montreal city directories as early as 1842; the 1852 directory and several subsequent issues registered J. Follenus as music master at the High School of Montreal. Documents do not refer to the type of instruction offered or the materials used, but he presumably followed the Wilhem fixed doh method, for an advertisement for a new publication entitled *Wilhem's Universal Method of Teaching Class-Singing* 'abridged and carefully arranged by John Follenus' appeared in the spring of 1851.[13]

There is no evidence of music instruction for younger students; however, in the authorized course which appeared in 1870, 'music was prescribed for all grades. The course for primary and intermediate students recommended 'simple airs, rounds and songs in two parts' – four lessons per week, a total of one hour and twenty minutes. Sefton's

Three-Part Songs – Canadian Series was designated for the upper grades.[14] The 1885 course of study listed *The High School Vocalist* and charts as the approved material for primary, intermediate, and senior grades. There was also mention of *The Franklin Square Song Collection*.

In October 1886 the Montreal Protestant board hired a Mr Dawson from Great Britain to give a course of thirty lessons in Tonic Sol-fa to teachers. They also issued an edict 'requiring each teacher in the future to take her own class in singing.'[15] This marked the beginning of a strong commitment to Tonic Sol-fa by the board. Dawson prepared a new course in Tonic Sol-fa, and in July 1887 he was appointed director of music for the common schools. Sets of Tonic Sol-fa charts were purchased, and a children's concert which illustrated the method and its results was presented. Dawson asked that academic credit be given for this study and requested that the board approve the use of a text he was preparing. When they refused to approve his book without first seeing the finished product, he resigned from his position. The board issued a testimonial stating, 'Mr Dawson goes attended by our best wishes, full of the vigour of early manhood, to a larger field of laborious usefulness.'[16] They found a replacement within three months.

Mr W.H. Smith, Dawson's replacement, was also a Fellow of the Tonic Sol-fa College and continued the work begun by Dawson. He received support not only from the Montreal board but also from the provincial Protestant Committee. In 1888 a subcommittee appointed by the dean of Quebec to study the subject of musical training in the Protestant schools recommended that the Tonic Sol-fa system be employed. They included the following reasons for their choice:

1) It [Tonic Sol-fa system] enables average pupils to read music more quickly, pleasantly and readily than is generally found when the system of training is that of the ordinary notation.

2) That while indubitably a first-rate teacher of the old system can produce as rapid results as one who follows the newer method, yet, that inasmuch as in our common schools, instrumental music is not generally thought of, it is wise to adopt the quicker and somewhat easier method of vocal teaching, especially inasmuch as teachers, not exceptional in their training capacity, can produce very satisfactory results under the Tonic Sol-fa method.

3) That, since the Normal School have given their adhesion to this latter system, it is certainly, for every reason, wise and desirable to adopt it in our Provincial Schools.

4) That the Tonic Sol-fa method of training, not only is not inimical to the old

staff notation, but rather leads the way to it, and that those who contemplate studying instrumental music, will not find that their training under the Tonic Sol-fa system places any obstacles in the way of their progress.[17]

The officials adopted the report of the subcommittee and authorized *The Canadian Music Course* by A.T. Cringan[18] and *The Code Music Drill* as approved textbooks for the course. Tonic Sol-fa was made a prize subject for intermediate and senior classes, and the board wrote to Smith in 1891 stating that the Tonic Sol-fa system might be regarded as permanently established in the city schools. Regulations for Protestant teachers in Montreal were changed to read, 'All female teachers are expected to be able to take their own classes in Tonic Sol-fa.'[19] This was later made more emphatic with the statement that teachers not qualified to instruct their students in Tonic Sol-fa would have ten dollars deducted from their annual salary. The reduction was increased to forty dollars by 1920.[20]

Various instructional materials were used in Protestant schools. In addition to those previously mentioned, these included *Young Voices*, Nos. 1 and 3, *The Notation Primer, Mann's Manual*, and *The Common School Song Reader*. After the turn of the century the approved list included *The Royal Songster, Blackbirds*, and *Ritter's Practical Method*; the volume *Infant School Songs* was listed under instructional materials for kindergarten beginning in 1892.

English-speaking communities in the Eastern townships had maintained traditions from both their British and American roots, including singing schools and other activities. Frequent references to the use of American textbooks in schools of this region are found; this probably included music texts as well. However, the Montreal board remained firm in its stand on the Tonic Sol-fa system and was not swayed by offers from publishers south of the border. In 1887 'Messrs. Ginn & Co. of Boston offered to send free of charge a man to explain and exhibit Mason's Music Charts. The offer was declined with thanks.'[21]

Although several private schools for English-speaking students were established in the nineteenth century, the Protestant board, unlike the Catholic school system, operated public high schools as well. Several private schools, including Stanstead College, Bishop's College School, and St John's School (later renamed Lower Canada College), offered music instruction. Most of these institutions resembled British schools and were denominational in origin. However, the High School of Montreal, established by a group of prominent citizens in 1843, 'looked to Scotland rather than to England for its inspiration,' and thus 'possessed democratic and non-conformist instincts, more inclined to accept boys from different social and religious backgrounds.'[22] In the 1850s this school became a department of McGill University, but in 1870 it was transferred to the authority of the Protestant board and thus became a public institution. Five years later public pressure led to the opening of a girls' division of this school.

The work begun by Follenus at the High School of Montreal in 1851 continued for several years. School reports during the 1880s referred to instruction in both vocal and instrumental music for girls, and in 1885 Guillaume Couture was listed as master of vocal music in the first and second forms for both girls and boys. Miss Macphee, his assistant, was in charge of instrumental music. In 1887 mental arithmetic was substituted for vocal music for boys in the senior school. Shortly after his appointment, W.H. Smith recommended that music be reinstated as part of the course for boys in the senior school, but this was not approved because the headmaster was opposed.

Reports after the turn of the century indicate that music was considered an important subject for girls, but there is no mention of any type of training for boys. Girls received individual as well as class instruction. One report stated, 'It is of the first importance that every girl should know enough of the subject to enable her to appreciate good music.'[23] A choir of selected voices met once a week under Couture, who remained in his post for several years. A special Couture singing prize was offered annually. The high school course emphasized Tonic Sol-fa but also introduced staff notation. This approach, known as the 'Dual Notation Course,' had been authorized for the schools of the Protestant board and was strongly endorsed by Couture's successor, Duncan McKenzie, a young Scottish teacher. Shortly after his appointment McKenzie gave a workshop for the Provincial Association of Protestant teachers, who reported: 'We were favoured at Quebec also by the presence of Mr. Duncan McKenzie, one of the staff of the McGill Conservatorium of Music, and superintendent of the teaching of singing in the High Schools of Montreal. Mr. McKenzie demonstrated with a class of pupils untaught in music, what marvellous results might be attained in voice culture in our schools with little attention thereto during the weeks. He also gave some very practical suggestions in regard to the Dual Notation Course which has been authorized for our schools and as yet very much neglected.'[24]

Although music was considered a 'special' subject in some respects, it was formally evaluated at the various grade levels in both elementary and high schools. It was stated in 1902 that 'tests [in singing] will be set from time to time by the Superintendent, Director of Music, and Principal, but must not be given later than the 15th of May of any year.'[25] A new, detailed course of study in music was issued in 1909 which continued the emphasis on the Tonic Sol-fa approach and listed *The School Song Book, The Empire Songster,* and *The Royal Music Reader* as recommended texts.

Smith made an effort to keep the public aware of his work in the schools in order to maintain community support for his program. Late in 1891 he was granted permission 'to form school choirs as long as they were optional and of no expense to the Board.'[26] The school children participated in massed choirs for many public events and celebrations such as the 1897 Diamond Jubilee: 'The assembled children, conducted by Mr W.H. Smith, and accompanied by the band, sang "The Maple Leaf," "The Red, White and Blue," "Victoria Our Queen" and other appropriate songs on the grounds of the Montreal Amateur Athletic Association.'[27] Similar events were often arranged for the celebration of Empire Day.

Empire Day was established on a national scale in 1898. Five years earlier, George Ross, minister of education for Ontario, had issued a volume of patriotic poems dedicated to the teachers of Canada which he hoped would 'direct the attention of teachers to the importance of cultivating a spirit of patriotism in their pupils by exercises of a patriotic character.'[28] This volume was distributed throughout Ontario; Hamilton was one of the chief centres to promote the idea, largely through the impetus of Clementine Fessenden. Feeling that this type of celebration should be instituted on a national scale, Ross decided to approach the Dominion Educational Association. He was unable to attend their 1898 meeting in Halifax, but in sending his regrets he requested that delegates consider 'the selection of some day during the school year, to be specially devoted to the cultivation of feelings of loyalty and attachment to our country, and to the institutions under which we live.'[29] Ross proposed that this occur on the school day immediately preceding 24 May; he gave several suggestions for titles but indicated that his personal preference was 'Empire Day.' His idea was adopted and Empire Day became a familiar event in Canadian school life for many years to come.

At the inaugural observance of Empire Day in Montreal 'a choir of nearly a thousand voices, selected from the public and senior schools, trained and conducted by Mr W.H. Smith, director of Tonic Sol-fa, rendered a program of national and patriotic airs.'[30] The ornate printed program of a similar event in 1903, featuring students from eighteen schools, was sent to school boards in large cities of the British Empire. The following statement was printed on the program: 'The Choir is *not* composed of picked voices, the only qualification being the ability to sing the Common Scale in tune. The entire programme was prepared without any instrumental aid whatever, the accompaniments not being introduced till the final rehearsals.'[31]

TEACHER TRAINING

Normal schools were established in Quebec in 1857 and eventually were developed in various regions of the province. In the Catholic system, only boys were allowed to attend these institutions. Girls studied at convent schools and, after their ninth year of study, took an examination from the Central Board of Examiners. This system remained in effect until 1937, when the Roman Catholic Committee granted certification to a number of convents.

Music instruction was given in the Catholic normal schools, often by well-known musicians. Before the turn of the century, these included Ernest Gagnon, who taught for many years at École normale Laval in Quebec; R.O. Pelletier, who taught for over forty years at École normale Jacques-Cartier in Montreal; and Guillaume Couture, who taught at various institutions in the Montreal area. Instruction consisted primarily of elementary music theory and Gregorian chant. In 1914 Parmalee stated that 'in all the Roman Catholic Normal Schools (Training Colleges) the practice and theory of singing are compulsory on all pupils, the staff notation being used.'[32] Materials included *Petit traité de solfège* by Charles Labelle, another outstanding teacher of the era.

A Protestant normal school was established at McGill University in 1857; this remained the only one in the province for English-speaking Protestants and was open to both men and women. Music was prescribed in the curriculum during the early years of the school. The music instructor was Professor R.J. Fowler, an English musician who had come to Montreal in 1848 and established himself as a choral director and teacher in the city. In 1886 J.J. Dawson was appointed as teacher of Tonic Sol-fa; he was replaced in 1888 by W.H. Smith. However, it would seem that Tonic Sol-fa was not the only method taught, for, according to reports, Fowler continued 'the work of teaching singing by the established notation' with 'undiminished faithfulness.'[33] In 1907 the McGill Normal School was moved to Macdonald College in Ste-Anne-de-Bellevue outside Montreal and became the Macdonald Normal School. G.A. Stanton was appointed resident instructor in music in 1914; he served as college organist as well as conductor of both the orchestra and glee club.

The regulation requiring all teachers employed by the Montreal Protestant board to teach music in their classes remained in effect, so it seems that it would have been necessary for most teachers to include music in their own training. In 1914 Parmalee referred to the work in the Montreal Protestant schools and normal school, stating that a specialist had been employed for the past thirty years who had 'achieved much success as a teacher of singing by the Tonic Sol-fa notation.'[34] However, he referred to the fact that this specialist trained the teachers who had 'an aptitude for this work.' This would suggest that the music classes at the Protestant normal school may have been elective.

PRIVATE TEACHING AND CONSERVATORIES

The influence of the clergy in the musical life of Quebec began to diminish following the British conquest. The arrival of British regimental bands and the great influx of immigrants from Great Britain, Germany, and the United States during the second half of the eighteenth century stimulated the growth of secular music in the province. Several of these new immigrants offered music instruction. One of the most noted was Friedrich Heinrich Glackemeyer, a German musician and bandmaster 'whose activities influenced and enriched musical life in Quebec to a great extent.'[35] During the winter of 1783 Glackemeyer served as music teacher for the daughters of Baron Von Riedesel, commander of one of the German mercenary regiments. Glackemeyer noted that his two pupils 'would have made great progress, had they had a better instrument [than] a miserable old spinet, which they had bought of Revd. Mons. Noiseux, curé at Belœil, at present Grand-Vicar at Three-Rivers; there being only one piano in Quebec.'[36] The following year he began to import printed music and instruments, and he placed an advertisement in the Quebec *Gazette* stating that he was available as a teacher 'on the Piano Forte, Guittar, Violin, Flute, Singing in French and English.'[37] In 1820 Glackemeyer became the first president and director of the Quebec Harmonic Society; he remained in

Quebec as a musician and teacher until his death in 1836. Although there were others who gave music lessons, 'musical pioneers of the type and quality of a Glackemeyer were rare.'[38]

During the second half of the nineteenth century there was an effort to standardize the quality of private music instruction. The musician Calixa Lavallée attempted to establish a conservatory based on the European model but was unsuccessful in obtaining funds from the Quebec government. A school of music was developed at l'Institut Nazareth, a co-educational institution for blind children established in Montreal in 1861. Many of Quebec's leading musicians taught at l'Institut Nazareth, which offered the first workshops in piano tuning in French Canada.

Two examining bodies for music were established in Quebec before the turn of the century; both assisted in raising standards throughout the province. L'Académie de musique de Québec was founded in Quebec City in 1868 by several local musicians, including Ernest and Gustave Gagnon. Incorporated in 1870, it began to give examinations the following year; Calixa Lavallée served as president during its early years. L'Académie, the first private institution to award music diplomas in the province, conducted examinations in various instruments, voice, and theory. It was privately funded at the outset and, despite some financial assistance from the provincial government, maintained its independence from all schools of music and political parties. Although l'Académie has never been a teaching institution, it has kept to its initial goals of promoting an interest in music and setting standards through a system of diplomas and certificates in all branches of music. The Dominion College of Music was incorporated in 1895 with the purpose of administering practical and theoretical examinations. Through affiliation with Bishop's University it offered diplomas, a BMus, and later a DMus, as well as silver and gold medals. Its operation was confined to private schools and convents in Quebec and Ontario in the early years, but it later spread to the Maritimes, parts of western Canada, and some places in the United States near the Canadian border. It ceased operation during the 1940s. Despite the existence of these examining bodies and the private music instruction available at various places throughout the province, there was still no institution which provided comprehensive studies in music. Therefore, the opening of the McGill Conservatorium in the fall of 1904 was a major event in the musical life of Quebec, particularly for the English-speaking community.

McGill University had been established in 1821 as a non-denominational institution in Montreal. The teaching of music was not introduced until 1884, and even then it was for women only. When the Royal Victoria College for girls was opened in 1899 it became responsible for musical instruction, and Clara Lichtenstein was brought from the Charlotte Square Institute in Edinburgh to be in charge of a music department. Around this time the music examinations of the Associated Board of the Royal Schools of Music[39] were instituted in Canada, primarily through the efforts of Charles A.E. Harriss, a wealthy Englishman who had established himself in Montreal as an organist/choir director, conductor, composer, teacher, and impresario. This effort by Harriss, the success of Clara Lichtenstein's teaching, and the financial support of Lord Strathcona led to the opening of the McGill Conservatorium in 1904. Harriss was appointed director of the Conservatorium as well as director of the board of examinations; Lichtenstein was appointed vice-director. The first session in the fall of 1904 was attended by 462 students. There were twenty-six instructors, all hired on an hourly basis, to give instruction in composition, theory, and performance. Harriss resigned from his (unsalaried) post of director in 1907 and recommended that a permanent chair be established for a full-time professor of music. The following year Harry Crane Perrin, former organist/choirmaster of Canterbury Cathedral in England, was appointed to the position, which he held for the next twenty-one years. The Conservatorium curriculum had from the beginning set out the requirements for a degree of Bachelor of Music and a further degree of Doctor of Music. Under Perrin's competent direction, the school presented its first graduate in 1910. She was Beatrice Donnelly, who later joined the teaching staff. The first Doctor of Music degree was given a year later to Charles Henry Mills who later became dean of music at the University of Wisconsin.'[40] During Perrin's first year at the Conservatorium he organized a system of music examinations in over fifty centres across the country, thus establishing autonomy for McGill by detaching it from the Associated Board. Despite this growing independence, a close liaison with British music institutions was maintained for many years. One example was the establishment of the Strathcona Scholarship in 1895, with Lord Strathcona as the sole donor; winners received free tuition at the Royal College of Music in London for three years as well as a substantial annual living allowance. The 1903 Cycle of Musical Festivals of the Dominion of Canada, initiated and organized by Charles Harriss, marked another example of close British ties.

This series of concerts in fifteen Canadian centres featured British choral and orchestral music under the baton of the Scottish musician Sir Alexander MacKenzie. According to Helmut Kallmann, 'Canadians responded with great enthusiasm to this display of imperial goodwill.'[41]

Meanwhile, more opportunities for advanced musical training for the French-speaking population arose both at home and abroad. In 1911 the Quebec government created a study grant known as the Prix d'Europe, which was offered annually to a talented young musician. Winners in the early years included Wilfrid Pelletier, who later influenced the development of music in Quebec. In 1905 le Conservatoire national de musique et de l'élocution was founded in Montreal by Alphonse Lavallée-Smith, a local musician, who directed its operation until his death in 1912. Lavallée-Smith was assisted by Edmond Archambault, who provided rent-free premises at his St Catherine Street music store. Le Conservatoire granted diplomas in music, diction, elocution, drawing, and painting from 1921 until 1951, when it was affiliated with l'Université de Montréal. Although music instruction was given by various religious institutions in Quebec City, a school of music was not established at l'Université Laval until 1922. Even then, formal music instruction was confined primarily to the study of liturgical music, reflecting the continuing dominance of the Roman Catholic Church in French-speaking Quebec.

2

The Maritimes

EARLY MUSICAL ACTIVITY IN THE REGION

The various folk traditions of the founding peoples of Canada have enriched the musical life of the country, particularly in Quebec and the Maritimes. The oral tradition of folk songs and the transmission of fiddling and bagpipe tunes from one generation to the next serve as early examples of informal music education. Although this practice continued for many generations in the Maritime region, during the late eighteenth century more formalized music instruction began to develop. This came about primarily in the port cities of Halifax and Saint John, which became the chief musical centres of the region. As Phyllis Blakeley notes of the Nova Scotia port: 'Halifax's reputation as a city which loved and encouraged fine band music dates to its founding when the British regiments stationed at this old seaport brought their bands with them. Besides providing stirring music for the troops and civilians, these bandsmen brought with them a knowledge and training in music from the old country.'[1] Another important factor, noted by Carleton Elliott, was the coming of the Loyalists in 1783: 'To perpetuate their culture in their new home, the Loyalist gentlemen of Saint John and, as their means permitted, those of smaller centres in the province, voiced abroad their desires for instructors and performers, and their wants were answered by adventurous British and European musicians.'[2]

By the beginning of the nineteenth century, private music instruction was offered not only in Halifax and Saint John but also in several other Maritime communities. This was primarily in piano, voice, and violin; the teaching of the theoretical aspects of music was often included. Concerts were given by many of the teachers and also by their students. In addition, there were performances by visiting artists from Britain and the United States. A music industry began to develop, for instrument manufacturing and music publishing on a small scale took place in both port cities.

Churches were important centres of musical life. From the earliest days of colonization in the Maritimes, the church has been associated with instruction in music. When Père Fléché first came to Port-Royal in the early 1600s he began teaching the Micmacs how to sing the simplest parts of the Roman Catholic service. In later years instruction in Gregorian chant was offered in several Roman Catholic institutions, and singing schools were established for the various Protestant denominations. Helmut Kallmann observes: 'The first people to teach music outside the Roman Catholic institutions were the singing Masters who appeared in the late eighteenth century, often from New England, and who organized so-called singing schools ... the singing schools appear to have flourished most strongly in the Maritimes.'[3] References to singing schools in existence before the nineteenth century include one operated by Amasa Braman in Liverpool around 1777, and another opened by Reuben McFarlan in Halifax in 1788. A sacred vocal music school was established in Saint John by the New Jersey Loyalist Stephen Humbert in 1796. Humbert was active in the early musical life of New Brunswick; he published his own collection of sacred music entitled *Union Harmony, or British America's Sacred Vocal Musick* in 1801. During the nineteenth century, singing schools opened in other communities throughout the three Maritime provinces. Although many of these were short-lived, some of them, like those of Andrew MacKay[4] in the Pictou area, lasted for several decades. The movement survived until the early years of the twentieth century.

Members of the clergy often played an important role in the musical life of the community. Notable in this regard was Bishop John Medley, who was active as a choral conductor, composer, and arranger during his tenure at Christ Church Cathedral (Anglican) in Fredericton, from 1845 until his death in 1892. He was also responsible for obtaining the first organ in Fredericton in 1848 for St Anne's Chapel; an organ was installed in the cathedral around 1860. Organs had existed in Maritime churches long before this time; St Paul's Anglican Church in Halifax obtained one in 1765, and Trinity Anglican Church in Saint John by 1801. During the nineteenth century, organs were placed in several other churches, including St Paul's in Charlottetown, for which the local resident Watson Duchemin built and installed a pipe organ around 1850. British and European organists were employed for many of these church positions. Most of them took an active part in community life and gave private lessons; several later became involved in school music instruction.

Numerous choral and philharmonic societies came into existence during the nineteenth century. Military and town bands were also popular, and many centres reported the existence of small orchestras. This activity was not limited to the larger centres. Smaller garrison towns such as Annapolis Royal benefited greatly from the presence of military musicians. Retired military personnel often participated in the musical life of the community and were sometimes invited to a new area to teach and direct performing groups. In the mid-1800s the newly formed Musical Society of Antigonish hired the retired bandmaster Herr Kaestner, who 'not only directed the society and gave music lessons to children and adults, but formed a band, taught the members how to play and arranged music for them.' Blakeley comments that 'as the children were not neglected, a solid foundation was laid for future musical progress in the community.'[5]

Ladies' Morning Musical Clubs played an educational as well as a social role in the community. A club was in existence in St Stephen, New Brunswick, at the turn of the century. The Ladies' Musical Club of Halifax, which took an active part in the musical life of the city, was formed in 1905. The club first followed a study plan outlined by the American National Federation of Music Clubs but soon broke away from this affiliation and developed its own program of activities. Performing groups for the members were also established.

PRIVATE SCHOOLS, CONVENTS, AND OTHER INSTITUTIONS

In addition to the instruction offered by independent teachers operating out of their own studios, there was music instruction in several private schools. Many were church-affiliated institutions. Among those established by Protestant denominations were two whose music departments have developed into university music schools. These were the Mount Allison Ladies' College, opened by the Methodists in

1854 in Sackville, New Brunswick, as a companion school to the Mount Allison Wesleyan Academy for Boys, and the Grand Pré Seminary, established by the Baptists in 1858, which in 1860 became the Acadia Ladies' Seminary in Wolfville, Nova Scotia.

The Mount Allison Ladies' College offered music instruction in its first year of operation, but diplomas were not awarded until 1874. As an outgrowth of this music department, one of Canada's first conservatories was opened at Mount Allison in 1885. Diplomas were given in piano, violin, and voice, with a choice of artist or teacher concentration. In 1891 a new conservatory building was opened and a music library established. A BMus degree was introduced in 1912 and first awarded in 1917. A system of local centre examinations in music for the Maritime region was initiated by James Noel Brunton, director of the conservatory, shortly after his appointment in 1911.

The Acadia Ladies' Seminary included music instruction in its early years and offered a licentiate diploma in music. In 1911 it introduced a BMus degree; this was not conferred, however, until 1928. In 1926 the seminary closed and the music department became the School of Music of Acadia University. Carl Farnsworth was appointed director; he was succeeded by E.A. Collins, who in 1928 became the dean of the School of Music.

Several Roman Catholic orders operated schools which became noted for their music. Among them were the Sisters of Charity and the Sisters of the Sacred Heart, two orders established in Halifax in the mid-nineteenth century; they later opened convent schools in other parts of the Maritime provinces. The Sisters of Charity arrived in Halifax from New York in the mid-1800s and began to teach young girls shortly thereafter. In 1873 they founded Mount St Vincent Academy, a college for Sisters which was also open to local girls. Writing in 1904, Hugo Talbot stated: 'The Academy of Mount St. Vincent has a reputation as a ladies' college of fifty years' standing. It is known as one of the leading schools of Canada, and its course embraces a thorough classical and commercial education. Needless to say, its musical department is a special feature and the Mount graduates play an important part in the musical life of Halifax.'[6] Private instruction in piano, voice, and various orchestral instruments was offered. A choir and an orchestra were formed and frequent recitals and concerts were given. In 1907 Mount St Vincent was empowered to confer degrees in music, and in 1925 it was chartered as a college, offering diploma and degree courses in performance and music education. The

Order of the Sisters of the Sacred Heart was also founded in Halifax as a teaching order in the mid-nineteenth century and established the Academy of the Sacred Heart in 1852. Talbot described this institution: 'All the usual branches of Ladies' education may be obtained here and it is needless to say that the moral as well as the secular training of the rising generation is equally cared for. Music is an important item in the curriculum, the piano and vocal departments being in [the] charge of Miss Elizabeth Page and Miss Ada Ryan respectively. There are eleven pianos in use in the building.'[7] The Sacred Heart Sisters also operated a public school, with music in all grades.

Other orders involved in music teaching in the Maritimes included the Sisters of Charity in Saint John, an order independent from the order of the same name in Halifax, and les Sœurs de la Congrégation de Notre-Dame from Montreal. The Notre-Dame congregation established several convents in the Maritimes, including one in Charlottetown as early as 1863, and Mount St Bernard in Antigonish in 1883; this later became affiliated with St Francis Xavier University. In 1885 three Sisters were sent from Montreal to Sydney to establish Holy Angels Convent. One of these, Sister St Helen of the Cross, was skilled in music; thus a music department was established at the outset. Twelve years later it was reported: 'Sister St. Joseph Calazance, the music teacher, took possession of the little music rooms just completed. What therapy for her head and ears! And what improvement for study for the pupils taking music.'[8] Among the male orders associated with education in the Maritimes, les Pères de la St-Croix, who established Collège St-Joseph in Memramcook, New Brunswick, in 1864, and les Péres Eudistes, who in 1890 founded Collège Ste-Anne at Church Point in Nova Scotia, have played an important role in music. Early in its existence, Collège St-Joseph founded a St Cecilia Society which included a choir, orchestra, and band. This college became well known for its musical training, particularly in the field of Gregorian chant. Collège Ste-Anne formed a band in 1893 which 'enjoyed considerable renown and was responsible to a large extent for the success of the Feast of St. Cecilia celebrations.'[9]

Music was a vital component of the curriculum at the Maritime School for the Blind, founded in Halifax in 1871. In 1886 A.M. Chisholm, a graduate of this school who had subsequently studied in Germany, became director of the music department, which offered instruction in pianoforte, cabinet organ, singing, writing and reading music, and pianoforte tuning. A large percentage of the graduates of this school pursued careers in music, primarily as teachers and piano tuners.

Toward the end of the nineteenth century, a feeling grew in the Halifax area that there was need for a non-denominational conservatory of music. This concern led to the founding of the Halifax Conservatory of Music in 1887. The aim of the promoters was 'to establish in Halifax and in connection with the Halifax Ladies' College a school of music complete in all essential departments and equipped to give the best instruction in all the branches of the art and science of music.'[10] The conservatory became affiliated with Dalhousie University, which granted a BMus degree to qualified candidates. The first director of the school was Charles Porter, a native of the United States who had studied at the Leipzig Conservatory. He had come to Halifax to assume the post of organist at St Matthew's Church. 'Mr. Porter was ... engaged Director of the Conservatory of Music, Halifax, which position he filled with unqualified success for ten years, combining his musical talent with an ability for business, seldom seen in a musician. He might aptly be called one of the Fathers of Music in Halifax, for it is through his patient and capable teaching that Halifax can boast so many home-reared artists in the piano and organ branches. There is no doubt that the conservatory suffered a great loss when this gentleman decided to turn his attention to a business career in Halifax.'[11] Several conservatory students took further training, some at the New England Conservatory, but most in Berlin or Leipzig. This close connection with Germany was stated in the calendar as one of the 'Advantages Offered for the Study of Music at this Conservatory':

Preparation for Berlin or Leipsig – It can hardly be questioned that the home of music at the present time is Germany. There are the largest and best equipped conservatories; from that land come the most celebrated musicians and performers; and it is to the schools of Germany that pupils from all parts of the world flock for the higher musical education. Many of the teachers of this Conservatory have received their musical education there, and it is to this centre of musical life and work, and especially to the schools of Berlin and Leipsig that we direct the attention of our pupils and offer them special preparation. Year by year ever increasing numbers of the pupils of this Conservatory are entering the Conservatories at Berlin and Leipsig.[12]

In 1900 a second school of music was established in Halifax by Max Weil: 'Mr Weil was brought to Halifax as head of the Violin Department at the Conservatory of Music in 1892, which position he held with great credit to himself and the college for eight years, when feeling the need of another school of music he inaugurated the institution now known as the Weil School of Music ... Mr Weil, as director of the Symphony Orchestra, has also been the means of bringing many artists of note before the Halifax public ... The Symphony Orchestra is an organization which Halifax is justly proud of, and its success is entirely due to the musical ability and untiring energy of its director.'[13] Privately run music schools were opened in various other places, including several in Saint John, but most, like the Weil School, were short-lived. However, a sense of pride in the educational opportunities now available was beginning to develop in the Maritimes. When the new conservatory of music was opened at Mount Allison, the catalogue of the ladies' college stated that 'the new conservatory would offer facilities unexcelled anywhere in Canada' and thus accomplish its aim 'to make it unnecessary for persons wishing to obtain a thorough and complete musical education, or to prepare themselves to teach music, to go outside of the Maritime Provinces.'[14] Similarly, Talbot stated, 'We may flatter ourselves that (judging from the number of prominent musicians educated entirely in Halifax) a musical education can be obtained here unsurpassable in the Dominion.'[15]

MUSIC IN NOVA SCOTIA SCHOOLS

References to the teaching of music in Nova Scotia schools can be found as early as 1819, when Bishop John Inglis of Halifax sent a letter to the Society for the Propagation of the Gospel in London describing his teaching at the National School: 'My experiment for teaching vocal Musick upon Dr Bell's plan of Instruction is undergoing a fair trial and answers beyond my expectation.'[16]

Music instruction was an optional subject in many private schools, particularly those for girls. In various parts of the province there were musicians who operated singing classes for adults and sometimes organized classes for children as well. Newspaper advertisements indicate that Wilhem's method (adapted by Hullah) was used for some of the classes in the Halifax area. One of these local musicians, Jacob Cunnabell, wrote to the educational committee of the House of Assembly in 1858 regarding an 'Illustrative Board' he had designed which could be 'successfully used' in common schools for 'Exercises in Arithmetic, Grammar, Composition, etc.' and with the addition of five lines 'for instruction in Vocal Music.'[17] There is, however, no evidence which indicates that this board was purchased for use in the schools. Neither is there evidence that *The Acadian Minstrel*, a book of songs and hymns for the classroom, was used extensively in the schools. This collection, published in Halifax in 1860, was compiled by a Mr Webster, a teacher at the model school in Truro.

Beginning in the 1860s and especially after the implementation of free schools in 1865, references to music are found more frequently in annual reports. In 1865 the inspector for Cumberland County in the northern part of the province stated: 'There are no schools in the county, with the exception of Advocate Harbor, where the science of music is taught; very few where singing is heard at all. It is quite unnecessary to affirm the importance of teaching music in our common schools as a distinct branch of study. The beneficial results, where this branch has been faithfully and persistently taught, are so apparent that it is with sorrow I have to record the fact of the general and lamentable deficience, as a community, in this respect.'[18] Music teaching was reported in Lunenburg, Shelburne, and Lockeport on the south shore and Pictou County in the east. In Lunenburg County the inspector made the following comment: 'Although not scientifically taught, [Vocal Music] is practised in every school in the county with but few exceptions, and wherever practised is attended with happy effects, both as a safety-valve for exuberant spirits, and a pleasing and judicious relaxation from the drier duties of the school.'[19] As described in one report, a local musician brought the matter of musical instruction to the attention of authorities in the Yarmouth region:

Last autumn Professor Charles E. Gates made the generous offer to give a week's course of gratuitous instruction to the teachers of this county on the subject of teaching vocal music to their pupils, provided the Council of Public Instruction would allow the time ... At the opening of the class, which assembled in one of the public halls of the town, there were 32 present, and the number rose during the first day to 46 ... Professor Gates illustrated his instruction during the course by reference to large and handsomely executed charts which could be read from every part of the hall. He informed his class that his object was to impart to them a knowledge of the general principles of vocal music, and the art of conveying that knowledge to others, so that they would be enabled to teach the pupils under their charge to read and sing ordinary music correctly ... and with the help of the charts to undertake the subject in their several schools ... the whole affair was a complete success.[20]

However, in provincial reports most attention was given to the work being done in the Halifax schools.

In February 1867 Jacob B. Norton was engaged by the Halifax school commissioners to train children in the schools to sing. Norton had already established a reputation as a singing teacher through private classes he had been holding for both children and adults. The *Acadian Recorder* noted this appointment and commented, 'Knowing of the success of Professor Norton during the past year in the practice of his profession we congratulate the commissioners on having obtained the services of so efficient a teacher.'[21] The inspector for Halifax County stated that singing had become a regular activity in all schools since the appointment of a professor of music: 'In the city, except in the schools taught by the Sisters of Charity, it was three years ago almost unknown.' He went on to say, 'When we consider that singing is not only intrinsically a necessary portion of an education but that it is also the very best means of promoting order in schools and a high moral instrument in the training of youth, I think we have reason for congratulations in the progress made during the past year in this department.'[22]

Norton had come to Halifax from Boston and had brought with him many of the ideas and methods in use in the Boston schools. He adopted the tradition of an annual public examination in music; one of the first, held in July 1868, was described in the Halifax *Citizen*:

> There were a large number of pupils present, who were examined in all the questions relative to the length of sounds, the distinctions in music, the different kinds of measure, the accent, how time was regulated, the diatonic scale, the chromatic scale. In the latter some of the pupils failed, not discerning the difference between chromatic intervals and a minor second. The minor scale was next taken up; very few failed in this. Then the transposition, and to see some of the boys and girls transpose from one key to another, proved that they not only had a smattering of rudiments, but that they thoroughly understood them; and not until the transposition of the minor scale, could the competitors be cut down to the number of prizes.[23]

This was followed by a special concert in the evening which featured students in a large chorus accompanied by a regimental band. After the 1870 examination it was reported: 'There were about fifteen hundred children partaking in the musical entertainment at Temperance Hall this morning who were exercised in music under the direction of Mr. J.B. Norton ... The appearance of the children, their gay and handsome faces, the evident interest each and every one of them took in the examination, was really pleasing to those who were present and decidedly shows that the services of Mr. Norton and the innovation of teaching music in the schools are acceptable on all hands.'[24] The program included choruses, duets, and solos as well as questions for the students on notation, scales, intervals, and other aspects of music theory. The students made a presentation to Norton at the conclusion of the exercises, and in his reply Norton lamented the lack of a suitable music book for the students and announced the recent publication of a text by him and his Boston colleague, W.O. Perkins. This work, entitled *The Dominion Songster for Schools, Classes, and the Family Circle*, was dedicated 'to the children of the public schools throughout the Dominion.'[25] He perhaps announced this publicly because he had received criticism the previous year from a parent objecting to his teaching of American songs and requesting that Norton be instructed to use British songs in the schools. Presumably Norton introduced his own publication in the Halifax schools, but he also employed the Mason Music Charts, which he had been using in his private evening classes. Norton was enthusiastic about these visual aids devised by Lowell Mason; he commented, 'By the use of them, nearly one half of the Music Teacher's time – which would otherwise be taken up with writing the lesson on an ordinary music board – is saved.'[26] He later commented on his work load: 'I have given lessons in vocal music to fifty-two departments per week, each lesson being from one half to three quarters of an hour in length ... there are several departments which I have not time to attend, and if the teachers would qualify themselves to teach the rudiments, as in some parts of Germany and the United States they are compelled to do, then the Music Teacher with such assistance could attend all the departments in the city without so much hard labour.'[27] However, the issue of assistance from the classroom teachers was left unresolved.

Norton continued to receive support from the school authorities and was frequently commended for his work with the children. In 1876 a supervisor asked: 'Ought we to expect a great deal from the efforts of one teacher with 3400 pupils? Let it be remembered that individual attention in this case is almost impossible.'[28] Frequently, it was simply stated that he was 'conscientiously laboring for the advancement of his pupils,' and that he was seeking the cooperation of the classroom teachers in his work. Two years later Norton took a trip to Boston to visit the schools and learn more about their music program. When he returned to Halifax, he informed the board that he wanted to adopt the

Boston syllabus and requested that the teachers assist with the music instruction. There is evidence in one report to indicate that he did adopt the Boston program in some schools: 'Yesterday afternoon a musical examination was held in the first department of Agricola Street School, when twenty-one pupils were examined on the "Boston Syllabus in Music for Grammar School" and all passed successfully.'[29] Norton had problems in obtaining cooperation from the teachers and there seems to have been minimal support for his proposal. In fact, when the board found themselves in financial difficulties in the early 1880s, they decided to abolish the position of teacher of music and informed Norton that his services would no longer be needed. He was given a certificate by the board stating the length of time he had been in their employment and indicating that he had been dismissed for economic reasons. There was no further testimony offered and his departure from the schools seems to have solicited very few comments from board members, teachers, or pupils. However, a letter was sent to the school board from the prominent Halifax musician Arnold Doane expressing regret 'at the abolition of the office of the musical instructor in the public schools, and referring at length to great good that resulted in other cities from the teaching of music to the school attendants.'[30]

Although the position of 'teacher of music' was not reinstated until after the First World War, interest in music instruction in the Halifax schools did not end with the departure of Norton. Education officials made frequent references to music and stated that 'music should be taught in every department to every pupil, not merely by rote but by theory.'[31] If teachers were unable to do this, principals were encouraged to arrange for an interchange of teachers. In 1888 a special class in Tonic Sol-fa was organized for teachers in the Halifax area to help them become more competent in music. One official expressed the strong feeling at that time that music instruction should be in the hands of the classroom teachers: 'It has been clearly demonstrated that children will acquire the art of reading music more readily under the daily instruction of their regular teachers than from the occasional visits to the school room of a musical teacher. Several of the teachers have followed the Tonic Sol-fa method with gratifying success. Better order has been one of the consequences and the hours of study have been enlivened with the melody of the children's voices in hymn and song. I consider that the ability to teach music should constitute an essential qualification of every primary-class teacher.'[32] It was further recommended that singing should be obligatory in all schools.

In 1882 the first course of study for Nova Scotia schools appeared. Until then there had been no provincially prescribed course of study for either the common schools or the county academies; teachers and trustees had usually determined the subjects to be taught. In this first course of study, teachers were urged to pay particular attention to hygiene, moral and patriotic duties, vocal music, gymnastics and military drill, correct forms of speech, proper intermissions, and outdoor exercises. Detailed outlines for these subjects were not given, however, and instructional materials were not always indicated. A new high school course was formulated soon after this, but music was not prescribed. Music instruction was given at many of the county academies, especially at the turn of the century, but this may have been on an extra-curricular basis. Vocal music was not listed as a high school course until 1902, and no references to instrumental music in the schools can be found, although it is quite probable that some of the county academies had performing groups.

Although there was some music instruction in parts of the province other than Halifax, it seems that the subject was still not given a prominent position, for in his report for 1888 David Allison, chief superintendent of education, stated: 'The important subject of music cannot be said to be on a satisfactory footing in our schools nor indeed to have ever been so. I am persuaded that the reported figures convey an exaggerated impression regarding the amount of attention which this branch really received, while of course they are even less reliable than indices of the nature and value of the instruction imparted. The matter has been pretty much left to take care of itself and teachers and local authorities should be held to account for the poverty of result accompanying this want of system.'[33] He indicated that the matter would be brought before the next meeting of the Provincial Educational Association and recommended that the schools of Nova Scotia 'should not be left without some tolerably specific instructions for their guidance.' He added, 'The claims of the Tonic Sol-fa system of reading music are deserving of careful consideration.'[34]

The Tonic Sol-fa method of teaching music became popular in many areas of the Maritime provinces during the last two decades of the nineteenth century; this came about primarily through the efforts of one man, Reverend James Anderson, a native of Scotland. Anderson was ordained as a Presbyterian minister in Halifax in July 1884 and given the charge at Musquodoboit Harbour, Nova Scotia. In November 1890 he demitted his charge in order to 'devote his skill and energies for some time to the work of the Tonic Sol-fa system of singing.'[35] For the next four years he travelled to various points in the region giving instruction in Tonic Sol-fa, wrote articles on this approach for the teachers' periodical the *Educational Review*, and taught special summer school classes. In 1894 he went to Toronto and then lived in several communities in Ontario before moving to the United States.

Anderson was appointed by the government of Nova Scotia to provide Tonic Sol-fa instruction to schools in various areas of the province during part of 1891. His work was well received by teachers and school authorities: 'No act of the Council of Public Instruction had apparently laid the foundation of such great results from a small outlay as the flying mission of Mr. Anderson through the counties of Nova Scotia to introduce the new musical notation to the attention of the leading teachers in the Province. We find fault with only one feature in the arrangement. Instead of half a year, Mr. Anderson should have been kept at work for a whole year at the very least.'[36] Anderson also taught at the Summer School of Science, a voluntary, interprovincial organization established in 1887, which held annual sessions in a different Maritime centre each summer. Many teachers obtained certificates in Tonic Sol-fa at these summer schools. In addition, Anderson taught special classes at the provincial normal school in Truro.

Throughout the 1890s educational authorities became more persistent with their recommendation that all children in the lower grades be given instruction in vocal music, and urged teachers to use the Tonic Sol-fa approach in their classrooms: 'Every pupil (excepting of course those known to be organically defective as respects music), should be able to pass an examination in vocal music before promotion to a higher grade. For the present the following minimum is prescribed for each grade. At least one simple song for its Tonic Sol-fa notation for Grade 1 ... Teachers musically defective may comply with the law by having these lessons given by anyone qualified.'[37] In subsequent years, teachers were given the option of using either the Tonic Sol-fa or staff notation. In 1894 the recommendation that all classes receive instruction in vocal music was stated much more emphatically: 'With respect to both Music and Drawing ... If there are teachers now who cannot see that their pupils obtain the privileges and advantages that the law intends they should have, they belong to the class who should no longer have indulgence granted them ... The loss of the Provincial Grant for *one* year will have a more awakening effect on these teachers than the *fifteen* years of recommendations and prayers, without enforcement.'[38]

Sessions on Tonic Sol-fa were given at regional teachers' institutes throughout the province by Anderson and various others who had been trained by him. Two of his pupils, Miss Hilton from Yarmouth and Ada Ryan from Halifax, assisted him in his teaching at the summer schools. Ada Ryan taught at St Mary's School in Halifax and was in charge of the vocal department at Sacred Heart Academy. She became the eastern Canada representative for the Tonic Sol-fa College, London, England, and also wrote a textbook for schools on the Tonic Sol-fa system entitled *School-Day Melodies* which was used in Nova Scotia schools for several years.

The Tonic Sol-fa method remained popular for many years; however, there were those who were opposed to this approach, mainly for practical reasons. Their objections are explained in the following excerpt from the normal school report of 1905 and express the feelings of many others involved in education: 'The Tonic Sol-fa method, which has been followed in this school, has largely failed to establish itself in the public schools of the province. Though admittedly easier of acquisition than the staff notation, tradition and the influence of the musical profession are nearly all in favor of the staff. Through the latter the youth of the community are instructed in piano, organ, and church music and in it alone is printed our popular vocal and instrumental music. Added to these circumstances is that of a ceaselessly changing corps of teachers, some unmusical, some musical ... generally untrained in sight-singing.'[39]

School music expanded in other areas of the province. At the 1904 meeting of the Teachers' Institute in North Sydney, it was reported that 'a remarkable demonstration of the successful music education of the public school pupils of North Sydney and Sydney Mines' was given. The *Journal of Education* declared that the teacher, Professor Chisholm, had 'put these towns in advance of any others in the Province in this respect,' and further stated that 'those who cannot sing should take up other professions than that of teaching in our common school grades, and those who can sing should be better trained than our minimum now requires.'[40] This program was short-lived, however, for the following year Chisholm left Cape Breton and seems not to have been replaced.

Music was included in the Amherst schools during this period; the teachers in charge gave sessions on music for the Cumberland County Teachers' Institute in which demonstration classes were given, with children chosen from the local schools taking part. At the turn of the century, a visitor to the French schools in the Yarmouth and Digby area commented on the role of vocal music: 'When called upon to vindicate their provincial Acadian musical talent, the children generally reply by a genuine gladsome smile, and no portion of their daily work seems to afford them greater pleasure than that which calls forth an expression of their innate love of music.'[41]

In 1912 a new course of study for grades one through nine appeared which included a detailed course in music. Two courses were listed, one using staff notation and based on the American textbook series *The New Educational Music Course*, and an 'Alternative Course' of Tonic Sol-fa with transition to staff notation. Emphasis was placed on voice training, ear training, and sight-singing in both courses. The text for the Tonic Sol-fa course was *School-Day Melodies*. In 1914 a program for rural schools with one teacher was issued. It recommended that simple songs be sung by rote at least three times daily and stated that 'inspectors should not accept any excuse for absence of singing in a school.'[42]

Music at the Nova Scotia Normal School and Educational Institutes

Music had been introduced as a subject at the provincial normal school in Truro shortly after it opened in 1855; the principal of the school paid the music teacher's salary out of his own wages until he was able to convince the authorities to provide a special grant for this purpose. For some time there was a new music teacher almost every year. The principal stated in his 1867 report:

> I have experienced considerable difficulty in supplying the place of Miss Hayes as Musical Teacher. Miss Hayes was succeeded by Miss McLeod, and Miss McLeod by Miss Rand, and now the situation is filled by a male teacher, Mr. Chessley, who seems in every way competent for the work ... Indeed he has evidently succeeded in infusing an enthusiasm in connection with this important branch of common school education. The cause of these changes in the conducting of this department arises from the smallness of the sum allowed by the Legislature not being sufficient to induce any celebrated musician to come to Truro for the purpose, so that we are in a measure tied up to employ any one who may chance to be in the locality for the time being.[43]

Although music was retained as a subject for all prospective teachers, many had had no previous musical instruction and felt insecure about teaching their own classes with the limited assistance they received during their brief period of training at normal school. Authorities, however, continued to press for a minimum proficiency in music as a requirement for certification: 'The Normal School is not expected to certificate teachers who do not show some ability to conduct singing in the common schools with at least the simplest musical notation – the Tonic Sol-fa ... As an example of what is being required in some of the other, even newer British Colonies than Nova Scotia, some of the musical examination papers of the Australian province of Queensland for the last school year are printed on a previous page. That may help to emphasize to doubters, how far we are yet behind the rest of the world in this department.'[44]

In addition to the instruction in Tonic Sol-fa given at summer schools and educational institutes by James Anderson and his students, there were other presentations. These included several sessions at the Hants and Kings County Institutes given by Miss N.A. Burgoyne and Mrs P.E. Parker, and presentations to meetings of teachers on the south shore by Father O'Sullivan, who had trained a very successful choir of boys from St Mary's School, Halifax, in Tonic Sol-fa.

Several of the inspectors felt that it was important to include music instruction for the teachers at these institutes. The need was emphasized in 1895 by C.W. Roscoe, the inspector of schools in the Wolfville area:

Music. This subject I would have taught at the Institutes as it is now taught to the teachers of the Summer School of Science. If possible to find the time, I would plan for two lessons each day while the Institute lasts. More teachers find it difficult to teach this, from lack of knowledge of the subject, than from any other cause. The teachers throughout the Province received such a scare on receipt of the *Journal of Education* for October 1894, that most of them began and did commendable work in learning and teaching music. As a rule, it is not well to frighten people, but here is an exceptional case. Those that have thus made a beginning are at a stage when some instruction would be very valuable and much appreciated. For these and for all teachers who have not entered upon the study, I would have the best teacher that can be obtained to give instruction at the Institute and have as many lessons as can be thoroughly given in the time, so that all teachers may go home with such a foundation laid that they can do good elementary work in their schools. Those, however, who have done the most and best work in teaching this subject, assure me that the time spent in learning to sing is more than compensated for in the increased ability for doing work which comes as the result of engaging in singing. There is no exercise so well calculated to drive away drowsiness and brighten up the pupils as this. It is found, after the music lesson, that the pupils' minds are active and that they can do their work rapidly and correctly. From personal knowledge I am prepared to corroborate this testimony, and, as far as possible, to provide that teachers shall be *instructed* and *give* instruction in music in all the schools.[45]

MUSIC IN NEW BRUNSWICK SCHOOLS

Instruction in most of the early schools of New Brunswick included primarily reading, writing, and arithmetic, but it is quite possible that singing was part of the day's activities. There was music in several of the Madras schools which operated in the province. The governor of the province supported the Madras system and often participated in school activities, notably music; Katherine MacNaughton writes of him, 'A talented musician, he often instructed the boys in the Central School in Saint John in singing, and when present at the opening of the school presided at the organ.'[46]

The problem of obtaining suitable textbooks was a constant source of concern. In 1846 the grammar school inspectors requested permission to obtain a series of school books prepared and published under the superintendence of the National Board of Education for Ireland. When these were procured from the education office in Dublin, the shipment included 'twelve sets of books, sheets, and tuning forks for teaching Hullah's system of vocal music.'[47] During the summer of 1850 Mr Duval, a schoolmaster in Saint John who operated a training and model school in that city, visited various American and Canadian cities to obtain information concerning their schools and methods of training teachers. Upon his return, he issued a report in which he made several comments about music instruction in the places he had visited.

In 1858 Henry Fisher, the newly appointed chief superintendent of education, spoke of his desire to have music as a subject in the elementary grades: 'I have also made preliminary arrangements for the introduction of Vocal Music, as an elementary branch of Education ... There is no doubt that the use of this delightful means of instruction will be as advantageous in New Brunswick, as it has proved to be on the continent of Europe, Great Britain, in the United States, and in some of the neighbouring Provinces. For the present, the Pupil teachers in the Training School are to receive at certain hours every week, instruction in this science; and I hope that in a few years Vocal Music will form a necessary branch of Education, in all our Parish Schools.'[48]

He had made a study of educational developments in other regions of Canada and elsewhere, and had also visited all the counties in the province, delivering lectures on education. MacNaughton notes, 'An untimely death made the new Superintendent's tenure of office so brief that no accurate estimate can be made of his views, or of his abilities as an administrator.'[49] Had he lived, formalized music instruction might have begun much earlier in New Brunswick schools.

Fisher was succeeded by John Bennet, who stated in his first report that the teacher training course included weekly lessons in vocal music, but made no mention of music in the schools. The branches of instruction were listed but music was not included. However, in the first report of the free schools of New Brunswick issued in 1872, singing was a 'branch of instruction' for common schools. According to this document only 12 per cent of the school population received instruction in music. By 1882 over half the school population was involved; this percentage increased very little until after the turn of the century. The statistics indicated the numbers studying singing 'by rote' and 'by note'; the number 'by note' was very low.

In the first course of study for common schools issued in 1879, singing was included under language. Instructions for Level I read, 'Rote singing – Simple songs selected chiefly from the first 14 pages of the First Music Reader.'[50] Rote singing was listed for all levels up to eight, with levels four to eight having the addition of optional singing by note from the blackboard and from charts. The materials prescribed were Mason's *National Music Readers* and *Campbell's Canadian School Song Book*.[51]

No special teachers of music were cited before 1900 so it is assumed that classroom teachers taught the singing. Instruction in music was given by a local musician, Professor E. Cadwallader, at the normal school in Fredericton, and several of the educational institutes scheduled sessions on music. During the late 1880s and early 1890s sessions on Tonic Sol-fa were given, including classes by Reverend James Anderson for teachers in Saint John. The 1889 course of study reflected this interest in Tonic Sol-fa, for the Mason text was replaced by the Curwen series, school music leaflets published in England by Curwen and Sons, and bound together into one volume by J. and A. McMillan, Saint John, with the title *Curwen's School Music*. Despite this, there is little evidence that the Tonic Sol-fa movement flourished in New Brunswick. In fact, the revised course of study issued in 1894 retained the Curwen series but reinstated the Mason *National Music Readers* as an approved series along with *Campbell's Canadian School Song Book*.

There was no course of study in music prescribed for high schools during this period, but musical performances, both choral and instrumental, were frequent. Both Saint John and Moncton had extra-curricular high school orchestras during the late 1890s. Music enhanced many of the special occasions in schools, and children often provided musical entertainment for community events; one newspaper looked forward to such an event as follows:

> The Floral and Musical Festival to be held in the Skating rink on the evenings of Monday and Tuesday next, under the directorship of Professor Norton [from Halifax], bids fair to be a great success, if we may judge of the fact by the progress made by the singers in their rehearsals. The main feature of the concert will be the attendance of something like a thousand children who will sing to the accompaniments of organ and piano a number of exceedingly pretty airs, many of which are quite new to St. John ears. They will be assisted and supported by a large number of ladies and gentleman amateurs – the best musical talent in the city – who have kindly promised their assistance. A distinguished musical gentleman from N.S., Mr. E.R. Weston, who took part in the Great Peace Jubilee at Boston, at present on a visit to this city, has also promised to perform on the organ. The proceeds go in aid of the funds of the Sunday School Union, a very deserving object.[52]

In 1887 school children participated in the Queen's Jubilee celebrations in Saint John, where they marched to King Square to listen to an address by the Lieutenant-Governor and then to sing the national anthem. They were accompanied by bands stationed at the four corners of the Square:

> Sir Leonard Tilley then called for the singing of the National Anthem, and the vast concourse of boys and girls, under the direction of Professor Max Sterne [a local musician], accompanied by all the bands, and sustained by the teachers, sang with splendid voice and all their hearts:
> Far from our mother land,
> Nobly we'll fall or stand
> By England's Queen.
> Through fields and forests free,
> Britons undaunted we
> Sing with true Loyalty
> God Save the Queen![53]

At similar patriotic events in later years the song 'My Own Canadian Home' was often featured since it was set by Saint John musician Morley McLaughlan to words by E.G. Nelson, who was also a native of Saint John. This work was sung by school children in various parts of the Maritimes. In fact, several inspectors reported receiving copies and placing these in every school room.

During the final years of the nineteenth century, several issues of the *Educational Review* contained articles advocating more music instruction in the schools. Some of these were rather humorous in nature:

> Why is it that Canadians are not distinguishing themselves more widely as musicians? The rugged Canadian physique is well known among athletes; the clear Canadian brain has caused its power to stir the world of literature; but the sensitive Canadian organism is scarcely known abroad among those who have waked sweet melodies. There must be some reason for this lack of musicians among us. Did it ever occur to you that perhaps it is partly due to the fact that our children as a rule, are not brought up with the staff as with the alphabet, and with the metronome as with the multiplication table?[54]

Recommendations for increased music instruction in New Brunswick schools also came from educational authorities, particularly Inspector W.S. Carter in Saint John, who frequently mentioned music in his reports and made many references to the instruction given in the schools of that city by the Sisters of Charity. In 1909 Carter was appointed chief superintendent of education for the province and brought with him to the post a great interest in music.[55]

Systematic instruction in music by a full-time music teacher was introduced into the schools of Moncton, Fredericton, and Saint John during the first decade of the twentieth century. Although several persons had been advocating this step, the actual impetus came from different sources in each case. In Moncton, initiative came from Mary McCarthy, a local music teacher who in the fall of 1904 asked permission to address the school board 'in respect to the introduction of the systematic instruction in music into the schools of the city.'[56] The board received her suggestions favourably and she began work on a six-month trial basis in January 1905. No expense for books or materials was to be incurred except that a staff-lined blackboard was to be provided for each school building. The experiment proved so successful that she continued in the position until 1915, when she retired and was replaced by Blanche O'Brien and later by Bertha Ferguson.

Yearly school board reports praised the work of Mary McCarthy, stating that she had 'succeeded in making the study and practice of vocal music in the schools deservedly popular,' and that 'the singing of the pupils in the various schools had shown marked improvement.'[57] She has been recalled by several former pupils as 'a petite, vivacious lady, who carried a small portable organ from class to class.'[58] She placed emphasis on singing as an enjoyable experience, but also included drill in Tonic Sol-fa and gave theory tests. She introduced merit cards for students who excelled in music and convinced a prominent local citizen to donate a banner to be awarded to the school achieving the highest general average in the music examinations. The work of Mary McCarthy was noted by the chief superintendent, who stated that Moncton had the distinction of being the first place in the province 'to provide regular instruction in vocal music to all the pupils of the schools, by employing permanently a professional teacher for that subject.' He continued, 'After an experience of over eighteen months, the Secretary reports that the teaching of music in the schools has proved an unqualified success.'[59]

The action of the Moncton school board sparked interest in other areas; the first place to follow their example was Fredericton, where the local teachers' association took the initiative. In 1907 the Fredericton Board of School Trustees 'decided to introduce regular musical instruction in the public schools under their charge,' an action described in a newspaper editorial as 'a wise and progressive measure' which, it was hoped, would be 'speedily followed in other communities.'[60] A local organist and music teacher, Frank Harrison, was appointed as music instructor for the Fredericton schools; he remained in this position until after the Second World War and greatly enriched the musical life of the community. By 1910 there was music instruction for all classes in the Fredericton schools, including the high school. The board members supported Harrison's work and the classroom teachers assisted him in his teaching. Sight-singing as outlined in the following was a primary objective of Harrison's program: 'Beginning with the first year in school, the elements of time, tune and notation, are presented and elaborated, grade by grade, through the entire school curriculum. In grades one, two and three the time is spent in teaching all the common scale intervals and reading melodies in rhythms of two[s], threes, fours and sixes, in which these intervals occur, all the work being done at the blackboard. In grade four music readers are placed in the hands of the pupils. Grade five, two part song is introduced. Three and four part song with all accidentals are taught in grade six, seven and eight. The easier oratorios, part songs, and glees, are taught in the high school.'[61]

In Saint John, where Inspector Carter had been advocating music instruction for many years, a teacher of music was appointed in Dufferin School during the first decade of the twentieth century; the work proved to be very satisfactory. The Women's Canadian Club was influential in having Catherine Robinson's program extended to other schools in the city. At a meeting of the Saint John Teachers' Institute held in 1915, Miss Robinson 'gave some illustrations of the system of teaching music' which she had 'so successfully introduced into the St. John Schools, showing the work done in Grades I, II and III.'[62] Like Harrison in Fredericton, she relied on the classroom teachers for assistance. Unlike his, however, her program did not extend to the upper grades.

Many aspects of the music program in New Brunswick were patterned after the one developed for the public schools of Philadelphia; at the 1906 meeting of the New Brunswick Educational Institute held in Chatham,

> Mr. E.W. Pearson, director of music in the public schools of Philadelphia, gave an address on the teaching of singing, which was greatly appreciated. He held that to make this successful, a definite course on the movable DO staff notation is necessary, and that the grade teacher, with good supervision, is the only one who can accomplish this. He gave a large number of instances in which it had been done, taking but twelve minutes a day, and answered satisfactorily a variety of possible objections. At periods of the institute where opportunity offered, he instructed classes in the elements of singing with the greatest interest to all. His enthusiasm and confidence in his method were catching.[63]

His presentation was followed by a report on the music program in the Moncton schools. A discussion led by Miss McCarthy and a school inspector from Nova Scotia followed.

Pearson had a significant influence on the development of public school music in New Brunswick. Frequent references to his method are found in reports, particularly in those for Fredericton. Frank Harrison studied with Pearson in Philadelphia and became familiar with his program in the schools. Pearson's influence continued for the next quarter century, for in a speech given in 1930, shortly before his death, W.S. Carter made reference to Pearson's 1906 address and stated,

'From this [presentation] dated our present method of teaching music in the school.'[64]

One of the main concerns of the three special music teachers was the need for a new music text. Although it had been emphatically stated by officials in 1900 that 'the Board of Education will probably prescribe before August next a suitable series of graded instruction books in singing,'[65] it was not until 1910 that the recommendation for the use of *The New Public School Music Course* by Charles E. Whiting was approved, 'subject to the substitution of a few patriotic Canadian and British selections for an equal number the books already contain.'[66] The Canadian edition of this series became the standard music text in New Brunswick schools and remained so for over twenty-five years.

There are also references to music in several of the new consolidated schools. At Riverside Consolidated School in Albert County it was reported: 'Miss Stella Crocker has charge of the music beginning with Grade six and has done much to cultivate a taste for music in the school. It is Miss Crocker's intention to continue her musical course at Teachers' College, New York, beginning Feb. 1st, providing a suitable substitute can be procured.'[67] Another report indicates that some of the music teachers in the consolidated schools were local musicians who were not paid for this service: 'Instruction in singing by note has also been included in our school work this term and that without any extra cost to the district. Mr. Ralph March, a former instructor of music in the St. Martin's Seminary, kindly offered his services and very satisfactory progress is being made by all the pupils and even better results are expected during the coming year.'[68]

Teacher Training in New Brunswick

There had been some provision for music at the provincial normal school in Fredericton since the 1870s, but apparently the subject was not taken very seriously by most of the students. In 1906 it was stated that 'only 38 out of 292 who received instruction during the session' were 'returned as qualified to teach rote singing, and only 13 of these' were 'qualified to teach theory.' The chief superintendent indicated that this was not to be interpreted as a reflection upon the competence of Professor Cadwallader, the music instructor; he stated, 'His skill as a musician is universally acknowledged,' and 'When students are singing in the hall in concert, it charms one to listen.'[69] Nevertheless, criticism about the limited music instruction for normal school students continued. The following lament by a school principal is an example: 'How long will it be ere our Normal School can furnish us with the teachers competent to perform this service?'[70] In 1913 Cadwallader retired and was succeeded by W.J. Smith, an organist who had recently come to Fredericton from England.

The matter of payment for teachers of music was an issue for several years. Although the Moncton school board wrote to the chief superintendent of education when they hired Mary McCarthy in 1905 requesting a provincial grant for her salary, it was not until 1913 that a regulation concerning payment was printed in the school law manual. The following statement then appeared: 'Teachers who devote their whole time to the teaching of music shall receive the full government allowance according to class of license held, but in no case shall the grant exceed that given to those holding licenses of the first class.'[71]

SCHOOL MUSIC IN PRINCE EDWARD ISLAND

As in many other areas of the country, the early efforts in formalized music instruction in Prince Edward Island were primarily associated with the church. Convent schools were opened by les Sœurs de la Congrégation de Notre-Dame in Charlottetown, Summerside, and Tignish in the 1860s; music played an important role in these schools from the beginning. An Anglican choir school was in operation in Charlottetown before 1900. The Methodists also opened their own private school in Charlottetown, and in 1895 the trustees of this school decided to open a kindergarten and a 'school of music.' Music instruction was available from private teachers, particularly in Charlottetown. Notable among these were Professor Vinnecombe and Professor Earle, who organized the Charlottetown Orchestral Club, which flourished in the 1870s and 1880s. Not all musical activities were limited to Charlottetown, however.

In the 1860s Père Belcourt, who had established a high school for young men in the Rustico parish house, 'secured the services of Israel J.D. Landry of Montreal, an experienced teacher and an excellent musician.' The curriculum of this school included 'Plain Chant and Music.' Landry also organized a band 'which, for many years, was the pride and glory of the parish.'[72] In 1865 this band performed at the closing exercises of St Dunstan's College in Charlottetown, and was given this tribute in the Charlottetown *Examiner*: 'The Rustico Band, under the direction of Mr. Landry, was present and added largely to the entertainment by playing lively French airs whenever there was a pause in the examination closing exercises. The members of the band, all dressed in white, presented a most creditable appearance. Although many of them were the merest youngsters, they performed their parts with an ease and skill worthy of practiced artists.'[73]

The early reports of schools for Prince Edward Island seldom mentioned music. However, by 1879 the chief superintendent stated that music was taught in fifty schools in Queen's County, but that both music and drawing were in 'secondary positions.' The course of study for common schools which appeared in 1883 listed singing and physical exercises under 'Miscellaneous' for grades one to four (theory of music was added for grade four). Music and physical and vocal culture were included under 'Miscellaneous' for grades five and six. The texts were *Campbell's Canadian School Song Book* for pupils and Mason's *The National Music Teacher* for teachers. There were few references to music in succeeding years other than occasional comments that more attention should be paid to the subject.

Music was listed as a department of study for student teachers at the Prince of Wales Normal School as early as 1878; one hour per week was allotted to this subject. In 1879 music lessons were given for Charlottetown teachers on Saturday mornings by Mr A.B. McKenzie, principal of Rotchford School, but very little was said about these sessions or their results. During the 1880s music was in the course of study for prospective teachers, but the major emphasis seems to have been on rudiments. By 1889 there was an increase in the number of students taking music at normal school. Professor F.E.J. Lloyd was appointed music instructor for Prince of Wales College and Normal School in 1890. His appointment was received with great pleasure by the normal school principal the following year: 'In enabling us to secure his valuable services, the Premier has not only conferred a favour upon the students who receive instruction in music but a boon upon the children in the various schools of the country who shall soon be placed under their care.'[74] Lloyd remained in this position for three years, during which time he gave several lectures on music at teachers' conventions; in 1893 he left Prince Edward Island. References to music at the normal school in the next few years state that it should not be neglected but do not indicate that it was taught.

In 1894 the Summer School of Science met in Charlottetown for the first time. Reverend James Anderson conducted classes in Tonic Sol-fa and also presided at a special round table session entitled 'Music as an Educational Factor.' For several years following this event the teachers in Charlottetown continued work in Tonic Sol-fa with the help of Inspector Stewart, who gave regular sessions for the teachers during the school year.

The inspector for the French-speaking Acadian schools suggested in 1893 that singing should be cultivated more generally in his schools. At the annual convention of Acadian teachers in July 1897 he gave a paper on the teaching of singing. There was also frequent mention in reports of music instruction at the convent schools in Miscouche and Souris.

By the turn of the century music seems to have gained more prominence in education. At the Eastern Teachers' Institute meeting in June 1900 Alice Willis gave a lecture on the role of music in the schools which was so well received that she was invited to repeat it at the Provincial Teachers' Institute in October of that same year. In 1904 the Summer School of Science met once again in Charlottetown. Professor Henry Watts, a local musician, provided musical entertainment with his orchestra. Watts was organist and choir director of First Methodist Church, served as director of their school of music, conducted the band of the 4th Regiment, and also taught music at Prince Street and West Kent Schools. At this meeting he also gave a lecture entitled 'Music in the Public Schools' in which, as one newspaper reported, he made 'an eloquent plea for its recognition as a curriculum study': 'Indifference in ethics is comparable to inertia in matter. To awaken the interest in music for the public schools was a matter of difficulty and time for Nova Scotia and New Brunswick while here in the Island we are not yet so fortunate as to have reached the point reached by our Maritime colleagues, but we have made a start and *nous arriverons*.'[75] It seems that music classes had been discontinued at these summer sessions, for he commented, 'Our august body has been lectured by Tonic Sol-fa-ists, lectured by old notationists until we relegated it off our Summer School of Science curriculum.' He continued later in his presentation, 'I simply explain your curriculum gave music no place and I but rise to protest at its absence.'[76]

Watts had been trained in Britain and had taught in Windsor, Halifax, and Moncton before moving to the Island. In an extensive article published in a Halifax paper in 1888, he outlined his views on 'this neglected branch of our children's education.'[77] His comments show that he was knowledgeable in the subject, familiar not only with the state of music education in his native Britain but also with the work being done in the United States. He seems to have been well liked by his students, one of whom in later years recalled his classes as follows: 'His Friday afternoon music sessions at West Kent School are among the most treasured memories of his pupils. Sometimes he would bring his cornet with him and would play the air on this instrument, at the same time improvising a lovely, running accompaniment on the piano with his left hand. If the singing wasn't to his satisfaction, he would often stop playing and shout, "Tutti", "Forte" or "Legato" and while we children didn't in the least understand the words, we always caught their meaning and responded to his wishes.'[78] Shortly after this summer session, Watts left the Island and settled in Edmonton.

In 1907 the chief superintendent wrote:

> There are two other subjects which I hope to see receive a greater share of attention than they have hitherto – Music and Drawing. The children are taught to sing in the schools of Charlottetown, Miscouche, and Summerside and a few other places, but I am certain that were the effort put forth and the student teachers trained to a certain degree, the exceptions would be the few schools in which the pupils did not sing. There is, I am sure, musical talent among the children and it is unfortunate that it should not have the opportunity of exercise and instruction. Every teacher who has employed it knows what a relief it is with young children to make them sing some bright and amusing children's song when they are tired, languid and their attention flags. The possibility of happy work in a primary room without music seems inconceivable.[79]

In this same report reference was made to the study of music at the new Macdonald Consolidated School. By 1914 it was stated that music was receiving its 'due attention,' but comments regarding the lack of music in the schools were frequent, and music was still not listed as a subject in the course of study. The following year reference was made to the excellent singing at the Souris Convent; the author of the report also commented on the need for patriotic songs: 'The schools are still keeping up this old custom. I think the singing of patriotic songs plays a leading part in the teaching of patriotism which will have to be taken up now on a greater scale than heretofore.'[80]

3

Ontario

Large numbers of United Empire Loyalists migrated to Upper Canada from the American states during the last two decades of the eighteenth century. As C.E. Phillips notes, those Loyalists not of English descent were often Dutch or German;[1] they were joined by an increasing number of immigrants from Great Britain commencing in 1800, when a group of Highland Scots settled in the Glengarry area. Colonial life was rough and rugged: 'The economy provided for the physical needs of ordinary people, but not much more. This condition, and the accepted opinion that only a minority could appreciate the finer things of life, were educationally effective in keeping aesthetic tastes and intellectual activity low.'[2] Characteristic of the rustic culture in this expanding pioneer society was what Helmut Kallmann calls a 'spontaneous and untutored music-making by the people in song, dance and instrumental playing.'[3] Despite the fact that there was little time for leisure or recreation, drinking and gambling were prevalent. Such excesses provoked strong reactions from those associated with the church, the institution which, in the context of colonial life, became the central influence in promoting the values necessary for a permanent and stable society. More specifically, the church exerted its will in the field of education and encouraged what it considered to be worthy pursuits for family and community life. The church choir became the natural vehicle of musical performance, opening the way for the musical societies which were formed later when urban communities emerged.

Just as choral music had its genesis in the church, instrumental music owed its existence to the presence of British regiments garrisoned in Upper Canada. The activities of militia bands extended far beyond the official exercises of military life to civic parades, concerts, dances, and other entertainments, thus providing incentives for the establishment of similar groups in the civilian domain. It was also auspicious that a large number of military personnel who had been stationed in Upper Canada remained in the new land, including some who used their musical skills as conductors, organists, and teachers. Many of the musical instruments available in the pre-Confederation years were left over from the garrisons, but even more important, the presence of military bands added momentum to cultural growth in general and to the development of secular music in particular.

Apart from military bands and church choirs, there were few institutions or organizations which advanced the cause of music and the arts. Contrasting musical traditions were brought to the predominantly rural settlements of Upper Canada by people of different denominations – Presbyterians, Anglicans, Methodists, and Roman Catholics. In Presbyterian churches precentors lined out the first verse of psalms, which were sung unaccompanied; many of these precentors also became singing teachers in the community and in the schools. The reluctance of Presbyterians to permit the use of organs or other instruments reflected their strong Calvinist ties. Anglicans steeped in English cathedral traditions were forced to accept the realities of the new world; only in large centres such as Toronto or Hamilton could they expect to find trained musicians. As Kallmann notes, some denominations restricted their musical pursuits because of an abhorrence for activities of a secular nature: 'Powerful opposition towards "ungodly" songs and dancing came from certain religious denominations, especially fundamentalist sects such as the Quakers and Methodists. These put popular music on a par with drinking, cursing and card-playing. The fiddle was condemned outright as a sinful instrument because it was the frequent associate of dance music. Only psalms, hymns (such as those of Isaac Watts and the Wesley brothers), and religious folk songs were recognized as legitimate music by these sects.'[4] The major Protestant denominations supported music in a nominal way, hoping of course that the level of congregational singing might be elevated to the point where it would be more conducive to worship; otherwise, there was little effort to attain purely musical or aesthetic goals.

The Children of Peace represent an exception, for this sect earned a widespread reputation for excellent vocal and instrumental ensembles. David Willson, their leader, came to Canada from the United States in 1801. A former Quaker, he left the Friends to establish a religious community of his own at Sharon,[5] a few miles north of Toronto. Willson had a strong predilection for music. In 1819 he organized a singing class and in the following year a band; the band not only played in the religious exercises at the temple but frequently marched in the streets of the surrounding communities and also gave a number of concerts in Toronto. Later known as the Sharon Temperance Band, it competed at the Philadelphia Centennial in 1876, where it was reportedly acclaimed as 'the best band in North America.'[6] David Willson's desire to cultivate music as an integral part of the religious rites at Sharon must have been intense, for he went beyond the membership of his own congregation to engage highly skilled musicians. Among several instrumental teachers and bandleaders at Sharon were Richard Coates, Jesse Doan, and J.D. Graham. Coates was also an organ builder; he constructed several instruments at Sharon Temple, including the first barrel organ to be built in Upper Canada. In describing the accomplishments of the Children of Peace, Emily McArthur notes that 'they also cultivated their talent for singing at a very early date, 1819, and had the best teachers engaged that were available at that time. The first Professor obtainable was Mr. Daniel Cory of Boston ... He commenced his duties January 11, 1846, and then a systematic training in all the rudiments of singing was engaged in with blackboard and all conveniences required. This continued for over two years. The surrounding country joined with the Davidites in the school exercises which were conducted in the large room above in the meeting-house.'[7] This unique form of music education among the Children of Peace could be regarded as a harbinger of American influence. But as intriguing as the Sharon community might be, it remains an isolated curiosity in the annals of Canadian music education.

As a general rule, music in traditional church settings did not command the prominence that it was given at Sharon. More characteristic of the times was the singing school movement, also of American origin but of far-reaching influence. Its main purpose was to teach people to read music as a means of improving the quality of congregational singing. Classes were usually held in the evenings and were attended by both children and adults. Sometimes they were conducted in schoolrooms and sometimes in church halls. Singing schools may have catered to the needs of the church, but they were essentially private enterprises, independent of religious affiliation. They represented a basic kind of music education though they were also outside the academic sphere of the school. In fact their appeal owed much to the social diversions they afforded. In her book on singing schools in Canada, Dorothy Farquharson depicts sessions held in a schoolhouse in the vicinity of Grimsby. This particular singing school attracted almost a hundred people, and there was a feeling that, whether or not you could sing, it was an escape from the humdrum life. Farquharson suggests: 'Here was an opportunity to meet the opposite sex. Chaperones were not deemed necessary since after all you were going to learn to sing sacred music!'[8] Her observations provide further insight into the nature of the singing school movement: 'The teachers were itinerant amateurs who probably only knew the basics of musical rudiments themselves but were willing to impart this knowledge for a small fee to supplement their income. Yet we owe a debt to these patient pioneers who shared the joy of music for very little remuneration. These men are hard to trace because in most cases they wandered from place to place, and in county directories or assessment rolls were never listed as singing school teachers because this was a wintertime sideline to some other seasonal occupation.'[9] One gets the impression that the singing school was more an activity than a learning experience, more a social occasion than a musical event. An 1831 advertisement in the Hamilton *Free Press* suggests that school teachers were expected to conduct such evening sessions. The notice called for 'a Master in Public School who understands the English Language, Writing and Arithmetic. If he can officiate as a Clerk in the Church, and teach a Singing School, he will be more acceptable.'[10] It may be that, compared to itinerant amateurs, school teachers were more resolute in purpose and more proficient in their methods.

This was certainly true in the case of Henry Frost, whose teaching manuals were discovered by Alastair Haig, music teacher at the Ontario College of Education. Haig writes: 'Sometime between the years 1835 and 1850, a young man named Henry Frost was teaching school on the Third Concession, King Township, in York County, Ontario. Frost was keenly interested in music, and wished to use it to vary the monotony of the three R's in his tiny school. Since he had no books or equipment, he resourcefully set about making his own ... He produced a set of twelve manuals, in all 192 pages, each page twenty by fourteen inches. The set constitutes a complete course in the rudiments of music, from the first lessons on notation and time to the reading of three- and four-part songs, the whole done by his own hand.'[11] Methodology was the salient feature of the Frost manuals; its organization implied an acquaintance with the work of leading educators of the day, including that of Pfeiffer and Nageli, musicians associated with Johann Heinrich Pestalozzi in Europe. The manuals incorporated a scale ladder – similar to one used by the Englishman, John Hullah – to illustrate intervals of the major scale. Moreover, the Frost manuals, unlike many school books of this vintage, included contemporary songs which were likely well known and loved by the pioneers in the area. Campbell Trowsdale points out that in this sense Frost 'showed an awareness of the need for relevance that was not evident in Ontario school music texts for many years.'[12] As early as 1846 Egerton Ryerson listed vocal music as a required subject for the common schools in Ontario and authorized John Hullah's method of music instruction. But it was 1871 before Henry Sefton, Ryerson's music appointee to the Toronto Provincial Normal School, published an adaptation of Hullah's text for use in Ontario schools. As Haig observes, 'it appears that our enterprising Henry Frost had beaten the official gun by several years.'[13] Frost must have operated an evening school, for it was recorded that when he died in 1851 his work in music was taken up by the local blacksmith.

Not enough attention was given to music as a school subject during the first half of the nineteenth century, partly because the curriculum of the grammar schools was predominantly academic and partly because educational authorities were preoccupied with more fundamental issues. Indeed, the most controversial development at the time was the transition from private to public schooling. In any event, prominent educators such as Bishop Strachan did not include music in their schools; neither did the politicians, with the exception of Charles Duncombe, who recommended the inclusion of music in his 1836 proposal for teacher training. It was left to Egerton Ryerson to affirm that music was a worthy subject for elementary education.

SCHOOL MUSIC IN THE RYERSON YEARS

The spirit of Pestalozzi's educational theories,[14] which had spread throughout parts of Europe, Britain, and the United States, held great promise for Egerton Ryerson, the first superintendent of education in Canada West. The idea that education could develop the moral nature of the person and could be directed to the whole of society motivated

Ryerson toward the ambitious task of producing a master plan for the public school system. The substance of this document was the result of extensive travels to New England, Great Britain, and several European countries, where Pestalozzian ideas were very much in vogue. This was an era when elementary education was being extended to the entire population, and although England had been slow in adopting the educational reforms taking place in Europe, there was a widespread conviction that much more effort was needed to alleviate the social conditions of the poor. A feeling of adventure and discovery permeated educational circles in many parts of the Western world at this time.

Vocal music was an essential subject in the process of education proposed by Rousseau and Pestalozzi, and its adoption in European institutions attracted widespread attention. It is also true that educational reformers, overwhelmed by the universal popularity of Pestalozzi's reputation, ascribed to his method 'teaching which owed little or nothing to his influence.'[15] However, music in education prospered as a result of this close identification with Pestalozzi. Ryerson was impressed by the quality of the Prussian educational system, which emphasized music for religious and cultural reasons. He was also influenced by David Stow, who had incorporated music methods as a regular part of teacher training at the Normal Seminary in Glasgow. Furthermore, Ryerson was aware of the acceptance of vocal music by leading educators in the United States and used statements by them to reinforce his own view that the ability to sing was not 'a highly restricted gift found only in a small number of children.'[16] To a great extent, Ryerson's interest in vocal music can be attributed to his background as a Methodist minister. Methodists had always been interested in the singing school movement both as an instrument for improving the quality of church singing and as an acceptable social activity. They were also committed to the Sunday School movement, in which music was used to nurture Christian virtues. The Methodist Book Store in Toronto, in addition to its religious publications, carried on a thriving trade in tunebooks and collections of sacred music. As a Methodist, Ryerson possessed a natural desire to make vocal music part of the day-to-day experience of school; as an educator, he perceived the public school to be a vehicle for promoting middle-class values; as a nationalist, he recognized the potential of music to foster loyalty and patriotism in Canadian life. He gave expression to these sentiments: 'I hope to see taught to the sons and daughters of our entire population – vocal music – an art and accomplishment which often converts the domestic fireside into a paradise, refines and promotes social feelings and enjoyments, and blesses the Churches of the land.'[17] Ever since he prescribed vocal music as a subject in the Common School Act of 1846, Egerton Ryerson has been regarded as the champion of music education in the schools of what is now Ontario. Yet this official endorsement in a document that became the foundation of the elementary school curriculum did not guarantee its implementation. Throughout Ryerson's stormy career, his preoccupations were often more political than philosophical, with the result that music continued to be only a minor concern. He could not always ensure that his intentions were carried out because 'his energies were strained by the great issues for which solutions had to be found during his time.'[18]

The justification for music in Ontario schools resembled the arguments for introducing music into public schools in the United States in the 1830s; they were based in both cases on extra-musical aims and objectives. In Boston, music had been considered under three categories – moral, intellectual, and physical. In Ontario, there was a wide range of claims, some relevant and others not: many of them had to do with classroom discipline; some referred obliquely to the effects of music on the emotions; others introduced notions of the moral and social benefits, including the practice of temperance; still others supported music because it offered a break from the so-called academic subjects. The majority of the claims advanced on behalf of music were vague, fuzzy arguments used in a society which sought practical results regardless of the nature of the subject. Trowsdale concludes that

> most of the attempts to justify music during the time of Ryerson were alike in this respect: the values which were presented, with the possible exception of its particular ability in discipline, were values which could be attributed to other subjects as well. The physiological argument, for example, could have been applied with even more justification to physical training; and its value for intellectual training simply placed it in the same category as subjects more easily defended on utilitarian or traditional grounds. Unfortunately, no arguments appeared pointing out the intrinsic values of music. Many of the values were essentially 'side effects' that bore little relation to the special qualities of music that deserved recognition.[19]

Although music managed to gain an initial foothold on the strength of its utilitarian appeal, educators neglected to formulate a convincing rationale that would guarantee the subject any permanent acceptance.

Ryerson, using his centralized powers to introduce music in education, decided that regular classroom teachers, rather than special music instructors, should teach music in the common schools; accordingly, he introduced the Hullah system as part of the training at the provincial normal school. In 1848 James Paton Clarke, a prominent Toronto musician, was engaged to give singing lessons to normal school students after regular school hours or on Saturdays. Clarke was paid five shillings for each lesson. Evidently there was considerable rivalry surrounding this part-time position, with the result that eight different teachers were contracted, in turn, within the first ten years. These frequent changes of instructors, often negotiated with reduced fees, made for little continuity and did not produce the desired results. Subsequently, in 1858, on one of his trips to Great Britain, Ryerson recruited Henry Sefton for the normal and model schools in an effort to increase the effectiveness of the Hullah system in Upper Canada. Sefton held this position for the next twenty-four years, during which time he also taught in the Toronto public schools and at the Mechanics' Institute.

Ryerson was able to exert considerable influence through his control of approved textbooks. It is possible that he chose Wilhem's method of teaching singing by John Hullah because it had been sanctioned by James Kay-Shuttleworth, a leading figure in the first state system of education in England. Trowsdale notes the significance of this decision, observing that 'England and her colony of Upper Canada passed over methods derived from Pestalozzian theory and utilized instead a music system developed especially for the monitorial schools of France.'[20]

Henry Sefton produced instructional materials while teaching at the normal school. His *Three-Part Songs* (1869) and *A Manual of Vocal Music* (1871) were designed to adapt the Wilhem-Hullah method to the Canadian situation and were in fact the first music textbooks written and published for Ontario schools. Ryerson likely welcomed the preparation of such texts as a means of adding momentum to the spread of vocal music. Sefton claimed to depart significantly from the Wilhem-Hullah method, but in fact there was a great deal of similarity. June Countryman gives some reasons for the weak impact of the Hullah-Sefton method: 'In both methods the teaching of music was approached from the standpoint of logic on paper rather than actuality in sound. And, taken as written, both methods kept the student verbalizing about music rather than making music until well into the course.

Music reading was the goal of both courses, but there were unsolved problems in each case: differentiating the quality of intervals, and indeed, the correct reproduction of any interval from its notated form; the reading in keys other than C major; and the whole problem of reading rhythms.'[21] Just as the fixed doh system used by Hullah encountered difficulty in England, so it did in Canada.

Ryerson's demanding schedule obviously allowed him little time to monitor the quality of instruction in every subject field. On the basis of his trip abroad in the mid-1840s, he was convinced that the Wilhem-Hullah method was the best available at the time. Had his visit been later, he might have been more impressed with the success of John Curwen, whose method eventually eclipsed Hullah's and emerged as the most effective approach to vocal music in England. In practice, instruction in Upper Canada was not confined to the Hullah method despite Ryerson's official support and Sefton's long term (1858–82) as music master at the Toronto Normal School. Given the unprecedented success of the method in Great Britain, it was inevitable that Curwen's Tonic Sol-fa would eventually be brought to Canada by British immigrants. It is doubtful that Ryerson was cognizant of the intense rivalry between these two methodologies, but his inquiry about the merits of Tonic Sol-fa drew a colourful response from Sefton, in a reply written in 1875:

Rev Sir,

The method of teaching Vocal Music, of which you ask for information, originated with a Miss Glover of Norwich, who compiled for her own use what she conceived to be a simpler means of representing musical sounds than those then existing, for teaching children vocal music.

About the year 1855, the Rev. Mr. Curwin [sic] following up the idea, modified and adapted the principles for general use under the title of the 'Tonic Solfa [sic] Method of Teaching Music'.

Its principal features consist of: 1) Dispensing with the music stave entirely; 2) The disuse of the ordinary symbols of notation; 3) The use of the *initial letters only*, of the syllabic nomenclature, – namely d-r-m-f-s-l-t-d-, instead of: do-re-mi-fa-sol-la-ti-do.

To illustrate which 'God save the Queen' would appear as under:

d:d:r/t:d:r/m:m:f/m:r:d:/r:d:t/d:-:-
s:s:s/s:f:m/f:f:f/f:m:r/
m:fm:rd/m:f:s/f:m:r/d:-:-/

These alterations are the only claim to originality contained in the method, the wisdom or necessity for which I think is at least questionable. The remaining features and advice given are common property, and are to be found in all musical systems.

If required, I shall be happy to give further personal information.

The method I have taught in the Normal and model schools, in many of its features [has] been approached by the Tonic Solfa.

By moveable diagrams of my own invention I venture to say that no method I have ever seen or read of presents to the eye so vivid a representation of sound, an impalpable medium; thereby securing the object and essence of the Tonic Solfa method without its eccentricities.

I remain, Rev Sir,
Your Obedient Servant
H.F. Sefton[22]

The *Journal of Education*, edited from 1848 to 1875 by Ryerson himself, was another powerful instrument in directing educational policies. Wily and shrewd to the core, Ryerson used extensive reprints from other countries to propagate his ideas. He had never been in favour of the influx of American school textbooks, yet he was not reticent about reproducing articles and speeches originating from New York State, Ohio, or Connecticut. Much of this material also found its way into his annual reports, such as the following excerpt from an address given by a so-called authority at the National Teachers' Association in Cleveland, Ohio:

Music should enter into Common School Education because,
1 It is an aid to other Studies.
2 It assists the Teacher in maintaining the discipline of the school.
3 It cultivates the aesthetic nature of the child.
4 It is valuable as a means of Mental discipline.
5 It lays a favourable foundation for the more advanced culture of later life.
6 It is a positive economy.
7 It is of the highest value as a sanitary measure.
8 It prepares for participation in the Church Service.
Through the medium of the Music Lesson the moral nature of the child may be powerfully cultivated. Music meets the demands of that nature; it infuses itself into his life; it entwines itself about his heart, and becomes a law of his being. Hence, his songs may more directly and powerfully than any other agency give tone and direction to his moral character; they may be made the

means of cultivating his nationality and patriotism; they may promote a love of order, virtue, truth, temperance, and a hatred of their opposites; they may subserve his Religious advancement, implanting lessons at once salutary and eternal. Regular Musical instruction is now incorporated with the School Studies of nearly every City and large Town in New England and the Northern and Western States, not only with the happiest musical results, but with marked good influence upon the health, general intelligence, capacity for receiving general instruction, and orderly habits of the youth so taught.[23]

There was scant information concerning vocal music in documents published by the government, and there were few references to the subject in circulars issued during the first twenty years of Ryerson's term. Even the new *Programme of Studies* (1871) described the music course in terms of 'simple songs,' for which there was a time allotment of one hour per week. It was not until after Ryerson's retirement that the first official course of study was issued. It was concerned primarily with rote singing and the rudiments of notation. As Countryman observes, 'no materials were suggested, and no mention was made of teaching music reading, which was the purpose of the officially-sanctioned Hullah Method.'[24]

References in annual reports indicate that Ryerson was aware of the reluctance of local authorities to act upon his suggestions, but he did not intervene in a direct way until 1871, when he asked inspectors to report on the state of vocal music. In 1872 an inspector from Frontenac County stated that in the majority of his schools 'not a note of music' was heard 'from one year's end to another,'[25] and lamented that this deficiency 'not only exercised a discouraging influence upon the welfare of Schools by removing cheerful influence from them' but had also exerted 'a damaging influence on public taste.'[26] As a result of Ryerson's renewed effort to combat local apathy, the reports in 1876 showed a definite improvement. Music was more conspicuous in the common schools by the end of Ryerson's term: as Trowsdale notes, 'seventy-six percent of city pupils, fifty-three percent of town pupils and twenty-four percent of rural pupils were studying vocal music.'[27] Although these results were disappointing, it should be pointed out that vocal music had done quite well when compared with its companion subject of art. Ryerson's leadership had been plagued with opposition on so many fronts that, given the claims on his time, any closer attention to the fortunes of music would have been difficult indeed.

The most successful programs in school music occurred in large urban centres. We are aware of them because of the colourful characters providing the leadership or, in some cases, because of controversies that arose over rival methodologies. Hamilton was one of the first cities to provide vocal music when it introduced the subject after school hours at Central School in 1853. Central was a well-known institution because it had expanded its curriculum in an era when most schools were offering little beyond the 3 Rs. The first music appointments were special teachers who apparently achieved little success and even less continuity; one teacher was criticized for frequent absences, and another, of European birth, was fired for his inability to communicate in the English language. Music was discontinued in 1861, reportedly for financial reasons, but in 1874 it was reinstated – albeit as an after-school activity – by Mr A.S. Cruikshank. Two years later it was scheduled in regular school hours under Professor Turney, a supervisor of music. With this rapid turnover of special teachers hired on a part-time basis, it is no wonder that progress was disappointing. The appointment of James Johnson in 1877 marked the beginning of a steady growth of school music in Hamilton. Johnson had emigrated from Britain in 1869 and, after serving as a precentor in Presbyterian churches in Guelph and Ingersoll, commenced a successful forty-year term as teacher and supervisor of music. He supervised the work of the regular teachers in the lower grades and taught the senior classes himself.

The earliest evidence of any music education in Ottawa (formerly Bytown) can be linked to such private operations as Mrs MacKenzie's Select Seminary for Young Ladies, which advertised instruction in needlework, music, French, and calisthenics. In 1838 a Mr J. Fraser opened a school for ladies and gentlemen in St Andrew's Church; it offered instruction from 7:30 to 9:30 every Monday and Wednesday evening, and in many respects resembled an American singing school. In the late 1840s the Sisters of Charity started a boarding school, which in 1865 changed its name to the Ottawa Convent. In the 1850s several institutions offered vocal music based on the Hullah system. Most private schools indulged in extravagant advertisements about the accomplishments of their distinguished teachers. This colourful aura surrounding vocal music in the private sector was in stark contrast to its drab beginnings in the common schools, where there seemed to be little activity and a conspicuous lack of leaders. The sporadic efforts that took place in the public schools were a result of the whim and fancy of classroom teachers who may or may not have had any musical expertise. Nevertheless, in 1859 'the subjects mentioned or implied as being taught'[28] included music, and according to the first clear statistical picture of the Ottawa school system, 687 students were engaged in vocal music at some time during the year. The qualifying reference 'at some time during the year' suggests that statistics from a Christmas concert or spring program may have been used to enhance the annual report, so it is unlikely that any systematic instruction occurred. This speculation notwithstanding, it is apparent that pupils were getting some exposure to the subject by 1869.

The leading musician in the Ottawa schools was William Gleed Workman. Originally from England, he moved from Cobourg to Ottawa in 1869 to serve as a precentor at Bank Street Presbyterian Church. Workman was expected to participate in the Sabbath School and prayer meetings as well as to lead the music in the regular services. He also had to teach singing to the congregation one evening per week, for which he received two hundred dollars per annum. Workman taught at the Ottawa Ladies' College and was also active in public school music, conducting a choir of approximately five hundred school children in 1872 to raise money for the purchase of pianos. He was on staff at the Ottawa Normal School when it opened in 1875 and at times taught at the model school. His work is described in a newspaper account of a reception for Lord Lansdowne in Ottawa on 26 May 1887:

When His Excellency had concluded his speech, the school children under the direction of Prof. W.G. Workman who occupied a very prominent position on a high stand opposite that containing the vice-regal party, sang the national songs arranged by the Professor for the occasion. The effect of the two thousand voices joined in the chorus was grand, the event being one of the most pleasant of the whole demonstration. Each child bore a miniature union jack the waving of which when singing the lines 'Thy banners make tyranny tremble / When borne by the red, white and blue' made an indescribably pretty scene. Cheers were then called for, for the Governor-General and next for Lady Lansdowne, and enthusiastically given by the great assemblage.[29]

For his efforts Workman received a pocket watch in an eighteen-carat-gold case with an appropriate inscription from the citizens of Ottawa. In addition to his responsibilites in church and school, he spent long hours teaching privately and in 1883 opened a music store under the name Workman and Bush. This busy life-style was essential because his normal and public school positions were part-time jobs which paid poorly. Obviously, in order to eke out a living as a musician it was necessary to be both energetic and enterprising.

London is another city with a long record in school music, dating back to 1862, when a teacher of vocal music was added to the staff of the Union School (also known as Central School). London was a garrison community, so it is not surprising that one of its foremost teachers was a musician from a regimental band. St John Hyttenrauch came to London in 1857 from Denmark, where he had studied at the Copenhagen Royal Conservatory. He was involved in almost all aspects of London's musical life: he was bandmaster of the 7th Regiment Band; he was organist at St Peter's Cathedral; he taught at two well-established private schools (Hellmuth Boy's College in London and Alma College in St. Thomas); and after starting a class at Central School in 1865, he served as music supervisor from 1876 to 1889. As in Hamilton and Ottawa, the first teachers in London were musicians or, in other words, music specialists. So much for Ryerson's original plan to train general teachers through the provincial normal school!

Music was introduced into Toronto's public schools on a casual basis, and according to a report in 1859 its success depended on the ability or inclination of the classroom teachers.[30] These conditions must have persisted because a report in 1871 stated, 'Vocal Music and Drawing are regarded more as School recreation, than as school work to be required.'[31] This attitude is apparent in the fact that in the school timetable music was relegated to late Friday afternoon. Following Ryerson's new Act of 1871, a school management committee in Toronto recommended several changes for music, including the appointment of two music teachers, and by 1873, 59 per cent of the pupils were receiving some form of music instruction. Using Yonge Street as a dividing line, the two teachers, A.P. Perrin and Henry Sefton, organized their work on an east-west division. As a result of their different interests, a curious situation arose: students east of Yonge Street were taught singing under Perrin while those in the west end were getting theoretical instruction from Sefton.[32] The schedule, however, still placed the music period in the late afternoon.

Robert Stamp observes that 'city school boards often led the provincial department in educational innovation.'[33] This was certainly true in Toronto, where James Hughes, inspector of public schools, who took office near the end of Ryerson's career, forged new educational programs during the tenures of several succeeding ministers of education. When Hughes surveyed the situation in Toronto, he was not satisfied with the quality of work in music. Irked by the different methods being employed east and west of Yonge Street, he contended that 'one competent teacher, who would instruct the teachers ... and who would adopt a natural and consecutive plan'[34] would be preferable. Hughes not only maintained that a music supervisor could organize the work for the regular teachers but was convinced that integrating music for 'fifteen minutes per day would produce much better results ... than a single lesson of an hour's duration once a week.'[35] He may have been influenced by American educators who had already adopted this 'supervisor' scheme. As Trowsdale indicates, Hughes had obtained instructional materials from the United States in the preparation of what was in 1876 'the first detailed course of study in Ontario for vocal music,' anticipating a 'comparable provincial outline by almost twenty years.'[36] Hughes eventually moved closer to the implementation of his comprehensive plan for music when he hired A.T. Cringan, a fellow Scot who was passionately committed to the Tonic Sol-fa method. In order to appreciate the full extent of Cringan's contribution it is necessary to divert our attention to the events which preceded his appointment.

METHODOLOGIES IN CONFLICT

Music seemed to receive less support from the central administration in the years directly following Ryerson's retirement. It is difficult to say whether this reflected apathy on the part of Adam Crooks, Ontario's first minister of education, or the prejudice of John George Hodgins, Ryerson's deputy, who continued to provide administrative leadership under the new regime. Evidently, Hodgins had not always shared Ryerson's enthusiasm for school music. In 1856 he wrote to his chief, who was in Great Britain recruiting, among others, a teacher of the Hullah method for the normal school: 'A Mr. Hickock of Whitby has sent a letter and some testimonials for the situation of Music Master. I do not suppose you intend appointing one. Our music teachers hitherto have introduced discord rather than harmony so that we are better without them – besides very few students wish to learn singing at all.'[37] On another occasion Hodgins expressed the view that 'Jurisprudence' in the normal school training courses was 'of far more consequence than either Music or Drawing, although both are useful in their place.'[38] The department of education produced its first course of study in 1877, but Trowsdale suggests it was 'possibly shamed by the initiative of Hughes in providing one for Toronto in 1876.'[39] It was not until 1882, the year before G.W. Ross became minister of education, that this provincial paralysis ended. In that year S.H. Preston replaced Henry Sefton as the music master of the Toronto Normal School, and the appointment signalled a new spirit of optimism.

The 1883 annual report referred to 'a great improvement' and added, 'The students now take up the study of Music with a great deal of enthusiasm.'[40] This new life which Preston breathed into school music derived much of its inspiration from the United States, in particular from the charismatic leadership of Hosea Holt. A strong advocate of note reading as opposed to the rote approach of his American compatriots, Holt garnered support on the claim that his was a 'scientific approach' designed for the classroom teacher. Since scientific approaches were much in favour then, it is obvious that Preston lost little time in introducing Holt's *Normal Music Course*[41] into Ontario in 1883. Furthermore, by 1885 Preston produced his own adaptation of this text for Canadian schools. Countryman observes that 'it is difficult to determine what adapting Preston actually did, the songs and exercises being those of Book 1 of *The Normal Music Course* (a five-book course) and the introductory chapter likewise drawn from Tufts and Holt, probably from their teacher's manual.'[42] Music teaching was stimulated even further when Hosea Holt spoke in 1885 at the inaugural meeting of the Ontario Music Teachers' Association (later called the Canadian Society of Musicians), of which Preston was a member. Holt's 'platform brilliance'[43] on this occasion was used effectively to win the future support of those in attendance, and subsequently the association recommended that the minister of education engage Holt as director of a summer school of music in Toronto. In a letter to the *Educational Weekly*, Holt hastened the impending controversy over methods by challenging the sol-fa enthusiasts to outline the principles of their pedagogy. Just as the combined efforts of Preston and Holt were gaining momentum, Alexander Thom Cringan arrived on the scene, proclaiming the virtues of Curwen's Tonic Sol-fa.

Curwen's Tonic Sol-fa had already appeared in Ontario. Trowsdale cites several references, one as early as 1869, which indicates that English immigrants were spreading the gospel of Curwen, and another in the London area, where a speaker declared: 'In all our colonies and even in Madagascar and China, books are being published in the sol-fa method, and children taught to sing from it ... some old dames who can scarcely read, spell out the Doh, Ray, Me most readily.'[44] In Toronto on 30 May 1872, Mr A.J. Arnold presented a concert featuring fifty vocalists trained on the Tonic Sol-fa system. In 1875 the Toronto *Globe* reprinted an address on the advantages of the sol-fa notation, given by R. McTaggart to the East Middlesex Teachers' Association.[45] There is evidence that a Miss Julie Porter had been using the method in Ontario since 1876. Moreover, in 1886, when Hughes appointed his new supervisor in Toronto, there were scores of Tonic Sol-fa teachers hoping to fill the position.

James Johnson, supervisor of music for Hamilton, had been using the Curwen method there long before he received his Tonic Sol-fa College certificate in 1885. John Spencer Curwen, during a visit to Canada, claimed that Hamilton in 1881 was the first Canadian city to use his father's system.[46] Notwithstanding some excellent results in the Hamilton schools, the board became embroiled in a public debate over the use of Tonic Sol-fa versus staff notation. The controversy arose in 1885, when the Hamilton *Spectator* published a letter to the editor entitled 'Tonic Sol-folly.' This letter, signed by 'Musician,' complained that school students who were learning Tonic Sol-fa would never use their musical skills in later life because there was no music published in sol-fa notation. The statement was challenged by another writer, who claimed to have in his possession all the major oratorios and large choral works published in sol-fa by Novello and Company. From the flurry of letters in the press it is apparent that school teachers preferred Tonic Sol-fa whereas private music teachers felt that all instruction should be given in staff notation. Sol-fa enthusiasts in the musical community cited the success of Curwen's method in the schools of England and pointed to hundreds of choral societies in Britain which had thrived on sol-fa training. The supporters of staff notation, including the majority of professional musicians, presented testaments from leading music educators in the United States in order to justify their opposition. The issue flared up again in 1893, when the *Herald* printed an article which endorsed Tonic Sol-fa and praised the work of James Johnson in the schools. The public debate went beyond the local musicians: Hamilton's major newspapers, the *Herald* and the *Spectator*, took opposite sides in the dispute, which continued intermittently until 1905. At that time Johnson informed the school board that the Hamilton Conservatory would be appointing a Tonic Sol-fa teacher. This announcement weakened the cause of the private teachers, for most of them were associated with the conservatory. Subsequently, the school board decided that Tonic Sol-fa would be taught in the lower classes but staff notation would be introduced in the junior third grade. As a result of this decision, the *Spectator* ceased its opposition and the furor subsided.

The point has been made that Cringan was not the first to introduce Curwen's method into Ontario, nor Toronto the first place where such a controversy erupted. However, having been appointed by Hughes to the Toronto school system, Cringan was thrust into a position of prominence in which he could not avoid the conflict over methods. Furthermore, he was thoroughly convinced of the efficacy of Tonic Sol-fa, and his Scottish passion would not allow him to yield to 'inferior' methods imported from the United States. Although there were significant differences between Holt and Curwen, 'it was the issue of notation,'[47] according to Countryman, that ultimately fuelled the controversy. A dramatic incident occurred in Toronto in 1886 when, at the second annual meeting of the Ontario Music Teachers' Association, Cringan and Preston staged a double demonstration of the rival methods, featuring their own student groups. These presentations were followed by an afternoon of intense discussion. Following this event strong views were expressed in several publications, and the *Musical Journal* added to the excitement by presenting 'all shades of opinion'[48] as received from a questionnaire. Even though Holt was supported by Toronto's professional musicians, who favoured traditional staff notation, Cringan was undaunted. He requested a public trial in which Tonic Sol-fa students with eight months' training would read, at sight, melodies prepared by an impartial musician, and he challenged students tutored in the Holt method for twice as long a period to submit themselves to a similar test. At every possible opportunity Cringan countered his opposition by addressing the same organizations which Holt and Preston addressed and by responding in kind to the tactics they used to promote their interests.

The methods dispute also surfaced at the first summer school of music, held in Toronto in 1887. George Ross had initiated this summer course after receiving reports from his inspectors that music was not systematically taught in many schools because of the scarcity of competent teachers. Ross asked for a representative teacher from each school where music was to be offered the next year, and the response was excellent. These summer schools, taught by Holt in 1887 and Cringan in 1888,[49] turned out to be showcases for the pedagogical prowess of each of the two systems. Teachers enrolled in summer classes in both groups were so convinced by the end of the course that each group in turn petitioned Ross to sanction its method as the official system for the province. Quite apart from the obvious benefit of improved teaching, the summer schools became focal points of professional concerns for the development of vocal music. Unfortunately, they ceased to operate after 1890 and were not reinstated until 1913. The methods controversy continued for many years without either camp gaining exclusive authorizations or textbook endorsements. In 1895 the Ontario Department of Education issued a music syllabus for public schools which in fact outlined two separate courses, one using Tonic Sol-fa and the other using staff notation.

It is regrettable that Ross did not sustain his initiatives to improve instruction in music. In a defensive way he attributed the demise of music to public apathy at the local level and argued that 'its educational value being not fully understood, too many regard the time given to its study as so much taken away from subjects ... more practical and useful.'[50] But closer scrutiny reveals that the department's record was not at all consistent: in 1893, efficiency reports required of inspectors did not even include the subject of music. There were also regulations in teacher training which in retrospect seem absurd. The department, for example, had initiated county model schools in 1877. These were ordinary elementary schools in which principals took on apprentices for approximately fourteen weeks of practical teaching experience; upon completion of this training, candidates received third class certificates. As Stamp points out, 'the system might have worked if the model-school graduates had later enrolled at either the Toronto or Ottawa normal schools to upgrade their certification and receive professional training. Yet only one-quarter of Ontario's teachers did so.'[51] In the meantime the model schools had overstocked the market with poorly qualified teachers. In 1887 Ross declared music a compulsory subject in the model schools but unfortunately left it optional for upgrading to a second class certificate. Such inconsistencies compounded the problems which already existed in Ontario's inadequate system of teacher training. Therefore, it is not surprising that several other subjects fared much better than music from 1877 to 1913. Vocal music was initially ahead of most optional subjects; however, as Trowsdale comments, 'art surpassed music in 1880; drill surpassed it in 1889, and temperance and hygiene in 1909. As an optional subject, it was dependent upon the whim of board, principal and teacher.'[52]

It is difficult to perceive any clear pattern of development in school music during the Ross ministry (1883–99) other than one of alternating growth and stagnation. This pattern was particularly true of smaller communities and county school boards where there were frequent changes in teaching staff. In a period of increasing urban industrialization, the interests of the public favoured expansion of the school curriculum toward practical and vocational subjects. Clearly music was not a high priority. Yet in spite of the inconsistency in department policy and the inadequacies of training in the normal and model schools, some teachers achieved progress on the basis of their own concerted efforts and abilities, especially in large cities which employed specialist teachers.

In London, Inspector Boyle reported in 1880, 'The question of music or no music still agitates the public mind.'[53] W.D.E. Matthews observes that, regardless of the instruction given by St John Hyttenrauch, most teachers were quite 'incapable of teaching even simple airs.' He adds, 'Furthermore, some of the boys appreciated music so little that the inspector was obliged to take a hand in settling some of the discipline cases that arose when they were required to participate in the genteel exercise of singing.'[54] The board undertook to sell the subject by having Hyttenrauch train approximately a thousand students to give a musical concert in the city's drill shed. The success of the event led to additional concerts, which must have served their purpose, as 'no further mention of public opposition can be found in the reports of the Board.'[55] In subsequent reports Inspector Boyle observed that music was one of the most popular subjects in the course.

In the late 1880s the Ottawa board advertised annually for a music teacher, and from year to year various teachers filled the position. There was some dissatisfaction with the manner in which these teachers followed their schedules, and whenever economic problems occurred the question of whether or not to retain a special music teacher was raised. In 1893, Ottawa discontinued music completely after reporting 100 per cent enrolment in the previous year. However, in 1905 a board delegation visited several schools in Toronto[56] and recommended that vocal music be reinstated and that it be modelled after the programs they had observed there. The next year James A. (Jimmy) Smith was appointed supervisor, and he immediately introduced the Cringan books, which incorporated Tonic Sol-fa methodology. Reportedly, 'this chubby little Scotsman was a veritable Santa Claus bringing a store of musical treats,' and over the years he 'brought untold enjoyment and delight'[57] to thousands of Ottawa pupils. By all accounts steady progress characterized his work in contrast to the sporadic pattern of the late nineteenth century.

Not only did music teachers have to be successful with their students, they had to show the public what was being accomplished. They often did so by mounting large-scale musical performances in which patriotic songs, sometimes composed expressly for the occasion, were featured. Music as a subject could not claim to have pragmatic applications, but it did have utilitarian appeal, which music teachers expediently turned to their advantage. For example, in 1889 James Johnson gave a concert with twelve hundred children in Hamilton's Crystal Palace, an event which included a demonstration of reading with Tonic Sol-fa hand signs. On other occasions his choirs performed for royal visits, and in 1914 he led a thousand-voice children's chorus at the Industrial Exposition. During his long career Johnson received various awards and honours from the community in which he had so faithfully taught music. Similar events took place in some of the smaller towns too; in 1887 W.J. Freeland, Stratford's first music director, led a chorus of a thousand children and a thousand adults in the skating rink. In the following year the *Stratford Times and County of Perth Gazette* advertised an entertainment as follows: 'A chorus of 1,200 voices will possibly be the greatest attraction ... Hand signs, tune names, and finger signs, telling tones by ear, sight test, etc., by the pupils, are sure to provide interesting demonstrations while the juveniles' singing of such hard-to-articulate words as "Rignumballidima-coymee" and "Aldiborontiphoscophornio," will also be worth hearing. Single fare tickets on the GTR are to be issued to parties desirous of attending Friday's concert from London, Woodstock, Seaforth, Listowel, Baden and intermediate stations ... The attendance is expected to be the largest ever seen at indoor entertainment in Stratford.'[58] A public drinking fountain erected in Freeland's honour attests to the high profile he once held in the Stratford community.

It usually took the combination of an outstanding musician and a dynamic administrator to produce superior results. This was the case in Toronto, where A.T. Cringan, championed by James Hughes, eventually provided the leadership and inspiration for school musicians throughout Ontario. Just two years after his arrival in Canada, Cringan published *The Canadian Music Course*, and ten years later, *The Educational Music Course*. He also prepared the *Teacher's Handbook of the Tonic Sol-fa System*,[59] which explained in great detail the principles of Curwen's pedagogy; through his instructional materials Tonic Sol-fa was systematically applied to classroom music. Cringan stood out among his contemporaries in that he was intrigued with the music of the Iroquois and was the first to record and transcribe native music in Canada.[60] His work was published in a series of archaeological papers appended to annual reports of the minister of education for Ontario; some of the material was used in his own songbooks.

Public performances were effective in gaining support for school music in Toronto. The May Festival Concert which Cringan inaugurated in 1886 became an annual event in the city. Among many special ceremonies, school children participated in the opening of Massey Hall in 1894, and a student choir of six thousand voices performed for the visit of the Duke and Duchess of York. Cringan's patriotic fervour was channelled into Empire Day celebrations, and his religious convictions were reflected in his activities in the Presbyterian church. Many of Ontario's politicians and educators were active in the temperance movement, so it is no coincidence that his massed choir was a feature of Children's Night at Massey Hall in 1897, on the occasion of the world convention of the Women's Christian Temperance Union.

Cringan was forceful in articulating a philosophy: 'Music is not now taught simply as a recreation, but as an instrument of value in the highest educational development and mental culture ... the pupil who masters this art must inevitably have formed definite habits of observation, comparison and reasoning, followed by decision and promptness of execution. In addition we must consider the refining influence of the effort to produce that which should be in itself artistically beautiful. This calls forth the finer sensibilities and emotions of child nature which might otherwise lie dormant.'[61] Donaldson Uhryniw comments that, although Cringan regarded his work 'with the serious zeal of the musical missionary, the importance he placed upon the artistic aspect ... caused him to be selective and critical of the material chosen.'[62] Cringan had strong opinions regarding quality of tone and expression and sought to avoid 'raw and tasteless renditions of tunes.'[63] Both his philosophy and his pragmatic objectives were adopted by many other teachers. As a frequent speaker at professional meetings and a contributor to educational journals, Cringan was an effective crusader in the advancement of music education. He extended his sphere of influence through in-service programs for the Toronto board and at local teachers' institutes throughout the province, and also as music instructor at the Toronto Normal School (1901–31). From 1913 to 1930 he was director of provincial summer schools of music and was the guiding spirit in the formation of the Music Section of the Ontario Educational Association. He also taught Tonic Sol-fa at summer schools in the United States. Cringan was the obvious choice when the department appointed a part-time provincial inspector of music in 1919 since he had already emerged as the undisputed leader in the province.

An emphasis on the development of reading skills remained long after the turn of the century, and as a result of Cringan's extensive influence Tonic Sol-fa proved to be the most enduring methodology. Although the excitement generated by the methods controversy had long since dissipated, an increasing number of music teachers and supervisors sustained the impetus for progress in the larger centres. They became local heroes in their own communities as they met the utilitarian demands of royal visits, Empire Day celebrations, and other civic ceremonies. Several commenced their lengthy careers just after the turn of the century: Llewellyn Rees (Toronto, 1903–21), E.W.G. Quantz (London, 1906–41), James Smith (Ottawa, 1906–41), and Whorlow Bull (Windsor, 1909–38).

The department of education initiated two programs after 1913 which gave further momentum to the efforts of the music teachers themselves. A summer school of music was established in 1913 to upgrade teachers and train music supervisors. In the first course, teachers with third class standing could earn certificates as teachers of elementary vocal music. In the second course, teachers with first or second class qualifications could earn certificates as supervisors of vocal music. It was in conjunction with this step that a grant scheme in 1915 provided financial incentives for boards to hire music supervisors who obtained certificates at these summer schools. In a sense this scheme was a tacit acknowledgment that normal and model school programs were not sufficient in themselves and that the department finally recognized the need for specialized training or supervision in the teaching of music. It also represented an attempt to establish certificates and formal qualifications. Trowsdale observes that, historically, 'musicians hired to teach in the urban centres did not require any certification or qualifications other than those demanded by the local board,' but that after 1913 'entrance to the new courses required provincial teaching certification.'[64] It is unfortunate that the department did not completely overhaul its training programs but merely added summer schools as an adjunct to the existing, inadequate system. Furthermore, the amount of money involved in the grant scheme was miniscule when compared with that of grants for military training, agriculture, and technical education. Obviously, the innovations in music compared with those in other fields were token gestures. For many years Cringan directed the summer schools, assisted by other well-known supervisors. These more competent teachers 'gradually began to revitalize music education in the province,' and 'along with the older city supervisors as a nucleus, they formed the first substantial corps of music educators.'[65] The exchange of ideas at summer schools foreshadowed the formation of the Music Section of the Ontario Educational Association in 1919, which became the official venue for the profession.

MUSIC IN THE HIGH SCHOOLS

The account of school music thus far pertains to vocal music in the elementary schools with roots in the common schools of Upper Canada. The historical traditions for music at the high school level were entirely different. Instruction in music was usually available in ladies' colleges and select seminaries, but it was not found with any frequency in boys' private schools, nor was it prevalent in the grammar schools, which were designed with professional careers in mind. As Stamp notes of the Crooks administration (1876–83), 'the universities played a dominant role in shaping the high school curriculum, and naturally shaped it to their own needs and interests,'[66] even though only 25 per cent of high school graduates went on to university study and professional careers. Teacher training in music had been confined for the most part to normal schools because, as an elementary school subject, music did not fall within the academic agenda or responsibility of the universities. Moreover, when alternative programs were developed in the late 1870s and 1880s, music did not fit into the practical or vocational scheme of things. In an increasingly urban, industrial society, music received little attention in the curricular expansion of secondary schools.

Despite the general neglect of high school music, there is evidence that the subject was taught in some schools. There may be two possible explanations for this apparent anomaly: annual reports indicate that music existed here and there, but the erratic, up-and-down pattern of the data suggests that statistics in music may have been reported on the strength of a school operetta, festival, or special event; the fluctuations may have occurred in situations where church organists and private teachers persuaded local boards to offer music on a trial basis. Few places sustained their enrolments from year to year, and even in cities such as Hamilton and London, where supervisors taught the senior work, the subject did not enjoy much popularity or permanence. A high school inspector wrote in 1878: 'There are but few certificated teachers who are qualified to teach music, and these are not as a rule, encouraged to pay much attention to it. On the other hand, special teachers of singing, who, under the present regulations require no certificate, are frequently wretched disciplinarians, and incapable of writing or speaking the English language with propriety.'[67] In 1881 one inspector recommended financial incentives for music, drawing, and drill, 'which ought to be taught in high schools but are too often neglected.' This neglect could be attributed to the fact that there were no intermediate examinations in these subjects. Furthermore, he noted that these three subjects had 'almost ceased to be taught since the grant for them was withdrawn.'[68] In the first year of W.G. Ross's term (1883–99), 26 per cent of the total high school population was reported under 'Music,' but in the last years of his term the figure was less than 1 per cent.

The department of education had never established any status for music in the high school, nor had there been adequate provision for the training of high school music teachers. It is understandable, therefore, that the growth of music in secondary schools by the end of the First World War had not materialized beyond isolated and temporary pockets of activity; music was crowded out of the picture by subjects that enjoyed higher political priority. In a practical, materialistic age, most people were content to let private teachers, churches, and community organizations provide music education beyond the elementary grades.

PRIVATE TEACHERS AND CONSERVATORIES

The contribution of private teachers has not been fully recognized because of the wide-ranging backgrounds, abilities, and artistic standards of those within their ranks. Such diversity made it difficult to demand professional qualifications. Furthermore, there were geographical and financial problems involved in organizing a large group of self-employed people. Private teachers have also been disadvantaged by the fact that they did not fall directly within the jurisdiction of a government ministry or under a bureaucratic umbrella. Consequently, there has been little, if any, official support for the work of private teachers, and the obstacles to their establishing professionalism have contributed to their sense of frustration. No useful purpose would be served in labouring over the uneven quality of private tuition. As a general rule, ladies' colleges and private schools offered music on an optional basis and charged additional fees for it. Such institutions had no difficulty in recruiting the better musicians as part-time staff; indeed, by the 1880s some of these schools had music departments that resembled conservatories. Albert College in Belleville, Hellmuth Ladies' College in London, and Alma College in St Thomas were among many schools that offered specialized diploma programs in music. The profusion of ladies' colleges declined as more young women entered regular high schools; at the same time there was an increase in the establishment of conservatories, many of which had their origins in ladies' colleges. The Brantford Ladies' College and Conservatory serves as an example. It was chartered in 1874 but renamed the Brantford Conservatory of Music in 1900.

Those conservatories which were independent of private school affiliations concentrated on music instruction and therefore attracted teachers formerly associated with ladies' colleges. A growing interest in performance standards led to intense rivalry among the major conservatories and the colourful personalities associated with them. Some schools were more pretentious than others, some more permanent than others, and as time passed the number of institutions dwindled, depending upon their fame and fortune. As early as 1876 a conservatory of music was operating in Toronto, and there were others in the city before the end of the decade. By the turn of the century Toronto, Hamilton, London, and Windsor could boast several such schools.

A few Ontario conservatories offered a full range of professional training and found it advantageous to be affiliated with a university. The Toronto Conservatory of Music (TCM) was affiliated with the University of Trinity College in 1888 and the University of Toronto in 1896. Two others were also affiliated with the University of Toronto: the Toronto College of Music in 1890 and the Hamilton Conservatory of Music in 1906. Such affiliations not only added prestige to the conservatory but also extended privileges to its graduates: university degree candidates who had already earned conservatory diplomas were exempted from the first and second levels of BMus examinations. Whereas the conservatories provided a comprehensive program of instruction, the universities were involved primarily in conducting examinations.

The Toronto Conservatory of Music[69] was founded in 1886 by

Edward Fisher, former director of the Ottawa Ladies' College. It opened in 1887 with an enrolment of two hundred students and a staff of fifty teachers. The subjects included theoretical courses and practical instruction in voice and individual instruments, not to mention a variety of other subjects such as 'elocution, foreign languages, public school music, acoustics, piano tuning and vocal anatomy and hygiene.'[70] Its programs were organized under two departments: the academic department catered to the needs of young students and amateurs, and the collegiate department offered courses and diplomas for senior students seeking professional careers as teachers or performers. By the end of Fisher's term (1886–1913) the enrolment had reached two thousand students, several branches were in operation, and local examination centres had been established in Ontario, Quebec, and the western provinces. In 1919 the TCM came under the control of the University of Toronto and within a few years absorbed most rival schools. Its distinguished faculty, its exacting standards in advanced work, and its development of a nation-wide examination system eventually enabled the TCM to assume the role of a national institution for English-speaking Canada.

The Canadian Society of Musicians, the first association of professionals, was founded in 1885 and claimed to have two hundred members. The society was comprised mostly of prominent musicians from southern Ontario, including a number of leaders in the field of school music. In the short span of the society's existence (1885–96) its members took an active interest in promoting music education. They sent several recommendations to the provincial minister of education with regard to textbooks, methodologies, and teacher training. However, this display of interest by professional musicians was short-lived, possibly because they were not given much scope to influence developments in education.

S.H. Preston of the Toronto Normal School taught a school music course for the Toronto Conservatory of Music and A.T. Cringan came on the TCM staff in 1897, at which time he was music director of the city schools. These part-time activities, however, were exceptional in that school musicians seldom worked with private teachers. Diana Brault makes reference to an incident in 1902 in which 'for one brief moment, the interests of both the professional musician and the teacher concerned with music but belonging to a general association, joined in a common cause.' Together, these groups suggested that 'a Music Teachers' Department be formed within the Ontario Educational

Association.'[71] Although this suggestion did not bear fruit, it implies that a sense of unity and cooperation existed within the musical community of Toronto at that time. Still, conservatories and independent institutions in general have been apathetic as regards school music, and private teachers have never formed close alliances with school musicians. This division among music teachers may have been a natural outcome of the jurisdiction of the department of education over school personnel, or it may have resulted from the difference in the methodologies of studio and classroom teachers. At times there seems to have been a lack of mutual respect, which may explain why the liaison between private and school music teachers has been so sporadic and tentative over the years.

The Examination Board Wars

As early as 1893 the Associated Board of the Royal Schools of Music (London, England) had received an inquiry from Montreal regarding the possibility of establishing local music examinations in Canada. When after a lapse of time the board took initial steps in this direction, its action gave rise to a series of acrimonious exchanges between representatives of the board and musical leaders in Ontario who opposed the idea. The larger conservatories feared that such an intrusion would drastically diminish revenues from their own examinations. Undoubtedly, the TCM added to the rancour when that institution questioned the artistic standards of the Associated Board. This, in turn, provoked statements defending the superiority of British institutions and exacerbated the feeling that Canadian musicians were regarded as colonials. These disputes or 'examination wars,'[72] as Gaynor G. Jones refers to them, reached a climax in 1899.

The spectre of competition from overseas eventually led to the formation of the Associated Musicians of Ontario, comprising 112 members – among them, the principals of the major conservatories and the leading music teachers of the province. It was at the urging of this group that the University of Toronto entered the field of local examinations. In 1899 the following proposal, moved by Mr F.H. Torrington, was unanimously adopted: 'That this meeting is in favor of practical examination in music, under the auspices of the University of Toronto, in co-operation with a council representing the musicians of Ontario.'[73] Appended to the proposal was a detailed syllabus for pianoforte, organ, violin, violoncello, and singing, each organized according to three levels of difficulty. The submission also recommended the holding of examinations in the local centres of Hamilton, London, Ottawa, and Toronto. Although the association had pledged to 'unite in supporting one common provincial standard of examination,'[74] only a small number of candidates registered in 1902, the year in which the university assumed its role as an examining body. Evidently, the various conservatories did not discontinue their own examinations, so the university found itself competing with those who had suggested the idea of a uniform standard for the whole province. In 1902 the Associated Board commenced its operation in Canada by holding examinations at McGill University.

MUSIC IN THE UNIVERSITIES

As early as 1844 King's College (renamed the University of Toronto in 1850) indicated its interest in creating a professorship with the intention of granting BMus and DMus degrees. James Paton Clarke, a well-known church musician, received the first BMus degree in 1846, but it was not until the 1890s that syllabi and examinations were established. George Strathy, the second person to receive a BMus degree in Canada, became the first professor at the University of Trinity College in 1853. There were recitals, occasional lectures, and private lessons, but universities did not give regular courses of instruction; consequently, music did not flourish as did other disciplines in the arts and sciences. The principal activity in these music departments was the administration of examinations for degree candidates, and individual faculty members seemed to be somewhat remote from the mainstream of academic work within their respective institutions. There are a few references to musicians at Trinity, but it is difficult to determine exactly what they did. In the case of Strathy, students in 1881 actually questioned his existence: 'We have seen nothing of him – no graduates – no lecture – no examinations – it is time for a change.'[75] For administrative purposes Trinity formally created a faculty of music later that same year, but courses were not established as a continuing or permanent part of the university curriculum. One of the most controversial events in Trinity's past is the appointment of Edward Kendall, a former mathematics professor, to serve as an acting registrar in England. Using several English organists as examiners, the university awarded a number of music degrees in London and New York during the late 1880s. There were questions raised about the legitimacy of this practice. Subsequently, an outcry from members of the music establishment in Britain – among others, C. Hubert Parry, C. Villiers Stanford, and Sir Arthur Sullivan – led to an organized protest in their journals, and a delegation approached the colonial secretary. In 1891 the awarding of degrees in absentia was discontinued.

Singing was a colourful aspect of campus life in the late nineteenth century. The University College (Toronto) Glee Club was formed in 1879 for the purpose of cultivating 'musical tastes by the study of songs and choruses, and the promotion of good fellowship among College men.'[76] In its first year, this ensemble sang at five organ recitals sponsored by the Literary Society. Rebecca Green's research on college songbooks affirms that the glee club required a varied repertoire for its broad range of activities: 'In the 1887–88 season, they performed at public and intercollegiate debates, an orphanage, several churches, the Lunatic Asylum, the Toronto Lacrosse Club, the Conversazione, and the public meeting of the Modern Languages Club ... Clearly, the University College Glee Club played a vital role in the songbook tradition at that university, and it is probably through this group that many U.S. college songs entered the Canadian repertoire.'[77]

The University of Toronto established a faculty of music in 1918; the first appointments were part-time positions held by people who also had responsibilities in the TCM. There was no effort to mount an intramural program of study with prescribed courses and lectures on a regular basis. Nor did other universities in Ontario introduce academic programs in music. This neglect of music instruction in higher education eventually changed, but it was a long time before universities directed attention to the needs of school music or even to music education for the general public.

The role of music appointments in higher education resembled that of kapellmeister, and university programs of study accommodated the needs of church organists or, to a lesser extent, private teachers. In the nineteenth century one person typically combined the functions of church musician and private teacher to round out a professional career. Music in higher education was patterned after British traditions and, if anything, was partial to the Anglican tradition, in which organist and choir assumed the main responsibility for the musical service. University musicians in general identified more readily with the elitism of private church schools such as Upper Canada College. Certainly their interests were not directed toward the needs of the public schools: from the time of Ryerson, school music had been more in tune with

Methodist traditions, in which there was a greater reliance on congregational singing.

Students seeking certification for teaching in Ontario high schools enrolled in faculties of education for their teacher training. Since music was not well established as a secondary school subject, the faculties of education at Queen's University and the University of Toronto did not need to provide methods courses in music. At Toronto, music instruction was given to students who chose elementary methods as an option leading to a first class certificate: Llewellyn Rees, director of music for Toronto schools, was hired in 1907 as a part-time instructor in this program; George N. Bramfitt, who was appointed in 1910 to teach diction and voice production, also taught music methods for elementary grades. The Ontario College of Education replaced the former faculties of education in 1920.

The developments described in this chapter indicate that the incidental forms of music education in pre-Confederation years found their destinies in a promising yet unsophisticated institutional framework by the end of the First World War: as urban communities emerged, church choirs were surpassed by large choral societies; singing schools disappeared, but music found its way into the public schools; though competent private teachers were few and far between in the pioneer period, artistic standards eventually improved, most notably in institutions such as ladies' colleges and conservatories. Official recognition of vocal music in Ryerson's plan for public education set a precedent for the future of school music in that many traditions and patterns established in Ontario were later transplanted into the western provinces by those who moved on to meet the challenge of new frontiers.

4

The West

MANITOBA

The efforts of the Roman Catholics, Anglicans, and Presbyterians comprise the main developments in education at the Red River settlements; the Hudson's Bay Company, which as early as 1808 had sent out teachers, was only too pleased to have the assistance of the churches. The first permanent school was established by the Roman Catholic Church in 1818. Bishop Provencher devoted much of his interest to education, and when he arranged for the Grey Nuns to come west as teachers, he specifically requested that 'at least one should have musical ability.'[1] Anne Loutit marvels at how they 'undertook the incredible, formidable difficulties and harassments of the 58-day voyage from Lachine ... in the freight-bearing canoes of the Hudson's Bay Company manned by none-too-smooth tongued voyageurs.'[2] Of the quartet of nuns which arrived in 1844, the musically gifted one was Sister Marie-Eulalie Legrave. She was a leader in arranging festive activities, adding to them 'immeasurably ... through her own solo singing and by the effective contributions of the choir which she soon organized.'[3] It was said of her work, which included the teaching of plainsong, that 'her pupils too were charmed, for she added to the more prosaic instruction the delights of music.'[4]

Subsequently, there were further requests for sisters trained in music. No doubt music was given a high priority because of its usefulness in nurturing both religious and educational aspirations. Much of the mission work was directed toward the Indians and Métis. Though the Grey Nuns were not a teaching order by tradition, their efforts were sustained right up until 1874, when they passed their work over to the Congregation of the Sisters of the Holy Names of Jesus and Mary; this order offered instruction in piano and theory at St Mary's Academy, a private girls' school which was established in Winnipeg.

The Earl of Selkirk tried to provide opportunities for schooling in his pioneer settlements. During the voyage of 1814, classes were held on board ship for the children of Scottish immigrants, but the first attempts to establish schools in the colony were not very successful. The main problem was finding a suitable teacher who was prepared to remain under the harshest, most difficult conditions. However, in 1820 a new beginning was made by Reverend John West, an Anglican clergyman. As time passed, a measure of stability was achieved, and by 1836 the Red River Academy was providing education for both boys and girls. The Presbyterians started to develop their own schools at Kildonan in 1847, operating for the first two years in the home of a settler; eventually they erected a log schoolhouse. Education in the Kildonan school was determined by public trustees, who were described by an early historian as 'plain, blunt men, whose own advantages had been limited.'[5] There is little wonder that teachers experienced difficulty in a system based largely on inspection by trustees and the public oral examination of students.

Music did not merit a dominant place in the Protestant schools, where basic subjects were given the highest priority. James Ross, who had been educated in Ontario, returned to the Red River community to teach in the 1860s. Reportedly, he used sol-fa syllables in his teaching, but apart from this scant information there is little evidence of music instruction in Anglican or Presbyterian schools. The settlers seemed to look to the church rather than the school for their musical development, as suggested by the abundance of church choirs around the time of Confederation. References in the late 1850s to 'teaching singing à la mode americain'[6] indicate that some music education was provided in evenings through singing schools. These must have been short-term endeavours – as transitional as the musicians who organized them and then moved on – because the singing school movement did not flourish to any great extent in western Canada.

Music was taught with greater purpose in the private schools of the

Red River settlement. At St Cross Ladies' School, Mrs Mills from England was in charge and the students were mainly 'daughters of what were termed the Hudson's Bay Company families.'[7] It was 'in the order of a European finishing school,'[8] with an emphasis on etiquette, music, modern languages, and handicrafts (especially embroidery). Mrs Kennedy, a leading figure in the 1860s, taught music at Miss Davis's School and was also organist/choirmaster at St Andrew's Church.

MUSIC IN THE COMMUNITY

When Manitoba joined Confederation in 1870, it was 'basically a French-English duality.'[9] But within a decade the population of Manitoba doubled: the first influx of people came from Ontario; they were followed in the mid-1870s by Mennonite and Icelandic groups; and a mass migration of Ukrainians commenced in 1896. According to W.L. Morton, these developments 'transformed the ethnic pattern from a bilingual to a multilingual one and profoundly affected the social, political and educational life of the province.'[10] The musical culture brought by settlers of European origin permeated many parts of Manitoba. The daily tasks and hardships of rural life were different from those of the towns and cities; hence, cultural and educational patterns of development did not give rise to similar traditions or even parallel the patterns of change that took place in urban centres.

Icelanders, 'among the most literate of Canada's early immigrants,'[11] settled at Gimli, on the shores of Lake Winnipeg, in the 1870s. Their commitment to choral music was rooted in the Lutheran service and Icelandic folklore. Bands and orchestras formed a vital part of their heritage too, though the instrumentation was seldom complete. A number of private teachers achieved fine results, most notably Olafur Thorsteinsson, who arrived in 1889 and continued to teach music for many years; by 1951 'he had successfully piloted over three hundred pupils through the Toronto Conservatory of Music examinations.'[12] The first Icelandic choral society in Winnipeg was The Harp, organized around 1880 in 'the home of Reverend Jon Bjarnason, whose wife was a trained musician.'[13] The existence of more than twenty Icelandic music teachers in Winnipeg by 1910 indicates the serious intent that characterized their cultural pursuits. One outstanding teacher, Jonas Palsson (1875–1947), has been described as 'a notable example of a person who by hard work and persistence surmounts the obstacles in his way': 'On his arrival in [Canada], about 1900, he first worked with pick and shovel on the railroad, on a ten-hour day, for $1.25 a day, and in winter he shovelled coal. He passed the Toronto College of Music examination in 1904 and established the Paulson Academy of Music.'[14] Concerts involved mostly church choirs in the prewar years, but in the 1920s community groups such as the Winnipeg Icelandic Choral Society and the Icelandic Male Voice Choir were formed.

The Mennonites in a striking way retained their individuality by holding on to musical influences from their communities in Russia and to their musical roots in German repertoire. What is characteristic of this group as a people is the diversity that existed within their ranks. Those who settled in Manitoba in the 1870s represented the poorest and least educated of the Mennonites who came to North America, but more telling from a cultural standpoint, they were extremely conservative in their religious views and customs even by Mennonite standards. Wesley Berg writes, 'Naturally, there was very little time in their first twenty-five years in Canada for cultural activities; the problems of establishing themselves on the open prairie, something that had been considered foolhardy, if not impossible, and of providing a basic education for their children, were difficult enough to deal with.'[15] Even so, the primacy of congregational music as an integral part of worship did lead to choral activities in the more progressive Bergthaler Church, where rigid traditions of singing old chorales in an extremely slow tempo gradually gave way to 'the formation of choirs, the use of quicker gospel songs, and the introduction of musical instruments.'[16] Outstanding among those Mennonites who advocated progressive musical ideas was a teacher from the United States, H.H. Ewert. As inspector of Mennonite schools and principal of the Gretna Normal School, he encouraged the formation of school choirs and, at Winkler, organized the first choral concert in southern Manitoba. Most conservative congregations did not permit choirs in the worship service or allow concerts in the church, so sometimes choral activities flourished initially in the schools. Ewert also introduced choral singing into the Sunday School movement, and evidently young people were encouraged 'to gather once a week for an evening of singing.'[17]

Developments in the Rosemorter Church of Saskatchewan were similar to those of the Bergthaler Church in that 'choirs were organized at a fairly early stage, and were closely linked to a concern for the welfare of young people.'[18] Moreover, after 1906, choirs performed on a regular basis at the annual conferences of these two churches held at various sites in Manitoba and Saskatchewan. Many Mennonites who had originally settled in the United States later moved to Saskatchewan, joining several small communities north of Saskatoon. Their liberal influence was reflected in the organization of a choral festival in 1905, a custom that had been followed by Mennonites in American settlements. This particular event featured sessions on music theory and the practical aspects of conducting. Such an educational emphasis was probably due to the leadership of Aron G. Sawatzky, who had conducted workshops in Russia before emigrating to Canada in 1903. In documenting festival events in 1906, Berg writes, 'What is remarkable is the fact that, in an area inhabited by farmers pioneering in the open, unbroken prairies, a choir directors' association was organized which sponsored increasingly numerous and complex activities for a period of almost two decades.'[19] Eventually Mennonite choirs from Manitoba also became members of this association, which remained active until 1923. At the request of the association, arrangements were made for visits between annual workshops by Sawatzky and his former student J.P. Wiebe. These musicians, who were both ordained ministers, invigorated choral singing in Mennonite communities across the prairies. On occasion, activities also involved choirs and leaders from the United States, as Mennonites in both countries maintained close communication through their conference publications. Indeed, so strong was their internal organization, based upon religious and social ties and transcending geographical borders, that years later British and Mennonite traditions in Manitoba had crystallized into two solitudes of choral music.

Ukrainian immigrants have retained their distinctive character most effectively in larger cities such as Winnipeg and Edmonton, where concentrations of their people enabled them to mount special events for national celebrations. In the initial stages they found expression in recreational activities that featured singing, dancing, and the use of various stringed instruments, including mandolins and guitars. It was largely their strong folk tradition that flourished in the new land. In the realm of religion, liturgical music was preserved by virtue of their membership in the Greek Catholic and Greek Orthodox churches of the Eastern rite. The full flowering of Ukrainian culture in Canada did not occur with the first generation of settlers, but as more refugees arrived the artistic climate improved. The influence of Olexander Koshetz in the community's achievement of high standards in choral singing is a striking example of the revival of Ukrainian culture. From

1941 to 1944 he trained conductors at special Ukrainian summer schools in Winnipeg. Such educational programs have been offered in parish halls and community centres and thus have helped Ukrainians preserve a strong sense of identity. As Paul Yuzyk notes, 'from a children's orchestra there often emerges an adult string or symphony orchestra.'[20] This self-contained infrastructure of musical training within the national community has been a significant factor in the development of Ukrainian music in Canada.

Musical Life in Winnipeg

The early settlers had to create their own amusement and forms of entertainment. In addition to choral activities these included dancing and fiddling as well as music provided for special occasions by military and civic bands. A band came out with the Wolseley expedition in 1870, and shortly afterward its instruments were obtained by the citizens, who formed a municipal band. The first band concert in Winnipeg took place in 1873. This event must have stimulated some interest, because a rash of band organizations is recorded in the 1870s. The first philharmonic society appeared in 1880, and throughout this decade operetta societies added to the city's concert life. Toward the end of the century the level of refinement was more promising, in that musical progress was not confined to ensembles; there seemed to be an effort to nurture individual performers as well.

The role of the private teacher became increasingly important in the ensuing years. Although the profusion of conservatories in Ontario did not extend to western Canada, interest in serious music study was stimulated through the conservatory examination system. At a practical level the Toronto Conservatory and the Associated Board of the Royal Schools of Music gave private teachers an incentive to raise their standards in the early twentieth century. The examinations conducted by various institutions provided a measure of direction and reinforcement which was encouraging to teachers who had to work in such geographic isolation; examination results served to recognize the most promising students and the teachers associated with them. In short, this practice of conducting local examinations was vital because it could rejuvenate the spirit and will of the teachers. In Lillian Scarth's words, 'back of all the musical developments of the west are its conscientious music teachers. Many of the best of them are from the old country, and one often experiences the pleasure of coming across these well qualified persons in quiet little towns as well as bigger centres, using their talents for the benefit of the community. Far removed from the old world "atmosphere" they work in a new land, less romantic, more materialistic maybe, but appreciative withal and eager.'[21]

The Women's Musical Club of Winnipeg, whose origin can be traced to 1894, advanced the cause of music by presenting visiting artists as well as sponsoring local performers. By 1907 their membership had reached four hundred, and in 1915 they launched a scholarship scheme in support of young artists. The Junior Musical Club, an affiliate of the Women's Club, was formed in 1901; it offered recitals and lectures to foster the appreciation of music among youth. In 1915 a group of prominent Winnipeg businessmen founded an organization that not only created performing opportunities for themselves but also contributed in many ways to the musical climate of the city. The influence of this fraternity, the Men's Musical Club, can be felt in the development of the city's major musical organizations; it was especially great in the period between the two world wars. Among the men at the forefront of this initiative were Joseph Tees, Ralph Horner, and J.J. Moncrieff. The sustained interest of the Men's and Women's Clubs improved the quality of musical life in Winnipeg to such an extent that by the First World War there were signs that the city was outgrowing the rather crude attempts of the late nineteenth century. By 1918 in Winnipeg there were several outstanding teachers established, whose high standards augured well for the future. Among them were John Waterhouse (violin) and Leonard Heaton (piano), both of whom were destined to have successful careers as private teachers and community musicians.

The Beginnings of Music at Brandon College

Whereas the Winnipeg College of Music (incorporated 1903) existed for only two years, the music department at Brandon College became a permanent influence in western Manitoba. Brandon College was founded in 1899 by the Baptist Union of Western Canada, and in 1905 a college band was formed to participate in evangelistic meetings and special services in churches within reach of Brandon. Alison McNeill-Hordern notes, 'By 1900, Brandon College had assumed a responsibility ... as patron and sponsor of the performing arts and ... within a few years [it] supplemented that role by providing music education and performances by faculty, students and outstanding visiting artists.'[22] The music department of Brandon College was established in 1906;

Miss Abbie Helmer, a piano teacher, served as its first director. A major factor in establishing Brandon as a musical community was the sustained influence of W.L. Wright, director of the music division at the college from 1907 to 1947. Brandon College gave faculty recitals in addition to an instructional program which prepared students in all grades leading up to the associate (ATCM) level.

MUSIC IN THE SCHOOLS

The Protestant Schools of Manitoba listed music in the official program of studies as early as 1876, but no specific details were provided as they were for other subjects. At this time the training of music teachers did not exist; indeed, training for general teachers was not yet in place. It was 1882 before normal school training was instituted, 'with a staff of one instructor and an enrolment of sixteen students.'[23] To appreciate the problem, one must realize that 'in 1883, fifty per cent of all teachers in the province, or sixty-six per cent in rural districts were without training of any kind.'[24] For years short-term institutes and other schemes were devised to cope with the shortage, but the brevity of the training remained a serious problem and specialized work in music was non-existent.

The cultural interests of Winnipeg's professional and business leaders formed a solid basis of support for the encouragement of music in the schools. This support was exemplified in the leadership of Daniel McIntyre, Winnipeg's superintendent of education, and W.A. McIntyre, who from 1893 to 1933 was principal of the Manitoba Normal School. Music instruction in the schools commenced in 1890, when Daniel McIntyre appointed Carrie Day as the first supervisor of music to provide singing as an obligatory part of the daily program. As did many other music teachers of that day, Miss Day presented a public demonstration, in which five hundred children took part, and thereby helped to widen the popular acceptance of music. According to one newspaper account, 'the children were learning to read music, and were praised for their volume and sweetness of tone.'[25] In 1894 Mrs S. Thompson, a graduate of the New England Conservatory of Music, became supervisor of music and also taught in the high school. Mrs Thompson had studied with Hosea Holt, so it is not surprising that *The Normal Music Course* (written by John Tufts and Hosea Holt) was used in Winnipeg around this time.

The influence of American educators is also evident in the work of the next music supervisor in Winnipeg, Laurence H.J. Minchin. Although a British church organist by background, he was committed to Holt's use of 'moveable doh' in methodology for elementary classes. Minchin was appointed as music supervisor in 1897 at an annual salary of nine hundred dollars. In 1898 a school management committee report stated: 'In a 20-minute exercise each day, music is taught as a subject that refines and sweetens life. A taste for good music is a safeguard against attractions of a lower order, and a subject that promotes morality.'[26] The report goes on to suggest that music was one of the 'best taught subjects in the programme.'[27] Later school board documents refer to Minchin as a special music teacher, and until 1904 he was registered in the city directory as a music dealer. Minchin seems to have left Winnipeg around 1905. This brief career notwithstanding, Minchin was the first person to compile school music books specifically for western Canadian schools, *The King Edward Music Readers*. The first of the three books in this series was written by Minchin and W.A. McIntyre. From 1903 on, four editions of these books were published by the Morang Educational Company of Toronto and were eventually approved for use in Manitoba, Saskatchewan, Alberta, and British Columbia. The series appeared in the Manitoba *Programme of Studies* up until 1913. In writing about music in the schools, Minchin stressed the need to develop reading skills and 'to cultivate in the pupil a love for music and a taste that will appreciate what is best.'[28] The development of taste was a common theme around the turn of the century. Minchin's co-author, McIntyre, resoundingly favoured repertoire over skills: 'Too much attention cannot be given to the proper singing of suitable school songs. It is to such singing rather than to the graded exercises of the music readers that we are to look for the best results. Better a few selections sung with feeling, than pages gone over in a heartless mechanical fashion.'[29] Actually, Book I of the *King Edward* series presented several pages of exercises before any songs were introduced, and even then the quality of the song material offered little help for the cultivation of taste.

Much of the support that school music enjoyed in Winnipeg can be linked to the interest and direct involvement of the McIntyres, who were prominent leaders with progressive ideas in education. Both held their academic positions for lengthy terms and travelled extensively in order to keep up with new developments in other places. In many aspects of education Winnipeg furnished the models for the rest of the province; certainly this was true in the field of music.

Principal W.A. McIntyre taught music himself at the normal school, and as editor of the *Manitoba School Journal* he wrote on several occasions about methods of teaching music in the elementary classroom. His deep interest is shown in his statements about the value of music. In reference to folk songs he stated: 'They are the birthright of all children. Just as we revere the old poets and painters and keep their productions before us even to the exclusion of the modern, so the old, old songs and selections that time has rendered precious, should claim first place in the education of the young. And this applies to Music in the home, the school and the church.'[30] In the same article he declared, 'It is a cause for congratulation that the teaching of Music is receiving such attention in the public schools.'[31] With such a strong commitment on the part of professional educators, it is not surprising that music in Winnipeg's schools was more firmly established than in most Canadian cities in the west.

Such positive beginnings paved the way for the dedicated career of Annie Pullar, who served the Winnipeg board for forty-two years, first as a teacher and from 1905 until 1937 as supervisor of music. Reportedly, for many years the other teachers referred to Annie Pullar as 'Dame Melody.'[32] Miss Pullar was a product of Winnipeg's own school system and a graduate of the provincial normal school. A vocal soloist in Grace Church and Old St Andrews, she was well known for her love of sensitive singing. Throughout her lengthy career she devoted herself to the day-to-day task of teaching and supervising singing from grades one to nine and was publicly commended for encouraging the participation of school groups during the early years of the competitive festival.

Music was listed in 1892 as a subject in the Manitoba *Programme of Studies* for high schools. Although it never found a secure place in the senior grades, high school choral activities seemed just as natural to Winnipeggers as did classroom singing in the primary grades. A literary and musical society was formed in 1890 at Winnipeg Collegiate (later known as Daniel McIntyre Collegiate Institute). Sharon Dueck reports that 'in 1898 school choirs, including a Glee Club and a Girls' Chorus, were officially organized. That year also saw the presentation of a "popular Saturday Night Concert," featuring choirs, instrumental soloists and an orchestra, held in Winnipeg's Board of Trade Auditorium.'[33] In 1912 Mrs V. Brostedt was appointed general instructor in music at St John's Technical High School. Responding to the criticism that high school music had been 'mostly chorus singing and that largely as an adjunct to entertainment,'[34] she recommended appreciation, history, and the organization of an orchestra, for a truly comprehensive program. Her article, 'Music in the High School,' concluded with the following statement: 'We are no longer a pioneer people. We are to become a mighty Dominion, and great things are demanded of us if we are to fulfill the destiny for which we were created. Let us teach the coming generation to sing and appreciate good music, which will tend to purer lives and a higher, nobler citizenship, keeping in mind that greatness does not consist of intellect alone, but in strength of character, high ideals, and a broad sympathy for all mankind.'[35] Such high hopes were not realized immediately, for high school music in Manitoba did not flourish until the period between the two world wars, and even then it was concentrated largely in a few schools in Winnipeg.

The first school boards in Brandon were also progressive and visionary in their policies. Carl Bjarnason writes:

This was no body of western-rustics, bent on merely the rudimentary essentials of the three R's. These trustees and the people they employed recognized with almost prophetic understanding the real ingredients of education, embodying the desire for growth, change and individual initiative. True, they possessed meagre funds and at the outset provided nondescript buildings; but seldom did these trail-blazers resort to the nostalgic habit of looking backwards, of making do, or of trying to perpetuate merely the rough-and-ready essentials of the pioneer town. On the contrary these hardy, first-generation Manitobans strove to nourish a tradition and a measure of culture. These they hoped would reflect the background which many of them had known in Eastern Canada or Europe. The early trustees were frequently professional people or men successful in business. For the most part they perceived above all, that the future of the raw, primitive, uncouth prairies depended on the development of education. Only with better schools could their children receive the opportunities now so far away, and only by education could the community enjoy a degree of culture, tradition and progress.[36]

In 1891, less than ten years after the city of Brandon had been incorporated, its school board decided that music instruction should continue even though 'resources at that time [would] not permit paying a music teacher the salary paid to a primary-teacher.'[37] Subsequently, a Miss Davidson was engaged to teach music at an annual salary of three hundred dollars. Alfred White was appointed music supervisor in 1904 and held that position until 1909, when he became superintendent of education. It is not surprising, therefore, that in 1911 Superintendent White recommended 'closing the schools to give school children the privilege of attending St. Paul's Symphony.'[38] A few years later an elementary school orchestra trained by Professor Williams proved to be a source of great interest.

Attitudes among Manitoba's educators were similar to those of their counterparts in Ontario regarding the nature of music, its importance relative to other subjects, and its place on the timetable. The following statements appeared in an article concerning an ideal primary school timetable: 'Thought subjects should be taken when the pupils are brightest (preferably in the morning), and should be followed by subjects which bring the presentative or representative powers into activity ... Subjects which do not require the exercising of the thought powers may be left until later in the day ... Writing should never be taken just after violent exercise ... Music is best after a recess in the open air.'[39]

The immigration of new Canadians to the west brought with it an infusion of European culture; the situation was of major concern to superintendents and school inspectors, who felt that the Canadianization of these peoples was essential to the future of the nation. Educators regarded music as an important means of accomplishing this goal and used patriotic songs in school assemblies, Empire Day celebrations, and other public events, including occasional visits from members of the royal family. W.A. McIntyre wrote: 'Music can also reach the national life through the school. When as in Winnipeg, as many as 30 nationalities meet in one building, it is no small thing that they unite in all the exercises of the day, and sink the differences of race, creed and language in order to become Canadians.'[40] The determination of ethnically British inspectors to Canadianize children of other ethnic origin was even more evident in the rural areas, where teachers were urged to use patriotic songs in schools with children of predominantly European background. Nevertheless, this somewhat utilitarian interest in music did not ensure that the subject was dealt with satisfactorily in every school. One rural inspector reported in 1902: 'There is more or less singing in all the schools, but comparatively little teaching of the subject. Constant changing of teachers and irregular attendance appear to affect this subject even more adversely than most of the other subjects.'[41] References in annual reports suggest that most people were pleased if rote singing was reasonably successful, and if the music instruction included some reading skills, this seemed to satisfy normal expectations. One could say that the philosophy of music education was simple and unsophisticated. Occasionally, however, school inspectors showed far-sighted vision by outlining aims and objectives which went beyond technical work and attempted to cultivate an appreciation of the art. It was often suggested that the gramophone should be utilized as a means of accomplishing such goals. The historian Keith Wilson observes that the problems of urban and rural districts were becoming increasingly disparate during the period from 1897 to 1916, and concludes that 'the province was fortunate in its educational leadership but unfortunate in its political leadership.'[42] To be sure, music in the Winnipeg schools thrived on the benefits of such enlightened educational leadership, but in rural communities the subject was taught only incidentally or, in many places, not at all. Winnipeg and Brandon were unusual in that much of the music instruction was assigned to special music instructors rather than general classroom teachers. This tradition has persisted although, in practice, there has never been any real consistency. The fundamental flaw in school music remained – normal schools did not provide the appropriate training for music specialists. The educational patterns and methodology found in Manitoba were derived from several sources: there was the influence of church music, particularly the British choral tradition, in the urban centres; later, some schools absorbed pedagogical ideas from the United States, and others were affected by teachers who had received their training in Ontario. Consequently, the repertoire used in music education in Winnipeg retained a British flavour, but the approach was modified to some extent by American school methods. Rural areas were less affected by British practice or customs and tended to preserve whatever ethnic traditions were represented in the community.

BRITISH COLUMBIA

CULTURAL LIFE IN VICTORIA

Before the 1870s there were few settlements of any consequence in which Europeans had established permanent communities in the west. In addition to the Red River district in Manitoba, there were the communities of Victoria and Nanaimo on Vancouver Island and the mainland settlements along the Fraser River from New Westminster to Lillooet.

Victoria's culture derived its early impetus from officials of the Hudson's Bay Company as well as from British military and naval officers. Parades, ceremonies, and military exercises were part of official life, but the military personnel, particularly those who were accompanied by their families, also initiated civilian activities that were traditions in the old country. Many officers and their wives were well-educated people with somewhat aristocratic backgrounds, and in trying to re-create the way of life of Victorian England, they indulged in entertainments that can be described only as pretentious for a frontier community. Thus, military leaders became patrons of the arts in these early settlements. The gold rush had lured a cosmopolitan population into British Columbia, so community life was enhanced by groups such as the Germania Sing Verein, a singing club of German residents, and a French group, Les Enfants de Paris, both established in 1861. Enthusiasm for the busy schedule of amateur performances was expressed, albeit in excess, by a writer in 1866:

> Isolated as we are from the great centres of civilization, driven to the verge of melancholy madness by the dull monotony of the times, ever and anon we need some enlivenment. Endless debates about constitutional law argued with any amount of ability and erudition, in the course of time grow wearisome, dismal statistics touching our commercial policy tortured to prove anything and everything, pall upon the appetite of the most enthusiastic devourers of news items, and even sensational robberies become 'flat, stale and unprofitable;' it is well, therefore, that we should occasionally recur to such innocent recreation, in the shape of theatrical and musical amusement, as the limited artistic resources of the colony will allow. In comparison with the population there are few cities on the Pacific Coast enjoy greater advantages than Victoria.[43]

Bands and orchestras were abundant in the musical life of Victoria. In addition to having the naval and military ensembles, citizens of Victoria formed their own musical groups, some of which date back to the 1860s. The Nanaimo Brass Band, founded in 1872, has had a long history; many others were in existence only for a short time as a result of the erratic patterns of some bandmasters of that day. It seems that instrumentalists were forever forming bands and regrouping under one conductor or another, sometimes in response to the charisma of a new leader and at other times in response to a shift in loyalty or a change of sponsor. What they may have lacked in refinement they made up for in spirit, colour, and enthusiasm. For example, in 1882 there was a band contest between the Excelsior Band of New Westminster and a Victoria band; musicians, one from each city, were to act as judges. A notice appeared in the Victoria *Colonist* shortly afterward: 'The Young Men's Amateur Brass Band challenge the Militia Band to compete with them before competent judges, non-residents of this city, for any sum from $250 to $500 aside. The challenged party to name the day.'[44] Nevertheless, it is clear from a perusal of Dale McIntosh's *Documentary History of Music in Victoria*[45] that band or orchestral performances were not always of a high order. An 1892 newspaper report reads: 'THAT ALLEGED ORCHESTRA: The audience at the Victoria Theatre last evening expressed in anything but whispers, their disgust at the music supplied by the so-called orchestra. The people went to the opera house last evening to see something out of the ordinary run of shows and they were not disappointed. They did not, however, care to have their pleasure marred by the alleged music between the acts. The gallery drowned the "noises" made by the orchestra in hisses, and they were heartily seconded by theatre-goers in other parts of the house.'[46] There was a plethora of colourful teachers in the early days of Victoria offering their services as purveyors of the arts. In 1862 Digby Palmer advertised:

MUSIC! MUSIC! MUSIC! Mr. Digby Palmer, the celebrated composer, teacher of the Pianoforte, singing and pianoforte teacher, late Band Master of the H[onourable] E[ast] I[ndia] C[ompany] Service, Bombay and London, would be happy to receive pupils for the pianoforte and singing. Pianofortes tuned and repaired in the most finished style. Digby Palmer is open to an appointment as organist, choir master, or harmonium player, at church or chappel. For list of Digby Palmer's own compositions and testimonials, apply at Messrs. Hibben and Carswell, Stationer's Hall.[47]

Some music teachers delighted in flaunting their international training and expertise. Mme De Meudon Dancourt advertised thus in 1874: 'Pianist and Teacher of Music offers her services to those in search of a musical education. Many years of successful experience as a teacher and performer are a guarantee of perfect satisfaction. Speaks English, German and French.'[48] Notwithstanding their idiosyncracies, private teachers were the leading spirits in many musical endeavours in the community.

Church choirs were the mainstay of vocal music, for their conductors, accompanists, and soloists were in the forefront of community choral societies, music clubs, operetta companies, and other performing organizations. Oratorios and large-scale concerts were often staged in churches by a cross section of the entire community, a practice which transcended the traditional denominational boundaries. Music drew the church into the centre of the city's social and cultural life. C. Herbert Kent recalled:

> In my boyhood days I practically lived among musical people, as all my friends of that time were gifted, and owing to my late mother possessing a beautiful soprano voice, which was always in demand for concerts, choir and church work, and scores of charitable events, it was my privilege and duty, when my age permitted, to accompany her to the rehearsals and performances, and I felt very important when asked by the accompanists of those days to turn the music for them ... One of the principal annual local events which was always looked forward to with eagerness and pleasure was the sacred concert held in the old St. Andrew's Presbyterian Church ... The choir of those days was up in a sort of gallery over which the minister sat, and it was from this lofty elevation that many of the oratorios were rendered in a most praiseworthy manner, practically all the principal singers of Victoria, regardless of the denomination [taking part in] this much looked forward to event.[49]

Many types of buildings were used for teaching, rehearsing, and staging entertainments and social events. In some cases the facilities were located in music stores, theatres, and hotels, particularly when the activity was secular, as in the case of minstrel shows, visiting operetta companies, and other travelling troupes. Rivalry among Victoria's musicians and teachers led to the establishment of numerous private schools and conservatories. Ladies' Collegiate, established in 1860, became Angela College in 1866, and despite a rapid turnover of teachers it enjoyed more continuity than most institutions. Many other schools were short-lived; some questionable financial dealings suggest they were not always founded by persons of the highest integrity. Victoria had been a bustling commercial centre in gold rush days, and in some aspects of its musical history it shows the character and colour of a boom town.

In 1862 the following notice appeared in the *Colonist*: 'Messrs. Jessop and Chisholm beg to announce ... that they have opened a Singing School for giving instruction in vocal music every Wednesday evening [from 7:00 to 9:00]. Terms ... $2 per month. Fees payable in advance.'[50] Although the identity of Mr Chisholm remains in doubt, we do know a great deal about Mr Jessop, for he later became the leading educator in the province. In 1865, when David Spencer organized singing classes in Victoria, there was specific reference to the new Tonic Sol-fa system. Spencer was a prominent dry goods merchant but he was also known as a vocalist and choir director of Metropolitan Methodist Church. A newspaper report in 1866 provides details on the scope of his project: 'SINGING CLASS: We had the pleasure of hearing Mr. D. Spencer's Sol-Fa class ... and were really somewhat surprised to find that they had made such progress, considering the short time the pupils have been learning. The class is composed of members of the Methodist Church, about 50 in number, ranging from the chubbiest little atoms of humanity to the full grown Basso Profundo.'[51] Within a short period of time another report appeared, containing evidence of the progress made by his singing class:

NEW TONIC SOL-FA SYSTEM at Victoria Theatre: A Music Festival ... under the patronage of His Excellency the Governor. Mr. D. Spencer's Tonic Sol-fa Class numbering 100 voices will sing an excellent selection of sacred, and secular pieces varying the entertainment with solos, duets, and trios. The proceeds of the evening are to be devoted to the purchase of books etc. for the better instruction of the class. The performers, who included young and old of both sexes, occupied seats on the stage in front of the drop curtain, the leader being mounted on a rostrum erected in front of the footlights ... Mr. Spencer explained the theory of his system through the medium of a little boy named Fox, who proved himself to be quite adept, and was loudly cheered by the audience.[52]

Other singing schools were conducted by Professor Rutan, a teacher who had graduated from the New York Institute for the Blind, and J. Millar, who organized a singing school of sacred music in 1877.

MUSIC AND EDUCATION IN THE PROVINCE

The rugged geography of mountains and rivers accounts for the scattered population and the remoteness of communities in the province of British Columbia. Because the patterns of cultural life in Victoria were not typical of those on the mainland, it is difficult to generalize about the overall growth of music education beyond a few references to individual communities. The first mainland settlement, at New Westminster, was influenced by the presence of the Royal Engineers. A number of them applied their musical talents to dramatic and musical entertainments, most notably Private William Haynes, who led a band and an orchestra. Arthur T. Bushby was a prominent civil servant whose versatile musical talents, both vocal and instrumental, stimulated the cultural life of the community. Choral music took on new life when Bishop Sillitoe and his wife arrived around 1880 and formed the New Westminster Choral Union. Although Vancouver was not an important centre initially, it experienced phenomenal growth after the announcement that the terminal for the Canadian Pacific Railway would be located there.

The first schools were organized by missionaries or clergy sponsored by the Hudson's Bay Company. The company brought Reverend Robert Staines to Victoria as schoolmaster and chaplain of the fort. Mrs Staines, his wife, was qualified to teach all subjects, including music, and may have been 'the first practicing musician'[53] on Vancouver Island. Another Anglican, Reverend Edward Cridge, arrived in 1855 to carry on the work in education. He was a keen cellist and participated fully in the musical life of the community. Though Cridge was superintendent of the public shools, he and his wife also operated a private boarding school for young ladies.

The Anglicans were prominent in the field of education and used music as a liaison between church and school, especially in their mission programs. Reverend James Reynard, who arrived from England in 1866, serves as an example; McIntosh notes that he 'was first associated with the Indian Mission and Christ Church Cathedral in Victoria. In 1868 he was posted to Barkerville where he assumed responsibility for the parish of St. Saviour in that rough and ready mining community.'[54] Wherever Reynard was sent, he organized brass bands, which performed for church services and community entertainments.

McIntosh finds that 'British Columbia Indian bands are actually of two types, those which developed in the Indian Residential and Day Schools, and those which were organized among the adult population of the various native villages.'[55] The first band of native players in a school setting was formed in 1864 at St Mary's Mission, near Mission City. This was a Roman Catholic school operated by the Oblates of Mary Immaculate.

William Duncan, an enterprising though somewhat controversial Anglican layman, pioneered several unusual educational projects in northern British Columbia. Among his schemes, he formed an adult brass band at Metlakatla in the 1870s. After 1898 the Salvation Army also cultivated brass bands in this region, and for years intense rivalries existed among native aggregations. Isabella Geddes Large, a graduate of the Toronto Conservatory of Music, worked among the coast Indians of northern British Columbia, where her husband served as a medical doctor, first at Bella Coola and later at Fort Simpson (later known as Port Simpson). Writing in 1912, she described the natives as 'a music-loving people, ready to come to any number of practices and to spend any amount of time on their music.'[56] Their musical efforts were channelled into bands, which furnished music for weddings, funerals, village feasts, and other celebrations, and choirs, which functioned according to the traditions of the Christian church. Her work was frustrating in other ways because, apart from four months in the winter, native people spent a great deal of time trapping, fishing, and working in logging camps. Nonetheless, in the fall of each year most Indian villages were busy organizing choirs to prepare carols and anthems for Christmas services and entertainments. Mrs Large wrote: 'They attempt very often more difficult compositions than they can do well ... but as they are a very proud people, resenting criticism, and fairly well satisfied with their own ability to manage things, one has to use infinite care and tact when trying to help them. Three years ago an Indian choir came over from one of the Alaska villages to visit Port Simpson, and gave the Messiah in its entirety.'[57] Evidently, she heard very little of their own native music, which to her ears 'consisted of a weird minor chant accompanied by the rhythmic beating of a drum.'[58] The legacy of the British traditions imposed by missionaries over a period of fifty years can be seen in the following account:

Their brass band is the best Indian band in the Province, numbering thirty-five pieces, and has taken prizes at several provincial competitions. They also enjoy the distinction of having played before His Majesty in Vancouver when he visited Canada as Prince of Wales some few years ago; and one of their number is the proud possessor of, and plays the 'pipes,' presented to him by Lord Dundonald, after visiting Port Simpson about 1904. This band paid a bandmaster from Prince Rupert to help them last winter, and under his baton gave a very good concert, playing the overtures from Zampa, and Semiramide, also Tannhauser March, as well as a few popular numbers. Several concerts were given in the village during the winter by various organizations, and while some of their attempts were amusing rather than entertaining, many of the people show marked native ability; and when we realize they are little more than a generation removed from the old heathen dances and barbarous customs ... we are surprised that with their very limited opportunities they have made such progress.[59]

The Sisters of St Ann have a long tradition in education and music in British Columbia. Four of them arrived in Fort Victoria in 1858 from Montreal via Panama, and by 1863 Sister Mary Praxede was teaching music at St Ann's Convent School. Their work in music was extended to New Westminster, where they offered piano instruction at St Ann's Academy, founded in 1865. The Sisters also taught music at academies in Nanaimo (established 1877), Kamloops (established 1880), and Vancouver (established 1888). The first piano in the city of Kamloops was purchased by St Ann's Academy, and even before the first public school existed, the Kamloops Academy was regarded as 'a centre of culture in the development of music and art';[60] without it, many of the early residents of the city would have remained uneducated. Music departments were among the strongest divisions of the academies, and piano instruction was usually their forte. They prepared students for examinations set by various institutions, among others, the Associated Board of the Royal Schools of Music and the McGill Conservatorium. The Sisters of St Ann were also involved with an Indian school on Kuper Island, where Father Gustave Donckele had started a boys' band in 1890 'to cultivate a taste for music and gradually have them do away with their baneful dances.'[61] Within a year twenty-five boys had learned to read and play many pieces of music. But not all schools offering music were under church auspices: one year before the Sisters of St Ann commenced their work in New Westminster, a Miss Joyce had opened a private school for young ladies in which French, music, drawing, and singing were available as extras. Fees were three dollars a month for older children.

Music in the Public Schools

Although there was an early tradition of public denominational schools in Victoria, free and non-denominational schools were not established in British Columbia until 1872, and then only after a long and bitter struggle. School attendance was a serious problem in the late nineteenth century. Up until 1888 the percentage of attendance was only slightly above 50 per cent, and before Confederation the schools were educating only 20 per cent of the school-age population.

John Jessop was a central figure in the development of public schools in British Columbia. Jessop came to Ontario from England in 1846 and attended the Toronto Normal School in 1853. After a brief teaching career in Ontario, he went west during the gold rush and in 1860 founded the *Daily Press* in Victoria. Jessop returned to teaching in 1861, when he opened Central School, his own private institution. As he was interested in music himself, it followed that Central should offer both vocal and instrumental music. In 1864 Jessop was appointed principal of Victoria public schools and eventually became the first superintendent of education (1872–8) for the newly formed province of British Columbia. Jessop sought advice and assistance from Egerton Ryerson, for whom he had 'an admiration verging on hero worship.'[62] Between them there was also 'the common bond of religion, Ryerson being the most prominent Methodist in Canada.'[63] Not surprisingly, Jessop's educational policies bore a close resemblance to those advocated by Ryerson. A strong justification for music in the schools was set out in his second annual report: 'A knowledge of vocal music is of more practical value than mathematics, yet there is no gainsaying the fact that probably nine out of ten persons of both sexes will find far more use, and derive greater benefit from, a fair knowledge of this subject than from mathematics beyond the simple rules of arithmetic. But its practical value in after life is but one argument, among many, why it should be carefully and generally taught. Its utility in the school room in maintaining order, in the enforcement of discipline, and as an incentive to study, cannot be overestimated.'[64] In concluding a lengthy discussion of music, he wrote: 'It might be argued that all teachers have not a taste for vocal music, probably not, neither have all teachers a particular bias for English grammar or algebra, yet all are obliged to teach the former at least. With the requisite amount of application, the theory of vocal music can be acquired and taught by all.'[65] But Jessop's desire to introduce music in the schools met with testy opposition from the editor of the *Colonist*: 'From the plan suggested by Mr. Jessop, the children will be taught to sing just about the time the Railway whistle is heard at Esquimalt on the arrival of the first through train from Canada … Unless Mr. Jessop can suggest some more feasible scheme than that suggested, he may consider the matter indefinitely postponed and that the subject of vocal music will furnish matter for a forthcoming Report on Education.'[66] In spite of public criticism, music enrolments soared in the two years following the 1873 report in which Jessop articulated his philosophy of music education; by 1875 more than half the school population was registered in music. In reference to Chilliwack, Jessop commented, 'The elements of music are efficiently taught, the whole school having considerable knowledge of the subject as far as transposition.'[67] The situation at Chilliwack was probably exceptional, as music instruction was concentrated in the schools surrounding Victoria, where Jessop's influence was strong. Moreover, this rapid growth was destined to be short-lived, for the 1876–7 report indicated that less than a third of the school population was enrolled in music that year. Despite the fact that Jessop listed music as a regular part of the curriculum, it is doubtful that the subject was actually taught in most schools. Like Ryerson, Jessop had so many concerns of a political nature that his plans for music in education were never fully implemented. He ran into considerable controversy over his Central Boarding School project at Cache Creek, and in 1878 the 'Ryerson of British Columbia' resigned when the government threatened to reduce his salary.

Enrolment in public schools escalated at an unprecedented rate from 1878 to 1900. During this period an increasing number of students enrolled in music, but the percentage of the school population involved in music declined from 36 per cent in 1878 to 25 per cent in 1900. School music in the 1880s and 1890s flourished mainly in Victoria, Esquimalt, New Westminster, and Chilliwack, and the most enthusiastic reports came from those places which hired special music teachers to give the instruction. The Victoria Girls' School was pleased with a trained musician who was skilled in the Tonic Sol-fa method, and authorities in New Westminster expressed great satisfaction with Professor J. Rushton for his work in their schools. An inspector's report reveals the attitudes which prevailed in 1892: 'Although singing is still an optional subject, the annual returns show that there has been a considerable increase in the number of pupils who have received instruction in this branch. Music is recommended on many grounds, especially as a means of securing wholesome and cheerful discipline. There is no exercise that children enjoy so thoroughly, and their joyous attention shows how their feelings have been stirred. In an altered mood they resume their studies, and pursue them with fresh zeal. Perhaps all our teachers do not see its utility in this light, or it may be that some have no musical talent.'[68] The reasons which prompted educational leaders to make music an optional subject apparently had more to do with the inadequacies of teachers than with the needs of students. In 1895 Inspector William Burns wrote: 'Music depends so greatly upon the individual ability of the teacher that it must always remain an optional subject. In many schools the children are taught singing by ear, in a few by the tonic sol-fa system, in each case this subject forms an agreeable change from the other school exercises.'[69] The superintendents who succeeded Jessop were not committed to the notion that music should be a compulsory subject, nor did they outline a course of study to be followed, as they did for other subjects. Eventually, in 1894, the department of education endorsed *Bannister's Textbook on Music*; this suggests that teachers were expected to go beyond the singing of songs and were encouraged to offer a more systematic form of instruction. There was also some lively dialogue concerning the place of music in education. When the Victoria Ministerial Association took up the torch for music in the schools, its action provoked an irate letter to the editor objecting to yet another 'ornamental subject.' The writer elaborated: 'The public having to pay for the instruction, will be entitled to the amusement – as also to the evils that may ensue. Put young people on the stage, no matter whether it be for a performance at a Sunday School room or in a theatre, and then after having tasted popular applause and seen themselves in fancy costumes and personages it will be found that they will hanker after more – but elsewhere. Is this desirable? May not the, of course, all-wise ministerial association, by aiming at one object, find they have missed it and led the young into another path altogether?'[70] This letter may not have reflected the general attitude, but it does testify to some strong feelings here and there. It is noteworthy that at the 1902 Kootenay Teachers' Institute in Nelson, Mr W. Elley presented a paper entitled 'Should Music Be Taught in Our Schools?' – an indication that there was some concern among teachers as well as among the general public.

A quickening of interest in school music took place after the turn of the century. In 1906 the Victoria school board considered the introduction of singing as a special subject and formed a committee to look into the relative merits of Tonic Sol-fa and staff notation. This initiative led to the appointment of William Dobson; originally from Birmingham, England, he moved from Toronto in 1907 to fill the Victoria position. However, the trustees were not easily satisfied and, after reviewing his work at the end of the year, decided not to renew the contract. In his place they hired Harry James Pollard for nine hundred dollars per annum, one hundred dollars less than Dobson's salary. A report in 1912 reveals that trustees were also divided in their support for Pollard. Some recognized the difficulties brought on by increased enrolments and in Pollard's defence contended that 'he had not neglected note singing, using the modulator, blackboard and hand signs'[71] – it seems that Pollard had incorporated the main features of the Tonic Sol-fa system. Initially he taught classes for fifteen to twenty minutes per week, but later on he became a supervisor. Since Pollard was not a certified teacher himself, one trustee was sceptical that he would ever get the cooperation of classroom teachers. Nevertheless, he supervised music instruction in Victoria schools until 1927. Normal schools in British Columbia did not provide music training before 1913, so Pollard was expected to conduct in-service sessions after regular school hours. Such heavy responsibilities over a period of nineteen years eventually brought on poor health and a forced retirement.

The appointment of George Hicks as Vancouver's first supervisor of music was a landmark for music education in British Columbia. Hicks and his brothers Gideon and William emigrated from Plymouth, England, and became active in choral societies in Westminster, Victoria, and Vancouver. The monthly salary offered George Hicks as supervisor of music was $83.35, which was less than school janitors were paid at the time. Nevertheless, his appointment was enthusiastically received by W.P. Argue, city superintendent, who conceded that the task was a difficult one. His report for 1904–5 stated: 'For one year music has been systematically taught to all intermediate and junior grade pupils. This year the work will be extended to include senior grade students. Very gratifying progress has been made. As many teachers were without musical training, it was necessary for Supervisor, Mr. Hicks, to organize teachers' classes in each school. With the instruction given in these classes, and with the assistance given by the Supervisor on his regular visits to the various rooms, the teachers have succeeded in making music both a pleasant and profitable study.'[72] The next year Hicks conducted an eight-hundred-voice choir of school children in patriotic airs as part of the Empire Day celebrations, and by 1907 he had established annual school concerts in the Vancouver Opera House in order to give the public an opportunity of seeing and hearing for themselves the excellent results of the work of his department. Ironically, the 1907–8 report also expressed regrets that the department of education was not yet prepared to give financial support for the teaching of music at the provincial normal school. George Hicks was typical of successful music supervisors in that he capitalized on every opportunity to promote the cause of school music. A most ambitious effort was undertaken when the Duke of Connaught, Governor-General of Canada, visited Vancouver in 1912. On this occasion Hicks assembled a choir of forty-five hundred school children and two hundred teachers on the Aberdeen School grounds for a magnificent city reception. He reported that 'they sang and cheered in such a manner as to bring forth most flattering comments from their Royal Highnesses, [who said] it was the best children's singing they had ever heard.'[73]

In the summers of 1908 and 1913 Hicks travelled extensively to several Canadian and American cities, Britain, and continental Europe, where he observed school music in other settings. Upon his return, he affirmed that music in Vancouver's schools compared favourably with the best programs he encountered abroad. The philosophical ideas in his report of 1908 reflect those espoused in Great Britain and New England in their stress on the physical and mental effects of music and on music as an educative force. Hicks believed that instrumental music for boys and girls would be 'much better for them than running the streets at night and frequenting places whose moral tone is none too healthy.'[74] His moral sentiments were reiterated in the 1916 report, in which he stated, 'More music and less pool and cards for our boys should be our watchword.'[75] On a practical level his goals were 'sight-singing and self-expression in song, through intelligent appreciation and artistic interpretation.'[76]

The work of George Hicks can be characterized as more systematic than that of many of his contemporaries in school music. *The King Edward Music Readers*, developed in Manitoba, had been authorized as early as 1907 for use in British Columbia. However, by 1909 Hicks had produced some of his own materials, and in 1913 he issued a 'Manual and Syllabus of Instruction in Vocal Music,' a teacher's handbook outlining a detailed course of study. Designed for the 'non-musical teacher,' the methodology dealt with rote songs, reading, ear-analysis, and technical work at various levels. There were exercises using Tonic Sol-fa syllables and many references to songs from *The New Educational Music Reader*.[77] In 1914 the *King Edward* series was supplanted by a Canadian edition of *The New Educational Music Course* published by Ginn. Close examination of Hicks's syllabus shows that he had meticulously organized materials for his teachers, but the manner of instruction suggested regimentation and the tone was pedantic. Under 'How to Use the Books,' teachers were directed as follows:

Do not sing with your pupils. (You may pattern for them). Be careful that the machinery of your music lesson runs swiftly and smoothly, and the same every day. Do not allow them to waste time. Do not teach too much; let your pupils learn instead. Do nothing for them that they can do for themselves – it is not music alone that you are teaching.

Teach your pupils to start when you say 'Sing.'

Teach them to keep going until they reach the end of the song or exercise, unless you say the word 'Stop.'[78]

A unique feature of music education in Vancouver was the night school program. In a 1911 report, Hicks wrote, 'Realizing that a large number of our pupils pass from the Public School out into the cold, relentless world, where they are confronted with so many evil and debasing influences, we are endeavoring to make some provision whereby they can still continue the study of the divine art, by establishing classes in connection with our Night Schools, and we are delighted to see so many young men and women taking advantage of the opportunity.'[79] As encouragement to teachers to improve their backgrounds, they were admitted free of charge. In 1910, 67 teachers and 26 normal school students enrolled along with others from the community. A total of 212 persons registered in various courses, including an orchestra class of 25 players. This was a boon both for in-service teacher training and for the development of musical culture in the community. In 1911 the choral music class of the night school formed themselves into the Vancouver Musical Society and with the orchestra presented large choral works for the general public. By 1915 they had performed Sterndale Bennett's *May Queen* and Handel's *Messiah*; Hicks claimed they were 'the most important and influential musical organization in the City.'[80] He even considered establishing classes in various parts of the city in order to reduce the cost of the car ride for a large number of the people who wished to participate.

In addition to being faced with the heavy demands of night classes, Hicks was overwhelmed with increased student enrolment in the day school operation and a corresponding influx of teachers. Since most new teachers had little background in music, it was up to the music supervisor to remedy the situation. In 1912, when a hundred new teachers were added to the Vancouver school system, the board appointed Miss Constance Butler to assist with music supervision in the junior grades; although this measure eased the work load for Hicks, the appointment was soon discontinued because of the financial restraints imposed by the war. A competitive festival was inaugurated in 1914 with twelve schools participating, its climax a grand finale in which a thousand students took part. There were three thousand children involved by 1917, but in the following year – again owing to wartime restrictions – it became necessary to have adjudicators visit classrooms individually. According to Hicks, much of the excitement was lost when the festival had to operate under these conditions.

Hicks worked diligently to promote instrumental music in the schools. As early as 1909 he organized a young people's orchestra composed of twenty-seven boys and girls and three adults. This project was integrated with the night school class and for several years furnished opportunities for adult participation. Hicks urged the board to introduce instrumental music as part of an overall plan to extend music instruction into the high schools. Almost annually he expressed regret that the lack of continuity from the elementary grades to the night school classes for adults left high school students without any real opportunity to develop their abilities in music. One of the first elementary school orchestras was organized in the Strathcona School during the 1918–19 year; it consisted of six violins, two cornets, one clarinet, one mandolin, a drum, and piano. Unfortunately, Hicks died during that same year and never did fulfil his dream of having instrumental music as a subject in the high school curriculum.

What Hicks managed to achieve in Vancouver was not characteristic of the entire province. Even in Victoria and in New Westminster (where F.T.C. Wickett was music supervisor from 1912 to 1922) music did not command much recognition as a subject. And in the province as a whole, school music neither flourished nor achieved any particular distinction, except in isolated cases in which good results may have been attained by extraordinary teachers. George Green summarized the situation: 'The subject of music has not received as much attention as other subjects on the curriculum for the following reasons: it was not a compulsory subject; no course in music was outlined until 1919; little expert instruction has been given to the subject in normal schools; few inspectors have had sufficient musical ability to inspect the schools in the subject.'[81]

HIGH SCHOOL MUSIC AND TEACHER TRAINING

Early in his term as superintendent, John Jessop recommended the establishment of high schools in British Columbia. One reason for opening high schools was that they could serve as teacher training institutions until a regular normal school was available. In initiating two such schools, one in Victoria and one in New Westminster, he had a three-fold plan, to have them function as high schools, training schools, and model schools. The curriculum of Victoria High School outlined by Jessop in 1877 included map drawing and music, and by 1880 the course of studies for high schools required all students to take music. Music was also specified in the curriculum of the junior division for the New Westminster High School, which opened in 1884.

Enrolment statistics for the province indicate that music was an established high school subject in the 1870s. This was so because a high school education constituted the academic prerequisite for a teaching career, and since Jessop felt that classroom teachers should provide music instruction, it followed that the subject should be obligatory in the secondary school curriculum. Before the founding of a provincial normal school, high school graduates could enter the teaching profession upon successful completion of the teachers' certification examinations. These were held annually over a period of several days in July. Jessop established a music component within the certification requirements, an examination which tested the candidate's knowledge of music theory and sometimes included a question on methodology. Jessop himself set and graded the music examinations, but they were discontinued during the next superintendency. When examinations were reinstated in 1888 by Superintendent S.D. Pope, they were not compulsory; candidates for a second class certificate could choose one of botany, drawing, or music. However, the music examinations for teacher certification were decidedly more difficult once they were put on an optional basis. The 1889 examination is shown below:

MUSIC, 1 and ½ hours, 200 marks (2nd Class, Grade B Certificate)
1) Define (a) Melody, (b) Interval, (c) Chord, (d) Harmony.
2) Explain the terms:
   (a) Tonic, (b) Mediant, (c) Dominant,
   (d) What is the harmonic triad?
3) Write the letters in the proper place on the staff, above and below middle C.
4) (a) What is Transposition?

(b) Explain fully why the signature of the key of D is two sharps.
5) Write the signatures of the flat keys on the treble staff.
6) (a) Write the different kinds of rests.
   (b) What is meant by ⅔ or ⅝ time?
7) Explain the following terms, and write the characters by which they are represented:
   (a) Tie
   (b) Appoggiatura
   (c) Shake
   (d) Turn
8) (a) Describe generally the Tonic Sol-fa System.
   (b) What are its advantages and disadvantages?
9) Explain the following terms:
   (a) Andante
   (b) Larghetto
   (c) Presto
   (d) Sforzando
   (e) Arpeggio
10) What are the characteristics of the following forms of musical composition, (a) Anthem (b) Cantata (c) Aria (d) Fantasia (e) Oratorio.[82]

A large number of those who attended high school did so with the deliberate purpose of entering the teaching field. In general, high schools in the late nineteenth century were oriented to the needs of future teachers and functioned like training schools rather than secondary schools in the modern sense.

In the post-Jessop years the status of elementary school music was changed from that of a compulsory subject to that of an optional one, and, increasingly, instruction was passed over to special music teachers. Once general teachers were not responsible for their own classroom music, the subject became less important as an academic course in high schools, and ultimately it declined. Whereas all students in Victoria had been registered for music until the mid-1880s, by the turn of the century the enrolment was negligible, and the role of music at this level changed in a fundamental way.

There was a long tradition of extra-curricular activities in Victoria High School. Rhymis Offerhaus was complimented 'for the efficient manner in which he conducted the musical exercises'[83] on the occasion of the Governor-General's visit in 1882; Howard Russell, a mathematics teacher and prominent choirmaster, founded a school orchestra in

1914; the school band played 'Rule Britannia' at the planting of the Kitchener Oak in 1917. Although there was an increase in ensemble activity, music as a curricular subject ceased to exist. In 1917 the inspector of schools for Victoria regretted that singing was not taught in the high school, especially since students who became teachers would eventually have to teach music in the classroom. J.H. Wormsbecker notes that in Vancouver's high schools 'music as an activity began in 1907 with the formation of girls' and boys' glee clubs and ... of a school orchestra in 1908.'[84] The first high school operetta was *The Flower Queen*, conducted by George Hicks in 1915. From 1913 until 1919, G.A. Ferguson directed a glee club at Britannia High School, and in 1914 Catherine McNiven formed an orchestra in the same school. By 1915 King Edward High School also had a glee club and an orchestra. A purely academic curriculum did not leave much room for other subjects, so by the end of the First World War music in the high schools of Vancouver had not progressed beyond these casual activities.

Of all the factors which thwarted the growth of public school music, the inadequacy of teacher training was seminal. Teachers' institutes were conferences held for two or three days in the summer or during the spring break. They were organized by the provincial department of education and provided a modicum of professional development before teacher training was initiated at the Vancouver Normal School in 1901. Superintendent S.D. Pope attempted to stimulate interest in music through a committee which arranged for musical entertainment as a regular feature of their meetings. Among those who gave papers was Mr A. Wilson, who presented 'The Necessity of Vocal and Physical Culture in the Schools' at the 1887 institute. But the appointment of Ethel Coney to the Vancouver Normal School in 1913 marked the formal beginning of teacher training in music. Coney held this position until her retirement in 1937. She also taught at summer sessions for teachers held in Victoria. Ida Morris, the first music teacher at the Victoria Normal School, was appointed in 1916, one year after the school was established. She returned to England after four years of service, and her position was not filled until 1922, when Miss G.G. Riddell was appointed. The general training given at these two institutions included rudimentary theory, some basic voice culture, and reading skills using sol-fa syllables. As time went on, the summer sessions held in Victoria offered more specialized training, and in the 1920s Coney was joined by other music teachers.

The University of British Columbia, incorporated in 1908, had been affiliated with McGill University before granting its own degrees in 1916. However, music in the university was virtually neglected until the period following the Second World War, when universities assumed more responsibility for teacher training, including the education of specialists in secondary school music.

THE NORTH-WEST TERRITORIES

The North-West Territories were formed in 1870, long before the establishment of Saskatchewan and Alberta as provinces; the territories were comprised of lands obtained from the Hudson's Bay Company. A few schools had emerged here and there in the territories as a result of the voluntary action of settlers or of Roman Catholic and Protestant missionaries. Schooling was a natural outgrowth of the desire to Christianize the native people, and the curriculum grew out of what George Sheane sees as an effort 'to give any useful kind of education to all classes.'[85] The initial attempts in education were centred in and around Edmonton, but only a few schools survived. The first permanent results were accomplished by the Grey Nuns, and, according to Sheane, 'the first school doing regular school work west of Manitoba was established at Edmonton in 1862 by Father Lacombe'; it was housed 'in a log chapel within the stockade of the fort.'[86] A number of Methodists came out in the 1860s from Upper Canada, including Reverend H.B. Steinhauer, a native Indian who had been influenced by Ryerson's work at Rama. Benjamin McKenzie, a graduate of St John's College in Winnipeg, taught in a Methodist school at Pakan on the North Saskatchewan River. He was a 'trained teacher with special ability in music,'[87] and from the forty half-breed, twenty Indian, and few white children he formed the first school choir in the North-West Territories. In 1883 Reverend James Turner taught at a Methodist mission school in Calgary. The Presbyterians organized a school in Prince Albert as early as 1866. Almost nothing more than these scattered efforts by religious groups existed before 1884, at which time the federal government created an administration that purportedly could deal more adequately with the needs of the people.

A normal school had operated in Manitoba since 1882, but the first public school teachers in the territories were certified by inspectors. It was not until 1889 that some basic teacher training became available in union schools,[88] and by 1893 a normal school had been established in Regina following the appointment of D.J. Goggin as superintendent of education for the North-West Territories. Before his appointment the curriculum had been nothing more than a list of textbooks. Goggin was educated in Ontario and until 1892 had been principal of the Manitoba Normal School; his revised curriculum of 1895 was modelled after the one which he had used there. It included music as a subject for elementary grades, prescribed textbooks which had been approved in Manitoba, and expected the normal schools to provide music training for classroom teachers. The strong similarity between the organization of music education in the North-West Territories and that in Manitoba can be traced back, through Goggin, to Ryerson's plan in Ontario.

The 1896 report of the superintendent of education contained a rather full statement on music indicating that Goggin valued the subject. He wrote: 'There is more or less music in every school but little systematic instruction. Rote songs are sung according to the taste of the teacher ... Music affords a culture for the soul as well as a training for the voice and only such songs should be learned as express noble and refining sentiments, for the taste can be educated downwards as well as upwards.'[89] There were serious problems in finding sufficient teachers in the territories because the population increased rapidly toward the end of the century. Furthermore, it was difficult to avoid attrition because rural teachers, especially those who came from outside the area, could not endure the rugged conditions and the loneliness of life among the foreign population. D.G. Scott Calder points out that 'the need for the home-trained teacher was urgent even before the province of Saskatchewan had been formed.'[90] The magnitude of the problem is shown in the following statistics: in 1886 the territories had 2553 students in 77 schools, and 84 teachers; in 1904 they had 25,191 students in 716 schools, and 1011 teachers.[91]

The first art and music instructor at the normal school was Miss Ellen Rankin, who had taught elementary school in Winnipeg. She was a graduate of the New York School of Art and frequently appeared at teachers' institutes, which Goggin promoted as a way of improving the quality of instruction in all subjects; most often her presentations dealt with the subject of drawing. The inadequate backgrounds of many of the new teachers probably offset whatever training in art and music Rankin was able to give; needless to say, music in the schools was not characterized by excellence or consistency. The music instruction offered by private teachers and other musicians in the community was, in general, superior to that of the public school programs, which were still in their formative stages. In 1887 a private school was established in Regina by Miss McReynolds, who was an organist at Knox Church. In addition to subjects such as English, French, and drawing, she taught vocal and instrumental music.

SASKATCHEWAN

MUSIC IN THE COMMUNITY

The first decade of Regina's cultural history was typical of the early history of prairie communities, in that there were musical clubs and societies offering a wide range of activities from sacred music to vaudeville and minstrel shows. According to the *EMC*, 'a Choral Society, formed in 1889, held weekly rehearsals and attempted to provide free instruction in vocal music and to assist at charitable entertainments.'[92] The residents of Regina also had the benefit of utilitarian forms of instrumental music provided by such ensembles as a North-West Mounted Police band and a brass band.

The building of the Canadian Pacific Railway had opened up the west for concert artists and theatrical troupes, and concert life improved with the advent of professional talent. Regina reached higher levels of performance after Frank Laubach arrived from Scotland in 1904 and, in Kallmann's words, 'became the undisputed leader in musical affairs until his retirement in 1922.'[93] Laubach organized the Regina Philharmonic Society, which was a large choral group; by 1906 he had also founded the first symphony orchestra as a regular part of the Philharmonic Society for performances of Handel, Haydn, and Mendelssohn oratorios. As early as 1907 there was a Regina conservatory of music with a staff of five teachers, including its two directors, Alfred Sturrock and Mrs Percival Dean. Its aim was 'to provide thorough, systematic and scientific instruction in music and such other subjects as may be necessary to develop the student mentally and physically, equipping him not only for the drawing-room and social circle, but also for concert, church and platform work, and for the teaching profession.'[94] It is not certain whether this institution had any connection with another Regina conservatory founded in 1911; the latter functioned as the music department of Regina College, an institution operated by the Methodist Church. In any event, in providing private instruction the conservatory helped to raise the calibre of music education in Regina. Musicians from the conservatory were often appointed as instructors in normal school and summer courses in music, and in this and other ways the institution became a focal point for the musical life of the community.

Unlike Regina, Saskatoon did not have one major conservatory dominating its musical life, but fortunately there were excellent private teachers and musicians active in the community. Some of them had emigrated from Great Britain, some had come from Quebec and Ontario, and a few had studied with teachers of international reputation; the quality of their work was a real inspiration in an isolated community like Saskatoon. F.W. Musselwhite, from the time of his arrival in 1903, was prominent as a choral director. Blanche St John-Baker was a piano teacher who had studied with Leopold Godowsky and Olga Varet-Stepanoff. She maintained a piano studio from 1908 until 1920 before moving on to Vancouver and Los Angeles to further her career. One of her students, Lyell Gustin, remained in Saskatoon for the duration of his career and received national recognition as an outstanding piano teacher.

Toward the outbreak of the First World War the city became a bustling centre of musical activity involving both local artists and international celebrities. The Saskatoon Philharmonic Society was established in 1908 and reached a membership of seventy-eight. The San Francisco Opera appeared in 1908, and from 1913 on there were annual productions of Handel's *Messiah*. The Toronto Conservatory of Music established a local examination centre in Saskatoon in 1911; shortly afterward, the Bell Conservatory and the Palmer School of Music opened teaching studios. During the First World War the Minneapolis Symphony Orchestra and Sousa's Band made visits to Saskatoon. One of the most dynamic organizations in the cultural community was the Women's Musical Club of Saskatoon, which was founded in 1912. This club required auditions because all members were expected to present papers and perform in recitals. It was only later on that associate memberships were available for those who were not active performers at the monthly meetings.

MUSIC IN THE ELEMENTARY SCHOOLS

The nominal support for school music which existed during D.J. Goggin's term as superintendent of education continued after Saskatchewan became a province in 1905. Educational leaders were always pleased to report musical activities which took place in the schools, but this token gesture of interest was never translated into any planned action whereby specific goals might be accomplished or uniform standards realized. Regina introduced music long before it was outlined as a subject of instruction in 1913 by the provincial department of education. Local officials were bursting with pride as they described their innovative action in the *Morning Leader*:

> Music and Drawing – As the educational metropolis of the new provinces, Regina evidenced its spirit of progressiveness and keeping abreast with the older educational centres, by the appointment this last year of a supervisor of art and music, this being the first such appointment in the new provinces, though other neighboring cities are following in the wake ... Art, including music, is not for the few, but is inherent and the rightful heritage of every individual; it is the basis of, and correlated with all other work, the highest and best form of self-expression. Where art training is omitted the child has not a fully rounded and developed life, but is mentally, morally and physically deformed.[95]

Miss Jessie Grier filled the new appointment in music. Two years later Miss Marie Lawson succeeded her as supervisor of music, and in 1909 the position was held by Miss L.A. Barrett. In Moose Jaw, Miss Lemon was designated as a special music teacher in 1906, and two years later Miss M.A. Stevenson became supervisor of music and drawing. The first music supervisor in Saskatoon, Miss Helgeson, was not hired until 1913, and then the appointment lapsed from 1915 until 1918, at which time Miss Sydney Aird assumed the responsibility for music. These early teachers did not remain in their jobs for very long, possibly because of the regulation that women had to resign as teachers once they married.

Annual reports implied that music instruction had progressed favourably in the towns, but there were frequent complaints about the teaching of music in rural schools. Comments invariably questioned the quality of teacher training, as in this excerpt from 1912: 'Drawing and singing [are] to a large extent neglected in the rural schools ... not because there is no time for teaching them, nor because the other subjects which are usually considered more important would be neglected, but because the teachers are not qualified to teach them, a defect which should be remedied as soon as possible.'[96] Saskatchewan's growth, like that of Manitoba, was in large measure a result of the influx of immigrants of many different European origins. Indeed, in 1911 almost half of Saskatchewan's population was of non-British stock. Usually the immigrants were from agricultural settings in Europe and were quite different from the sophisticated Europeans who frequented the international concert stage during this era. Furthermore, they were extremely practical in their interests and not always sympathetic to the value of education, especially in times of economic depression. Yet school inspectors, who were mostly of British ancestry, felt strongly that the schools should promote patriotism. One inspector reported, 'Several teachers in my foreign schools, as well as elsewhere, devote considerable time to the teaching of patriotic songs and from the appreciative manner in which the children sing I believe this is no mean step in nation building.'[97]

Although there were references to a new music course in 1907, the first description in the annual reports did not appear until 1913. Rote songs were prescribed and great emphasis was placed on voice culture. The course also called for the singing of scales and intervals using syllables, names, and pitches. *The King Edward Music Readers* – Book I for grades one to five, and Book II for the senior grades – were authorized. In the larger centres a special music teacher, usually trained in music but with little understanding of classroom techniques, came once a week to administer drills and exercises in sight-singing and ear training. Tonic Sol-fa was used extensively. However, the study of rudiments seemed to be the main preoccupation of the senior grades, for by 1919 'grade eight students were required to pass an examination in music theory in order to obtain their Grade eight diploma.'[98]

The 1919 music curriculum was identical, word for word, to the 1913 document, but the authorized texts had been changed to include *The Common School Book of Vocal Music, Dunstan's ABC of Musical Theory,* and *The New Normal Music Course* by John Tufts and Hosea Holt.[99] What is significant about this change is that the *King Edward* series, written for the western provinces and published in Canada, was being supplanted by British and American materials. Although *The New Normal Music Course* was published by a Toronto firm, it was actually a Canadian edition of a well-known American textbook.

MUSIC IN THE HIGH SCHOOLS

Music instruction took place mostly at the elementary school level, but toward the First World War there was an increase in extra-curricular high school activities. In 1911 there was a glee club in Regina, and there were more and more attempts to form orchestras, sometimes to accompany hymns in school assemblies or to present musical selections at oratorical contests and literary society meetings. Orchestras were also organized to enhance operetta productions, which were extremely popular at the time. Occasionally, adult instrumentalists were drawn from the community to bolster a struggling school orchestra in an operetta or theatrical presentation.

Nutana Collegiate in Saskatoon had a long and cherished tradition in music. R.N. Anderson, a commercial teacher, organized a school orchestra, and A.W. Cameron, an English teacher who was enthusiastic about choral singing, developed a number of musical activities in the school. In 1913 Cameron formed the Pauline Music Club, which produced annual operettas and presented choral concerts in the school and community. The club distinguished itself by winning several shields in the competitive festival; it also attracted members through its music appreciation activities. Later, when Cameron became principal of Nutana Collegiate, he was unable to continue this extra-curricular work in music. Like many other principals in Canadian schools, Cameron promoted music in the high school before education officials approved the subject for study and long before music teachers as such were appointed.

In 1917 Nutana's students raised the issue of music as a curricular subject in their publication the *Collegiate Hermes*: 'The Department of Education has expressed its intention to have music as a subject of study during each year of the Collegiate Course, and our students should be in a position to take full advantage of the opportunity.'[100] Although this suggestion was not implemented, sensitive educators such as A.W. Cameron fostered the desire for more music through their leadership in extra-curricular organizations. The introduction of music in the secondary schools of Saskatchewan, however, was not destined to take place until much later.

THE ROLE OF THE UNIVERSITY

The decision to locate the university in Saskatoon resulted in a wide range of benefits to the citizens of that city. Walter Murray, the founding president of the University of Saskatchewan, ardently supported the cause of music education in several ways. In 1909, F.W. Chisholm, a local musician, wrote to Murray regarding the place of music in the university curriculum, and received the following reply: 'The question of music has been brought before the University Senate, but no definite action has been taken. It is quite improbable that any provision will be made for instruction in Music, but it is possible that the University may follow the example of Toronto, and provide a syllabus for examinations and issue certificates to candidates who have passed the University examinations ... I think it important for the University to make some effort to stimulate the study of Music. The interest shown at the last Music Festival, and the need for something to fill up the long winter evenings is surely sufficient reason to justify the University in taking up this work.'[101] Some years later President Murray took the initiative in the establishment of the first music department among the universities of the west and was a leading spirit in organizing the Western Board of Music.

In 1916 the Saskatchewan government commissioned Dr Foght of Washington, DC, an expert in rural education, to make recommendations to the legislature regarding the provincial education system. Anticipating some major changes, R.A. Wilson, principal of the Regina Normal School, tried to enlist the support of Walter Murray. Wilson suggested to him that music should be given consideration as a high school subject, especially as an alternative for girls: 'It seems to me not much short of a tragedy to see a girl say of 17 years of age with very little talent for mathematics and a considerable talent for Music, struggling with the higher work in mathematics prescribed for the Senior Matriculation, hoping to get a bare pass, and with the intention of throwing aside the books forever when the examination is over, and all this time is obliged to abandon her Music on account of the pressure of work.'[102] A number of others urged President Murray to assist in recognizing the educational value of music through private study. In 1917 he supported a recommendation to the department sent by the Saskatchewan Provincial Musical Association that music be approved as an elective in collegiates and high schools. This support was typical of his keen interest in music, and had the result that educators and musicians throughout the province looked to him frequently for leadership and inspiration in cultural matters.

THE SASKATCHEWAN PROVINCIAL MUSICAL ASSOCIATION

Through the collaboration of Frank Laubach and F.W. Chisholm, the music festival movement in Saskatchewan commenced in 1909 with 400 participants and an audience of 1500 people in attendance at the final program in Regina. In 1912, 750 participants competed in Moose Jaw. Lloyd Rodwell records that on that occasion the city was 'gaily decorated with bunting and Main Street as far as Zion Church was hung with colored lights.'[103] For many years the festival movement embraced people of all ages – it was truly a community affair, and only in recent years have its participants been primarily school children and relatively young performers. Rodwell's research reveals that the social aspects of the festival contributed immeasurably to the spirit and enthusiasm of the singers, young and old: 'In 1914, the festival was held in Saskatoon. Eight coaches of competitors, including 65 members of children's choirs and 310 adult singers, came from Moose Jaw. The Moose Jaw group occupied nearly all the first floor rooms of the Flanagan Hotel. A total of 22 sleeping coaches were used by other contestants from the south, many of whom used the sleepers as hotel rooms while in Saskatoon.'[104] As time passed, the University of Saskatchewan furnished office accommodation on campus for Nelson Palmer, secretary-treasurer of the Saskatchewan Provincial Musical Association, and President Murray created a position in the university bookstore for him. Evidently Palmer was relieved of his regular duties from 15 April to 30 June every year 'to enable him to carry on the work of the ... Association.'[105] The success of the provincial festival was undoubtedly linked to the forceful personality of Walter Murray. In spite of his busy schedule, Murray took a personal interest in the competition and served as president of the association. Thus, he was directly involved with two British traditions which left an imprint on music education in the prairie provinces, namely, the competitive music festival and the local centre examination system. The competitive festival was an English phenomenon tightly woven into the fabric of western Canadian culture. It was not just the adjudicators who were British; many choir leaders and teachers seemed to thrive on sentimental ties with the old country, and they revelled in the annual festival as a social event, embracing it as a form of entertainment.

TEACHER TRAINING

Educational leaders engaged either trained musicians or certified school teachers as music instructors in normal schools. It is doubtful that officials had determined what kind of background and experience would be ideal, since there was no consistent pattern in the hiring practice. Ellen Rankin taught at the Regina Normal School from 1902 until 1912, when she was transferred to the normal school in Saskatoon. She taught music and primary methods during her first years but eventually concentrated on drawing; unlike her successors, she held a full-time position. It was not unusual to engage church or community musicians as part-time instructors in normal schools: in 1913 Dr J.E. Hodgson and Professor Golam Hoole of Regina College taught the music course at the Regina Normal School, and in 1915 Hoole offered a summer course, which was satisfactorily completed by eight women teachers. It appears that the next appointee was a school teacher, because the 1916 report stated that Laura Caldwell worked at the model school and also taught on the normal school staff. W.E. McCann, vice-principal of an elementary school in Regina, was in charge of music activities at the 1917 summer school for teachers held at the university in Saskatoon. By 1919 he had become supervisor of music in Regina and was teaching a full music course at summer school.

Madame Helen Davis Sherry was appointed to the Saskatoon Normal School in 1917 and in that same year commenced her thirty-year term as the director of music at Knox Presbyterian Church. Of British birth, she had received her musical training in Britain and later in Toronto, where she made her Canadian singing debut in Massey Hall as a guest artist on the CNR Classical Music Hour. After a short stay in Neepawa, Manitoba, she settled in Saskatoon, where she was highly acclaimed as a performer and voice teacher. It was not uncommon to encounter this combination of British training and previous contact with central Canada in those who assumed musical leadership in the west. It is clear that Madame Sherry was appointed to the normal school staff for her expertise in music rather than for experience in classroom methods; nevertheless, all reports on her work were resoundingly favourable, and her service as a part-time instructor at the Saskatoon Normal School lasted until 1944.

The major problems in education were related to the supply and training of teachers and were compounded by an increase in population after Saskatchewan became a province. In 1906, there were 31,275 students, and 188 teachers trained in Saskatchewan; in 1915, there were 119,279 students, while the number of teachers trained in Saskatchewan had risen to 1222.[106] Normal school programs were not of sufficient length or academic depth to give teachers-in-training any real musical expertise. Much more than with other subjects, the quality of music instruction depended upon the ability, confidence, and interest of the individual teachers. Although inspectors complained about superficial training, these programs were not altered significantly to improve the situation because normal schools were already struggling to cope with the supply of regular teachers. The magnitude of that problem was more compelling than the seemingly trivial nature of the concerns in music.

ALBERTA

MUSIC IN THE COMMUNITY

The rivalry that grew up between the two major cities of Saskatchewan was paralleled, perhaps even surpassed, by the competition between Calgary and Edmonton. Yet in terms of cultural development these two cities have a great deal in common. Both demonstrated vigour and enthusiasm in their attempts to achieve a measure of artistic refinement in spite of their rugged origins and the ungrateful conditions of pioneer life. Church and community choral groups contributed immeasurably to the quality of life around the turn of the century, as did bands, orchestras, and troupes associated with the theatre or other popular entertainments. In recalling early days in Calgary, Annie Broder wrote:

> With the coming of the railway and the gradual growth of Calgary in civic importance music began to be of value as a medium of social intercourse, no gathering being complete without a sing-song, or some instrumental contribution – mouth organ, parlor organ, piano, fiddle or flute. Whoever had a gift was glad to use it, many must have been the merry meetings of oddly assorted talent hailing from the East or the Old Country – some of it remarkably good – that contributed to the joy of life, most people being indisposed to venture upon what is elegantly described as 'high brow' music. Even when small choral societies and clubs came into existence the proceedings were usually to end in a dance.[107]

There was a great tradition of bands in Calgary. The community was favoured by the presence of the first North-West Mounted Police band, organized in 1877.[108] The popularity of the RCMP band conducted by Fred Bagley from 1886 to 1899 may account for the formation of numerous other bands before the turn of the century: the brass bands of the Calgary Fire Brigade, the Odd Fellow's Lodge, and the Salvation Army. There were also attempts before the First World War to develop an orchestra of high calibre. A number of professional people, including prominent doctors and lawyers, were active as amateurs in the musical circles of Calgary. The Calgary Women's Musical Club and the Philharmonic Society both date back to 1904, and church musicians such as J.J. Young, Frank Wrigley, and P.L. Newcombe rendered yeoman service in advancing the cause of choral music. Understandably, Calgarians have been proud to claim as their own outstanding instrumentalists such as Kathleen Parlow (violin) and Gladys Egbert (piano); others, such as Annie Glen Broder, who had studied with Sullivan and Stainer in England, might be thought of as imported musicians.

Motivated by its own set of musical leaders, Edmonton also made great strides in music after the turn of the century, when the flow of immigration brought musicians such as Vernon Barford and W.J. Hendra to the city. Among others, these two men helped transplant British traditions in church choral music, oratorio, and operetta. Percy Hook, Beatrice Crawford, Jackson Hanby, and Arthur Putland also made valuable contributions, and before the First World War several new organizations stimulated the musical life of the city. The Edmonton Choral Society was founded in 1904 and the Ladies' Musical Club in 1908, and, according to the EMC, an 'orchestral society of about 15 players is known to have flourished as early as 1913.'[109] In the short fifteen years after Alberta became a province, the musicians active in Calgary and Edmonton helped these cities attain a level of musical proficiency that had required a much longer period of development in eastern Canada. They made their contributions through the churches and community performing organizations, and through musical societies, which at that time served as surrogates for music education.

Two institutions with a long record of service in music had their origins in the Methodist Church: Alberta College in Edmonton and Mount Royal College in Calgary. The former commenced operation in 1903. Vernon Barford was one of the first teachers at Alberta College; W.J. Hendra was on staff for over fifty years as an instructor of viola and voice. Before the First World War this school prepared students for examinations conducted by the Toronto College of Music. Alberta College teachers were not salaried but were part-time appointees who received their income from lesson fees. Mount Royal's music department opened in 1910 under the direction of William Oaten with a staff of five teachers and an enrolment of almost a hundred students. For years the music departments of these two schools were centres of private instruction drawing upon the most competent teachers in their respective communities. In general, their traditions were more closely aligned with those of private than those of public schools, and the role they played in music education enhanced the efforts of studio teachers, particularly those dedicated to reaching higher performing standards. Whereas the public schools tried to give a basic musical literacy to everyone, these two institutions catered to individuals desiring specialized or more advanced training.

THE ALBERTA MUSIC FESTIVAL

The history of the competitive festival movement has an interesting link with the history of music education in Alberta, in that the festival held in Edmonton in 1908 was the first of its kind in Canada. But the suggestion that musical competitions did not take place before 1908 is hardly true, for band tournaments, to mention one example, thrived in the late nineteenth century. Nevertheless, two aspects of the Alberta festival are significant. First, it was modelled after the British prototype, with a strong orientation toward adult choral groups such as church choirs and community ensembles. Second, the Edmonton organization enjoyed a longevity that many others did not. The competitive festival movement was reinforced by the addition of similar festivals in Saskatchewan, Manitoba, and British Columbia. There is no conclusive evidence, however, that these owe their beginnings to Edmonton. People of British origin re-created the traditions of their homeland, and since most cities had strong pockets of English and Scottish people, a competitive festival was a natural development in communities such as Regina, Saskatoon, and Winnipeg. What did bring these festivals into closer contact was the cooperation in 1919 between Winnipeg and Edmonton in hiring adjudicators. Arrangements growing out of similar cooperation on the part of all the western provinces were made in 1923 and eventually led to the formation of the Canadian Music Competition Festivals.

To return to the situation in Edmonton, Rodwell describes the circumstances leading up to that historic first festival: 'At the inauguration ceremonies of the province of Alberta a concert was arranged to conclude the celebrations. Attending the concert was the Governor-General, Earl Grey, who subsequently suggested that a Dominion-wide Festival should be established for music and drama. Earl Grey sent letters making such a suggestion to the Lieutenant-Governors of each province. In Edmonton the letter was given to three musicians who, not being as interested in a Dominion-wide contest as they were in something of a more local nature, decided to hold a competitive festival similar to those they had known in England and Scotland.'[110] Vernon Barford, Howard Stutchbury, W.J. Hendra, Jackson Hanby, and Beatrice Crawford were involved in planning the original festival. Thirty entries were adjudicated by J.W. Matthews and Rhys Thomas, both of Winnipeg. Over the years the festival kept expanding its syllabus to accommodate individuals and groups of all ages, and its appeal to performers from church, school, and community was reflected in annual increases in the number of participants. Its success was also manifest in greater audience attendance. School groups first appeared in the Alberta Musical Competition Festival in 1911. In response to repeated suggestions that this event should not always take place in Edmonton, the provincial executive agreed in 1920 to hold future festivals on a rotating basis in Edmonton, Calgary, and Lethbridge. As a vehicle for improving performance standards and fostering a general interest in music, the competitive festival has had a vital and lasting influence. But the romance of the festival, with its unique blend of the social and the artistic, transcended the practical values and gave it an almost legendary significance in the large cities of western Canada.

MUSIC IN THE ELEMENTARY SCHOOLS

Ada Dowling Costigan was one of the first teachers to introduce music in the Calgary schools. She arrived in 1887 from Fredericton, New Brunswick, where she had been organist at St Dunstan's Church. After teaching in the public schools, she accepted an appointment at St Hilda's College as a piano teacher. This college, the first Protestant girls' school in the North-West Territories, was operated by the Anglican church as a private institution. Ada Costigan also taught privately, and reportedly her piano was the first grand piano to appear in Calgary. Mrs Costigan and Annie Glen Broder were both on the original staff of Western Canada Boys' College, which operated from 1903 until 1926. The order of the Faithful Companions of Jesus opened a Catholic school in Calgary in 1885. Mother Greene and her Sisters brought old-world culture to the pioneer settlement, for many of them had spent several years on the Continent. According to one account, 'music, vocal and instrumental, was taught not only to the children but to a large number of adults of all denominations.'[111]

Music made its appearance as a subject in the curriculum in 1892 despite a fear that this 'frill' might occupy too much of the pupils' time to the detriment of the more essential subjects. To alleviate this concern, it was pointed out to Calgarians that music was taught in French schools and in all Ontario towns with a population over five thousand. Time and time again in the annals of Canadian history, crusaders in education used this tactic of appealing to local pride through comparisons with other communities. Claims of this sort were not necessarily substantiated; indeed, they were frequently exaggerated for the sake of the desired results. Citing the example of Ontario may have been persuasive, for Frank Fenwick was appointed as a part-time singing teacher in February 1892 at a salary of three hundred dollars per annum. Fenwick resigned in the following year, and Mrs C. Booth, who came from Milwaukee, Wisconsin, was appointed in 1903; she served as a music teacher until 1907. Her successor, Miss E. Comben, formerly of Sackville, New Brunswick, held the music position until 1914. The knowledge of where these teachers came from can furnish clues as to possible influences in methodology, repertoire, and teaching traditions. Alberta recruited a large number of teachers from other provinces in the first decade of its existence; many others came from Britain and the United States. Several inspectors felt that British teachers were better trained in music than those from Alberta or the eastern provinces. There was a wide variety of background and training among Calgary's teachers, but unfortunately no one music teacher or supervisor remained long enough to leave an indelible stamp on school music. As a further frustration to progress, the Calgary school board dispensed with music teachers in 1914 in response to the economic hardships brought on by the war. Music instruction, however, was resumed in 1918 with the appointment of Dr J.E. Hodgson, a well-trained British organist and a former director of Regina's Conservatory of Music. Hodgson served as supervisor of music until 1922.

James McCaig, Edmonton's first superintendent of education, was a progressive, though somewhat controversial, leader. Some of his school principals thought the introduction of vocal music would interfere with the academic progress of the senior students. However, the board overruled them, and in 1895 music was introduced into College Avenue School for half an hour each day; with the support of Superintendent McCaig the subject gained acceptance at a time when the curriculum was still rigid and severe. Kate Chegwin, John Barnett, and E. Butterworth were involved as itinerant teachers and supervisors in the early years, but the development of music in Edmonton's public schools entered its most vigorous period with the hiring of Norman Eagleson in 1912. By virtue of his education and experience, Eagleson was on the leading edge of his profession, especially during the early stages of his career. He had earned a music degree from the University of Toronto and had taught at normal school in North Bay, Ontario, for three years. During his years in Edmonton, he attended summer sessions in Chicago and Boston, so he was well aware of the state of music education in the United States as well as Canada. Eagleson was by all reports diligent and energetic in his work and organized an extensive schedule of in-service courses in the evenings to ensure that classroom teachers were realizing the objectives of his program. Teachers in Edmonton remember him as an austere, intimidating personality moving from school to school to inspect those who were giving the daily instruction. Norman Eagleson was not easily persuaded in matters about which he had strong convictions. For example, objecting strenuously to salary decreases at the time of the First World War, he reminded the board at every opportunity of the heavy burden he carried in the music department.

That Eagleson had formulated a systematic approach to classroom music is obvious in his article 'First Grade Music Methods,' published during the 1918–19 academic year. The article also affords a glimpse into the methodology that supervisors were using for in-service work with general classroom teachers: 'Before entering school little children have had aural musical experiences of varying kind and extent. Few have used their singing voices except in a detrimental way. Many have heard a considerable amount of good music – the band, the phonograph, the choir, the pipe organ, mother or father singing at home. These have all left their musical impressions – subconscious though they be. It is now for the primary teacher to organize these impressions and give the child a vocal experience. This experience must be gained through songs learned by rote from the example of the teacher.'[112] It was expected that fifty songs would be learned in grade one, carefully chosen according to range, melodic and rhythmic qualities, form, and general interest. Approximately twenty of these were to be memorized so that they could be sung with 'good tone and apt expression.'[113] Eagleson advocated a light head tone and was painstaking in describing posture: 'If the desks are of proper height, the forearms should rest on the elbow points to the finger tips, the palms downwards, hands far apart. It is essential that the backs be straight and the shoulders well settled down. This is a restful position and insures good breathing.'[114] Teachers were to be vigilant in identifying those who could not sing on pitch; in Eagleson's terminology they were the 'good listeners,' not the 'poor singers.' Practical instructions were offered: 'Ascertain who is the best singer in each row, place him in the back seat, the second best in the next seat and so on down to the monotone or "tone dull" in the front seat. The back is the seat of honour in singing.'[115] His instructions indicated strong preference for a concert C tuning fork, with a closing comment that 'pitch pipes are not to be recommended, chiefly on sanitary grounds.'[116] Eagleson had firm opinions regarding the use of phonographic recordings and machines. He maintained, 'The best records are not those reproducing a children's song sung by Madame This or Madame That, celebrated though she may be.'[117] It was his view that the quality of tone demonstrated by a class of children would be more ideal; therefore, until such records were available, 'better leave the phonograph alone.'[118] It appears that there was a concentration on reading and the development of musical literacy in middle and upper grades. Eagleson's style was disciplined, logical, and highly organized, as shown by his series of sight-singing books, which was based on the Tonic Sol-fa approach but used staff notation. An examination of these books suggests that he was probably influenced by A.T. Cringan, who had established Tonic-Sol-fa in Ontario's schools. Eagleson was able to accomplish a great deal in Edmonton, partly because of the length of his term as supervisor of music (1912–49) and partly because of his strong, single-minded personality. Suffice it to say that music was firmly implanted in the Edmonton schools as a result of Norman Eagleson's long and dedicated service.

Calgary and Edmonton were not the only cities in Alberta to introduce music into the public schools before the turn of the century. As early as 1891, Miss A.A. McKibben was hired by the Lethbridge school board after she responded to an advertisement for 'a female teacher in possession of a second-class Normal Certificate and able to teach kindergarten songs.'[119] The Lethbridge school trustees decided in 1906 that music should be assigned to a specialist teacher, and in 1912 the board appointed Miss Lombard as director of music. In reference to drawing and music, the 1909 provincial report noted, 'In Medicine Hat and Lethbridge these subjects are under the supervision of specialists and the results are gratifying.'[120] Although some of these early appointments in Alberta were discontinued during the First World War, the question of whether or not to reinstate music often arose in connection with festivals or civic celebrations. Audrey Baines Swedish describes a measure taken in Lethbridge: 'News of a music festival to be held on May 23rd, 24th, and 25th, 1916, reached the trustees and a committee was appointed to interview the principals with regard to entering school choruses in this event. Early in March arrangements were made to hire Miss Layton from March 1st until the day of the festival, during which time she was required to give two hours per day to the work involved.'[121]

THE STATUS OF SCHOOL MUSIC

When Alberta became a province in 1905, the school system inherited the curriculum which D.J. Goggin had revised in 1902 for the North-West Territories. It reflected the thinking of a man who had travelled extensively and had formed strong opinions regarding the aims of education as a preparation for life. Briefly stated, Goggin valued music and drawing as subjects which would exert a refining influence. The first curriculum generated within the new province was drawn up by a committee and implemented in 1912. Though it was basically similar to its predecessor, it did give more attention to certain subjects, including music:

> Scope – The course in music is made up of rote singing, progressive mastery of the mechanics of music, systematic voice culture and sight singing.
>
> The object is to teach the right use of the voice by exercise in tone production and to develop an appreciation of melody and harmony. Incidentally, music should aid language by improving articulation and by giving flexibility and expressiveness. It gives force to the sentiment of poetry.
>
> General Method – The rote singing of the lower grades should give the child an appreciation of melody and rhythm. The essential features of voice training in the lower grades is the securing of voice control by soft singing. The soft use of voice is likewise the beginning of appreciation and taste. Formal teaching of rudiments should be introduced from the beginning. Rounds should begin with the fourth grade and two part songs with the fifth. The poetry should likewise be progressive beginning with the kindergarten or game songs and season songs and ending with glees and patriotic songs ... At the end of the public school course pupils should be able to sing music of ordinary difficulty at sight. The minds of the children should be at work during the music lesson. In the lower grades free use should be made of music at other than regular periods to give change and relief to ordinary work.[122]

The course of study was based upon *The King Edward Music Readers*, which were still listed in provincial documents in 1912. However, there was a preponderance of British books recommended as reference materials for teachers. Even though music was outlined in some detail, it was not one of the 'examination subjects' required for entrance into high school. It follows, therefore, that it was often neglected by teachers and inspectors who were preoccupied with examination results. But if music failed to get official support on academic grounds, it certainly was encouraged and even exploited for its extra-musical value. As in other prairie provinces, the tremendous influx of non-British immigrants was a major concern of the educational authorities. They had ulterior motives for encouraging singing; one inspector reported in 1906: 'Those teachers that have musical ability are doing excellent work ... The tone of the schools is improved by the singing of appropriate and patriotic songs.'[123]

There was a continuous effort by the provincial department of education to establish consolidated schools, but the public showed little enthusiasm for the idea. According to Sheane, 'these schools permitted the teaching of the newer subjects such as manual training, domestic science, school gardening, music and art.'[124] It is disconcerting that 'by 1918, when fifty-four consolidated schools had been established,'[125] music was still regarded as a 'newer' subject even though it had been on the books since 1884. In the rural schools, rote songs were enjoyed if the teacher could sing, but, according to one annual report, 'with one or two exceptions, no attempt [was] made to giving systematic instruction.'[126] Among inspectors it was a common complaint that the better teachers gravitated to the cities and towns. The 1918 curriculum revision embraced a philosophical swing back to the 3 Rs, and unmistakably, the guiding principle was support for essentials before frills. Norman Eagleson, probably the most prominent music educator in the province, complained that music always had to struggle for recognition: 'Music is included in the Course of Studies for the Province of Alberta. In the list of subjects stated therein it will be found on the last line – sitting out on the back doorstep, as it were. There is a suggestiveness of relative values in such a list to which the teacher fresh from Normal School is susceptible; and, if she happens to take a school lying in the district of an unmusical inspector who has the reputation of passing this subject up, there will be little music taught.'[127]

To satisfy interest groups not involved in the Alberta Musical Competition Festivals, a local school festival was inaugurated in Claresholm, Alberta, in 1917 by W.G. Moffatt. This event gave rise to similar ones in other small communities. Department of education circulars indicate that these festivals encompassed singing, instrumental music, recitations, art, and woodwork. After a preliminary competition, successful performers competed in a final round, but, as Olive Fisher notes, 'the crowning glory was an evening performance for which admission was charged to provide prizes.'[128] The Claresholm

Festival brochure described its aims: 'To promote artistic singing and reciting among children, to bring rural and town schools into co-operation with one another working with the same object in view, viz.: "cultivation of taste for the beautiful in tones, colors, and form." It also is an endeavor to bring school and home into closer acquaintance.'[129] School festivals flourished in those places which were beyond the sphere of the provincial competition. Evidently, during the first few years of the school festival movement, its success was used to persuade the department to place a greater emphasis on music in its program of study. In response to a report in 1919, the minister of education expressed positive interest, indicating that a meeting would be called to discuss future plans for music. The school festival movement also elicited a zealous plea from a rural inspector of Welsh origin who lobbied for music in the high schools:

> If the teachers of music follow instructions and study carefully the Gen'l Statement, I see the day not far distant, when Alberta will be a land of song. This intensive study of music in our schools will ultimately make us less dependent on European countries. Our own students will become composers of note, I hope, and Western natural phenomena, the story of mountain, field and forest, will be given to music, as they are to prose and verse. I have often wondered what a splendid orchestra theme a three-day Western blizzard would make. Then there is the calm and peace of the prairie with its wide expanse. Rural communities will derive great benefit from this course not so much musically as socially, and I look to this as a strong factor in Canadianizing people from other lands. It has been said that in music people forget their nationality.[130]

Some inspectors were directly involved in organizing school festivals and, in many cases, seemed more eager about special events than they were about the day-to-day music instruction. The school festival movement continued to be effective in rural Alberta throughout the 1920s and 1930s.

There was evidence of official goodwill on the part of the department of education in the form of special grants to support school music. Yet Mary Buckley concludes that 'music education in Alberta appears to have been at two extremes; either good, as in the city schools, or poor, as in the majority of rural schools.'[131] She describes the situation thus: 'The most encouraging change was the realization, by 1918, that music education should be enjoyable, emotionally satisfying, and free from drudgery. Unfortunately, the pedantic details of the course description did not include any concrete suggestions as to how to achieve those goals. A teacher who followed the course outline faithfully would probably have had difficulty in avoiding drudgery and monotony in music classes.'[132]

Music in the High School Curriculum

The high school curriculum was designed for students interested in teaching or continuing their education at university; therefore, courses were essentially academic and music occurred only on an extra-curricular basis. In the years leading up to the First World War there are isolated references to operettas, glee clubs, and, in a few city schools, orchestras. Musical efforts such as these usually were under-taken wherever an interested principal or teacher provided the initiative. For example, a science teacher organized an orchestra at Crescent Heights School in Calgary, and by 1916 it had grown into an ensemble of sixteen players. There was also a high school orchestra operating in Lethbridge by the early 1920s. Generally, almost any instrumentation was tolerated because school groups had to rely upon players who studied privately or received training in local bands. A pianist was essential in a school orchestra; having a piano was one way of compensating for an instrumentation that was invariably incomplete. Music was not officially recognized in the high school *Programme of Studies* until 1919. Even then there was little evidence of any music activity other than the awarding of academic credit for private music study outside the school. Nevertheless, it augured well for the future that in the 1920s 'the Department was anxious to grant external credit for music to as many students as possible.'[133]

TEACHER TRAINING AND HIGHER EDUCATION

Although music education in the large cities had a degree of individuality as a result of the influence of specific leaders, institutions, and local traditions, annual reports on music in the rural districts contained a common theme. Rural inspectors maintained that poor results in music reflected the varying abilities of the classroom teachers. Even in situations in which the normal school instructors were excellent musicians, one has to question the efficacy of the normal training in preparing candidates to be competent teachers of music.

The first normal school in Alberta opened in Calgary in 1906, just one year after the province had been established. In general, elementary teachers did not stay in the profession long, and normal schools consequently were hard pressed to keep up with the heavy demand for teachers. A second normal school was established in Camrose in 1913 and another in Edmonton in 1920; those candidates who were university graduates usually attended the Edmonton institution. A report in 1907 stated, 'It is impossible to deal with such subjects as manual training, music, drawing.'[134] This comment, often repeated, should not be surprising: the normal school course was only four months long; even after it was extended to eight months, in 1919, it was not considered adequate.

Most music instructors in normal schools were hired on a part-time basis, and many served for relatively short terms. Mrs C. Booth was the first music teacher on the Calgary staff. Of all the music instructors in Alberta's normal schools, Madame Ellis Browne was truly outstanding. Unlike many others, she was a musician rather than a certified elementary school teacher. Her career extended from 1909 to 1936, and as well as a teacher at the Calgary Normal School she was a widely respected singer, voice teacher, and choir director, of First Baptist and later of Knox Church. Madame Ellis Browne had been born in Wales and trained in England. In her emphasis on voice culture and Tonic Sol-fa she serves as an example of the British influence in Canada. In addition to giving class instruction, she organized operettas and occasionally formed an orchestra of normal school students. Her reputation was not entirely local, in that she also taught at a summer school session for teachers in Victoria, British Columbia.

Teachers' institutes and conventions were organized in the early years to help those who had been trained locally and to integrate more effectively teachers from other provinces. Commencing in 1913, summer courses for classroom teachers were held annually at the university in Edmonton, but music was not offered. It was in response to repeated requests that a course was eventually given, in 1918, under the title 'Music and Games.' The University of Alberta (founded 1906) opened its doors in 1908, but a music department was not formed until 1945. In 1909 Vernon Barford took over the glee club which L.H. Alexander[135] had organized during the opening year of the university; around the same time, 'a Mr Graham conducted the university orchestra.'[136] By 1912, as Barford recalled, the glee club consisted of 'a group of about twenty young men who met weekly.'[137] Because the training of elementary teachers was confined almost exclusively to normal schools, the University of Alberta had little influence on music education beyond what came within the scope of its campus cultural clubs until the 1930s, when its extension department forged a number of innovative programs in the arts.

PART II

GROWTH AND EXPANSION

5

The Role of National Institutions

Before the Second World War there were very few national institutions, organizations, or agencies which were equipped to nurture the growth of music in Canadian society. As a young country Canada was beset with problems, and as a land characterized by rugged terrain, great distances, and isolation, it had to contend with the reality of sparse population. Of even greater concern were the racial and linguistic divisions of the founding nations, not to mention the subsequent immigration of ethnic peoples, who ultimately contributed to the formation of the multicultural society commonly referred to as the Canadian mosaic. Progress in music education, as in other spheres of national development, was in some respects adversely affected by the British North America Act, which relegated education to a provincial responsibility. The provincial-federal division of jurisdictions impeded the cultural growth of the nation as a whole, and the absence of an umbrella organization for the arts prolonged its state of dependency on others. It is disconcerting that Canadians came to rely upon external agencies such as the Carnegie Foundation of New York for the funding of many cultural projects during the period between the two world wars.

THE CANADIAN BROADCASTING CORPORATION

Technological advances in radio transmission made Canada vulnerable with respect to cultural sovereignty, for, as Keith MacMillan observes, the majority of Canadians chose 'to live along the southern fringe, within easy electronic reach of the world's most clamorous broadcaster, the USA.'[1] The CNR and CPR were pioneers in the field and produced music programs on a national scale in the late 1920s. However, with the coming of the Depression the railways 'were forced to abandon broadcasting and a public clamour grew for a reorganization and consolidation of public broadcasting.'[2] In 1932 the Canadian Radio Broadcasting Commission was formed, and in 1936 it was superseded by the Canadian Broadcasting Corporation, an event which proved to be as vital to Canada's cultural unity in the 1930s as the construction of the CPR had been to Canada's economic survival in the 1880s. Certainly, the dearth of national institutions in music and the arts imposed an exceedingly heavy burden on the CBC – one of fostering a national consciousness within the diversity of Canada's regions and communities.

The CBC has made an enormous contribution to music in Canada. Through talent competitions, recitals, and special programs, the corporation has discovered and promoted solo performers from all parts of the country, not to mention the many artists and musicians who have been involved in regional orchestras, opera and ballet productions, and countless other projects. Composers, too, have been well served by programs featuring Canadian compositions, by the commissioning of new works, and by the production of recordings in a period when the commercial industry was extremely wary, if not sceptical, of their merit. Music educators entered into an informal partnership with the corporation in the late 1930s, when the resources of CBC were utilized to add variety to classroom instruction through a wide range of radio programs. Music broadcasts originating from the United States served as models for Canadian experiments. One of these, Walter Damrosch's 'Music Appreciation Hour,' was carried over CBC in 1938, and the CBS series 'School of the Air' was carried over CBC's Ontario stations in 1940–1. Eventually, in response to a desire for material specifically designed for Canadian schools, CBC initiated productions of its own. Following a conference in 1942, the corporation established an advisory council and appointed R.S. Lambert as national supervisor of school broadcasts. This administrative structure helped to solve problems that typically arise when national projects are extended to individual provinces, each of which has its own educational jurisdiction.

Those involved in school broadcasts were not always school teachers or supervisors; many were semi-professional musicians or private teachers, and, as time passed, the more sophisticated programs required specialists to prepare scripts and manage other aspects of production. CBC facilities and expertise were often made available for local and regional projects. Some of the country's finest musicians and media specialists were enlisted for national programs; their efforts advanced the quality of music instruction and thereby helped to reduce disparities in the rural schools. Indeed, CBC has had a direct impact on school music, and the magnitude of its influence in promoting artistic standards in the performing arts is inestimable.

THE HART HOUSE STRING QUARTET

In 1931 an advertisement in *Musical Canada* billed the Hart House String Quartet as 'a national institution.' There is no doubt that the quartet, fully supported by the Massey Foundation, enriched Toronto's concert life through regular series at the University of Toronto's Hart House and Convocation Hall. But the quartet reached an even wider audience through radio broadcasts and concert tours: 'By 1938, it had undertaken 12 Canadian tours and had given some 30 concerts in New York and over 100 throughout the U.S.A.'[3] In 1927 Hector Charlesworth described its contribution thus: 'Canada as a whole may well take pride in the Hart House Quartet which, though Toronto is its home, has made the whole country its field and is winning enthusiastic recognition clear across the United States.'[4]

Extensive tours across the country took this premier ensemble into Canada's small and remote communities and provided a musical baptism for many who were unfamiliar with the string quartet genre. Concert engagements on its 1927 tour ranged from the Ladies' Friday Morning Club in Regina to Ottawa's Chateau Laurier Hotel, and in 1932 from the Scout Hall in Vernon, BC, to Trinity United Church in Charlottetown, PEI. Such activities encouraged ordinary music lovers to become astute listeners in the realm of chamber music. In general, Canadians sensed the high standards of artistic performance offered by the Hart House Quartet, as did international audiences during the ensemble's European tours in 1929 and 1937. In the words of Augustus Bridle, these distinguished figures were 'the high priests of perfect art in the most refined of all forms of music.'[5] Another critic portrayed the quartet's influence in more practical terms: 'What the British adjudicators do by precept at the great western music festivals towards the maintenance of high standards, the [Hart House] Quartet does in practice by its actual performances.'[6]

Although the individual players were not Canadian by birth, they made a concerted effort to contribute to music education in their adopted country. While on tour they did this by playing afternoon concerts in high schools before their evening engagements. At the University of Toronto they established an annual series for university and high school students, and reportedly a thousand undergraduates took advantage of these concerts in Convocation Hall in 1930. The quartet also enhanced the cultural growth of the country through its repertoire, for as one writer observed, 'possibly no other musical organization in Canada has done more to introduce to Canadians the work of contemporary American composers.'[7] Although the membership changed over the full span of its existence, the artistic quality and commitment of the group remained consistent. A historical account of music education would be incomplete if it failed to recognize the unique role of this ensemble; as an emissary of music both at home and abroad, the Hart House Quartet attained the status of a national institution.

THE TORONTO CONSERVATORY OF MUSIC 1886–1947 / ROYAL CONSERVATORY OF MUSIC OF TORONTO 1947–

In recognition of its vital role in music education, the Toronto Conservatory of Music (TCM) was renamed the Royal Conservatory of Music of Toronto (RCMT) in 1947. However, long before the change of name received royal assent the conservatory had become a mecca for musicians throughout English-speaking Canada. Its national eminence can be attributed in large measure to the strong leadership of Augustus Stephen Vogt (principal, 1913–26) and his successor, Ernest Campbell MacMillan (principal, 1926–42). Vogt expanded the TCM's network of local examination centres into a nation-wide operation and, as the first dean of the Faculty of Music (1918–26), clarified the relationship of these two musical units within the University of Toronto. In 1919 the university took control of the TCM, and in 1924 purchased the Canadian Academy of Music (which had already amalgamated with the Toronto College of Music in 1918); this meant that all rival music schools in Toronto had been eliminated, with the exception of the Hambourg Conservatory. Vogt furthered the reputation of the school through his leadership of the Toronto Mendelssohn Choir, establishing high standards for church and community groups to aspire to. His commitment to choral music was echoed by Ernest MacMillan in 1932 at a conference in Chicago: 'A sure indication ... of a musical community is an interest in choral singing.'[8] Whether the training was in church, community, or school, Canadians regarded choral music as the basic foundation of music education.

MacMillan's vision and energetic leadership brought the TCM to new prominence in music education. Not surprisingly, private teachers in Canada looked to this institution for leadership and inspiration. As performers, examiners, adjudicators, scholars, and commentators, the conservatory's leading musicians became celebrities not only in Ontario but in other provinces as well. By the late 1920s the TCM staff included most of Toronto's outstanding teachers, among them several highly trained musicians from Great Britain and Europe, who added a distinctive old-world flavour to the institution. Its three main areas of operation were 1) instruction of young children and amateurs, mainly through private lessons (as of 1905, the TCM had established several branches in the Toronto area); 2) training of advanced students interested in professional careers; 3) examination of students of all levels in practical and theoretical subjects (by 1923 more than ten thousand local examinations were being held in centres throughout the Dominion).

Prominent as the TCM was, it did not have a monopoly throughout Canada. As only one of several examining bodies, it competed with the Associated Board of the Royal Schools of Music, Trinity College of Music, the McGill Conservatorium, and a number of others which did not function on a national scale but engendered strong loyalties in their particular regions. The conservatory's instructional operation was concentrated in Toronto and adjacent Ontario communities. For many years the Hambourg Conservatory (1911–51) also attracted a fine staff of teachers, some of them from Europe. As well, there were a few musicians in Toronto who maintained their own teaching studios. One notable teacher was Mona Bates, a performer of international renown, who taught many outstanding Canadian pianists during her forty-year career. Such exceptions notwithstanding, the TCM dominated music education in Toronto and its examinations had an influence across the nation. The conservatory's graded syllabi gave teachers a common curriculum and a systematic guide for instruction and evaluation. Through major revisions of examination requirements in the mid-1930s, MacMillan introduced more rigorous demands in theory, ear training, and sight-reading and established the system of grades still in use. National examining boards have been effective, up to a point, in establishing levels of attainment for generations of private teachers who have urgently needed such help and direction. But there has been a pervading criticism that teachers followed examination requirements with a fidelity that bordered on the slavish. On one occasion MacMillan responded to this criticism:

> No one can pretend that the result of an examination, limited in point of time and conducted under conditions which frequently render pupils very nervous, is in every case infallibly just. The institution controlling the examination can only ensure that it shall be as just as circumstances will allow, and, having announced examiners' decisions, uphold them. If teachers and parents would only realize that the work put into the preparation of examination requirements is of much greater importance than the result of the examination (although in the vast majority of cases I doubt not the examiner's decision is reasonable), there would be fewer heartaches and indignant letters to the institution. On the other hand, there are cases in which teachers take up cudgels on behalf of their pupils in order to save their own faces; they would be better employed in examining their own shortcomings and endeavoring to overcome them.
>
> Another disadvantage of examinations is that no curriculum can be absolutely exhaustive. Some teachers stick so closely to the requirements that their pupils never receive a hint of the great world of music which lies outside. An examination syllabus should not be looked upon in the light of the scriptures of the Old and New Testament which, we are told, contain 'all things necessary to salvation.' In such cases it is not the system which is at fault but the teacher.[9]

The system has helped rank-and-file teachers; for example, conservatory publications have recommended standard editions and thus discouraged the use of less reliable versions of repertoire and study materials. Among those conservatory teachers who wrote instructional books, Frank Blachford, Healey Willan, Leo Smith, Ernest MacMillan, Boris Berlin, and Frederick Horwood became household names for young Canadian musicians. The TCM has not confined its operation to private lessons and practical examinations; other specialized programs, courses, and lectures have been offered, including summer sessions for teachers. Probably the first systematic method for the teaching of young children available at the TCM was the Fletcher Music Method, which was introduced around the turn of the century. Another, the Kelly Kirby Kindergarten Method, published in 1936, was used internationally; its author, May Kelly Kirby, joined the staff in 1910 and continued to teach there for seventy years. Through its workshops and publications the TCM became widely known for its work in pre-school instruction.

Not all the enterprising schemes at the TCM have enjoyed the longevity of the Kelly Kirby system. For example, a department of school music was announced in 1922 under Duncan McKenzie, director of music for Toronto schools. The newspaper notice indicated that lectures would be given on Saturday mornings and explained: 'These classes have been formed to meet the demands of students and teachers from all over the dominion who wish to equip themselves to take charge of music in the public and high schools. At present no such school exists in Canada, except the summer school held for six weeks in Toronto under the authority of the provincial department of education.'[10] In spite of its ambitious beginnings, this proposal did not develop into a permanent project. Yet there have been many successful ventures over the years. In 1927 Madeleine Boss Lasserre joined the conservatory, and for fifty years she gave instruction in Dalcroze eurhythmics, solfège, and improvisation. In 1934, in recognition of her work, the Dalcroze Institute in Switzerland authorized the TCM to award elementary certificates in Dalcroze training.

Among those who have influenced music education in Canada, none has rivalled the distinguished Sir Ernest MacMillan. His professional expertise, prestige, and magnetism thrust him into almost every sphere of music in Canadian life. MacMillan was Canada's consummate musician: a performer of chamber music, a conductor, a composer, an accompanist, and an organist of extraordinary talent. He gave annual performances of St Matthew Passion with the Toronto Conservatory Choir and in 1947 succeeded H.A. Fricker as conductor of the Toronto Mendelssohn Choir. In 1931 he became conductor of the Toronto Symphony Orchestra, a position he held until 1956. As a composer MacMillan produced several major works and numerous pieces for didactic purposes; he also wrote and edited many books, articles, and performing editions. An administrator of unusual ability, he was principal of the TCM (1926–42) and dean of the Faculty of Music, University of Toronto (1927–52). Later, MacMillan was influential in such national organizations as the Canadian Music Council, the Canada Council, the Canadian Music Centre, and Jeunesses musicales. But even more amazing was his personal involvement in ordinary musical events. On many occasions he took the time to serve as an adjudicator in music festivals; he participated in events sponsored by the MacMillan Fine Arts Clubs in British Columbia; he addressed music education conferences in both Canada and the United States. He was in constant demand as a speaker, radio commentator, and panelist. What is most impressive is that he accommodated so many people at the grass roots level even while administering several major musical organizations.

Sir Ernest MacMillan was consulted at all levels of Canadian society concerning music, the arts, and various aspects of education; in some ways he became more of a national institution than the organizations to which he devoted his service. Certainly, the pre-eminence of the TCM was due largely to his commanding stature in Canadian musical circles, not to mention his wide international reputation. It would be difficult indeed to chronicle all the ways in which he encouraged, advised, and influenced the cultural growth of the country.

It was not by official sanction or predetermined plan that the TCM evolved into a national institution; perhaps it was owing to its extensive examination system, through which teachers and students came to identify with the conservatory and its staff. The TCM struggled valiantly to meet the needs of musicians from all provinces. In the absence of a national school with adequate federal funding, the conservatory bore the burden of providing advanced musical training within the financial structure of a private, provincial university. The economic restraints brought on by the Depression precluded any real expansion or long-range planning at the TCM. Its financial position was improved somewhat in 1944, when Frederick Harris, who had become the exclusive publisher of conservatory instructional books, turned over the company's assets to the university, with profits to be used for scholarships and bursaries. Even so, because there were no extensive resources for developing the kind of programs offered by American and European institutions, many Canadians continued to go abroad for professional study and advancement. Concern about this state of affairs led to a study in 1937. It was requested by the university president and the conservatory board but funded by the Carnegie Foundation of New York. Ernest Hutcheson, president of the Juilliard School of Music, undertook the task of examining the operational structure of the TCM within the university. He did so at the time of a triumphal visit to the city during which he was the featured soloist for the opening of the TSO's 1937–8 season under the baton of Ernest MacMillan. In reviewing the concert, critic Augustus Bridle noted that Massey Hall was full to capacity and that 'traffic on lower Yonge Street was as slow as round the Maple Leaf Gardens on a hockey night.'[11] In his report Hutcheson stated: 'The tuitional system of the Conservatory, though not altogether unusual, invites some comment. The Conservatory acts less as a school employing a faculty than as a clearing-house for private teachers, providing them with studio facilities and in return receiving a percentage of their fees.'[12] He recommended, among other things, 'a more compact faculty, fewer in number, individually better paid, with gradual elimination of weaker elements,' and the expansion of a senior division which would prepare students for professional employment. He also advocated the 'assignment of teachers by the directorate rather than by choice of the students'[13] in the graduate division. In commenting on the functions of the TCM, Hutcheson said:

> Broadly speaking, the Conservatory, because of its standing, history and ideals, must be a leading agency in the development of Canadian music. It should continuously graduate musicians of all kinds, creative, interpretative, and pedagogic, to sustain a vigorous musical life and growth, and it should diffuse a love and appreciation of the art among all classes of the people.
>
> The Conservatory, then, should in the first place operate as the most prominent national establishment for the training of Canadian musical talent. The flight of native talent to the United States and Europe for advanced study is seriously to be deplored, and can be prevented only by demonstrating its needlessness.[14]

There is no question that the spectre of another world war played a role in preventing the main recommendations of this report from being implemented until 1946. Other reasons for the delay will emerge later, for the implementation of the report was connected with the expansion of the university's Faculty of Music and, in turn, with the future of music in higher education.

THE CANADIAN GUILD OF ORGANISTS 1909–20 / CANADIAN
COLLEGE OF ORGANISTS 1920–59 / ROYAL CANADIAN
COLLEGE OF ORGANISTS 1959–

One of the first national associations with a specialized function in music education was the Canadian Guild of Organists. It changed its name in 1920 to the Canadian College of Organists and at that time incorporated Canadian members of the American Guild of Organists. Its fiftieth anniversary, in 1959, was marked by the addition of the word 'royal.' The Royal Canadian College of Organists (RCCO) has attempted to set professional standards through the granting of fellowships, associateships, and other diplomas on the basis of examinations in organ, choral conducting, and theory. The college also has established scholarships for aspiring young organists. Through its national executive and network of local chapters, the RCCO continues to offer a full range of activities for professional development: annual conferences, competitions, workshops, recitals, and choral festivals.

The RCCO has been associated informally with church music, particularly that of the established denominations in which the traditional practice was to install pipe organs and hire trained organists and choir directors. The college has served as a forum in which selected aspects of organ playing and church service can be addressed. It has undertaken a number of practical projects from time to time, such as the preparation of *The Employment of a Church Musician: A Guide for Canadian Churches*, a brochure which recommends a range of appropriate salaries and fees for church work. Despite the fact that the major religious denominations are perceived as national entities, church music by and large has not been institutionalized or structured according to uniform patterns. Even in those denominations with a highly centralized structure, local musicians have exercised a high degree of independence or autonomy within their own congregations. The Salvation Army, because of its administrative framework, has been an exception to this general rule. It is also exceptional in its use of a brass band instead of an organ to accompany congregational singing.

THE SALVATION ARMY

Ever since the Salvation Army (SA) 'opened fire' in Canada in 1882, proclaiming its gospel message on the street corners of towns and cities, music has been woven in a unique way into its religious and social life. The rapid spread of this movement was astonishing, for Salvationists were visible in all provinces even before the turn of the century. Hallelujah bands, composed primarily of tambourines and drums, and minstrel groups, which gave entertainments reminiscent of the British music hall, were spontaneously formed as part of a strategy to attract converts to the faith. The first instrumental combinations which played under the banner of the Salvation Army may have been unworthy of the term 'brass band.' Gordon Moyles notes: 'The oft-asserted claim that among those who threw rotten tomatoes at Salvation Army marchers were genuine lovers of music might indeed have been true. In time, however, with an influx of knowledgeable bandsmen from England, the band of the Salvation Army was often the best (and not because it was the only) musical group in town.'[15] Steps had already been taken to ensure some degree of uniformity among bands in Britain: 'By 1881 regulations governing the formation of bands had been firmly established, and the Army began publishing its own brass-band music.'[16] The Household Troops Band from England must have sparked considerable interest during its visit to Canada in 1888, for Canadian officers formed a similar group of their own. By 1895 local congregations (corps) had been established from coast to coast, and invariably the formation of a brass band followed shortly after each congregation was organized on a permanent basis. The Salvation Army – a religious denomination rooted in Methodist traditions – appealed directly to the working class and tended to flourish in those areas where there was a concentration of British people, most noticeably in Ontario and in large cities across its Canadian Territory. It is understandable, then, that when the SA introduced derivative forms of British culture, it found a strong following among recent immigrants. Moreover, the Army was an international organization which emphasized loyalty to the main tenets of the British Empire. Possibly more than any other denomination in Canada, the Army, with its centralized authority and quasi-military administration, determined or, more often, dictated the rule and manner in which music was to be used.

The Salvation Army band on the street corner has been a familiar sight on the Canadian landscape since the turn of the century. To outsiders, the most visible musical unit has always been the brass band. Those intimately acquainted with the Army, however, would contend that vocal music has been equally important in its musical heritage. From the standpoint of numbers the SA's brass band movement reached a climax in the 1930s. But from a musical standpoint it did not realize its full potential until after the Second World War, and even then progress was confined to a comparatively small number of bands. The Salvation Army in Canada retained its British connection, and Canadian corps purchased brass instruments from the SA's own manufacturing plant in England. These instruments, which were pitched higher than the standard A440, could not be used in 'outside' bands, and it was not until the early 1960s that the instruments were converted to standard pitch. The differential from standard pitch had the effect of preventing Salvationists from playing in bands outside the organization; hence, their members constituted a musical fraternity of their own. The music used in both junior and adult ensembles was printed by the Salvation Army Music Publishing Department in England, and according to regulations other music was not allowed. Young People's Bands, for many years restricted to boys, served as the training ground for senior bands. Singing Companies were predominantly female in membership, serving as feeder groups for the senior choir, which was known in Army parlance as the Songster Brigade. Junior groups functioned in Sunday School meetings and other youth activities, whereas senior groups handled the music for worship services, marches, and open-air meetings. Since dancing, movies, and entertainments of a worldly nature were not permitted, the social life of the Salvationist usually centred around meetings, concerts, and special gatherings in which music became almost paramount.

There was a remarkable uniformity in the manner in which the Salvation Army sustained its musical traditions, not only in Canada but around the world. SA youth in Canada were given training or playing experience on brass instruments long before instruction was available in public schools. This fact is significant when one realizes that, for economic reasons, private lessons were not possible in most working-class families. The training was insular and casual in some ways but highly structured in others. Such as it was, the instruction was designed specifically to meet the SA's needs, and it operated as a self-contained system. A beginner was usually tutored by a senior bandsman, at least until the budding player could be absorbed into a Young People's Band; sometimes this instruction involved little more than being taught to produce a tone on the cornet or memorize the correct fingerings of the C scale. Any further training normally consisted of ensemble experience in junior and senior bands. Perhaps the most notable development in this musical training – and one which predated comparable developments in other organizations – was the introduction of summer music camps. In 1940 a one-week camp was held at Jackson's Point, Ontario. Following the Second World War the Salvation Army established similar programs in other regions and eventually had music camps in virtually every province. Instructors were drawn from the larger corps bands and songster brigades, and over the years summer programs have become more intensive in scope and more effective in their methods.[17]

Hundreds of Canadian brass players received their early musical training in the Salvation Army. Not all of them, however, remained in the ranks of the organization. Invariably the brass sections of service bands during the Second World War were dominated by Salvationists, many of whom became soloists and conductors, particularly in RCAF units. Many SA musicians pursued careers in music education, particularly in the postwar years, when the rise of instrumental music opened up greater opportunities for music teachers.

THE CANADIAN BUREAU FOR THE ADVANCEMENT OF MUSIC

The Canadian Bureau for the Advancement of Music (CBAM) was an unusual music agency operating on a national level. The bureau was initiated in 1919 by the Canadian Piano and Organ Manufacturers' Association as an outgrowth of their 'Music in the Home' campaign and until 1922 was directed by John A. Fullerton. It was fashioned after its American counterpart as a non-profit organization designed to stimulate general interest in music and to promote specific projects in music education. Since 1921 it has been closely linked to activities at the Canadian National Exhibition such as CNE Music Days, recitals, and competitions.

In the Canadian context the CBAM enjoyed its heyday under the leadership (1922–54) of J.S. Atkinson, who travelled across the country promoting a wide range of schemes: the Music Memory Test, essay contests, competitive festivals, and community music weeks. However, the bureau's major impact was in the realm of class piano instruction, an innovation which had already gained widespread acceptance in the United States. Class piano instruction was established in Kitchener in 1925 under the auspices of the local school board. Hope Kammerer, one of the earliest exponents of the method, gave demonstrations at teachers' conferences, and within a few years the CBAM introduced this branch of its work. To establish the bureau's programs in communities across Canada, Atkinson usually worked through public school boards with the cooperation of their music supervisors, who distributed information and application forms to parents. School facilities were made available after regular school hours, but the actual instruction was given by local private teachers, who were required to take special training prescribed by the bureau. During the Depression many parents were pleased to enrol their children in class piano, since this type of instruction was less expensive than private tuition. Atkinson was forceful and optimistic in articulating its advantages: 'By the class method the pupils naturally lose somewhat in individual attention from the teacher, but on the other hand, the class method offers them many splendid advantages, such as the opportunity to compare their work and progress with that of others; the privilege of hearing others' work criticized or commended, and the great advantage of the group enthusiasm and friendly competition which is engendered. This leads to the pupils in class work willingly and cheerfully practising, when too often pupils taking instruction from individual teachers have to be driven to practise.'[18] Although school facilities were used and local private teachers gave the instruction, this extensive enterprise was facilitated and controlled through a national office in Toronto; the CBAM's role was primarily one of administration. Yet school officials and music supervisors were quite willing to be identified with these piano classes, often representing them as supplements to the regular classroom work. In other words, the opportunity for good public relations was not overlooked. It may have been partly owing to its special nature that class piano never became an integral part of the musical life of the schools. The bureau's attempts to expand class instruction in violin never flourished; the popularity of the violin class was minute compared with that of the piano class. Atkinson claimed that 'the piano class method, with its reduced expense to pupils' would motivate many to begin and subsequently 'continue their instruction under private teachers.'[19] But private teachers in general were somewhat negative about group instruction and probably resented having to compete with the CBAM for beginning students. Admittedly, some of their reactions may have stemmed from the close connection between CBAM and the music industry, which cast a shadow over the bureau's real purpose and motivation. Such opposition notwithstanding, CBAM has continued to operate class piano programs for more than fifty years, though its declining importance in music education is reflected in reduced enrolments and in the termination of many programs since the Second World War.

6

Progress on the Prairies

Even though it lasted only a few years, the general prosperity which prevailed in the prairie provinces immediately after the First World War provided a favourable climate for the expansion and improvement of music and the arts. In urban communities the people of British origin continued to preserve many of their traditions, often relying upon immigrants from the old country to provide the leadership. This was especially true of the large Protestant churches, which more often than not engaged organists and choir leaders from Great Britain. However, with each passing decade local musicians became more confident, and the ratio changed, albeit only gradually, in favour of a generation of musicians who had grown up in Canada.

Women's musical clubs in larger cities continued to be the patrons of the arts through scholarships, concert series, and recitals by visiting artists and local performers, but there was less performance by club members themselves. The Saskatoon club resisted this general trend by restricting its membership to active musicians. In 1933 Mary Mitchner affirmed: 'We all work energetically and our efforts are more along the line of study than for entertainment. New members are only accepted after performing before a committee and it has sometimes been their sad duty to turn down some would-be aspirants. The Club is not for social purposes, therefore tea is never served and one never sees that rush for tea cups that is so obviously the important part of many clubs.'[1] The Calgary Women's Club sponsored an unusual project, a concert featuring music by local composers. This annual event was first held in 1921, and thereafter for more than twenty-five years.

By international standards the music scene during the 1920s was still insular, but the initial taste of artistic progress had furthered aspirations to higher levels of performance. Entertainment and concert life flourished here and there on the strength of celebrated artists and professional touring groups; as well, local performers were becoming more conspicuous on the concert stage. An indication of this trend is given by the popularity of the Fred Gee Celebrity Series: it originated in Winnipeg in 1927 and, from 1934, was also produced in Regina, Saskatoon, Calgary, and Edmonton. By 1938 its subscription series at the Winnipeg Auditorium reached thirty-five hundred; reportedly, it was 'the largest concert series on the North American continent.'[2]

Whereas orchestras around the turn of the century had been organized to accompany large choral performances or to provide accompaniments for theatrical productions, the orchestra emerged from the inter-war period with a sense of artistic independence. Most orchestral organizations did not enjoy longevity, yet there were attempts to establish a legitimate instrumentation and to program standard orchestral repertoire. Serious efforts to develop good community ensembles took place in Calgary (1913, 1928), Edmonton (1920), Winnipeg and Regina (1927), and Saskatoon (1931). These endeavours indicate that prairie cities were cultivating a more sophisticated palate with respect to instrumental music. Moreover, progress was aided throughout the 1930s by the availability of music through radio programs. Orchestras appealed to the elitist ambitions of the cities, bands to the general population. People from a wide range of national backgrounds in both urban and rural settings looked to the band to provide opportunities for musical participation as well as entertainment. In the instrumental realm band music was the music of the common folk, for even with the rise of the 'big name' bands on radio, the concert in the park and the band on parade retained their popularity.

Cultural activities in rural areas often took place in the local church or one-room schoolhouse. Folk traditions were preserved in rural areas, but because most of the activity was amateur at best, this aspect of western Canadian life did not attract much attention beyond the immediate community. Much of the music was in a popular vein without any distinctive ethnic origin. In describing local orchestras, Lorraine Blashill writes: 'Many were family groups, that usually included a violin or piano, perhaps a guitar or banjo. Later there were drums and saxophones and the occasional trumpet ... With the building of community halls to accommodate ever growing numbers of dancers, these orchestras were in greater and greater demand. Often playing by ear rather than music, some tunes sounded much like others. But when you're having fun, and it's 1935, who really notices?'³

Of the many European peoples who settled in the west, the Mennonites were unique in preserving a musical life of their own. Canadian communities were augmented in the 1920s by an additional twenty thousand Mennonites, who emigrated to Canada to escape persecution in Russia. Many of their musical leaders came from this new wave of settlers, which included teachers and others with well-defined intellectual interests. According to Wesley Berg, wherever they settled, in new locations or established communities, they 'had a stimulating effect on cultural life among the Mennonites already in Canada.'⁴ In the meantime, some of the original settlers were moving to Mexico to achieve greater freedom in education. Berg comments: 'The influx of immigrants from Russia beginning in 1923 brought many people to Canada who had been accustomed to singing in choirs and attending choral festivals. The departure of many Old Colony Mennonites from villages in Southern Manitoba, and their replacement by immigrants from Russia, meant that within a few years an enormous change had taken place in the general attitude to choral singing in the Manitoba Mennonite settlement.'⁵ For the new generation of Mennonites the expanding network of music festivals, workshops, and church celebrations became a way of life in which social patterns reflected a close bonding of church, school, and community; given the realities of a strict religious life, music festivals could be exciting affairs for young people who had to endure taboos on dancing and worldly entertainments. Still, a few progressive leaders working within the Mennonite community challenged the inward-looking views of their predecessors by introducing 'art' music. Such musical ambition went well beyond the old parameters of chorale settings and other sacred pieces, and those who extended the repertoire often created tensions among the more conservative element. In noting Franz Thiessen's predilection for performing Mendelssohn's *Elijah*, Berg observes that 'this classical music aroused consternation, and it was frequently only Thiessen's stature as a minister and man of God that allowed him to get away with the programs he presented.'⁶ Cantatas and oratorios, many of them performed in German, were to become standard repertoire for massed choirs on festival occasions. With this growing interest in choral singing, there were also attempts to improve the expertise of choir directors, as well as a conscious effort to make music an essential part of education. One of the most prominent leaders was Kornelius H. Neufeld, who had received his education in Russia and had had professional chorus experience in opera. Neufeld came to Manitoba in 1923 and for years directed choirs in Winkler and Altona, communities that were to become renowned as centres of Mennonite culture. In 1928 Neufeld transformed the Mennonite Collegiate Institute school festival at Gretna into a large-scale celebration featuring choirs from several surrounding communities, and in 1932 he organized a competitive festival, the first of its kind in southern Manitoba. He worked as a lay leader for the Manitoba Mennonite Youth Organization (established 1942) and helped popularize its festival movement. These accomplishments were not realized without opposition from the church. In Ben Horch's words, 'the pragmatic, mission-minded Mennonite Brethren could simply not accept Neufeld's casual references to the Moscow Opera and other worldly institutions, and were offended by his dramatic approach to music.'[7] Because of his imposing presence at choral events from Ontario to British Columbia, Neufeld was called the 'Wandering Conductor from Winkler.'[8]

David Paetku, who arrived from Russia in 1926, was influential in the Rosthern district of Saskatchewan. He served as a choral director in the church and in the Rosthern High School, where he developed a systematic approach to the instruction of music. Among Mennonite musicians, John Konrad was notable for his work as an instrumentalist. He was a violin teacher in Winkler and later in Winnipeg. His special mission was the development of orchestras, not only in Winnipeg but also in the rural areas, where he continued to teach violin. Konrad broke out of the shelter of the Mennonite musical community in 1937, when he became head of the string department at the Bornoff School of Music. Eventually he took over this school, renaming it the Konrad School of Music in 1950. He was also the founding head (1947–54) of the music department at the Canadian Mennonite Bible College. Typical of most Mennonite musicians, he was first of all a choral director; he was associated with several Mennonite churches in Winnipeg and served as a workshop leader for the Mennonite Youth Organization.

Ben Horch came to Canada from Russia in 1909. Unlike other leaders, he grew up in Winnipeg in a family that was originally of Lutheran persuasion. He had early contact with Ethel Kinley in the schools, encountered British adjudicators at the Manitoba Musical

Competition Festival, and sang in the Winnipeg Male Voice Choir. His was a decidedly cosmopolitan background by Mennonite standards. Commencing in 1928 Horch worked for seven years as choral director and theory instructor at the Winnipeg Bible Institute, later known as the Winnipeg Bible College. He organized the Wayside Chapel Orchestra at the North End Mennonite Brethren Church, the congregation his parents had joined, and was active in Winnipeg as a baritone soloist. His long career as a workshop leader began in 1934, but in the period 1939–43 he studied at the Bible Institute of Los Angeles. Berg observes, 'He returned in 1943 equipped to play a key role in shaping the direction in which Mennonite music education and church music were to go in the second half of the century.'[9] Horch built a fine school orchestra during his tenure as a teacher for the Winkler school board and also established a music department in 1945 at the Mennonite Brethren Bible College in Winnipeg. An influential teacher and a free spirit, Ben Horch opened up new vistas and so challenged a number of time-honoured traditions. Many factors, of course, contributed to change, but none were more pervasive than new opportunities in education. Music training in Mennonite Bible colleges along with greater access to higher education increased the tendency of Mennonite musicians to leave their denominational cocoon for professional careers in music. Horch, who was in the vanguard of this transformation, secured a position in the CBC, and some of his students have done likewise. While retaining their identity collectively, a number of individual Mennonites have moved into the mainstream of Canadian life in the second half of the century, especially in the field of choral music.

MUSIC AND THE MEDIA

Technological advances provided greater access to music in Canadian society. There were improvements in the gramophone, and according to the EMC, 'player pianos could be found in thousands of private homes.'[10] Progress in radio broadcasting in the 1930s did much to minimize the geographic isolation that had affected, if not dictated, the social patterns of western Canada. Music on radio became an everyday experience in Canadian households and enriched the quality of family life; nowhere was it more appreciated than in rural areas, where the remoteness had been most severely felt. From a cultural standpoint the railways helped to open up the west. The CNR pioneered in the development of radio stations, and the CPR produced numerous broadcasts from its large hotels, which often housed broadcasting facilities. With the establishment of the Canadian Broadcasting Corporation in 1936, a vast country was finally linked together by a communication system that could unite the nation by fostering a cultural consciousness. The sociological changes brought by radio magnified the potential of music to be valuable in society and widened the horizons for music education in the broadest sense. At the same time they resulted in less singing in the home and may have precipitated the eventual decline in church choirs.

PRIVATE INSTRUCTION

Private teaching has been directed and shaped to a great extent by the local examination system. The Associated Board of the Royal Schools of Music conducted examinations in the western provinces; the McGill Conservatorium and the Toronto Conservatory were also active in the early decades of the twentieth century. As early as 1910 Walter Murray wrote to the McGill Conservatorium suggesting a national board of examinations in music. There was a strong feeling in the west that it was time for a change – if possible, an amalgamation of the various examining bodies. Western leaders recognized the need for more uniform standards, hoping at the same time to direct financial returns to the prairie region. There was an exchange of correspondence between Harry Perrin (McGill Conservatorium), Ernest MacMillan (TCM), and senior administrators in the western universities.[11] But at this preliminary stage, the established boards in eastern Canada seemed reluctant to enter into an equal partnership, and although invitations were sent to the University of British Columbia, their representatives never joined in the negotiations. Eventually, the three prairie provinces formed their own inter-provincial examination board. The basis for this arrangement was established at a meeting of representatives from universities and provincial departments of education on 13 April 1934 in the Hotel Saskatchewan in Regina; the one musician in attendance was Arthur Collingwood. The agreement was completed at a meeting in the Bessborough Hotel in Saskatoon on 28 April 1936. The original board consisted of the three university presidents, three deputy ministers of education, and a trio of music representatives, Eva Clare (Manitoba), Arthur Collingwood (Saskatchewan), and Gladys Egbert (Alberta). Even after the establishment of the Western Board of Music (WBM), the Toronto Conservatory retained its local examination centres, and right up to the present day the rivalry has led to the development of strong loyalties among private teachers.

Examination boards produced graded syllabi for both practical and theoretical examinations and through their various services attempted to set high standards. Private teachers relied heavily upon.the evaluations and critical comments of examiners. Moreover, the publication of repertoire and study materials was of great benefit to teachers, as were the workshops, recitals, and other forms of professional development designed to stimulate and inspire musicians engaged in private instruction. Eva Clare was one of the outstanding performers and teachers in the west. She moved from Regina to Winnipeg in 1918, studied in Europe, and returned there for concert tours in the late 1920s. In addition to her initiative in the formation of the Manitoba Music Teachers' Association, she worked with Gladys Egbert of Calgary and Leonard Heaton of Winnipeg in compiling the first graded books for the WBM. Her Wednesday Morning Musicale, established in 1933, offered monthly concerts by local performers and often premiered works by Manitoba composers. Eva Clare won an international award for her book *Musical Appreciation and the Studio Club*,[12] which was published in New York by Longmans and Green in 1924.

Private teachers in Winnipeg assumed much of the leadership in church music and in community activities sponsored by the Women's and Men's Musical Clubs, including the Manitoba Musical Competition Festival. They also cooperated with the provincial department of education, so that commencing in 1919 students in Manitoba could receive credit for their private study as a music option in junior and senior high schools. When a provincial music option board was created, private teachers helped to prepare a syllabus and served on its board of examiners. These arrangements remained in place until the university assumed responsibility for the syllabus under the aegis of the WBM. The Manitoba Registered Music Teachers' Association[13] developed into a strong organization, enabling teachers to act as a body while at the same time maintaining independent studios. Private instruction in Winnipeg was not as concentrated in conservatories or institutional settings as in other Canadian cities; the majority of teachers operated on their own. That is not to suggest that there were no private schools in Winnipeg. A conservatory founded by William H. Shinn in 1922 continued to operate until 1967. One of the most enterprising institutions was the Bornoff School of Music and Associated Arts, which opened in 1937. It functioned as a conservatory, offering private instruction in vocal and instrumental areas, with a vigorous schedule of recitals and performance evaluations. Its initial enrolment of seventy students had grown to beyond six hundred by the 1940s, and an emphasis on string instruction reflected the background of its founder, George Bornoff. In 1938 a day school was established so that music students could combine general education with a specialized training in music. This unusual day school 'came under the official supervision of the Manitoba Department of Education'[14] in 1941, but it did not survive into the 1950s. After 1945 Bornoff studied at Columbia Teachers' College in New York, where he further developed his methodology in string class materials as a graduate student and an instructor.

Musical activity in Regina was closely associated with the Regina College Conservatory of Music and its teachers. Dan Cameron, appointed in 1923, taught voice and was active in church and community choirs; Knight Wilson, also appointed in 1923, taught violin and conducted the Regina Symphony; George Coutts, a pianist who taught in the city from 1921 to 1931, was well known as conductor of the Regina Choral Society. Darke Hall, erected in 1929, became one of the musical centres of the city. There were sixteen teachers on staff in 1931, when Cyril Hampshire (director, 1928–36) claimed, 'It is recognized as the leading institution of its kind west of Toronto.'[15]

In Saskatoon the University of Saskatchewan became a focal point for musical activities. Several private teachers who opened studios called them conservatories; however, none of these enjoyed the central place that the Regina Conservatory had achieved in its community. Lyell Gustin was renowned for his success as a piano teacher. He initiated many special events in the community and, in connection with his own studio, developed a summer school of music in Saskatoon. From time to time Gustin was also engaged to teach courses and participate in musical activities at the university.

The leading music school in Edmonton was Alberta College. From 1910 to 1926 this school had music departments on both its north and south campuses. Among the administrators of the music division, Herbert Wild had one of the longest tenures; he was director for more than thirty years. Vernon Barford and W.J. Hendra served for many years as members of its teaching staff. Edmonton, like most Canadian cities, probably had its share of weak teachers, but it could also claim some of the best: Jenny Lerouge LeSaunier, for example, opened a piano studio there in 1922 and drew international acclaim as a performer and teacher.

The Mount Royal College Conservatory of Music became an important centre for music instruction in Calgary. It affiliated with the University of Alberta in 1931 and offered courses leading to a diploma in music. The Mount Royal 'Baby Symphony,' an orchestra of children aged four to twelve, was organized in 1937 by Jascha Galperin. With her fifty-year teaching career (1914–64), pianist Gladys Egbert stands out among the private teachers in Calgary. She developed a program for comprehensive music instruction at her Associated Studios of Music and played a major role in establishing the Western Board of Music.

Private teachers made progress between the wars in organizing their own associations. The first attempts were in Winnipeg (1919), Regina (1925), and Edmonton (1932); later, each of these city groups expanded into a province-wide operation. Provincial associations were formed in Manitoba in 1921, in Saskatchewan in 1930, and in Alberta in 1934. In 1935 the four western provinces led the way by organizing the Canadian Federation of Music Teachers' Associations, and were later joined by other provinces. Private teachers have directed their efforts toward the improvement of music education in general, but they have also sponsored projects designed to promote young artists and to raise performance standards. The licensing of teachers and the establishment of professional qualifications, however, have been of primary concern to the membership, consuming a great deal of its time and energy at meetings and conferences.

Music teachers in the west probably valued the competitive festival more than did their counterparts in other regions of Canada. The place it held for them was an outcome of the geographic and demographic realities of the prairies. But it also reflected how predominant was the influence of British organists, choir leaders, and private teachers in the larger cities, the competitive festival being originally a British phenomenon. Piano and voice teachers especially used this annual event to direct their students toward goals defined by the festival. For many Canadians the Rose Bowl became a prized symbol of musical achievement. The festival paralleled in some ways the practical work of the examination boards. For example, many teachers chose their repertoire from graded examination requirements or festival syllabi. Examinations were private encounters between performer and examiner, with the teacher having access to the written assessment after the event. But a competitive festival could be more dramatic because it was so public – not only the performance itself but also the marks, ranking, and verbal comments of the adjudicator. Its wide appeal to students, teachers, and parents can be seen in table 6.1.

TABLE 6.1
Participation in the Manitoba Musical Competition Festival, selected years 1919–1934

Year	Days	Classes	Entries	Individual competitors	Estimated public admissions
1919	4	38	274	2,500	2,000
1924	6	86	454	6,100	8,500
1929	12	156	833	7,828	22,000
1934	13	187	1,171	11,301	31,000

SOURCE: George S. Mathieson, *Crescendo: A Business Man's Romance in Music* (Winnipeg 1935), Appendix E, 100

The Manitoba Musical Competition Festival was the most successful in Canada, owing in no small measure to the dynamic involvement of its sponsor, the Men's Musical Club of Winnipeg. Other cities such as Regina and Edmonton also had strong citizen groups which built public interest and served as a support system for music teachers in their respective communities. The competitive festival nevertheless has been controversial in music education and has met with criticism on occasion. In 1942, when the philosophy of progressive education was at its height, education officials in Alberta recommended that school groups enter only non-competitive classes in which marks were not assigned. The pros and cons of this long-standing debate aside, however, the festival movement made such a strong impact that it became an intrinsic part of the musical culture in prairie cities.

MUSIC IN THE PUBLIC SCHOOLS

An emerging philosophy of education in the United States left its imprint on Canadian schools between the wars. Innovative work in the area of child development and in the junior high school curriculum was so compelling that the interest of the student became the paramount concern. Learning, as opposed to teaching, became the main goal. As a logical extension of this philosophy, the psychology of education called for more insight into how children develop through various stages of their maturation and how curricula, materials, and methods could be better directed toward ideal outcomes. Some practical features of the educational reforms were introduced into the Winnipeg schools by Daniel McIntyre immediately following the First World War, but it was not until the late 1930s that education in Canada was widely influenced by the progressive education movement. Music teachers did not respond immediately; it will be seen later in this chapter that there was resistance to innovation, and certainly it was a long time before new approaches were implemented in practice. Even inspectors, who were notorious for putting the best face on the situation, furnished no convincing evidence in their annual reports that school music had changed in any fundamental way.

There was a simple, straightforward emphasis on beautiful singing in the elementary schools of Winnipeg during Annie Pullar's lengthy term (1905–37) as supervisor of music. She had attended normal school back in the 1890s and since that time had devoted herself to music in the classroom without introducing any striking innovations. Pullar urged her teachers to participate in the annual competitive festival, in which good performances were reinforced by the comments of adjudicators. Otherwise, the day-to-day work continued in a rather predictable way. The first detailed music curriculum in Manitoba did not appear until 1928. It listed *The Progressive Music Series*, a popular American songbook, as the approved textbook. The success of this book was owing to its careful sequencing of rhythmic and melodic patterns in a child-oriented song repertoire of high quality; its pedagogy was based largely on the rote approach. *The Progressive Music Series* had been recommended in the 1922 *Course of Studies* for Alberta and was also being used in the other provinces of western Canada. Widespread acceptance of these books marked the beginning of a persistently strong influence of the song method, with its roots in the United States. An examination of its content reveals that the so-called Canadian edition of this text (published by Gage in 1921) bore a striking resemblance to the original American edition of 1914. Compared with *The King Edward Music Readers*, the sophisticated repertoire of *The Progressive Music Series* was more compatible with the goals of the child study movement.

The situation in Regina was similar in many ways to that in Winnipeg. William McCann, a former elementary school principal, became supervisor of music in 1919. The province of Saskatchewan also sanctioned *The Progressive Music Series*, and school music programs there invariably emphasized the singing of songs. Education officials and parents alike seemed to equate accomplishment in music education with festival results to such an extent that the reputation of a music supervisor often rested upon the comments, positive or negative, of a visiting adjudicator. The Reverend R.H. Adcock, an Anglican rector in Regina, was fanatical in supporting music in the schools. The degree of his interest can be explained in part by the fact that he had personal experience as a choral conductor and adjudicator. Moreover, he was not at all reticent about criticizing the city's schools when festival results did not meet his expectations. Adcock was irked by the lack of school choirs representing Regina in 1928, and at the annual meeting of the Saskatchewan Provincial Musical Association, the organizing body for the festival, he complained, 'Not enough time is being spent in the musical education of the children in Regina public schools.'[16] His comments, made in Moose Jaw, were reported in the Regina *Leader*: 'In 1927, when the Musical Festival was held in Regina, only one choir performed and this year, none. Moose Jaw, a city which has not the paid experienced man at the head of affairs as in Regina, entered 19 choirs this year, while Yorkton, a city of 5000 brought three choirs to Moose Jaw at an expense of $1200. What I claim is needed, is the loyal support of all school principals and every member of the school board to enlarge this work. I am of the opinion that singing in the public schools should not be an adjunct or a frill, but placed on the curriculum as an absolute necessity.'[17] Reverend Adcock pledged that 'he would hold himself ready at any time to assist principals, teachers or school board in order to put over a large musical program during the coming season.'[18] Subsequently, the teaching of music came under review: a small delegation from the festival association (Reverend Adcock, John Fenstein, F.W. Chisholm, and A.L. Wheatley) met to thresh the matter out with the school board and, they hoped, to clear the air of any misunderstanding; members of the board, two principals, and the music supervisor were in attendance. The delegation recommended that the competitive element be encouraged in the schools and that the board hire teachers willing to lead choruses and do musical work. Later that year Adcock campaigned successfully to become a school trustee and, among other things, devoted himself to the expansion and improvement of school music. Board minutes revealed that one of the most marked budget increases was in 'music' – from $244 to $1000 – and the board made plans for the future purchase of high-quality phonographs. But Adcock's missionary zeal was channelled primarily into music for the festival. Evidently he made good his offer of assistance, for in November 1930 the *Leader-Post* reported: 'Eleven choirs from public schools were entered in the Saskatchewan Music Festival held in May, and Connaught school choir was awarded the highest possible marks for school choirs. In this connection, Mr. Adcock visited every public school in the city, to test voices and select entrants for the festival. In preliminary competitions for solos and school choruses, Mr. Adcock acted as adjudicator last May, and in the same capacity the previous Spring. As chairman of the music committee, Mr. Adcock has made periodic visits to the public schools, examining voices and offering suggestions and advice to the teachers giving instruction in music.'[19] McCann did not receive any direct criticism as music supervisor – indeed, Adcock even praised his efforts on occasion – but he must have felt the pressure of having such an ardent supporter of the festival on the school board. This emphasis on festival performance probably precluded any major change in the teaching of music as a school subject. When McCann resigned unexpectedly in February 1935, Adcock offered to carry on 'the music' until the festival was over.

The elementary curriculum as revised in 1931 by the Saskatchewan Department of Education did give more substance to the music course, but the course was designed with attention to the acquisition of musical skills rather than being based on principles of child development and growth. Cyril Hampshire, principal of the Regina Conservatory, became music supervisor for the public schools in 1935. He drew rave reviews at the annual festival and by all reports accomplished high standards of performance during his four years in this post. But there is little doubt that an organist/choirmaster trained in England would have been concerned more with musical achievement than with the subtleties of progressive education. In 1939 Hampshire moved to Ontario, where he served as principal of the Hamilton Conservatory; later he pursued a successful career as director of music in the public schools there.

As in Regina, references to music in Saskatoon dwell on the music festival. In 1929 C.A. Oulton, superintendent of schools, wrote: 'A decided attempt has been made to improve the teaching of Music to our children and with a very considerable degree of success. In almost every one of the schools there is at least one thoroughly qualified teacher who organizes and directs the teaching of this subject, and the results obtained have been very gratifying. At the Musical Festival held in this city in May 1929, seven choruses from the public schools competed: all acquitted themselves very creditably. One was successful in winning one of the two School Chorus Shields offered.'[20] His report more than ten years later indicates that the number of students and teachers had increased but that the program was still focused on the festival: 'There has been a decided improvement in the quality of music instruction given in the schools. At the music festival held in this city in May 1940, 39 teachers directed the singing of more than 2000 school children in 62 choruses or singing games. There were entries in all of the 13 competitions and every school was represented.'[21] Although Oulton considered this event to be 'a festival rather than a competition'[22] and maintained that marks were not of great importance, he was precise in noting the results. He concluded, 'Participation in the festival is to quite an extent responsible for the great interest in music in the schools.'[23] Generally speaking, schools in the small communities and rural areas of Saskatchewan were not caught up in the provincial competition, but they did have their own local festivals, in which a music contest was often organized as an integral part of an exhibition or special event. The preoccupation with competitions and public demonstrations persisted even after the 1931 curriculum revision, and only on rare occasions do inspectors' reports indicate that their expectations for the subject went beyond the mere participation of students in fairs, festivals, or field days. In 1932 the chief inspector conceded: 'In music, the progress has been very slow. The teachers are quite inadequately prepared to carry out the recommendation of the new curriculum.'[24] However, he sounded a note of optimism later in this report: 'I have been greatly pleased with the splendid attitude of many of my teachers in spite of greatly reduced salaries. It has been remarkable to note the number who are taking music lessons in an effort to improve their standard and place themselves in a position to better interpret the curriculum and to teach this subject as it should be taught.'[25] Music generally was perceived as an extra-curricular activity in rural schools, though from time to time inspectors suggested that the musical demonstrations reflected the regular work of the classroom. A report in 1935 shows the range of extra-curricular events: 'A number of oratorical contests, musical festivals, school exhibitions and union school picnics were held. Preparations are under way for a local musical festival and physical training competition. The festival is simply a public demonstration of the work done in the classroom. The songs selected are those from the prescribed outline. Parents are enthusiastic. The one difficulty is to get all schools to participate. Those in which only fair work is done in music are diffident about giving a public demonstration. The Christmas concert looms large in the minds of our people.'[26]

Music supervisors in the large cities were frequently church musicians by training rather than teachers equipped to deal with music in education. In Calgary, Dr Frederic Rogers, organist at Central

Methodist Church, held the supervisory position from 1922 to 1926. He was succeeded by Captain H.S. Hinton, who was organist at one of the large Baptist churches. Hinton's credentials, however, did include a Tonic Sol-fa certificate from England. During his twenty-four year term, Hinton held annual school demonstrations, which were expanded into four-night affairs. These demonstrations were broadened to include drama, physical education, and choral speech and served as excellent public relations activities. A major part of his job was to provide in-service training for teachers, including work in the preparation of curriculum materials. Hinton stated that the aim of the supervisor was 'to develop community singing in the schools and so help children to understand and appreciate some of our National Songs, Folk Songs, and other great songs.'[27] Hinton's reports to the board did not vary much from year to year. Furthermore, there is little evidence that his brand of theory and music appreciation embraced the integrated approach, which took into account student growth and motivation; its absence is conspicuous in a province which by the mid-1930s was breaking new frontiers in progressive education.

Music in Alberta's separate schools remained for many years in a comparatively neglected state. In 1928 Father Boltz became the first supervisor of music in Calgary, but it was not until 1933 that Father Leo Green was appointed to a similar position in Edmonton. Green, a trained singer from England, arrived in Edmonton in 1927 and served as choir director for thirty-five years at St Joseph's Cathedral; his church activities paralleled his work in the schools. During his tenure as supervisor (1933–68), Leo Green laid the foundation in Edmonton for what eventually became one of the strongest music programs in Canadian separate schools. Father Green was also involved in drama and other cultural endeavours during his colourful career, and in recognition of his work one of Edmonton's elementary schools was named in his honour.

Norman Eagleson's term as supervisor of music in Edmonton's public schools extended from 1912 to 1949. He was tireless in his efforts to expand the music program; he introduced class piano and non-competitive festivals, and even proposed a plan for regional orchestras in the city to be trained by professional musicians. Eagleson wrote a series of instructional books in the 1930s entitled *777 Graded Exercises in Sight Singing for Schools.*[28] These books were designed for elementary, intermediate, and high school classes, and the methodology, 'moveable do in staff notation,' was explained in meticulous detail in a published teacher's manual. Early in his career Eagleson had visited American cities to keep abreast of the latest developments in music, but by the time he retired his pedagogy had not kept pace with the innovations that had permeated Alberta's educational programs. It does not follow that Eagleson's work was inferior because he was not part of the new generation. He had a long-standing interest in music reading, and like many other teachers in Alberta at that time he was reluctant to sacrifice the traditional emphasis on skills for the purpose of correlating subjects toward general social goals. In this controversy, which was rampant in educational circles, music teachers were usually slow to relinquish traditional values related to performance.

The Advent of Progressive Education

Alberta was in the vanguard of educational reform in the late 1930s. Columbia Teachers' College in New York and the University of Chicago, the main centres for progressive education in the United States, had a strong philosophical influence on western Canada. Innovative ideas were promoted through graduate programs at the School of Education at the University of Alberta. Donalda Dickie gave leadership at the grass roots level by implementing new methodology in Alberta's elementary and secondary schools. Dickie's influence was spread through her teaching at the university and through her curriculum work for the provincial department of education. Simply stated, the new approaches purported to teach the whole child rather than the subject, and much of what the controversial American educational theorist John Dewey advocated was transformed into the so-called progressive education movement. The synthesis of history and geography in social studies is an example of the increasing interest on the part of educators in integrating subjects. The idea of projects by small groups and individuals, a feature of what was sometimes referred to as the 'enterprise' system, captured the imaginations of teachers seeking more sophisticated approaches in the motivation of students. The notion of the efficacy of active rather than passive learning was particularly relevant to aspects of the teaching of music. From the time of its initial acceptance, however, this philosophy had a polarizing effect among the ranks of educators. Those who retained a discipline-oriented approach scrutinized the implementation of the new ideas, holding fast to the importance of content; by way of challenging the new order, they demanded convincing proof in the form of practical results. Whether it was regarded as reform or rhetoric, educators at all levels were vitally concerned with the tenets of progressive education.

Curriculum development in Alberta had been daring in seeking the opinions of lay people and in experimenting with new schemes for a rural population. But music in rural education had never known widespread success, and new curricular models accommodated the subject in only a superficial way. Moreover, traditional school subjects in the 1930s were discarded for a modern organization based on the psychology of learning, and in this context music was integrated with other subjects until its intrinsic value and purely artistic vitality were at risk. Much of the momentum generated in curriculum revision penetrated the realm of music through *The Music Hour*, a revised version of *The Progressive Music Series*. New pedagogical ideas were demonstrated by Maude Garnett, one of two Americans brought on staff for the 1939 summer school at the University of Alberta. Most attempts to revolutionize music learning probably fell short of the desired expectations. Yet as the stages of child development took on increased importance, there was less emphasis on sight-singing but more effort to bring variety into music programs of an eclectic nature. These practical applications of progressivism were introduced in Alberta through the use of American song series and were directed primarily toward music appreciation. In Manitoba, however, appreciation was rooted in song material, and although substantial listening units were developed, the emphasis remained on expressive singing. American books which correlated music with other subjects were not embraced so enthusiastically in this province. Ethel Kinley provided the musical leadership in Manitoba's educational system; she was music supervisor in the Winnipeg schools but her influence was province-wide. Miss Kinley, who was inclined toward British song material, compiled *The Manitoba School Song Book*[29] in 1940. It was a collection of carefully chosen songs which made no attempt to include formal appreciation lessons or other supplementary material found in American texts of that vintage.

Although the circumstances were different from those in Alberta, the seeds of progressivism implanted in Saskatchewan had far-reaching societal effects there too. Teachers in that province were deeply affected by the hardships endured by the rural population during the Depression years. Many of them were leaders in the formation of the CCF political party. This party formed the provincial government in 1934, and its reform programs in education reflected the ideals of the progressive movement. Still, changes were slow to manifest themselves in school music. *A Song Book for Saskatchewan Schools*[30] was adopted; it was Ethel Kinley's *Manitoba School Song Book* published under a different title. Moreover, there was a continued commitment to the festival movement, for in general, British traditions in music were not crowded out by the pedagogical experimentalism which had been cultivated in Alberta. Saskatchewan did not feel the full effects of progressive education in music until Rj Staples became an adviser to the department of education in the 1940s. Staples's influence can be seen in the music curriculum of 1947, but his impact was even more direct and powerful when he became provincial director of music in 1949.

Junior High School Movement

The junior high school was the product of an attempt to liberalize the rigid curriculum that existed before the First World War. The movement reflected a growing recognition that schools should address themselves to the motivation of students – through activities and projects which appealed to students themselves – rather than to their mastery of prescribed subjects. To realize these objectives, teachers possessing specialized expertise were selected to develop more fully the potential of students at this level. The western provinces experimented with junior high schools long before they were introduced elsewhere. Curricular programs in Manitoba and Alberta were eventually organized into three levels, elementary, intermediate, and high school. Even though some school boards did not establish junior high schools as such, this three-level plan was implemented across the province for purposes of instruction. The patterns and traditions associated with music education in the west are significantly different from those in other parts of the country. To a certain extent these differences can be attributed to the three-level structure which had its conception in the junior high movement.

Ethel Kinley was appointed music teacher at Earl Grey Junior High School in Winnipeg, one of the first of its kind in Canada. From 1919 to 1925 she presented auditorium sessions dealing with folk songs, directed annual Gilbert and Sullivan operettas, and, through the Manitoba Musical Competition Festival, stimulated interest in school choirs. Her immediate success won recognition both from her own principal and from Daniel McIntyre, director of education. McIntyre had introduced the junior high school concept after studying similar schemes in several American cities; the idea of rotating classes had been inspired by the Gary, Indiana, plan. Kinley expressed her philosophy of music education in the *Manitoba Teacher* in 1924. With regard to the values of music, she asked, 'What could be better than a listening lesson, where a musical theme is to be followed through its repetitions and variations; or an ear-training lesson where a simple melody or rhythm heard must be remembered and translated on paper?'[31] Ethel Kinley was in frequent demand, often demonstrating music methods at teachers' meetings and designing new curricula for the province. In commenting on her work with adolescents, she wrote: 'This is the age of disturbing emotions, when the desire for self expression and the creative impulse asserts itself, when the love for team work is so strong. The singing of beautiful songs provides a legitimate outlet for the emotions, and a delightful medium for self-expression.'[32] She held strong convictions about the quality of music necessary for achieving goals in music appreciation: 'This is the period, too, when tastes are being formed; hence the possession of a repertoire of good songs, which never fail to satisfy, will leave no place for the cheap and unworthy, which in this age of "jazz" will crowd into every unoccupied space. The lesson in music appreciation ... should, by enlarging the child's knowledge of the best in musical literature (through the medium of the gramophone, other means being lacking), open up vistas of loveliness later to be more definitely explored.'[33] The junior high organization was introduced in Calgary in 1934 and two years later was adopted throughout the province. Cornelia Higgin was one of the first music teachers appointed to junior high schools in Calgary, where the curriculum was structured according to compulsory and optional subjects. Music (both choral and instrumental) was listed as an option along with dramatics, household economics, general shop, junior business, art, agriculture, French, typewriting, and elementary sociology. Over the three years students were expected to sample at least four of these exploratory subjects. Although instrumental music was listed, it did not become established with any widespread success or continuity until the 1950s. Nevertheless, there was a freedom to experiment in junior high schools, and at times, formal instruction gave way to activities in which learning was more experiential.

Music Appreciation

Music appreciation became the most discussed aspect of school music during the inter-war years, and it was in this realm that the greatest expansion of the curriculum took place. Whereas music instruction up to the First World War had been primarily concerned with singing and basic musical literacy, in this period there was a philosophical shift toward appreciation. Even if music appreciation in the real sense of the word did not always materialize, at least educators were exploring the idea. Instruction in music appreciation appeared at various levels and in many different forms. Sometimes it grew out of song material but placed emphasis on aesthetic qualities and on sensitivity. In other cases it was designed as a separate listening program leading to the formal study of musical genres or the lives of great composers. Perhaps the best examples of this type were broadcasts on radio which were designed as supplements to classroom activities. Indeed, technological advances in radio broadcasting and in the recording industry accelerated the philosophical shift toward appreciation and opened up possibilities for enhancing the quality of musical experience within the classroom. Phonograph companies prepared instructional materials to be used with selected recordings. These were produced in albums dealing with historical periods or with instructional units on songs, symphony, or the instruments of the orchestra. The larger companies in the United States appointed distinguished teachers such as Frances Clark to design instructional materials, and the quality of these commercial projects drew an enthusiastic response from teachers. Music appreciation lessons prepared by Mabel Rich of the Victor Talking Machine Company were recommended to those schools in Manitoba which had procured gramophones or victrolas.

But not all music appreciation material originated with commercial companies. An unusual project was undertaken in Saskatoon, where Lyell Gustin conducted appreciation sessions for the public schools from 1931 to 1938. Each year he presented a series of five programs in which live performances were enhanced by introductory comments. The series was repeated in various sections of the city and then a sixth program was presented in Third Avenue United Church. In 1933 the superintendent of schools reported: 'Arrangements were made by which all the children of the upper grades attended these concerts. They were encouraged to write notes on what they had learned from Mr. Gustin's talks, and to give their impressions as to interpretations given by the assisting artists. More than 200 notebooks were thus compiled and prizes were awarded for the best of these. At the final concert, which was broadcast, over 1600 children were present, and their keen interest and rapt attention gave evidence that the purpose of the whole series had been well fulfilled.'[34] Gustin, an outstanding private piano teacher, organized this series for the school board without receiving any remuneration. The performers were either Gustin's own advanced students or colleagues who shared his altruistic desire to extend music appreciation to the whole student population.

Music appreciation was offered in Regina schools in the late 1930s through regular radio broadcasts by Cyril Hampshire, who, according to Earl G. Drake, 'modelled his half-hour program on those of Walter Damrosch in the United States.'[35] In Calgary, Captain Hinton used the proceeds from annual school demonstrations to stock a central library of music, books, and gramophone records. He referred every year to the great advantages which his teachers derived from the use of this fine collection. In commenting on the revised courses for Alberta in 1936, Norman Eagleson declared that music appreciation had been given new prominence at all levels, even down to the rhythm band activities in the lower grades. He found the outlines were 'much more enlightening than was the case with all former statements issued by the Department.'[36] The objective was no longer 'the child's acquirement of a fluent technique' but 'the generation of his love for music shown in continued favourable reactions.'[37] Eagleson's expressions of enthusiasm, however, were counterbalanced by the following: 'Because appreciation has not been mentioned specifically as a "course" in the older statements, it does not follow that it did not exist. It is always an indefinable residue from any active musical experience whether choral, solo or instrumental ensemble. Indeed there are those who contend that appreciation through musical activity is of more value than that accruing from the passive listening lesson.'[38] Music appreciation as it was outlined in Manitoba's 1939 curriculum was substantive and comprehensive, reflecting Kinley's strong views that the essence of music was inherent in its performance. The functions of singing, listening, and creating were identified as the means by which music's intrinsic values contributed to a genuine understanding and appreciation of the art. It was a curriculum which derived its vitality directly from musical experience. Ethel Kinley's long-standing family ties with Ivan Shultz,[39] the minister of education, enabled her to influence the shape and direction of school music with the full weight of political power behind her. Curricula developed in Alberta in the late 1930s reflected sophisticated forms of progressive education, as exemplified in the 'enterprise.' In the 1936 curriculum the cultivation of music appreciation was sought through the integration of music with other subjects; the approach was derived from an educational orientation with its primary concerns in child development. Those teachers who were not conversant with the new ideas had to adapt music as best they could, and, in the course of events, the extrinsic aspects probably became more important than the intrinsic values of the subject itself.

School Radio Broadcasts

Radio broadcasting helped to expand the scope of school music, and though broadcasting made its greatest contribution in the area of appreciation, there were radio programs that dealt with other facets of music. P.G. Padwick, for example, used a small orchestra in Winnipeg to conduct rehearsals over the radio on Saturday mornings. As early as 1930 Ethel Kinley presented radio broadcasts on topics such as art songs, folk themes, and composers. She also conducted school choirs on radio programs featuring songs or carols in the Christmas season. Elizabeth Harris, Beth Douglas, and Muriel James were among the teachers in Manitoba who developed music appreciation programs in the 1940s. In Alberta, radio sing-song sessions by Agnes Davidson were carried over station CJOC in Lethbridge, and in 1938 Janet McIlvena introduced a series for elementary grades. Her association with such programs lasted until 1958, and she became well known throughout Alberta for her school music broadcasts. Cooperative programming had commenced in the four western provinces in 1941, but apart from the early efforts of Cyril Hampshire in Regina, most school radio programs in Saskatchewan originated in Manitoba or Vancouver. Later, the most prominent person in Saskatchewan was Rj Staples, who after his appointment as provincial supervisor of music made radio broadcasting the highlight of his career.

High School Music

Students taking private lessons on an instrument (or in voice) were granted external credit which could be used as a music option in junior and senior high schools. Such regulations were in operation in Manitoba and Alberta by 1920. To satisfy the requirements students had to present certificates from accredited examination boards, and in addition to obtaining certificates for practical examinations students were also expected to do theoretical work. Provincial departments of education conducted their own written examinations initially, but later on conservatory certificates for theory were accepted. The external credit arrangement was a form of support for music students and their private teachers. It also set a precedent for having music as an optional subject at a time when there was no music other than in extra-curricular activities. The province of Manitoba extended credit for music courses taken within the school in 1933; similarly, Alberta established high school music courses in 1937. Only a small number of students requested external credit for music study in Alberta, but music enrolment rose sharply once courses were available within the schools.

Following the First World War there was a growing interest in activity as a valid part of the educational process. This idea formed a cornerstone of the junior high philosophy and was also applicable to extra-curricular programs at the senior high level. Even before music was offered for academic credit, there was an increase in the number of glee clubs, orchestras, and operetta productions as part of the social life of the school. This flowering of interest was often owing to the efforts of enthusiastic principals or teachers who were amateur musicians prepared to sponsor these clubs and activities. In many cases they had to call upon local church organists or bandmasters to direct groups that had begun casually but later required more musical expertise. Instrumental music in most schools was confined to extra-curricular orchestras, which accommodated students who had already received some training. These ensembles enjoyed support from principals and boards because of their utilitarian rather than their educational value. They provided music for school assemblies, parents' nights, graduation ceremonies, public speaking contests, and a host of school functions involving the community. The school orchestras of this era were characterized by incomplete instrumentation and dubious repertoire. Nevertheless, their efforts were appreciated to the point that many students and parents expressed interest in making instrumental music part of the instructional program.

The formation of a provincial orchestra in Manitoba during the 1920s was a remarkable accomplishment given the undeveloped state of instrumental music in Canadian schools at that time. This ambitious enterprise owed its genesis to Percy Graham Padwick, a British teacher who came to Winnipeg to teach Latin, French, and mathematics at St John's College Preparatory School; his extra-curricular duties involved music and cadet training. Padwick applied four times before he finally secured a position in the Winnipeg public schools in 1920. In his first school, Lord Roberts, he organized an extra-curricular orchestra. He transferred to Kelvin High School in 1926, where he taught Latin, mathematics, and music, and in the following year, as Leonard Takoski notes, he 'gathered seventy-five young musicians from the schools of Winnipeg and outlying municipalities to form a broadcasting orchestra.'[40] For the next eleven years he sent orchestral parts to students, who rehearsed by playing along with his radio program in their own homes. Saturday morning sessions carried on station CKY served as preparation for full rehearsals in Winnipeg, where the massed orchestra would present its final concert during Easter week; these live concerts were also broadcast across the province by radio.

In 1929 Padwick formed the Winnipeg Junior Symphony Orchestra, of approximately a hundred players. Its concert debut in 1934 'was carried from sea to sea over the national network of the former Canadian Radio Commission.'[41] A few years later, he renamed his ensemble the Western Canada Junior Symphony Orchestra. 'Its membership was drawn from cities, towns, villages and farms as far east as Kenora, Ontario, and as far west as Moose Jaw, Saskatchewan.'[42] Not surprisingly, Padwick experienced a nervous breakdown and had to take a leave of absence. However, shortly after he resumed teaching he accepted responsibility for carrying on and extending the orchestral work in the schools of Winnipeg. This involved the personal direction of thirteen orchestras and the supervision of conductors in three other schools. The highlight of his hectic career came in 1938, when he conducted more than four hundred students in a grand concert held in the Amphitheatre Rink, not long before he died. The press covered the event, and his efforts were aptly summarized in the Winnipeg *Tribune*:

Tonight ... the dream of P.G. Padwick will reach a climax ... the long and short of it is that Paddy, God bless him, is a passionate educationist at heart. He is a school teacher, a task fit only for idealists, and it was out of this devoted labor that his notion of music as a great uplifter and inspirer grew. When broadcasting came along, with its power to reach over vast distances and into innumerable homes, he was carried away by his enthusiasm. Music – carried over the vast prairies, creeping into humble farm homes to comfort and inspire! It was almost too good to be true. Paddy went for it, body and soul. Week after week, month after month, hammering the rudiments of music into them, pleading, haranguing, urging – it has been a tough grind for Paddy.[43]

The large ensemble which Padwick had directed was reorganized in

1938 and officially named the Manitoba Schools' Orchestra. As part of the reorganization a number of junior ensembles were formed to help develop younger players. Ronald Gibson (1938–41) and Filmer Hubble (1941–53) in turn served as conductors in a concert schedule which included extensive tours to smaller communities throughout the province. As representation from the rural areas diminished, activities shifted toward the specific needs of city students. This change was duly recognized in the 1961–2 season, when the organization was renamed the Greater Winnipeg Schools' Orchestras and Band. Padwick's project was ahead of its time, and orchestral programs in individual schools were slow to develop. Indeed, it was not until 1957 that instrumental music was authorized in Manitoba's official program of studies.

The Edmonton Schoolboys' Band was formed in 1935. It was an extra-curricular ensemble which initially drew its members from Victoria and Technical Schools but later recruited players from all city schools. The band was initiated by T. Vernon Newlove, a part-time teacher of mechanical drafting and building construction at the old Technical High School. He received a grant of three hundred dollars from the school board to purchase music and a few used instruments. After several months of rehearsal, the band was busily engaged at the Technical School's Open House, the laying of the cornerstone of Eastwood High School, the Edmonton Exhibition Parade, and the Beverly sports day; its first concert took place in 1936 in the Canadian Legion Hall. Although the band was an extra-curricular enterprise, both Newlove and O.W. Murray, his assistant conductor (1941–59), were given released time in the afternoons to compensate for their evening rehearsals. Eventually, Newlove became a full-time bandmaster.

The Edmonton Newsboys' Band, a precursor of the Schoolboys' group, had been sponsored by John 'Mike' Michaels, the proprietor of a downtown news-stand. Michaels started this project in 1914 as a social outlet for newsboys, and originally his wife served as its musical director. Ever popular with the citizens of Edmonton, the Newsboys' Band reached its peak when it performed for the British Empire Exhibition held at Wembley Stadium in London, England. By 1936 the school board was sufficiently impressed with Newlove's Schoolboys' Band that they negotiated with Michaels for the purchase of instruments and uniforms from the Newsboys' organization, which had been defunct since 1928. In that same year Newlove enlisted approximately sixty boys from junior high schools as a training ensemble for the senior band. Two-week summer music camps were held in Banff for ten consecutive seasons commencing in 1937. The boys travelled to the first camp in a Wilson Transport van equipped with four rows of benches, and by all reports thoroughly enjoyed the adventure of tenting out. In their second season, 'a staff of four undertook to handle a camp of 120 boys, with Mrs. Newlove as chief cook, nurse and camp mother.'[44] According to M.A. Kostek, 'their biggest thrill came in 1939, when the 132 boys paraded at the CNR station to welcome King George VI and Queen Elizabeth to Edmonton.'[45] The band toured extensively after the Second World War. Newlove's aggregation functioned independently of the music department, retaining its own budget and schedule of events. This administrative anomaly rankled the supervisor of music, Norman Eagleson, and led to strained relations between the music department and the band. It was not until 1970, a year after Newlove's retirement, that girls were also admitted into the band, at which time it was renamed the All City Band.

The introduction of music as an optional subject in junior high schools opened the way for general acceptance of the subject at the high school level; it was a logical step to extend music to grades nine and ten in senior high once a precedent had been established for a grade nine course in junior high. The courses typically consisted of singing, music appreciation, and some work in the rudiments of theory. After a successful term at Earl Grey Junior High School, Ethel Kinley transferred to Daniel McIntyre Collegiate Institute in Winnipeg. She succeeded Miriam Armstrong, who had already accomplished a great deal in music at this school. Kinley remained in this position from 1925 to 1937, and Daniel McIntyre Collegiate set the pace for other schools such as Kelvin and St John. Indeed, high school music in Winnipeg gained an outstanding reputation in the years leading up to the war. Most schools were noted for their operetta productions. They were also renowned for their choirs and seemed to thrive on the accolades which British adjudicators on the 'chain' threw their way at the annual Manitoba Musical Competition Festival. The formation of graduate choirs in several high schools became a tradition which lasted for several decades, a testament to the success of high school music in Winnipeg.

The overall growth in high school music during the period between the wars was modest. Any expansion which did take place was found in urban communities, and even in those centres there was usually one school which served as a model for others. For instance, interest in music at Crescent Heights High School in Calgary can be traced back to

1915, when James Fowler organized a small orchestra. This ensemble was developed from 1921 until 1938 by Edgar J. Smith and was much appreciated when it provided accompaniment for school operettas. The school also had an interesting background in choral music, in that William Aberhart, leader of the Social Credit Party, conducted the school's glee club in 1923; later he became premier of Alberta and served as minister of education. In 1938 Norman Pickard assumed responsibility for the music at Crescent Heights and established a tradition which reached its climax in the 1960s under the direction of Lloyd Erickson. In Alberta, music emerged as a bona fide subject when major curriculum revisions in the late 1930s finally approved academic credit for music courses. An immediate rise in the music enrolment for 1938 suggests that student interest was substantial. Mary Buckley attributes an increase in 1940 to the fact that for normal school entrance 'a high school course in music became a compulsory requirement.'[46]

Progress in getting music into the high schools of Saskatchewan seemed to be slower than in other prairie provinces. There were the harsh economic conditions of the 'dirty thirties,' and there was the fact that Saskatchewan did not adopt a junior high school structure, which in Manitoba and Alberta led to a more varied curriculum with optional subjects. When Rj Staples was appointed to Regina's Central Collegiate in 1933, he found an outmoded state of affairs in that the boys in grades nine and ten took spare periods while the girls went to their music classes for theory, twice a week. However, Staples was too energetic to accept the confinement imposed by such a restrictive program:

> After almost five full years of arguments, persuasions, and negotiations, Staples managed to have a large room in the basement of Central Collegiate allotted for a music and art room, and to arrange for all grade(s) nine and ten students (male and female) to elect either music or art as a non-compulsory subject area. Staples taught music and art during his sojourn at Central ... and, until the last few years, other subjects such as English and French ... so he had no spare periods. This heavy schedule was implemented despite the fact that there were over 1,000 students enrolled in the school, and practically all his extra-curricular work ... orchestra, band, glee club ... was done at noons, after school, evenings, and weekends.[47]

The Staples story was typical: many schools depended upon an aggressive, skilful teacher to break through the complacency of school administrations. To their credit, a few music teachers accomplished remarkable results even though most of their work was relegated to noon or after-school rehearsals. It was also common for music teachers to be assigned to basements, annexes, or temporary 'portable' class-rooms so that any disturbance of sound to academic classes would be avoided. Achievements in such anything-but-ideal acoustical situa-tions eventually convinced administrations to provide the improved music facilities and equipment that are characteristic of many Canadian schools today. Frequently teachers had to raise money through con-certs and other projects in order to produce musical shows or acquire instruments for their ensembles. For example, Staples and his students collected over five thousand recordings during the Second World War for the RCA Victor Company. The company melted these recordings to provide shellac for the manufacture of munitions, and for their efforts the students received one of the company's best radio–record players. The enterprise and drive shown in Staples's career was typical of those teachers who were determined to break new ground in high school music.

Although progressive education made inroads into a curriculum that had been almost exclusively academic, the period leading up to the Second World War was a transition at best. Instrumental music re-mained an extra-curricular activity, disappointingly so, in that edu-cation was undergoing major philosophical changes which could have brought music into more prominence. Instrumental music as a second-ary school subject was not firmly established in the prairie provinces until the late 1950s. More often than not, music penetrated the life of the school because of its universal appeal as entertainment. For stu-dents in the inter-war years, music and sports provided a welcome relief from the rigours of an academic curriculum which had been designed as a preparation for university or teachers' college. Therefore the pleasing sounds of a glee club or the excitement of an operetta lent a touch of cultural and social life. As impressive musical groups emerged, the results of their efforts were demonstrated not only in the communities but also at professional meetings, where principals and administrators became aware of what could be accomplished. In time, other schools tried to emulate these models. Thus, music expanded not as a result of any educational philosophy, administrative decision, or well-conceived plan, but rather through the imitation of a few success-ful programs which had been created by highly motivated individuals.

MUSIC IN HIGHER EDUCATION

Music in the university was regarded as a peripheral activity rather than as a fitting academic discipline. University people were not hostile toward music, but they perceived it merely as something to enhance campus life, in the form of glee clubs, operetta societies, and the like. At the University of Manitoba, a small singing group formed in 1925 developed into the University Glee Club and in 1928 presented its first operetta, *The Mikado*. Annual Gilbert and Sullivan productions, with Winona Lightcap as music director, enjoyed widespread popularity in the community, and in 1937 a university symphony orchestra was established. Conductors over the years included Ronald Gibson, Frank Thorolfson, and Filmer Hubble. Eva Clare, appointed director of music in 1937, served as representative on the WBM and coordinated the university's musical activities, but courses were not offered until 1945, when music electives were accepted in general arts programs.

In 1925 the University of Alberta installed a pipe organ in Convocation Hall and offered Sunday afternoon recitals by local organists. However, most of the cultural developments at this university came as a result of visionary leadership in adult education and extension programs. The Extension Department, through a grant from the Carnegie Foundation of New York, enlisted music adjudicators and provided administrative assistance for school festivals in smaller communities. This department also pioneered the use of radio as a medium for education in rural regions. Its own radio station, CKUA, commenced operation in 1927 and accommodated a wide range of interests. According to one account, 'they had their own orchestra of twenty pieces; their own radio players; a wealth of lecture talent; one of the finest pipe organs in the country (the memorial organ in Convocation Hall) and the co-operation of student groups in debating, mixed chorus, opera and sports.'[48] Through the efforts of E.A. Corbett, director of the Extension Department, and a Carnegie Foundation grant, the station procured 'a very large record player and a library of over 900 recordings of classical music.'[49] Corbett recalled: 'This enabled us to go on the air every evening with an uninterrupted hour of the world's greatest music, and as a result the station became something more than a source of information chiefly of interest to farm people. It began to acquire a large listening audience of music lovers throughout the Province and beyond.'[50] Corbett also forged the beginnings of the Banff School of Fine Arts. Initially operating as a summer theatre school, it was supported by a thirty-thousand-dollar Carnegie grant in 1933. Music began informally in 1934 with sessions in folk singing conducted by Jocelyn Taylor and Wally House of New York University Drama Division. Corbett recalled, 'They were both accomplished guitarists and their repertoire of folk songs represented every part of North America and many European countries.'[51] Donald Cameron became the first director (1936–56) of the Banff School, providing vigorous leadership in establishing it as an international centre for the arts. Formal instruction in music was first given in 1936, at which time Viggo Kihl of the Toronto Conservatory of Music taught piano for two summers. He was succeeded by Jacques Jolas of the Juilliard School in New York and, in 1941, by Max Pirani, who taught intermittently until 1950. Glyndwr Jones taught choral music in 1937, and eventually a string program was introduced by Clayton Hare, in 1951. With reference to piano instruction in the early period, David Leighton comments: 'Although all were outstanding teachers, they had difficulty filling their classes. The annual reports of the Department of Extension for those years refer repeatedly to the disappointment at the enrolment. Yet, to its credit, the School did not abandon the effort. After all, it was a School of Fine Arts, and no such school would be complete without music.'[52] Before the Second World War, Banff was one of few summer schools in Canada where talented musicians could pursue advanced study in music.

The University of Saskatchewan (founded 1907) was the first in the west to establish a music department in which courses and degrees were integrated into the academic program of the university. This milestone was reached through the good offices of President Walter Murray. As early as 1930 he inaugurated a chair in music with financial support from the Carnegie Corporation of New York. After considering three candidates, all of whom were from Great Britain, he appointed Arthur Collingwood, an organist from Aberdeen, Scotland. Collingwood, like the other candidates, had visited Canada as an adjudicator on the festival chain. Motivated by President Murray, Collingwood busied himself in stimulating the development of all facets of music in the province. He introduced a full range of courses within the university, including evening and summer offerings; for a number of years instruction was administered by the Faculty of Music. The University of Saskatchewan awarded its first BMus degree in 1934. Collingwood also created a conservatory, which listed nine local teachers as part-time instructors, and the university cultivated a close affiliation with the Regina Conservatory. Collingwood organized and conducted the Saskatoon Symphony Orchestra in 1931–2, attempted to develop a more comprehensive program in the schools of the province, assumed responsibilities in the WBM, and was also involved in the provincial music festival. Clearly, the duties associated with this university post became extremely heavy and diversified. In his first report to the Carnegie Foundation (1931–2), Collingwood wrote:

> The Music Department is being increasingly regarded as a general inquiry bureau by teachers and students: budding composers, teacher inquiries concerning music, students with professional ambitions, embryo conductors of choirs and orchestras regarding the technique of conducting, anxious parents seeking good teachers for their children, women's musical clubs re: courses of study – right down to the confessedly self-taught banjoist who found it impossible to play in time and in tune at the same moment – would the Professor of Music, if he was able, tell him what to do.[53]

Collingwood perceived himself as a provincial ombudsman, for in this advisory role he received enquiries 'not only from all parts of the province but from every province in Western Canada.'[54] Upon closer scrutiny it appears that Dean Collingwood's early enthusiasm ran ahead of his actual accomplishments, for by the time his term ended, such ambitious plans had not been consolidated into a permanently large or distinguished department. The destiny of music at this university may have been too firmly in the hands of President Murray, who retired in 1937. The University of Saskatchewan, nevertheless, did better than most western institutions, in that it was responsive to the musical needs of the greater community and took the initiative in establishing music as a university discipline.

Departments of music were eventually established at the University of Manitoba in 1944 under Eva Clare and at the University of Alberta under John Reymes King in 1945. Their growth and sphere of influence was modest, not venturing beyond an administrative function in the WBM and a general contribution to the cultural milieu through student activities or projects funded by the Carnegie Foundation. It was not until the 1960s that they assumed a vital role within their academic communities by expanding course offerings to full professional degrees.

TEACHER TRAINING

In 1919 a conference of principals from the normal schools of western Canada recommended a number of changes for the improvement of teacher training. Their most urgent concern surrounded the length of the normal sessions, which in some cases lasted only two months for third class certificates and four months for second class certificates. There was no immediate impetus resulting from this conference. Nevertheless, the 1930s was a transitional decade in which provincial departments of education gradually relinquished teacher training to the universities. A number of changes were made in the early 1940s, when colleges of education within the universities were reorganized into faculties of education. Eventually these new faculties subsumed elementary school training.

In music, results remained sporadic in teacher training during the inter-war years, for there was no consistent policy in hiring instructors. Moreover, expectations remained vague and diffused. The issue as to whether the instructor should be primarily a certified teacher or a trained musician was never resolved. A number of accomplished musicians held normal school positions: W.J. Hendra (Edmonton, 1920–2), Mrs F. Barber Smith (Edmonton, 1930–3), and Filmer Hubble (Winnipeg, in the 1930s). Their terms were relatively short, sometimes because the demands of a music career took first priority. Conversely, there were situations in which experienced classroom teachers lacked the musical expertise required for an ideal balance of music and methodology. These general circumstances not only resulted in many part-time positions but also led to frequent changes in staff. Those whose tenure and commitment were more enduring included Madame Ellis Browne (Calgary, 1909–36), Madame Helen Sherry (Saskatoon, 1917–44), R.T. Bevan (Moose Jaw, 1930–42), Cornelia Higgin (Edmonton, 1940–55), and Beth Douglas (Winnipeg, 1943–56).

Provincial departments of education and universities co-sponsored summer courses for teachers interested in upgrading their backgrounds and qualifications. Summer schools did not remedy in any fundamental way the inadequacies of teacher training, but for those who took advantage of them they were valuable supplements to the general programs of the normal schools and were effective as short-term solutions. Saskatchewan was the first prairie province to offer music instruction in the summer. The courses held occasionally from 1913 to 1919 did not attract large enrolments or become annual events, and between the wars there was very little summer work devoted specifically to music education in the province. In 1918 there was a course in Alberta entitled 'Music and Games,' but not until the late 1930s did summer courses in music make a strong impact. When the department of education introduced curricula associated with the progressive education movement, Alberta's summer schools attracted a large number of teachers. The increased activity was stimulated by the University of Alberta's Extension Department and the School of Education. These units became renowned for innovative programs which brought guest lecturers from abroad to implement new methods and approaches. Maude Garnett of Oswego College in New York used a demonstration group of fifteen students, aged five and six, to introduce the *Look and Play* song series written by an American, Osborne McConathy. The methodology in this series emphasized the 'sound before symbol' principle and was compatible with Alberta's new curricula, which treated music as an exploratory course. Garnett also taught at the Edmonton Normal School for part of the 1939–40 academic year, just before the appointment of Cornelia Higgin from the Calgary school board. Higgin was a graduate of the University of Montana; the combined efforts of Garnett and Higgin made for a strong thrust of American influence.

Summer schools of music in Manitoba took on a decidedly British influence under the leadership of Ethel Kinley. According to Sharon Dueck, 'Miss Kinley's experience dated back to 1928 when she attended the Scottish Summer School of Music, and studied with Hugh Roberton and George Dodds.'[55] In 1929 Ethel Kinley conducted a summer music course for the provincial department of education designed to help teachers cope with the revised curricula for grades one to six (1928) and seven to nine (1929). Kinley was again invited in 1939 to develop summer courses in methodology and in music appreciation. These were focused on curriculum revisions to which Kinley had already contributed her musical expertise, teaching experience, and personal charisma. The success of these summer courses led to even more ambitious plans, facilitated to a great extent by Kinley's influence with Ivan Schultz, the minister of education (1936–44). In 1941 Kinley operated a summer music camp at Singoosh Lake in Duck Mountain Provincial Park on the site of a former lumber camp. Although the physical and geographical environment was rugged, the musical milieu was of extraordinary refinement. Winnipeg church musicians Ronald Gibson and Filmer Hubble were in attendance, and a resident string quartet provided daily chamber music. Through the resources of the department, Kinley was able to add British adjudicators Frederic Staton and Steuart Wilson to her staff. (Because of the war they had been unable to return to Britain after 'making their rounds on the Canadian Festival Chain.')[56] Marjorie Horner described events at the 1941 camp:

> For a series of lectures on various aspects of school music, we sat under Dr. Frederic Staton, that most sincere and purposeful gentleman, who understood so well our class-room problems, and shared with us so lavishly the rich store of his own musical knowledge and experience. There were illuminating talks on accompanying, conducting technique, boys' choirs and interpretation.
>
> Then for another interesting and productive course we had as lecturer our good friend, the erudite and brilliant Steuart Wilson. With him we made an exhaustive study of English vowel sounds. In yet another course under Mr. Wilson we sought to analyse the complexities of Elizabethan music, and sang, under his direction, many lovely examples of the fascinating music of this period ... The recreation period over, we were again ranged upon those unyielding benches in the pavilion, to sing, under Dr. Staton, that most eloquent and moving composition of Holst, 'Hecuba's Lament.'[57]

Staton returned to teach for four consecutive summers, and, as Dueck notes, in 1944 he teamed up with John Goss to give a course tracing 'the development of painting, architecture, literature and music from the 15th to the 19th centuries, an ambitious venture undertaken with the aids of gramophone records and an epidioscope.'[58] Owing to 'petrol rationing' the 1943 camp was held near Gimli, only fifty miles north of Winnipeg.[59] In 1944 it was held in the city, at St John's Theological College.

The pattern and character of the summer music courses in Alberta and Manitoba were entirely different. The Alberta course derived its momentum from general educators in the United States whose priorities were methods-intensive. The Manitoba course was based on a musical foundation with strong ties to British choral traditions. Manitoba's curriculum procedures were less sophisticated, and the musical substance of the course reflected the background and priorities of Ethel Kinley, who completely dominated music education in her own province.

7

A Swing of the Pendulum in British Columbia

Vancouver was on the international performing circuit in the period between the wars, and celebrities became a regular part of concert life. Its audiences enjoyed performances by Sergei Rachmaninoff in 1923 and 1931; Maurice Ravel appeared during the 1927–8 concert season; Paderewski, Heifitz, Kreisler, Lily Pons, and Dame Nellie Melba were among those who performed in Vancouver during the 1920s and 1930s. Many touring artists also played in Victoria, stimulating its musical growth as well. But the more isolated communities were less fortunate, and except for occasional visits small towns had to rely upon local and regional people for their concert fare.

Choral organizations, operatic societies, and, to a lesser extent, community orchestras were formed on an ad hoc basis, sometimes merely to satisfy new or ambitious conductors; consequently, many of these groups proved to be short-lived ventures. Few orchestras managed to attain any degree of longevity, and bands were even less successful. In spite of their instability, however, bands remained a genuine expression of popular culture and continued to be valued for utilitarian reasons, particularly in the remote parts of British Columbia. Many community ensembles functioned as training grounds for young people who for various reasons did not receive music tuition from private teachers. A generation of boys had their musical debuts in juvenile bands in Vancouver with British bandmasters Jock Parle and William Sarah-Hoskin or in New Westminster with C.J. Cornfield.

Later, a steady stream of young players came up through the ranks of the Kitsilano Boys' Band, which Arthur Delamont directed from 1928 until the 1970s.

PRIVATE TEACHING

The academies operated by the Sisters of St Ann developed excellent music departments. The work of this religious order in British Columbia, dating back to the 1850s in Victoria, later expanded to several other places, such as New Westminster, Nanaimo, Kamloops, and Vancouver. In addition to an impressive record of private teaching, their recitals and public lectures contributed to the musical life of these communities. Otherwise, there was an absence of reputable conservatories or private music schools surviving long enough to have a telling influence. Outstanding work in studio teaching can be attributed to many people who not only gave private instruction but also fulfilled leadership roles in community organizations. There were many fine teachers in Victoria: Gwendoline Harper, Gertrude Huntly Green, Stanley Shale, and Marie George. Among the outstanding teachers in Vancouver were Mrs Walter Coulthard, J.D.A. Tripp, Avis Phillips, Nancy Paisley Benn, Gideon Hicks, Phyllis Inglis, Barbara Custance, and Ira Swartz. Typically, in most smaller communities there were two or three dedicated teachers who without recognition or fanfare worked long hours at inconvenient times for modest fees. Many of them were church organists and choir directors, and it was not unusual for a local teacher to operate the only music store in town. The majority of music teachers, especially those outside the major cities, relied upon examiners' comments or adjudicators' praise to renew their spirits for yet another season. Consequently, examination boards – the Associated Board of the Royal Schools of Music, the McGill Conservatorium, the Toronto Conservatory of Music, and Trinity College of Music (London) – represented an essential support system for private instruction.

Private teachers formed professional associations in the hope that they could raise musical standards and, through licensing, improve the status of studio teaching. The Vancouver Men's Club was formed in 1913. A rival group, the Vancouver Music Teachers' Association, was organized in 1920 with H. Roy Robertson as president, and in 1932 it expanded to become a provincial organization. In 1935 similar groups from all four western provinces took the initiative in forming a national body which, joined by other provincial organizations in the 1940s and

1950s, ultimately led the way for the incorporation of the Canadian Federation of Music Teachers' Associations. The first conference of these founding associations took place in Vancouver in July 1936. The agenda covered a wide range of topics, including music as a school subject. Delegates raised questions regarding the decision of British Columbia's department of education to allow credit for private music study as a high school matriculation subject. They noted that in the new regulations successful work in piano (or violin) and theory could be used in lieu of Latin, French, or other optional subjects. Concerns were also expressed with respect to the qualifications of high school music teachers as compared with those of private teachers. At one point in the conference, a teacher from Kamloops challenged the value of competitive festivals. She declared, 'The festivals have just about run their course of usefulness'; in her experience, students were 'discouraged by unfavorable comparisons.'[1]

Competitive festivals could add a dimension of excitement to music making, not only for the students but also for their teachers. Yet not all adjudicators called forth a positive response, for some teachers despised the arrogance and acrimony which occasionally characterized the style of these visiting dignitaries. Dale McIntosh notes that 'the first competitive music festival held in the province was organized by A.E. Waghorne at Lynn Valley, now part of North Vancouver, in 1912.'[2] By 1916 this event had attracted five hundred contestants, who were adjudicated over a four-day period by Frank Wrigley, a church musician from Calgary. The Lynn Valley competition was the progenitor of others, some of which did not last very long; for instance, an ambitious festival inaugurated at New Westminster in 1919 was held for one year only.

The British Columbia Musical Festival began in Vancouver under the auspices of the Knights of Pythias in 1923 and, in its first year, consisted of forty classes involving approximately a thousand competitors. The Knights of Pythias sponsored this annual event until 1960, when the Vancouver Kiwanis Club assumed responsibility for its operation. There was a dramatic increase in the number of festivals and participants during the inter-war years. The Okanagan Valley festival commenced in 1926 and the Victoria festival in 1927, and by 1930 the West Kootenay and the Yale-Cariboo festivals were also in operation. A large registration of school choirs in Vancouver probably reflected the British choral background of the music supervisors themselves, namely, Fred Dyke, Charles Findlater, and Fred Waddington. It is also noteworthy that British adjudicators were used almost exclusively in the major festivals until the restrictions of wartime travel made it impossible to engage individuals from overseas. This practice of using British musicians was virtually enshrined by an organization which became known as the Federation of Canadian Music Festivals.[3] The federation had representation from the four western provinces, but its administrative work was carried out in Winnipeg through the office of the Men's Musical Club. Members of this club were not reticent in justifying their preference: 'These British adjudicators, who have graced the Canadian festivals ... are musicians of the highest standing on both sides of the Atlantic, gifted and trained for their peculiar tasks, men whose integrity and honour are beyond question, and whose decisions have been given without fear or favour.'[4]

SCHOOL MUSIC

The music syllabus contained in the courses of study issued by the provincial department of education in 1922 outlined the work for the elementary grades. It placed an emphasis on vocal training and competency in sight-reading, recommending the use of sol-fa syllables, hand signs, and modulator chart, followed by simple exercises in staff notation. The first and second readers of *The New Educational Music Course*, Canadian Edition (Ginn and Co.) and the *School and Community Song Book* by Vogt and Willan (W.J. Gage and Co., Toronto) were listed as the approved textbooks.

In 1925 J.H. Putman and G.M. Weir[5] were commissioned to conduct a survey of education in British Columbia. They found the school system to be extremely conservative and, in many ways, irrelevant to the needs of the province. Their report contained no specific recommendations for music, although it suggested that the subject should be given more importance. Presumably, the aesthetic nature of music opened up possibilities beyond regimentation and drill for Putman and Weir, who contended that the curricular framework of education should be more responsive to the individual interests of students. The document was particularly critical of rigid academic requirements in secondary education and advocated much more flexibility in school curricula. Such philosophical ideas were beginning to enjoy universal acceptance in educational circles throughout North America and abroad. Perhaps the most striking outcome of the Putman-Weir survey was the introduction of junior high schools in Vancouver. There, music gained acceptance in innovative programs, and in 1930 the subject became obligatory for grades seven and eight and was offered as an elective in grade nine. Otherwise there was little evidence of a transformation in the philosophy or methodology of music education as a result of the provincial survey.

It is clear that major improvements would have required a completely new approach to the training of music teachers: in fact, no drastic changes were implemented. The normal school, which operated under the provincial department of education, was in a strategic position to effect change, and according to the 1927–8 report the basic tenets of progressivism had already been endorsed by the 'establishment': 'The old emphasis on "teaching" has given place to the larger and more fruitful concept of "learning" and once again the child himself occupies the centre of the educational stage. The old notion of imparting information to the child is now entirely obsolete. In its place has come the concept of individual growth in a social environment. These all-important principles are coming more and more to be recognized, and acted upon in our training schools.'[6] However, in recognizing the inherent problems facing normal schools, the report sounded a note of realism: 'The same complaint is now made by our Normal School instructors that has been voiced from time to time ever since the Normal Schools began – namely, insufficient knowledge of the subject matter of instruction in the various elementary school subjects. It must be obvious that in a one-year Normal course professional training for the highly technical work of teaching cannot be fully achieved if a large proportion of the time has to be given to what might be termed academic subject preparation.'[7] Certainly this was true for music in the normal sessions held during the academic year. It was only at summer schools, where teachers came to upgrade their qualifications, that any real progress was shown. Ethel Coney and F.T.C. Wickett were music instructors at summer sessions held at the Victoria Normal School in the 1920s. Coney was music mistress of the Vancouver Normal School from 1913 to 1937; Wickett, a former supervisor of music in New Westminster (1912–22), was a church organist who also taught at Brentwood College, a private school in Victoria. Initially summer courses consisted of vocal music and harmony, taught by Coney and Wickett respectively; in 1922 there was an enrolment of only twelve teachers in music.

The New Canadian Music Course,[8] a five-book series by Coney and Wickett, was authorized for schools in British Columbia in 1925; its organizational plan served as the basis of the summer course. The series was advertised as 'a graded course of instruction in singing, designed to teach the reading of music, to develop an appreciation of rhythm, and to provide a large selection of songs suitable for all grades.'[9] The song repertoire, use of modulator drills, and complete outline of theoretical details reflected the traditional British background of the authors and furnished a systematic approach for elementary teachers. But it was neither new nor progressive. What materialized in the aftermath of the Putman-Weir survey was a trend toward specialization. With the addition of new courses in summer schools, enrolment reached a high point in 1929; a report lists these figures: 'Vocal Music, 31; Choral Music, 80; Music Supervisors, 29; Art of Singing, 42; Class Piano Teaching, 25.'[10] A number of special projects were introduced in summer sessions in the late 1920s. One of the most successful was a demonstration school in which Fred Waddington, a manual training teacher, rehearsed and conducted a chorus of boys and girls. He established this workshop on an annual basis, and, according to reports, the high standard of singing impressed both teachers and the general public. Waddington, whose choral pedigree was of British origin, eventually shifted his teaching from manual training to music, and in 1927 he was appointed supervisor of school music in Victoria. Activities at the Victoria summer school also revealed a growing interest in instrumental music: a juvenile symphony orchestra comprising thirty-five players 'met each morning for instruction and practice'[11] during the summer session of 1930. This ensemble was composed of pupils from the ages of eight to sixteen years as well as a few school teachers. By all accounts the adult members of the class were amazed at the ability of the juniors. The annual report concluded, 'Not only should the orchestra be continued next year, but the subject of how to train an orchestra would be a fitting one for music-teachers.'[12]

Many events at the 1929 summer school were broadcast on radio, and for several years Mabel Rich, a representative of the Victor Talking Machine Company, came from Toronto to give a series of lectures on music appreciation. Summer schools also sponsored recitals and concerts, sometimes featuring guest artists. Ira Dilworth, principal of Victoria High School, was one staff member who encouraged such artistic activities and at times performed as a pianist himself. Indeed, the Victoria summer school was much more than a series of courses for teachers; it evolved into a festival of the arts in which a final concert of choral and instrumental music was enjoyed by audiences of more than a thousand people. Despite such efforts at summer sessions, school music did not change significantly – apart from the introduction of the rhythm band; in the words of a report, 'We also introduced last year the rhythmic band or toy symphony orchestra as recommended by the highest musical authorities, and an afternoon concert was given to demonstrate how young children may cultivate the musical sense of rhythm and time by natural and interesting means.'[13] The momentum generated by summer sessions ended abruptly in 1931, when for financial reasons the Victoria summer school was discontinued. A summer school was held in Vancouver, however, in which students were expected to pay for their own tuition. In 1932 Victoria resumed its operation on similar terms, but the excitement of breaking new ground had ended and projects such as demonstration choirs and orchestras were not resurrected. It is not surprising, then, that Coney and Wickett were still teaching Vocal Music I and II in the summer of 1935, albeit to a declining enrolment. A description of Vocal Music II in the annual report claimed that 'the study of rudiments of music was treated exhaustively, a good knowledge of which was deemed essential.'[14] C.E. Findlater, supervisor of music in Vancouver from 1928 to 1931, taught choral singing at the summer school held in that city. Again the course description stressed 'the necessity for all theory-work in the class-room when teaching music or leading a school choir.'[15] Even at summer schools, where presumably the staff consisted of outstanding teachers, methodology in music did not reflect the idealism of the Putman-Weir report, other than to laud the value of music appreciation and to popularize the percussion band in primary grades. In short, the swing of the pendulum toward progressive education had not yet affected music as a school subject.

It was not until the late 1930s that music at the Victoria summer school enjoyed a renaissance. The escalation of summer training was a response to major revisions in music curricula; it also reflected a growing need for more specialized teaching in junior high schools. A new generation of music educators assumed the leadership for summer courses: in 1936 Stanley Bulley, newly appointed music supervisor in Victoria, joined the staff, and in 1937 Mildred McManus, Coney's successor at the Vancouver Normal School, and Burton Kurth, supervisor in Vancouver, commenced lengthy terms as summer school teachers. F.T.C. Wickett, however, who had been involved since the summer of 1922, remained on staff until the end of the Second World War.

Vancouver

Progress, or the absence of it, in school music was not always mirrored in the rise and fall of summer schools, for as in other provinces the larger cities often led the way with ideas which provincial departments later formally adopted in their policies and programs. Vancouver achieved considerable success as a result of the continuity in the terms of its music supervisors: George Hicks, 1904–19; Fred Dyke, 1920–8; Charles Findlater, 1928–31; Fred Waddington, 1931–7; and Burton Kurth, 1937–55. The majority of these men were of British background and training. Even Burton Kurth, who was born in Buffalo, New York, had been steeped in a British choral tradition in Winnipeg. Most supervisors in Vancouver, like their counterparts in other cities, were experienced musicians rather than graduates of teacher training institutions. Therefore, their notions of child development were not rooted in the psychology of education. Some supervisors compensated for their deficiency in this area by persuading the school board to appoint assistants for the primary/junior grades, usually female teachers who possessed normal school qualifications. These assistant supervisors helped to alleviate the burden of in-service training by conducting workshops and preparing guidelines for classroom teachers. As a general rule, school boards must have had a predilection for male supervisors, for they rarely promoted the female teachers who served so efficiently and faithfully in these 'assistant' roles.

Grade eight students were required to pass provincial examinations for entrance into high school. Teachers, therefore, were under pressure to ensure that students were well prepared for this annual ordeal. As a consequence, music, which was not an examination subject, received only token support from inspectors, principals, and teachers. Music teachers traded on their successes in competitive music festivals to get recognition from their superiors, and supervisors used public demonstrations and civic celebrations to strengthen support for their work. For example, in 1921 Fred Dyke organized six thousand children for a performance in Stanley Park on the occasion of the fiftieth anniversary of the province. In 1936 Fred Waddington produced a Golden Jubilee program which featured a massed choir of two thousand voices, comprised of high school choirs (400), senior elementary choirs (1000), and junior choirs (600); also participating in this program were an orchestra conducted by Ifor Parfitt and a composite schools band under the direction of Arthur Delamont. The music programs at

Magee, John Oliver, and Kitsilano High Schools indicate that some progress had been made at the secondary level. Among the prominent school musicians in this period were Mildred McManus, Ifor Roberts, and Sherwood Robson.[16]

The appointment of Burton Kurth as supervisor of music ensured the primacy of choral work in Vancouver's schools. Having been a voice teacher in Winnipeg, he was aware of several fine school choirs there and the close relationship between the Manitoba Competition Festival and the public schools. Kurth came to Vancouver in 1929 as choirmaster at Chown Memorial Church and, from the time he accepted the school supervisory position, filled his two roles with energy and enthusiasm. Kurth collaborated with Mildred McManus on several school songbooks, and he composed approximately a hundred songs, many of which have been used in festivals and competitions. In the mid-1940s two city-wide choirs flourished under the leadership of Alfred Hewson and Sherwood Robson, and McIntosh notes that 'a fifty-piece string orchestra with players from many schools was directed by Priscilla Long.'[17] As well, a number of excellent performing ensembles, both choirs and orchestras, were developing within individual schools.

Victoria

School music in Victoria did not enjoy the vigorous leadership which proved to be so beneficial in Vancouver. Although he was supervisor for almost twenty years, Harry James Pollard did not build a strong tradition, nor were his efforts in the final years, when he was in poor health, crowned with distinction. And Fred Waddington, appointed in 1927, remained only until 1931, when he became music supervisor for the Vancouver schools. Unfortunately five years passed before the Victoria school board filled the position, and in the meantime classroom teachers were left to their own devices in music. It is evident that music education suffered from the economic constraints of the 1930s.

Stanley Bulley was a British organist who had been at Christ Church Cathedral in Victoria since 1930. In 1936 he gave an address to the University Women's Club in which he advocated music as a compulsory subject in the schools and, moreover, insisted that instruction should be in the hands of specialists. Bulley's rationale, based on a notion of the importance of cultivating good taste in music, was expressed thus: 'A storm of indignation would rightly arise if our classrooms were decorated with undesirable pictures or our libraries stocked with pornographic literature ... we may yet see such a storm arise if music which possesses the same destructive influence be presented to our children in the schoolroom, the movie or through the radio.'[18] Shortly after his criticism of music in the public schools, Bulley was hired as music supervisor for Victoria, and subsequently he served on a provincial committee which was responsible for a new elementary school curriculum (grades one to six). Bulley claimed that his 'devastating critique of the curriculum resulted in a complete revision,'[19] a project which enabled him to visit educational leaders in England for extensive consultation. Bulley also negotiated a Carnegie Foundation grant to procure a record collection together with 'mechanical aids'; this equipment was used for music appreciation in regular classes and in night school classes for adults. Through this grant, NBC school broadcasts by Walter Damrosch were made part of a scheme that furnished free teacher manuals and student workbooks. A highly trained musician, Bulley was strong in purpose and opinion, so it is not surprising that he met resistance in carrying out some of his plans; his term as supervisor did not last through the Second World War.[20] Another break in the continuity of music supervision occurred, for Harry Bigsby, Victoria's next supervisor, was not hired until 1946. The vocal program at Victoria High School was directed by G. Jennings Burnett in the 1920s and by Frank Tupman in the 1930s. McIntosh notes that 'by 1940 the school could boast a fine aggregation of singers when Norma P. Douglas, teacher of music and Latin, developed a fine mixed choir at this school.'[21]

There were other places throughout the province where school music seemed to be taking hold: in 1922 Celeste Page held a full-time music position in Penticton; in 1927 Mabel Willcox was music supervisor in Vernon; and by 1925 J.P. Humphreys had developed an orchestra of about thirty-five players in Chilliwack. Yet there is no discernible pattern in the gradual spread of music to the less-populated areas – in most situations it happened simply because a reliable teacher or musician was available to initiate some form of instruction or musical activity. Opinion regarding the quality of school music was often determined by results in competitive music festivals. Inspectors congratulated winning schools in their reports and even noted the names of the successful teachers. By the late 1930s, however, the British Columbia Department of Education had recommended the elimination of marks at music festivals on the strength of the new educational values. A controversy erupted as a result of comments made by the British adjudicator Sir Hugh Roberton at the 1938 festival in Victoria. Roberton stated publicly, 'Standing in a non-competitive festival is not and cannot be anything like what it is in a competitive festival.'[22] Subsequently, the Honourable G.M. Weir, minister of education, 'issued a stinging rejoinder'[23] pointing out that Roberton was neither an educator nor a psychologist. The newspaper account observed: 'The high standards of the past to which reference was made were a delusion. They meant a high nominal standard for a few and the neglect of others.'[24]

MUSIC APPRECIATION AND SCHOOL RADIO BROADCASTS

Some of the most enterprising programs in education were devised as experimental approaches in music appreciation, especially in the early days of radio. Even before the advent of radio programs Miss A.E. Fraser had pioneered an extra-curricular appreciation course at King Edward High School in Vancouver. But the most dynamic exponent of music appreciation was Ira Dilworth, an English teacher at Victoria High School. When Dilworth became principal of that school, he invited soloists and groups such as the Hart House Quartet to perform, and used the gramophone in music appreciation assemblies which he conducted himself before the entire student body. Peter Lawson Smith says of Dilworth, 'With a passion that approached missionary zeal, he embarked on a plan to give music and drama a central place in the life of every youngster in his charge.'[25] Dilworth eventually became Pacific regional director of CBC and, in this post, encouraged the production of school broadcasts for the purpose of extending music appreciation into classrooms which did not have a music teacher.

The use of music in school radio programs was initiated by Miss Ellen Lloyd Roberts, assistant supervisor of music for Vancouver's elementary schools. Each of twenty-four schools produced a sixty-minute program of songs, educational games, and helpful lessons in the 1927–8 school year. Not appreciation lessons in the strict sense, these were well received by students and adults alike. In his book on school broadcasting, Richard S. Lambert notes that 'the most marked response came from country teachers who in many instances arranged for groups of students to gather in a home where there was good radio reception, to listen and learn. Some children came as far as fifteen miles to attend, while in one locality children came in rowboats across deep channels through narrow fjords. Such was the lure of radio in those early days!'[26] A series of six music appreciation programs originating from a Kelowna radio station in 1936 created sufficient interest to motivate the provincial superintendent toward a more ambitious plan, an experimental program in which Mildred McManus and CBC staff collaborated to produce 'Musical Pathways.' This was a series of ten programs which offered practice in the singing of songs familiar to the schools by inviting participation from the classroom audience. By 1938 plans had materialized for the establishment of 'The British Columbia Radio School,' and with Ira Dilworth on the provincial school radio committee the future of music in educational radio was assured. Another initiative in music appreciation began as early as 1934, when arrangements were made for secondary school students to attend the final rehearsal of the Vancouver Symphony Orchestra before each of its public concerts. Interest was stimulated through preliminary information and annotated programs. This project, one of the first experiments with a live orchestra, attracted as many as twelve hundred students.

The Sir Ernest MacMillan Fine Arts Club, British Columbia's unique venture in music education, was conceived in 1936 by Marjorie Agnew and was named in honour of Canada's leading musician.[27] The idea grew out of noon-hour recitals presented by student groups at Templeton Junior High School in Vancouver. The purpose, to nurture an appreciation of the arts, was realized through the formation of chapters in individual schools and was supported by special events which Miss Agnew organized on a provincial scale. Within a short time MacMillan clubs spread to other schools throughout British Columbia and in parts of Alberta. Agnew was a teacher of boundless energy, and through a succession of inventive projects she managed to bring students together in a common purpose. For MacMillan Club members these cultural pursuits were characterized by a spirit of discovery and adventure. In 1937 fourteen chapters took part in the first fine arts festival. Later, mammoth rallies were staged in Stanley Park, and radio programs featured activities of the clubs. Student members also worked as ushers at the Orpheum Theatre and Denman Auditorium. Close communication between schools was maintained through a newsletter, which contained reports and announcements from various clubs, thereby giving students a sense of identity within an arts community of their own. Commencing in 1940 the 'MacMillan Club Radio Quiz' became an extremely popular program. It was broadcast live before a packed studio audience at 6:00 p.m. on Thursdays over the Pacific stations of the CBC. Each program featured two school teams from either elementary, junior, or senior high levels fielding questions drawn from music and the arts; in the words of one account, 'in music, questions ranged from Gershwin to Chopin or Sinatra to Tschaikovsky.'[28] Ira Dilworth, the inspiration behind many cultural developments in British Columbia, made this ambitious undertaking possible, and his own musical expertise added much to its continuing success. Occasionally Sir Ernest MacMillan himself acted as quizmaster. This was a congenial arrangement because he had a marvellous rapport with young people, and they in turn found his sense of humour irresistible. He was also greeted enthusiastically when he appeared in Stanley Park as guest conductor for arts festivals. Such personal contacts inspired and reinforced the efforts of Marjorie Agnew and her assistants, with the result that Sir Ernest became a national hero to a generation of students in British Columbia. 'Agnew was the club's driving force throughout its 40-year existence,'[29] according to the EMC, so it is not surprising that with her failing health the club fell dormant in the mid-1970s.

INSTRUMENTAL MUSIC

As supervisor of music in the Vancouver schools, Fred Dyke organized violin classes in 1924. The program involved three hundred students and six teachers in eleven different schools. Classes varying in size from ten to twenty pupils were held between 3:30 and 6:00 p.m., and students were charged fifty cents for two half-hour lessons per week. The annual report stated: 'A great deal of interest was manifested in this venture from its inception – most of it friendly, a little the reverse. The latter manifested itself in a protest against additional expenditure, but, when it was shown that the classes could be conducted at no expense to any one save the parents of the children enrolled, all opposition ceased.'[30] The report also noted that good results were found only when medium-sized classes, of approximately ten students, were held immediately after the close of regular classes in the students' own schools and conducted by teachers who could give class as well as individual instruction. The Canadian Bureau for the Advancement of Music (CBAM) negotiated with several school boards in British Columbia to offer class piano instruction. The bureau, operating out of Toronto, made its arrangements in Vancouver through the supervisor of school music. In 1930 the report for the Vancouver schools noted an enrolment of 470 pupils, 70 per cent of whom continued their study to the close of the year.[31] Among similar programs in the smaller communities, CBAM introduced class piano instruction in Kamloops in 1932.

George Dyke, the brother of Fred, organized the Victoria Boys' Orchestra in 1922 and introduced violin classes in the schools of Victoria in 1927. Just as versatile as his brother, George had operated one of the first music stores in Vancouver, established several private music schools, and held positions as choirmaster, critic, orchestral conductor, and impresario. Apart from string classes in Victoria, he was not directly engaged in public school work but functioned primarily as a free-lance musician. Victoria High School had a rich musical tradition dating back to 1914, when E.H. Russell,[32] a mathematics teacher, formed a school orchestra. It was reorganized in 1919 by T.S. Whittemore and in 1926 by Principal Ira Dilworth. Alfred Prescott conducted the orchestra commencing in the 1930s. For a number of years it was augmented by players from outside the school and was known as the Victoria Junior Symphony.

Conversely, in Kamloops a community orchestra which began under the sponsorship of the Canadian Legion was later integrated into the school. This unusual development arose from the apparent misfortune of Nelson 'Archie' McMurdo. McMurdo had come to the Kamloops area from Scotland, but experiencing little success as a farmer, he acquired work in a music store and in due course was persuaded to teach violin to a few private students. In 1931 McMurdo formed a small community orchestra of ten players, which grew in numerical strength and musical maturity. The success of his musical endeavours was demonstrated in 1939 at the music festival in Vancouver, where much to everyone's surprise, the orchestra from Kamloops was declared provincial champion. Dorothy Hopgood, one of McMurdo's first students, helped to keep the orchestra functioning during his absence in the Second World War; after graduating from UBC, she taught music in Trail and for many years was on the staff of Victoria High School. McMurdo, upon his return from war service, persuaded school authorities to incorporate his community ensembles into the school. By so doing, he placed this type of musical training on a more systematic basis. McMurdo's programs eventually included both orchestra and band. Rex Potter was another person who pioneered instrumental music in the Interior. His appointment to the Trail-Tadanac High

School in 1938 marked the beginning of a thriving program which involved bands and orchestras; by 1944, 550 students, more than half the school population, were enrolled in music.

Arthur Delamont formed an extra-curricular band in 1928 at the General Gordon School in Vancouver. Shortly afterward, Delamont, who was a band director rather than a certified teacher, severed his connection with the school system, and the band became known as the Kitsilano Boys' Band. For over fifty years he provided intensive instrumental training in this community band which was geared more toward competitions and international tours than toward purely educational goals. Later, he resumed his school band work in several programs, including those at West Vancouver High and Point Grey Junior High. A number of professional players received their early musical instruction from Delamont, so it is not surprising that he became a legendary figure among wind players in British Columbia.

Several instrumental music programs originated from school bands. McIntosh reveals how the evolution took place in one situation:

In the Interior, the movement started as early as 1938, when Fred Turner began a school band at Testalinda Creek Elementary School (just south of Oliver) without the knowledge of his superintendent. Students from his class were absorbed into the Oliver High School Band under Gar McKinley in 1939. The ensemble claims to be the first school band with regularly scheduled classes within the school day, and it can boast a continuous history from 1939. Initially band classes were scheduled with one period in school time and a second after school, but in 1941, by which time McKinley was also vice-principal of the school, band classes were scheduled for three periods per week, all within the school day. Factors that precipitated the move, at a time when most instrumental programs in the province operated on an extra-curricular basis, included serious transportation problems for students who lived long distances from their school, and a sympathetic school administration. That McKinley was vice-principal of the school was a distinct advantage.[33]

School orchestras were more common than bands before the Second World War because the instrumentation of the orchestra could absorb almost all instruments, including a piano to cover missing parts. Bands were sometimes formed as useful adjuncts to cadet corps and generally had a strong appeal for boys who were attracted by uniforms, parades, and other extra-musical features. More often than not, teachers relied upon the success of extra-curricular ensembles to elicit support for instrumental music as an accredited school subject. The violin classes introduced by the Dyke brothers in the 1920s had been attempts to establish instrumental music instruction, yet orchestras remained as extra-curricular organizations and flourished or floundered from year to year according to the availability of accomplished players in each school. With few exceptions, it was not until the 1950s that a system of group instruction was developed in which full-time, certified teachers were operating within the regular school schedule, thus ensuring a steady supply of instrumentalists and a more consistent level of achievement within individual schools. Canadians who went to the United States for degrees in music education brought back pedagogical practices and instructional materials which they had encountered in American schools. Such refinements in the methodology of music education aided the future growth and development of instrumental music in the postwar period.

MUSIC IN HIGHER EDUCATION

Musical activity in the formative years of the University of British Columbia consisted mainly of performances by the UBC Musical Society, founded by E. Howard Russell, a mathematics professor. The society was a student organization which from its inception in 1916 offered choral concerts as a regular feature of campus life. With the arrival of Ira Dilworth, who taught English there from 1934 to 1938, there was a surge of interest in music inspired by his personal involvement in the arts. One practical outcome of his initiative was the acquisition of a Carnegie record collection, which formed a nucleus of music holdings for the library. The first music instruction offered at UBC was a music appreciation course given by Ida Halpern in 1940. She later worked as a music critic for the Vancouver *Province* and also used her musicology background, a PhD degree from Vienna, in researching the music of British Columbia's native peoples. But it was not until 1946 that music was formally established as a discipline at the university. At that time Harry Adaskin was appointed to a new chair in music, which was endowed by the Vancouver brewer Robert Fiddes. Pianist Frances Marr Adaskin and composers Jean Coulthard and Barbara Pentland were among the first instructors. Their presence at UBC stimulated the artistic environment of the institution, but on a purely pragmatic level their musical inclinations were somewhat removed from the vocational needs of school music teachers. Students interested in pursuing music beyond secondary school had two main alternatives: they could enrol in liberal arts programs at UBC and continue their practical studies in music through private tuition; or, if it was within their means, they could go outside the province to earn music degrees. Of course, there were limited opportunities for studying music anywhere in Canada, and many Canadians were enrolling in universities in the United States. Indeed, the lack of professional degree programs within British Columbia dictated that for years to come many of the leadership positions in the province were filled by musicians trained or qualified elsewhere.

8

A Period of Transition in the Maritimes

Despite the problems of recovery from the First World War and the economic hardships brought on by the Depression, there were improvements in the cultural and educational life of the Maritime provinces between the wars. Music was a major part of this development. Although churches of the region continued as important musical centres and church musicians were often involved in the activities of the community, many cultural ventures were completely independent of church support.

Community Concert Associations were formed in several towns and cities of the three Maritime provinces during the 1930s. These were affiliated with Columbia Artists Management, Inc., in New York City. In some centres concerts were held in church halls and gymnasiums. Such was the case in Halifax, where, following the demolition of the Academy of Music in 1929, various church halls, the auditorium at the School for the Blind, and the Dalhousie University gymnasium were used. In other areas, however, such as Moncton and Saint John, new high schools were constructed containing large public auditoriums which are still used as concert halls.

The establishment of Community Concert Associations did not mark the beginning of concert activity in the Maritimes; travelling artists had visited the region previously under individual sponsorship, and this practice continued. One of the most frequent attractions during the period between the wars was the Hart House String Quartet. The quartet visited many Maritime communities during yearly tours from 1931 until its dissolution at the end of the Second World War. These tours were sponsored by different groups, including the Halifax Philharmonic Society, ladies' musical clubs, IODE chapters, Rotary clubs, and students' associations, and there were also some private sponsors. The members of the Quartet felt that it was important to give concerts in the small communities as well as the large centres. The violist Blackstone said after their visit to the Maritimes in 1931, 'I'm often tempted to chuck it and stay at home, but when I think of all those splendid audiences to whom we are the only visiting musical attraction, I know it our work.'[1] After their 1934 tour Blackstone commented: 'People of Ontario have no idea of the musical progress that is being made in the Maritimes. If we think we have a mortgage on Canadian culture in this Province, we are mistaken. I do not hesitate to say that Canada is breeding a race down by the sea who will eventually make their mark on the musical history of the world.'[2] Local performing groups also added to the concert life of the communities. The Halifax Philharmonic Society, conducted by Harry Dean, gave performances of oratorios in Halifax, Truro, and New Glasgow. This group also sponsored spring festivals from 1925 to 1931 which often featured soloists from the United States. Others active in this city included the Halifax Choral Union (which later developed into the Halifax Choral Society, under Ifan Williams), the Halifax Madrigal Society, and the Ladies' Musical Club. Choral groups were prominent in several other communities as well. Gilbert and Sullivan productions maintained their popularity. In Charlottetown, Roberta Spencer Full and Lillian MacKenzie mounted productions using singers from the local schools as well as St Dunstan's and Prince of Wales Colleges, and in Sackville, New Brunswick, Harold Hamer established a long-standing Gilbert and Sullivan tradition at Mount Allison University.

Instrumental ensembles, in addition to those affiliated with philharmonic societies, included both small orchestras and town bands. An editorial in the 1931 issue of *Musical Canada* remarked: 'The largest instrumental ensemble ever organized in the Maritimes was heard in concert at the Capitol Theatre, Moncton, last month ... One hundred and twenty-seven players constituted this unique orchestra including forty violins, nineteen clarinets, sixteen saxes, two string basses, six French horns and brasses and woodwinds in due proportion.'[3] The concert was presented under the auspices of the Moncton branch of the Canadian Legion, with support from the Women's Musical Club. The orchestra was conducted by Percy Belyea, head of the music department of the T. Eaton store in Moncton. Belyea was director of an orchestral group in the city which later became the Central United Church Orchestra, under Ernest Freeborn.

Several private schools, convents, and church-affiliated institutions expanded their offerings in music between the wars. The Halifax Conservatory, under the leadership of Harry Dean, provided an impetus for the musical life of that city. A new two-year program leading to a certificate in public school music was introduced. However, in 1934 Dean left the conservatory to establish the Maritime Academy of Music, taking some of the staff with him. Ifan Williams assumed the headship of the conservatory, which maintained its affiliation with the Halifax Ladies' College. Both these institutions offered various diplomas and a BMus degree through affiliation with Dalhousie University.[4] A BMus degree was also offered by Mount St Vincent, Acadia, and Mount Allison Universities.

During the 1920s and 1930s the Carnegie Corporation of New York made significant contributions to the Maritime provinces, particularly in the field of medical education. Its generosity extended to the arts as well, for gifts of music study materials, including scores and recordings, were presented to Acadia University in 1933 and to the Halifax Ladies' College and Mount Allison University in 1936.

The role of the private music teacher became increasingly important during the inter-war period. Many teachers prepared their students for external music examinations offered by the Toronto Conservatory, the McGill Conservatorium, Trinity College, and the Associated Board. In 1930 Mount Allison revived the local centre examination system introduced by James Noel Brunton before the First World War. Piano classes for school children were organized in several centres under the auspices of the Canadian Bureau for the Advancement of Music during the early 1930s; they provided inexpensive instruction to a large number of students who could not otherwise have afforded to study music.

Although much of the private instruction at this time was in piano, voice, and, occasionally, violin, there were also more opportunities for young people to learn to play other orchestral and band instruments, both through extra-curricular instruction in the schools and through private study with musicians in the community. A few musicians, such as the Burbanks in Moncton, organized their own ensembles for young people. Maude Burbank and her husband, Arthur, who had been vaudeville artists in the United States, came to Moncton in the 1920s and played in the orchestra for silent movies. With the advent of the 'talkies' Arthur Burbank turned his attention to real estate and a few small instrumental groups in the city, but his wife began to teach music to young people and established an extensive, independently financed band program which continued in the city for over thirty years. The Maritime Band Festival, held annually in Moncton, is named in her honour.

Local music teachers' associations were organized in several communities and were sometimes affiliated with women's musical clubs. They sponsored recitals, small festivals, and competitions. In Halifax, several members of the local chapter of the Canadian College of Organists who were also active as private teachers proposed the formation of an organization which would embrace all branches of music teaching. It was through the initiative of these members, under the chairmanship of Harry Dean, that the Nova Scotia Music Teachers' Association was formed in 1937. From the outset this group addressed issues concerning music in the schools as well as matters related to private instruction.

The advent of radio during the 1920s made significant changes in everyday life and in education. Several radio stations were established in the region during this decade, and local musicians as well as groups of school children began to perform for the new audience. In 1924 Mount Allison became one of the first Canadian colleges to broadcast a program of music. An account of convocation week-end activities stated, 'The number of those who have enjoyed the various programs has been enlarged through the establishing of a radio broadcasting station in Beethoven Hall.'[5] The music for these broadcasts ranged from various piano, vocal, and violin solos and ensembles, to a performance of the overture to *Der Freischutz* by the conservatory orchestra, directed by Cladie Smith, and selections for chorus and orchestra by Sir Edward Elgar, conducted by Professor Brunton. When the new CNRA station opened in Moncton in the fall of 1924, Mount Allison made arrangements to use their broadcasting equipment by means of the telephone wires between Sackville and Moncton. This new transmitting studio in Moncton, built by the CNR, offered many programs of music for its listeners.

Henry Munro, superintendent of education for Nova Scotia, became interested in the introduction of school broadcasting in Britain in 1927 and soon recognized the advantages of using the new medium for educational purposes in his own province. In the spring of 1928, with the assistance of Victor Seary, an experimental school program was broadcast over the Halifax station CHNS. This two-hour broadcast consisted of a variety of items, including selections by the Harmonica Band of St Patrick's (Boys') School in Halifax, directed by Cyril O'Brien. The enthusiastic response to this broadcast encouraged officials, and in the fall of that same year Nova Scotia set in place what Richard S. Lambert identifies as 'the oldest continuous system of local school broadcasting in Canada.'[6] These weekly programs, broadcast on Friday afternoons, were designed for junior and senior high school students. 'The two hours were divided into 15-minute periods covering six different topics interspersed with brief musical interludes and announcements. All the subjects were treated as supplementary to class-room teaching, using the techniques in the British school broadcasts. They included talks, readings, dramatizations, French language lessons, and vocal and instrumental music, including performances by high school orchestras.'[7] B.C. Silver and his Wolfville School Orchestra were often featured. The broadcasts did much to encourage instrumental music in the schools, and were also appreciated by listeners far beyond the Halifax vicinity. The first broadcast 'drew a letter of congratulations from a group of lumbermen in northern New Brunswick who had been thrilled to pick up the performance by chance in their camp.'[8] Friday afternoon school broadcasts continued in Nova Scotia for the next nine years. In 1930 a series was initiated over station CJCB in Sydney to serve the schools of Cape Breton Island. By 1937, however, Gerald Redmond recommended a change of policy which would shift the emphasis to rural and village schools; these schools had been making more extensive use of the series than had those in the urban centres.

The other Maritime provinces began to take an interest in the work being done in Nova Scotia, but it was not until 1943 that the first school broadcasts were launched as a joint venture of the provincial departments of education and the CBC Maritime network. According to Lambert, the purpose was to present programs which would 'provide new interests and appreciation and help in building desirable attitudes and ideals,' and the programs themselves were designed to 'supplement the work of the classroom teacher on the imaginative side.'[9] Two music programs were included, 'Junior School Music' for grades one to three, given by Miss Irene McQuillan, assistant supervisor of music for the Halifax schools, and 'Music Appreciation for Junior High School,' given by Harold Hamer of Mount Allison University. Both programs continued for several years and were made extensive use of by teachers in the region. Irene McQuillan's program won an Ohio State award in 1943.

Henry Munro had several purposes in mind when he inaugurated school broadcasts for his province; among other things, he hoped to 'keep alive the local and national songs of the people of Nova Scotia.'[10] His concern for preserving the folk traditions of the people indicates his awareness not only of the effects of the radio and the gramophone but also of the developing sophistication of music instruction in the region. Oral traditions were rapidly disappearing. Fortunately, this trend was recognized by others as well, particularly Roy MacKenzie, Helen Creighton, and Louise Manny, whose pioneer work in collecting the folk songs of the region has helped to preserve its cultural heritage.

MUSIC IN THE SCHOOLS

Following the First World War several centres began to pay more attention to the teaching of music in the schools. In 1919 Bessie McNeil was appointed singing teacher for the Halifax schools, the first music teacher since the dismissal of Jacob Norton in the 1880s. Subsequently, considerable attention was given to the music program in annual reports, one of which describes the procedures followed: 'Each teacher receives at the beginning of the month, a copy of the course of study to be followed during the month in the classroom, and she is expected to make herself sufficiently familiar with it by careful study, to teach it to her class [twenty minutes per day] ... The Director visits each class twice a month, and gives a model lesson to the children out of the monthly course laid down by her for the teacher's guidance. She helps to classify the voices, and aids in smoothing away any difficulties encountered by the regular teacher.'[11] The text used in this program was *Music in the Public Schools* by E.W. Newton, published by Ginn and Company.

This arrangement in the Halifax schools, whereby an itinerant teacher was responsible for music in all the elementary schools, remained in place for many years. The program was thus dependent upon the classroom teachers, who in certain cases contributed greatly to the musical development of students. However, during the Depression years, the position of music teacher was once again discontinued, and it was not reinstated until 1942, with the appointment of George Little to the post. Irene McQuillan was appointed his assistant and assumed the post of director after Little's departure the following year.

The Ladies' Musical Club actively supported the school music program in Halifax. In 1915 the members had written to school board officials concerning the need for a teacher of singing. After the reinstatement of the position they assisted by sponsoring music competitions for school students, giving monthly concerts in the schools, and, later, providing books on music for school libraries. They also supported the music program at the School for the Blind and invited students to their monthly programs, which were sometimes held in the auditorium of this institution.

Music instruction expanded in other places as well. The 1921 report of the Nova Scotia Book Bureau stated that many music texts had been distributed. Truro schools hired a music teacher shortly after the First World War; a 1923 article stated that the 'fundamental musical instruction in the schools started on a small scale in Truro about four years' previously had now developed and enlarged.[12] This program was under the direction of Harry Wellard, a British organist who had come to Truro in 1913. Both Wellard and his wife were graduates of the Royal Academy of Music. Soon after his arrival he was appointed to the music position at the normal school, and subsequently he was invited to design and implement a program for the Truro schools. He also played an active role in the town as church organist, private teacher, and director of the Truro Philharmonic Society. He was highly regarded as a community leader; one report reads: 'Harry Wellard's very superior capacity and artistry as a musician and teacher, and his fine qualities as a citizen and gentleman are well known. In its truth, skill, and reach, his contribution to education has not yet been surpassed in our province.'[13] Wellard placed emphasis on sight-singing but felt that music was to be enjoyed by all students. He included theory, history, and music appreciation in his program, relying upon the assistance of regular teachers, who remained in the classroom during his weekly visits.

During the 1920s, Frank Harrison continued his work in the Fredericton schools, while James Browne and Alice Harrison assumed similar posts in Saint John and Moncton respectively. All three influenced the development of music instruction in New Brunswick schools for the next two decades. In addition to their school responsibilities, these musicians held church positions and taught private piano students.

James Browne had come from England to an organ post in Saint

John, having received his musical training at the Hereford Cathedral School and the Royal College of Music. Much of his work had been with boys' choirs and Tonic Sol-fa, and he brought these traditions with him to Canada. Alice Harrison, the daughter of a Methodist minister, had received her musical training at Mount Allison Ladies' College and then had continued her studies in London, England. She served as church organist in several centres and also held the position of Children's Work Secretary for the Maritime Religious Education Council before accepting the music position for the Moncton schools. Although the influence of Enoch Pearson from Philadelphia was still present (particularly with Frank Harrison), James Browne and Alice Harrison modelled their programs more on the work of Edwin Barnes of Washington, DC.

Edwin N.C. Barnes, director of music for the Washington schools, was a New Brunswick native who had studied in the United States and Britain but who had maintained an active interest in his native province. Barnes made frequent visits to a summer home on the Saint John River, where he 'conducted voice instruction on an itinerant schedule ... at Williams Wharf, Oak Point.'[14] James Browne met Barnes during one of his summer visits to New Brunswick and later studied with him in Washington. When Browne organized special music classes for teachers in Saint John shortly after his appointment in January 1924, he was able to arrange that certificates from Washington College be issued for all who passed an examination. Browne continued to rely upon the assistance of classroom teachers throughout his years of teaching in Saint John. Alice Harrison first met Edwin Barnes around 1920, when she was working as an organist and private piano teacher in Fredericton. She studied privately with him for one summer and was able to qualify as a teacher of music for the public schools; she began work in the Moncton schools in 1924. Classroom teachers were cooperative, and weekly plans were left with each teacher for practice between lessons. Alice Harrison walked from school to school, often carrying a large phonograph, but as the school population grew, her schedule became more complex, and arrangements were made for a standing order with a local taxi company which enabled her to move quickly between schools. A firm believer in the advantages of community singing, she encouraged singing in large groups whenever possible and often combined classes in the assembly halls. In 1926 she prepared a special radio show involving six hundred children, which was broadcast from the assembly hall of Edith Cavell School by the local radio station. A newspaper reported that 'a short address on Music Week and what it meant was also given by Miss Harrison'[15] as part of this broadcast.

Other schools in New Brunswick, including schools in Sackville, Rothesay, St Stephen, and St George, began to introduce music into their regular course of studies throughout the 1920s. Special teachers were often employed to give the instruction. A new course of study for New Brunswick schools was issued in 1928. There was no change in the music textbook, which was that of Whiting, and very little change in the brief outline of the music course. One added feature was a list of approved additional materials for teachers. These included *Twice 55 Community Songs*, *Canadian Folk Songs* by Gibbon, and *British Songs for British Boys*. For the first time, a French publication was listed for music, *Recueil de chants acadiens*, available through L'Évangéline publishers in Moncton.

Throughout the Maritimes members of the various religious orders offered music instruction, both privately and in classes. Some members taught in the public schools, but there were also convent schools, which placed an emphasis on music. Convent schools made a particular contribution in Prince Edward Island, where as late as the 1920s very little music instruction was given in the public schools. A 1923 report refers to the two academies operated by les Sœurs de la Congrégation de Notre-Dame in Charlottetown (Notre Dame Academy) and Summerside (St Mary's Academy), and also to the convent schools: 'At the convents at Tignish, Miscouche, St Augustine, (Rustico) Souris and St Joseph's (Charlottetown) in which free, common, public schools are now operated, instruction is given in music in special classes, this subject not being included in the public school course of study.'[16]

The following year music was listed for the public schools – 'Singing, daily if practicable,' for grades one through ten, with a few specific suggestions for the younger grades. Under 'Aids to Public School Teachers,' Vogt and Willan's *School and Community Song Book* was listed with the comment, 'Teachers using this book will make a judicious selection of the songs to be sung in school.'[17] By 1929 music and manual training were 'receiving a due proportion of attention as in former years'[18] in Charlottetown schools, but elsewhere there seems to have been very little music except in the convent schools. As late as 1942 an inspector stated, 'Singing is becoming a lost art in our province.'[19]

In 1939 the Kelvin Grove Women's Institute helped to secure the services of a qualified music teacher for their local school. The inspector reported favourably on the progress being made, stating that five schools had been provided with organs and commenting, 'I hope the day is not far distant when instruction in singing and music appreciation will be given in all schools by travelling music teachers provided by the Department of Education.'[20] The music program at Prince Street School in Charlottetown, initiated at the turn of the century by Professor Watts, was maintained throughout this period. Lillian MacKenzie served as music teacher at this school for many years. The work of this school was commended in several reports, including the following:

> A special tribute needs to be paid to the teachers of Prince Street School for this contribution to the development of a music program in their school. That Prince Street has had continuity in its music program for many years is largely the result of the efforts of its teachers. Several years ago they, on their own initiative, decided to underwrite the annual cost of a special music teacher, employed on a part-time basis. Largely because of this concrete evidence of the genuine desire these teachers had to improve the quality of music instruction in Prince Street School, the Charlottetown School Board and the Provincial Department of Education have since been persuaded to assume the cost of music instruction in Prince Street as well as the other three schools.'[21]

Music in the High Schools

Formal music instruction in schools throughout the Maritimes, except for certain private schools, was confined primarily to the elementary grades. A notable exception to this was the program in Fredericton under the direction of Frank Harrison, which since 1911 had included instruction for all grades, from elementary to high school. A report indicates that in 1922 'a public exhibition of community singing was given by the different grades on the grounds of the High School, and the satisfactory manner in which the pupils acquitted themselves attested to the excellence of the instruction given by Professor Harrison.'[22] The previous year the board had purchased a phonograph for use in the high school, and several years later a twenty-piece orchestra was begun by a member of the high school staff, Clarence Burden. The high school program thus included music appreciation, theory, choral singing, and instrumental ensembles.

Saint John and Moncton had performing groups at the high school level, but music was not included as a regular subject of instruction. In Saint John, Professor Bowden conducted an orchestra at the high school, and in Moncton a similar ensemble was directed by a local organist, Dr George Ross, who later became director of music at the high school. In Halifax, an extra-curricular music program was developed at St Patrick's Boys' School which attracted attention through a series of articles published in the *Journal of Education* by Cyril O'Brien.

Several other high schools and county academies throughout the region had choral groups, and a few had small instrumental ensembles, but generally music was 'absolutely abandoned at the high school period.'[23] The chief inspector of schools for Nova Scotia, David Soloan, commented: 'The argument, as one might suspect, is that there is not time; meaning that there is not time except for the crassly material element in schooling. The June examination makes many an otherwise competent teacher, a timid drudge, and any loosing of the examination screw that can be accomplished promises to set free a flood of imprisoned genius in both teachers and pupil.'[24] In 1931 he stated that music was 'an art so neglected that the choral efforts of young Nova Scotia when heard on football or hockey excursions are usually little short of shameful.' He did indicate, however, that there had been some improvement:

> School music has received special attention this year in Middleton, Annapolis and Digby, these towns each employing a paid supervisor of singing who gives a weekly or semi-weekly lesson in each of the grades, including the high school. Instruction in music has for years past been given by a professional in Yarmouth and Truro. In Sydney, Mr. Campbell of the Academy staff has organized the high school as a glee club, as have Mr. Silver in Wolfville and Miss Evelyn Wood in Stewiacke. Good school orchestras are maintained in the first two mentioned schools, and Mr. Clark of the Yarmouth Academy staff is engaged by the school board to devote a number of hours weekly to choral singing and orchestra training in the high school.[25]

David Soloan was principal of the provincial normal school as well as chief inspector of schools and was a strong supporter of the arts in education. Some of his arguments are reminiscent of the singing school movement and its influence on the beginnings of school music in the United States in the previous century. He contended that music and drawing were receiving too little attention in the lower grades to permit satisfactory achievement in the high schools. Admitting that there were a few towns in which both 'effort and result' were 'commendable,' he added: 'In general, neither community nor teaching staff displays more than a step-motherly interest in the arts, and this is often true of towns which pay generous salaries to church organists and choir masters. Is it not probable that better church music, and, particularly, better congregational singing would result if some of this money were diverted to the musical needs of the children of school age?'[26]

During the 1930s there was discussion of high school credit for music in both Nova Scotia and New Brunswick. In 1936, the chief superintendent of education for Nova Scotia stated that music was already on the school course and indicated that it was being taught in several areas at both the junior high and senior high school levels. The *Journal of Education* published details concerning these music courses. Students were divided into two groups: Class A, those studying music in institutions especially devoted to the teaching of music, and Class B, both those studying music in schools where music was given as part of school studies and those studying music under private teachers. Students in Class B were to 'follow the syllabus and take the examinations of some recognized examining board or institution.'[27] Instruction was recognized for pianoforte, organ, voice, and the regular woodwind, brass, and stringed instruments of the symphonic orchestra. A subsequent journal article stated, 'Marks assigned by public school teachers are not recognized for credit in this subject.'[28]

In New Brunswick there was also discussion, but action was not taken on a provincial basis. In Saint John, the Women's Council lobbied for music as an elective subject in high school, and in 1935 the executive of the New Brunswick Teachers' Association passed a motion concerning this issue. The editors of the *Educational Review* commented on the opposition from some quarters: 'Those who criticise the suggestion as impractical are evidently unaware of the fact that this very thing is being done in other places. In Winnipeg, for instance, pupils are allowed to substitute Music for a Science on the Matriculation examinations. Of course only the standard examinations in Music (such as McGill) are accepted.'[29] In 1938 the Moncton school board approved the conditions under which credit would be given for 'Music – Theory and Practice': 'The course to (be) laid down and examinations to be carried on by the Director of Music, but the teaching to be done by any qualified teacher, provided such examinations be given only to the pupils who have elected music as a subject of the course ... The cost of the lessons to be borne by the parents entirely, no individual teaching at school ... Pupils who take music will be allowed study time in school hours on the other subjects equivalent to five forty minute periods a week to compensate for the time required for music lessons and practice out of school hours.' The board also approved the following, with respect to 'Chorus, Orchestra, Cadets': 'In all courses a bonus to be given for satisfactory work if practical.'[30] They later passed a resolution, 'That the Board confirm the Regulations Governing the Granting of Credits for Choir, Orchestra and Cadet Work, with the addition that these credits are not to count in the awarding of prizes.'[31] This regulation remained in effect for many years. However, only boys were eligible to join cadets, so while girls could receive credit for music, boys could receive credit for both music and cadets.

FESTIVALS AND COMPETITIONS

In both Halifax and Truro impetus was given to the school music program by choral organizations which sponsored special competitions. A report in 1922 noted the following concerning Halifax: 'The Philharmonic Club, which has always taken a warm interest in music in the schools, offered a handsome shield to be competed for annually by the common schools.'[32] Each school sent a choir of forty voices; the choir sang a two-part song chosen by the teachers and also a unison song chosen by the Philharmonic Society. The 'best all-round choir' won the shield. The 1925 issue of the *Journal of Education* stated that in the two previous years 'the Choral Society of Truro, under Miss L.A. Richardson, Secretary, and Professor H.A. Wellard, Conductor, held Annual School Music competitions, which greatly interested the public and splendidly stimulated the cult of vocal music in the town and the important educational institutions within it.'[33] These events developed into the Truro Music Festival, one of the oldest festivals in the Maritime region.

James Browne organized a school music festival in Saint John shortly after he assumed his position. In 1929, according to a report, 'the Ladies' Morning Musical Club offered to donate a prize of $50 to stimulate interest in music in the city schools. The offer was accepted, and a competitive musical festival was held on Saturday, May 10th, with twenty-six Choirs competing ... The Supervisor of Music, Professor James F. Browne, recommended that an exhibition be held for the schools who had won foremost place in the music competition, and this exhibition was held in the High School Building on Friday, May 23rd.'[34] The festival was continued, and in 1931 it was broadcast over the local radio station. Similar events were organized in other centres, including Fredericton and Moncton. A report indicates that a few years later in New Glasgow 'fourteen schools entered the singing competition sponsored by the Ladies' Music Club ... whose object [was] to improve the singing in the rural schools of Pictou County.'[35]

Music festivals and exhibitions became popular in other places as well, including several rural regions, where folk song and folk dance festivals were held. These events were supported in Nova Scotia by the Rural Division of the department of education. Dora Baker described one of the festivals in 1933:

> The most ambitious musical program yet attempted in the schools of the province was the Music and Folk-dance festival held in Kentville on June 2nd, [1933] as the opening feature of Nova Scotia's first Apple-Blossom Festival ... Nearly two thousand children from the schools of Hants, Kings and Annapolis Counties participated in this activity with distinct success, winning credit for themselves and their leaders. The chorus of 1200 children who met on that occasion under one baton, had experienced but little musical training previous to the intensive work for this event. Massed on the grandstand, and led by an orchestra of sixty pieces, their voices rang out blithely, tunefully, and in perfect accord, reaching the huge outdoor audience without the aid of amplifiers. The notable success both of the choral and part-song numbers constitutes a triumph for their teachers, local leaders, and especially for their conductor, whose indefatigable and enthusiastic leadership made it possible. To those who witnessed the performance, the picture presented was one arresting by its sheer beauty: The blue sky over the green sunlit field in its frame of blossom-laden trees, and then the wave of dancing children so absorbed in the joy of lilting motion as to be oblivious to the audience.[36]

The folk music and folk dance festival was viewed as a means of encouraging cooperation among schools, training students in constructive ways of filling leisure hours, and acquainting them with their cultural heritage: 'Cape Breton and the eastern counties of the mainland have never relinquished the folk-dances of their ancestors. In many a sheltered cove and secluded hamlet the folk-songs persist despite the modernizing influence of the radio. Other parts of Canada hold their choral competitions and their mammoth gymnastic exhibitions;

but Nova Scotia, without fanfare of trumpets, has inaugurated a co-operative festival which should have a far-reaching effect in preserving, extending, and reviving the folk-ways of the past for the education of her youth, and the leisure and pleasure of her communities.'[37] In 1934 the inspector for Richmond and Inverness South in Cape Breton reported that, 'notwithstanding the strong wind that prevailed,' Miss Cameron, 'with her wonted thoroughness,' successfully conducted a musical rally at Whycocomagh, 'participated in by schools from both North and South Inverness.'[38] Rural festivals on a smaller scale were later held in both New Brunswick and Prince Edward Island.

Another important influence on music education at this time was the School Music Contest held at the annual Provincial Exhibition in Nova Scotia. The eight categories in 1938 were practical performance, measurement of latent talent, musical memory, music appreciation, tonal memory, melody, written music, and demonstrations. The contest was open to both individuals and groups. Two scholarships of forty dollars each were awarded to winning contestants, one award for a pupil from Halifax and one for a pupil from another part of the province. The regulations stated, 'The two prizes aforementioned will be awarded solely upon the basis of native musical talent and not upon what one already knows or has accomplished thus far.'[39] The introduction of this contest reflects an interest in the tests and measurement movement in music, for the regulations further stated, 'While generally the most musical pupils will be found in musical institutions and centres, it is quite possible for a talented one who has never studied music to outstrip his or her confreres in a psychological test.'[40]

The need for a festival of much broader dimensions, open to both solo and group participation by students of all ages, had been recognized for several years by musicians in Nova Scotia and New Brunswick who were aware of the development of the British system of festivals in the Canadian west. Such an event was organized in Halifax in 1935 as the first Maritime Competitive Musical Festival, under the auspices of the Halifax Conservatory. It later became known as the Halifax Music Festival. James Browne requested permission for the Saint John schools to compete in this event but was informed that the cost would be too high. A non-competitive festival was held in Saint John in May of that year; two years later a province-wide festival was initiated, which became known as the New Brunswick Competitive Festival of Music. Festivals were also established in other Maritime centres, including an extensive one in Yarmouth under the initiative of Catherine Allison. A provincial festival was founded in Prince Edward Island in 1946, sponsored by the Women's Institute. Many prominent musicians adjudicated at these festivals, among them Sir Ernest MacMillan, who visited all three Maritime provinces.

TEACHER EDUCATION AND CURRICULUM DEVELOPMENT

Although sessions on music were frequently given at teachers' institutes and articles on music continued to appear in periodicals, officials and teachers alike felt that the training was insufficient and that skills in music could not be acquired in the short space of time allotted to the subject in normal school. The appointment of Harry Wellard to the Truro Normal School was well received, but it seems that much of the program was still recreational in nature; one account reads, 'A piano and an Edison gramophone have been purchased and placed at the disposal of the students, who have been glad to organize under the direction of the teaching staff, regular periods for music, dancing, receptions and school games.'[41] The principal obviously felt that more attention should be given to music training for teachers, that it was 'fully time to insist on a standard adopted practically all around the world in English speaking countries.'[42]

A few years later, largely through the influence of the Provincial Council of Women, music was introduced as a requirement for the Minimum Proficiency Qualifications certificates for teachers in Nova Scotia. Under the heading 'Helpful Notes on the Preparation for the M.P.Q. Music Examination' was the statement 'There are other occupations than teaching in elementary schools suitable for those who cannot give instruction in singing.'[43] This music examination was short-lived, however, and it was proposed that certificates from 'well known musical schools' be accepted in its place, with the first year of the 'Music Supervisor's Certificates of the Halifax Conservatory of Music ... rated at 100.'[44] Other vocal music certificates were rated on the basis of how their standards compared with those of the conservatory. The two-year conservatory course included rudiments, harmony, ear training, sight-singing, voice culture and singing, pianoforte playing, the history of music, and conducting, as well as class methods for both elementary and high school grades.

In 1927 a special committee on public school music appointed by the Nova Scotia Department of Education submitted several recommendations, including one on teacher education in music. The music committee also assisted in the development of the new program of studies for grades one to six which appeared in 1933. This was a detailed, child-centred curriculum which had an extensive section on music incorporating many of the recommendations put forth in the 1927 report. The opening statement of the music section read:

> Music is the art which gives expression to the emotions by means of tones arranged rhythmically, melodically and harmonically. Its tendency is to create international goodwill. In all institutions of civilization – the home, the school, the vocation, the church, and the state, it has a value. Music trains the eye and ear, develops intellectual power, stimulates creative impulses, and stores the memory with uplifting material for emotional expression. It enriches and purifies the feeling, and affords a new outlet for the pent-up emotions of the child. Where a lasting appreciation of good music is aroused in boys and girls, it provides for the proper use of leisure time, not only for the performers, but also for those who listen. It is the universal language.[45]

The recommended texts were *The New Canadian Music Course* (five volumes) by Coney and Wickett, published by Gage in Toronto, and *The School Teacher's Music Guides* by Venables, published by Curwen and Sons in England. A list of suggested songs was included in the document, but a suggestion that teachers give special attention to 'British, French, Canadian and Nova Scotian Folk Songs' notwithstanding, the songs on this list were primarily British in origin.

It is difficult to assess the extent to which this program was followed in the Nova Scotia schools. The lack of adequately trained teachers makes it unlikely that the program was implemented in many areas. Two years previously David Soloan had commented that few teachers were 'able to worry out the melody from a new piece of staff notation or of Tonic Sol-fa.' He had continued, 'The Normal School is in a position to give a start to the formation of the music teacher, but not more.'[46] The following year Soloan recommended that more opportunity be given to teachers to study music at summer schools and that there be provision for the continuance of the instruction during the succeeding year. He maintained that such a step was essential because 'the mastery of music teaching lies by no means entirely in intellectual comprehension, but also in drill sufficient to produce a response automatic, or, as the psychologists call it, secondarily automatic.'[47] He also stated his views regarding the employment of trained musicians as teachers in the public schools: 'It would be a mistake to consider the average graduate in musical theory and instrumental or vocal technique as competent to do effective teaching in a school. In no other branch of the school curriculum is special pedagogical training so necessary, for its technique cannot be mastered simply by reading about it.'[48]

Harry Wellard died suddenly in 1930 and was replaced in his normal school position by Douglas Baker, another British organist. Baker, like Wellard, emphasized choral singing and frequently had his choir participate in the Halifax Music Festival. His teaching of methodology was considered innovative by many. One report notes, 'All students were required to prepare and take with them to their schools, an anthology of songs suitable for every grade, and also for school concerts and special occasions.'[49] The 1927 recommendation concerning an expanded music program for the normal school was not fully implemented, however, until Catherine Allison was appointed to the normal school staff in 1957.

The establishment of a Rural Education Division in Nova Scotia under the direction of L.A. DeWolfe resulted in more educational opportunities for the smaller centres in the province. One of the innovations implemented by DeWolfe, a system of 'helping teachers,' was of great benefit to music, for it was recommended that these helping teachers be capable of assisting with the singing in the schools. They played an important role in many of the rural rallies and festivals.

Although the work of Professor Smith at the New Brunswick Normal School in Fredericton was frequently praised, most who attended his classes felt that their exposure to the subject was far too brief and that the background they brought from their own school experience was weak. The main emphasis was on choral singing, and this activity showed noted improvement within a few years. Smith seems to have had great success with the young men as well as the young women, for reference was made in a report to the improvement in singing of the male students as 'worthy of special mention': 'A higher percentage among those have received certificates to teach singing in the last few years than among the young ladies.'[50] A third of the students received certificates to teach music; however, in order to receive a certificate, students had simply to teach a song to a class in the model school and pass a brief theory examination, so most of them still did not feel qualified to teach the subject. Instruction in music was given in their own languages to both English- and French-speaking students; the account of the opening of the new building in 1930 mentions that 'the choruses by the students, especially those by the French students, under the direction of Professor Smith, were much enjoyed.'[51] Those wishing to teach music in the public schools who had not received their training at normal school were required to teach music classes at the model school in the presence of the instructor of music for the normal school.

In Prince Edward Island, the chief superintendent reported in 1930, '[The] lack of music teaching in the Normal School is a cause of much regret, but school singing led if necessary by a pupil should be a regular practice in all schools.'[52] In 1942 this lack of music teaching was still lamented. The following year, Professor John Inch offered instruction, but the classes, held apparently in a cold, drafty auditorium, were poorly attended.

Both New Brunswick and Nova Scotia offered grants for those employed as special teachers of music. The requirement that the teacher be employed at least ten hours per week often meant that rural areas were excluded from taking advantage of the grants. David Soloan commented in 1930, 'The only regret is that the smaller towns which are willing to pay for music instruction in their schools are not eligible for any part of the special provincial grant for music, for it is not in reason to expect them to employ a full-time teacher.'[53]

Music was offered at several summer sessions between the wars, especially during the 1930s. These were sometimes sponsored by the provincial departments of education and other times by private institutions or organizations such as the Canadian Bureau for the Advancement of Music, which provided sessions in class piano instruction for teachers. In Nova Scotia, music instruction at department of education summer schools was given by teachers from the province; later, specialists from other parts of the country, including Ethel Kinley from Winnipeg, were invited as instructors. Music teachers from the Maritimes also attended summer schools in Ontario and the United States.

In New Brunswick, Harold Hamer of Mount Allison offered instruction in music to teachers, both at summer schools held in Sackville and at the New Brunswick Summer School of Education held in Saint John in the late 1930s. This provincial school was organized by the newly appointed director of educational services for the province, Fletcher Peacock, who felt that it was imperative to have a teacher training service that would 'produce and maintain an adequate supply of teachers that are skilful, cultured, and dynamic.'[54] He described the first summer school in 1937: 'This was a purely professional school attended by 350 alert teachers who gave intensive study to the practical problems of our schools under the guidance of expert leaders. The central and undivided interest of the summer school was to improve education in New Brunswick, especially in the rural and primary schools.'[55] Teachers did not receive credit for these courses but neither did they pay tuition; a new plan for licensing teachers which would require summer school attendance was being considered. Work had already begun on a new course of study for the schools, and these summer sessions were held in an effort to introduce teachers to the new methodologies which the committee had been exploring.

During the 1938 summer school, which was attended by over six hundred, teachers were introduced to the materials which had been developed during the past year. Over fifty teachers throughout the province had cooperated in this effort. The course offerings had been expanded to include more music, art, drama, and handicrafts. Nine courses in music were given; the instructors included Harold Hamer from Mount Allison, William Bowden from Saint John, and Maude Garnett from Oswego, New York. The music section of the new course of studies was drafted in the summer of 1938 and then refined during the school year, and when the new program of studies for grades one to six was published and officially approved for use throughout the province in the fall of 1939, twenty pages were devoted to music.

This new program of studies, like the one published in Nova Scotia a few years earlier, was child-centred and placed emphasis on the training of citizens for a democracy. In the music section, there was a marked departure from the previous single emphasis on singing and sight-singing. Considerable attention was given to music appreciation and the need to 'foster the creative impulse.' One of the most welcome changes for teachers was the authorization of new classroom materials for music. The Whiting text, which had been the approved material for over twenty-five years, was replaced by a Canadian series, *The Singing Period* by Harry Hill. *The Music Hour*, a Canadian edition of an American series, was also approved and was suggested for rural schools. However, despite this official authorization of materials which teachers had been recommending, and despite the appearance of detailed courses of study in music for both Nova Scotia and New Brunswick, it would be several years before any substantial effects of these written documents would be seen in the schools of the Maritime region.

9

Denominations and Dichotomies in Quebec

In the years following the First World War opportunities in the arts increased for both Protestant and Catholic young people in Quebec. More teachers were available for those who wished to study music privately. There was growth in both semi-professional and amateur music-making through church choirs, community groups, and organizations affiliated with educational institutions. New performing ensembles in both the orchestral and operatic fields were formed, and several managed to survive despite the financial hardships brought on by the Depression. Most of these organizations were based in Montreal, a trend which reflected the urbanization of Quebec to which the developing business sector had given impetus. There was also considerable activity in Quebec City and in the Eastern Townships.[1] The influence of the Roman Catholic clergy, particularly in efforts to maintain a rural, family-based society, was maintained throughout this era.

Private schools continued to provide music instruction for their students. Several Roman Catholic orders expanded their work to include more remote areas of the province, thus extending music opportunities to the French-speaking rural population. In 1920 Sœur Marie-Stéphane was appointed director of a music program for young girls in the houses run by les Sœurs des Saints Noms de Jésus et Marie. In 1932 this order founded a special school in Montreal, known as l'École supérieure de musique d'Outremont, which became affiliated with the Faculty of Arts of l'Université de Montréal. The aims of the school were 'to promote the art of music, to teach music and singing in regular courses, to give lectures, concerts and recitals, to organize competitions, to set examinations, and to grant certificates and diplomas.'[2] Many prominent musicians, including Claude Champagne, were engaged as teachers, and the school earned an enviable reputation in the field of performance. In 1951 its name was changed to École Vincent-d'Indy.

The McGill Conservatorium continued to play an important role for the English-speaking population, as did Bishop's University and the Eastern Townships Conservatory at Stanstead. In 1917 the Montreal philanthropist Sir William Macdonald presented a large endowment to the McGill Conservatorium which led to the establishment of the Faculty of Music in 1920. Harry Perrin combined his role of director of the conservatorium with the new position of dean of the Faculty. In 1930 Perrin was succeeded by Douglas Clarke, who attempted to raise the profile of the institution. Following his appointment there was a marked increase in musical activities of interest to the public; these included a special series of Sunday evening concerts by prominent musicians and several guest lectures by such scholars as Edmund Fellowes and Percy Scholes.

A school of music was created at l'Université Laval in 1922 within the Faculty of Arts. The curriculum gave priority to religious music, but courses were offered in solfège, harmony, theory, and history, and instruction was given in several practical areas, piano, organ, and violin. A department of sacred music was established in 1932; it played an active role in the revival of liturgical music and later collaborated with les Bénédictines de St-Benoît-du-Lac in offering summer courses in Gregorian chant. Although l'Université de Montréal did not establish its own faculty of music until 1950, it granted diplomas and external-examination certificates in music as early as 1921.

In 1942 le Conservatoire de musique du Québec was founded in Montreal; two years later a second branch was opened in Quebec City. This institution, which subsequently opened branches in five other centres, offered professional music training along the lines of the Paris Conservatoire system and was entirely subsidized by the state. It was known officially as le Conservatoire de musique et d'art dramatique du Québec. Although instruction was free, the students had to compete for admission. Sir Wilfrid Pelletier served as director from 1942 until

1961, with Claude Champagne as assistant director for most of those years. The initial offerings included work in various instruments, theory, solfège, and dictation. Vocal instruction was added a few years later, and the offerings have gradually expanded to include chamber music, symphony orchestra, jazz, and electronic music.

Various organizations and specially formed clubs contributed to the musical life of the province. One of the most enterprising among these was the Delphic Study Club of Montreal, composed of 'broad-minded and progressive women'[3] who, in the early 1920s, turned their attention to music and initiated plans for a special Music Week modelled after similar events in Chicago and New York. The first Music Week, using the theme 'Give More Thought to Music,' was held in March of 1923. A series of free concerts and lectures formed the basis of this event. Many diverse organizations and performing groups were involved: private students and teachers, church organists, the Metropolitan Choral Society, the Old Country Choir, the YMCA Orchestra, the Catholic Women's League, and the Montreal Women's Club. In the words of the founder, this event 'was begun with abundant faith and a treasury too small to pay postage, and a few workers who took the lead, while others took the side lines and didn't even cheer.' However, 'it went over the top with overwhelming success' and continued for several years, expanding its events and later offering scholarships for promising young artists. Although Music Week was generally well received by the public, there were some who felt that these events should not be 'all piled up in one week' because 'an appetite for music needs to be satisfied more than once a year':[4] 'It would surely be more useful if the energy put into music week could be devoted to giving concerts, at intervals through the season, – and especially concerts for children, – at prices that would compare with those of the moving picture shows. Children should come to them, unless they are very different from children in other parts of the world, and the ultimate value to music in Montreal would be far greater than that of many music weeks.'[5] During this first Music Week the Toronto Mendelssohn Choir visited the city as guest of the Rotary Club, and conductor H.A. Fricker gave a special address on music. The performances of this choir in the St Denis Theatre drew to the attention of the Montreal audience the need for a large concert hall. One member of the audience who had heard this choir previously in Massey Hall in Toronto wrote to the newspaper about the matter of the 'much-talked-about-but-not-yet-forthcoming concert hall.'[6]

Concerts known as Soirées Mathieu were held periodically in Montreal from 1930 to 1952. These were given in various locations, including the Windsor and Ritz-Carlton Hotels and le Cercle universitaire; they were under the auspices of the Canadian Institute of Music, founded in Montreal in 1929 and directed by Rodolphe Mathieu. Orchestra concerts became more frequent in the 1930s and 1940s, and special events for young people took place. The Montreal Orchestra under Douglas Clarke held series of concerts for children in the ballroom of the Mount Royal Hotel. Its rival group, the Montreal Symphony Orchestra, with Wilfrid Pelletier as artistic director, inaugurated a series of concerts for French-speaking young people entitled Matinées symphoniques pour la jeunesse. Several years later, after the demise of the Montreal Orchestra, Pelletier's group initiated a second series of young people's concerts for English-speaking students.

Although Wilfrid Pelletier returned to his home province to conduct the Montreal Symphony Orchestra and later to direct le Conservatoire and conduct the Quebec Symphony Orchestra, he did not relinquish his position as conductor with the Metropolitan Opera in New York City; he held this post until 1950. He directed the Metropolitan Opera Auditions of the Air for many years, and 'his abiding interest in young people led him to conduct the Children's Concerts of the New York Philharmonic.'[7] Nevertheless, Pelletier took an active interest in the development of music in Quebec and initiated several special projects. One of these was the summer Festival de musique de Montréal, which developed into the Montreal Festivals supported by the Honourable Louis-Athanase David and his wife. The inaugural concert was held in June 1936 featuring a performance of Bach's St Matthew Passion followed the next evening by Beethoven's Symphony No. 9. For these performances the Montreal Symphony Orchestra under Pelletier was joined by Christ Church Cathedral Singers, directed by Alfred Whitehead, and les Disciples de Massenet, directed by Charles Goulet.

School music instruction in Quebec between the wars continued to follow different paths for Protestant and Catholic children. Private music instruction became more readily available for French-speaking Catholic children in convents and classical colleges, and a special program in solfège devised by Claude Champagne was instituted in the elementary schools supervised by the Montreal Catholic Commission. The school program for English-speaking Protestants, particularly in Montreal, expanded its music offerings to include more music at the high school level, instrumental work, and classes in music appreciation.

MUSIC IN PROTESTANT SCHOOLS

George Stanton resigned his music post at Macdonald College Normal School in 1919 in order to assume the position of supervisor of music for the Protestant schools of Montreal. Stanton continued the program developed by his predecessor, W.H. Smith, with its emphasis on Tonic Sol-fa, and expanded the work at the high school level. Two new teachers, D.M. Herbert and Irvin Cooper, were appointed to high school music positions in Montreal during the 1920s and became prominent in the field.

In describing the music program in the Protestant schools, Stanton commented: 'Education for leisure is one of the most serious problems at the present time ... Music is such a vital constituent of the life of the community that, if the school is to fulfil its function honestly, it must include in the curriculum some provision for music study.'[8] He then described the program:

> Under public school conditions, the musical activities of the classroom, aiming to lay a solid foundation on which an artistic superstructure can be built, (limited only by the child's capacity and opportunity.) include (1) inculcating right vocal habits, (2) acquiring a useful vocabulary of worthwhile songs, (3) ear-training, (4) notation and sight-singing. Each of these topics must be taught artistically and related to the others in a unified whole. This is the framework on which the course of study is built.
>
> In application, the six-year-old child is concerned with organizing his first experience in rhythm and pitch, and in learning to express himself in very easy songs, nursery rhymes, singing games, and so forth. In the primary grades his experience is extended, his knowledge made more definite, and he associates simple facts in tone with their printed symbols. Complexities are added in careful gradation in the elementary grades; knowledge and skill go hand in hand; eye and ear are co-ordinated; and the balance between thinking and feeling aimed for. In the high school grades the process is continued in a similar progressive manner, with greater emphasis on the aesthetic side, appreciation, rendering, modern composition. Music in the high schools is taught by specialists, but in the elementary schools by the class teacher.[9]

The work of Stanton and his staff was respected by school authorities and also by others not directly involved in education, such as Thomas Archer, music critic of the *Gazette*: 'Valuable pioneer work has been accomplished this season in the musical education of children. In addition to the series of illustrated lectures being given over the radio by the Victor Talking Machine Co. of Canada, ground-work has been laid by the Montreal High School authorities and by a comprehensive course on music given Saturday mornings during the month of March in Tudor Hall under the direction of G.A. Stanton.'[10] Stanton was a strong supporter of the music appreciation movement and encouraged teachers to stress the aesthetic aspect of music. He warned that in teaching music the intellectual difficulties often obscure the aesthetic objective: 'Too many lessons in the "cultural" subjects are so concerned with the bare facts that the intrinsic spiritual values are lost. Our children cry for bread and we offer them a stone.'[11] He was also supportive of the annual Delphic Study Club Music Week, as this account indicates:

> Music Week was celebrated in Montreal from April 2nd to April 8th [1933] by an elaborate programme of broadcasts, a festival of school choirs and special programmes in individual schools. The Delphic Study Club arranged for radio receiving sets to be lent to the schools for one week and for a series of educational musical programmes to be broadcast. The programmes included junior and senior programmes on 'Songs and Singers', 'How Music is Built', 'Stringed Instruments', orchestral concerts from the Eastman School of Music, [Rochester], New York, and a musical appreciation series by Dr. Damrosch. There was also a choral programme by high school choirs, and a festival of school choirs which sang numbers of their own choice with an added programme of instrumental music by the Montreal High School Orchestra. This ambitious programme was carried through enthusiastically and has done much to encourage the practice and appreciation of music by school children.[12]

The American music appreciation series by Damrosch was broadcast in the province of Quebec throughout the 1933–4 school year. There were four separate series for various grade levels, from grade three through to high school and college. A notice in the *Educational Record* announced that these programs were being broadcast in the province through station CFCF of Montreal. After listing the dates, the notice concluded, 'Teachers desiring full information should send 25 cents to the National Broadcasting Company, Inc., New York for a copy of the instructor's manual, giving most interesting information in regard to each programme.'[13] In 1945 the Montreal Protestant board began to use the Ontario school broadcast series 'Music for Young Folk.'

The inclusion of music listening in the Montreal school program was not new in the 1930s; it had been part of the course of study for several years. As early as 1924 a writer for the *Teachers' Magazine* stated:

> The need for training in musical appreciation is, at the present time, particularly urgent. The plague of the silly and the primitive in popular music has not come uninvited. We have, as a people, sought it by our persistent neglect of music in its more ennobling and more intelligent forms. To a certain extent to-day is the age of music – we eat to music, we reduce to music. Radio has also played its part in creating an entirely new interest in this, the most popular of the fine arts. The phonograph, at last, has come into its own, not only in popular favour but in the approval of the entire body of music-lovers. The time when it was fashionable for musicians to regard it with contempt, or, at least, tolerant indifference has passed away. It now has a place in educational work.[14]

Stanton's concept of music appreciation included live concerts for school children. He felt there was 'room for a regular series of attractive educational concerts, designed especially for young audiences.'[15]

Short articles on school music programs in the neighbouring municipalities of Lachine and Westmount were published in the 1931 *Montreal Music Year Book*. Reportedly, there had been improvement in music teaching in the Lachine schools; W.J. Hislop, the author of the article, credited this improvement to two main sources, the influence of the lists of songs compiled by Stanton and the establishment of a music library. Frederick Whiteley, supervisor of music for Westmount, dealt with the issue of the major purpose of music in the schools: 'Music appreciation is occupying a prominent part in our present day life, but the writer is firmly of the opinion that if we all develop into devotees of music appreciation, no one will be left to provide the music to appreciate.'[16] The first necessity was 'to encourage song in the pupils,' combining it with a practical understanding of the elements of music theory. He referred to the formation of classes for instruction in pianoforte and violin but felt that there was need for much more attention to music in the public schools: 'One's first thought is to utter a deep-throated growl of protest against the inflexible rule of allowing the minimum time for study of this subject.'[17] However, he was not totally negative in his outlook and indicated that there was a move toward granting music a more important place in the curriculum.

Stanton was also optimistic; in discussing the progress being made in this own schools, he mentioned 'signs of an awakening interest in school music in other parts of the Province.'[18] Stanton's optimism was not justified by any great developments during his own tenure, for the 1938–9 report of the Protestant Commission stated that music was perhaps the least well taught of all the special subjects and that the course of study was infrequently followed. Two years later, however, Stanton's successor Irvin Cooper wrote: 'At the present time, music in the schools of this province, and particularly on the Island of Montreal, is experiencing a forward surge, owing to three factors: (1) the progressive attitude of the Director of Protestant Education and the Protestant Committee; (2) the actively sympathetic attitude of a great majority of superintendents of various school systems; and (3) the enthusiasm and energy of the recently formed Provincial Association of School Music Specialists.'[19] He described the growth of music as a school subject, stating that in 1923 the staff had consisted of 1 supervisor of music for the city of Montreal and 5 music specialists, 3 full-time and 2 part-time, but that it had increased to 5 supervisors, 17 full-time specialists, and 6 part-time instrumental teachers by 1941.

Music in High Schools

The matter of credit for music in high school was mentioned in the report of the Protestant Commission for the 1925–6 school year. A new course of study which allowed for more options, including credit for instrumental and theoretical music studied with a private teacher, was being introduced at that time; pupils were to take one of the examinations offered by the McGill Conservatorium. In 1928, certificates of the Eastern Townships Conservatory of Music at Stanstead were recognized in the same way as those of McGill. Examinations given by the Toronto Conservatory were also recognized for credit toward the School Leaving Certificate.

In the 1931 *Montreal Music Year Book* Stanton praised the high school choirs in the city. This volume also contained a short article on the West Hill High School Choir directed by Irvin Cooper. Cooper was an Englishman who had come to Montreal in 1923 and was appointed to this school shortly after his arrival. He soon formed a girls' choir and then a mixed choir, which gave frequent performances, including some radio shows. Cooper later did extensive work on the boy's changing voice and became known throughout Canada and the United

States for his writings on this subject and for his special arrangements for teen-age choral groups. He served as supervisor of music for the Montreal Protestant schools from 1938 until 1947.

Baron Byng High School also possessed a fine choral program directed by D.M. Herbert, a British musician who taught for many years at the school. This institution served a predominantly Jewish population, with most of the students first and second generation Canadians. There was strong parental support for the arts, for these were 'people who revered anything of the soul and spirit that reminded them of the old country.' The art teacher, Anne Savage, who worked with Herbert at Baron Byng, further commented, 'We lived in a wonderful period; there were so many clever and talented children there – very, very able.'[20] In 1928 J.L. Yule, director of music for Guelph Collegiate, visited Herbert's school. He referred to this visit in *Musical Canada*: 'Although the school had been in session less than a month, the entire programme was given from memory. The Quality of tone in all the choirs was exceptionally good, that of the boys with changed voices being particularly outstanding. Messers Astbury [the principal] and Herbert are to be congratulated on having a High School music department that has few equals in Canada.'[21] The following year Herbert was invited to speak to the Music Section of the Ontario Educational Association. In his opening remarks he quoted from the course outline for high schools in Montreal, stating that the aim of music instruction is to cultivate a taste for good music and that this aim can be best attained through a course in vocal music. Herbert explained that the course was directed toward the large majority of students who go out into the world 'not as performers but as listeners' and who should have 'a keen and lively interest in at least one of the arts to help them along in their everyday toil.' His comments regarding his philosophy and concept of the role of a teacher give some indication of the reason for his success at Baron Byng: 'The music of the high school should be in the hands of not only a competent teacher but one who has boundless enthusiasm for his subject and endless patience. Without the latter he is doomed to failure. He should be given a free hand to carry out any courses of instruction he may deem suitable, and no matter what weird noises may be heard emanating from the music room, the principal and staff should realize that all is well within – a breaking voice can perform some weird and wonderful vocal gymnastics.'[22] In the course of his remarks he also commented on the need for a well-equipped music room, to which pupils should have free access 'at all reasonable times.'

In describing the course content, Herbert explained that classes met for two half-hour periods per week for the first and second years, and one half-hour period for the third year. Sight-reading and ear training were stressed; he referred to the advantage of a strong background in Tonic Sol-fa. The materials used included British, American, and Canadian publications. Listening lessons on 'works of the greater composers through the use of the gramophone'[23] were incorporated. Singing was an integral part of the class activities rather than a separate exercise. Herbert stressed that adequate preparation by the teacher was imperative, especially in a situation in which little time was available for music: 'Much can be accomplished if the teacher knows exactly what he proposes to do in any given lesson period. Without a well-prepared lesson the pupils lose interest, the lesson is a failure, and the teacher becomes discouraged. Keep the pupils well occupied all the time ... let the pupils' listening be active, not passive; let them not only listen to but for something.'[24] He also made a plea for students and staff to sing together as often as possible: 'Great is the power of such united singing to refresh the mind and give a new meaning to the words "The School Spirit" – all for one and each for all.'[25]

Presumably, the special music course described by Herbert was taught in selected high schools in Montreal. According to Cooper, by 1931 this course was in danger of being cut as an 'unnecessary frill.' He gave the following account:

> In order to offset this action, the high school music specialists worked out a new course in music, obtained the approval of a large number of prominent educationists and presented the course to the Protestant Committee, with a request that music be placed on the regular course of study and accorded credit as an optional subject for School Leaving Examinations which are conducted for students at the end of four years in high school. The Matriculation Board of McGill University was also approached with a request to include the course as an option for matriculation into Arts and into Science. In due course both these bodies accepted the recommendations. From that moment the term 'frill' was forgotten, and music now enjoys equal status with other credit subjects.[26]

Cooper described this high school course as a 'listener's course,' not a 'performer's course,' explaining that at the conclusion of the fourth year, students had a clear understanding of orchestral and band instrumentation, form, elementary theory, and history of music, and 'a first-hand acquaintance with the better-known, symphonic works of the great masters.'[27] The final examination was in two parts, written and oral, and made extensive use of gramophone recordings.

In addition to the elective course, extra-curricular choral and instrumental groups were popular at many high schools. Cooper was a great believer in combining these various groups in order to attract public support. In 1941 he organized a special project known as the High Schools Opera of Montreal. Ten senior boys and girls from each high school in Montreal district were 'welded into an opera group for the purpose of presenting *The Mikado* for three evenings during the Teachers' Convention in October.'[28] Twelve school music specialists were involved in the project, which was financed by the Provincial Association of Protestant Teachers. High school music instruction was not confined to the Montreal area, but it was uneven throughout the province. In 1945 it was reported, 'Excellent results are being obtained by music specialists in the High Schools of Arvida, Richmond, Shawinigan Falls, Lennoxville and Coaticook, but the results obtained in many high schools leave much to be desired.'[29]

Instrumental Music

In 1926 the Montreal High School Orchestra played at a meeting of the music section of the Provincial Association of Protestant Teachers, but no details about this performing group were given in the report. During the 1920s there were several references to harmonica bands in various Montreal schools. Later, rhythm bands became popular and were 'organized in elementary schools as extra-school work'; the report added, 'This measure is very agreeable to the students and enables them to appreciate deeply both rhythm and harmony.'[30] In his 1931 article Stanton mentioned that orchestral music had made a successful beginning and also referred to classes in piano and violin, which were conducted in a number of schools, out of school hours, by the McGill Conservatorium. These classes were initiated through the Canadian Bureau for the Advancement of Music.

Instrumental music became popular during the late 1930s in the schools in Montreal, Westmount, and Montreal West. These boards purchased a large number of instruments and were offering after-school classes for grade five and upwards. Students used school instruments, as in high schools, but paid thirty-five cents per week for instruction. Cooper reported thirty-five classes in operation by the end of the decade, as well as six school bands, three school orchestras, an all high schools' band, and an all high schools' orchestra. In the fall of 1940, instrumental music was authorized as an optional course for credit in grades eight through eleven and was available as a credit for a high school leaving certificate. The aim, according to Cooper, was 'not to develop outstanding performers, but to teach young people that great enjoyment can be obtained in co-operative effort in music making.' He commended the provincial department of education for foresight which made 'the ideal effective in practice.' They had inserted a clause in the high school leaving requirements for instrumental music, to the effect that 'prior to the examination, the candidate must submit to the examiner a statement signed by the school principal testifying to regular attendance and satisfactory performance at band or orchestra rehearsals.'[31] Legislation was adopted providing for two music options in the high school leaving examinations, making it possible for 'a talented music student to obtain credits as for two full subjects, one for his work in the high school elective course and one for his instrumental studies.' A student engaging in pianoforte work with a private tutor could thus 'obtain another credit by submitting work in the high school elective course in music.'[32]

MUSIC IN ROMAN CATHOLIC SCHOOLS

In the report issued for the 1918–19 school year by the inspector of 'superior schools' for the Catholic Commission, it was stated, 'Lessons in singing form part of the exercises in nearly all the schools.'[33] However, in the following year a discussion of the new course of study for the elementary grades contained no references to music. Singing was listed as optional.

The words and music of 'O Canada' were published in the October 1920 issue of the teachers' periodical L'Enseignement primaire, and an editorial was included encouraging teachers to sing this selection frequently in their classrooms. In 1922 the Catholic Commission adopted the resolution that '"O Canada" be sung at least twice a week.'[34] One inspector who found four schools which could not fulfil this requirement reported that he did not grant them the customary holiday. However, this was not the situation in all areas of the province, for the inspector for House Harbour, Havre Aubert, Étang du Nord, and Île Coffin [Îles de la Madeleine] reported, 'The little Acadians sing with heart and soul the French Canadian anthem, O Canada, as well as the Ave Maris Stella and the songs of Evangeline.'[35]

Music was included in the curriculum of many of the convent schools. Instructional materials were prepared by several of the orders, including a series entitled *Le Chant à l'école*, published in 1926 by les Sœurs de la Congrégation de Notre-Dame in Montreal.

Most classical colleges also included music in their course of study. In 1928, 'the Catholic Committee, after having consulted the Bishops present at the meeting, who stated that solfeggio, a compulsory subject of study in classical colleges, is everywhere taught by competent professors, thanked the Honourable Provincial Secretary for the generous offer made by him to contribute towards the expenses for teaching of this subject.'[36] Instrumental study was also offered at certain Roman Catholic institutions. Among those mentioned in reports were De La Salle Academy at Trois-Rivières, in existence for over eighty-eight years, 'with six hundred pupils, thirty-five brothers and several servants in cramped quarters,'[37] and St-Louis-de-Gonzague Academy, operated by the Ursulines in Grand'Mère.

There seems, however, to have been little music instruction in the Catholic elementary schools during this period. Music was not a compulsory subject, and it was left to the classroom teacher to determine what time and effort would be expended in this area. The lack of music at this level was recognized by some of the school authorities, however, for in 1929 the president of the Montreal Catholic School Commission invited the composer Claude Champagne to submit a proposed course of study in music for the elementary grades. Champagne had recently returned from Paris, where he had been studying composition, and was seeking employment at a rather difficult time. He obtained part-time teaching positions at various institutions in the Montreal area and had to relegate his composing to his spare time, but he did accept this invitation.

In his report Champagne urged the adoption of a solfège program which stressed a reliance on ear training and intuitive response as opposed to rote learning. Champagne felt that students should eventually be able to read in all clefs and that plainchant should serve as a basis for learning. His ideas on the subject reflected those of André Gedalge, with whom he had studied in Paris. In a study of Champagne and his work with the Montreal Catholic schools, Gilles Pilote made this comparison: 'Ce qui differencie les deux, c'est que Gedalge adopte un style d'exposition, sinon intellectuel, du moins complexe, tandis que Champagne se distingue par une extrême simplicité.'[38] Champagne's report was favourably received and he was subsequently appointed 'surveillant du chant choral dans les écoles.' He established a program of studies 'comprenant toutes les années du cours primaire' which stressed the use of Gregorian chant as described in recent papal encyclicals and also elements of 'folklore canadien.'[39] He wrote manuals to be used by the students and teachers and organized training sessions for the teachers. It seems, however, that he did not have a large enough staff to carry out the program successfully, and that the regular classroom teachers did not have enough background to give sufficient help to their students. He resigned in 1942 in order to assume the position of assistant director of the newly formed Conservatoire de musique du Québec. He was succeeded by Raoul Paquet, who served until his death in 1946, when Alfred Mignault was appointed to the post.

Champagne was active in music education for all ages before his appointment to le Conservatoire. In 1941 the 'Radio Collège,' intended as a high school supplement but designed for adults as well, was broadcast on eight French radio networks. The weekly series 'Invitation à la musique' was prepared and hosted by Claude Champagne until 1945. The work of Champagne in promoting singing and solfège was noted in the annual reports, but few details were given: 'The Commission has given a remarkable impulse to the teaching of singing, solfège, and physical culture. The progress already noticeable seems to have justified its initiative.'[40] There was also mention of a new course of study for Catholic high schools and English-speaking Catholic schools, but no details on music were included. The report did state that 'singing and gymnastics' were generally taught in the 'town' schools and that the teaching of these subjects was well done in convents and classical colleges, but that it was 'practically nil' in the rural school.

Music instruction in the Catholic schools was not recognized as a success by those outside the Catholic Commission either, for in a 1941 article entitled 'School Music in Quebec' Irvin Cooper dismissed the music program in the Catholic schools in one short paragraph: 'Organized curricular music in the French Catholic schools is practically non-existent, with the exception of a few choirs and bugle bands; and in the English Catholic Schools the Supervisor of Music, Miss Beatrice Donnelly, is engaged in a determined effort to win for it the recognition it deserves, and to establish a definite curricular status for music. Consequently, this article will confine itself to music in the Protestant schools.'[41] Reference has already been made to the appointment of

Sœur Marie-Stéphane as director of music for les Sœurs des Saints Noms de Jésus et Marie and the subsequent establishment of École Vincent-d'Indy. In 1936 la Congrégation de Notre-Dame created the position of director general for music studies in all its houses. The same year les Sœurs de Ste-Croix also appointed a music director and established both a school and a college of music. These schools run by the various orders, along with l'École de musique at Laval, the classical colleges, and the newly formed Conservatoire, provided many more musical opportunities for the French-speaking Catholic population of the province.

TEACHER EDUCATION AND PROFESSIONAL ORGANIZATIONS

Programs for Protestants

Macdonald College continued as the chief training centre for Protestant teachers in the period between the wars. There was a close liaison between the college and the Montreal Protestant board, for when George Stanton resigned, the principal stated, 'His skill and knowledge, however, are not lost to the province, as he has been appointed to the important position of supervisor of music in the Protestant Schools of Montreal, where his cooperation will still prove valuable to our students in training.'[42]

R. Birkett Musgrove, a graduate of the Tonic Sol-fa College, London, England, was appointed to succeed Stanton and held this position until 1939. The program for teachers continued to emphasize the Tonic Sol-fa approach, but instruction in conventional staff notation was also given in keeping with the 'Dual Notation Course' offered in the schools. Certificates in both approaches were granted each year. This practice lasted until 1932, when the course of study was expanded to reflect changes in the school music curriculum: 'New music certificates were instituted during the year with an improved course of study of greater value to teachers. Certificates of various grades in music were obtained by 98 students. This would appear to justify the innovation of a Music Certificate given by the Department of Education of this Province.'[43] An explanation of these changes in music certificate requirements and the rationale given for them suggested that the existing requirements were possibly out of date and that their rigidity discouraged teachers. Before this, 'a candidate for Tonic Sol-fa College certificates had to reach a satisfactory standard in every detail, or bear the stigma of total failure.'[44] There were four grades of music certificates established under the new system. The same five categories were tested, with increasing levels of difficulty for each certificate: songs, rhythm, sight-singing, ear training, and knowledge. In each grade the candidates were classified according to their degrees of achievement by a letter system. The requirements stipulated: 'A candidate must attain A or B rank before offering herself for the examination for the next higher certificate; but a candidate attaining C or D rank may enter again in the same examination to obtain an A or a B rank. This should provide an incentive to teachers to continue their studies in the subject, and should serve to indicate more closely their musical ability.'[45] It is evident that Montreal had been considered a stronghold in the Tonic Sol-fa movement, for when this change in curriculum took place it was noted in the *Musical Times* in London, England, 'It is greatly to be regretted that the education authorities at Montreal have decided to abolish the Tonic Sol-fa notation from their schools, not only because this decision is based upon false assumptions, but also because they are thereby inflicting a decided injustice upon each scholar under their control.'[46]

Special summer schools were given for Protestant teachers at Macdonald College during the 1930s. Teachers were able to work toward an advanced elementary or an advanced intermediate diploma; music was one of the elective subjects offered in these programs. In addition to general classroom choral work, the teachers were introduced to the use of radio for music appreciation and the study of school bands. Summer courses were also offered for Protestant teachers at McGill University and at Bishop's College in Lennoxville. In addition, the Montreal Protestant board provided special instruction in music for its classroom teachers. Cooper described this program:

Generally speaking, music in the Protestant elementary schools is taught by the class teacher. A regulation of dubious utility, in use in some districts here, requires the class teacher to teach music or suffer a deduction of $40.00 annually. As a result, all but the musically bereft, and in some cases even these, attempt the teaching of music to their classes. When it is borne in mind that a large number of these teachers received their education in rural schools, in the majority of which no music was taught, and that nine months in normal school comprise the sum total of their musical experience prior to embarking on a teaching career, some rough idea may be gathered as to the state of music in many classes. However, classes are offered each session at no cost to the teacher, and the attendance is most gratifying. At lectures held in the city of Montreal during the past session, seventy-eight per cent of all elementary school teachers attended whatever series affected their own particular grade.[47]

Cooper also mentioned a teachers' choir of nearly a hundred voices which met weekly, courses in music appreciation for teachers which were well attended, and a teachers' band which was to be organized in the fall.

The music section of the Protestant Teachers' Association sponsored sessions on music at annual meetings, and articles on various aspects of music instruction appeared in the periodical of this organization, the *Educational Record*. In 1932 'several delegates from the Province of Quebec attended the Music Supervisors' National Conference in Cleveland, Ohio ... among whom were Mr. George Stanton, Montreal, Mr. James Small, Montreal West, Dean Laird, Macdonald College, Mr. Hanson and Miss Dodds of the McGill Conservatorium of Music.'[48] A few years later a small group of music teachers from the Montreal Protestant school board formed a professional organization which became known as the Provincial Association of School Music Teachers. Irvin Cooper was elected president. Beth Newell notes that 'up to 1960, the membership of the group never exceeded fifty and the quarterly meetings were, in the main, social gatherings or concerts by its members.'[49] It later became affiliated with the Canadian Music Educators' Association, and the name was changed to the Quebec Music Educators' Association (QMEA). An association of private music teachers, known as the Quebec Music Teachers' Association, was founded in Montreal in 1942 at a meeting organized by Mary Covert, piano teacher, music critic, and correspondent for the *Musical Courier*. In 1945 this organization affiliated with the Canadian Federation of Music Teachers' Associations.

Programs for Roman Catholics

The 1921 course of study for Catholic normal schools listed singing along with politeness and hygiene and devoted one hour per week to these subjects. Singing was described as 'solfeggio, religious hymns, popular and national songs.' The course of study also stated that teachers should use songs which were 'traditional and which the school should help to keep alive,' and that teachers should develop 'lessons of good taste to combat the introduction of rowdy songs, whether from the United States or elsewhere.'[50] It seems that music was offered in most of the numerous Catholic normal schools; the success of these programs no doubt depended upon the ability and enthusiasm of the teacher in charge. By 1930 there were forty-five regular professors and fifteen special professors of 'singing, music, and gymnastics' in these schools. The inspector general was a strong supporter of the music program: 'Solfeggio and singing are held in high honour in every scholasticate. Such exercises develop taste, encourage better speaking, introduce an ideal note in school circles. Instrumental music is also part of the programme. Gregorian chant, especially, is carefully studied, as is liturgy. These two closely connected studies give a better idea of the beauty of Catholic worship, instil an enlightened piety, lift up the souls of the young and improve their minds by revealing to them all that Christian liturgy contains of nobleness, dignity, and grandeur.'[51] This emphasis upon music for the liturgy of the Catholic worship service was of paramount importance in the minds of most authorities in the Catholic system, and members of the religious orders were often engaged to teach music. The Hull Normal School reported in 1931: 'A professor of Gregorian chant has been added to the staff in the person of Rev. Philippe Montour, of the Ottawa Seminary. Let us hope that our future teachers will become apostles of sacred chant in schools.'[52] In remoter areas the instruction was not always as regular, as at the Gaspé Normal School, where a Reverend Ethelbert Thibault gave instruction in Gregorian music 'from time to time.' Mention was also made of instruction at Iberville, Athabaska, and Rigaud, where 'piano, organ, singing and band lessons completed the esthetic education of our young Brothers.'[53] Students were usually charged extra fees for these private lessons.

Frequent references to normal school students' singing for church services are found, and by 1934 music examinations for special certificates were being given at certain schools. Despite this, the teaching of music does not seem to have improved to any great extent in the Catholic schools, particularly those in rural areas. A discussion of the new course of study in 1937 shows the low regard in which music was still held by certain officials: 'Less important subjects, such as singing, gymnastics, manual work, even agriculture will gradually be better taught. There is nothing complicated in the manner of teaching these subjects.' Later in the same report, however, one of the inspectors expressed quite the opposite view: 'The course of study, as revised last year, has still provisions that are hard to apply ... solfeggio supposes certain natural aptitudes in teacher and pupils.'[54] He emphasized that he felt the subject should have remained optional.

The report for 1938 referred to the work of the Montreal Catholic School Commission in giving 'a remarkable impulse to the teaching of singing, solfège and physical culture' and stated that the classroom teachers had 'responded very well to superiors by following special courses and putting in practice the principles taught by specialists.'[55] These special summer courses were not limited to the Montreal area; in 1938 summer courses in solfège were instituted at several normal schools throughout the province, including one at l'Université Laval, and many of the religious orders offered special instruction for their members. In 1942 it was stated: 'For the fourth year, a certain number of religious and lay female teachers have been asked to qualify for teaching solfeggio according to the course of study. Quebec, Sherbrooke, Baie-Saint-Paul and Chicoutimi have in turn during a week gathered groups of fifty to a hundred teachers who took lessons under the direction of specialists in the practice of solfeggio, in order to obtain a certificate of qualification.'[56]

More specialized training in music was also available for Catholic teachers. A normal school for music associated with l'Institut pédagogique de Montréal was established by les Sœurs de la Congrégation de Notre-Dame in 1926. This institution, along with its school of liturgical singing, played an important role in training teachers for music instruction. By 1939 there were forty religious and lay female teachers enrolled in l'École normale de musique, 'thirty of whom received certificates, four a teaching diploma, and one the baccalaureate in music.'[57]

FESTIVALS

Several music festivals were held in Montreal between the wars, but many of them seem to have been short-lived. The previously mentioned Music Week, sponsored by the Delphic Study Club, continued for many years. Several years after its inauguration the club initiated a scholarship competition in conjunction with this event. In 1923 a competitive choral festival was held in Montreal under the sponsorship of the Metropolitan Choral Society conducted by Mr G. Vanderpoll. This choir had successfully participated in choral competitions in Ottawa, and its members and conductor felt that a similar competition should be held in their own city. The festival was planned as an event which would involve solo piano and violin playing as well as choral classes, and was proposed with the aim of encouraging participation from both language groups; the *Daily Star* commented, 'Such a competition should prove effective in stimulating artistic effort among our resident musicians, both professional and amateur, and as the plan is sufficiently broad to give ample place to French-speaking organizations side by side with English-speaking bodies, there may develop out of it a more secure entente cordiale, and a firmer unification of music interest, than has yet been established.'[58] This event also brought together groups from various parts of the province, as noted by the same newspaper: 'If the Montreal Musical Festival had done nothing else, it would have been worthwhile for the amount of good material brought to notice and for the convenient means it opened up for musicians from different cities to get in touch with each other. A choir from Quebec, for example, made everyone sit up; and the fact that contestants from other cities than Montreal carried off not a few prizes indicates the scope of the competition.'[59] A Canadian Folk Song and Handicraft Festival was held in Quebec City for several years beginning in 1927 as part of the special CPR Festivals held in various parts of the country. This city, 'with all its ancient charm,' was considered by the organizers to be 'the perfect background for such a gathering'; they felt it was a city which had 'grown old gracefully, like one of the ancient chansons, without losing any of its old world beauty.' The 1928 festival was under the direction of Marius Barbeau of the National Museum of Canada and Harold Eustace Key, musical director of the CPR. The program booklet indicates that children were involved in the event: 'Children's songs, dances and games, as they have been sung and danced and played for centuries in the convents of Canada, will add a delicate touch to the programme. Madame Duquet and some children of Quebec will interpret two groups. The children will wear the costumes of the last century, the little girls hoops and pantalettes, the boys the dress of the soldiers and gentlemen of that period. In some of the rondes, such as the "Ronde du loup" and "La souris gris" the children will be attired as animals.'[60] In 1937 a special festival known as the Festival-concours de musique du Québec was held in Montreal in which more than fifty-four hundred young musicians participated. This festival continued for four years and had many prominent adjudicators, including Father Bernier and Sir Hugh Roberton. In 1939 there were twelve thousand competitors.

Music festivals seem to have been held periodically for the Protestant schools; Cooper recorded that 'the elementary schools wound up the school year 1940–41 with a Festival of School Music in which eighty-four choral groups participated, giving five regional concerts, a final concert, and three radio broadcasts.'[61] In 1941 Cooper was invited to Toronto to be a guest conductor in the Varsity Arena Concert, sponsored by the Music Section of the Ontario Educational Association. This event seems to have inspired him to propose a similar venture in Montreal, for in the spring of 1942 the School Music Specialists' Association presented a special concert in the Montreal Forum under the sponsorship of the Provincial Association of Protestant Teachers. Cooper described the motive behind the venture: 'The city of Montreal and various parts of the province of Quebec need to be made conscious of the wealth of musical ability that is present in its young people ... to be awakened to a new pride in the musical accomplishments of their children, and, furthermore, made to realize the importance of good music in a well-rounded education. It is with this object in mind that the school music specialists are pooling their resources and efforts for a mass demonstration next spring. They are determined to break down the benevolent tolerance associated with music in schools, and to replace this with a profound respect for music in education and for those engaged in its development.'[62] Similar events known as Victory Loan School Rallies were held at the Montreal Forum throughout the war years. Following the Second World War, Cooper turned his thoughts to an even larger undertaking, that of the International Festival of School Music held in Montreal in 1947 under his leadership.

10

Politics and Public Relations in Ontario

If musical maturity in Ontario can be measured in a valid way by progress in Toronto, then the emergence of a permanent symphony orchestra in the 1920s was indeed a milestone, since Toronto's musical tradition had hitherto revolved around its choral aggregations. Although there had been forerunners, the New Symphony Orchestra formed by Luigi von Kunits in 1922 was the first instrumental ensemble to enjoy an enduring existence. It was renamed the Toronto Symphony Orchestra in 1927 and has continued as one of the major musical organizations in the city. In its early years concerts were scheduled in Massey Hall at 5:00 p.m. to accommodate the many musicians engaged in theatre orchestras during the heyday of silent movies. Von Kunits had had a thorough training in his native Vienna, including personal contact with Brahms, Bruckner, and Hanslick; at one point he was offered a position as conductor of the Philadelphia Orchestra. Appointed to the Canadian Academy of Music in 1912, he was a valuable addition to the musical life of the city. As a conductor he established the standard orchestral repertoire for Toronto audiences, and as a violin teacher, according to the EMC, he 'shaped a generation of string players, some of whom continued to play with the Toronto Symphony in 1980.'[1]

From a musical standpoint the orchestra was secure by the time Ernest MacMillan was appointed conductor in 1931, and it eventually became the prototype for future orchestras throughout the dominion.

Several EMC articles refer to Ernest MacMillan and Reginald Stewart as rival figures in a lively flow of orchestral activity. Stewart conducted the Promenade Symphony Concerts, which took place weekly in Varsity Arena during the off-season (May–October). Among others, Donald Heins and Ettore Mazzoleni, both associated with the TSO and the TCM, were also prominent as conductors in this formative period of orchestral development.

Efforts to build a permanent opera company in Toronto did not prove to be successful except for a few organizations which specialized in Gilbert and Sullivan and light opera: the Savoyards (1919–28), the Eaton Operatic Society (1932–65), and the Canada Packers Operatic Society (1943–55). Membership in the latter two societies was comprised of employees of the firm which sponsored the amateur group. Several local companies attempted to establish grand opera around the mid-1930s. The efforts of the Canadian Grand Opera Association (1935–7) and the Opera Guild of Toronto (1935–41) did not bring lasting results because of inadequate financial support and, at times, more rivalry than the situation could tolerate. Dorith Cooper observes that 'during the war years, the public's attention temporarily turned away from opera,'[2] with the exception of a production in 1941 at a promenade concert in Varsity Arena, which attracted an audience of six thousand. The void was partially filled, however, through the regular radio broadcasts of the Metropolitan Opera Company of New York, which have been heard in Canada since 1931. Concerns regarding cultural domination notwithstanding, this is one of many benefits which Canadians enjoyed as a neighbour of the United States.

The development of opera in Toronto was nurtured by TCM musicians involved in opera training at that institution. Early in his term as principal, MacMillan engaged Countess Laura de Turzynowicz to conduct classes in operatic ensemble, and in 1928 he established the Toronto Conservatory Opera Company.[3] Although the conservatory company had several successful seasons, it ceased operation in 1930. The TCM revived its interest in 1936 by giving opera classes at its summer school. The most significant link between training programs and professional activities, however, took place in 1946, when an opera school was formed within the new senior school of the TCM. Arnold Walter, Herman Geiger-Torel, and Nicholas Goldschmidt contributed immensely to the success of this venture, and the professional company which ultimately became the Canadian Opera Company was a direct outcome of the opera school.[4]

In spite of a rising interest in orchestral music, Toronto's long-standing tradition in choral music was sustained throughout the inter-war period. H.A. Fricker succeeded A.S. Vogt as conductor of the Toronto Mendelssohn Choir in 1918 and extended its reputation internationally by presenting large-scale works, accompanied on occasion by leading American orchestras. Fricker also conducted the CNE Chorus, which in 1925 was reputed to be 'possibly the largest choir in North America.'[5] MacMillan, whose TCM choir had offered annual performances of St Matthew Passion, assumed the mantle of the Toronto Mendelssohn Choir in 1942 and joined forces with the TSO in oratorio, including annual presentations of Messiah. Among other choral societies, the Toronto Bach Choir flourished under the direction of Reginald Stewart, and numerous church choirs maintained ambitious schedules of their own. It bears repeating that several generations of musicians in Ontario received their initial musical training as members of church choirs.

The state of musical maturity was uneven throughout the other parts of the province. Cities such as Hamilton and Ottawa could boast of excellent choral societies, but overall their musical offerings were pale in the light of Toronto's accomplishments. This is understandable, for the presence of CBC, the Toronto Mendelssohn Choir, TSO, and other organizations of national stature attracted outstanding musicians to Toronto, where they could pursue an interlocking pattern of professional opportunities; frequently such free-lancing involved some teaching at TCM or, in later years, at the University of Toronto's Faculty of Music. TCM was a focal point for music throughout the province, functioning at times as a central bureau or unofficial headquarters; for music, people automatically thought of the 'Con' in the same way that rural people identified with the CNE or hockey players with Maple Leaf Gardens. TCM's imposing stature aside, there were other institutions operating in places outside of Toronto whose presence and independence deserve recognition.

A plethora of conservatories existed in Ontario cities before the First World War, many of which were merely glorified studios of short duration. Among the few schools that lasted as centres of private teaching were the Hamilton Conservatory of Music (1897–1965, known as Royal Hamilton College 1965–80) and the Western Ontario Conservatory of Music (1934–). Both institutions had been formed from precursors bearing different names, and though they affiliated with major Ontario universities, they granted diplomas and conducted their own examinations through most of their existence. Two outstanding principals, William Hewlitt (Hamilton 1918–39) and Harvey Robb (Western Ontario 1938–57), attracted some excellent teachers to their respective institutions and fostered musical growth in ways that national institutions, however prestigious, were not able to accomplish in local areas. One might assume that in larger cities the conservatories institutionalized private instruction. But a great deal of teaching took place in domestic settings within neighbourhoods, and apart from registering students for conservatory examinations many teachers operated in relative isolation. In some cases they avoided direct contact with conservatories because examination marks could be embarrassing and examiners' comments even more devastating.

Perhaps the impetus to form local teacher groups was born of the solitude experienced by private teachers, especially those who taught in their own homes. They felt the need for an exchange of ideas and welcomed the inspiration provided by guest speakers and recitalists. The desire to improve their professional status intensified in the late 1930s. Conservatory staff and a few independent teachers provided the leadership and initiated the political action. A large segment of the membership benefited from professional development which was designed to improve standards, but, of course, many incompetent teachers did not register with these organizations. Several local teachers' groups were in operation when W.B. Rothwell took the initiative in forming the Ontario Music Teachers' Association in 1936. In 1942 this body joined the Canadian Federation of Music Teachers' Associations, and in 1946 it was incorporated as the Ontario Registered Music Teachers' Association.

PRIVATE SCHOOLS

Music education thrived in private schools, seminaries, and convents. In fact, music became a strong department in many institutions which were originally founded as ladies' colleges. Private schools offered individual lessons in both practical and theoretical subjects, and students received academic credits under the department of education's equivalent certificate program by completing the appropriate conservatory examinations. The quality of teaching in private schools was often on a par with that of the leading conservatories. Indeed, many of TCM's outstanding teachers also taught at schools such as the Ontario Ladies' College in Whitby and Alma College in St Thomas. Music instructors at Upper Canada College included such distinguished musicians as Ettore Mazzoleni and Arnold Walter. Because music teachers in private schools were usually part-time staff members, music instruction remained a special, separate entity. Consequently, aside from general appreciation classes, music education in these schools did not develop along the lines commonly found in the public school system. Whereas the emphasis in private schools was on individual work, the emphasis in public schools was on ensemble activities.

Private music instruction has been a point of pride in Windsor's convent schools such as St Mary's Academy, founded in 1864 by the Sisters of the Holy Names of Jesus and Mary, and the Ursuline School of Music, established in 1915. The Sisters of Loretto had music departments at schools in Toronto, Hamilton, and Stratford; many of their students were successful in completing examinations with TCM. At St Michael's, the Roman Catholic cathedral in Toronto, Monsignor John Edward Ronan instituted a day school program in 1937 which combined specialized training for boy choristers with a general academic curriculum. Modelled after church choir schools in Europe, this program required daily participation in worship services as part of the training. The St Michael's Cathedral Choir School started with 18 boys in grades seven and eight, but by its fiftieth anniversary it had an enrolment of 373 boys in grades three to thirteen. Most other attempts to develop this type of school in Canada have been short-lived or have resulted in modified versions at best.

THE ONTARIO SCHOOL FOR THE BLIND

Music can claim a special place in the history of the Ontario School for the Blind (OSB) in Brantford. From 1872 to 1913 the school was known as the Ontario Institute for the Education of the Blind. Its first public concert was presented on 23 December 1872. The program featured Professor B.F. Cheesbro, the school's music director, as well as a number of his students. W. Norman Andrews served as music director from 1907 to 1918. On a typical day in the 1920s the national anthem would be sung at 8:30 a.m. to the accompaniment of the pipe organ in the assembly hall. Margaret Chandler describes the routine in the assembly which followed the news of the day: 'A few records from the best artists are then placed on the victrola, or perhaps a selection is played on the player-piano, and the day is thus started with the melody of sweet music ... At 9 o'clock the literary, musical, sewing and knitting classes commence.'[6] Several teachers served relatively short terms before Frederic Lord became director of music in 1924; he remained at the school until 1945. Lord emigrated from England, where he had been a church organist; his training also included piano study in Switzerland. Active in both church and community choral work, he achieved recognition as conductor of the Canadian Choir of Brantford (1928–45), a group which competed in England's Blackpool Music Festival and toured extensively. Frederic Lord is also remembered for his achievements at OSB, where he and others prepared many students for conservatory examinations. Most teachers at the school were private teachers in the Brantford community, including Lord's wife, Dorothy, who taught violin there for almost forty years.

Students at OSB were encouraged to perform outside the school. A quartet of girls trained by Susie Miller maintained a busy schedule of concerts, as did the school orchestra led by Lord. Both groups performed at Toronto's Eaton Auditorium in 1938 in a concert sponsored by the National Council and Women's Auxiliary to the Canadian National Institute for the Blind. Frederic Lord was keen to enter his students in competitions: the OSB Madrigal Ensemble won a gold medal at the Stratford Music Festival, and in 1937, the first year of the Brantford festival, thirty of the forty-five students from OSB won awards. But perhaps the most remarkable accomplishments during Lord's twenty-one years of service were the operettas, which began in 1932 with a production of *Princess Ju Ju*. The school's operatic tradition reached its zenith with the Gilbert and Sullivan productions of Lord's successor, George Smale; a number of these were staged in such places as the Eaton Auditorium and the Royal York Hotel. Smale gave up his position as director of music for Brantford's public schools to become music director at OSB in 1945. During his twenty-five year tenure he developed a comprehensive program which demonstrated the effectiveness of music in educating the blind, and eventually the music position was elevated to full-time status. Piano tuning was taught in OSB's vocational department by James O. Ansell from 1915 to 1947. Through this practical training the school provided students with skills for employment, and for years Canadian communities have been well served by piano technicians who graduated from this department. The Ontario School for the Blind was renamed the W. Ross Macdonald School in 1974.

A PERIOD OF TRANSITION IN SCHOOL MUSIC

From 1919 to 1945 the Music Section of the Ontario Educational Association (OEA) was an annual barometer of the climate in school music. Diana Brault's account of OEA proceedings reveals that members were concerned with pedagogy, programs, and politics, The suggestion for a music section within OEA arose at a banquet on 20 February 1919 at the King Edward Hotel in Toronto; reportedly, this banquet was sponsored by the Canadian Bureau for the Advancement of Music. Hollis Dann, an eminent American music educator, addressed the gathering, which was made up of more than sixty people, including music supervisors, normal school instructors, professional musicians, and two representatives from the department of education, namely, Dr H.J. Cody, minister of education, and John Waugh, chief inspector of schools. In Brault's words,

> Dann exhorted Canadians to avoid mistakes made by Dann's own countrymen in granting insufficient time and creating inadequate standards for the training of music supervisors in the various states. Training should be rigorous and of a depth which would develop musicianship on the part of the prospective supervisor and an ability to handle the complexities of instrumental and vocal music at both elementary and high school levels. Declaring the importance of music for the individual child and for the society as a whole, Dann advocated the teaching of music in the high school and supplied information concerning New York State's new regulations of the current academic year for the granting of credits for music courses.[7]

While still under the spell of Dann's stirring address, the music supervisors resolved to convene as a group at the forthcoming Easter convention of OEA. At this inaugural meeting they elected A.T. Cringan of Toronto as chairman and E.W.G. Quantz of London as secretary. Inspector Waugh spoke to the group on this occasion, encouraging them 'to organize discussions regarding the teaching of Public School Music, and to pass on to the Department any requests or recommendations of theirs to better the teaching of music.'[8] Subsequently, their practical concerns were embodied in seven recommendations:

> First: That the regulation relating to the compulsory teaching of music be made active throughout the Province, and that a minimum of one hour per

week be required by the Department to be devoted to the study of Vocal Music.

Second: That a Supervisor of Music for the Province of Ontario be appointed to stimulate an interest in music, particularly throughout the rural districts and towns where the subject is not now taught in Public and High Schools.

Third: That the duties and relationships of Supervisors of Music to the school be clearly defined by the Department of Education in the Departmental Regulations.

Fourth: In view of the lamentable conditions of music in the rural districts – it being found that 88 per cent of all students entering Normal Schools have had no previous training in singing – we would strongly urge the appointment of Supervisors of Music for rural districts, as provided for by regulation, and that this recommendation be carried into effect as promptly as practicable.

Fifth: That phonographs, and band and orchestral instruments for school use only, be put on the approved school apparatus, in order that they may be subject to the same exemption from Customs Duties as other school apparatus.

Sixth: That we recommend the granting of credits for outside music study in the High School Course, as soon as the Department deems it expedient.

Seventh: In order to give teachers-in-training an opportunity to hear the best music, and in order that they may receive training in music appreciation, we would recommend that gramophones be placed in Normal Schools, in English-French Training Schools and English Model Schools of the Province.[9]

The original Music Section was a group of approximately thirty members. Many were supervisors in large cities: H. Whorlow Bull (Windsor), E.W. Goethe Quantz (London), Bruce Carey (Hamilton), James Smith (Ottawa), P.G. Marshall (Simcoe), Emily Tedd, Duncan McKenzie, and Benson Collier (Toronto), Harry Hill (Kingston, and later Kitchener), and Alwilda McKenzie (Leamington). Among the membership were normal school music teachers: A.T. Cringan (Toronto), T.A. Brown (Ottawa), Charles Percy (London), James Bottomley (Stratford), and Harry Stares (Hamilton). These people were leaders in their fields, but, even more significant, a number of them were activists who used the annual meetings to discuss issues and air their concerns.

A.T. Cringan was appointed in 1919 as a part-time provincial inspector of music, and eventually most of the other recommendations of the Music Section were implemented in some form or another. More important, the department of education altered its policies to extend the scope of music as a school subject in the 1920s. The government's policies were not always effective or its programs entirely successful in achieving their goals, but there was evidence of genuine interest on the part of senior education officials, and by 1924 the teaching of music became obligatory in Ontario's elementary schools. Despite Ryerson's original plan to use classroom teachers for music instruction, the department recognized the value of specially trained music teachers and supervisors. Moreover, local boards were given incentives to hire music specialists. The department acted on its commitment to employ qualified staff by offering summer school training and improving the system of music grants. The number of special music teachers and supervisors increased from 79 in 1925 to 219 in 1930. As supervisors assumed more responsibility and leadership, they looked enthusiastically to new methodologies as means of improving the quality of music instruction.

The Impact of the Song Method

The influence of American educational philosophy can be seen in discussions pertaining to the song method. A younger generation of supervisors voiced enthusiasm for the rote approach coupled with more song repertoire and less drill. Music for enjoyment became increasingly important, to the extent that there was less commitment to reading skills. There was also a feeling that song repertoire should be suitable to the interests of students and compatible with the psychological principles of child development and growth. Such sentiments were embodied in James Bottomley's articles, in which he praised the work of several Americans, most notably that of Thaddeus Giddings.[10] But in practical terms, the song method was implanted in Ontario when Bruce Carey introduced *The Hollis Dann Music Course* into the Hamilton schools in 1919. Carey studied with Dann in the summer of 1918 at West Chester, Pennsylvania, and found his work appealing because it combined 'elements of tonic sol-fa and note-reading methods with the philosophy of the song method.'[11]

No one was more outspoken about methodology than Harry Hill. He attended summer sessions in music and psychology at American institutions, where he encountered such exponents of progressive education as W.H. Kilpatrick and James Mursell of Columbia Teachers' College in New York. As editor of the 'School Music Bulletin'[12] and as president of the Music Section of OEA, Hill chided those who were opposing change. He contended that 'in other educational circles the new ideas are constantly being scrutinized for what is better than that which is in vogue,' and concluded, 'Why should we as school musicians not be open to the latest ideas in teaching and the latest findings in psychology?'[13] After attending an OEA board of directors' meeting, Hill wrote: 'It was very evident that many persons interested in education still look upon music in the school as an addition, and a not altogether welcome one. It seems to be all right to fill in on a programme, or for state occasions when pupils are expected to perform for admiring parents, but as for taking it as a serious subject to hold its place with the three R's, why that is another thing entirely ... in Canadian circles we are at least fifty years behind the times in this regard.'[14] The feelings inflamed by diverse pedagogical views became so hostile that the following appears in the minutes of the 1931 meetings: 'The morning was spent in one of those useless discussions for which the Music Section is noted. Those who are convinced that all which is old is right, spend their time trying to offset the efforts of those who would try many things which are new. Thus the Section chases itself in circles and school music in Ontario suffers as a result. The unfortunate part is that so many people take these discussions as a reflection upon themselves, and as yet the section has to reach the point where it can discuss two sides of a question in an impersonal and dispassionate way.'[15] The methods controversy can be best understood by means of a comparison between *The New Canadian Music Course* (1932) of Cringan and Marshall and two series that followed, namely, *The Singing Period* (1936) by Harry Hill and *The High Road of Song* (1939) by G. Roy Fenwick. As Campbell Trowsdale sees it, the Cringan text 'had been excellent in its day but its arteries had hardened and its visions had remained unchanged. It had not grown and evolved sufficiently to keep pace with changes in educational thinking.'[16] Apart from the fact that it used staff notation throughout and relied more on songs than exercises, it was merely a revised version of Cringan's other books, which had a pedigree reaching back to Curwen.

Hill produced *The Singing Period* in collaboration with Arthur Putland (Fort William), Leonard Richer (Oshawa), and Edna Dunning (Ottawa).[17] This series was based on the song method, and, according to June Countryman, 'much of the structure and content of Hill's method [came] directly from *The Progressive Music Series*.'[18] Yet the repertoire was not extracted from American texts, for much of it was composed by Hill himself and, in general, incorporated songs of British origin.

Having had an opportunity to contemplate the strengths and weaknesses of *The Singing Period*, in 1939 Fenwick introduced *The High Road of Song*, which was based on the work of Hollis Dann and Robert Foresman of the United States. Dann had published a celebrated song series, and Foresman had compiled songbooks for use in elementary schools. Fenwick studied with Dann in the summer of 1923, so it should not be surprising that Fenwick's books favoured a number of American pedagogical ideas. Whereas Curwen's Tonic Sol-fa method began with the intervals of the tonic (d, m, s) and dominant (s, t, r) triads, Dann's method began with the stepwise movement of the major scale. Hill retained the chordal approach, but Fenwick used the scale and so took a significant departure from the Curwen tradition. But perhaps neither series was more American than the other; Countryman finds: 'Both song series were influenced by the American song method, with Hill's series coming closer to the ideals of that method. Fenwick's series used rote singing experiences to prepare for future cognitive learning, and in this respect utilized one aspect of the song method. On the other hand, his series kept sight reading and song singing as separate activities, a practice that was not part of the song method philosophy.'[19] The sentiment recurred throughout the methods controversy that although American materials were more progressive, Ontario needed a series of its own which would preserve aspects of music education which were distinctively Canadian. Though influenced by *The Progressive Music Series*, Hill relied mostly upon his own original song material – in fact, one criticism of his songs was the 'predictable, formula-like sound'[20] in Books One and Two. Any weakness in the Fenwick books could hardly be attributed to their originality: the methods were based upon Hollis Dann's, and many of the songs were taken from Foresman's books, even to the point of appearing 'in the same order as they did in the original series.'[21] Apart from the addition of a few patriotic songs, *The High Road of Song* was anything but distinctively Canadian.

The influence of American education was evident in the 1937 *Program of Studies*, which stressed enjoyment and appreciation in the elementary grades. Countryman observes that 'despite the Department of Education's stated support of a progressive philosophy of music education, and despite the availability of American song series which gave practical form to this philosophy, in practice music educators in Ontario continued to be pre-occupied with the rote singing/

music reading program.'[22] The controversy of the late 1880s had been waged over the kind of notation used in vocal music, but that of the 1920s and 1930s was concerned with the song method, a creature of the progressive education movement. Specifically, the dissension arose over such things as the importance given to the rote approach as opposed to note reading, the preference for songs over drills, and the priority assigned to appreciation even, if necessary, at the expense of performance skills and technical development. What was common to these two controversies was the fact that Ontario teachers were divided in choosing between British and American methods. It is evident that Tonic Sol-fa, which had flourished under Cringan's leadership, did not hold its own between the wars. By shifting the momentum in favour of the song method, a new generation of music supervisors prepared the way for greater American influence in Ontario.

The question as to who should teach music in the schools was not satisfactorily resolved either. Historically, special teachers of music drifted into supervisory roles as a logical extension of the in-service training which they conducted for regular classroom teachers. Most of them were experienced musicians who, like Carey, Fenwick, and Hill, had demonstrated their skills in church or community activities, but few supervisors had attended normal school for basic training in educational methods. Not surprisingly, in its first five years the Music Section 'focussed on the nature of the music supervisor's work, his status and duties within the school and the community, and his interaction with the classroom teacher and with his school inspector.'[23] The department recognized the need for better supervision by offering special courses at summer school. Cringan had directed the Toronto school for many years, and Charles Percy was in charge of another which operated in London during the 1930s. These were administered within the summer school and extension departments of the University of Toronto and the University of Western Ontario; however, the instruction was given by supervisors and normal school teachers, who dominated the Music Section. This inner circle of leaders represented the establishment in the field of school music during the inter-war years.

At Music Section meetings there was a preponderance of topics concerned with the development of musical competencies and expertise. The boy's changing voice was a recurring topic, and certain others concerned with music reading, ear training, and other performance skills seemed to surface in a cyclical pattern every two or three years.

Demonstrations in music appreciation and instrumental music heralded new methods, equipment, or instructional materials to stimulate the group with fresh ideas and enthusiasm. OEA members discussed the need for more music in the high schools, the admission requirements for normal schools, and policy changes designed to expand music as a curricular subject. Thus, the Music Section of OEA functioned not only as an academic forum but also as a political lobby forging strategies for strengthening school music throughout the province.

The Festival Movement

The spectacular massed concerts which were staged for royal visits and other patriotic occasions before the First World War became less frequent in the 1920s. Instead, music supervisors and teachers turned to the festival movement in the hope of motivating students and, at the same time, garnering support from parents and educational leaders. Newspapers added a measure of encouragement through references to the festival as 'an important element in the school music movement.'[24] Of those teachers participating in festival activities, the majority seemed to favour the competitive type. This preference was often reinforced by inspectors who believed that higher standards were achieved whenever competitive festivals were held. Those opposing them did so on the grounds that an emphasis placed on competition ultimately recognized the prowess of the teacher rather than the needs of the student. Competitive festivals in Ontario were not directly linked to the movement which commenced in Edmonton in 1908, for, whereas the western festivals involved the entire community, many competitions in Ontario operated within the schools. James Bottomley organized the Stratford public schools' music contest in 1901; Llewellyn Rees, Toronto's music supervisor (1903–21), founded a similar festival in 1909; Bruce Carey, Hamilton's director of music (1918–22), introduced a competitive school festival there in 1919.

An attempt in 1923 to initiate an Ontario competitive festival met with less success than did its precursors in the western provinces. Captain J.S. Atkinson of the Canadian Bureau for the Advancement of Music was the organizing secretary for a festival which was staged in Toronto's Massey Hall and Elm Street Church, with British adjudicators Granville Bantock and Harry Plunkett Greene officiating. In describing the event, Greene declared: 'The musical establishments were benevolently neutral officially – they wished very naturally to be sure of their ground before encouraging their students to enter. The public, in the absence of "scare" headlines, looked upon it at first as some mild musical beano, while the Press, with the exception of one lady representative who attended all the sessions ... either boycotted it or sat gingerly on the fence.'[25] Bantock, who acknowledged that 'only on the last day was there any appreciable audience in the large Massey Hall,' also said, 'There is no reason for doubting the eventual success of this festival in the near future.'[26] Bantock's prediction notwithstanding, the Musical Competitive Festival was discontinued after 1924.

A flurry of local festivals appeared in the late 1920s, some primarily for schools and others for the entire community, including both competitive and non-competitive types. The Perth County Music Festival was one of the most enduring; it was later known as the Stratford Music Festival and most recently as the Kiwanis Music Festival. By 1928 there were seventeen festivals established in Ontario and by 1940 more than fifty.

G. Roy Fenwick, throughout his term as provincial director of music (1935–59), used festivals as a means of stimulating music instruction in rural districts. In pamphlets circulated by the Music Branch, he not only gave instructions for organizing festivals but also presented arguments in favour of competitive and non-competitive types. Fenwick revealed his own preference when he suggested that 'a non-competitive festival is about as exciting as a non-competitive baseball game.'[27] By stressing the primacy of class singing and by forming a festival choir for the final concert, Fenwick tried to translate the goals of the festival into direct benefits for the rural school. He chose festival pieces from textbooks which were already in the schools, frequently from his own *High Road of Song* series – and for this he was sometimes criticized by his colleagues. Reportedly, he adjudicated many festivals in their first year of operation without a fee and with travel expenses paid by the department. With the help of good media coverage Fenwick managed to inveigle local residents into supporting new festivals. A rural inspector in eastern Ontario reported, 'His adjudications, full of kindly sympathy, were responsible to a large extent, for the success of our first festival, and for the insistent demand from the public that the festival be made an annual event.'[28] Since Fenwick's adjudications reached out to 168 centres, it is no wonder that 'the number of festivals in Ontario increased from 25 in 1936 to 125 in 1950, with more than 50,000 pupils participating.'[29] Ironically, the competitive festival movement flourished during the late 1930s and the 1940s, when exponents of progressive education were advocating creative approaches designed to nurture personal initiative, self-expression, and individuality. If teacher-centred activities such as school choirs competing in a festival seem to be incompatible with the spirit of the 'new education,' the suggestion is that music teachers were either oblivious of the philosophical thinking of the time or, possibly, reluctant to give up activities which elicited strong community support. While the provincial department espoused the new philosophy in a revised curriculum, its own Music Branch channelled more and more support toward the festival movement. Whatever the explanation, it is evident that methodology in music was fashioned to a great extent by the demands of competitions, and that the philosophy permeating the 1937 program of studies did not have a profound influence on the day-to-day practice of music teachers.

Music Appreciation

Music appreciation became a household term in the period between the wars. Indeed, it became so popular that its over-exposure contributed to its downfall. By the end of the Second World War, music educators who had previously cherished the term were already starting to despise it. Music appreciation meant different things to different people. For some, it became an ideal which required changes in methodology for the elementary grades. In the new order of priorities, supervisors and teachers spent less time with modulator drills, focusing attention instead on the expressive nature of the repertoire, both in singing songs and in listening to recordings. In 1923 Mae Skilling, an Ontario elementary teacher, encouraged classroom teachers to capitalize on the value of music in 'illuminating and making realistic the work in geography, literature, history and art.'[30] Even rhythm bands at the primary level were regarded as an introduction to the orchestra and hence an aspect of music appreciation. Skilling wrote: 'Music is now being brought to all the people everywhere, and in no way is this being done so effectively as through the phonograph. In the settlement houses, in community gatherings, in the home, and most of all in the schools, the harmonizing, uplifting, cultural influence of good music is being spread ... By means of the phonograph and records the folk songs and dances of the people, old chants, ballads and instrumental compositions ... all give new life and meaning to what heretofore has been confined to the printed page.'[31] A few years later, the Columbia

Phonograph Company sponsored sessions at OEA conventions in which Skilling displayed methods for using the grafonola in the music class. Similarly, Mabel Rich, educational director of the Victor Talking Machine Company, demonstrated the victrola as a teaching aid for music appreciation at the 1928 and 1929 conventions.

Even before the First World War, phonograph companies in the United States had established educational departments to produce instructional materials for the schools. Albums, teacher guides, and student workbooks were designed to solve musical problems for classroom teachers and proved to be popular among those who were insecure about sight-singing, ear training, and vocal technique, the traditional fare in classroom music. It is clear that the use of the phonograph, supplemented by suitable instructional materials, affected the evolution of classroom music to such an extent that methods at normal schools changed. Normal schools not only explored programs which included listening but also used the phonograph to help teachers who could not sing. James Bottomley of the Stratford Normal School claimed: '[The phonograph] sings amazingly well, and new records of children's songs are available, while the children, guided by the teacher, can learn from the record. The model is perfect, and it can be repeated as often as necessary.'[32] But not all normal school instructors agreed. In discussing aspects of ear training, A.T. Cringan stated: 'During recent years the introduction of phonographic instruments has tended to simplify the teaching of [ear training] by making it possible to present complete musical sentences as subjects for analysis and criticism on the part of the pupils. It would be unwise, however, to depend entirely on this means for the training of the perceptive faculties.'[33]

Music appreciation served as a stepping stone for getting music into the high school grades. As educational leaders revised the curriculum to accommodate student interests, the potential of music became attractive, and more obvious as the popularity of glee clubs and orchestras increased. In the meantime teachers argued that music education should include appreciation as well as performance activities, and used this rationale in lobbying for the acceptance of music as a full-fledged curricular subject. Sometimes music appreciation was organized in the intermediate or senior classes as a separate component within a general music course. Depending upon the teacher's background, there might also be some singing, theory, and history to comprise a comprehensive course of study. Although phonograph recordings were valuable aids for incorporating listening activities, too much attention was given to composers and their historical background; the distinction between music history and music appreciation was not always clearly made. Education journals in the 1930s attracted no end of articles on methods and materials pertaining to music appreciation; it was a topic that yielded both positive and negative comment.

Ernest MacMillan vented his own negative sentiments at the 1928 meetings of the OEA, where he presented 'Suggestions For A Course of Music Study for High Schools.' In underlining the need for intelligent listeners in society, he commented on the planning of courses in music appreciation: 'I detest this term, by the way, as I detest the term "musical theory" ... but it is difficult to find suitably comprehensive equivalents, so we may let them stand for the present. The danger is that we may come to regard music as a sort of purgatory through which we may enter the heaven of "Culture".'[34] Among high school teachers Leslie Bell became an authoritative exponent of the subject. His articles first appeared while he was teaching at Parkdale Collegiate. Some were written to explain the new departmental courses in grades nine and ten, but perhaps his most profound statements were those in 'The Failure of Music Appreciation,'[35] published years later in the *Canadian Music Journal*. His opinions reveal the intensity surrounding teaching methods in the late 1930s:

> This tendency to pigeon-hole music activities has frequently had unfortunate results in the case of so-called 'music appreciation'. The term is considered as applying to a specific subject, taught by means of putting aside one period a week for the purpose of listening to recordings, after which nothing is said about 'appreciation' till that period again recurs. But music appreciation does not mean merely listening to records. It means much more than that. Appreciation is, or should be the goal of every activity in music education. We do not have our pupils sing because we want them to become professional performers; we do not teach them theory merely to sharpen their wits. Our purpose in the case of all such subjects is to instil in the child a fuller understanding and love of music.[36]

In whatever context it was found, music appreciation symbolized a growing interest in something beyond the mere acquisition of technical skills. In recognizing the expressive nature of music as a humanizing force, educators perceived music appreciation to be compatible with the philosophy of progressive education. Yet because of its multi-faceted nature, music appreciation was never well defined, and consequently much time and energy were dissipated without teachers' being able to demonstrate convincing evidence of success.

Orchestral Concerts for Students

As early as 1914 a live orchestral concert for children was given by the first Toronto Symphony Orchestra in Massey Hall. This experiment, scheduled as a matinee with an admission price of fifteen cents for children, was most successful: 'Within the hall', reads one account, 'the scene was as remarkable as it was inspiring. Tier upon tier of radiant children packed into every available seat, and all around the platform some four thousand young patrons of classical music.'[37] Richard S. Warren, TSO archivist, observes that 'although the review gave indications of promise for the future, there is unfortunately no record of further concerts.'[38] A number of students' concerts did occur in other places: during Bruce Carey's regime in Hamilton, the Detroit Symphony gave a concert in that city, in 1920; E.W. Goethe Quantz, London's music supervisor, engaged the Cleveland Symphony Orchestra in 1922 for a special matinee for school children; in 1925 H. Whorlow Bull, supervisor of music in the Windsor schools, arranged for students to attend a series of five concerts in Detroit; and during Music Week in 1929 the Toronto Symphony Orchestra performed for 'collegiate, senior public and separate school pupils in Guelph.'[39]

The frequency of live orchestral concerts tailored to the needs of elementary school children increased as music appreciation became more fashionable. The New Symphony Orchestra offered a series of concerts in 1925, initiated by the home and school association of Brown Public School. This series was planned by Luigi von Kunits, the orchestra's conductor, and Miss Emily Tedd, assistant supervisor of music. Moreover, Duncan McKenzie, director of music for the Toronto schools, gave a short talk before each number was played. In the 1926 season the orchestra performed 'one movement from Beethoven's Fifth at each concert, and at the last of these the children were given a musical quiz, for which prizes were awarded.'[40] Contests similar to the Music Memory Test were administered at various concerts; the Women's Committee took on the onerous task of marking the papers, and winners were announced at later programs. The TSO Children's Concerts lapsed after 1926 but resumed in 1930 under the direction of

Sir Ernest MacMillan and Emily Tedd.[41] In 1941–2 the Toronto Transit Commission objected to the number of children using the transit system during rush hour, and subsequently these 4:15 p.m. matinees were discontinued. In lieu of live student concerts, the TSO became involved in 'Music for Young Folk,' a CBC radio series inaugurated in 1943. The commentators for many of these forty-five-minute programs were Ernest MacMillan and Ettore Mazzoleni.

Requests for TSO concerts specifically designed for high school students date back to 1938. A series launched in 1942 was given added impetus by the formation of a students' council comprised of two representatives from each high school in the greater Toronto area; teachers also assisted with the promotion and publicity for secondary school concerts. However, the most dedicated supporters over the years were the TSO women's committees, which accepted administrative responsibilities for these and other projects in which the orchestra served the community.

Music Education and Radio

Radio had a life of its own in the evolution of music education, following close on the heels of the phonograph, which was already enjoying great popularity. Those who recognized the value of radio did so on the strength of its potential for communication. Roy Fenwick presented 'Musical Homework,' a weekly fifteen-minute program, on Wednesday evenings over a local Hamilton station. A showcase for solos, small ensembles, and choirs from representative schools, it had more in common with public demonstrations than with music appreciation programs. Parents were encouraged to send comments to the station, and the Hamilton board reported the series to be 'an incentive to improved classroom work and a means of interesting the parents and public generally in school music.'[42] A portion of the 1935 OEA concert in the Eaton Auditorium was broadcast over radio, and in the following year the CBC network carried a half-hour segment of the OEA concert held in Massey Hall. The 1936 OEA concert featured an all-Ontario orchestra, a public school chorus, and, for the first time, a provincial high school chorus. Throughout the late 1930s music educators welcomed any opportunity to display the accomplishments of their performing groups on the CBC network or local stations.

Music appreciation programs originating in the United States were broadcast in Canada, but there was a growing feeling in some quarters that school programs should be rooted in Canadian culture. According to the EMC, 'pressure was applied by the Ontario Educational Association, the Ontario Federation of Home and School, the CBC, and other interested groups on the hitherto indifferent and unresponsive Ontario Department of Education.'[43] Shortly after the election of Premier George Drew (who also assumed the education portfolio), the Music Branch received funding to work with CBC in expanding radio broadcasts. Experimental programs were produced with the participation of Sir Ernest MacMillan and the TSO. Leslie Bell prepared the scripts for 'Music for Young Folk' (1944–60), a series which for thousands of Ontario children became synonymous with music appreciation, and one which was closely identified with the soothing, gentle voice of commentator G. Roy Fenwick.

Just as teachers have been concerned about television and, more recently, the computer, so were they disturbed by the impact of radio. Emily Tedd cautioned her colleagues in 1934 that 'the advent of radio carried with it the glaring need for most teachers to instill a discriminating taste in students.'[44] Supervisor Harry Hill was less guarded in a speech to the Kitchener-Waterloo Rotary Club in 1935 in which he referred to 'the kind of piffle which pours forth daily from our radio' and added, 'High school students want a distinctly jazzy type of music.'[45] He concluded his tirade by charging that 'the average taste of the university graduate never gets beyond the kindergarten.'[46] These remarks had been provoked by an incident in which a committee of staff and students at Kitchener Collegiate had attempted to choose the repertoire for assembly singing. When the popular song 'Cheek to Cheek' was proposed, Hill had objected vehemently. He pointed out to the Rotarians that musical taste could not be fully developed because there was scarcely any music in the high schools, and that little attention was paid to the subject by the universities. In making his case, he contended that the United States was far ahead of Canada in developing high school orchestras. Not only did Hill's hyperbole draw a sharp response from his own school board, it also got reactions from London and Toronto, some supportive and some otherwise. Whereas Sherwood Fox, president of the University of Western Ontario, applauded his bold stand, prominent musicians in Toronto considered the statements to be too sweeping and extravagant. Sir Ernest MacMillan remarked, 'Hill's criticism was made along too general lines to warrant comment.'[47] Even Emily Tedd, a crusader for more music in high school, would not concede that the musical taste of Canadians was lower than that of children across the border. The incident enjoyed considerable publicity. Preoccupation with the development of musical taste was often a response to films and jazz. Leslie Bell in 1943 mused, 'Perhaps nothing worries the present day music teacher more than the adolescent's craze for popular music' and his apparent contempt for the 'classics.'[48] Bell's caustic description of the situation probably applied to the majority of teachers, but it is unlikely that they shared his ideas, for in these Bell was ahead of his time.

Early Attempts in Instrumental Music

Music appreciation derived much of its momentum from the use of the phonograph and radio, but school programs were expanding in other directions too, most notably toward instrumental music. The earliest ones appeared at the elementary school level in the form of string instruction scheduled outside regular school hours. One of the most ambitious efforts was made in Ottawa by a professional violinist, Donald Heins, who grew up in England and received formal training at the Leipzig Conservatory. He was persuaded to come to Canada in 1902 by his brother-in-law, Harry Puddicombe, who had opened the Canadian Conservatory in Ottawa. Heins conducted a conservatory orchestra which later became the Ottawa Symphony. In 1918 he initiated string work in the public schools by training classroom teachers to play the violin. Classes two hours in length were conducted every Saturday morning, with preference being given to teachers who had previous experience in violin or piano. Classes for pupils commenced in 1919, using *The Mitchell Public School Violin Class Method*. Pupils were expected to provide their own violin outfits, and by an arrangement with local music stores these could be bought at a cost of less than thirty dollars. Toward the end of that year Heins organized a master class of approximately twenty pupils. It consisted of a few players from each school, and after receiving advanced instruction they formed the nucleus of an Ottawa public school orchestra. Heins gave the following report: 'In June, 1921, this class performed publicly the first movement of Schubert's *Unfinished Symphony* with great success. The violin sections were made up entirely of public school pupils: the remaining sections were augmented by members of the Ottawa Symphony Orchestra.'[49] By 1923 there were 420 receiving instruction from Donald Heins and 15 assistant teachers in classes of approximately 22 students. With a rapid increase in enrolment it became necessary to engage violin teachers from outside the school system. The Ottawa Public School Orchestra in 1923 also included a flute, two clarinets, two cornets, and drums. Heins indicated in an OEA presentation, 'To this will be added the balancing instruments from outside sources.'[50] This program continued under Heins's leadership until he moved to Toronto in 1927, where he taught at TCM and became concertmaster of TSO. Drury Pryce was hired to carry on violin classes, which were held in Ottawa's public schools until 1942. Harry Hill, who replaced James Smith as supervisor of music, explained in his 1942 report that the violin classes had been discontinued owing to difficulty in obtaining string instruments and supplies.

Ottawa also offered tuition on wind instruments, given by Lieutenant W.B. Finlayson, who was hired as a part-time teacher. In 1927 James A. Smith reported that provision had been made at five elementary schools and that 126 students had received instruction. Finlayson organized the Ottawa Public School Boys' Band, which gave annual concerts in Lansdowne Park or the Coliseum. A junior boys' band was also in existence by 1930, but it was not until 1938 that girls were enrolled in these programs. In 1934 Finlayson started the Capital City Boys' Band, composed of fifty-six graduates of the Ottawa Public School Boys' Band. They won several prizes in CNE band competitions in Toronto, an achievement that was duly noted in the 1939 annual report on music. Ottawa may have had some influence on other places because the violin program was outlined in some detail at the 1923 OEA convention and Heins demonstrated string class techniques at the 1928 meetings. As a way of fostering local pride, it was traditional at OEA conventions to feature musical numbers from the school board of the current president, especially in general sessions in which music could provide welcome relief from laboured introductions and long-winded speakers. It was, therefore, appropriate that the choir of Glashan Intermediate School (director, Lillian Johnson) and the Ottawa Public School Orchestra (director, Drury Pryce) should perform at the General Association meetings in 1932, the year when J.H. Putman, chief inspector of the Ottawa Public Schools, was president of OEA. His commitment to progressive education and his personal interest in music prompted Harry Hill to exclaim, 'O, for dozens of inspectors who feel about music as does Dr. Putman, then indeed would the future of school music in Ontario be bright.'[51]

The Hamilton board of education did not approve Bruce Carey's proposal for instrumental music in 1919. However, violin classes were begun there in 1924, and a similar program was organized in London by E.W.G. Quantz in the late 1920s. There may have been other schemes, but they were not sustained long enough to influence development beyond their own local regions. Aside from the Ottawa program, the one in Hamilton was the most successful. It was directed by Jean Sutherland, a vocal music supervisor who was also an accomplished violinist. Sutherland was required to carry on her vocal supervision in the mornings but was allowed to offer violin instruction after 3:30 p.m. She formed classes of approximately twelve students, and, as in Ottawa, the formation of a city orchestra became the major attraction. After the violin program had been operating for five years, Fenwick, then supervisor of music in Hamilton, reported that not all the students who had applied could be accommodated; unfortunately, this program fell victim to the economic restraints of the Depression.

Extra-curricular High School Orchestras

The impact of Jean Sutherland's work may have been reflected in Hamilton's extra-curricular activity, which was enthusiastically described in a speech recorded in the minutes of the 1927 OEA convention:

> Before calling on the Symphony Orchestra from the Hamilton Collegiate again, I would just like to say a word or two ... I thought I was going to have dinner with a group of Hamiltonians who were coming over here to entertain this audience, a small ... ordinary size of orchestra, and I was simply astounded when the first one of those large buses came up and about twenty-five or thirty got out of it and they had no more alighted from the bus when a second bus came up equally laden. I concluded that our friends from Hamilton – Ambitious City, as it is called – wished to make a good showing and collected all the different orchestras they could get in Hamilton and merged them together for the occasion and were trying to palm off a real good orchestra on us to-night, but I ascertained I was entirely wrong ... this orchestra that has entertained us ... is the orchestra of the Central Collegiate Institute in the City of Hamilton. It is composed of all bona fide boys and girls, students of the Institution, and some sixty-four pupils are taking part in this orchestra. They are under the leadership of Captain Cornelius and they are a real credit to the City of Hamilton.

The minutes conclude: 'The rendering of "Poet and Peasant" was received with such thunderous applause by the audience that another selection had to be rendered.'[52] Such performances by school choirs and orchestras became more frequent in the 1930s, a fact indicating that music educators recognized the power of OEA audiences to make educational leaders aware of their accomplishments.

Edward Johnson, world-renowned tenor of Metropolitan Opera fame, showed an interest in providing opportunities for the youth of Guelph, his native city. In 1928 he pledged five thousand dollars annually for five years to establish a department of music within the collegiate-vocational institute and public schools. The board announced that St John's school would be re-opened and 'fitted up as a music headquarters,'[53] and indicated that all piano and instrumental classes would be held there. Accordingly, a program of string instruction was introduced by J.L. Yule, the newly appointed director of music.

These early attempts to establish instrumental music in Hamilton and Guelph were extraordinary. But what Leslie Bell encountered in Toronto's Parkdale Collegiate may be more typical of Ontario schools in the 1920s:

I entered high school with a pretty vague memory of any previous school music training. True, we had been given some sort of music course but it had not left much impression ... At high school there were not even doh, me, sohs. This was the place for the serious business of Latin and Algebra. A program of music would have been considered as out of place as a course in contract bridge. I remember on one occasion I ventured to talk to the literary society about musical instruments and as a result was considered a bit strange. When I eventually joined a dance band I was abandoned as a lost soul. My chief school music training was the result of the determination of our French teacher to organize a school orchestra. This courageous man had a good tenor voice and played drums as he said 'by ear.' There was no attempt to grade or reject the applicants for the orchestra. It was a question of taking what could be had. Eventually there was assembled a group consisting of a piano, two violins, a trumpet, seven ukuleles, three Spanish guitars, a mandolin and myself. The majority of the group did not read music. When a poll of the instrumentation was being taken and I said that I owned a clarinet, a general gasp went up. The teacher gasped at his good fortune in discovering such a rare instrument and the rest gasped because they did not know what a clarinet was. No one asked how well I could play. It was enough that I was there.[54]

Despite the crude state of school orchestras, efforts were made to encourage players who owned instruments, particularly if they had already received some training or experience. In 1930 there was reference to a concert featuring a combined school orchestra and a band held at Central Technical School. The report stated that 'the concert was unique inasmuch as it was the first of its kind in Toronto,' and also observed, 'The School Orchestra has long enjoyed an enviable reputation ... but the Band is quite a new venture.'[55] Throughout the late 1930s and early 1940s Emily Tedd, director of music (1926–42), and her successor, Eldon Brethour (1943–58), rehearsed a combined Toronto schools orchestra on Saturday mornings to give students experience beyond their own schools, where they seldom had an ensemble with full instrumentation. Joseph Maddy conducted an all-Toronto secondary school orchestra at the 1931 OEA convention, one of many occasions on which American leaders were invited to promote the introduction of instrumental music in Ontario.

A number of teachers were well known for their instrumental ensembles in the late 1930s: Leonard Richer (Scarborough and later Oshawa), I.W. Lomas (Westdale Collegiate, Hamilton), Leslie Bell (Parkdale Collegiate, Toronto), and Brian McCool (Harbord Collegiate, Toronto). There were also long traditions for high school orchestras and other extra-curricular activities in Timmins, Owen Sound, St Catharines, and Niagara Falls. Indeed, the proliferation of orchestras in larger towns and cities just before the Second World War was so extensive that the existence of a school orchestra became the rule rather than the exception. In Brockville, the initiative came from the principal; in St Catharines, a vocational shop teacher was the driving spirit. In many places, the music supervisor conducted the orchestra even though he was not on the high school staff. Orchestras often received support from boards and principals because of their utilitarian benefits in accompanying hymns and providing musical selections for assemblies, commencement exercises, and other school events. But their function was essentially one of entertainment. Still, it was generally felt that extra-curricular organizations might offer something which would persuade students to remain in school until graduation. On the basis of these and other extrinsic values, performing organizations were encouraged within the bounds of extra-curricular status, but economic restraints during the Depression prevented any universal acceptance of the idea of instrumental music for credit; as a secondary school subject its time had not yet come.

There was one breakthrough, however. In 1936 the Ontario Department of Education passed new regulations permitting the study of instrumental music in vocational schools. Special grants were offered as incentives to schools interested in participating in this new scheme, and instrumental courses were established at the department's summer schools for teachers, in both Toronto (1936) and London (1937). Although the provision for music in technical and commercial schools produced rather modest results, this recognition of instrumental music as a secondary school subject set an important precedent, for it enabled the Music Branch to extend such grants to all secondary schools in 1945. The effects can be seen in the postwar years, when instrumental music in collegiates and high schools grew at an unprecedented rate.

OEA Concerts in Massey Hall

The difficulty of getting music approved as a high school subject did not demoralize music teachers. Enthusiastically, they channelled their efforts into provincial projects. Annual evenings of music became a special feature of the OEA conventions held in Toronto during Easter week. Brault notes that it was 'an excellent opportunity to make an impression not only upon teachers drawn from the full range of academic disciplines, but upon those well able to influence the character of educational priorities – the trustees, principals, and officials of the Department of Education.'[56] The first OEA concert was held in Massey Hall in 1933 and relied almost entirely upon choirs, orchestras, and soloists from the Toronto schools. In the following year the concert presented choirs from many parts of Ontario, and the featured instrumental group was the Little Symphony Orchestra of the High and Public Schools of Oshawa, conducted by Leonard Richer. The 1935 concert was a landmark, in that a provincial high school orchestra of a hundred players was formed on that occasion with students representing twenty-four communities. To mount this large-scale ensemble, preliminary rehearsals were conducted in London, Hamilton, and Toronto by E.W.G. Quantz, Captain J.R. Cornelius, and A.T. Wilkie respectively. Leonard Richer assumed the leadership at the convention, but H.A. Fricker (conductor, Toronto Mendelssohn Choir) and Ernest MacMillan (conductor, Toronto Symphony Orchestra) each conducted a rehearsal, an indication that Toronto's most distinguished musicians supported this innovative project. That a segment of this concert was broadcast over radio was significant because it set a precedent for subsequent broadcasts of OEA concerts.

The Music Section had used radio in 1931 and had been the first OEA group to do so. On that occasion the Kitchener-Waterloo Collegiate

Glee Club, directed by Harry Hill, shared a forty-five minute program with Dr Joseph Maddy, who spoke at length about the evolution of music in American education. With special reference to instrumental music, Maddy commended the idea of giving full academic credit to the subject and stressed that it should be scheduled during regular school hours. At the 1941 musical evening held in Varsity Arena, the all-Ontario orchestra numbered two hundred players, and the provincial public school and secondary school choirs each comprised five hundred voices. For music educators this event may have been the pinnacle of success in projecting their presence through OEA concerts. The all-Ontario orchestra provided incentives to students and teachers: several students who participated in OEA orchestras became professional musicians in the postwar years. Needless to say, the inspiration of these annual events revitalized teachers and reminded inspectors, principals, and trustees of the potential for further development.

It took the efforts of many people in OEA to keep music in the forefront of educational thinking. For several years Benson Collier, Vera Russell, and Leslie Bell assumed major responsibilities in organization and production, and G. Roy Fenwick placed the full support of the department behind these annual events. It was unfortunate that travel restrictions during the war brought an end to provincial orchestras. However, the Harbord Collegiate Orchestra and the Barrie Collegiate Band were invited to participate, a fact suggesting that a measure of maturity had been realized in some schools. The introduction of instrumental music courses at departmental summer schools also added to the surge of interest in orchestral work. A statistical summary of music organizations in Ontario's secondary schools in 1945 revealed the existence of 92 orchestras, 33 bands, 62 bugle and pipe bands, and 283 choirs. It was also reported, 'In 87 schools, 172 operas or operettas were presented during the past three years.'[57] These data indicate that school orchestras were more prevalent than school bands, and though there was a quickening of interest in cadet bands in the years leading up to the Second World War, concert bands did not appear in great numbers until the 1950s and 1960s.

Choral Music in Secondary Schools

High school choirs and glee clubs flourished in the late 1930s and the 1940s. To a great extent this growth was linked to the popularity of school concerts and shows, for in Ontario the Gilbert and Sullivan

tradition reached its peak during these years. Schools were proud of
their choirs, and principals were well aware of the enthusiasm to be
derived from operetta productions. Music teachers promoted choral
music as well as instrumental through the OEA concerts in Massey Hall.
A provincial high school chorus made its debut in 1936 under the
direction of P.G. Marshall of Simcoe. In addition to radio coverage,
these concerts drew enthusiastic praise from Toronto newspaper
critics. The reviews covered details of the performance, but, even more
encouraging to the Music Section, they often commented on the value
of music in education. Teachers were also appreciative of the support
which parents showed, collectively and individually, for school music.
A provincial home and school choir performed at the 1936 convention
under the leadership of Reginald Stewart. In succeeding conventions
Georgina Barton organized a home and school mothers' choir, which
performed in Massey Hall under G. Roy Fenwick as guest conductor.

As extra-curricular activities gained support with the general public,
teachers became more vocal in pressing for music as a legitimate
subject. They realized that even better results could be accomplished if
music instruction were to be approved for credit and scheduled in a
regular classroom period. The crusading spirit demonstrated in local
communities by individual supervisors and teachers was also evident
in discussions at meetings of the Music Section. Members felt that
good beginnings in the elementary grades were being wasted because
students could not continue their study of music in high school.
Moreover, a secondary school education was a prerequisite for admission to normal school, and there was a recurring complaint that normal
music training, superficial at best, was forced to become even more so
when the majority of students did not have sufficient background in
music. Brault observes that 'hardly a convention went by without some
speaker pressing for high school music or for a more intensive music
training at Normal School.'[58] In 1933 George Bramfitt of the Ontario
College of Education was blunt in his analysis of the situation:

In High Schools the teaching of music is not exactly prohibited, but is
certainly damned with faint praise, for if given, it must be in addition to the
obligatory and other optional subjects and carries no credit towards promotion. Few, therefore, there be that find it. No wonder 85% of candidates for
Public School certificates in Normal and O.C.E. have had no training in
music whatever. Yet at the close of their professional course (say 60 hours
for Normal, 18 hours for O.C.E.) they are certified teachers of music in

public school! So we go 'round in a vicious circle: teachers, being incompetent in music, cannot teach it; inspectors, being untrained, cannot insist, still less offer any help; pupils, receiving no training, give no assurance of improvement in the next generation of teachers and inspectors. Granted there are most satisfying exceptions in a few individuals and localities, but of the Province as a whole the picture here painted is not too dark; and this 80 odd years after Ryerson insisted that the state owed every child a rudimentary education in music![59]

Community singing, which it was felt engendered a feeling of unity and a national spirit, was encouraged in the context of the high school. Music was introduced in the auditorium either as a singing period for the entire student body or as part of an assembly program along with public speaking, announcements, student council activities, and the like. Mimeographed song sheets or lantern slides were the teaching aids of this era. Some principals scheduled assemblies on a regular basis, others organized them according to the availability of guest speakers. Music supervisors, whose main responsibilities were in the elementary grades, were sometimes recruited to lead the singing in high school; in some cases teachers who taught other subjects conducted the assembly singing and in due course shifted over to the teaching of music, as exemplified in the career of Don Wright.

A graduate of the University of Western Ontario in classics, Wright also possessed a good musical background. His mother was a pianist, and his father founded the Wright Piano Company in Strathroy. Don Wright was well known throughout Ontario because the Wright Brothers' Orchestra played at leading dance spots such as the Embassy and the Brant Inn. While working as a classics and history teacher at Sir Adam Beck Collegiate in London, Wright demonstrated a flair for conducting music assemblies, in which he taught appreciation, four-part choral singing, and other aspects of music education. Assemblies at Beck were more than sing-alongs in the community tradition. Stimulated in these auditorium sessions, student interest in music was eventually directed toward instruction in classes; as a result of Wright's outstanding results in both vocal and instrumental activities, he became director of music for the city schools in 1942. There is no doubt that Don Wright's remarkable career was due in large measure to his scintillating personality and boundless energy. But it was his success in dealing with boys' changing voices that extended a far-reaching influence, through publications such as *The Collegiate Choir* and *Youthful*

Voices. That the service rendered by music supervisors has not always been fully appreciated is illustrated in the following incident. Wright purchased a small English car shortly after the war in order to save gasoline in travelling from school to school. Ever vigilant on the taxpayers' behalf, the London board of education felt obliged to reduce his travel allowance accordingly. Wright admitted that it was the board's gesture, rather than the actual loss of remuneration, which hastened his decision to leave school music to become a professional musician.

Typical of many teachers, Wright was heavily involved in community service. He organized an all-city air cadet band during the Second World War and conducted and arranged music for troop shows, a task which entailed three performances every week. His dedicated, patriotic service thrust him into public life, and he later became manager of radio station CFPL. His professional career was as meteoric as his teaching career had been. The Don Wright Chorus was featured for years on both Canadian and American radio networks, and the Don Wright Singers on television. He composed commercial jingles as well as music for television shows and films. But his phenomenal success in the profession did not diminish his devotion to school music. Not only through compositions for schools, workshops for teachers, and guest conducting, but also through the Don Wright Charitable Foundation he has supported music education by establishing permanent annual scholarships in thirteen Canadian universities from coast to coast.

Leslie Bell's career paralleled that of Don Wright in many ways. Bell's university degrees (BA, MA) were in English, but he had studied music privately and had considerable experience in dance bands. He taught English and history at Parkdale Collegiate, where he was also acclaimed for his fine choirs and orchestras. His leadership in OEA conventions and articles in the *School* contributed further to his high profile in secondary school music. In 1939 he was appointed to teach music at the Ontario College of Education, the institution which published the *School*. Successful high school teachers like Wright and Bell knew how to deal with boys in vocal music classes. In one of his many articles, Bell wrote:

Probably the most difficult problem that the teacher of music in grades IX and X has to face is that of handling singing in boys' forms. In many cases, the boys either refuse to sing or else turn the lesson into a burlesque, which has serious effects upon discipline. Some teachers have simply avoided the difficulty by turning to music appreciation or theory, but this is scarcely satisfactory. Really good results can be obtained, if the problem is handled in the right way.

First of all, it is necessary to understand the reasons for the boys' attitude. The primary one is that, in most cases, the voice of the boy entering secondary school is just changing. He has lost the self-confidence that he possessed in elementary school and fears ridicule. Secondly, there is the curious fact that most boys in their early teens consider singing an effeminate or 'sissy' practice, only to be attempted by girls. The main task, then, is to break down the attitude of the pupils and inspire confidence and enthusiasm.[60]

Bell published *The Chorister: Theory and Sight Reading for Vocalists* in the late 1940s and taught choral techniques at the University of Toronto's Faculty of Music from 1946 to 1953. The Leslie Bell Singers, a female choir which began as a group of former students from Parkdale Collegiate, became popular for its troop shows, radio programs, and concert tours across Canada. Bell's success as a professional musician, like Don Wright's, eventually led to a career in radio, television, and films. Later, while working as a free-lance writer, broadcaster, and musician, Bell combined his many talents in serving as executive director of the Canadian Music Educators' Association.

Brian McCool, Alastair Haig, and Harvey Perrin were among others in the prewar years whose successful work in their respective schools helped blaze the trail at the secondary level. These teachers entered the profession before specialized degree programs in music education were available; for them, there was no clearly defined procedure whereby music teachers could prepare academically for a secondary school career. In most subjects, honours degrees were prerequisites for specialist programs at the Ontario College of Education; in music, teachers qualified with general degrees and gathered whatever expertise they could through private music study, summer courses, or on-the-job experience. In fact, secondary school music was already established before an adequate training scheme was implemented. Whatever progress Ontario realized in music education was due to the valiant efforts of teachers rather than to the work of senior officials, who failed to provide vision, leadership, and planning for the future.

A number of educational leaders in Ontario had embraced many principles of the progressive education movement by the late 1930s. The new philosophical spirit was founded upon a psychology of adolescent development and favoured curriculum expansion into learning activities which had potential for realizing societal goals. The swing of the pendulum in general education was a positive influence in that it reduced the resistance to non-academic subjects. Whether or not music teachers fully understood the subtleties of progressive education is open to question, but there is little doubt that music was introduced more readily because of the flexibility – or, in the words of its critics, the permissiveness – that characterized the 1937 curriculum. There were also political factors which aided the cause of music: 1) resolutions passed by the Music Section were forwarded to OEA for its endorsation; this provided a mechanism for recommending changes to the minister of education; 2) home and school associations supported music in the schools and helped to organize activities at the local level; 3) the creation of a Music Branch in the provincial department of education ensured that music teachers had representation within the bureaucracy.

The Status of Music in Secondary Schools

Music as a secondary school subject was established in an official sense when the subject first appeared on the list of Ontario departmental examinations for middle school in 1927 or 1928. According to Bramfitt, 'this concession by the Matriculation Board followed a request by the staff of the Toronto Conservatory for some relief for students seriously following music during their high school course.'[61] Representations had been made for the obtaining of credit for private study in voice, piano, and orchestral instruments. It was difficult, however, to standardize evaluation in performance because practical examinations were administered individually, and there were questions as to whether all conservatories demanded equal standards. Ernest MacMillan reported that 'it was not found possible at the time to institute more than a written examination'[62] but expressed hope for better recognition in the future. At the 1934 OEA convention the Music Section forwarded a resolution that music become a matriculation subject. It is difficult to know what political pressure such a resolution carried, because several years passed before this recommendation became a reality.

High school principals wielded a great deal of power within their own schools in implementing, or working around, regulations by the provincial department. It is not surprising, then, to find music thriving in a few schools long before departmental policies were enacted. In 1935 Principal John S. Jackson offered music in Simcoe High School by taking one period a week from the time allotment for English literature. But the status of music was secured beyond the whim of individual principals when a new regulation in 1937 required all students in grade nine to choose either art or music. This requirement was part of a general curriculum revision carried out by Duncan McArthur, deputy minister of education. In liberalizing education through the introduction of cultural subjects, he hoped to develop the emotions as well as the intellect. From a practical standpoint, these curriculum changes can be viewed as Ontario's alternative to the junior high movement. In 1938 the department announced a grade ten music course as an option for those wishing to continue the subject beyond grade nine. It was a general course of one or two periods a week in which singing, theory, and music appreciation were combined at the discretion of the teacher. As principals differed widely in their scheduling of music classes, Leslie Bell cautioned: 'Curious situations may arise. In some cases Grade X music will be taken as an extra subject by brighter pupils, and in other cases as a substitute for subjects which pupils have been forced to drop. It may be necessary for the teacher to frame different courses for these two types of student.'[63] Music was officially approved as an option in grade thirteen, effective in the 1943–4 school year. This development was a milestone, in that universities accordingly agreed to accept music for admission into many of their programs, thus giving it an academic prestige which previously it had not enjoyed. Fenwick noted that in 1943, 68 per cent of all secondary schools offered music but admitted that 'in the majority of these schools, music courses did not extend above Grade X.'[64] With the establishment of a grade thirteen music course he felt the way was now open 'to continue music instruction upward through the Middle and Upper School Grades of Ontario secondary schools.'[65] As usual, Fenwick was not only optimistic, he was also prophetic.

School Bands

Much of the enthusiasm for school bands was generated by groups and organizations outside the framework of education. The Canadian National Exhibition and the Waterloo Musical Society are two examples. In 1929 the Ottawa Public School Boys' Band played at the CNE's Music Day at the invitation of the Canadian Bureau for the Advancement of

Music. C.F. Thiele was zealous in organizing competitions and sponsoring band activities at the CNE. Before emigrating from the United States in 1919 to become conductor of the Waterloo Musical Society Band, Thiele had directed a family musical troupe on the Chautauqua circuit and had been involved in several leading American bands. He quickly earned a reputation in Canada as a cornetist and conductor. Moreover, he was president of the Waterloo Music Company, founder of the Ontario Amateur Band Directors' Association, and publishing editor of *Musical Canada* from 1928 until 1933, ever displaying versatility and flamboyant showmanship in a host of enterprising projects. In 1932 Thiele established the Waterloo Band Festival, which became an annual gathering of bands in Ontario. His varied experience, as band conductor, organizer, and music dealer, eventually converged in the promotion of instrumental music as a novel adventure in education, at just about the time when the popularity of town bands was flagging. Coincidentally, the Waterloo Music Company had been forced to seek new markets, for when the era of silent movies ended there was a decline in the sale of sheet music. Following the success of Harry Hill's *Singing Period* for elementary schools, Thiele shifted the company's operations more and more toward music education. Almost instinctively he turned to the band, a field which showed a promising market potential and one in which his own expertise was widely respected. The Waterloo music festivals and, later, the Waterloo band clinics were designed to get schools involved in band work. For thousands who attended these events, Thiele was an impressive figure as he conducted massed bands clad in his white uniform accented with gold braid; a colourful link with the American town band heritage, he rejuvenated an old tradition, which was transplanted to the schools with renewed life and spirit.

In an entirely different way Martin Chenhall acted as a catalyst in the promotion of bands in the Toronto schools. Chenhall, though lacking Thiele's panache, did share his enthusiasm for and obsession with bands. His designated position, 'band instructor,' was unique; as an itinerant musician, Chenhall travelled tirelessly from school to school in a station wagon loaded with instruments, band uniforms, supplies, and equipment. In 1937 he presented a proposal to the Toronto board for an expansion of instrumental activities. Although the board made no formal commitment, he continued to campaign and to coax individual principals in order to keep the idea of school bands ever in mind. Chenhall conducted a North Toronto boys' band at the 1939 OEA meetings – 'the first appearance of a band at a Music Section session,'[66] according to Brault – and he also formed several cadet bands during the war years. The 1945 OEA concert in Massey Hall included two marches by a composite band from various Toronto schools under his direction. Because he was on staff at the board's music department, Chenhall was not associated permanently with any one school but worked on an ad hoc basis wherever he could provoke action. Again in 1946 he submitted a proposal for the expansion of instrumental music, even though the board had not responded to his earlier requests. In fact, instrumental classes had begun that year at North Toronto Collegiate under Jack Dow; they were initiated by Principal Houston as an experiment in his own school. Houston's action demonstrates once again that secondary school principals could launch pilot projects before they were formally approved by provincial authorities or by the board. From this casual beginning at North Toronto Collegiate emerged an impressive instrumental music program. In commenting on these early developments, Jack Dow paid tribute to the persistence of Martin Chenhall, whose efforts contributed to the success at North Toronto and at other schools which followed North Toronto's lead.[67]

The development of a curricular wind program at Barrie Collegiate by W.A. Fisher predated the North Toronto enterprise. Fisher, because of his background and training, always referred to himself as a history teacher, yet he was a pioneer in the teaching of instrumental music and for many years was head of both the history and music departments in Barrie. In 1939 he organized a school orchestra, but after experimenting with wind classes he decided to concentrate his efforts on the band. At the Music Section of the 1940 OEA convention, Fisher gave a demonstration entitled 'Instrumental Music as a Practical Classroom Subject.' He explained in a subsequent article that instrumental music in Barrie was an optional subject scheduled for four periods a week in the regular school timetable. As a solution to the problem of equipment, students were expected to provide their own instruments, although percussion and tuba were furnished by the school. Fisher wrote: 'We have been favoured with loans from local service clubs and fees from entertainment projects ... This has made it possible to set up a fund to aid those pupils who were forced to pay for an instrument by random earnings.'[68]

The high cost of instruments was a major obstacle to the introduction of instrumental music. Otherwise, more programs might have been started in the Depression or during the war years. Fisher limited his instruction to woodwind and brass instruments because of his feelings about 'the futility of beginning the study of strings in a secondary school.'[69] In his inimitable style, he asserted, '[Any] violinist worthy of the name knows that the study of his instrument should begin at the primary school age.'[70] North Toronto and Barrie went their separate ways: though their bands encountered each other at the Toronto Kiwanis Music Festival, North Toronto devoted itself to orchestral work while Barrie specialized in bands. The first performance of the Barrie Collegiate Band at an OEA concert took place in 1942 at Massey Hall; it was just one of many occasions on which this premier band served as an inspiration for others. Unquestionably, Allen Fisher has had an incalculable influence on the growth of instrumental music in Ontario.

THE MUSIC BRANCH

In 1919, long before the creation of the Music Branch (1935), the provincial department of education appointed A.T. Cringan as 'inspector of the teaching of music.'[71] He held this part-time position concurrently with his appointment as music master at the Toronto Normal School. Trowsdale observes: 'This turned out to be a strange appointment for the use of the word "inspector" was scarcely justified. So far as the Department was concerned, he was not really an inspector, for his name does not appear in the inspectoral lists of the annual reports, nor was his work of a province-wide nature.'[72]

Cringan saw inspection as a means of ensuring high standards in school music, but by 1935, when G. Roy Fenwick was appointed provincial supervisor of music, regimentation was already giving way to a new spirit in education, and inspection was assuming the guise of supervision. In a full-time appointment Fenwick was able to exercise greater authority and had the resources to go well beyond the role of inspection. The Music Branch functioned as a central bureau, providing information, advice, and overall supervision for music in the public schools. This was no small undertaking in a province where local trustees, unwilling to forfeit their power, had resisted the creation of large school districts, which could have facilitated educational opportunities in a more equitable manner. It is little wonder that Ontario's one-room schoolhouse remained part of the landscape even after the Second World War. The 1935–6 annual report revealed that 'although there was singing in most classrooms ... in only 57 per cent was any effort made to present a well-organized course.'[73]

The conditions in most rural schools in the 1930s had not changed appreciably from those of the previous decade as described by Robert Stamp:

> While the urban high school of the 1920s forecast future developments in Ontario education, the rural elementary school confirmed the ever-present conservative tradition – a remembrance of things past. Every morning from early September till the end of June, some 200,000 country children arrived at the schoolhouse door – to learn their lessons, play with friends, and receive their social and moral preparation for responsible adult life. The school buildings had changed little in the half-century since Ryerson's retirement. Most were plain, rectangular structures of brick or stone, consisting of one class-room together with a small entry hall or cloak room where the children hung their coats and stowed their lunch boxes. The familiar wood stove dominated the back of the class-room, with teacher's desk and blackboard at the front. Depending on the annual harvest and the inclination of the trustees, a few dollars might be spent each year on interior or exterior painting, new library books or maps. A major change for many rural schools in the 1920s was the switch from double to single desks. But comforts such as central heating and indoor toilets were usually dismissed as too expensive or apt to spoil the children. The surrounding school-yard was usually a half-acre in size, containing two outdoor privies, a well and an iron pump, often a woodshed, but no play apparatus.[74]

In his first year with the department, Fenwick visited 105 inspectorates, where he also took opportunities to address teachers, trustees, and service clubs and to attend school fairs, concerts, and festivals. His 1935–6 report claimed that music instruction had been introduced to an additional 895 rooms. The Music Branch actively promoted local festivals in order to interest rural schools in music. Guidelines offered help in organizing either competitive or non-competitive events, lists of songs suitable for both festival and classroom were circulated widely, and adjudicators were recommended upon request. Fenwick himself served as an adjudicator, thus kindling community spirit for the festival as an annual event. Department regulations were amended in 1939 so that festival participation could be allowed as regular school attendance without any loss of revenue. Fenwick had never attended a normal school; he secured the supervisor's job in Hamilton on the strength of his private teaching and experience as a church soloist. After accepting the Hamilton position, he attended the summer session for music supervisors at West Chester State Normal School in Pennsylvania, and later, in 1927, he earned an extramural MusBac degree from the University of Toronto. Fenwick was not reticent in recruiting others like himself into school music: he endorsed the appointment of church organists, piano teachers, or town bandmasters who possessed sufficient background to provide music instruction in rural areas. They travelled from school to school either teaching classes themselves or supervising regular teachers. Many itinerants lacked formal qualifications but were granted 'letters of permission' from one year to the next and were expected to attend the department's summer courses. Fundamental to the success of the Music Branch was its system of grants, designed to pressure boards into hiring competent musicians. Financial incentives were also available for teachers who upgraded their certificates at summer music courses. In effect, Fenwick exerted a measure of control by issuing grants only when specific conditions were satisfied. 'Teachers from other subjects resented the special grants for music and art,'[75] according to Bradley, but, more significantly, the success of these programs led to increasingly high costs. Consequently, the department discontinued the grants to teachers in 1940, and the special music grants to boards were absorbed in general instructional funding as of 1945.

Fenwick did not confine his attention to problems in the rural schools. He recognized the importance of teacher training and put great effort into departmental music courses, which historically had revitalized the system whenever competent teachers were urgently needed. Two summer schools were operating throughout the 1930s, the original one in Toronto under P.G. Marshall of Simcoe and another at the University of Western Ontario under Charles Percy, assisted by E.W.G. Quantz. In the late 1930s Fenwick directed the London school himself.

Ontario universities in the 1930s had not yet developed specialized programs for music teachers, so it was left to the Music Branch to furnish advanced work beyond the general training of the normal schools. Because most summer instructors were supervisors, normal staff, or outstanding teachers from the public schools, these courses were weighted toward methodology. By 1936 three summers were required to complete the cycle of courses for supervisors' qualifica-

TABLE 10.1
Enrolment in summer schools of the Music Branch, Ontario Department of Education,
1935–40

Year	Toronto	London	Total
1935	264	145	409
1936	362	191	553
1937	481	238	719
1938	614	356	970
1939	597	413	1,010
1940	554	342	896

SOURCE: AR (Ont.), 1935–40

tions, and by 1937 an instrumental music course was being offered at both schools. Eventually, as many as nine different certificates were issued for summer work. The vocal course covered practice teaching, vocal training, music appreciation, ear training, sight-singing, and choral conducting. In the 1940s the methodology was closely related to that of *The High Road of Song*. The instrumental course stressed methods and materials as well as arranging, conducting, and orchestral training. The extent of the summer operation can be seen in table 10.1. The sense of accomplishment that pervaded summer sessions inspired a generation of teachers. For those who gave the instruction it was stimulating to work each year in an environment in which new methods and ideas could be channelled into a common cause. The good feelings culminated in a final program, which featured the entire student body as a massed choir in public performance. The department discontinued summer schools in 1941 owing to the restrictions of the Second World War, and recurring resolutions from the Music Section urged department officials to reinstate these courses. Fenwick expressed concern in his music report for 1942–3: 'Fifty-five Elementary and 26 Secondary school teachers are teaching or supervising music by reason of special temporary permits issued by the Department. Many more hold a lower certificate than is required by the regulations. This situation will tend to become worse, and no remedy is possible until the Departmental Summer Courses are re-established.'[76] Summer schools resumed in 1945; nine courses were offered, with a total enrolment of 327, but the momentum that had built up to 1939, when the enrolment exceeded one thousand, had been sacrificed to the demands of the war.

The Music Branch assisted teachers through its circulars, pamphlets, courses of study, booklists, and other resource materials. There were guidelines dealing with Empire Day programs, festival participation, music appreciation, and songs for wartime use, and suggestions for producing Gilbert and Sullivan operas. Fenwick maintained a steady flow of publications as he perceived needs in the field. Teachers must have appreciated the department's film library, for Fenwick reported in 1945 that music films were seen by 158,094 children and 29,380 adults. In cooperation with CBC, the Music Branch sponsored a series of eight radio programs featuring elementary and secondary school choirs from Toronto, Hamilton, Ottawa, Windsor, and Kitchener. The series was extended further afield to present school groups from North Bay, Port Arthur, and Fort William. In 1939 three programs of Christmas music prepared by schools in Hamilton, Toronto, and London 'were heard over the entire Canadian network of the CBC, and the Columbia chain in the United States.'[77] By and large these broadcasts were publicity efforts designed to show off excellent choral groups from the schools of Ontario. Some of the first educational radio programs were music appreciation series carried over CBC but produced by the large American networks. Once the department of education started to produce its own programs in 1942, this creative activity added prestige to the Music Branch and placed its director, G. Roy Fenwick, in the forefront of school music.

Joseph Beaulieu was appointed assistant supervisor for music in the French-speaking schools in 1943. Originally from the Ottawa area, he was renowned for his work with boys' choirs and published a great deal of music for schools. As a member of the Music Branch, Beaulieu operated out of North Bay, 'visiting rural, urban and normal schools' as well as meeting with 'inspectors, teachers and school boards.'[78] The longer he was in the job, the less contact he had with the Toronto office, and it appears that the lines of communication broke down, for although Fenwick's annual reports were polite, they contained few details from the French sector.

Ontario teachers gained a great advantage in having a provincial director within the department as a spokesman for music – someone to articulate a philosophy, someone who could stimulate the system through innovative and strategic programs. G. Roy Fenwick performed these functions admirably from 1935 to 1959. An astute politician, he carried out his duties with confidence and dignity. Not only could he finesse the support of senior officials in the department, he could also win enthusiastic cooperation from principals, teachers, and the public at large.

NORMAL SCHOOLS

Stamp describes teacher training as 'that perennial backwater of the Ontario educational system.'[79] This and other references suggest that normal schools were the most maligned institutions in the province. Contributing to this general attitude were specific criticisms regarding instruction in music. Normal school instructors themselves complained that they did not have sufficient time to provide the basic music background upon which teaching methods could then be developed. This being so, each wave of graduates was only superficially equipped to carry out instruction in music. Given the insular nature of these institutions and their ultra-conservative programs, it is not surprising that questions were raised concerning the appointment of music staff. Too often local musicians such as church organists or private teachers were hired on a part-time basis. In some cases they did not have classroom experience and, being unfamiliar with school problems, devoted what little time was scheduled for music to the teaching of rudimentary theory. This aggravated music supervisors, who had to compensate for the lack of practical work by conducting in-service training for new teachers. To make matters worse, part-time instructors did not enjoy the same status as full-time appointees, who, designated as masters, participated in shaping the academic policies and programs of the normal schools.

Although local musicians were pleased to augment their earnings through part-time work, music educators were chagrined by the fact that the subject was not given high priority by those in charge of normal schools. It was inevitable that normal school students likewise considered music to be of little importance. Early in the 1930s the Music Section used panel discussions, study committees, and resolutions to campaign for improvements in teacher training; as editor of the 'School Music Bulletin,' Harry Hill was relentless in his attacks on the system. Fenwick also recognized inherent weaknesses in the general programs as a preparation for classroom music, but since normal schools fell within the department's teacher training division, it was not easy for him, as director of the Music Branch, to effect major changes. Therefore, he sought improvements through music courses at summer school, where he was personally in charge of content and the hiring of staff. Fenwick directed his efforts toward supervisors and itinerant music teachers and, by exerting his will through the Music Branch, shifted the department's priorities in favour of specialist training. To ascribe negative results to the entire network of ten normal institutions would be an injustice to some who held full-time appointments and, in spite of the system, had outstanding careers in their respective institutions. Several distinguished music teachers served on the staff of the Toronto Normal School: A.T. Cringan (1901–31), Charles Percy (1931–7), and Vera Russell (1937–64). Cringan's publications and leadership have already been noted in detail; Charles Percy was well respected as a teacher at both the London and Toronto normal schools and as director of the London summer school; Vera Russell, originally a rural school supervisor in Halton County, was a prominent executive member of the Music Section and had great influence through the *Songtime* series and her book *Teaching Music in Canadian Schools*. James Bottomley (1908–23) and William Rothwell (1923–50) of Stratford and T.A. Brown (1899–1925) of Ottawa also enjoyed long terms as normal school instructors. Though normal schools were renamed teachers' colleges after the Second World War, their traditions lingered on. Neglecting to make any real changes in teacher training, the department flirted simultaneously with general classroom teacher and music specialist without ever making a commitment to one or the other.

THE ONTARIO COLLEGE OF EDUCATION

Secondary school training was centralized in 1920 when the faculties of education at Queen's University and the University of Toronto were superseded by the Ontario College of Education (OCE). In addition to methods in secondary school subjects, there was also an elementary option available which included some general work in music. George Bramfitt was in charge of elementary music until 1939, at which time Leslie Bell joined the staff as a high school music specialist. As a result of Bell's dynamic personality, music took on a new vitality at OCE; indeed, his leadership in establishing the subject at the secondary school level was felt across the province. He remained in this post until 1948.

MUSIC IN THE UNIVERSITIES

Music in the universities of Ontario did not change dramatically in the period between the wars. At Western University, later renamed the

University of Western Ontario, there had been proposals to establish music programs from time to time, but in most cases these attempts did not come to fruition. It was indeed a long while before music became an integral part of the academic life on this campus. A.D. Jordan, a local organist and choir leader, proposed a music school in affiliation with Western University in 1919. Later that year, having received no response from Western, he founded the Institute of Musical Art, in affiliation with the University of Toronto. Most of the city's finest teachers joined the staff, and the institute 'soon assumed the leading place in musical education in London.'[80] In 1922 it amalgamated with its rival, the London Conservatory of Music, which had been struggling financially for over twenty years. Jordan continued as principal until 1932, even though he had moved to Toronto to be organist of Timothy Eaton Memorial Church in 1925. The University of Western Ontario (UWO) seemed more interested in music by 1924. At that time the university invited Dr Albert Ham of Toronto to establish a music department: he, however, declined the offer. Sherwood Fox stimulated music at UWO during his term as president (1927–47) by encouraging more activity at summer schools. Fox consulted with Edward Johnson to find outstanding musicians for voice classes and workshops in the 1930s and, to a large extent, relied upon grants from the Carnegie Foundation of New York for special projects in music. Western's Extension Department cooperated with the Ontario Department of Education in administering summer courses for school teachers. In 1934 the London Institute of Musical Art was incorporated as the Western Ontario Conservatory of Music, with Frederick Newnham as its first principal. Harvey Robb, who succeeded him at the conservatory, was appointed director of music for the university in 1939. Robb's energetic leadership led to a closer affiliation between the two institutions, and in 1943 he introduced courses for credit within the Faculty of Arts. One of the most ambitious projects at UWO was the creation of Music Teachers' College in 1945. As an affiliate of the university it functioned like a conservatory, providing special training for private teachers through a two-year diploma course in music pedagogy (MusGPaed). Max Pirani and Ernest White were among the outstanding musicians recruited during Robb's term (1939–57). It was not until 1956 that degree programs in music were introduced – a BA with music options – and at that time Music Teachers' College was integrated into the Faculty of Arts and Science.

Music at Queen's University was not connected with a conservatory operation, though 'the need for a music department had been debated at the turn of the century.'[81] Music instruction was initiated in the summer of 1932 when Eduardo Petri of the Metropolitan Opera Company gave a summer course in vocal music; he also returned for one or two succeeding summers to train choirs. The appointment of Frank Llewellyn Harrison in 1935 marked the beginnings of music within the university's academic program; at Queen's, music was treated primarily as a cultural subject, fulfilling its role as one of the humanities. As a resident musician Harrison taught appreciation courses and founded choral and orchestral societies. In 1938 music became a full-fledged credit course, and in 1942 Harrison was given a regular staff appointment. Summer courses in the newly formed School of the Fine Arts commenced in 1942. Leslie Bell conducted the orchestra in 1943 and taught on the summer staff until 1945. Graham George succeeded Harrison in the full-time music position in 1946.

The University of Toronto had two distinct interests in the realm of music. Because of its early involvement in administering practical examinations, the university had been drawn into competition with conservatories and subsequently took steps to exercise more control in this field. Early in his term as principal of TCM, A.S. Vogt worked toward closer ties with the university and, in his dual role as principal of TCM and dean of the Faculty, attempted to clarify the place of music within the university. However, the division remained unclear because the university and the conservatory shared physical facilities, equipment, and teaching staff. The University of Toronto's other vested interest, the granting of degrees, was an exclusive function of the Faculty of Music. As of 1904, when it entered into federation, the University of Trinity College had relinquished its degree-granting power in music, leaving the University of Toronto as the only Ontario university offering MusBac and MusDoc degrees. The University of Toronto had no rivals in this sphere of music education, and consequently the Faculty settled into a comfortable, conservative existence.

By and large British traditions prevailed at the University of Toronto. Consequently, the university was concerned with theoretical subjects – harmony, counterpoint, music history and form, the academic requirements for degrees – whereas the conservatory was involved in practical work, mainly performance as prescribed in requirements leading to diplomas. The students working toward diplomas (associate and licentiate) outnumbered by far those who were pursuing degrees. It follows that most of the student activity was associated with the TCM; there, a large corps of teachers worked for an hourly wage, but relatively few held salaried positions. Only a small complement of conservatory teachers held academic positions in the Faculty of Music, which was established in 1918. The original faculty consisted of Dean A.S. Vogt and four part-time lecturers: Albert Ham, Herbert Fricker, Healey Willan, and F.A. Mouré, the university's organist and bursar. During the 1930s this inner circle of faculty dwindled to three: Dean Ernest MacMillan, Healey Willan, and Leo Smith.

Despite the fact that degrees were offered, little instruction was available apart from private tuition. There was an annual series of lectures on a wide range of subjects commencing in 1919, but Earl Davey notes that 'the lectures were not designed to provide the student with the knowledge and skill required to successfully complete the degree examinations; they were intended, rather, to supplement the private study undertaken by the student.'[82] For many years the MusBac and MusDoc remained as extramural programs. Degree candidates made their own arrangements with private tutors in preparation for written examinations and, in most cases, did not have much interaction with other students. The original lecture series initiated in the Faculty of Music had continued without significant changes until 1934, when the first formal courses were offered to students registered in the Faculty. There were two: the first course, as described by Davey, was 'similar to the traditional lecture series, though possibly more oriented towards the examination material than had previously been the case';[83] the second course, provided by the conservatory, consisted of a tutorial in harmony, counterpoint, and fugue, as well as work in ear training, music history, and form.

The prevailing concept of music in higher education was expressed by Ernest MacMillan at the 1932 Music Supervisors' National Conference in Cleveland:

> To the average musician a judiciously arranged university course is of great value, especially when it involves some real contact with university life, and some insight into the university point of view. The degree in most cases not only stamps a man as a musician; it is also an indication that his general education has reached a definite standard. We need such men as leaders in music education, and we are going to need them more as time goes on.
>
> The problem of the university course in music lies in the fact that it must on the one hand give a student something which no purely musical college can provide, and on the other hand must be of practical value to him as a

musician. The problem is complicated by the prevailing impression in the public mind that music is essentially a matter of performance. This attitude is reflected in certain forms of phraseology. We speak of *practical music* as opposed to *musical theory*. Practical music means, as a rule, playing some instrument or singing; theory appears in many cases to mean merely something that one must 'pass' in order to get a diploma. It is on this so-called theoretical side that a British or Canadian university course lays great stress, and, I think, rightly so. The danger is that students may come to regard such subjects as harmony and counterpoint as a variety of musical mathematics or even as a sort of jig saw puzzle. The real function of such studies should be, of course, to enable students to think in musical terms: to apprehend a composer's intentions; to separate essentials from nonessentials; to view various types of music in historical perspective, and, in so far as technical knowledge and practice can insure it, to become composers themselves.

The value of a university course in music may be judged according to its success in reaching these objectives, but in addition it must in some way secure to the student something of that broad detached outlook which is rightly or wrongly considered to be characteristically academic. If it fails to do this, the university degree in music is, so far as I can see, practically indistinguishable from the diploma of the musical college, except for the difference in the letters which a student may add to his name. Our courses, therefore, aim at developing all around musicianship and not at specific training in performance.[84]

It was not until 1936 that an intramural program was introduced in the form of an honours BA degree in music. It was similar to the extramural degree in that it concentrated on courses in music history and theory; it was different in that it did include electives in arts and science. Earl Davey observes: 'The musical instruction, which involved four to six hours per week in each of the four years, was provided by members of the Faculty of Music. This marked the beginning of the acceptance of musical studies as part of the Bachelor of Arts programme.'[85] Evidently the university thought this an ideal program for prospective high school teachers and, to add a measure of practical training, included choral training on a casual basis. Yet people in the secondary schools felt the amount of choral work was negligible as preparation for a career in music education. Their dissatisfaction was still prevalent in 1943, when a senior official of the Ontario Department of Education informed Sir Ernest MacMillan that 'Mr. Fenwick and others found the university music course still lacking in pedagogy, mainly because none of the instructors had a background of practical work in school music.'[86] Subsequently, it was agreed that Leslie Bell would be in charge of choral techniques at the Faculty of Music in addition to his regular work at the Ontario College of Education. Otherwise, no major changes were made at that time.

It is evident that music supervisors and teachers were becoming more familiar with music education in the United States and were incorporating American ideas and patterns in their school programs. But during this period Canadian universities remained impervious to developments in their American counterparts, thus retaining decidedly British traditions with an emphasis on academic subjects. Increasing criticism from some quarters, most notably the Ontario Department of Education and the Music Section of OEA, maintained that universities were not responsive to the practical needs of specialized school music teachers. A series of informal discussions regarding music in the universities and secondary schools took place in 1941; 'with Sir Ernest MacMillan as chairman, the group consisted of Dr. H.J. Cody, representatives from other Ontario universities, Professors Healey Willan and Leo Smith, and Roy Fenwick.'[87] Undoubtedly the most far-reaching outcome of these meetings was the decision to recognize grade thirteen music as a university admission subject, and although it was several years before grade thirteen enrolments grew substantially, this agreement released an academic adrenalin which helped to extend music to the senior grades.

As the demand for secondary school music teachers increased, more pressure was applied to the University of Toronto to revise its degree programs accordingly. But it was not until 1946 that advanced levels of training were introduced: a school music degree within the Faculty of Music, and performance programs within a new senior school of the TCM. At first glance this breakthrough might be attributed to the long-awaited implementation of the Hutcheson Report; however, the impact of political pressure from the department of education and the school music profession in challenging the inertia which had characterized music in higher education should not be minimized. Plans for postwar rehabilitation placed new hope in cultural and humanitarian values, as the nation's leaders attempted to create a more ideal society. Adventure and optimism were in the air, as servicemen returning from overseas and aspiring young musicians from across Canada converged on Toronto to take advantage of new opportunities for professional training. It seems clear that, along with all these other forces, the collective aspiration of Canadian musicians by the end of the Second World War could not be held back any longer. The progressive steps taken at the University of Toronto marked the beginning of an era which saw the rise of instrumental music in the secondary schools, followed by an unprecedented growth of music in higher education during the 1960s.

11

The Traditions of Newfoundland and Labrador

When the other nine provinces joined Newfoundland and Labrador in 1949, Canada inherited a culture dating back to the adventure of Sir Humphrey Gilbert in the late sixteenth century. Newfoundland's intriguing history is one of struggle and celebration inextricably bound up with certain geographical, political, and economic realities. Only those who are well acquainted with this history can appreciate the extent to which rugged conditions, isolation, and problems of transportation have dictated the social patterns of the sea-girt isle. In 1937, long before union with Canada had been consummated, Joseph Smallwood expressed the heroic spirit of its people:

Newfoundlanders are great battlers. They must be great battlers: they have been battling against this or for that ever since the first settler landed here. Battling for the opportunity of getting a berth on one of the West-Coast English fishing-vessels coming on a summer voyage to Newfoundland in the early days of the Island's discovery; battling for an opportunity to desert the vessel before she returned to England with her cargo of codfish in the autumn of the year; then battling to hew a humble home out of the virgin forest that grew to the salt water's edge in some small cove far along the coast out of sight or knowledge of the English fishing-vessels coming to our coast each summer in those early years; battling against Nature and the elements to wrest a living from the sea and the forest while they were building homesteads; battling against the dreaded surprise attacks of pirates,

English men-o'-war, 'Fishing Admirals'; battling against the merciless, ruthlessly determined efforts of the early fishermen: against official stupidity and private greed; against betrayal, treachery, double-dealing and downright theft: against all these and many other evils had the early Newfoundlanders to battle ... The much-advertised English bull-dog courage and the equally publicised Irish love of a fight have both found their greatest need of expression here in Newfoundland, from the dawn of our history to the very present.[1]

From these adversities unique traditions have survived in the richness of Newfoundland's folklore, in the character of its institutions, and in the lives of those who shaped its progress. Such traditions give Newfoundlanders good cause to be proud of their past. The legacy of tragedy and hardship, kept alive in religion, language, song, and legend, has permeated the consciousness of the people, who have, moreover, shown intense determination to preserve what is deemed valuable for future generations. Music has been at the heart of this heritage in that the treasury of folk song in Newfoundland today, according to one description, not only 'documents what is lost and forgotten, but also celebrates what has survived, and thrives.'[2] This music has had a central place in the life and education of a people whose traditions, dreams, and aspirations are now part of Canada's inheritance. It is most fitting that the tune 'Squid-jiggin' Ground' was 'played on the Peace Tower carillon in Ottawa to mark the entry of Newfoundland into the confederation of Canada in 1949.'[3]

MUSIC IN FAMILY, CHURCH, AND SOCIAL LIFE

Music plays a role in religion and worship; it can arouse feelings of national pride; it provides pleasure and entertainment. It has done all these things in Newfoundland, and it has also claimed its own niche in the educational system, first of all as an informal activity and eventually as a regular subject in the curriculum.

As difficult as it is to document in any detail how missionaries used music in working among native peoples and the first settlers, we cannot deny its existence, nor should we underestimate its importance. According to Paul Woodford, in some of the earliest settlements – among them, Renews (1617) and Ferryland (1621) – there are references to priests who celebrated mass every Sunday and 'used all other ceremonies of the church of Rome, in the ample manner as it is used in

Spain.'[4] It has also been suggested that music was practised in the French settlement of Placentia: 'At least three priests were there as early as 1662 and the Franciscan Friars took up residence in 1689.'[5] One account of the pirate Peter Easton, who frequented the Harbour Grace area from 1612 to 1673, claimed that 'this king of pirates operated in style, often taking minstrels and trumpeters with him to herald his attacks.'[6] Given the facts that permanent settlement was forbidden by law and that piracy was a constant threat, it should not be surprising that there is scant evidence of music in communities whose energies were wholly taken up with survival. In all likelihood, music played a more prominent role in the missions which the Moravians established in Labrador. At Nain, a community which has maintained continuity since its beginnings in 1771, the Moravians incorporated both vocal and instrumental activities. A hymn book was introduced and natives were taught to sing chorales and motets in four parts; instrumental music included work in both brass and strings. Music in the Moravian missions reached its peak in the nineteenth century but suffered a decline in the twentieth. As will be seen, the initial efforts of the missionaries foreshadowed a continuing commitment to music education by leaders of the church.

Comparatively little is known about music among the population on the Labrador coast. One is reminded of the isolation and rugged conditions in the following reference to an Englishman at St Fraser's Harbour in the late 1840s: 'Mr. Saunders, who has been living here one and twenty years was married in England last winter, and brought out his lady in June. I believe she is the first lady who ever visited this coast, and as far as I know, is the only female who has come from England to dwell on the Labrador ... Mrs. Saunders has brought a piano, as great a novelty as herself on the Labrador, and she kindly played for us some church music.'[7] Of the Newfoundland fishermen who frequented this area, very few moved their families to Labrador on a year-round basis, and there is scant evidence of musical activity, certainly nothing to compare with the traditions associated with the Moravian missions. The posting of a military garrison in St John's influenced the social milieu over a range of entertainments and cultural pursuits. In his colourful history of St John's, Paul O'Neill writes: 'It is not difficult to imagine what it must have been like in the 1700s as damsels of flawed virtue, their eyes flaring like St. Elmo's fire, sought out the large number of soldiers, sailors and fishermen who, drink-inflamed, staggered about the paths anxious to share what Lord Byron was later to call, "a love for beauty and sin" ... The only real competition known to these frolicsome wenches came from cards and demon rum.'[8] But the presence of the military invariably introduced some form of instrumental activity, whether utilitarian or recreational. Such was the case with a military officer who was accused thus by the Reverend John Jackson: 'He hath often gone about the harbour on the Lord's Day with his fiddle on purpose to divest people from coming to church, the rest of the day he revell's away with his companions in dancing and rioting.'[9] This infamous officer, Captain Thomas Lloyd, 'also played flute in the same wanton manner.'[10] A great deal of the entertainment in St John's was associated with taverns. By 1726 the number of establishments had reached forty-six: 'Each with its own gaily painted signboard ... beckoned customers to such centres of social intercourse as W. Best's Bunch of Grapes ... John Cahill's Tavern for All Weathers ... the Jolly Fisherman, Dooling's Red Cow, or Michael Hanlen's Shoulder of Mutton, to name but a few.'[11] Nevertheless, some taverns in the late eighteenth and early nineteenth centuries were much more than drinking establishments. The Globe offered theatrical performances and the proprietors of the Crown and Anchor 'dabbled in the arts'; those who boasted a more elegant touch catered to 'officers of the garrison, the clergy and wealthy merchants.'[12] The London Tavern, operated by one Cornelius Quirk, 'was the scene of many memorable events' during a short existence of ten years.[13] In 1806, 'a group of Irishmen, mainly Protestant, founded the Benevolent Irish Society over dinner at the inn ... The Society for Improving the Conditions of the Poor held an annual breakfast at the tavern, attended by the governor, at which collections were made on behalf of charity. There were forty-seven business and government leaders at table for the farewell dinner tendered the retiring Roman Catholic bishop, James O'Donel, before his departure for his homeland.'[14] O'Neill writes, 'We are told of the famous old inn that nothing could exceed the friendship and conviviality of the evening ... as Barbara Allan, Hearts of Oak, and Bonnie Dundee were rapturously encored.'[15] Toward the middle of the nineteenth century, a movement was organized to counter the increasing number of grog shops and the adverse effect that alcohol consumption was having on society. Accordingly, in 1841 Michael Anthony Fleming, the Roman Catholic bishop, denounced the evils of drink and proclaimed a grand temperance movement open to people of all faiths. O'Neill gives the following account:

The crusade received a boost on Sunday, November 20, when Father Murphy of Ferryland took the pledge at the foot of the altar, then rose and spoke in such glowing terms that six hundred signed it then and there. The group of zealots held their first annual parade on 6 January 1843, which was known as the 'Tee-Total Procession.' It included one hundred farmers on horseback, two by two, the garrison band, two amateur bands, and a portrait of Queen Victoria. At Government House the procession was greeted by His Excellency. By the end of 1844 over ten thousand had signed the pledge.

While the Catholics were taking the pledge, in aid of temperance, their Protestant brothers were taking tea. *The Times* of 8 February 1843 announced a Temperance Festival under the auspices of the Church of England Total Abstinence Society and the patronage of His Excellency the Governor. According to the newspaper, 'the members and other friends of the above society will DRINK TEA TOGETHER in the upper room of the factory [behind the present Synod Hall] on Queen's Road on the eve of Tuesday the 14th, at 6 o'clock. The Band of the Royal Newfoundland Companies will ... be in attendance.'[16]

These events in nineteenth-century Newfoundland account for the frequent or habitual references to organizations, buildings, and streets such as the Total Abstinence and Benefit Society, Temperance Hall, the Juvenile Total Abstinence Fife and Drum Band, and Temperance Street. Yet not all entertainments were associated with taverns; there were also private family gatherings and activities, especially toward the latter part of the nineteenth century. Frederick Rowe depicts the tenor of social life in the following passage:

Although the consumption of rum appeared to decline considerably after 1850, it was still a very common commodity especially when festive occasions such as a wedding (or in some places even a funeral) required special observance. When rum was lacking 'home brew' was often available. Prior to the advent of radio, the long winter evenings were characterized by spontaneous gatherings in private homes where 'forty-fives' or 'one hundred and twenty' (card games) were regular features. Other groups gathered to hear one or the other of the local patriarchs repeat tales of adventure and misfortune, almost invariably connected with the sea; and the ballads or folk-songs of Newfoundland, some of them – the 'come all ye's' – possibly composed by himself or one of his audience, and sung lustily to the accompaniment of a mouth organ or accordion. In most Newfoundland outports the two-week Christmas period saw a vigorous practising of the ancient English art or game of mummering, usually among the younger element but not infrequently among the older people as well. The players, disguised by masks and bizarre forms of dress, went from house to house where they danced, sang or otherwise disported themselves in return for treats of one kind or another, while residents of the house endeavoured to guess or deduce the identities of the mummers.[17]

Of the few communities outside St John's which enjoyed a high level of culture, Harbour Grace was pre-eminent. For instance, in 1851 Mr J.F. Myers, a graduate of the Queen's Musical Academy in Toronto, delivered a lecture entitled 'The History of Music' at the Commercial Room. The Harbour Grace Literary Institute sponsored concerts and in 1893 presented the cantata *Eva* with an accompanying orchestra; its Total Abstinence Band participated in temperance parades, and in 1852 Harbour Grace had 'a pipe organ installed in the Roman Catholic Cathedral.'[18] Church musicians in Harbour Grace, Brigus, Carbonear, and Twillingate were often active as school teachers and, in some cases, also gave private lessons. The more remote places thrived on a strictly church-centred life, especially the predominantly Methodist communities. In fact, the relationship with the church became so narrow in the tiny outports that people spent virtually every night at a church function, whether a prayer service, a lodge meeting, a concert, a social, a dance (where the denomination permitted it), or a hot supper.

The primacy of church choirs in the musical culture of Newfoundland, both in the outports and in the city of St John's, has been a widely accepted fact. Although church music was ostensibly sacred in nature, organists and conductors in St John's extended their concerts and recitals well beyond the needs of the worship service itself. The repertoire in the churches could become decidedly secular or at times even cosmopolitan. Hence, musicians used the church choir as a nucleus for large choral societies in the community. In the latter part of the 1800s, there was a marked increase in the number of grand entertainments which featured local talent – choral groups, vocal soloists, and instrumentalists. Concerts were often given in aid of charities or educational organizations.

A Handel and Haydn Society was formed in St John's in 1838, and another choral society followed in 1848. Initially these choral aggregations presented excerpts from oratorios and featured guest pianists or vocalists, but as the musical leadership improved there was a higher incidence of complete works. The more ambitious undertakings involved instrumental accompaniment. At first, bands were used to accompany large choirs, but later on, when the repertoire became more sophisticated, orchestral accompaniments were much in vogue. The St John's Choral Society became the most renowned musical organization in the city. It was formed in 1878 and performed regularly until 1887. During its existence this society registered a total of two hundred members and, through presentations of complete oratorios and major choral works, reached unprecedented levels of artistic achievement. The large Protestant churches of St John's attracted well-trained organists and choral directors from Great Britain. These musicians were also engaged as teachers in their respective denominational colleges. Unfortunately, many of them did not remain in Newfoundland but chose to further their careers in Canada or the United States. The Roman Catholic churches followed the practice of hiring local musicians. In several cases, Charles Hutton and Patrick J. McCarthy among them, these musicians went abroad for advanced training. But more important, these local people provided for a greater measure of continuity in the musical growth of the Catholic churches and schools, and indeed, of the community at large. One of the most respected musicians in Newfoundland was Charles Hutton, a native Newfoundlander whose work as organist and choir director at the Roman Catholic cathedral was complemented by his accomplishments as teacher, composer, and impresario.

The military personnel in port at St John's may have quickened an interest in bands, just as they did in Victoria, BC, and other garrison cities. Bands of a sort furnished accompaniments for theatrical presentations, parades, and a colourful array of civic events. In 1822 a band played selections from *The Beggar Girl* for the cornerstone ceremony of a theatre in St John's. Bands were in attendance at the laying of the Atlantic cable on 27 July 1866, at the consecration of the Roman Catholic basilica in 1873, and at the inauguration of train service on 29 June 1882.[19] A plethora of bands operated under the auspices of fraternal lodges, civic societies, militia units, schools, and even church organizations. The instrumentation of these bands was by modern standards dreadfully incomplete and, by and large, reflected traditions from the old country. As one example, Salvation Army bands, which have endured since 1889, were based upon the British brass band model. The Roman Catholics and Methodists had quasi-military cadet movements which for utilitarian purposes sponsored their own bands. The Anglican counterpart was the Church Lads' Brigade, formed in 1892 by Major H. Rendell, an ensemble which competed in the All-Canada Band Contest held in Ottawa in 1907. Professor David Bennett, often referred to as 'the Sousa of Newfoundland,' directed bands of all types over a period of fifty years. Another bandmaster, James Power, trained ensembles in St John's and in a number of smaller communities. He worked with the Mount Cashel Orphanage Fife and Drum Band from 1898 to 1909. Sister Kathleen Rex notes that Power performed on clarinet at Placentia, where 'for sometime past he had been teaching juvenile and adult bands for the Star of the Sea Association.'[20] Bands of various types thrived well into the twentieth century, providing a training ground for the majority of instrumentalists in Newfoundland.

The violin had been a popular instrument from early times, yet orchestras approximating a full instrumentation did not emerge until very late in the 1800s. The formation of the St John's Orchestral Society in 1890 signalled a period of advancement, owing in no small measure to the leadership of its founder, Charles Hutton. Peter LeSueur was another reputable musician who founded his own choral and orchestral society. A church organist who also taught music at Methodist College, LeSueur left Newfoundland in 1905 to become director of a conservatory in Erie, Pennsylvania.

Of all the arts organizations which flourished in the last half of the nineteenth century, the Athenaeum was by far the most impressive. It grew out of the St John's Library Society (founded 1823), the Mechanics' Institute (1849), and the Young Men's Literary and Scientific Institute (1858). In 1861, 'these institutions amalgamated and a building was completed on Duckworth Street by 1879 featuring an auditorium with seating capacity for 1000.'[21] According to Louise Whiteway, the Athenaeum 'had gathered up in itself various strands of the country's culture viz. library, lecture, entertainment and maximized all, giving greater continuity, more conscious total direction to the culture of the country.'[22] For many years, lectures, recitals, and concerts were regular features of the Athenaeum movement, and after 1880, weekly lectures were interspersed with alternating evenings of reading and music. Other groups sponsoring similar entertainments in this era were the Ladies of St Vincent de Paul, the Benevolent Irish Society, the Ladies' Methodist Benevolent Society, the Academia Club, the Dorcas Society, and the Star of the Sea Association. An event of unusual fascination was a demonstration of Edison's Speaking Phonograph or Talking Machine at Mechanics' Hall in 1880. The advertisement claimed, 'It speaks, it sings, it laughs, it plays cornet solos,'[23] and local people were encouraged to have their voices recorded on this miracle of sound reproduction. Among the buildings used for cultural entertainments in St John's were the Total Abstinence Hall, the Old Factory, the Benevolent Irish Society Hall, Fishermen's Hall, Masonic Hall, and the Athenaeum. Unfortunately, the great fire of 1892 destroyed almost every major theatre and concert hall in the city.

During the nineteenth century, secular entertainments in St John's shifted from the tavern to the theatre. The first opera presented in the city was *The Duenna; or, the Double Elopement*. Newspaper notices indicate a dramatic increase in the number of operatic troupes and theatrical companies which visited St John's in the 1860s, and minstrel shows became popular box office attractions too. But St John's did not establish a tradition of its own in opera production until the 1880s. The impetus for this came from the visit of Miss Clara Fisher of Boston, who performed selections of Offenbach and Gilbert and Sullivan at the Athenaeum in 1879. She decided to reside in St John's and later that year played the leading role 'in the Josie Loane Dramatic Company production of H.M.S. Pinafore.'[24] This first complete presentation of a Gilbert and Sullivan operetta in Newfoundland prompted local musicians to organize two other Pinafore companies. The fever for operatic fare was sustained well into the twentieth century. Throughout the next ten years Clara Fisher performed frequently with Charles Hutton, who directed and produced operettas annually 'over a career spanning sixty years.'[25] Hutton also appeared on occasion as an accompanist for Twillingate Stirling, Newfoundland's 'Queen of Song.' Employing a French version of her name, Mlle Marie Toulinguet made her international debut at La Scala and subsequently toured as a concert and opera star in Europe and North America. She also made a phonograph recording shortly after the turn of the century. Unfortunately, her career ended prematurely, when she encountered serious problems with her voice.

Hutton dominated the operetta and concert scene in St John's. He formed the Academia Minstrel Troupe in 1883 and also sang leading roles on occasion, one of which Woodford describes as follows: 'The grandest operatic success ever witnessed in Newfoundland, *The Bells of Cornville* by Jean-Robert Planquette, a joint production of Charles

Hutton and Peter LeSueur, was presented at the Total Abstinence Hall towards the middle of September, 1896. A comic opera in three acts, the production was the largest ever performed in Newfoundland and utilized a large orchestra and fifty performers, with imported costumes. Charles Hutton played the role of Gaspard, a miser, while LeSueur directed the orchestra.'[26] But Hutton's own productions of Gilbert and Sullivan drew the highest artistic acclaim and secured him a reputation as 'Newfoundland's greatest musician and dramatist.'[27] In 1894 he staged no fewer than four Gilbert and Sullivan shows. A 'Grand Complimentary Concert' on 12 October 1896 was tendered by Miss Stirling and an Irish tenor, Mr Joseph O'Shaughnessy, with the assistance of local musicians. According to newspaper reports, the audience for this event was the largest ever seen at local entertainments, and Hutton was honoured after the performance: 'It is only those who have permanently resided in St. John's for the past fifteen years who can understand the bounds and leaps which the local drama, opera and concerts have made under your training and control. The present number of high-class musical artists in St. John's, the culture and high tone which the opera and concert have attained, all speak more eloquently in your behalf than any words of ours.'[28]

GENERAL EDUCATION

Missionaries who worked among the early settlers did so with the tacit blessing of the government and the powerful merchant class. And in the ensuing years the patterns of general education in Newfoundland were profoundly influenced by religious denominations and church organizations. By the nineteenth century, Newfoundland society was substantially made up of an English upper class and a large population of poor, many of whom had emigrated from Ireland between 1750 and 1850; for the most part, the former were Anglican and the latter Roman Catholic. A middle class was almost non-existent. The impetus to provide schooling for the poor during the early eighteenth century came from the Society for the Propagation of the Gospel, whose headquarters was in England. According to Frederick W. Rowe, its record of achievement in education was anything but impressive, and after 1825 it 'devoted its energies entirely to purely religious activities.'[29] Two local societies attempted to improve the situation in the early 1800s: the Society for the Improvement of Conditions of the Poor in St John's established charity schools, and the Benevolent Irish

Society founded an orphan asylum school. But of all the voluntary organizations it was the Newfoundland School Society, established in 1824, which proved to be the most effective in assisting the disadvantaged.

Children of well-to-do families either attended private schools or received private instruction at home; a number went abroad for an education. The reasonably high quality of instruction in the private schools probably helped to enshrine the tradition of denominational schools in the province, and the absence of a large middle class reduced any urgency on the part of authorities to improve opportunities for schooling. Not until the First Education Act of 1836 did the government furnish state aid to schools. In 1843 funds were distributed simply between Protestants and Roman Catholics. A government scheme to create one academy for all Protestant groups in St John's was aborted, as were other attempts at a non-denominational system. The Education Act of 1874 granted funds according to the ratio of denominational affiliations and approved the appointment of denominational inspectors. The Education Act of 1892 recognized the Salvation Army as yet another Protestant board. Whether by default or by decision, the government had to give up plans to create a non-denominational framework; it seemed more difficult to resolve political differences than to solve the problems of a fragmented, denominational structure. Legislation in 1903, however, did allow for the possibility of amalgamated schools. In 1920 a provincial department of education was established, and in the following year a non-denominational normal school. Since 1949 there have been several procedures introduced for denominational cooperation. Education in Newfoundland has evolved into a state-financed system in which denominations may administer their own schools according to academic standards established by the government, most notably in matters of curriculum, textbooks, and the professional qualifications of teachers.

MUSIC IN EDUCATION

The Moravians in Labrador were probably the first to introduce music as an integral part of the school curriculum. They taught the Inuit at Nain and at other small communities on the Labrador coast. According to all accounts, the Inuit had a great capacity to learn music. By 1804 the Moravians were teaching hymns in their mission schools, and a report in 1824 noted, 'Violins have been introduced, and French horns, and a few of [the Inuit] accompany the voices with great precision.'[30] In

1827 L. Morhardt, who held the dual title of schoolmaster and music director at the Hopedale mission, was requesting more violins and a violoncello. Woodford observes that 'the Inuit were taught not only to sing and play musical instruments but also to read music notation.'[31] The instruction continued for several generations; it must have been thorough, for an Anglican clergyman who visited the Labrador missions in 1899 remarked on 'the musicality of the Inuit' and noted that 'most adults could sight-sing simple melodies.'[32] The communities at Nain and Okak developed fine brass bands which often participated in special events. The Moravians incorporated musical activities into all facets of life; indeed, it is not easy to differentiate between music in the school and in the community in these highly integrated settlements. It is clear, nevertheless, that the Moravians were interested in music education primarily for its utilitarian value. Working to Christianize the native peoples, the missionaries translated their European hymns into Inuktitut but showed a total lack of interest in the music of the indigenous people. Since the mid-twentieth century, the Inuit have sought to rediscover their own musical heritage, and few vestiges are left of a proud tradition of accomplishment in vocal and instrumental music of European derivation.

The major influences in Newfoundland education have been English and Irish, in music as in general education. The Presentation Sisters of Ireland commenced their distinguished record of teaching in Newfoundland schools in 1833. Each day began and ended in the convent schools with the singing of hymns. Referring to Mother M. Josephine French, Sister Kathleen Rex writes, 'A Presentation Sister of rare musical powers arrived in Newfoundland from Galway in 1846, to share her musical talent as a volunteer missionary.'[33] The Presentation order extended its work to several communities outside St John's within the next few decades. It was said that the graduates of the school in Witless Bay from 1860 to 1883 'occupied the schools of the surrounding settlements,' and that the school had 'sent graded teachers to fill similar positions in other parts of the country.'[34]

The Sisters of Mercy arrived in Newfoundland in 1842 and in the following year accepted their first piano pupil. In 1892 there was evidence of their work, as described by Rex:

The Mercy Convent School in St. John's presented the Junior Grades in a concert on January 14. The exhibition included exercises in Callisthenics, Tonic-sol-fa [sic], and Drill, followed by the operetta, 'The Crowning of

Virtue.' A critique of the performance stated: 'The opening chorus and Tonic-Solfa [sic] exercises were nicely rendered, displaying the ease with which a knowledge of vocal music can be imparted by this system and the proficiency of the pupils in it; the fresh young voices harmonized well and the effect was very pleasing.' After a second appearance, a reviewer wrote: 'Every person present, on either or both of these occasions, must have felt that with an Institution which can make such a creditable display, it is no longer necessary to send children out of the country to educate them.'[35]

Musical activity was encouraged in several Roman Catholic schools for boys. As early as 1861, Father Carfagnini formed a band at St Bonaventure's College in St John's. Thomas Mullock, organist and choirmaster at the Roman Catholic cathedral, served as a professor of music at St Bonaventure's; other music teachers included a Professor Brace and Professor David Bennett. Bennett used the Tonic Sol-fa method and directed a school chorus and band until well into the 1880s. In 1885 'the students of St. Bonaventure's presented the operetta *Music in High Life* at the Star of the Sea Hall.'[36] The Irish Christian Brothers assumed control of this school in 1889. Among those on the music staff was David Flynn, who taught there from 1897 to 1910. His work was highly commended in 1898: 'The Tonic Solfa [sic] class, under the direction of Professor Flynn, has in a short time accomplished much. There are about 90 pupils in this class and all receive three lessons per week, each lesson being about 35 minutes. There is no more refining influence in the formation of character than a good selection of songs well taught, and learned with due appreciation ... This can only be done under the tuition of a skilful teacher who has mastery both of the theory and practice.'[37] It was reported in 1892 that 483 students were taught music at St Patrick's Hall and Holy Cross, and in 1894 a Reverend Mr Brennan, the music director for both schools, conducted a chorus of 140 voices in music and physical drill. The first half of a 'Grand Vocal and Dramatic Entertainment' by the boys of these schools featured the 'Huntsman's Chorus' from *Der Freischutz* 'by a tonic sol-fa [sic] class of sixty.'[38] Evidently all North American candidates to the Brotherhood before 1916 received Tonic Sol-fa training in Ireland.

There was rarely any music instruction in the remote communities of Newfoundland. What was typical was the attempt to have a concert or Christmas program of hymns, carols, and songs interspersed with an occasional instrumental solo or duet. But apart from the convents, which frequently gave music lessons to Protestant children, relatively few schools outside St John's had incorporated much music. By the 1920s, as Sister Kathleen Rex notes, even some schools in the city neglected music education: 'Other than schools where the church organist worked in the schools the music program consisted of the students assembling in the auditorium or gymnasium of the school to hear a recording of classical music once a week.'[39]

Shortly after 1893, the Council of Higher Education, which dealt with the secondary level, approved music examinations in an arrangement whereby local professors were authorized as examiners. Much of the private teaching in St John's was associated with convent schools or private denominational colleges operated by Roman Catholics, Anglicans, and Methodists. These so-called colleges – St Bonaventure's, Church of England Academy, Wesleyan Academy – provided secondary education both as day schools and as boarding schools for out-of-town students. However, such institutions also accepted elementary students and not infrequently became denominational private schools for all grades. Individual instruction in piano, organ, voice, or violin was available at these institutions on an optional basis; competent church musicians were usually hired as specialist teachers for the more advanced students. Music students in denominational schools received tuition for practical and theoretical examinations administered by Trinity College of Music, London. After 1902, examiners came annually from England to several local centres in Newfoundland. This development marked the beginning of a long tradition; Trinity College as an examining body has been more pervasive in Newfoundland than in any other province. In 1964 Trinity College awarded Sister Mary Loretto Croke of the Presentation order an honorary fellowship in recognition of her more than forty years of music teaching.

The differences between private and school teaching were not so clear in Newfoundland as in other provinces because the two types of music instruction already co-existed at denominational institutions. Though some private teachers maintained studios in their homes, a large number of them worked in institutional settings with church affiliations. The music departments in these schools functioned almost as small conservatories. As a consequence, private teaching in Newfoundland was never concentrated in one main conservatory, nor did private music teachers form a professional organization until 1987.

References gleaned from newspapers and school reports verify the existence of choral groups and music classes in the Protestant schools of St John's. Music instruction in the Wesleyan Training Schools was given by a Mr and Mrs Hamilton beginning in the 1850s; in the 1870s Mr Hancock, a church musician trained in England, taught at the Wesleyan Academy. The incidence of Tonic Sol-fa instruction was as high in Protestant institutions as it was in Roman Catholic schools and convents. In the late 1880s, George Rowe was commended by the bishop of Newfoundland: 'Your thorough knowledge of the tonic sol-fa [sic] system, as well as your long experience with the Old Notation, in voice culture, are a guarantee to parents and the public generally of the solid foundation for "future singing power" laid by you in your course of training.'[40] James Walker, who taught at St John's Methodist Academy until 1892, had credentials from the Tonic Sol-fa College in London, England. But Charles Hutton was undoubtedly the foremost music teacher in Newfoundland and received universal acclaim for his results in various Roman Catholic schools. An assessment of his work at St Bonaventure's College in 1902 read:

Fresh impetus has been given this year to the teaching of vocal music in our college. Large classes have been formed, and a regular course of graduated lessons suited to the capabilities of each is systematically followed. This course, which is in the hands of a fully qualified teacher is conducted on the principles laid down by the highest authorities on Tonic-Sol-fa [sic] teaching and comprises: Imitation of phrases which have been carefully patterned by the teacher; 2) singing from hand signs (tune); singing from finger signs (time); 3) 'blackboard scheme' and 'modulator scheme' practice; 4) ear training, the pupils telling from ear the Sol-fa names of the notes that have been sung or played; 5) voice training – a regular course of voice training exercises for the cultivation of pure vocal tone (Klang), as recommended by Bhenke and other celebrated voice specialists. We note with pleasure that already there is a marked improvement in the quality of the boys' voices, and, judging by the very severe test examination which has just been held in this subject, we may confidently look forward to the happiest results in this department of our work.[41]

Up until 1920 Hutton taught vocal music and elocution concurrently at St Bon's (Bonaventure's) and at St Bride's Academy, Littledale; these schools, for boys and girls respectively, also functioned as teacher training institutes. He also directed school music activities at St Patrick's Hall and Holy Cross. Near the end of his career Hutton worked at the Mount Cashel Orphanage, where among his other feats he directed a summer program which included training in singing, elocution, dancing, and choreography. Beginning in 1927, vocal students and members of the band were coached in preparation for their fall productions. Woodford gives this picture: 'The operatic troupe, itself, consisted of about fifty to sixty orphan boys and after each summer of hard work it was taken on tour by train across the island of Newfoundland to present some twenty-five to thirty performances ... each annual tour was very much like that of a circus with sets constructed and groups rehearsed.'[42] Hutton initiated several innovative projects during the inter-war period. In 1922 he produced a phonograph recording of Newfoundland compositions through the Brunswick-Balke-Collender Company. In the same year he was also involved in the first commercial radio broadcast in Newfoundland. His music store sponsored radio programs in the 1930s featuring local talent, and in the 1927 summer school for teachers held at the St John's Normal School, Hutton introduced the Foresman Music Records. These were teaching aids developed for class singing in the United States.

Charles Hutton was the first music instructor at the non-denominational normal school established by the Newfoundland Department of Education in 1921. The normal school staff consisted of a principal and four visiting instructors, who taught approximately a hundred students for the duration of one semester. After 1934, the school was absorbed in the newly created Memorial University College as a teacher training department, and the course was extended to a full year. In 1946 the department was fully integrated into the university as a department of education offering a three-year program of studies. It is clear from Hutton's own comments that the course in music covered only the basics: 'While it is not possible for the students to become (in such a short time) good sight readers and good vocalists, they were taught the proper method of imparting these two subjects to the children which, after all, is the most important part, and I feel sure, if those who intend to take up singing in their schools will persevere, not alone will the children benefit by their tuition but the teachers themselves will become proficient in the divine art.'[43] Woodford summarizes this aspect of Hutton's career in music education: 'Hutton had devoted twenty years of his life to the training of Newfoundland's teachers, many of whom later brought his teachings back to their homes in remote communities. During that period from 1921 to 1940 every pupil-teacher attending the regular school sessions at the Normal School and Memorial University College received instruction in voice production and singing from Charles Hutton.'[44] The visit of

Maud Karpeles, an English collector of folk songs, was of historic importance. She lectured in the summer school of 1929 and subsequently published two volumes of Newfoundland folk songs. In league with Canadian folklorist Marius Barbeau, Karpeles encouraged the organization of the Canadian Folk Music Society in 1956. A number of others were involved in music at the normal school and at Memorial University College. R.T. Bevan, organist at the Anglican cathedral, taught at the 1926 summer school and until 1930 gave lectures and recitals during the academic year. He was in the forefront of the music appreciation movement, placing more emphasis on music literature and history. Bevan left St John's in 1931 to join the normal school staff in Moose Jaw, Saskatchewan. Eleanor Mews was appointed to the normal school as visiting lecturer in 1933 and directed a large glee club at Memorial College, which gave annual campus concerts such as 'Springtime in Song' and 'Carols by Candlelight.' Fred R. Emerson offered non-credit music appreciation courses in the 1940s, using the resources of the Carnegie record collection. In this era, assemblies and evening courses were effective means of expanding music education at Memorial.

The mantle of leadership which Hutton had taken on in the early 1900s was assumed midway through the century by one of his distinguished students, Ignatius Rumboldt. In 1936, not long after Rumboldt had excelled in operettas at the Mount Cashel Orphanage School, he succeeded his teacher as organist and choirmaster of the Roman Catholic cathedral. He also followed in Hutton's footsteps as a music teacher in various schools operated by the Irish Christian Brothers; in 1952 he accepted a part-time appointment at Memorial University, where Hutton had introduced music methods as an instructor in the normal school. Rumboldt's musical achievements were as manifold as those of his mentor. His church, school, and community choirs set high standards of artistic performance, and in collaboration with Gerald S. Doyle, Newfoundland's foremost folk-song authority, Rumboldt did a great deal to publicize the wealth and beauty of Newfoundland folk songs through broadcasts and recordings of his CJON Glee Club. A part-time appointment to Memorial University in 1952 enabled Rumboldt to develop musical activities at the university level; after 1960 he held a full-time appointment in the university's Extension Services. In these two positions he made an impact which was province-wide, thereby demonstrating the urgent need for a full-fledged department of music in Newfoundland. Like his predecessor,

Ignatius Rumboldt was the recipient of many awards and tributes, including an honorary degree from Memorial University. In the citation Otto Tucker asked: 'How can we describe the inspiration which "Nish" Rumboldt has brought to Newfoundland and Labrador through his choirs, bands and orchestras? What words shall we use to praise him for the dignity he had brought to our folk songs and traditional music?'[45] The citation went on to suggest that in the future this cultural era would be referred to by Newfoundland's musicians as 'The Rumboldt Years.'[46]

In nineteenth-century annals, there are references to school bands in St John's and in some of the outlying communities in Conception Bay, such as Placentia and Harbour Grace. References to orchestras are fewer. Although the incidence of instrumental ensembles rose around the turn of the century, there is no reason to suggest that there was anything more than casual activity; now and again such groups did exist but not as an integral part of the school instructional program. They served mainly as a musical outlet for those who had their own instruments without necessarily having any real training or skill. More than anything else, the calibre of an ensemble depended upon the availability and resourcefulness of its director, and reliable ones were few in number. A small orchestra was formed at the College of Our Lady of Mercy in 1921. By 1928 it consisted of seventeen violins, five cellos, two pianos, bells, drums, and effects. Even by 1955 this school and St Bride's, Littledale, 'were the only girls' schools in St. John's to have orchestras.'[47] St Bonaventure's College had an orchestra which included brass and woodwinds, and the Mount Cashel Orphanage Boys' School operated a band.

The Salvation Army's inclination toward brass bands provided the springboard from which Eric Abbott, a teacher at the Salvation Army College in St John's, initiated instrumental music in the Protestant schools. Abbott commenced his work on an extra-curricular basis with elementary and secondary students enrolled at this training institution. He used music which the Salvation Army published exclusively for its own brass bands. It was during a period of transition, when Salvation Army students were absorbed into the Avalon Consolidated Schools, that these activities became an integral part of the school program.

Roman Catholic schools, with their long tradition of orchestras, offered instruction in strings, brass, and woodwinds in their classes. But the most striking aspect of their development was the fact that new programs were shaped by influences from abroad. Service bands stationed at United States air force bases in Newfoundland during the Second World War opened the way for a strong American influence. These bases were retained long after the end of the war, so their impact on local musicians was significant, particularly in the performance of contemporary band repertoire and jazz. Eventually, instrumental music in the schools adopted pedagogical patterns and characteristics which were typical of programs in the United States.

As one of the oldest regions of Canada, Newfoundland has sustained strong traditions in music education, especially in vocal music. Folk songs, Tonic Sol-fa methodology, and Gilbert and Sullivan operettas are examples. However, geographical isolation and strong denominational currents in education have produced the marked characteristics which distinguish Newfoundland from other provinces. While having the advantage of a rich folk heritage, Newfoundland remained comparatively undeveloped in some aspects of music education until the 1970s.

Newfoundland was relatively late in establishing competitive music festivals. The first Kiwanis Music Festival in Newfoundland was held in St John's in 1952. Among a succession of others, the Central Newfoundland (Kiwanis) Music Festival (established 1961) in Grand Falls and the Corner Brook Rotary Music Festival (established 1963) have served their communities well. In fact, competitive festivals assumed such significance in the 1950s and 1960s that many people in Newfoundland equated music education with the festival movement. Members of festival committees did much of the prodding in their communities to develop music both in the schools and in the community. This prodding was, in large measure, reinforced by contacts with adjudicators from the mainland, for in the normal course of events committees invited suggestions from adjudicators for improving future festivals. Frequently, the recommendations went beyond the scope of the festivals and addressed in a more fundamental way the role of the schools, the university, and the cultural community. In the formative years, the festival was indispensable in motivating individual players and school and community ensembles. But more recently the standard of musical performance has risen as other organizations and institutions have contributed to the growth and maturity of music education.

Going abroad to complete an education was a long-established custom among the affluent families of Newfoundland. For some, it meant advanced study in England, and for others, enrolment in reputable schools on the mainland or in the eastern United States. This practice had not changed by the end of the Second World War. In local parlance, musicians from 'the Rock' went away to schools such as Mount Allison and Acadia and to Toronto in order to earn music diplomas and degrees. Even though Memorial College assumed full university status in 1949, coincidentally with the union between Newfoundland and Canada, it was another twenty-five years before professional music degrees were available on the Island. In the remaining chapters, in which recent developments in Newfoundland are discussed concurrently with those in the other provinces, it will be seen that Ignatius Rumboldt and Donald Cook have been leaders in shaping many of the institutions and organizations which constitute the present framework for music education in Canada's tenth province.

PART III

NEW DIRECTIONS

12

Diversification in the Postwar Years

Support for Canada's social and cultural institutions moved in a new direction shortly after the close of the Second World War. Fundamental to this change was the emergence of a federal policy designed to strengthen and nurture national development in the arts. Gradually Canadian cultural life was transformed from a state of adolescence to one of growing confidence and maturity. It is unclear whether the arts would have flourished without government involvement, but it is evident that those innovative structures and strategies which eventually coalesced into a national policy were a major force in improving the cultural life of the country.

A ROYAL COMMISSION

The first impulse toward a new national policy took place even before the end of the war. In 1944 a parliamentary committee on postwar reconstruction looked at education and the arts among a broad range of practical concerns for the future. Those concerns, as they pertained to cultural life, were investigated with even greater resolve by the Royal Commission on National Development in the Arts, Letters and Sciences, appointed by the federal government in 1949. Known in some circles as the Cultural Commission, it was chaired by Vincent Massey, chancellor of the University of Toronto and long-time patron of the arts. Its report was a landmark in the history of Canada, if for no other reason than the fact that the recommendations led to the founding of the Canada Council in 1957. The Massey Report defined culture as 'that part of education which enriches the mind and refines the taste,' and continued: 'It is the development of the intelligence through the arts, letters, and sciences. This development, of course, occurs in education. It is continued and it bears fruit during adult life largely through the instruments of general education.'[1] Although commission members recognized education as a provincial jurisdiction, they did not exclude it entirely from their investigation, contending that adult education fell within the terms of reference. Moreover, they regarded the universities as vital participants in the future of Canada:

> The universities are provincial institutions; but they are much more than that. It would be a grave mistake to underestimate or to misconstrue the wider and indeed universal functions of these remarkable institutions. We are not here concerned with them as units in a formal educational system or as representing the final stage of an academic career. We are convinced, however, that we cannot ignore other functions so admirably performed by Canadian universities. They are local centres of education at large and patrons of every movement in aid of the arts, letters and sciences. They also serve the national cause in so many ways, direct and indirect, that theirs must be regarded as the finest of contributions to national strength and unity.[2]

Although commission members were optimistic about artistic achievements in the context of postwar reconstruction, they were troubled by particular trends, including the loss of talented musicians to other countries. They were 'repeatedly told that this exodus would reach catastrophic proportions were it not for the CBC,'[3] which was doing everything it could for Canadian music within its limited resources. After the 450 briefs and public sessions held in major cities, the Royal Commission felt that 'it had heard the voice of Canada,'[4] and in presenting its recommendations declared:

> We have been more and more impressed by the timeliness, indeed by the urgency, of our inquiry. If, at the outset, we were convinced of the importance of what we were to do, as we proceeded this conviction deepened. The work with which we have been entrusted is concerned with nothing less than the spiritual foundations of our national life. Canadian achievement in every field depends mainly on the quality of the Canadian mind and

spirit. This quality is determined by what Canadians think, and think about; by the books they read, the pictures they see and the programmes they hear. These things, whether we call them arts and letters or use other words to describe them, we believe to lie at the roots of our life as a nation.[5]

A major concern arising from this investigation was the increasing influence of American broadcasting, particularly with the advent of television. A belief in the importance of the electronic media was reflected in recommendations that gave the CBC sweeping new powers in broadcasting and communications. Programs featuring Canadian artists and young amateurs became more frequent, including the 'Sunday Concert' series for young soloists performing with orchestra. The CBC Opera Company was founded in 1948 to present opera performances on the 'CBC Wednesday Night' series; the CBC Light Opera Group specialized in Gilbert and Sullivan productions. In addition to its regional radio orchestras, the corporation formed the CBC Symphony Orchestra (1952–64) in Toronto. The CBC Talent Festival, initiated in 1959 and first broadcast in 1960 over both the English and French CBC networks, introduced many promising Canadian musicians to the nation.

A CORNERSTONE OF SUPPORT

Among the imaginative and far-sighted ideas of the Massey Report was that of creating a permanent agency to administer state support in a context that would be free from political interference. For people in the arts it was to be a parallel to the National Research Council, formed in 1916 to serve the needs of the pure sciences. The Canada Council was established as a crown corporation in 1957 with a mandate to encourage and support the arts, humanities, and social sciences through funding programs for artists, scholars, and organizations. The Council 'has defined its mandate broadly. It helps everything from children's theatre to publishing houses, across the whole range of cultural activities.'[6] In performing such essential service, it has assumed an increasing burden within the constraints of inadequate funding, often in the midst of highly political criticism.[7]

The National Film Board of Canada (NFB) is another organization dedicated to the idea that Canadian culture is unique and should be preserved. Created by the federal government following the adoption of the National Film Act in 1939, it was given the mandate 'to produce and distribute films serving the national interest and intended specifically to make Canada better known both to Canadians and to people of other countries.'[8] In 1942 a production and animation department was created with Norman McLaren in charge; he perfected a method of composing music directly on film. The first music director, Louis Applebaum, was appointed that same year. Other music directors included Eugene Kash and Robert Fleming. The production centre moved to Montreal in 1956, and two autonomous sectors, French and English, were created. The NFB has produced a wide variety of works: documentaries, short features, educational films, animated films, and full-length productions. Music has been the subject of many of these films; composers have been hired both on permanent staff and on a contract basis, and Canadian performers have been featured. The NFB's viewing centres and free lending service have made its films available as tools for teaching and learning, and over the years many of these works have been used at both community and school events.

The establishment of agencies to support Canadian culture is the result of government action, but the vision and drive of people in the field provide the stimulus for this action. Marius Barbeau and Sir Ernest MacMillan represent two people with such vision and drive. Barbeau, whose work at the National Museum began in 1911, is considered the father of professional folklore studies in Canada. He influenced the founding of several groups such as the Canadian Folk Music Society (1956), and his research led to the establishment of a significant body of texts and songs, preserved at the Canadian Centre for Folk Culture Studies.[9] Barbeau's collecting, transcribing, and publishing of folk material encouraged others to continue exploration in this field, so an ever-growing resource is available to scholars, educators, musicians, and the community at large.

Throughout the period extending from the deliberations of the national reconstruction committee in 1944 to the creation of the Canada Council in 1957, Sir Ernest MacMillan was the dominant voice within the music community. In response to the Parliamentary Committee on Post-War Reconstruction, he hastily assembled a music committee, comprising 'a group of prominent and mutually accessible musicians – to speak for their confreres throughout the country.'[10] Two years later this committee established itself as the Canadian Music Council and became an even more compelling influence through its written brief to the Massey Commission; those parts of the published report which dealt with music drew heavily, almost word for word, on MacMillan's written submission. The goals of the Canadian Music Council were to coordinate and communicate with the 'various regional and provincial organizations interested in promoting the cause of music in Canada,'[11] and to provide liaison with other countries with respect to Canadian music. It also functioned as the music constituent of the Canadian Arts Council, established in 1945.[12] Sir Ernest MacMillan was chairman of the Canadian Music Council for more than twenty years; John Cozens served as its secretary from 1944 to 1976. From its inception the Canadian Music Council was severely limited to ad hoc sources of funding, and, undoubtedly, members were disappointed that it was not incorporated in 1957 as the 'music arm' of the Canada Council. Although it was destined to be what the EMC calls an 'unofficial voice of Canadian musicians,'[13] the Canadian Music Council's projects and activities were of inestimable value, for its executive remained vigilant in raising the salient issues concerning many aspects of future development. Its literary projects led to several major publications, including the *Canadian Music Journal*, which during its brief existence (1956–62) maintained a high quality of journalism in the field of Canadian music.

The establishment of the Canadian Music Centre (CMCentre) in 1959 was, up to that time, the most ambitious undertaking of the Canadian Music Council. The proposal came originally from the Canadian League of Composers in 1956 and, according to Helmut Kallmann, 'was due largely to a blueprint drawn up by [John] Weinzweig and [John] Beckwith.'[14] It was made possible through funding from the Canada Council and the Composers, Authors, and Publishers Association of Canada. The CMCentre has facilitated the dissemination of Canadian music, both nationally and internationally, through a full gamut of library services, recording projects, and special enterprises. More recently, the establishment of facilities in Montreal, Calgary, and Vancouver has brought Canadian music into closer contact with regional activities. The CMCentre focused attention on the neglect of Canadian music in school programs through a project launched by John Adaskin, executive secretary from 1961 until his death in 1964. Early in his tenure Adaskin began work on what Karen Kieser identifies as 'his own area of highest priority – that of music education.' His interest 'had been piqued by the kind of material his own daughter brought home from her high school music class. He fully realized that Canadian music had to make inroads at the school music level in order to be appreciated by the public later on.'[15] A Canada Council grant was obtained to fund the first stages of the Graded Educational Music Plan, designed, in Coleen Orr's description, 'not only to make composers aware of a source for performance of their works, but also to arouse the interest of progressive music educators in performing more contemporary music, particularly Canadian music.'[16] This goal reflected Adaskin's vision of having 25 per cent Canadian music content in schools within five years. Four months before his death, Adaskin was successful in bringing more than twenty school music teachers and supervisors from the metropolitan Toronto area into contact with fifteen Canadian composers – Harry Somers, John Weinzweig, R. Murray Schafer, and Clermont Pépin, among others – in order to bridge the gulf between teachers and composers. His efforts also led to the commissioning of new works written expressly for school ensembles.

Keith MacMillan, who succeeded Adaskin in 1964, maintained the momentum of the Adaskin project by challenging the Canadian Music Educators' Association (CMEA) to share responsibility for its continuation and expansion. MacMillan organized a second seminar in 1965, at which time the project was renamed in Adaskin's memory. As part of MacMillan's challenge to music educators and musicians in general, he initiated a special policy conference in 1967, which was open to all interested persons involved in music. Invited speakers included John Davies, assistant director of the Contemporary Music Project in the United States, and Peter Maxwell Davies, an English composer involved in innovative teaching in a Gloucestershire grammar school. This three-day meeting gave delegates an opportunity to hear reports of the 'composer in the classroom' activities and to discuss the future of the project. A recurring point of discussion at this conference was the need for greater use of creative approaches in the classroom which would help develop the full potential of students and also help sensitize both students and teachers to music written in a contemporary idiom. Several individuals have considered this emphasis on creativity to be one of the most important. George Proctor states, 'The most original contribution that Canada has made to music education has been through the work of R. Murray Schafer, whose approach emphasizes original creative work in developing musical sensitivity and the use of all types of sound, including environmental ones, as material for musical organization.' Schafer has written extensively on this subject; his 'books (The Composer in the Classroom, Toronto, 1965, and others) deal with the young and musically unsophisticated, and bypass the traditional theoretical approaches.'[17]

Since the beginnings of the original Graded Educational Music Plan in the 1960s, much effort has gone into the selecting and grading of repertoire appropriate for school groups and the commissioning of works suitable for young performers. Although there was a period of inertia following the 1967 policy conference, Keith MacMillan's challenge to CMEA finally resulted in the appointment of Patricia Shand of the University of Toronto as coordinator of the project in 1973. Responsibility was henceforth shared by the CMEA and the CMCentre. One tangible result of this cooperation has been the publication of Shand's resource aid, *Canadian Music: A Selective Guidelist for Teachers*.[18] Attention has also been given to the selecting and grading of contemporary repertoire suitable for use by private studio teachers. This was undertaken by members of the local branch of the Ontario Registered Music Teachers' Association, who established the Contemporary Music Showcase Association in 1967 and held their first week-long festival three years later. The festival has continued as a biennial event dealing exclusively with Canadian music; a graded syllabus of contemporary music is published along with each of the festival programs.[19]

The success of the 'composer in the classroom' aspect of the John Adaskin Project encouraged other agencies to bring professional performers – musicians, dancers, and actors – directly into the schools. One of the most successful of these endeavours has been the Prologue to the Performing Arts, founded in Toronto in 1966. It was meant to serve as a liaison between boards of education and the Canadian Opera Company, the National Ballet of Canada, and the Young People's Theatre and 'to present in intermediate schools live productions planned jointly by the performing companies, the prologue organization, and the education authorities.'[20] Although artists from other provinces were sometimes employed, the actual performances have been limited to Ontario. In the 1970s a similar agency, Educanima, was established in Quebec.

The idea of 'artists in residence' has been used to good effect in a number of different situations. During the 1969–70 academic year, the Festival Singers of Canada, directed by Elmer Iseler, was the 'choir in residence' for the Scarborough board of education, offering six workshop sessions spaced throughout the year. Professional artists with an interest in teaching have also worked with general music classes on a more long-term basis – as in the case of the bass player Gary Karr, who taught in Halifax schools in the early 1970s. Musicians have been involved in the Creative Artists in the School (CAIS) program sponsored by the Ontario Arts Council. According to Orr, however, 'because of the nature of the program, which neither encourages performance nor pedagogical activities, CAIS programs have had less impact in music than in other fields.'[21]

AN ERA OF OPPORTUNITY

The development of audiences to appreciate and support the arts in Canada became a major concern in the postwar years. Jeunesses musicales du Canada (JMC) has been an effective force in this regard. The parent project, founded in Brussels during the Second World War, developed into a world-wide movement that reached Canada in 1949, largely through the efforts of Gilles Lefebvre in Quebec. At a special organizational meeting convened in St-Hyacinthe, Lefebvre suggested 'linking all the existing societies devoted to cultural activities among young people and submitted a plan of action calling for concert tours, new lines of administrative co-operation, scholarships, a summer camp, a permanent home, and exchanges between young performers.' Consequently, 'an association called Helicon was founded, comprising the musical clubs of the Quebec towns of Grand-Mère, Mont-Laurier, St-Hyacinthe, Shawinigan, Sherbrooke, and Trois-Rivières.'[22] This group affiliated with the international Jeunesses musicales organization and held its first national congress in Trois-Rivières in 1950. Lefebvre was elected president for a four-year term and in 1953 became director general of the Canadian organization, Jeunesses musicales du Canada.

In addition to the sponsorship of tours and international exchanges of young artists, one of JMC's initiatives was the establishment in 1951 of a summer camp, which has developed into the JMC Orford Art Centre in Quebec's Eastern Townships. Other activities have included the publication of a journal, the sponsorship of national competitions, the production of recordings, and, more recently, the introduction of workshops for schools. Gilles Lefebvre also participated in the world-wide organization of Jeunesses musicales. An international congress was hosted by Canada in Montreal in 1955 and again twelve years later, during Expo 67, when JMC was in charge of the pavilion 'Man and His Music.' During this congress, an international orchestra of young musicians from many countries was organized; led by Zubin Mehta, these young people performed Beethoven's Symphony No. 9 at Place des Arts. Three years later the Jeunesses musicales World Orchestra was created on the initiative of Gilles Lefebvre and JMC.

The operation of JMC has expanded beyond Quebec. In 1955 Sir Ernest MacMillan commented, 'Les Jeunesses Musicales has of recent years succeeded, through its international affiliations, in effecting exchanges between Canadian and foreign artists on a more equitable basis, but its activities are at the moment largely confined to French-speaking Canada.'[23] A decade later, however, the situation had changed, for his son Keith observed: 'Almost seven hundred concerts and recitals were given during the 1966–67 season to young audiences totalling close to 90,000 in cities across the country from St. John's, Newfoundland, to Vancouver, British Columbia ... Although admittedly Les Jeunesses Musicales du Canada originates in the Province of Quebec and is most active in French Canada, a healthy percentage of its membership is English-speaking. The organization has apparently never felt the necessity of adopting an English title.'[24] Arnold Walter wrote in that same year: 'Whether competitive festivals can or cannot help us to build the right kind of audiences – Les Jeunesses Musicales certainly do. Their work has been called "the most important thing that has happened in Canada (in the field of music) because it is aimed at the next generation of musicians and listeners. It is Canada's musical future."'[25]

A host of music competitions was initiated in the postwar decades. In 1961 JMC launched a national competition for young pianists, and during 1967 it organized three national competitions for performers as well as an international composition contest. The Winnipeg-based Federation of Canadian Music Festivals (founded 1926) expanded to include eastern provinces and was formally constituted in 1949. It has grown from a membership of nineteen festivals in 1950 to a total of 225 in 1980. In 1967 this federation, with financial assistance from the Centennial Commission, collaborated with the Quebec Music Festivals in sponsoring a national festival in Saint John, NB. This event was not continued, but both sponsoring bodies later established independent national competitions. In 1970 the Canadian Music Competitions was founded with headquarters in Montreal. Claude Deschamps, who had directed the Quebec Music Festivals association since its inception a decade earlier, became managing director of this successor to the Quebec group. Two years later the Federation of Canadian Music Festivals initiated the National Competitive Festival of Music, held annually at the Canadian National Exhibition in Toronto with the cooperation of the Canadian Bureau for the Advancement of Music and financial support from the Canadian Imperial Bank of Commerce.

Recently, this festival has been held in a different part of the country each year.

A number of projects have been initiated by private teachers, both provincially and nationally. As early as 1942 the Canadian Federation of Music Teachers' Associations (CFMTA) established a Young Artists Series to provide touring experience for promising performers. In the early years this project was confined to western Canada. Canada Music Week was established by CFMTA in 1960 'to support Canadian composers and performers, to introduce Canadian contemporary music to students, and to sponsor competitions for student composers.'[26] This special week was also designed to acknowledge and bring public attention to the role of the private music teacher in Canada.

MUSIC IN THE COMMUNITY

Many people across the country, professional musicians as well as talented amateurs, have influenced the development of community music-making in their own regions. Lyell Gustin in Saskatchewan, Ignatius Rumboldt in Newfoundland, and Ira Dilworth in British Columbia serve as examples. In Quebec, George Little concerned himself with many aspects of music; one effort was his work in the formation of CAMMAC (Canadian Amateur Musicians/Musiciens amateurs du Canada).

In 1953 George Little and his brother, Carl, along with their wives, Madeleine and Frances, founded the Otter Lake Music Centre northwest of Montreal. Their purpose was to establish a place where amateurs interested in group music-making, instrumental or choral, could gather together in a holiday atmosphere. The camp operated for several weeks each summer, offering instruction in solfège and choral singing; recorder playing was also available, under the direction of Mario Duschenes. Concerts by professional musicians as well as those by amateur performers were included in the camp program. The name was later changed to CAMMAC, and the association began to function as a non-profit organization on a year-round basis. Winter meetings held in Montreal featured sight-reading of choral works such as Bach cantatas. As membership grew, branches were formed in other regions of the country, and CAMMAC established a music lending library for amateur musicians. By 1962 the offerings of the summer camp included recorder playing, chamber music, madrigal singing, folk dancing, and French and English conversation, as well as instruction in voice, viol, classical guitar, and the Orff approach. The camp was later moved to Lake MacDonald. A special feature since 1957 has been the addition of a summer program for children aged four to twelve, as well as classes for the entire family. Several guided tours to ISME congresses were organized by CAMMAC under the direction of George and Madeleine Little.

Not all those who have influenced community music have had the training and breadth of experience of George Little, nor have they all been native born. In New Brunswick, David Thomson, a musician with very little formal training, was influential in awakening an interest in music in several areas of the province. Thomson's family had moved from their native Scotland to Saint John when David was a young man. Although he worked in several office jobs, Thomson spent his evenings and week-ends pursuing his first love, music. He conducted church choirs, played for silent movies, led a male quartet, and formed his own group, the Carriden Choir. In his choral work he was inspired by his uncle, Sir Hugh Roberton, conductor of the Glasgow Orpheus Choir; Roberton visited the Thomson family during his trips to Canada as an adjudicator.

Shortly before the Second World War, weekly sing-songs led by Thomson were established at the Capitol Theatre in Saint John. These events became very popular; people travelled from various parts of the province to participate. During the war Thomson was appointed district supervisor of the Canadian Legion War Services for New Brunswick to provide recreational activities for servicemen. In 1946 he was approached by Dr Fletcher Peacock, director of educational services for the province, concerning a project to help further the cause of music instruction in the schools, particularly in the rural areas. Thus it was that the 'Let New Brunswick Sing' project, sponsored by Kiwanis Clubs throughout the province, was initiated. For the next three years Thomson visited many communities, giving music instruction for school children during the day and meeting with parents and school officials in the evenings at special 'community gatherings.' He recalled:

I would talk about the importance of music in every-day life and in education in particular; there, I would demonstrate the joy to be gained from the making of music by having everyone engage in rousing community singing; encouraging soloists, duetists, trios and quartettes to take part in the programme. In some areas, instrumentalists were unearthed. Old and young men would arrive, vainly trying to hide the fiddles and guitars they carried; shyly they would conceal them under chairs and then, gradually, they would be coaxed into taking part and *then* the hall would fairly jump with the rhythm of country music provided by natural musicians playing violins, guitars, harmonicas.[27]

Thomson also spoke to service clubs, home and school associations, teachers' groups, and women's institutes. As a result of this effort and a great deal of lobbying by various groups and individuals, David Thomson was appointed as New Brunswick's first supervisor of music in 1949.

Summer Programs

Summer activities for both young people and adults have increased remarkably in the years following the Second World War. The programs at Banff and at the Royal Conservatory, as well as courses for teachers at several universities and normal schools, continued to attract students each season. During the 1950s, summer music camps designed primarily for young people were initiated in other parts of the country. In addition to JMC at Mount Orford in the Eastern Townships and CAMMAC in the Laurentians, these included the International Music Camp on the border between Manitoba and North Dakota (1956), the Mount Allison Instrumental Music Camp in Sackville, NB (1959), and the Okanagan Summer School of the Arts in Penticton, BC (1960). Sometimes music was only one element of a wider arts program. At the Tatamagouche Festival of the Arts in Nova Scotia, musical performances were a vital feature of the program from its inception in 1956. A few years later, the Nova Scotia Music Educators' Association sponsored a music tent at the festival as part of an expanded component of instruction for children.

As music camps and summer schools grew in number and in size, there was a variety of sponsoring agencies. Most projects have been privately funded, but in some cases governments have provided financial assistance. This has been so in both Saskatchewan and Alberta. The Saskatchewan Arts Board (established 1948) subsidized numerous projects and celebrations, among them the Saskatchewan School of the Arts, founded in 1962 at the Echo Valley Centre near Fort Qu'Appelle. Its counterpart in Alberta, under the sponsorship of Alberta Culture, dates back to 1960. These summer camps were held in various places in Alberta until 1967, at which time they became permanently located at Camrose.

In 1960 a special 'seasonal school' was created for young Canadian instrumentalists. Established as the National Youth Orchestra (NYO), it has evolved into an organization which operates independently and which, according to the EMC, 'despite the name "orchestra," is in fact a summer school for the intensive conditioning of talented instrumentalists in the techniques and traditions of ensemble playing.'[28] It has received funding from both federal and provincial governments. The NYO was formed as an orchestra workshop in the summer of 1960 in Stratford, Ontario, with James McIntosh as manager and Walter Susskind and Harman Haakman as co-directors. Players were auditioned from across the country. A second training session was held during Christmas week of the same year, leading to the debut of the NYO on 31 December 1960 at Massey Hall, with Victor Feldbrill and Sir Wilfrid Pelletier as conductors. The NYO has presented concerts in major cities in Canada and has performed in the United States and Europe. 'Besides winning critical and public acclaim, the NYO has contributed to the development of a generation of Canadian musicians.'[29] Its success has undoubtedly strengthened the resolve of provincial and city groups to form youth orchestras in their own communities.

Independent Schools and Community Projects

In addition to the expansion of summer programs and special opportunities for private instruction, there has also been an increase in the number of community music schools. Community and provincial arts councils have sometimes been leaders in the establishment of these institutions, as was the case with one of the earliest of such groups: 'Indicative of a new emphasis on education in the broadest sense was the founding in 1946 of the Community Arts Council of Vancouver, with Ira Dilworth as its first president. Although not an educational body, the council, as a source of well researched ideas, encouraged ... the opening in 1969 of the Community Music School of Greater Vancouver.'[30] This school has promoted several new approaches to music teaching, including that of Suzuki, which became known in Canada in the 1960s. The Suzuki approach to violin teaching, developed by the Japanese violinist and educator Shinichi Suzuki, was introduced to western Canada by Thomas Rolston, who founded the Society for Talent Education in Edmonton following a trip to Japan in 1964. In 1965 John Kendall, who had been instrumental in bringing the Suzuki approach to the United States, gave two sessions at the CMEA convention held in Calgary. That same year programs were started by Claude

Letourneau in Quebec City and by Jean Cousineau in Montreal. Cousineau had visited Japan to consult Suzuki about the publication of a teaching manual; upon his return he founded l'École des petits violons in Montreal. In 1967 the women's committee of the Hamilton Philharmonic Orchestra established the Philharmonic Children's School as a centennial project. Directed by Marta Hidy, this school offered training in violin and cello incorporating the principles of the Suzuki method. Suzuki programs have been established in various other parts of the country, and some have also offered flute and piano instruction. Suzuki visited Canada on several occasions: Montreal in 1966, London and Winnipeg in 1972, and Edmonton and Montreal in 1977.

The institutional framework for music education became increasingly complex as professional musicians and community groups felt the need for specialized teaching beyond what was available in the public schools. With each succeeding decade, more conservatory-type schools have been providing studio instruction and ensemble experience, particularly at the preparatory levels. This growth has occurred not only in metropolitan areas but also in the smaller cities, including several in remote regions. Some schools were initiated by local orchestras or parents' organizations; some were sponsored by private academies or church groups; others have been administered by regional cultural centres or community colleges as a function of their mandate to serve local needs; and a few have been developed in cooperation with the public school system. Although the proliferation of specialized schools has improved opportunities across a wide spectrum of interests, it has nonetheless led to a tangled web of competing programs, many of which are struggling to survive in the face of inadequate resources and lack of funding. Apart from the conservatoire system in the province of Quebec, there is no single vision of how this realm of music education should be structured and coordinated in an orderly way, or how independent non-profit institutions should be reconciled with the funded programs of the public schools and universities.

An Emerging Music Industry

The music publishing industry in Canada has grown extensively since the Second World War. Several people associated with music publishing firms have taken personal interest in the educational process and have played active roles in both community and school music. Notable in this regard have been Gordon V. Thompson and John Bird of the

Thompson Music Company and C.F. Thiele, Fred Moogk, Frank Daley, and Howard Underwood of the Waterloo Music Company. The Frederick Harris Music Company in Oakville, Ontario, has been particularly supportive of the private piano teacher and the church musician. In the west, Empire Music Publishers in New Westminster, BC, began to issue educational materials in the mid-1950s; they have since then expanded their operation by opening branches in Ontario and the United States. Music schools directly associated with the music industry have been established in centres throughout the country, most of them locally operated. A few, however, such as those run by Yamaha, are international.

CENTENNIAL COMMISSIONS AND CELEBRATIONS

As the country emerged from the Second World War, a period of affluence together with the heightening debate over biculturalism caused many people to reflect upon the nature of the Canadian experience. The spirit of this new nationalism found expression in the centennial celebrations of 1967, which, in the words of Proctor, 'brought forth a flurry of activity at both the local and the national levels, not the least of which were many musical presentations, new concert halls, and new works by Canadian composers ... For six months Expo 67 in Montreal served as the focal point for performances and commissions through its World Festival of Music and the Canadian Pavilion's Festival Katimavik, while the Centennial Commission's Festival Canada stimulated Canadian music throughout the country.'[31] Instruments of official support for the arts reinforced the insistent efforts of spokespersons and of local, regional, and national groups who were too vigorous to be ignored. Indeed, as J.L. Granatstein and others observe, 'the developments on so many fronts seemed to mark the passing of a colonial and derivative culture and to portend the emergence of a culture that would be uniquely and distinctively Canadian.'[32]

The establishment of a music division as a separate branch of the National Library of Canada was yet another sign of progress. This facility was organized in 1970 under the direction of Helmut Kallmann, Canada's foremost historian in the field of Canadian music. In the short span of a decade Kallmann developed this facility into a major repository for music materials of Canadian interest: imprints, literature, sound recordings, manuscript collections, and bibliographic tools. It provides a full range of services to musicians and scholars, including liaison with other libraries and resource centres. The prominence of the music division has been enhanced by Kallmann's own career as librarian, author, and archivist. Before his appointment to the National Library he had been with the CBC for twenty years, and from 1962 until 1970 was supervisor of the CBC Toronto music library. Kallmann's *A History of Music in Canada 1534–1914*, published in 1960 by the University of Toronto Press, was the first authoritative account of Canada's musical heritage. He has also been prolific as an author of articles, essays, and bibliographic works and has spearheaded *The Canadian Musical Heritage* project.[33] Kallmann's achievement in preparing the *Encyclopedia of Music in Canada*, with co-editors Gilles Potvin and Kenneth Winters, marked a high point in the nation's quest for cultural identity.

The erudite interests of Kallmann have been shared by the composer John Beckwith, whose creative work, music criticism, and scholarship have fostered a growing sense of independence in Canada's musical development. Beckwith's impact on music education can be attributed to his teaching and administrative leadership at the University of Toronto's Faculty of Music, where from 1970 to 1977 he served as dean and in 1984 was appointed as the Jean A. Chalmers Professor of Canadian Music and founding director of the Institute for Canadian Music. Together with Keith MacMillan, Beckwith edited *Contemporary Canadian Composers*. In his diverse roles with the CBC, the CMCentre, and the University of Ottawa, MacMillan has also been vigilant in pursuing projects of national concern. Kallmann, Beckwith, and Mac-Millan, regarded by many as the leading exponents of music in Canadian society, have provided insight and initiative in working with organizations and professional groups which have championed the cause of the performing arts.

The developments outlined in this chapter reveal how the diversification of activities in the arts brought about profound changes in the postwar years. Many of these changes were accomplished through institutions and instructional programs which hitherto had been unavailable or had been left to chance. For a relatively young nation it had been a coming of age; the success of Expo 67 and of a multitude of centennial projects symbolized an escalating pride in Canada. Such idealism was needed as the high hopes of the 1960s faded during the 1970s, a decade in which economic constraints hampered cultural activities almost as much as earlier prosperity had fostered them.

13

The Evolution of Vocal Programs
in the Schools

Music in Canadian elementary schools did not change significantly in content or approach in the years immediately following the Second World War. Programs were expanded to reach students not only in the urban centres but in rural areas as well. Educational authorities at all levels were forced to deal with the increasing enrolment created by the postwar 'baby boom'; they responded by providing additional summer instruction for teachers, in-service training, and assistance from individuals with musical expertise. In larger centres music supervisors worked with classroom teachers or with music specialists, when these were available, in an attempt to have elementary students participate in some form of musical activity. Massed singing in the annual spring concert with its 'cast of thousands' performing in one large auditorium became the trademark of many music education programs across the country.[1]

Leadership in elementary school music was usually provided either by those who held supervisory positions, with responsibilities for an entire board or city-wide system, or by those who were appointed to teacher training institutions. Some of the leaders held their posts as a result of successful teaching careers in the classroom; others were appointed because of their musical background and training. The question of who would do the teaching, music specialist or classroom teacher, was one of the most pervasive issues. There was often more than one system in operation, and rural areas differed greatly from urban centres. Even where there was a desire to have music taught by a trained musician, the situation usually necessitated the use of classroom teachers to at least some extent because of the lack of qualified specialists. Throughout the country supervisors provided extensive in-service training within their boards and also helped to design provincial curricula. Beth Douglas in Manitoba, Cynthia Downe in Alberta, and Frances Tyrrell in Nova Scotia serve as examples.

Before the Second World War, Ontario was the only province which had a government official responsible for music in the schools. The appointment of Roy Fenwick in 1935 did not cause other provinces to take similar action, and it was not until the late 1940s that similar positions were created in two more provinces, Saskatchewan and New Brunswick. Rj Staples was appointed special music consultant for the Saskatchewan Department of Education in 1945. Four years later he was given the position of full-time provincial supervisor of music; he served in this capacity until 1969. David Thomson became the first supervisor of music for the province of New Brunswick in 1949. His post became part of the physical education and recreation branch of the department of education. Thomson held this position until 1965; following his retirement Gloria Richard was appointed to the provincial music post.[2] In the other two Maritime provinces, music supervisors were not appointed until the 1960s. In 1961 Christopher Gledhill, a British organist who had been teaching in Montreal, was named supervisor of music for Prince Edward Island. Three years later, Nova Scotia hired another British musician, Peter Hinkley, as the first 'music inspector.' He was succeeded in 1967 by Paul Murray, a New Brunswick native who had served as organist/choirmaster and music teacher in both Saint John and the metropolitan Toronto area. In 1965 the Montreal musician George Little became the first head of the music division for Quebec's newly created ministry of education. Four years later, following the publication of the Rioux Report on the state of the arts in Quebec, Little was appointed head of the arts division for the ministry of education. Newfoundland appointed its first provincial music consultant in 1970, when Sister Paschal Carroll of the Presentation order was named to the post. Thus, by 1970, provincial directors of music had been appointed in all Canadian provinces except British Columbia, Alberta, and Manitoba. However, Ontario closed its Music Branch in 1965 as part of a major restructuring within the ministry of education, and in a more decentralized system, the ministry established regional offices.[3]

Classroom Methods and Materials

The most common approach in elementary school music during the 1940s and 1950s was some version of the song method, with emphasis on the enjoyment of singing. Many educators continued to stress the importance of music reading, but it was not unusual for teachers to incorporate a variety of activities including listening, movement, and the playing of classroom instruments. Roy Fenwick's *High Road of Song* maintained its stronghold as an approved music series in Ontario for many years. Fenwick's second edition, *The New High Road of Song*, with its two volumes of sight-singing exercises, was adopted in several other provinces, including New Brunswick, Nova Scotia, and English-speaking Quebec. The teacher's manual for this series frequently served as the outline for the music curriculum. Harry Hill's *Singing Period* continued to be used in such widespread regions as the Maritimes and British Columbia, and *The Music Hour* also retained its popularity.

Although several music books in use at this time came from Ontario, educators in other parts of the country also published instructional material. Ethel Kinley's *Manitoba School Song Book* went through fourteen reprintings between 1940 and 1964. It was also published under three other titles: *A Song Book for Saskatchewan Schools*, *A Song Book for Ontario Schools*, and *A Song Book for Schools*. The contents were the same in all four books, and they were used from coast to coast. Other teachers in western Canada associated with publications include Burton Kurth and Mildred McManus in Vancouver, Lola MacQuarrie and Beth Douglas in Winnipeg, and Rj Staples in Saskatchewan.

Staples advocated numerous activities in his 'music exploration' courses. In addition to classroom singing, these included the use of classroom instruments, particularly the flutophone, recorder, and autoharp; he also placed great emphasis on music appreciation lessons. Staples made extensive use of radio broadcasts in order to reach students in the rural areas, and through a special cooperative arrangement these broadcasts were used in all four western provinces. He produced a series of school broadcasts for which he prepared teachers' booklets and recordings; for non-unison choral numbers there were separate recordings of each part as well as a recording of all parts sung together. Staples was the inventor of several 'teaching devices and curiosities,' including 'a scale and chord pattern ruler, a chord indicator, and a record indicator ... which could locate and isolate any particular selection on a recording (78rpm).' He also designed a simplified cello 'to encourage children's interest in string music.'[4] Staples had a flair for mounting spectacular productions, never missing an opportunity to open new channels for music education in the province. In 1955 he produced the pageant 'Salute to Saskatchewan' to celebrate the Golden Jubilee. For this event he compiled the songbook *Saskatchewan Sings of Jubilee*, representing 'the various ethnic groups who had contributed to the development of the province.'[5] Staples taught these songs over a weekly radio program and incorporated them into his pageant. Reportedly, an estimated hundred thousand people were united in this celebration broadcast, which was carried across the province. An even more elaborate program was telecast for the Diamond Jubilee in 1965. On that occasion he also featured a provincial school orchestra. Again, students, assembled in their local areas, 'simultaneously participated by singing and dancing ... through the synchronization of their television sets.'[6]

Instructional books were also prepared by educators in the eastern part of the country. Gifford Mitchell, supervisor of music for the Montreal Protestant school board, assisted in the compilation of the three-volume set *Songs of Praise for Schools*, 'prepared by direction of the Protestant School Board of Greater Montreal in fulfillment of an obligation to provide religious instruction in the schools under their care.'[7] New Brunswick musicians R.C. Bayley, Janis Kalnins, Douglas Major, and David Thomson produced a volume entitled *Songs for Junior High*[8] which was adopted as the grade seven music text in New Brunswick.

In describing elementary music texts used in Ontario between 1935 and 1959, June Countryman notes that 'the activity in ethnomusicology in Canada had virtually no effect on school music materials up to this point.' She cites two major reasons: 'a lack of awareness on the part of educators of the importance of using indigenous folk materials in music education, and a lack of involvement of school music publishers with ethnomusicological materials.'[9] One exception was the Waterloo Music Company's *Folk Songs of Canada*, which Richard Johnston selected, arranged, and edited in collaboration with Edith Fowke.[10] Published in 1954, this was one of the first folk-music publications to enjoy widespread use by music educators.

Several music series prepared especially for Canadian schools appeared in the late 1950s and the 1960s, reflecting a change in focus and an expansion of musical activities in the classroom. While the ability to read music was still regarded as important, it was now only one component of an increasingly diversified program. 'Concern for the tastes of young people was taken into consideration ... Beautifully illustrated, easy-to-read materials taught them about the structure and theory of music by encouraging exploration, creativity, and problem-solving.'[11] In addition to *Songs for Today*,[12] these series included *Songtime*,[13] *Basic Goals in Music*,[14] *Music for Young Canada*,[15] and *Music 7* and *Music 8*.[16] Some Canadian works, both folk songs and new compositions, were featured; their inclusion signals the beginnings of a concern to have more repertoire drawn from Canada's traditions and culture.

Developments in the United States continued to have a strong influence on Canadian programs. With the exception of Ontario, which had a stricter policy regarding Canadian texts, the use of American instructional materials was widespread. Most programs made use of bright, attractive students' texts, detailed teachers' manuals, and good-quality recordings. To a great extent, these materials determined the pedagogy adopted in music classrooms because teachers embraced what Countryman calls the American ideal of 'multi-faceted, enjoyment-oriented programs with life-embracing correlations and individual problem-solving experiences as important features.'[17] Canadian supervisors and teachers absorbed the ideas which they encountered in summer schools in the United States or at MENC conferences. Moreover, a steady stream of American music educators came to give workshops in Canada, sometimes sponsored by teachers' organizations and sometimes by music companies promoting new publications. Canadian editions of some American series were prepared, but the changes consisted primarily in the substitution of suitable patriotic selections.

There were major changes in the philosophy of music education in the United States during the 1960s. According to Countryman, the Yale Seminar in 1963 and the Tanglewood Symposium in 1967 'provided forums for dialogue where leaders in the field of music education articulated a discontent with the quality of current programs. Influenced by the educational theories of Jerome Bruner, these leaders argued that the elements of music must become the focus for instruction.'[18] Leaders in American music education began to advocate a more conceptual approach focusing on the understanding of musical elements as a means of developing aesthetic sensitivity. In the context of these reforms, the principles of comprehensive musicianship were enthusiastically endorsed by the majority of Canadian music educators. This led to an increased emphasis on the interrelationship of the arts, and the choice of repertoire became more global, to include song materials from all eras of Western music as well as selections from various world musics, North American and British popular music among them. With the advent of open area classrooms, music educators were faced with yet another challenge, one which brought about an increase in individualized instruction. Subsequently, a number of schools created special 'music corners' in classrooms and resource centres.

Music for French-speaking Students

A number of publications for French-speaking students featuring materials from their own traditions appeared during the 1950s. Most of these were volumes of songs for classroom use, produced at minimal cost and thus of a more modest appearance than many of the casebound books produced in English. Additional volumes in the series entitled *La Bonne Chanson* were published in St-Hyacinthe, Quebec, for French-speaking students; they were also used in Acadian schools in the Maritimes. The first volumes in this series were published by Père Charles-Émile Gadbois following the 1937 French Language Congress in Quebec City, 'which emphasized the value of song as a vehicle for the preservation of culture and language.'[19] Recordings were issued to accompany the song albums, and a radio program featuring this material was produced in Montreal from 1939 to 1952. Materials were also prepared by les Sœurs de la Congrégation de Notre-Dame in Montreal, and special solfège books were published by l'École Vincent-d'Indy in Montreal.

A series of songbooks for the French-speaking schools in Ontario, entitled *Mon école chante*,[20] was prepared by Joseph Beaulieu. Although he was a member of the Music Branch under G. Roy Fenwick, Beaulieu operated out of an office in North Bay, devoting his efforts to northern Ontario and the Ottawa region. Despite the appointment of Beaulieu, the French-speaking schools have not had the same benefits as their English counterparts. Trudy Bradley observes, 'The Music Branch was the only area of the Department of Education which was responsible for its subject from kindergarten to grade XIII in both the French and

English sectors, yet when Beaulieu retired in 1965, his position was not filled by a Francophone.'[21]

Education in French-speaking Quebec did not change as quickly as it had in other parts of the country. Although vocational and commercial training were available to students, most French-speaking education officials in the province were still following the model of classical education offered in France, and it was not until the 1960s that educational developments taking place on the North American continent had any significant impact on the schools of French Canada. The lack of a well-developed music program in the French Catholic system was recognized by some in the province, who brought it to the attention of the CMEA. The minutes of the national executive meetings held in Vancouver in 1962 record that a letter was sent by CMEA to the secretary of the Catholic Committee in the Department of Public Instruction urging that music instruction be given more attention in the elementary schools under their jurisdiction.[22] The revised program of studies set by the department of education the following year contained the statement 'Music will be taught from Grade I to XII inclusive in all French-language schools of the Province.'[23]

The implementation of the Parent Commission's recommendations following the release of its report in 1964 brought about major changes in Quebec's educational system. The jurisdiction of the church in educational matters was greatly diminished, and there was less emphasis on a classical education. An entire chapter of this commission's report was devoted to the topic of musical training. It cited the need for many changes and recommended the appointment of a provincial coordinator of music. When George Little was appointed to this government post in 1965, he became the architect of a transformation in music education, particularly in the French Catholic schools. A few years later the Rioux Report on the state of the arts in Quebec advocated further changes in music education.

Music was valued as a vehicle for cultural expression among French-speaking Acadians in the Maritimes. Chorale de l'Université St-Joseph, founded by Père Léandre Brault in 1946 'with the aim of developing interest in Gregorian chant,'[24] became known throughout the country and won the Lincoln Trophy on four separate occasions during the 1950s. In 1953 Père Brault left for Montreal to help organize a choir school founded to serve the needs of St Joseph's Oratory; he was succeeded by Père Roland Soucie and later by Père Neil Michaud.[25] Educational opportunities for young Acadian women improved in the years following the Second World War. To the convent schools were added special classical colleges for girls, founded in the 1940s and 1950s. Several institutions became well known for music, particularly École Notre-Dame-d'Acadie in Moncton, operated by les Sœurs de Notre-Dame-du-Sacré-Cœur, a French-speaking order established in Memramcook in 1924. The choir from this school, directed by Sœur Marie-Lucienne, received national acclaim; they were awarded both the Lincoln and Mathieson trophies on a number of occasions, and they represented eastern Canada at the first Canadian Music Educators' Association meeting in Toronto in 1959.

Music instruction also became more readily available for young Acadians as programs in the public schools expanded. Several school groups which were formed for the Acadian nationalism celebrations held throughout the Maritimes during the 1950s stayed together as performing organizations, and their doing so helped to preserve the heritage of folk material and also to establish a strong choral tradition in Acadian communities. One example was Chorale Beauséjour, a girls' choir formed in Moncton in the 1950s. In 1969, Sœur Gallant, the conductor of this ensemble, founded Chorale d'Aberdeen, which later changed its name to les Jeunes Chanteurs d'Acadie and earned an international reputation. Classroom music instruction in the French-speaking schools also increased. A school broadcast series for French-speaking students was prepared by Sœur Marie-Lucienne in Moncton. The method of music instruction developed by Maurice Martenot in France, employing the use of fixed doh, has been used in many of the French-language schools in the region.

School Music in the Northwest Territories

Apart from singing activities in church-operated schools, music instruction was neglected in the education of native peoples in the Northwest Territories. A House of Commons Standing Committee on Indian affairs reporting in 1971 on the state of education concluded that the schools have tended to emphasize and propagate values evolved by the middle-class majority of the south and, even more regrettable, that the system has denied native peoples the possibility of nurturing their own culture. The National Indian Brotherhood responded in 1973 and, among other recommendations, requested greater opportunity for native peoples to make their own decisions. Historically, general education in the Northwest Territories had been left to a loosely organized collection of public and private schools under the auspices of churches, local governments, commercial companies, and the federal government. Not until 1955 was a program of formal schooling introduced. In 1968 a new department of education was established. The first elementary school curriculum was distributed to all territorial schools in 1971. This document was generated in the territories with the express purpose of utilizing materials which relate to a northern environment. To arrest the one-way process of acculturation which had characterized schooling in the past, officials recognized that curricula should be revised to provide relevant courses in native culture, music, and art. Educational leaders also acknowledged that special training was needed for those instructing Indian and Inuit children, including a program to develop native teachers. These new policies, reinforced by recent commitments to the preservation of aboriginal languages and cultures, augur well for the future.

FESTIVALS

Both competitive and non-competitive festivals have motivated and challenged young musicians in Canada. During the postwar years the competitive festival movement grew in the eastern provinces as it had done earlier in the west, providing an incentive for many school programs to remain performance-oriented. Numerous solo entries, classroom choirs, choral speech ensembles, and rhythm bands were included, as well as highly selective choral and instrumental groups of various ages and abilities. By the early 1950s all four Atlantic provinces had established provincial festivals as annual events. In 1957 the Halifax Music Festival, which had been suspended during the Second World War, had a total of 15,000 entries in 347 classes. Over 40,000 young musicians were involved in the Quebec Music Festivals in 1968. Similarly, in Newfoundland, where competitive music festivals were initiated with the support of the Kiwanis Club, the number of competitors in the St John's Festival grew from 1400 in 1952 to more than 12,000 in 1974.

Non-competitive festivals also grew in number, especially in rural areas. A 'Little Festival' movement was initiated by David Thomson in New Brunswick shortly after his appointment as provincial supervisor of music. 'They would start as one-day events and invariably grow to two-day events the second year ... after the second festival, the local parents would start to agitate for a music teacher in the school and, as always, when the people *want* something, the local school board listened.'[26] Thomson estimated that approximately fifty thousand school children participated annually in these events.

Saskatchewan had a unique form of festivals. The idea was developed through the efforts of Rj Staples, who had strong negative feelings toward competitive activities. He organized 'Music Meets' – usually held in the spring – which involved both classroom performances and massed singing. These events flourished in the rural communities, whereas the competitive festivals retained their own traditions in the cities.

TEACHER EDUCATION

The structure of teacher education in Canada changed in the years following the Second World War. Although training was still in the hands of the normal schools or teachers' colleges, these institutions were gradually integrated into the universities. This transition was further complicated by an increased demand for qualified teachers to accommodate the tremendous rise in public school enrolment. Fenwick, Staples, and Thomson all attempted to extend music instruction into the rural areas. To help accomplish this aim they organized special summer schools for teachers. Sessions sponsored by the Ontario Department of Education attracted a large number of teachers from Ontario and from other parts of the country. Similar ventures were undertaken in other provinces as well. At the British Columbia summer schools held in Victoria under the direction of Burton Kurth, a traditional choral approach was retained. Similarly, Beth Douglas helped to sustain a high level of choral singing throughout her career in teacher education in Manitoba. During the early 1960s, both school programs and teacher training became more comprehensive in nature. Institutions such as the University of British Columbia (UBC) and the University of Alberta developed large music divisions within their Faculties of Education.

Instruction in many parts of Canada reflected the philosophy and pedagogy of James Mursell and other leading educators at Columbia Teachers' College in New York City. Their approach, rooted in the child development movement, was committed to the song method. Its proponents designed instructional units to stimulate the musical growth of students through movement, listening, the use of classroom instruments, and other activities featured in eclectic programs. Irvin

Cooper and Rj Staples were among those who embraced Mursell's philosophical views. After the appointment of Lloyd Slind to UBC's Faculty of Education in 1956, this influence became more widespread, for Slind had been closely associated with both Cooper and Staples. The ties between Columbia Teachers' College and the University of Alberta have been very strong in the field of general education. In music, the Columbia influence has been sustained through the work of Elizabeth Filipkowski at the Faculty of Education, University of Alberta. Frank Churchley was another Canadian who had a direct link with Columbia Teachers' College. He did graduate work there leading to a doctoral dissertation entitled 'The Piano in Canadian Music Education.' Following a two-year term at Macdonald College (McGill University), Churchley initiated courses for the preparation of teachers at several universities in western Canada: Calgary, Regina, and Victoria. Some of these curricula were established as combined programs in fine arts and education. At UBC, Donald Gibbard, Campbell Trowsdale, and Sandra Davies contributed to various aspects of teacher training within the Faculty of Education. Frank Gamble, another member of this faculty, devoted special attention to the use of the recorder in classroom instruction.

A revitalized program for the training of music teachers was begun in Nova Scotia in 1957 with the appointment of Catherine Allison to the normal school in Truro. It included music classes during pre-service training and additional summer schools to familiarize teachers with the provincial curriculum. Several Nova Scotia teachers, including Irene McQuillan Murphy and Vernon Ellis, taught at these special summer schools, which Catherine Allison directed for twenty-five years. She also brought guest instructors from outside the province, Ethel Kinley and Beth Douglas from Winnipeg and Garfield Bender from Kitchener, Ontario. Appointments made at other normal schools in the country included that of Janis Kalnins, a Latvian composer, who was appointed to the New Brunswick Normal School in 1951. Kalnins played a prominent role in the musical life of the province as a teacher, organist, and composer, and also as a conductor of several ensembles, including the New Brunswick Symphony Orchestra.

Neither Prince Edward Island nor Newfoundland offered extensive training for school music teachers until the 1960s. According to reports, there was no music taught at Prince of Wales College in Charlottetown, either in the academic courses or at the normal school, in 1960. In Newfoundland, a special workshop was held at the first meeting of the

Music Education Council in 1966, at which the provincial department of education engaged the services of Elizabeth Filipkowski from Alberta. Sister Kathleen Rex notes that for music educators in Newfoundland 'this was the first united attempt to employ the efforts and talents of all musicians in the province for the purpose of establishing music as a subject in the prescribed curriculum for all schools.'[27]

In-service training and special events were of great benefit to teachers in the Montreal region. The 1961 Canadian Music Educators' Association convention in Montreal featured many distinguished guests whose lectures and demonstrations stimulated interest in current developments. In 1966 Shinichi Suzuki visited Montreal and gave a special workshop for teachers. For French-speaking Quebec, l'École normale de musique de l'Institut pédagogique has made an important contribution to teacher education. In 1954 this institution, on the initiative of Sœur Marcelle Corneille, introduced a series of summer sessions on new methodologies in music education, focusing initially on the nursery school and lower elementary grades. For the first ten years these courses were available only to members of religious orders, but in 1964 the institution was authorized to grant a special music licence to teachers, and lay teachers were permitted to attend the summer sessions. Teachers at the summer schools have included Maurice Martenot, Marcel Corneloup, and Jacquotte Ribière-Raverlat.

NEW INTERNATIONAL INFLUENCES

In addition to American influences, pedagogical approaches developed in other parts of the world have had an impact on Canadian music education. Historically, Curwen's Tonic Sol-fa from England and various methods from France have been pervasive. The work of Émile Jaques-Dalcroze became known in North America in the early years of the century with the establishment of the Dalcroze school in New York in 1915. In Canada the Dalcroze approach has been developed primarily through classes in eurhythmics, solfège, and improvisation offered at the Royal Conservatory of Music (RCMT) and l'Université Laval. In the French-speaking parts of the country the approach of Maurice Martenot has been used in teaching music to young children. Profound developments in elementary school music took place during the late 1950s and the 1960s, when Canadians became aware of the European approaches developed by Carl Orff and Zoltán Kodály. These innovations coincided with the emergence of the International Society for

Music Education (ISME), which helped to make music educators throughout the world community more aware of developments in other cultural settings.

Both Orff and Kodály were influenced by the work of Dalcroze; all three dealt with the development of basic musicianship, but each had a different means of achieving his goals. Their approaches demanded intensive training for teachers and generally assumed that instruction would be given by music specialists rather than by classroom teachers. The initial thrust toward these specialized approaches to elementary music education came from university faculty members who were assuming greater responsibility for teacher training. Many music supervisors and leaders within the teaching profession also supported the trend toward more creative and sophisticated modes of music instruction.

In 1954 Arnold Walter, director of the Faculty of Music at the University of Toronto, arranged for Doreen Hall to study in Germany with Carl Orff and Gunild Keetman.[28] Upon her return in 1955, Hall introduced the Orff-Schulwerk to North America. This approach, known as Music for Children, combines speech, movement, singing, and the playing of instruments. Classes were initiated at the RCMT and in 1956 Doreen Hall was appointed to the Faculty of Music at the University of Toronto as lecturer in elementary music education. The following year an Orff summer course was introduced, the first of many sessions given in Toronto and later in other parts of Canada and the United States. With the assistance of Arnold Walter, Doreen Hall prepared the first English adaptation of the Orff-Keetman five-volume *Orff-Schulwerk*, called *Music for Children*, and wrote a teacher's manual outlining the basic philosophy and methodology of the approach.

Keith Bissell, who had returned from Edmonton to become director of music for the Scarborough school board, was a strong supporter of this new approach; through his writings in the *Canadian Music Educator*, he made many Canadian teachers aware of the changes taking place in the field: 'I know that many teachers share my skepticism of the various "banging and blowing" systems of music education involving tonettes, toy harps, and rhythm band gadgets, because the sounds produced are not musical, the musical material employed is invariably trifling, and the end results are vague. The Orff method must not be confused with such musical aberrations. I suggest, that in the Orff method, we have an approach to elementary music education which in its scope, breadth of imagination, and proven effectiveness, presents itself as a desirable alternative to our traditional approach with its obvious and serious limitations.'[29] Bissell recommended that all teachers, supervisors, and others genuinely interested in elementary music education undertake a serious study of this approach. Following a visit to Orff in Germany, he stated that it seemed that the 'most serious flaw' in the present system of music education was 'the narrowness of its scope': 'Because of the grievous lack of first-rate music literature for schools, our young people are constantly exposed to inferior music written or arranged by second rate composers, and monotonously nineteenth century in idiom.'[30] He explained how Orff's Music for Children takes the child back to the beginnings of music, using the so-called elemental approach: 'through a colorful and varied program of music-making' the child is 'carried through the centuries up to the contemporary music scene.' He continued: 'Orff achieves this with no concessions to cheapness or vulgarity; the music is all first-class, with the emphasis placed on the folk song, which has through the ages been the chief source of the world's greatest music. I believe that Orff has pointed the way, and that in this direction lies the future salvation of school music.'[31]

Laughton Bird, who later became supervisor of music for the North York schools, praised the Orff approach, and also spoke of the work of Keith Bissell, who, he hoped, would 'be encouraged to publish settings of suitable music from our own sources in the Orff idiom.'[32] Keith Bissell has indeed made a significant contribution to Canadian music education, not only as an arranger of folk material, much of it for Orff ensembles, but also through original choral and instrumental compositions for young performers. The Orff approach spread gradually to various regions of Canada. Workshops in other parts of the country included one at Mount Allison University in New Brunswick in the summer of 1957. The following year the National Film Board released a documentary entitled *Music for Children*. By the late 1950s the Waterloo Music Company had begun to place advertisements for the specially designed Orff instruments in music publications, and the Leeds Music Company was promoting the Hall-Walter edition of *Music for Children*, published by Schott. Bissell gave an Orff presentation at the Alberta Music Educators' Association convention in Edmonton in 1961. In the summer of that same year an Orff program directed by Doreen Hall was included as part of the Nova Scotia Festival of the Arts in Tatamagouche.

Sessions on the Orff approach surfaced periodically in CMEA conventions. At the 1961 Montreal convention Doreen Hall gave a demonstration lecture, in which she was assisted by the Montreal musician Mario Duschenes, who has been associated with the Orff movement through his expertise on the recorder. Two years later Richard Johnston presented a lecture in Halifax entitled 'The North American Folk Song in Orff's Music for Children.' A demonstration group led by Joan Sumberland from Scarborough shared the session with Johnston. That same year her students were heard on CBC radio in a three-part series featuring this approach entitled 'Living through Music.'

A special two-week summer course in Music for Children with both elementary and advanced levels was held in 1962 in the new Faculty of Music building of the University of Toronto. Carl Orff himself attended this conference and presented the keynote address and several lectures.[33] This summer school attracted teachers from both Canada and the United States. Two separate courses, one for the private teacher and one for the school music teacher, were offered. The staff included Lotte Flach and Barbara Haselbach, members of the Orff Institute in Salzburg, in addition to Canadian instructors Doreen Hall, Laughton Bird, Keith Bissell, and Hugh Orr, a recorder specialist. The event included a three-day conference on elementary music education with Orff and Walter as speakers, as well as Vally Weigl on music therapy and Richard Johnston on North American folk songs; demonstration classes were led by Doreen Hall.

New teaching methods were also introduced to French Canada. L'École normale de musique in Montreal, under the direction of Sœur Marcelle Corneille, offered courses in the Orff approach. One of the instructors was Miriam Samuelson, a Montreal native who taught for many years at the Orff Institute in Salzburg.

The Orff movement has enjoyed widespread recognition throughout Canada. However, despite the fact that a national organization was formed in the United States in 1963, it was not until 1974 that a similar association was founded in Canada, with Doreen Hall as its first president. The first convention of Music for Children–Carl Orff Canada–Musique pour enfants was held in Toronto in 1975. The organization has developed extensively, sponsoring national conventions and regional workshops, maintaining a publication for its members, and offering scholarships for young teachers.

Almost a decade after the introduction of Orff-Schulwerk to Canadian educators, another European approach appeared on the horizon. During the summer of 1964 the sixth ISME conference was held in Budapest, Hungary. The composer Zoltán Kodály, honorary president of this organization, delivered the welcome address, in which he gave a brief history of Hungary and the development of its education system. He remarked, 'You will have occasion to get acquainted with the modest results of our efforts,' and indicated that the Hungarian delegates were interested in learning 'everything which may be useful for our purposes.' He went on to say, 'We are deeply convinced that our mutual work will contribute to prepare a more beautiful and happier life for all humanity.'[34] Earlier that same year, University of Toronto theory professor Richard Johnston had visited Budapest during a study leave in Europe. Johnston was the first representative of a Canadian institution to observe the Kodály approach. Upon his return to Canada, he initiated Kodály instruction at the RCMT and at the Faculty of Music. He was assisted by Ann Osborn, a graduate student who subsequently spent three years in Hungary studying this approach. Johnston made music educators aware of his experiences in Hungary in an extensive article published in the *Canadian Music Educator* in the spring of 1965. He began with an appraisal of the current situation in Canadian music education: 'For ten years or more, we have had the example of *Music for Children* of Carl Orff on our doorstep; his materials and teaching examples are here for the understanding ... I am one of those persons who believe in Carl Orff as a composer and educator. I believe that his Music for Children is historically and musically correct. And I believe that it cannot possibly make the proper impact on our children unless it is taught by persons who are thoroughly trained as musicians and as teachers.'[35] He went on to say, however, that he was not totally uncritical, for he felt that the lack of a systematic approach to the teaching of music reading was a serious omission. 'The reader can then imagine the enthusiasm I feel for the work done in music education in Hungary which I was fortunate enough to see intimately during a visit to that country last March.'[36] Johnston described the classes he had observed in considerable detail, explained the techniques employed by Hungarian teachers, and also commented on the origin of the method. Kodály had visited England during the 1920s and had been so impressed with the choral work there, based on the Tonic Sol-fa system, that he had it incorporated into the course of study for Hungarian schools. Johnston ended with these remarks:

In Canada, we do not often achieve the standards in music which are possible and which we deserve to achieve, but this is simply because we have not paid our greatest art its due homage at the most elementary level. We, therefore, cannot hope to reach the summit. I cannot call loudly enough for serious attention to the work of Carl Orff, Zoltán Kodály, and their associates as examples of what can be done in our schools and of how to do it. The picture is there for all to see. We must not be blind to the fact that in both cases the leadership has been given by dedicated creative artists: men who are 'en rapport' with the well-springs of their art and who have troubled themselves to show others the way.[37]

At the CMEA convention held in Calgary in 1965 Mary Helen Richards of California, author of the *Threshold to Music* series, presented workshops in music reading and ear training, using sets of charts she had devised from her study of the Kodály method. During the summer of that same year Erzsébet Szönyi of the Liszt Academy in Budapest was invited by l'Université de Montréal to give introductory summer courses at l'École normale de musique. The following summer Kodály received an honorary doctorate from the University of Toronto and delivered the annual CAPAC-MacMillan Lectures.[38] He also observed Kodály classes at the RCMT summer school before travelling to Michigan, where the seventh ISME conference was taking place at Interlochen.

Although Richard Johnston has not been directly involved in the public school system, he has been an active participant in the school music field, both in Toronto and, later, in Calgary, where he served at the university as dean of the Faculty of Fine Arts. Johnston often assumed the role of catalyst. Kenneth Bray has mused, 'His varied activities in musical circles coupled with his propensity for expressing refreshingly candid opinions have earned him the designation of a "disturbing influence" by some of his close friends.'[39] Johnston's interest in Kodály influenced Harvey Perrin, director of music for the Toronto school board; Perrin visited Hungary with Johnston during 1966. They were both members of a music subcommittee whose task was to produce a new music course for primary and junior schools which would reflect recent developments in elementary education. Through this research project, funded by the Ontario Institute for Studies in Education, materials were prepared and piloted in several classrooms in Metropolitan Toronto schools. The project resulted in the publication of the two volumes of *The New Approach to Music*. The authors (Harvey Perrin, Nan Allin, Betty Kovacs, and Frank Daley) had been impressed with Kodály's emphasis on the development of music literacy at an early age; as they indicated in the following, they were also influenced by other approaches: 'Several specific studies in music education have proven that the optimum period for acquiring basic music-language skill occurs much earlier than was formerly recognized. Zoltán Kodály with the children of Hungary and Mary Helen Richards' adaptation for American children, Carl Orff's *Music for Children* and, closer to home, Kelly Kirby's kindergarten piano classes all have evolved fresh techniques which make possible a much earlier introduction of music symbols.'[40] The Ontario Ministry of Education offered special summer schools in the Kodály method. The first Hungarian to teach these sessions was Ilona Bartalus, who subsequently taught at the University of Western Ontario (UWO). However, *The New Approach* received 'little official recognition from the Ontario Department of Education,'[41] and although certain local boards have developed programs based on this document, it has never officially been adopted by the province.

During 1967 Jacquotte Ribière-Raverlat, 'a French educator who was responsible for an authorized French adaptation of the Kodály principles, headed an experimental venture in the province of Quebec.' This venture consisted of 'training courses for teachers, supervision of student teachers, and later a pilot project at the elementary level at the Villa-Maria Convent in Montreal.'[42] A four-volume French adaptation of the Kodály method for teachers and pupils, *Lisons la musique*, was prepared in 1967 by the Hungarian composer Thomas Legrady, who taught at Loyola College, McGill, and l'École normale de musique. Pierre and Margaret Tsé Perron introduced elements of the Kodály approach in the radio series 'Faisons de la musique,' prepared for French-speaking students in Quebec. Despite these examples of the use of relative solmization, the majority of French-speaking teachers throughout the country have continued to employ the European fixed doh approach, which has been taught by members of the various religious orders in classical colleges and convent schools for well over a century. The fixed doh system has also been employed by English-speaking teachers from time to time. In fact, the use of both fixed and moveable doh systems, the former indicating absolute pitches and the latter emphasizing intervallic relationship of pitches, has led to a great deal of confusion and controversy in music education throughout Canada.

Shortly after Paul Murray's appointment in Nova Scotia, the *Threshold to Music* series was adopted as the provincial program. Its author, Mary Helen Richards, was invited to teach at the Nova Scotia summer school in 1968 and 1969. In subsequent years, two Hungarian music educators, Aniko Hamvas and Katalin Forrai, were brought to Nova Scotia not only to teach the summer sessions but also to work with a committee of teachers developing new curriculum guides. Sarah Connor observes that 'as a direct result of these Summer School courses interest among educators in the Kodály method grew and curriculum committees established by the Department of Education wrote three provincial music curricula based on the Kodály method.'[43] For several years the work being done in this area of the country received little recognition elsewhere in Canada; however, it was known in the United States. Mae Daly remarked, after attending the Kodály Musical Training Institute in Boston in the early 1970s, 'I discovered that there had also been a course in Nova Scotia, Canada, that I had not heard of until I went to the United States.'[44] Nova Scotia has retained its commitment to the Kodály movement. In 1977 the Third International Kodály Symposium was held in Wolfville on the campus of Acadia University under the co-chairmanship of Kaye Dimock and Vernon Ellis.

As the Kodály movement in Canada continued to grow, the need was perceived for a national organization; in 1973 the Kodály Institute of Canada was founded with Gordon Kushner of Toronto as president. For several years the institute operated a head office in Ottawa with Mae Daly as executive director but later changed its name to the Kodály Society of Canada. The organization issues a publication and holds workshops and national conventions in various parts of the country for its membership, which has increased from coast to coast. Other recent developments in the Kodály movement include the introduction of courses directed by Lois Choksy at the University of Calgary.

The influence of both the Orff and Kodály approaches has been manifested in different ways in different places. Some teachers have adopted one of these approaches in a fairly complete manner, whereas others have merely incorporated certain aspects into already existing programs. The Kodály structure, with its emphasis on choral singing and music reading, has appealed to teachers who value these aspects of music instruction, especially in regions which have had a long choral tradition and an emphasis on Tonic Sol-fa. For others, Orff's concentration on improvisation and the development of creativity has been welcomed as a means of introducing students to contemporary composition. The Orff movement has kindled a greater interest in recorder playing and also in the interrelationship of the arts. Both movements have focused attention on the importance of integrating Canadian folk materials into instructional programs. Orff and Kodály both advocated beginning music experience at an early age and have thus contributed to the development of early childhood education in music. Their approaches have been incorporated into enrichment programs for gifted children and have also been used in programs for mentally and physically disabled children. In the mid-1960s Lois Birkenshaw was invited to use her Orff training with students at the Metropolitan Toronto School for the Deaf. She has subsequently worked with various institutions, at the same time helping to train other teachers. She has given courses and workshops on music in special education in various parts of North America as well as abroad and has numerous publications in this field. Although Orff and Kodály programs have flourished in some parts of the country, Canadians have not taken full advantage of these international influences, especially where music instruction is left to general teachers. Initiatives in Orff and Kodály training came originally from university teachers, but these specialized approaches have not been emphasized in programs designed for the training of regular classroom teachers.

Despite these developments, and despite the existence of some excellent music programs for young students, elementary music education has not realized its full potential in Canada. The question 'Who should do the teaching?' remains a problem. And so does the implementation of adequate training programs. Furthermore, the time allotment for instruction is still often inadequate. Across the country the situation varies from province to province, from board to board, and sometimes even from school to school. In general, however, the provinces in the Atlantic region have attempted to place instruction in the hands of music specialists, whereas other parts of the country tend to rely more heavily upon classroom teachers. Nevertheless, the need for adequate training, both pre-service and in-service, continues to be a major concern for those providing leadership in elementary school music in Canada.

VOCAL PROGRAMS IN JUNIOR AND SENIOR HIGH SCHOOLS

The emergence of full-fledged music courses in junior and senior high schools has been described in previous chapters dealing with the period between the wars. It was not until several decades later, however, that music was introduced beyond elementary grades in some provinces, and even then it was often in the form of choral activity rather than formal instruction. Many of these music courses might well be described as 'vocal/general,' for although the majority of them placed an emphasis on choral singing, they also incorporated both theory and history as well as listening activities. These courses were most common in junior high schools and in grades nine and ten of secondary schools. The balance among performing, listening, and written work differed widely, according to the inclinations of individual instructors, but successful programs, where they did occur, usually reflected the enthusiastic drive of an outstanding teacher. There were strong traditions in Winnipeg associated with Daniel McIntyre and Kelvin High Schools; the teachers involved were Lola MacQuarrie and Gladys Anderson Brown respectively. These institutions were renowned for their fine choirs and excellent operetta productions. In Vancouver, Sherwood Robson at John Oliver High School and Harold King at Magee High School set high standards for others to follow in that city. The popularity of events organized under the auspices of the Sir Ernest MacMillan Fine Arts Clubs heightened student interest in music, thus contributing to the expansion of secondary school programs throughout the province of British Columbia.

The vigorous state of high school music in Montreal's Protestant schools was evident in the number of schools involved in the city's annual festival of choral and instrumental music; there was also keen participation in the Montreal Competitive Music Festival. During the late 1950s, Montreal's English Protestant schools offered a multiple-channel course in high school involving singing, playing, or listening. As a general rule, enrolment in senior classes was higher in those provinces which had a matriculation or high school leaving examination in music. By the 1962–3 school year 575 pupils were registered for the high school leaving examination in music in these various channels. Among several successful programs in Montreal, those at Rosemount High School (Ruth Schiller, and later Helen Hall) and Lachine High School (Ted McLearon) were noted for their choral work. In 1957 the Lachine High School Singers performed in an all-Canadian program at MENC, held in Atlantic City. A comprehensive program at Monklands High School which offered choral, band, and orchestral work was maintained for many years by Grant Blair. A CBC television network show in 1961 featured choirs from ten Montreal high schools as well as an interview with Gifford Mitchell. Following the passage of controversial education legislation in Quebec, however, music in the English-speaking schools suffered a period of decline.

Ontario, unlike most other provinces, could boast of thriving programs at schools in a number of smaller communities, Simcoe District High School (Lansing MacDowell), Listowel District High School (Lorne Willits), and Kingston Collegiate Institute (George Maybee), among others. The fact that the majority of Ontario's schools had vocal music in the late 1940s can be attributed to a provincial regulation dating back to 1937 which stipulated that grade nine students choose either art or music as an optional subject. Clearly, this requirement stimulated the growth of secondary school music. So did the grade thirteen music course, which was introduced in 1943. Such decisions on a province-wide basis gave official status to music as a high school subject.

Music teachers in Toronto had the added advantage of a supervisory staff which provided leadership, resources, and a wide range of inter-school activities. Eldon Brethour served as director of music from 1943 to 1958, and Harvey Perrin held this position from 1958 to 1971. The Toronto board of education maintained a close liaison with the Toronto Symphony Orchestra. TSO concerts for secondary school students were held in Massey Hall from 1941 until 1957. This annual series was of inestimable value to both students and teachers, especially in seasons during which the orchestra programmed works prescribed for study on the grade thirteen matriculation examination. From year to year Sir Ernest MacMillan made a point of featuring student soloists; among these promising young artists was the pianist Glenn Gould. The TSO's city-wide students' council participated in the planning and promotion of concerts, and once a year they staged a 'Symphony Week' in the schools, including a 'Tag Day' to raise funds for the orchestra. The council met each Thursday evening preceding their Tuesday night concert for previews, which were, in effect, music appreciation sessions based on the music to be performed at the next concert. In 1951, CBC aired a radio quiz program which was also used to introduce the repertoire for each student concert; the questions for the quiz were submitted by the Symphony Student Council.[45] The TSO Women's Committee, which did much of the organizational work, was convinced that such projects were valuable links between school and concert hall: 'It is a thrilling experience to go to one of the Students' Concerts and see row after row of interested young people anxious to see and hear good music. They are a very critical audience indeed – and well they might be – as they are the concertgoers of a few years hence who will, through the musical training in their schools and the many concerts they have attended, be a much more understanding and appreciative listening group than their parents ever were.'[46] An indication of the respect commanded by this series was the fact that Toronto's music critics reviewed these secondary school concerts on a regular basis.

Of the Toronto teachers in the postwar years, Dawson Woodburn was unquestionably the most intrepid. He built an extensive music department at Riverdale Collegiate in which there were vocal and instrumental classes in the timetable as well as extra-curricular ensembles both at junior and senior levels. James Robbins conducted bands, Kenneth Bray orchestras, and Woodburn was in charge of the choirs. William Bailey, the principal of Riverdale, was appointed to Lawrence Park Collegiate in 1957 and, as part of this transfer, took the head of his music department with him. Together, Bailey and Woodburn mounted the most comprehensive music department in the province; within four years over 50 per cent of the student body of approximately thirteen hundred were enrolled in music. Woodburn's forte was choral music, but he believed it was essential to have both vocal and instrumental music within the same school. He accomplished this feat at Lawrence Park by capitalizing on the tremendous support of his principal, and through the assistance of Natalie Kuzmich, whose orchestral work complemented the excellence of Woodburn's choirs. Wherever Dawson Woodburn went he was a force in combatting complacency among his colleagues and in chiding administrators for not giving more support to school music. Not satisfied with success in his own school, Woodburn strove to improve music throughout the province; in effect, he became an unofficial leader of music teachers in central Ontario. It is not surprising, then, that through the 1950s and 1960s Woodburn became a dominant voice in the Ontario Music Educators' Association. He taught for many years at the department of education's summer school and was conspicuous at events such as the annual Kiwanis Music Festival. In 1965 Dawson Woodburn was appointed to Althouse College of Education, where his strong presence at the University of Western Ontario was largely responsible for an expansion of music education in the southwestern part of the province.

It is unfortunate that the paucity of trained teachers in many provinces restricted the growth of secondary school music. Not only was there an insufficient number of competent teachers in regions where specialized training was not yet available, but it was always difficult to attract them to small, isolated communities. As recently as 1959 a survey in Alberta concluded that 'the scarcity of qualified and competent teachers' was 'a serious problem'[47] contributing to the low status of music in the overall curriculum. The teacher shortage was less severe in the late 1960s, for by that time more Canadian universities were committed to professional training and were starting to graduate competent teachers. In the prairie provinces, a few schools in the main cities served as models for others to follow, and as a general rule those schools which had music scheduled on the timetable also developed excellent performing ensembles. Lloyd Erickson was a prominent high school teacher in Calgary. His Crescent Heights High School Choir performed at CMEA conferences held in Vancouver in 1962 and Calgary in 1965. The choral program at Viscount Bennett High School in Calgary reached a high standard under Marilyn Perkins; her choir was featured at the 1963 CMEA conference in Halifax and again at the 1967 centennial conference in London, Ontario. The Meistersingers of Swift Current was one of several choral groups directed by Alastair Browne; this ensemble appeared at CMEA conferences in Regina in 1969 and in Edmonton in 1975. Even so, it must be acknowledged that strong vocal programs were few in number and outstanding groups which appeared at conferences represented the exception rather than the norm.

The awarding of academic credit for the study of music outside the school, an issue in many parts of Canada before the Second World War, received attention in the eastern regions of the country. But music in the school was typically based on extra-curricular activity. Performing groups existed in many schools in the Atlantic provinces, and several institutions presented a yearly operetta or musical. The high school choir or glee club became an important part of the community; extra-curricular instrumental groups also functioned in schools throughout the region. But music was not offered as an in-school subject in most situations. Indeed, it was not until the late 1960s that a high school credit course in music which combined practical performance with theory and history was piloted in New Brunswick. It met daily and was offered at the grade ten, eleven, and twelve levels. Tom Morrison of Fredericton High School and Ernest Freeborn of Moncton High School worked with provincial consultant Gloria Richard on the design of this course, which made use of recordings, slides, and workbooks. Similar courses were later introduced in other schools of the region.

In 1960 Howard Brown, head of the music department at Mount Allison University, organized a conference entitled 'Music in the Schools of the Atlantic Provinces.' Individuals from many organizations and institutions were invited to this two-day gathering, which addressed the problems facing schools and reported on special projects already in existence. This included an account of the activities of the Halifax Symphony Orchestra, which for the past eight years had been touring schools throughout Nova Scotia: 'Each year 20 to 25 concerts are heard by 10,000 to 12,000 school children in 15 to 20 cities, towns and rural centres. Reports from the schools indicate a total audience of well over 35,000 pupils in the last three years alone.'[48] Speakers from outside the provinces were also invited to the Mount Allison conference; the Canada Council granted an award of four hundred dollars, 'making it possible for Dr. G. Roy Fenwick, former Director of Music, Ontario, Dr. Frederic Fay Swift, Hartwick College, Oneonta, New York, and Mr. E.J. Fergusson, Director of Music, Oxford-Waterloo (Ontario) District High School, to come to the conference.'[49] Bruce Attridge, national supervisor of children's programs for the CBC, was also a guest speaker. The discussions focused primarily on teacher training, instrumental music in the schools, and music in the senior grades as a matriculation subject.

Whenever instrumental classes were introduced – and it differed widely from province to province – the common complaint among teachers was that instrumental music was crowding out the vocal programs. It was not easy to maintain string, wind, and choral streams in one school unless its population was large. However, it was possible for a school principal to structure optional subjects in a way which not only guaranteed sufficient enrolment but also ensured a good distribution across the various music classes. Attracting students into secondary vocal courses was particularly problematic in situations where students had not been motivated by their previous experiences in vocal music. Lack of interest in vocal courses was characteristic of students from elementary schools in which the instruction had been left to general classroom teachers who felt inadequate or insecure. Presumably, the novelty of instrumental music, a subject not usually offered in elementary grades, gave a decided advantage to instrumental programs at the high school level.

Vocal music was also plagued by the problem of the boy's changing voice. While this problem did not daunt some teachers, others regarded instrumental music as the easiest solution in their efforts to cope with boys. Such difficulties notwithstanding, the truly talented teachers were able to survive the powerful trend toward instrumental music. It is regrettable, nevertheless, that instrumental music became so popular in the postwar years that its widespread growth was often at the expense of vocal music. In many situations vocal music as a school subject was discontinued, even though most schools maintained a choir on an extra-curricular basis. The tradition of teaching girls and boys in separate classes was retained in a number of Canadian school systems. Free from the problem of changing voices, many teachers who worked strictly with girls produced a high calibre of performance. This was certainly true in Newfoundland, where several Roman Catholic schools for girls have received national acclaim for their superior choirs.

The success of vocal classes paved the way for the acceptance of instrumental music as an accredited secondary school subject. Invariably, an expansion to instrumental work followed in the wake of demonstrated success in the vocal field. Hence, instrumental music owes a great deal to the generation of teachers who opened up new frontiers in secondary education through the successful development of vocal courses. Some of these teachers shifted their interest to instrumental music or, in many instances, assumed the responsibility for both vocal and instrumental instruction.

The high school vocal programs, which had crystallized in the late 1930s, were less dependent upon American methods and materials than were their instrumental counterparts. Vocal music books produced by Don Wright and Leslie Bell were still widely used in the 1950s. Of a more recent vintage, *For Young Musicians* by Bray and Snell[50] met the needs of teachers who retained theory as an integral part of their general programs, and *Let's Explore Music*, a series of booklets by G. Roy Fenwick, Richard Johnston, and others,[51] focused on topics in musical form and understanding. But at conferences and workshops music teachers were preoccupied with the complexities of instrumental music, and there seemed to be a consuming interest in sessions presented by instrumental specialists from the United States.

The establishment of a special high school of music was proposed in the city of Toronto as early as 1962. This idea became an extremely controversial issue, and subsequently, several versions of the original proposal fell victim to political struggles. Quite apart from differences of opinion among administrators, music teachers themselves have been divided as to their support for special high schools for the performing arts. Such schools have been developed in other areas, particularly in the province of Quebec, but not until later did they emerge in the Toronto area. By the 1980s, many school boards had experimented in establishing special schools for the arts, including several at the elementary school level.

14

The Rise of Instrumental Music

Music in secondary schools had a remarkable growth following the Second World War. Nowhere was this more dramatic than in the field of instrumental music, where instruction on band and orchestral instruments became an integral part of the school curriculum. Although teachers had been pressing for this change throughout the late 1930s, the exigencies of war interfered with any progress in making the idea universally accepted in Canadian education. Before the war the need to exercise financial restraint, a legacy of the Depression, had served as an obstacle, and during the war was added the difficulty in procuring instruments – indeed, it was only after the war that these problems could be solved with a view toward offering the study of instrumental music. But the resistance to instrumental music had not been entirely on a practical plane; philosophical considerations had posed problems in themselves. In the late 1940s, however, educational authorities seemed receptive to the idea as part of a national resolve to realize reconstruction through the strengthening of humanitarian values. Instrumental music came in on the crest of a spirit of hope for the future, and the earlier reluctance to venture into the so-called frills seemed to recede, at least temporarily.

QUEBEC

In schools under the jurisdiction of the Montreal Protestant board, great emphasis was put on combined instrumental groups featuring students from several schools. According to director of music Irvin Cooper, the rationale for this centralization of activities had been partly financial. However, by the 1943–4 school year, conditions appeared to favour decentralizing this work, placing it in each of several high schools as an integral part of the school program. By 1947 it was reported that most schools had at least one choir, band, or orchestra. The board supplied the instruments and paid for the instruction. Special grants were made to Montreal West and Mount Royal High Schools to enable them to provide more instruments, and instrumental music was introduced at Lachine High in the 1946–7 session.

An International Festival

Irvin Cooper was energetic and resourceful in devising schemes for the expansion of music programs in the Protestant schools of Montreal. His most ambitious undertaking was the International Festival of School Music, which took place in the Montreal Forum in 1947. As part of the planning and promotion of this event, he made a presentation at the eastern division of MENC, encouraging colleagues from nearby American states to bring their school groups to the festival. Billed as an opportunity to foster international peace, this shared experience in musical activity brought thousands of young people together in a busy schedule of rehearsals, parades, and concerts. Members of the visiting groups were billeted in the homes of Montreal students. The festival attracted school choirs, bands, and orchestras from Quebec, Ontario, and the eastern region of the United States. Many of them performed as solo groups; there were also several combined or 'sustaining' choirs from the schools of Montreal, and in the final program three large ensembles whose members were drawn from all participating schools: an international schools chorus (conducted by J.F. Williamson), a schools band (conducted by J.J. Gagnier), and a schools orchestra (conducted by Albert Wassell). The festival received extensive coverage in the media, of which the following is a sample:

Montrealers gave 12,000 visiting school musicians an ovation last night in the Forum where the opening concert of the mammoth International Festival of School Music proved to be a sensational display of the advances in recent years of school music. Students from 80 cities and towns of the United States and Canada assembled here for the three-day music meet ... including a street parade of visiting school bands, from the Forum to the

Currie Gymnasium at McGill University. Splendid uniforms were displayed by some of the United States scholars, scarlet and gold and all manner of colours. One choir wore gowns which made them look from a distance like a row of black and white exclamation marks.[1]

The newspaper reports also alluded to problems which arose in coping with the magnitude of the operation:

> The proceedings at the opening concert of the International Forum, while spectacular from the point of view of uniforms, and pleasing to the eye, were rather spoiled by the late arrival of many of the audience during the first half hour, and by the noise of walking [in and out] after the long program had been under way for a couple of hours.
>
> Though none of the music could be well heard in all parts of the building, and some of it hardly heard at all, the sounds which reached the far end of the building carried conviction that they were caused by good singing and playing. The best heard part of the program was of course the singing of the big 'Sustaining Choirs' which filled the whole of one end of the Forum. These on Thursday were senior choirs, and their singers came from twenty-seven Montreal schools, both French and English.[2]

There was an overwhelming representation of American school bands: Barrie Collegiate Band was the lone entry from Ontario, six groups came from Montreal schools, and the remaining thirty-seven bands came from the United States. The instrumental ensembles attracted a great deal of attention: 'The young audience seemed to like the bands even better than the choirs, and a band from Medford, Massachusetts, was so much applauded that it added two of Sousa's marches to its three pieces on the program.'[3]

The most publicized aspect of the International Festival was a dispute which arose between Irvin Cooper and the Music Guild of Montreal, the local chapter of the musicians' union. Cooper had planned to produce recordings for those students and teachers who wished to retain 'portions of the festival for educational purposes.'[4] But most of the school accompanists were not members of the American Federation of Musicians, and consequently, the union placed a ban on the sale of festival recordings. The confusion and strong public reaction generated by this incident gathered the momentum of a storm during the festival. At the height of the drama, Cooper told the Montreal *Star*: 'I fail to see why a festival of school children's music originating in a

Canadian city has to be subject to a ruling from a United States authority who has nothing at all to do with education.'[5] In the same issue appeared the following:

CZAR PETRILLO BANS RECORDING OF 12,000 VOICES AT FESTIVAL – ONE OF MOST VALUED FEATURES DOOMED AS CANADIAN MUSICIANS BOW TO ORDER.

Their voices shall not be preserved for posterity. James Petrillo of Chicago, who has assumed the role of czar of North American professional musicians, now desires to assume the role for school students. He has issued a ban, through an agent in New York, against the recording of the voices of 12,000 students at the first International Festival of School Music, whose opening concert is scheduled for Thursday evening in the Forum.[6]

The *New York Times* reported that Cooper withdrew from the union over this issue, and the incident commanded international attention even on the diplomatic level, for United States congressmen Carroll Kearns and Richard M. Nixon were sent to Montreal to investigate.

Further Developments

The international festival drew attention to aspects of American school music which had not yet been developed in Canada. However, apart from the Barrie band and three choirs from Ontario, this window into American music education was opened mostly to residents of Montreal. And any direct impact on school programs in Montreal may have been diminished by the fact that Cooper resigned from his Montreal post to become director of the Eastern Townships Conservatory in Stanstead, Quebec. Nor was there evidence of any immediate expansion in instrumental music. By 1950 instrumental instruction was being given on a rotating system during the school day, with participants excused from regular classes. To avoid depriving students of essential classroom work, the board decided to schedule these music classes after regular school hours. Lessons were given in a number of designated schools from 3:00 p.m. to 6:00 p.m. on school days and from 9:00 a.m. to 12:00 noon on Saturdays. A non-refundable tuition fee of five dollars was charged and a special instrumental report card was introduced. Lewis Elvin served as a special string teacher in the schools. He also established the Montreal Junior Symphony, for players of eleven to nineteen years, and from 1947 until his resignation in 1971 he used this city-wide organization to provide ensemble experience for school musicians as well as private students.

The Young People's Symphony Concerts, directed by Wilfrid Pelletier, gave the more advanced students orchestral performing experience. In 1956–7 sixteen members of school bands and orchestras performed with professional players both in open rehearsals (rotated among various high schools) and in the final concert. In the following year student soloists played concertos, and thirty-three senior students performed in orchestral works. A junior advisory council with two representatives from each high school assisted with the programming. This practice of using student soloists and having students perform with the symphony orchestra lasted for several years.

An important step was taken in 1952 when class instruction was integrated into the regular timetable of the Westmount Junior High School. The initiative followed upon a visit to North Toronto Collegiate by Gifford Mitchell and Morley Calvert.[7] As the North Toronto courses were designed for outstanding students, it is not surprising that the Westmount program was based on a similar rationale: that time could be allotted for music because gifted students could manage with fewer periods in their academic subjects. The Westmount program was eventually extended to the senior high level, and thus it paved the way for other schools in the Montreal area, such as Montreal West, Westhill, and several in suburban West Island.

High school teachers have often looked beyond the intrinsic nature of music to motivate students. Typically, school band directors in Quebec, like their counterparts in other provinces, resorted to special events to stimulate interest in their programs. It was not unusual for school ensembles from Montreal to compete in the Ottawa Music Festival or to participate in band exchange trips with schools in the New England area. In 1958 Grant Blair of Monklands High School taught an instrumental course as part of the board's summer school. For many summers Morley Calvert operated the Monteregian Music Camp on Lake Memphrémagog for high school students, and in the 1960s he conducted the McGill University Concert Band. The surge of instrumental music activity in the Protestant schools of Montreal coincided with the growth and development of music education courses at McGill University.

George Little endeavoured to establish more uniform standards throughout Quebec under a new centralized structure which was less susceptible to church domination. Much of his attention was focused on the French Catholic schools of the province which had not yet developed strong music programs. Instrumental music was included in a comprehensive plan which covered all aspects of music instruction throughout the elementary and secondary school levels. The goals implicit in the Parent and Rioux Reports were also reflected in progressive changes which Lucien Brochu incorporated in music education at l'Université Laval. Yves Bédard, who joined the Laval faculty in 1961, was also associated with these reforms. He collaborated on briefs submitted to the Parent and Rioux Commissions and formulated new programs of instruction, including initiatives in instrumental music. It was indeed the dawn of a new era for school music in Quebec.

ONTARIO

In Ontario the conditions necessary for a significant breakthrough in instrumental music seemed to converge immediately after the Second World War. G. Roy Fenwick noted: 'While there has been provision in the regulations since 1936 for the teaching of instrumental music, prior to 1945 instrumental music lagged far behind vocal music in the schools. This was due to lack of funds, shortage of trained teachers, and the impossibility of obtaining instruments during the war.'[8] Fenwick was referring to legislation which 'permitted vocational schools to teach instrumental music as a shop subject'[9] and authorized the department to give grants in support of this scheme. In 1945 relatively few vocational schools were offering the subject, but under a new system of grants, funding was made available to all types of secondary schools. In order to receive such grants, schools had to meet with the satisfaction of secondary school inspectors with respect to the certification of teachers, the allotment of class time, accommodation, facilities, and equipment. Instrumental music entered a period of vigorous growth as a result of these new financial incentives. Fenwick had consolidated the support of senior officials in the Ontario Department of Education during the war years. Not only had he expanded music up to grade thirteen, but he had also prevailed upon the University of Toronto to improve degree programs for school music teachers. Moreover, the appointment of Major Brian McCool in 1945 as assistant director of music for Ontario added further impetus, for McCool was assigned specifically to the secondary school field.

The decision of Principal Walter Houston to introduce instrumental music as an optional subject at North Toronto Collegiate in 1946 was a landmark in the annals of school music in Ontario. His unstinting support for instrumental music reinforced the efforts of music teacher Jack Dow, who became a veritable workaholic in building the North Toronto program. In 1951 Leonard Dunelyk joined the staff as a string specialist, and within a few years these two teachers developed orchestral ensembles which set high performance standards for the rest of the province.

This program was an experiment in which 'music was to be treated like any other subject,'[10] and as a result of this directive the administrative framework for instrumental music classes was permanently established in Ontario. Although North Toronto Collegiate was not the first school to form instrumental music classes, its success was so phenomenal that it became the prototype in a widespread expansion of the subject over the next three decades. Students were selected on the basis of high academic achievement and a simple aural test administered in grade eight. Music, like other optional subjects, was scheduled every day in a forty-five minute period in classes of approximately thirty-six students, and the mark assigned for music was averaged with those for other subjects for regular academic credit. At North Toronto the routine organization of 'home form' classes dictated that enrolment in instrumental classes was limited. The first phase required separate classes for strings and winds in grade nine, and students were required to maintain a 65 per cent average in all subjects for progression into grade ten. In grade eleven, wind and string players were grouped together to form an orchestral ensemble, and this arrangement was retained in grade twelve. To preserve a normal class size, only the best wind players were allowed to continue in grade eleven; such decisions were also governed by the need for a balanced instrumentation. These restrictions probably added prestige to the subject, which from its inception had carried overtones of elitism. The grade thirteen music course did not involve performance activities because its content was determined by a province-wide matriculation examination, one which dealt with theory, history, and a detailed study of four prescribed works.

To a large extent, extra-curricular activities provided the motivation for the entire program, in that the senior orchestra and band afforded rewarding experiences to both students and teachers. These large ensembles drew their players from grades eleven and twelve and were augmented by instrumentalists from grade thirteen. For North Toronto students, their annual spring concert known as 'Maytime Melodies,' the Toronto Secondary Schools Festival in Massey Hall, and the Kiwanis Music Festival were the musical highlights of the year. This highly successful program, dual in nature, serves to illustrate the truth of the statement that 'instrumental music in an Ontario secondary school is a composite of two sub-programs, one curricular and the other extra-curricular.'[11]

Prominent among the major figures who advanced the cause of instrumental music was Brian McCool. As a former Latin teacher at Toronto's Harbord Collegiate, he was well known for his extra-curricular orchestras and Gilbert and Sullivan operettas. His distinguished war record and personal contacts in military circles contributed to his effectiveness in dealing with secondary school principals, many of whom had also served overseas. Principals exercised a great deal of authority in administering the curriculum within their own schools; from a political standpoint the appointment of Major McCool to the provincial department of education was indeed an astute move. He not only projected his influence as an inspector but, on frequent occasions, served as a public relations member of the Music Branch. In his first year of service he visited 177 schools. Trudy Bradley observes: 'McCool's efforts in instrumental music paralleled Fenwick's efforts in vocal music. Although they were entirely different in personality and worked in a different manner, they were similarly successful.'[12]

Under a project called the Ontario Department of Education Concert Plan, McCool organized concerts for the smaller communities. Some of these performances were given by young, rising artists, others by professional groups, and a few by school organizations. The plan was launched in 1946 with an annual budget of ten thousand dollars and operated until 1952. Two school ensembles which toured under the concert plan were the Barrie Collegiate Band and the North Toronto Collegiate Orchestra. It was a simple enough strategy, designed to promote secondary school music. McCool tried to show communities that cultural life could be enriched by establishing instrumental music courses in their schools, and in administering these events he frequently asked principals and community leaders to act as sponsors and local organizers. In 1946 the Barrie band toured for a week in eastern Ontario, presenting concerts to both schools and communities. They were billeted in the homes of local students and by all reports created a most desirable impression under the leadership of W.A. Fisher: 'The members of our school and the citizens of Peterborough who packed our auditorium last night were thrilled with the excellent music ... and it proved a great inspiration to our students here, when they saw and heard what can be done with musicians of their own age.'[13] Similar tours were undertaken by the Barrie band to northern and central Ontario in 1947 and 1948 respectively.

While McCool was promoting music in secondary schools, the University of Toronto was training a new generation of teachers in an innovative degree program called 'school music.' Sir Ernest MacMillan was dean of the Faculty of Music when this program was inaugurated in 1946, but he delegated much of the planning and administrative detail to Arnold Walter. Though of European training himself, Walter was partial to the North American type of university music school, which provided both the practical and the theoretical aspects of music education. As a consequence of Walter's interest in the programs at schools such as Juilliard and Eastman, the new MusBac program at Toronto was modelled along similar lines. This American influence was reinforced by the appointments of Robert Rosevear in 1946 and Richard Johnston in 1947, both graduates of the Eastman School of Music, University of Rochester. Through their contact with university students and their continuing leadership in the profession, Rosevear and Johnston played major roles in shaping various aspects of music education in the postwar period.

Rosevear, an expert in the instrumental music field, introduced Canadians to instructional books and ensemble techniques which had been developed in the United States. He also invited prominent American educators to conduct workshops at the University of Toronto as a means of improving instrumental class methods in the schools. At this juncture studio teachers at the conservatory were sceptical about the feasibility of group instruction. Similar workshops were eventually integrated into the in-service activities of OMEA, and this influence was thereby extended beyond the Faculty of Music to instrumental teachers throughout the province, many of whom had never received university training themselves. Rosevear became the first chairman of the music education department at the university, and was conductor (1946–50) of the RCMT Symphonic Band, (1953–9) of the University of Toronto Symphony Orchestra, and (1962–74) of the University of Toronto Concert Band.

McCool's success in opening up school programs complemented the effectiveness of Rosevear's work at the University of Toronto and vice versa. The reciprocal benefit may have been more by chance than by design, for McCool and Rosevear represented diverse backgrounds and did not share a common philosophy. There was a long-standing attitude in the department of education that the university's program in music education was inadequate. On the other hand, university faculty members questioned the value of the department's short-term summer courses, in which the emphasis was placed on methodology. In spite of the tensions between these rival systems of training, the combined efforts of McCool and Rosevear did a great deal to establish instrumental music as a subject in the secondary schools of Ontario. The momentum was further reinforced by impressive results at Barrie and North Toronto Collegiates, the former specializing in winds and the latter in a full orchestral program.

North Toronto had an immediate effect on other schools. By 1949 all secondary schools in Toronto had launched instrumental music courses, and Martin Chenhall – functioning as a resource person for the entire system – facilitated this expansion by attending to the day-to-day needs of teachers. The board assumed the responsibility of furnishing instruments and equipment, consistent with its treatment of instrumental music as any other optional subject. Initially, several music dealers offered a 40 per cent discount on instruments as an incentive to school boards to establish instrumental music classes. The industry expected that, in the future, students would purchase or rent their own instruments, as was the practice in the United States. However, the initial arrangement between music companies and school boards remained in place, much to the chagrin of the dealers, who found it difficult to withdraw the discount in the face of competition. This historical accident or misunderstanding worked to the benefit of those students who could not afford to buy their own instruments, and Ontario teachers were spared the administrative headaches that American teachers had experienced with rental/purchase plans. Among the Toronto schools which developed orchestral programs, Riverdale Collegiate (Ken Bray) and Oakwood Collegiate (Bruce Snell) reached high levels of performance. These two schools also maintained fine choral groups, under the direction of Dawson Woodburn at Riverdale and Earl Davison at Oakwood. Not all Toronto schools achieved well-balanced programs; at North Toronto, choral work was not given a high priority, and Malvern Collegiate was unique among the Toronto schools in that it confined its instruction to band classes.

Instrumental music seemed to flourish more naturally in collegiates than in vocational schools. The response to the 1936 circular offering the subject in vocational schools had met with limited success. Likewise, a special program introduced into Central Technical School in 1955 did not fulfil its intended purpose: it was designed to prepare students for a Bachelor of Music program, which in turn could lead to careers in secondary school music or professional work in radio, television, orchestras, or bands. The idea of a concentration, in which music was treated as yet another trade, did not attract many students to this vocational program at Central Tech. On the other hand, an increasing number of students took music as an optional subject within the academic programs of collegiates and secondary schools.

The expansion of instrumental music was not confined to the city of Toronto; curricular programs also spread rapidly throughout the metropolitan Toronto area and the industrial central region of the province. Among the teachers in the forefront of these early developments were Ed Bartlett (Owen Sound), Robert Cringan (North York), Wallace Laughton (St Catharines), Donald McKellar (Ottawa), Allan McKinlay (Scarborough), John Murdie (Ottawa), and Earl Simard (Sudbury). Alan Smith summarizes the extent of music in Ontario's 359 secondary schools in 1954–5: '260 Ontario secondary schools offered instruction in music, 224 offering vocal music, 89 curricular instrumental music, and 178 extra-curricular instrumental music.'[14] He also lists ninety-nine schools in which no music was offered; most of these were continuation schools or high schools located in smaller communities.

The Toronto Kiwanis Music Festival began in 1944, just before the ground swell of instrumental ensembles in the schools. George Peacock of the Salvation Army and music publisher Gordon V. Thompson were among several Kiwanians who promoted the idea of a competitive festival, one which would serve a wide spectrum of participants from private studios and church, community, and school groups. At first the school entries were mostly choral, but by the 1950s an increasing number of bands and orchestras were gravitating each year to the instrumental sessions held in the Eaton Auditorium. This annual event proved to be a motivation for those who thrived on competition, for long after festivals were established in other centres – Hamilton, Ottawa, and London among them – many teachers continued to participate in the Toronto Kiwanis festival. Although the Toronto festival was never intended to serve as a provincial competition, it attracted choral and instrumental ensembles from many parts of Ontario and became a veritable showcase for school music. The Kiwanis Clubs usually held a post-festival meeting of Toronto teachers in order to consider suggestions for changes and improvements. As one outcome of these meetings, the festival committee agreed to engage either Americans or Canadians to adjudicate orchestra and band classes because it was felt that British adjudicators on the 'chain' were not familiar with the structure and standards of school instrumental ensembles in the North American context. A few festivals outside Toronto were sponsored by other service clubs or independent organizations. However, for several generations of young Canadian musicians the term 'Kiwanis' refers as much to their experiences in competitive festivals as it does to the service club per se. This cultural phenomenon exists from coast to coast as a tribute to the unique contribution of service clubs to music education.

Instrumental music as a curricular subject was so well established by the late 1950s that, as schools were constructed in new suburban areas, almost automatically music rooms were included in the building plans. And so it became difficult to find certified music teachers, with the result that the quality of instruction suffered from too rapid an expansion. It might even be suggested that instrumental music became the victim of its own success. Although there were difficulties with scheduling, equipment, and rehearsal facilities, none of these were as detrimental to long-range progress as the shortage of competent, well-trained teachers.

The first music education graduates of the University of Toronto did not enter the profession until 1950. In the meantime school boards were already hiring teachers who lacked the appropriate credentials. It was virtually impossible for one university to train enough graduates to meet the increasing demand for music specialists. University-trained music specialists were certificated in other subjects by virtue of their professional study at the Ontario College of Education (OCE). High school principals therefore enjoyed a great deal of flexibility and could hire a music specialist even before the school required a full teaching load in the subject. Many music specialists did indeed teach other subjects, with the result that the pool of music teachers was reduced even further. Inevitably, the department of education adopted a wide latitude in accommodating schools which wished to offer music and, in so doing, approved instructors of dubious ability through letters of standing, letters of permission, and various means of upgrading basic teaching certificates to specialist standing. The majority of these people did not possess degrees, and some who upgraded through vocational certificates had not even completed a high school education. Most of them were certified through the department's summer school. This led to a situation in which the Music Branch was operating the largest training program in the province and was supplying far more music teachers than the universities. Not until the late 1970s was this practice discontinued.

Summer school staff usually consisted of school teachers who were experienced in teaching methods, but for prospective teachers who needed a thorough understanding of music the short-term courses offered in the summer were cosmetic at best. A large number who qualified through the department's summer school were former bandsmen from military or town bands or, in some cases, players with a dance band background. Bandsmen were usually more secure teaching instruments related to their own background and experience; therefore, relatively few of the new programs introduced in the 1960s included string classes. In fact, even among those schools which had begun full orchestral programs, many discontinued strings and retained only their brass and woodwind classes. The incidence of bands was even higher in district high schools located in rural regions. Smith, writing in 1956, offered an explanation: 'In these small communities, the band is frequently considered to be the music organization *par excellence*. Town councils, in many of these communities, sponsor town bands directed by members of the community or, as in three cases, by the secondary school music teacher himself ... Brought up in such musical traditions, the townsfolk are apt to consider string instruments unsuited to their *mores*. On the one hand, they associate the violin with the country fiddler whose function is more entertaining than educational. On the other, they associate the string orchestra with cosmopolitan city life which does not accord with their own hardy traditions.'[15] The extent of the trend toward bands can be seen in table 14.1.

The department of education brought George Bornoff to its summer school from 1958 through 1960 to conduct intensive workshops in string teaching. His participation was designed to promote the teaching of strings at a time when the majority of schools outside Metropolitan Toronto were dealing primarily with wind classes and extra-curricular bands. McCool in particular was most eager to develop comprehensive programs with both strings and winds. He felt that Ontario could ensure its own, independent traditions by avoiding the predominance of bands he saw in the United States. Bornoff came originally from Winnipeg but had studied and taught at Columbia Teachers' College in New York and later joined the faculty at Boston University. He was one of few Canadians whose instrumental materials in group instruction have

TABLE 14.1
Extra-curricular orchestras and bands in Ontario secondary schools, selected school
years 1946–47 – 1966–67

School year	Orchestras	Bands
1946–47	98	34
1949–50	78	47
1954–55	87	87
1958–59	85	119
1960–61	81	150
1966–67	89	270

SOURCE: AR (Ont.), 1945–66

been used in the United States. To a great extent Bornoff's books, *Finger Patterns* and *Fun for Fiddle Fingers*,[16] shaped the direction of string instruction in these formative years.

The department's efforts to redress the imbalance between bands and orchestras did not reverse the trend. Numerous reasons could be advanced as to why wind programs thrived and flourished. It is generally agreed that wind players can acquire performing skills quickly and thus be allowed almost immediate participation in an ensemble; by comparison, strings demand time and patience before students experience the rewards of orchestral performance. Recently, educators have become cognizant of the need to start instruction at an early age when psychomotor skills can be acquired more readily. The possibilities inherent in early instruction have been demonstrated in a convincing way by the Japanese teacher Shinichi Suzuki in his Talent Education program. In retrospect it seems that string programs might have enjoyed greater success in Ontario if they had been introduced at an earlier level.

Historical relationships suggest that the practice of commencing instrumental instruction at the grade nine level was the result not of a conscious decision based upon pedagogical principles but of administrative policies. Traditionally, there has been a sharp division between elementary and secondary education in Ontario. This can be seen in the bureaucratic structure of the department with respect to curriculum and supervision, but nowhere was it more apparent than in certification and teacher training. To be certified in elementary education, students attended normal schools, later called teachers' colleges, for one year of training in teaching methods. This program, which led to a teaching certificate, was designed to prepare generalists for elementary school classrooms. To be certified in secondary education, students were required to earn a degree and then to take one year of professional training at the Ontario College of Education (OCE). In short, teachers' colleges were associated with general training for elementary schools whereas OCE was identified with specialized methods for secondary schools. The sequence of events which placed the specialized methodology for instrumental music at OCE reinforced the perception of instrumental music as a secondary school subject.

In 1937 the provincial department had introduced curriculum changes which required students to choose either art or music as an option in grade nine. Subsequently, Leslie Bell was appointed as music instructor at OCE to develop a new methods course for secondary school teaching. University of Toronto graduates of the honours BA in music could proceed to OCE for this professional training, which qualified them for an interim Type A Specialist's Certificate in vocal music. But following intermittent criticism from both the provincial department and the Music Section of OEA, the university in 1946 introduced a three-year degree in school music, one which was of a more practical nature. Graduates of this program were admissible to an expanded music course at OCE which included methods in the instrumental field. These arrangements enabled a University of Toronto graduate in music education to obtain a Type A Certificate in vocal and instrumental music on a par with specialist certificates in other secondary school subjects. In the deliberations between Fenwick and senior officials of the department on the one hand and MacMillan and his university colleagues on the other, there was always the assumption that improvements in instrumental training would be directed toward secondary education. Consequently, instrumental music was entrenched as a high school subject because its teacher training was placed within the existing structure, which had been devised for teacher training in other secondary subjects. It appears that beginning instruction in instrumental music was assigned to the grade nine level without there having been any questioning of the nature of music and of the pedagogical implications. To be sure, other factors had a bearing too.

It has already been noted that instrumental music as a school subject was an outgrowth of the extra-curricular musical activities which flourished in secondary schools during the 1930s. It should also be noted that the Music Branch and the majority of music supervisors regarded the vocal music requirement that applied up to grade eight as a sacred trust and were not eager to have it replaced by instrumental work. In all likelihood they were more receptive to the idea of instrumental music as a high school option. There were also practical reasons why instrumental programs were not initiated at an earlier grade level. Secondary schools were generally larger, autonomous institutions with more extensive budgets; therefore, it was easier for a high school principal to absorb the cost of offering instrumental music. Smith's research indicates that 'curricular instrumental music was offered most frequently by schools with a larger than average enrolment.'[17] If the size of the institution was a critical factor, then the elementary school may have been too small to support a full instrumental program under normal conditions. Again, the circumstances surrounding the evolution of instrumental music indicate that instructional patterns were determined, if not dictated, by the administrative structures of general education rather than by principles based upon the psychology of music teaching and learning.

Instrumental Music in Elementary Schools

Instrumental music at the elementary school level was financed and administered in most places as a city-wide project rather than as an instructional program within individual schools. The music department of the Toronto board introduced free violin classes at the grade five level in 1949. Ten students were selected from each of five elementary schools which had shown a decided interest in orchestral work. Only students with high academic and musical ratings were enrolled in this pilot project. A memorandum to the board recommended violin classes for several reasons: 1) the low cost of violins – thirty dollars (compared with seventy-five for trumpets or eighty-five for clarinets); 2) the ease with which violin class instruction and ensemble playing could be realized, in comparison with a varied instrumentation; 3) the need to begin string instruction early if full instrumentation was to be achieved at the high school level. Leonard Dunelyk was hired as a part-time instructor to teach half-hour lessons to each class twice a week during regular school hours. After demonstrating success with these classes, Dunelyk joined the North Toronto Collegiate staff to pursue a career in secondary school teaching. Don Wasilenko filled the itinerant violin position in 1950 and has devoted more than thirty-five years to Toronto's elementary school program. He was given a permanent full-time position in 1965 as a special consultant in instrumental music and has directed his expertise primarily to string classes. Eventually, group instruction was offered in violin, viola, cello, and double bass. In addition, ensembles were formed in many schools to provide orchestral performing experience. Even so, these programs were not as visible as those in the secondary schools, partly because instrumental music at the elementary level was supplementary to the regular curriculum, in which vocal music was an obligatory subject. Initially, instrumental instruction was given by itinerant teachers who were specialists on their own instruments but did not hold Ontario teaching certificates. For this reason their involvement was on a casual basis. Yet pedagogically it made good sense to begin string instruction early in the student's development; it also furnished a source of advanced players for secondary schools. In 1959 the board expanded its instrumental instruction to include wind classes, and in that same year an all–public schools orchestra conducted by Jack Dow, then assistant director of music, made its debut at the annual May Concert in Massey Hall. The instrumental work in elementary schools has become an important aspect of the Toronto program; by 1965 there were two thousand pupils in 238 classes and a staff of eleven itinerant teachers.

The departmental regulation requiring vocal music to the end of grade eight was generally observed, if not enforced, during Fenwick's years as director of music. Therefore, the inclusion of instrumental music was considered a supplementary program in most situations. The vocal music requirement was relaxed, however, when junior high schools were introduced into suburban areas such as East York, North York, and South Peel. Instrumental music, a grade nine subject in junior high, was extended down to grades seven and eight, and thus a precedent was set for strings or winds as optional courses in senior elementary schools. By this sequence of events instrumental music became an option beyond grade six, sometimes in lieu of vocal music. The incidence of instrumental music in the senior elementary grades increased rapidly in the late 1960s in both curricular and extra-curricular activities, opening up the way for elementary teachers to become involved in a field which hitherto had been restricted to teachers with music degrees or specialist certificates. Gradually, without too much attention being paid to this transition, the instruction was subsumed by elementary teachers, many of whom had never received specialized training. Secondary schools in the 1950s had very little difficulty in recruiting grade nine students for instrumental courses, perhaps simply because of the novelty of the subject.

However, as more students have begun their instrumental study in the elementary grades, fewer have been inclined to continue it in secondary school, especially among those whose first experiences have been unrewarding. Not surprisingly, a provincial task force in the 1980s concluded that 'in some parts of the province teachers in Grades 7 and 8 do not have sufficient instrumental background to provide satisfactory instruction.'[18]

Philosophy and Practice

Fenwick regarded the instrumental music course as a parallel to the general vocal class, in which the allotment of time was singing, 40 per cent; appreciation, 40 per cent; and theory and sight-reading, 20 per cent. With this format in mind, he proposed that the singing component could be replaced by instrumental performance. Official documents expressed the view that class work should not be used primarily to develop fine orchestras or bands, but rather to emphasize the cultural aspects of the subject. Smith comments, 'It was expected that bands and orchestras would improve after its introduction, but this improvement was regarded as incidental to the main purposes of the curricular program.'[19] But to articulate a philosophy for the guidance of teachers is one thing, and to ensure that the appropriate balance of activities is adhered to is another. Whether Fenwick changed his views or simply adjusted the official policy to match what teachers were actually doing is not clear. The 1954 departmental curriculum was more specific in prescribing instrumental music, and although it did not increase the time allotment of 40 per cent, it offered a description that seemed to swing in favour of performance: 'The courses of studies outlined in the present publication constitute the official requirements for each grade ... the performance of music is, above everything else, the most important activity that can be carried on in the name of music in any curriculum.'[20] There has been little agreement among teachers themselves with respect to the relative merits of performance and broad cultural goals, and principals have tended to value extra-curricular ensembles for their usefulness in performing at school and community events. Smith observed in 1956: 'Being aware that administrators favour the development of fine bands and orchestras, individual teachers have tended increasingly to stress the performance component of their teaching. They have made the curricular program the servant of the extra-curricular program by carefully selecting their students for special talents, by practicing the band and orchestra repertoire in curricular classes, and by virtually abandoning musical knowledge classes.'[21]

Throughout the 1950s instrumental music teachers were preoccupied with the challenge of 'how to teach,' and a disproportionate amount of class time was spent on technical drills which were designed to develop performance skills. Teachers, eager to find materials suitable for group instruction, flocked to workshops and conventions seeking improved methods and techniques. In attempting to prove that good results in ensemble classes are possible, too often they stressed performance to the exclusion of cultural aspects.

The launching of Sputnik in 1957, with its ensuing 'shock of Russian space achievements,'[22] unleashed a critical assessment of education in the United States. The process of self-examination was taken up by Canadians with similar severity. In music education the recurring question of 'how to teach' gave way during the sixties to the question 'Why?' School subjects labelled as frills in the past were forced, yet again, to justify their existence, in an environment in which the philosophical pendulum was swinging in favour of cognitive learning. It is not surprising, then, that music educators, out of political expediency, attempted to balance performance-oriented programs by providing content in history, theory, and music literature. Those responding in this way did so on the basis that music was an academic discipline; they argued that both scholastic work and performing experience were vital to an understanding of the art. Still, these endeavours to refine and balance curricular programs were not embraced by all teachers. Many continued to operate performing ensembles with an emphasis on the development of technical proficiency. Moreover, there was a widespread feeling that performance standards would be lowered if substantial class time were given over to theory and appreciation. Such fears notwithstanding, the calibre of performance improved in the 1960s. Duane Bates concluded that 'the amount of instructional time provided for music was little changed,' but that 'it was being used to better advantage by 1970.'[23] An on-going dialogue concerning the educational objectives of school music took place within OMEA, especially among members with careers in supervisory or leadership roles. These concerns surfaced with increasing frequency at professional meetings and at working sessions of curriculum committees. Similar discussions predominated at the 1966 Ontario Music Conference at Couchiching[24] and at events associated with the John

Adaskin Project. There is no doubt that philosophical statements were seldom translated into significant changes in day-to-day instruction, yet many music educators felt changes were in the air.[25]

In the first two decades of instrumental music, teachers functioned in highly individual modes because official course outlines had not been developed. Curriculum content was usually determined by whatever band or string class method books were used; in wind classes these were exclusively American publications geared to a grade five or six starting level. Instruction in the senior grades invariably revolved around repertoire chosen for commencement exercises, Christmas concerts, competitions, and school shows. A provincial committee of supervisors and teachers was formed in 1964–5 to prepare a curriculum for instrumental music classes. By the time this publication was issued in 1967, the ministry of education had decentralized its operation and the Music Branch as such was dismantled. The ministry continued to produce guidelines outlining general policies, but the main responsibility for selection and organization of course content was transferred to local boards. Relatively few teachers have been conscientious or consistent in implementing provincial guidelines. A common complaint has been that these documents are not sufficiently specific. More recently, guidelines committed to aesthetic values have called for strategies in which performing, listening, and creating are integrated in a more systematic way. The mixed reactions to these innovations give a reason for reaffirming the belief that 'the distinctive aesthetic values of music education, in order to be understood by the public, must first be understood and accepted by music educators themselves.'[26]

BRITISH COLUMBIA

The rise of instrumental music in British Columbia can be attributed principally to the determined efforts of individual teachers. Many embryonic ventures took place in widely scattered communities even though close communication was impeded by the natural barriers of British Columbia's mountains and rivers. In Ontario, instrumental music spread from the urban centres out to the rural regions, but in British Columbia, the pattern, if one is discernible at all, was the reverse: much of the pioneering took place in small, remote communities; towns such as Kamloops, Kelowna, Kimberley, and Powell River did not wait for Vancouver to lead the way. Developments in Ontario were regulated and expedited by a provincial director of music, but individual teachers in British Columbia did not enjoy a similar advantage. In the absence of centralized leadership or political will the burden was placed on teachers to shape their own destinies in developing this specialized subject; more often than not, instrumental music originated as an informal enterprise and lacked official status until a measure of success was demonstrated. Only then could the instrumental music teacher expect administrators to support the subject by providing the structure and resources necessary for its continuance as a legitimate component of education.

Another way in which British Columbia differed from Ontario was in the starting grade level of the early programs. Although it is difficult to generalize, it might be said that instrumental music in British Columbia grew out of the junior high curriculum, which historically had been more flexible in accepting activity-type learning as valuable, educational experience. It should be conceded, however, that the extension of instrumental music into the secondary curriculum was aided in some situations by the existence of extra-curricular ensembles in high schools or in the community. Those schools which provided some kind of instrumental instruction during the war continued to gather momentum as individual teachers persuaded principals and boards to initiate programs. The potential of this scattered activity rose dramatically in 1954, when Fred Turner organized the first BC High School Band Conference, held at New Westminster Junior High School. On that occasion seven bands performed in a busy schedule of concerts, clinics, a parade, and a dance. It was particularly enlightening for students and teachers to see what was going on in other places. The participating bands were Kelowna High School (Mark Rose), Kimberley High School (Ralph Yarwood), Oak Bay High School (Gordon King), Oliver Southern Okanagan High School (Gar McKinley), Powell River High School (William Cumming), Summerland High School (John Tamblyn), and S.J. Willis Junior High School of Victoria (Howard Denike). Other bands represented were Castlegar High School (Ted Eames), Gladstone High School (Jack Cuthbert), Trail High School (Rex Potter), and Victoria High School (Rowland Grant). This event was also significant in that teachers attending the festival took the opportunity to form an organization called the BC Schools Instrumental Teachers' Association (BCSITA). A second festival took place in New Westminster in the following year, with John Tamblyn as chairman.

BCSITA devoted itself to the improvement of teaching through special events, curriculum projects, and grants, and from its inaugural meeting the association sought official clarification concerning the certification and status of instrumental teachers. This was yet another situation in which growth was taking place long before appropriate training programs were established by the authorities responsible for teacher education. Members of BCSITA regarded Dr J.F.K. English as a friend of music. He and his wife had been involved in the music festival in Kamloops, and as director of education in Victoria he had extended the scope of instrumental music there. Invariably, Howard Denike was the member designated to communicate concerns, requests, or recommendations during the period when Dr English served as deputy minister of education. Among its many causes, BCSITA lobbied for the appointment of a provincial director of music and urged the University of British Columbia to develop courses for instrumental music teaching.

A remarkable growth in the late 1950s can be observed in the annual festivals sponsored by BCSITA. The 1956 festival took place in the Victoria Memorial Arena, under the organization of Howard Denike. Close to thirty ensembles participated, not only bands but also orchestras, as well as bell-ringers from Castlegar. The HMCS Naden Band and the Victoria Symphony Orchestra also performed in this program of extravagant length, and it is noteworthy that the minister of education was on hand to present trophies. Plans for the fourth festival were announced in the *Canadian Bandmaster*:

> On May 10th and 11th, boys and girls from all over B.C. will converge upon the beautiful Okanagan Valley. Some 1500 students will be billeted in Vernon, Rutland, Kelowna, Summerland and Penticton. The Occasion will be the fourth annual Band and Orchestra Conference sponsored by the B.C. Schools Instrumental Teachers' Association ... While the conference is non-competitive, each band and orchestra receives a taped record of its playing together with an adjudication by the chief consultant. Men of distinction from both sides of the border will be on hand to act as clinicians for the various instruments.
>
> Besides taking part in the clinics and playing for adjudication, each band will have an opportunity to play for the others, parade through Kelowna's main street, see some outstanding musical films, attend the dance, and take part in the gigantic public programme on the final night. The young musicians will certainly go home from this conference filled with inspiration for the coming year.[27]

Mark Rose organized this ambitious event. It featured a euphonium soloist and a guest conductor from the United States, and the printed program noted, 'Miss Swanee Wood, majorette consultant, will perform during the evening.'[28] But it was not until 1958 that the BC Schools' Band Conference was held in Vancouver, on the campus of UBC. By this time the annual festival had grown to such a size that alternative arrangements had to be considered for the next year; it was estimated that thirty-two hundred students would be involved in the 1959 festival, if it were held. The need to find billets for so many people restricted the choice of location, and concerns were raised about student behaviour and supervision. It was suggested that the number of ensembles be limited, that the number of students from each school be reduced, and that regional rather than provincial festivals be held. These proposals met with mixed reactions, and consequently there was no festival held in 1959. Instead, BCSITA members scheduled their annual meeting during a conference of the BC chapter of the Canadian Bandmasters' Association (CBA) in Victoria.

The Chilliwack Conference in 1960, entitled 'Nights of Music,' was the last annual festival sponsored by BCSITA. Individual school bands were not invited on this occasion. The Royal Canadian Engineers' Band shared the program with the Burlington-Edison High School Band from the state of Washington on Friday evening, and the Saturday concert featured the Oak Harbor High School Choir and a BCSITA conference band representing schools throughout the province. In 1954 only twelve teachers had been present, but in 1960 there were forty. CBA expressed interest in establishing affiliation with BCSITA. There were a number of teachers, however, who favoured amalgamation with the BC Music Educators' Association (BCMEA), which had been founded in 1957. At the 1959 meeting Gar McKinley commented on the history of BCSITA, and said, 'In the long-term view there will be, in time, only one organization and ... the name Music Educators is superior.'[29] Lloyd Slind was also influential in drawing BCSITA into the music educators' organization. BCSITA had become effective in mobilizing the efforts of individual teachers throughout the province. Indeed, their collective leadership became the main drive behind the growth of instrumental music, until they merged with BCMEA. This amalgamation, which was formalized in 1962, strengthened the position of school music teachers and enabled them to deal in a unified way with all aspects of music education.

Until the 1950s, course outlines were left to individual teachers, but eventually the ministry of education formed committees to prepare curriculum materials. Dorothy Hopgood Evans, Rowland Grant, and Howard Denike were among those who worked on the instrumental syllabus. This was an important stage in the consolidation of a field which had from its inception relied upon the initiative of individuals. By 1956 the ministry approved the idea of a music major within the programs offered in secondary schools, and the general state of instrumental music appeared to be secure and promising. But the optimism felt by a growing circle of music teachers ended abruptly when the report of the Royal Commission on Education in British Columbia[30] was released in December 1960. This commission, conducted by Donald Chant, recommended sweeping changes which relegated music to a peripheral position in secondary education and reduced its accessibility to students proceeding to programs in higher education. It would be an understatement to say that music educators were disenchanted with this report. In recommending the overall structure of the curriculum, the document reserved top priority for 'the word and number subjects and their later forms, Literature and Mathematics,'[31] asserting that 'because they are essential in modern living and prerequisite to all further learning these core subjects must take precedence over subjects which may be temporarily attractive or useful.'[32] Even more disturbing was the omission of music from the inner zone surrounding this core, which Chant categorized as 'pre-eminently school subjects: History, Geography, Science and Languages.'[33] The document divulged its position with regard to music as follows:

> In an outer zone are groups of subjects rightly included in schools but which can be taught elsewhere, namely, those contributing to intellectual versatility and aesthetic appreciation such as Art, Music and Drama, and the serviceable subjects such as Agriculture, Commerce, Industrial Arts, Home Economics and others. Since the Commission believes that the primary aim should be intellectual development it is recommended that this order of priority be used in defining the scope of the school curriculum and the apportioning of school time.[34]

Chant was critical of repetition in the curriculum and recommended that the 'spiral of learning' principle be discontinued. It was disconcerting for music teachers to read that 'students are three times as likely to get an "A" grade in Music as in Social Studies and seven times as likely to fail in Mathematics as in Music.'[35] The report commented further: 'Such disparities give the pupils an impression that less effort is required in some subjects than in others. Subjects that require little or no effort have no place in an academic programme.'[36] If the criticism of music in the general sections discouraged music educators, the specific suggestions under 'Art, Drama and Music' must have put them in a state of shock: 'These subjects extend intellectual development into fields of aesthetic appreciation. Other agencies are available for doing this and the school reorganization recommended reduces the amount of school time devoted to these subjects in elementary schools and retains them as options in secondary schools. Quality of instruction is more important than time allotment. The Commission recommends that those having professional qualifications in these subjects be considered suitable for instructing in their specialties without the necessity of obtaining further qualifications.'[37] Lloyd Slind of UBC's Faculty of Education responded to this last point: 'Notwithstanding the Commissioners expressed view that the present program of teacher training will aid in obtaining suitable, qualified instructors, the Commission paradoxically decided that "those who have professional qualifications in the field of art, drama and music be considered suitable for conducting instruction in their specialties in the public schools without the necessity of obtaining any further qualifications." Applied to other subjects, this would imply that accountants could instantly take over as mathematics teachers and novelists and writers take over duties in the teaching of English, and so on.'[38] Slind's rebuttal also raised the question of the utilitarian demands imposed upon music teachers:

If the above views are to be taken as acceptable, it seems clear that the schools have, by and large, failed in their mission to make music a worthwhile, meaningful and educative subject. Whether or not this is true in part or in full, the indictment stands.

In searching for possible causes for such views it is plausible that, among others, there has been an overemphasis upon performance as opposed to educative (aesthetic-intellectual-creative) values. No other subject lends itself to exploitation as much as does music. School music teachers are very often under considerable pressure to provide music for (1) school public relations purposes (2) community affairs, and (3) semi-professional or social appearances, in addition of course, to their work as educators.[39]

Because of the impending danger of losing whatever gains they had made in the postwar years, music educators united in a vigorous group following the Chant Report. This renewal of purpose was particularly intense among instrumental music teachers. Subsequently, Mark Rose and Tom Furness played vital roles in representing the views of BCMEA during the hiatus in which many recommendations of the Chant Report were implemented. Curriculum revision was accelerated during the 1960s as part of the implementation process. Only after much procrastination did the ministry form a music advisory committee as a means of minimizing restrictions imposed by the Chant reforms. These restrictions were particularly severe in the academic stream, which prepared and qualified students for university admission. The wide swing of the philosophical pendulum in general education from the Putman-Weir Survey (1925) to the Chant Royal Commission (1960) was devastating. Naturally, music educators reacted in a defensive manner to a reordering of priorities in which music was not valued highly. And as a consequence of the report, they had to expend a great deal of their energies in justifying their subject to administrations and in selling it to students and parents.

The annual festivals, regional conferences, and special events by means of which BCSITA promoted band and orchestral activities were subsumed by BCMEA and other sponsoring groups. The first CMEA conference to be held in the province was organized in Vancouver by Lloyd Slind in 1962. On this occasion a concert by an all-province band, chorus, and orchestra gave music teachers an opportunity to display what had been accomplished in the region. More important, an infusion of ideas from other parts of Canada and the United States rejuvenated teachers at a critical time, when the future of music education in British Columbia seemed so uncertain.

In 1964 BCMEA staged a provincial conference in Victoria. The Thursday evening program consisted of composite choirs, bands, and orchestras at elementary, intermediate, and senior levels from the Greater Victoria schools. This array of ensembles within one school system was an indication of what had transpired since the first provincial festival of bands held in 1954. On Friday evening, an all-province choir, band, and orchestra presented 'Youth in Harmony,' with guest conductors from the United States. Another indication of growth and maturity was the improved standard of repertoire as compared with that of earlier festivals. The first school programs in the Interior encompassed bands and orchestras, reflecting the musical backgrounds of early teachers such as Archie McMurdo and Rex Potter. Many of those who subsequently entered the field continued to offer instruction in both winds and strings.

String classes were introduced into the Victoria elementary schools in 1949 as a deliberate effort to provide sufficient players for the senior ensembles. Harry Bigsby stated, 'This plan will enable high school orchestras to grow out of the haphazard stage.'[40] George Bower, Dorothy Hopgood Evans, Howard Denike, and Rowland Grant were among the instrumental teachers who taught in Victoria. In Vancouver, music education reflected British traditions, with an emphasis on choral work. That is, most instrumental ensembles during Burton Kurth's term as director of music (1939–55) were orchestras, and his successor, Ifor Roberts (1955–63), maintained this priority during his tenure too. But there was a shift of emphasis when Fred Turner became director of music in 1963, for he had been more directly involved in instrumental music than his predecessors. Moreover, his graduate work at the University of Washington had brought him into contact with American methods and materials, especially in the realm of bands. American influences became prevalent in Vancouver and throughout British Columbia as more teachers went to universities in the United States for professional training and graduate study.

If the department of education was reluctant in providing teacher training for instrumental music, it was intractable in its refusal to appoint a director of music who could coordinate activities on a provincial scale. In the meantime teachers' groups had to devise their own means of professional development and from time to time expressed the need for an expansion of music at the university level. Those who were engrossed in teaching instrumental music were looking for specialized courses dealing with practical problems in group instruction, an idea encountered in the United States. However, their concept of what should be done was not shared by UBC's music department, whose commitment to teaching music in a liberal arts tradition was directed toward general cultural growth. This situation changed when Welton Marquis, an American theorist, became head of the music department in 1958. He expanded the curriculum to include professional programs and developed a summer music session in which activities ranged from a 'school of opera' to a high school band and orchestra workshop.

A faculty of education was established at UBC in 1955, and a number of faculty appointments were made in music. Much of the instruction was directed toward the general student, of whom the level of achievement required was lower than in the case of a music major. Music instructors in the Faculty of Education took an active interest in school music teachers, their programs, and their concerns: summer courses and workshops

were offered; a number of university teachers gave leadership in professional journals; some served on BCMEA executives and committees.
Among others, Mark Rose and Allen Clingman taught instrumental
methods in the Faculty of Education. In the formative years, tensions
between UBC's music department and Faculty of Education impeded the
university's effectiveness in facilitating the instrumental music movement
in the schools.

The University of Victoria first offered music instruction as an outgrowth of the teachers' college, and more recently its programs have
spanned the Faculties of Education and Fine Arts. Although its music
division did not come into operation until 1967, Victoria has extended its
influence through a vigorous expansion of programs in music education.

MANITOBA

In 1946 Ethel Kinley participated in the Music Educators' National
Conference in Cleveland and the Canadian Federation of Music Teachers' Associations conference in Toronto. During her trip she observed
group instruction in orchestral instruments both in American cities and
in Toronto, and on the basis of these experiences she concluded that
Winnipeg was lagging behind in instrumental music. Coincidentally, a
recommendation from the Manitoba Schools' Orchestra, a city-
provincial organization outside the school system, urged 'that the
schools assume more responsibility for instrumental music instruction.'[41]
The executive of the orchestra indicated that they 'wholeheartedly
approved of any move that would develop musicians in the schools of
Greater Winnipeg.'[42] It was in this context that Ethel Kinley submitted
a proposal in 1947 to Winnipeg School Division No. 1 for string classes
as an integral part of the elementary school program. The school
board, reportedly for financial reasons, did not implement Kinley's
plan within regular school hours, but they did hire several teachers to
conduct violin classes, of approximately eight students, in a number of
elementary schools. Arthur Fraser, appointed as a full-time instrumental music teacher, coordinated much of this activity; he was also
expected to develop winds in six schools and to direct seven orchestras
and two bands. A newspaper account of the program in 1949 reported:
'Only those who are starting study of the violin for the first time are
permitted to enter the school's group instruction. The beginner's
course, set for the grade 4 level, is given over a two-year period within
school time. Instruction from the three violin teachers, Miss Frances

Port, Lloyd Blackman and Richard Grymonpre is given free of charge. Students are asked to pay a portion of the cost of the music. Since the classes were started in the spring of 1947, they have grown from 12 to the establishment of groups in 36 schools in all parts of the city.'[43] Each child was allowed no more than two years of free instruction. Arthur Fraser estimated, however, that 'about half of the school orchestra players also take private lessons.'[44] It was evident that many students were attracted into these classes by the prospect of eventually getting into the provincial orchestra. The expansion of instrumental work during Marjorie Horner's term as supervisor of music was such that in the early 1950s there were as many as fifty classes, requiring four full-time and two part-time instructors. But the preponderance of violins meant that school orchestral groups were not well balanced, even within their string sections. In short, this program furnished players for the Manitoba Schools' Orchestra, but it was less successful in developing instrumental ensembles within individual city schools. In 1955 the board imposed a charge of fifty cents per pupil for each group lesson, and the instruction was reorganized as an extra-curricular activity. It was reported in 1963 that 'the classes have continued, but on a greatly reduced scale.'[45]

From 1945 to 1964 the Manitoba Schools' Orchestra visited twenty-nine towns and, by means of annual tours during Easter week, stimulated interest in music education beyond the urban centres of Winnipeg and Brandon. Horner recognized the close relationship between the orchestra and the Winnipeg school system: 'Our music staff and our students are very active in the Manitoba Schools' Orchestra, both its junior and senior divisions; this is so much the case that our school programs are consciously integrated into the program of that organization.'[46] Winnipeg school teachers who served as conductors in the postwar years included Glen Pierce, Eric Adams, and Frances Port. A change of name to the Greater Winnipeg Schools' Orchestra in 1962 was an acknowledgment that most of the students were from the Winnipeg region. From the inception of instrumental music, Winnipeg's dynasty of music supervisors – Ethel Kinley, Marjorie Horner, and Lola MacQuarrie – stressed string instruction as the best means of building orchestral ensembles in the schools, but undeniably the priority was reserved for choral music, a field in which Winnipeg was renowned.

Art Buss started a band at Elmwood High School in 1956, though he was originally hired to do orchestral work. At Elmwood, academic credit was given for band instruction, and the school not only supplied instruments but also scheduled classes in regular school hours. The immediate success of these classes convinced Buss's principal to retain the program despite the unsympathetic attitudes of supervisors who associated bands with jive and swing. The Elmwood School Band also functioned as the Blue Bomberette Band in affiliation with the Winnipeg Blue Bombers football organization. Needless to say, Buss achieved a high degree of popularity among his students, as the band maintained a busy schedule of football games, parades, and other entertainments.

Fred Merrett was also active in brass and woodwind teaching in Winnipeg. He taught at Machray Elementary School and later started a band at TechVoc School. Merrett was bandmaster of the Winnipeg Citadel Band of the Salvation Army and for many summers was on staff at the International Music Camp, situated near the border of Manitoba and North Dakota. This camp provided motivation for young instrumentalists during the summer period; in 1956 there were only 6 Canadians in attendance, but by 1963 the number had risen to 257. The formation of a Manitoba Schools' Concert Band was an added incentive for wind players and set a standard for school bands to follow; the executive of the provincial orchestra noted in 1961 that the imbalance of instrumentation in favor of strings had been reversed. Certainly the momentum in building band programs increased throughout the 1960s.

Instrumental music as a school subject received token recognition in 1957. The music curriculum for senior high school grades was outlined in a mimeographed publication, *Music I, II, III* (grades ten, eleven, twelve): 'Music could be studied in three ways: 1) As a general option (Music I, II, III); 2) As a "special activity" (e.g. festivals, etc.); 3) As a private music option.'[47] The general option consisted of (a) theory (30 per cent) as required for Grade III, University of Manitoba School of Music, (b) participation in choral or instrumental groups (20 per cent), (c) history of music (50 per cent). The course outline described various genres and composers, to be taught only by a teacher holding a specialist certificate in music. According to Lola MacQuarrie, music supervisor for Winnipeg School Division No. 1, 'the course [had] not been taught for at least thirty years, and several of the [school] principals were not aware of its existence.'[48] In 1962 the department of education mounted new general courses for the entire province. As part of this project, Lola MacQuarrie and a group of music teachers prepared the *Program for Senior High School General Course in Music*.[49]

This revision called for music theory (20 per cent), music appreciation (30 per cent), and participation in choir, band, or orchestra (50 per cent). Although the time allotment for performance had been increased, the content of the curriculum consisted largely of repertoire and musical styles to be covered in the listening program. The unsophisticated nature of the departmental documents reflected an apathy with respect to the performance facet of music education. Officials relied upon Winnipeg to lead the way, and it was a long time before instrumental music was described in any detail in the provincial curriculum. In Winnipeg, performance was translated loosely to mean participation in the competitive festival, probably because that had been the focus in choral music.

Fred Merrett investigated the status of instrumental music in Manitoba during the 1962–3 school year. His research furnished data on school programs as well as activities affiliated with church and community groups, many of which provided the only opportunity for instruction in strings and winds in remote areas; typical of these ensembles were the small brass bands operated by the Salvation Army. Group lessons accounted for 32.5 per cent of the instruction in areas outside Winnipeg. Moreover, Merrett's findings confirmed the popularity of bands over orchestras in rural Manitoba and left little doubt concerning the uneven quality of teaching by people with inadequate musical training. Merrett identified 16 orchestras and 43 bands operating outside the school systems but found only 12 different schools involved with orchestras and 9 with bands. Even fewer schools had integrated their instrumental work into the regular part of the curriculum. Simply stated, there were only two or three schools with sufficient enrolment to justify the term curricular instrumental programs. It may reasonably be assumed that the success of the Manitoba Schools' Orchestras (and Band) diminished any urgent need to nurture instrumental programs within the individual schools of the greater Winnipeg area. This 1962–3 survey also revealed that

> conditions in which instrumental music was taught in the schools of Manitoba varied from school to school. An instrumental program operated wherever there was a teacher or individual who was willing to give the time and energy necessary to keep it going despite such deterrents as school board lethargy, principal or teacher opposition, competition with sports activities for the time of students, and lack of equipment or practice room facilities. Very seldom was music instruction the result of organization on

the administrative level, or of pressure from the local school board. The influence of public opinion was ineffective because there was no organization through which parents or interested people could channel their desire for instrumental music opportunities for their young people.[50]

Given this state of affairs, there was little demand for qualified instructors and 'no incentive whatsoever for young teachers to take on the complicated routine of teaching music under adverse conditions.'[51] The absence of leadership on the part of any government department, educational association, or parents' group had all but predetermined that too much would be left 'to chance or to the isolated efforts of a few enthusiasts.'[52] Such apathy notwithstanding, instrumental music in Winnipeg grew during the 1966–76 period, when Glen Pierce was supervisor of music. He extended performance opportunities beyond the scope of the Greater Winnipeg Orchestra's organization so that eventually instruction and ensemble activities were localized within each school.

The growth of instrumental music could have progressed in an orderly, systematic way if the universities had been more enterprising in the field of teacher education. Brandon College was the first institution to offer a BMus degree in Manitoba, but its small number of graduates did not meet the increasing need for instrumental music teachers. At the University of Manitoba, students interested in school music could take practical methods in the Faculty of Education, but these courses were general in nature and traditionally had been confined to choral techniques. The situation looked promising when the University of Manitoba established a school of music in 1964, with Leonard Isaacs as director. However, its programs – with their emphasis on theory, history, and performance in piano and voice – reflected British rather than North American traditions. In the absence of advanced instrumental training, school teachers had to rely upon professional development and in-service training as their careers required it. The Manitoba Music Educators' Association responded to teachers' needs by featuring guest conductors at Easter conventions and separate orchestra sessions (1960–7) at annual workshops held in Brandon. The clinicians for these events were often imported from outside the province.

Instrumental music had been introduced into Manitoba schools at about the same time that new beginnings were being made in Ontario and British Columbia, but, by comparison, progress in Manitoba was slow. The original program, which emphasized strings in the elementary grades, was supplementary at best. It ameliorated the programs of the Manitoba Schools' Orchestra, which ultimately served an elite group of aspiring musicians, but it did not lead to curricular programs in most secondary schools. The continuation of strong choral programs and the close affiliation of the provincial orchestra with school staff members had the effect of mollifying demands for instrumental music as a regular option in general education. Nor did the administrators in the department of education foresee the need for policies based upon a sound philosophy of education. In lieu of appointing a provincial director of music, the department leaned on Winnipeg's supervisors to give direction and assistance. Too often this help was in the realm of yeoman service rather than participation in long-term planning. For many years, instrumental music in Manitoba remained in a state of inertia, broken occasionally by excuses from the provincial department of education, the school boards, the teachers' college, and the universities. Merrett maintained, 'Unless the adults who control our educational system ... can become convinced that instrumental music should be a part of every child's general education, there is little hope that they will ever demand that our colleges provide qualified teachers for the classrooms.'[53] More recently, the division of responsibilities between the Faculty of Education and the School of Music at the University of Manitoba has hampered the immediate implementation of specialized programs which were needed during the 1960s. Consequently, instrumental music has developed along American lines, for the obvious reason that failure to train qualified teachers in Manitoba necessitated the hiring of graduates from colleges south of the border.

ALBERTA

Because of Alberta's sparse population, the province sustained a number of small high schools, and conditions were not ideal for the development of instrumental music. In most situations progress can be attributed to a few resourceful and aggressive individuals who forged ahead before there was any official sanction or support for this branch of school music.

In Calgary, Lloyd Erickson organized a band at Balmoral Junior High School as early as 1950 and was in the forefront of band and orchestral activities throughout the decade. His work at Crescent Heights High School set the pace for other schools; Elgar Carter was associated with developments at Central High School. From these informal beginnings the Calgary board proceeded to offer instruction in many junior and senior high schools. Official endorsation of instrumental music as a curricular activity took place shortly after Cyril Mossop was appointed supervisor of music (1951–72). In 1951 he 'requested funds to organize a 20-piece band in a senior high school.'[54] Although his request was not granted until the following year, it marked the beginning of a comprehensive program at all levels. He described the program as follows: 'Rhythm band classes are encouraged in the first three grades, melody instruments in grades 4–6, with school orchestras and bands creating harmony at the junior and senior high level. Of course recorder classes playing in two, three or four parts are also encouraged in the junior high schools, particularly in grade 7, as a preparation for the study of the real orchestral instruments in grades 8 and 9.'[55] Mossop recalled later that a number of secondary school principals, 'recognizing the educational value of such a program,' saw fit to 'schedule band, orchestra, and string classes in school hours, thus avoiding conflict with the extra-curricular physical education programs.'[56] These new ventures were inspired by participation in festival competitions and, later, in other community projects. One of the most impressive of these projects was an all-city junior philharmonic orchestra, which operated on Saturday mornings. It was 'sponsored jointly by the Public and Separate School Boards, Mount Royal College, and the Calgary Philharmonic Society.'[57] This ensemble was established in 1957 and was conducted in turn by Captain F.M. McLeod, Jack Mirtle, and Frank Simpson. By the 1960s it had grown into a three-level organization (Junior, Intermediate, and Southern Alberta Youth Orchestra), with Haymo Taeuber, conductor of the Calgary Philharmonic Orchestra, acting as its overall artistic director. As in other regions, military bands stimulated interest in instrumental activities through their concerts in school assemblies. Presumably, these concerts were part of armed services recruiting campaigns, but by and large they fullfilled an educational purpose by performing music from the standard band repertoire. The Princess Patricia's Canadian Light Infantry Band and the Royal Canadian Air Force Band of Edmonton appeared frequently in Calgary schools. By 1966 Mossop reported that there were instrumental groups functioning in twenty-nine of the fifty-two junior high schools: '(a) band programs in sixteen junior and eight senior high schools; (b) orchestral programs in two junior highs and one senior high school; (c) string programs in seven junior high schools.'[58]

In Edmonton the Schoolboys' Band had provided a form of instrumental music since its formation in 1935. It began as an extra-curricular activity, but in the late 1950s academic credit was given to its members, who came from various city schools. Rehearsals were held in the evenings under the leadership of T.V. Newlove and his assistant, O.W. Murray. Band engagements included concerts, tours, and parades, among them appearances at the Calgary Stampede and the Grey Cup games in Vancouver and Toronto. This organization gained the support of parents and band enthusiasts, but it held less appeal for those interested in activities of an educational nature. Inasmuch as the band was allowed to maintain its own independent budget, the board's music department exerted very little influence over its policies and operation; more significantly, music supervisors in Edmonton did not regard the band as an entirely satisfactory medium for purposes of music education. Keith Bissell, who succeeded Norman Eagleson as music supervisor in 1949, was more committed to orchestral training and experience. Accordingly, he organized the Edmonton Junior Symphony (later renamed Youth Orchestra) in 1952 and served as its conductor until 1955. The existence of a city-wide school band and junior symphony in Edmonton may have lessened any feeling of urgency to offer instrumental instruction in individual schools, for it was not until the late 1950s that Alan Rumbelow (music supervisor 1955–72) formally introduced instrumental music as a secondary school option. In 1958 the Ross Sheppard Composite High School in Edmonton had the largest orchestral enrolment in the province, with a total of sixty-nine members; smaller orchestras were in operation at Eastglen, Bonnie Doon, and Strathcona Schools. Instrumental classes were incorporated into junior high schools in 1961; Ron Stephens served as assistant supervisor during this period of unprecedented expansion. By 1962–3 such classes were operating in thirteen junior high schools and five out of six secondary schools, and the annual 'Night of Music' was used effectively to make the public aware of progress and achievement. Father Leo Green initiated instrumental music in the Edmonton separate schools in 1956 by offering brass and woodwinds commencing in grade ten. Paul Bourret succeeded him as supervisor in 1968 and expanded the program to include string instruction beginning as early as grade four.

Not all early developments took place in the cities. In 1953–4 Harry Lomnes mounted a band program at Wetaskiwin High School, where he was principal. Lomnes prodded the department of education to give more encouragement to instrumental work, and as a founding member of the Alberta Chapter of the Canadian Bandmasters' Association (CBA), he was involved in band workshops and festivals. A number of special events were coordinated by the CBA (Alberta Chapter) and the Cultural Development Branch of the provincial government. The latter organization also sponsored provincial summer band workshops for high school students from 1958 to 1969. In Alberta the cultural division of the provincial government was more helpful to teachers in supporting projects of a practical nature than was the department of education; even more discouraging to teachers was the fact that the department ignored periodic pleas for the appointment of a director of music to coordinate affairs on a province-wide basis. In a survey conducted in 1958–9, Lomnes reported: 'Music is not a part of the curriculum in 296 Alberta high schools. Only ninety-three high schools have found a place for music courses in the curriculum and only 6.1 per cent of the total enrollment of Alberta high school students receive classroom music instruction for credit.'[59]

Instrumental instruction represented a small part of the overall musical activity in Alberta, and not until 1958 did the department of education sanction an instrumental music course as such. In a new document music electives for grades ten, eleven, and twelve were outlined under four categories: 'General: Music 10; Choral: Music 10, Music 20, Music 30; Orchestra: Music 10, Music 20, Music 30; Band: Music 10, Music 20, Music 30.'[60] This official endorsement of the subject added momentum to the growth of band and orchestral classes.

The universities in Alberta took over all teacher training after the Second World War, but they did not anticipate the increasing need for instrumental specialists in the 1960s. And even if they had, university administrators were reluctant to act quickly, especially when confronted simultaneously with similar pressures from other disciplines and professions. Seldom was music high on any university's list of priorities. Yet music education was as well served by Alberta's institutions of higher education as it was in most provinces in western Canada.

Degrees in music education were offered through the Faculty of Education at the University of Alberta in Edmonton; Richard Eaton, head of the fine arts department, initiated practical courses for students pursuing careers in school music, including a variety of offerings in summer school and extension programs. The music education courses, however, reflected Eaton's own choral background, and only a small number of graduates were prepared at an advanced level for instrumental careers. That teachers in the profession were not satisfied with the seemingly indifferent response of educational authorities was manifest in the Lomnes study: 'The teacher-training program of Alberta evidently does not take care of the demands of a growing instrumental program. The need for more instrumental music teachers is imperative. Some revision of the policy of the Department of Education and of the University of Alberta could do much to alleviate the shortage.'[61]

Alan Smith's unique approach to the training of instrumental music teachers at the University of Alberta was in the nature of a music education laboratory (MELAB) organized within the Faculty of Education in 1963. Although originally conceived as a laboratory band for purposes of teacher training, it was later expanded to include work in orchestra, choir, and general music. MELAB was designed 'to train teachers rather than to produce Grade VII bands and orchestras.'[62] Smith described the set-up: 'The student teachers attend lectures on general music methods and on the instruments and techniques of the band and orchestra. They also participate in instrument laboratories where they learn to play all of the instruments of the band and orchestra. The sequence of study in each of these courses closely parallels the activities in the workshop, thus providing a continuing academic background for the "inquiry processes" motivated by the workshop.'[63] Yet some educators raised questions concerning the unusual procedures employed in MELAB. To answer the question 'How is it possible for modestly qualified student teachers to teach in all areas of MELAB simultaneously?' Smith wrote: 'Concurrent with their MELAB teaching assignments, all student teachers are enrolled in lecture courses dealing with instrumental techniques, band and orchestra ensemble techniques, and curriculum and instruction in music. They are also enrolled in laboratory courses where they learn to play all instruments of the band and orchestra. The scope and sequence in these lecture and laboratory courses is closely related to the development of the MELAB bands, orchestras, and choruses. This has resulted, of course, in a radical re-structuring of the content of the courses.'[64] Specialized training was also introduced on the Calgary campus of the University of Alberta with the creation of a fine arts department in 1959. Frank Churchley was its first chairman; he was succeeded by Malcolm Brown in 1964. The Calgary branch became an autonomous university in 1966 and in that same year entered into affiliation with the

Banff School of Fine Arts. The University of Lethbridge opened its
music department in 1967.

The universities fell behind in supplying teachers with expertise in
the instrumental field. In situations where specialists were not readily
available, school boards hired teachers trained in the United States or
others who had experience in community bands and orchestras. In
addressing the shortage of music teachers, Harry Lomnes posed the
following solution:

> Due to the prevalence of professional service bands in Canada, bandsmen
> are gradually leaving the services on retirement. Most of these men have
> been excellently trained within the services, where they spend full time on
> music and are required to study and write examinations to gain promotions.
> A number of them are being sent overseas to Kneller Hall where they receive
> intensive training as conductors. The Navy Band School at Esquimalt,
> British Columbia, is training excellent musicians for service in Navy bands.
> Many of these professional conductors and bandsmen plan to take school
> music positions upon retirement after twenty years. Why not take advan-
> tage of these fine musicians as the opportunity arises?[65]

Whatever satisfaction may have accompanied the growth of instrumental music, there was still cause for concern regarding the quality of
the teaching personnel. Although a number of the instructors were
adequate musicians, some were deficient in applying goals and objectives as professional educators. Their disparate backgrounds may have
contributed to the demise of the Alberta Music Educators' Association,
which was formed in 1957 but dissolved in 1969. At the time of the
dissolution music educators were offered membership in the Alberta
Fine Arts Council; instead, many instrumental teachers aligned themselves with the Canadian Band Directors' Association. In a similar way
choral teachers were attracted to the practical activities sponsored by
the Alberta Choral Directors' Association. Consequently, music teachers in Alberta have splintered off into special interest groups, leaving
themselves without a unified voice to express their collective views on
philosophical and political issues.

Post-secondary institutions can yield special benefits to a community
at large, especially if the faculty includes artist performers, scholars,
and teachers aware of current research and pedagogy. As an example,
Professor Thomas Rolston introduced Shinichi Suzuki's string method
into Canada in 1964 with the establishment of the Society for Talent

Education, Alberta. By 1968 more than two hundred young violinists and cellists were enrolled in this program, with the result that string players in Edmonton and Calgary were receiving advanced training and experience well beyond the level available in public school classes. The project also brought Suzuki's pedagogical principles to the attention of private studio teachers and challenged school musicians to examine its applications to group instruction. The University of Alberta String Quartet became a resident ensemble in 1969. Its performances stimulated the musical environment of the university, and the quartet's commitment to contemporary repertoire, including numerous Canadian compositions, contributed to the cultural maturity of the community. This surge of string activity on the Edmonton campus not only established the university as an important centre for music education, it also renewed enthusiasm in string performance at all levels. Rolston's presence at the University of Alberta and later at the Banff Centre School of Fine Arts represents the kind of leadership that is vital to the inspiration of teachers and the artistic growth of talented students.

SASKATCHEWAN

Saskatchewan was later than other western provinces in developing courses in instrumental music. The fact that Saskatchewan did not incorporate junior high schools in a three-level structure might account for this; certainly, in other provinces the flexibility associated with the junior high curriculum was a salient factor in expediting the acceptance of music as a subject beyond the elementary grades. And yet Saskatchewan was the only western province to appoint a provincial supervisor of music. At least the government recognized the need for systematic planning, consultation, and coordination. This position was advantageous for music teachers in that it placed a spokesperson inside the department to represent the interests and concerns of music in policy decisions.

The choice of Rj Staples for this post was a natural one. He had proven himself as an innovative teacher at Regina's Central Collegiate, and while there he had assisted the department of education on curriculum matters. In 1945 Staples became music director at Moose Jaw Teachers' College and part-time consultant for the department. He was subsequently engaged as full-time music supervisor in 1949 and in this capacity became the driving force behind school music in Saskatchewan for the next twenty years. One manifestation of Staples's presence was a 1948 regulation permitting students to earn 'credits towards high school standing through participation in school sponsored bands, orchestras and glee clubs.[66] The development of orchestral work was closely linked to events at Regina's Central Collegiate, where Staples had become legendary for his bustling schedule of extra-curricular activities. Lloyd Blackman, a violinist, placed increased emphasis on curricular instruction, particularly on strings, during his term at Central (1950–61.) He became a prominent figure in the orchestral field, well known not just in his own school but also in the city by virtue of his supervisory roles, and as conductor of the first provincial orchestra. This ensemble performed in the celebration for the 1965 Saskatchewan Diamond Jubilee, which was broadcast as a province-wide extravaganza under the leadership of Rj Staples. Although it was primarily a choral production, the enthusiasm which it engendered in the public undoubtedly added support for instrumental music as well. Don Cowan pioneered instrumental work at Scott Collegiate long before the subject was described in any detail in provincial curricula. Later, he taught at Sheldon-Williams, before his appointment to the Regina Teachers' College and the University of Regina. Cowan was widely respected for his publications: textbooks in general music, method books for the recorder, and original compositions for solo flute and saxophone.

City-wide instrumental aggregations were often the precursors of instructional programs within individual schools. In a striking way the emergence of wind programs in Saskatchewan's city schools has been inextricably linked to community bands sponsored by service clubs. In Regina Mrs A.B. Mossing reorganized her Queen City Band as the Regina Junior Lions in 1943. Eventually, this ensemble evolved into a training system of bands at various levels of development. Her son D'Arcy organized a band in 1950 under the auspices of a parents' group within the Regina separate schools; its members were recruited from four elementary schools. Another son, Robert, has spent many years building an elaborate community band organization under the auspices of the Lions Club.

Mikel Kalmokoff, a high school mathematics teacher in Saskatoon, initiated action there by forming the city-wide Saskatoon Collegiate Cadet Band. Growing out of this project was an affiliation in 1954–5 between the Saskatoon school board and the Lions Band; the board provided practice and storage facilities, while the service club furnished funds for instruments, uniforms, and travel expenses. Under this joint sponsorship the board approved a half-course academic credit for participating school students, and in the curriculum revisions of 1961, band members were allowed full-course credit for instrumental music in each year of high school.

Staples recalled that there were only two school bands in the province when he became provincial supervisor; by the time he retired there were over 150 bands. The Sturgis school unit was the first in a rural area to develop a band program. Initially, the board was asked to consider instrumental work because a fledgling band in the community had become defunct. With the help of a provincial grant and permission to hire a musician who was not a certified teacher, the board began the program in the early 1950s under Bud Haffsteinn. His position was designated that of supervisor in order that he would qualify under department of education funding regulations. He taught instrumental groups in several schools in an extra-curricular arrangement that brought players together for band rehearsals. At the close of the school year in 1956, a massed band concert was held in the Sturgis arena. Rural boards in many provinces experienced difficulty in recruiting and retaining music teachers, and Sturgis was no exception. Cyril Lacey succeeded Haffsteinn in 1957 but remained for only one year. In 1958 the board advertised for a band leader in England and subsequently hired Leonard Camplin, who served as supervisor until 1961. An oboist with Kneller Hall training, he provided instruction in both elementary and secondary schools; by 1960 students were receiving academic credit for their band work. Another British army bandmaster, Captain E.R. Wragg, took over the program in 1961. Sturgis served as a model for rural Saskatchewan. Joanna Weweler notes that 'Staples arranged for the Department to pay the expenses of sending this Sturgis Band to play a concert at the provincial School Trustees Convention in Saskatoon. The trustees were very impressed and this sparked many of them to emulate Sturgis in their areas.'[67] The band won widespread recognition in the late 1960s under the direction of Duane Emch, whose background and training were American.

There is no doubt that Staples favoured the general music approach outlined in his 'music exploration course,' which encouraged activities such as creative listening. Nevertheless, he did promote instrumental music through provincial grants, workshops, and summer courses. For years before the universities offered specialized instrumental training, summer schools were vital for those teachers who were inadequately prepared for band and orchestral work. In 1949 six-week sessions superseded the one-week crash courses which Staples had given for many summers at the request of the Faculty of Education, University of Saskatchewan. Commencing in 1956 the venue for summer music courses was shifted to the resort setting of Fort Qu'Appelle, and the instruction for teachers became more advanced. Summer camps for students were effective in raising performance levels and in motivating promising instrumentalists who had little instruction beyond the limited expertise of their classroom teachers. In 1963, 160 bandmembers attended the second annual music camp, which took place at Qu'Appelle under the direction of Frank Connell, conductor of the Moose Jaw Lions Band. This program was supported by the Canadian Bureau for the Advancement of Music, the Canadian Bandmasters' Association (Saskatchewan Chapter), the Saskatchewan Arts Board, and the provincial department of education.

Orchestral clinics involving students from grade seven and up were held in the 1960s during the Christmas vacation period. These sessions were used to select players for the provincial orchestra and to rehearse music for performance at SMEA conventions. The busy calendar of events for school bands and orchestras reinforced the growth of instrumental music. That is not to imply that all of these activities were educational or even intrinsically musical in nature. For example, the Moose Jaw International Band Festival (established 1949) was a colourful cavalcade of concerts, competitions, parades, and band drills with an entertainment appeal that prompted festival organizers to refer to the city as the 'Band Capital of the World.' The fusion of community and school band activities in Saskatchewan is an outcome of historical relationships which stem from the 1950s. During this decade instrumental music in the schools began to spring up in advance of an adequate supply of competent music teachers. The annual report in 1957–8 stated that 'the recurring problem of helping administrators to secure qualified school music specialists' had been 'greatly alleviated by the engaging of persons from the United States and Great Britain.'[68] As instructors became available, school programs multiplied in both the cities and the rural areas, and eventually Staples found the burden of work so heavy that he was given an assistant. In 1967 Herbert Jeffrey, former director of the Princess Patricia's Canadian Light Infantry Band, was appointed as provincial band consultant. Although Jeffrey did not bring extensive school experience to this job, he had received musical training at Kneller Hall in England as part of his military career. The name Kneller Hall had a magic ring, especially among educational authorities who had had military service in the past, so it is not surprising that graduates of this institution were hired for instrumental programs in many parts of Canada. A number of projects were undertaken in 1967–8 to promote the development of school bands: a provincial youth band was organized in 1967, and grants were made to twenty-seven schools to assist in the purchase of instruments. In that same year sixty-four special clinicians were engaged for twelve workshops held in various places throughout the province.

Much of the momentum in instrumental music can be attributed to new developments at the university level. David Kaplan was appointed to the Faculty of Education of the University of Saskatchewan in 1960. A woodwind specialist from Indiana University, Kaplan gave leadership in a variety of ways: through his revision of the woodwind syllabus of the Western Board of Music, through his articles on the pedagogy and literature of woodwind music, and through his involvement in the formation of the Saskatchewan Arts Council. He also conducted the Saskatoon Symphony from 1963 to 1969. Later on, Dwaine Nelson was appointed to the University of Saskatchewan; he stimulated the growth of school bands through instrumental workshops and festivals in many parts of the province. Howard Leyton-Brown provided leadership in the realm of private studio instruction and community string ensembles. He served as conductor of the Regina Symphony Orchestra (1960–71) and director of the Regina Conservatory (appointed 1955), and initiated several projects to further the advancement of instrumental music. As secondary school programs have flourished, there has been a corresponding rise in admissions for university degrees in music. Over the years the universities have assumed greater responsibility for musical training, to the extent that the province gradually has become less reliant upon specialists from outside Saskatchewan.

THE ATLANTIC PROVINCES

According to a survey by Arthur Fraser in 1950–1, 'instrumental music was one of the weakest aspects of the music programs in schools across Canada.'[69] Survey results are seldom complete and therefore are only approximate in their statistical accuracy. Nevertheless, Fraser's conclusion appears to be valid for the Atlantic region on the strength of his comparative figures for all provinces. But the indomitable efforts of those whose accomplishments predated the sanctioning of instrumental music as a curricular subject should not be overlooked. Such isolated attempts paved the way for future acceptance of instrumental programs. In Edmundston, NB, Leo Poulin, a bandmaster from Maine, had established an instrumental program during the 1930s which featured an all-girls high school band. A variety of instrumental ensembles enhanced the school life of several institutions in the Atlantic region; these activities were often under the direction of private teachers, church organists, or regimental musicians from the community rather than certified school teachers.

In 1955 a member of the Board of School Trustees of Saint John wrote to the Canadian Education Association in Toronto inquiring about academic credit for music as a subject in the high school curriculum. It is clear from the contents of the letter that instrumental music represented uncharted waters at that time. There had been instrumental ensembles at the Saint John High School and the Vocational School for many years under the direction of William Bowden, but there was no instrumental program on a city-wide basis until 1955, when Paul Murray became supervisor of music for the city schools. During his term (1955–61) he took steps in organizing a practical framework for instrumental music in the curriculum. The board made three thousand dollars available for a band program in 1957, and string instruction based on the Bornoff system was introduced in 1960. Bruce Holder from Saint John and Adolf Krack and Heini Henkes from Germany were hired as instrumental instructors. The first concert of the Saint John Youth Orchestra was given in 1963, under the direction of Peter Hinkley, Murray's successor. The success of the work in Saint John sparked interest in other Maritime centres, but it took several years for programs to develop. When Boyd Neel, dean of the Royal Conservatory of Music, visited the Maritimes in 1957, he expressed concern regarding the lack of instrumental instruction in the schools:

On my recent visit to the Maritimes, I was struck by the enormous interest everywhere in music. The recent formation of a full-time symphony orchestra in the City of Halifax has no doubt done a lot to stimulate such interest among the public. Hitherto, it would seem that concentration has been more on vocal and choral work than on instrumental work, especially as regards the schools, where I found that little attention has been paid in the past to instrumental performance of any kind, other than the playing of the piano. The results of this neglect of instrumental music generally can be seen in the Halifax Symphony itself, where, in order to start the orchestra at all, it was necessary to import about nine or ten players from the United States to fill the key positions, no Canadians being available for the posts.[70]

The conference 'Music in the Schools of the Atlantic Provinces' held at Mount Allison University in 1960 was an important event in that it enabled music teachers to find out what was happening in other parts of the region. They shared their experiences of trying to make progress and formulated ideas for the overall development of music education. Instrumental music was one of the major concerns in their discussions and deliberations. There were initiatives in several quarters, both before and after the conference, that augured well for the future. The report from PEI stated that there was a 'military band for selected students at Queen Charlotte High School, operated and sponsored generally by the Reserve Army,' but 'no school orchestras on the Island.'[71] At this time, however, Gabriel Chaisson in Summerside and William Conkey at the nearby air force base were involved in instrumental activities. Although these initiatives were outside the academic sphere of their respective schools, they were the embryos of instrumental music in this province. Elizabeth Murray spoke at the Mount Allison conference about her work in the adult education division of the department of education in Nova Scotia:

> The main concern of the Adult Education Division is with leaders and participants in community music activities, but assistance is also given in in-service music courses for teachers. Last year more than 800 adults took courses held in twenty-eight places. All of these courses were co-sponsored by such organizations as Home and School, Women's Institutes, teachers' study clubs, Music Festivals, Nova Scotia Music Educators' Association, etc. Two projects were carried on directly by the Division, one a course for recorder players, and the other the music portion of the School of Community Arts at Tatamagouche, where courses in choral and instrumental music are given in a school following the Nova Scotia Festival of the Arts.[72]

The content of this report suggests that, as yet, the curriculum branch of the department had not made a commitment to instrumental music as a bona fide school subject.

In the summer of 1966 a second seminar on music education in the Atlantic region was held in Charlottetown, sponsored by the Charlottetown Festival and the Fathers of Confederation Building

Trust. These sessions were chaired by John Fenwick, conductor of the Halifax Symphony Orchestra and assistant artistic director of the Confederation Centre in Charlottetown. His father, G. Roy Fenwick, was again featured as keynote speaker. Delegates discussed a number of issues, but much of their time was spent on the topic of instrumental instruction. It was recommended that 'a common board of examiners be set up to assess the qualifications of potential instrumental teachers from among ex-service bandsmen.'[73]

The establishment of Mount Allison's summer music camp provided a gathering-point for young Maritime instrumentalists, many of whom came from places where instruction and ensemble experiences were limited. It also afforded Mount Allison an opportunity to identify talented players who might pursue music at the university level. At a time when instrumental music was struggling to earn widespread acceptance and practical support, the presence of the Lawrence Park Collegiate Orchestra at the 1963 CMEA convention, held in Halifax, was of inestimable value. Stellar performances, both technically and artistically, by a school orchestra with a complete instrumentation left a lasting impression on convention delegates and the general public. More often than not, school music has expanded on the strength of such demonstrated achievements rather than as a result of any philosophical determination that it should be part of the curriculum. Putting it simply, the proof is in the performance. In like manner the New Brunswick Youth Orchestra, formed in 1966 (conductor, Stanley Saunders), served as a continuing incentive to young instrumentalists. Coupled with the Mount Allison summer camp, it channelled an otherwise fragmented pattern of activity into an effective aggregation of young musicians. It was a logical progression to move from these province-wide projects to instrumental programs within the individual schools.

There were summer sessions initiated by other universities in the Atlantic provinces. The School of Music at Acadia University sponsored a summer school in Wolfville, NS, which began in 1967 under the direction of Janis Kalejs. An instrumental music camp was held in Newfoundland under the sponsorship of the Extension Service of Memorial University in 1972, with Donald Cook as its founding director. It was not until 1975 that a youth music camp was initiated in Prince Edward Island; Hubert Tersteeg was its first director. These summer projects did a great deal to reinforce neophyte programs in the schools. The establishment of the Maritime Band Festival in Moncton in the late 1960s also encouraged instrumental instruction throughout the region.

Like many parts of the country, Nova Scotia owes much of its early development in the area of instrumental music to servicemen who became involved in community groups. Wilf Harvey was posted to the Greenwood Air Force Base in the Annapolis Valley in 1944. Shortly thereafter he assumed the post of bandmaster of the Middleton Concert Band, which for many years also functioned as the West Nova Scotia Regiment Band. Harvey also started a drum and bugle band for the air cadets which gradually evolved into a full-fledged brass and woodwind ensemble. During the 1960s he organized instrumental classes for school students, which met during activity period on Wednesday afternoons and on Saturday mornings. This led the way for classes to be held during school hours, and in 1967 Wilf Harvey was hired as a full-time instructor for Middleton, which thereby became one of the first areas in Nova Scotia to have instrumental music as part of the school curriculum. Harvey taught at summer schools for teachers sponsored by the department of education and also contributed to the development of an instrumental curriculum for the province. Two years later Ken Elloway, a British musician who had come to Canada as director of the Royal Canadian Artillery Band, was hired as coordinator of instrumental music for the Dartmouth schools. Ron MacKay, who was stationed with the Royal Canadian Navy Stadacona Band in Halifax, offered instrumental instruction in Truro in the late 1960s and became director of instrumental music for the Truro schools.

There had been extra-curricular instrumental groups in several Halifax schools for many years, but they were not part of the curriculum. Irene McQuillan Murphy had seen a need to expand instrumental instruction; upon her retirement in 1967, J. Chalmers Doane was appointed as supervisor of music. 'At the end of Doane's five-year plan (1967–72) for upgrading the program, there were 50 full- and part-time music teachers serving 55 schools and 26,000 students.'[74] Many of these teachers were instrumental specialists who travelled from school to school training players for all-city performing ensembles. An important aspect of this scheme was its inclusion of adult classes to ensure parental and community support. String instruction under the direction of Ninette Babineau reflected Bornoff principles; both Babineau and Doane had worked with Bornoff at Boston University. Doane's innovative use of the ukulele became an integral part of the Halifax program and later spread to other parts of the country.

There were visible signs of instrumental music in Newfoundland associated with the Salvation Army, in activities such as Christmas serenading and at open-air meetings and special musical events. These activities were not school-oriented but they were related to church ministry and outreach programs. But the Salvation Army, one of the four major denominations operating schools in Newfoundland, did introduce instrumental music into its schools. Not surprisingly, the instrumentation was confined to brass instruments, for the Army's heritage was rooted in the British brass band movement. Eric Abbott, one of the foremost Salvationist musicians in Newfoundland, commenced his teaching career in 1948 and incorporated instrumental classes at Booth Memorial School in the late 1950s.

Instruction in the Roman Catholic schools grew out of orchestral and concert band traditions. Lester Goulding was involved in the early programs in St John's. More recently, Leo Sandoval has been the driving force in the field of instrumental music. He came to the Island as a United States serviceman in 1955 and, after marrying a local woman, commenced his career as a teacher in 1964. Sandoval introduced methods and materials into Newfoundland which had their origins in the United States. His music program at St Pius X School became the model for several other schools which began instrumental instruction in the 1970s, and many of his former students became teachers during this period of expansion. Following his success as a high school teacher, Sandoval was appointed to the Faculty of Education at Memorial University.

A small group of enterprising students in St John's formed the Calos Youth Orchestra in the late 1960s. They felt the need for such an ensemble because at that time orchestras had not yet been developed in individual schools. The organization reached a membership of fifty players during its ten-year existence and was sponsored by the Extension Department of Memorial University. This ensemble created widespread interest in orchestral music through public concerts and performances on radio and television. In 1971 they 'made a large contribution to the cultural life of the less fortunate communities when on an Opportunities for Youth grant, they completed a ten-day tour of Eastern Newfoundland.'[75]

Ewald Hajek was a central figure in the establishment of instrumental music in the Corner Brook area. He was a violinist of Austrian background, and in addition to giving private instruction he directed band and orchestral ensembles in Regina High School, a Roman

Catholic school for boys. During the late 1960s, before school authorities approved an adequate schedule for class instruction, Hajek had to rely upon his own private students to maintain these ensembles. Needless to say, he worked long hours, both in and out of school, in order to produce results with his school groups. Hajek also conducted a community ensemble, the Memorial Extension Service Orchestra, and, later in his career, taught string classes in St John's. The high school band of the Harmon Air Force Base frequently competed in the Corner Brook Rotary Music Festival. This base was operated by the United States, and consequently its school produced an American style of band performance. Their frequent participation in the Corner Brook music festival undoubtedly helped to motivate the local school bands, which at that time were still in an early stage of development. Brother Bellows, principal of St Michael's High School, pioneered the work in Grand Falls in 1956, but the development of a strong band program in this school can be attributed to the efforts of Ray Alyward, who joined the staff in 1962.

The competitive festival in Newfoundland played a vital part in motivating individual players as well as school and community ensembles, for even in the 1960s there was no institutional structure to ensure a systematic development of music education. More recently other organizations have provided the impetus and direction; the Newfoundland Music Council (affiliated with the Newfoundland Teachers' Association) and Memorial University have accelerated progress in school music, the former through professional development and the latter through teacher training.

RECENT DEVELOPMENTS

The inclusion of jazz and other forms of popular music is a recent trend in Canadian schools. Whereas dance bands had traditionally been on the periphery of school programs and were often left to the initiative of student enthusiasts, gradually teachers became more directly involved with these groups. Consequently, in the 1970s, jazz ensembles became an integral part of music education. In the context of a modern high school, the dance band has become known as the stage band. Its instrumentation has been standardized on the model of the big bands of the 1940s, and various aspects of technique and style have been developed within the framework of the instructional program. Improvisation has received special attention, and the acceptance of popular music as a legitimate part of musical training has been shown by the increasing incidence of stage band performances at school concerts and competitive festivals. It is ironic that the schools rescued the concert band at a time when its popularity was flagging in community life, in the 1950s. Similarly, schools embraced the stage band long after the demise of the big name band as a popular form of entertainment. There is some validity in the notion that the recent growth of the stage band movement has been fuelled by organizers of the Canadian Stage Band Competition (later known as Musicfest). This annual competition has been promoted by interests in the music industry and has achieved a high profile in the first few years of its operation. In the 1970s there was also an increased number of guitar classes, but interest in other instruments – those not found in bands or orchestras – has been quite limited.

In retrospect, instrumental music has undergone a remarkable transformation since the Second World War. Although it began with a somewhat precarious existence as an extra-curricular activity and was supported chiefly for its utilitarian values, within recent years it has become a permanent part of the school curriculum. The instructional patterns of instrumental music have varied from one province to another, depending upon the social and geographical character of the region and the attitudes prevalent within the provincial department of education. The traditions of local institutions have influenced the shape and direction of instrumental activities. However, the most significant factor in the rise of instrumental music in Canadian schools has been the teacher, for in every province two or three outstanding individuals have provided the leadership and set high standards for others to emulate.

15

Music in Higher Education

The rise of music in higher education following the Second World War represents one of the most impressive developments in Canada's cultural growth and possibly the consummate chapter thus far in the history of music education. The initial stirring of musical endeavour in a few scattered institutions inspired a widespread awakening of interest in music and the performing arts in higher education until it became exceptional for a Canadian university to be without a department or faculty of music. It should be remembered that music was only a small part of an educational macrocosm in which universities had to cope with spiralling enrolment, owing initially to the return of veterans and later to the postwar population boom of the 1960s. Virtually all disciplines experienced increases in enrolment, yet this phenomenon could have taken place without the occurrence of major changes in the performing arts, for music as a discipline in Canadian universities had been 'on the periphery of the academic community'[1] for a hundred years.

It will be seen, moreover, that music was destined to make gains in universities because of its role in professional education, or more precisely, in teacher training. The magnitude of these gains can be appreciated in light of the phenomenon that 'the growth of full-time enrolment in education in Canadian universities between 1940 and 1960 [was] one of the most striking characteristics of the period, an increase from 667 in 1940–41 to 10,473 in 1960–61.'[2] It has already been noted that universities were pressured into expanding programs for secondary school music specialists. A cyclical effect ensued, as students from school programs, particularly instrumentalists, formed a new wave of young people interested in pursuing music at the tertiary level. And later, in an entirely separate development, there were far-reaching consequences for music when Canadian universities began to assume greater responsibility for the training of elementary teachers. This took place at the University of Alberta in 1945 and at the University of British Columbia in 1956. Eventually, almost all normal schools or teachers' colleges were absorbed into university faculties of education throughout Canada. Thus, the teaching of music methods for elementary school teachers found its niche in Canadian universities. By the 1980s Nova Scotia Teachers' College in Truro was the only surviving institution of the earlier vintage.

Whatever role practical developments may have played in the proliferation of music in post-secondary education, one should not minimize the favourable cultural conditions brought about by the formation of the Canada Council. The Council's programs, in concert with those of arts organizations, contributed incalculably to the stabilization and well-being of the arts. The history of music in higher education is a complex one, its very complexity arising from the fact that beyond non-credit activities – choirs, glee clubs, bands, orchestras, concert series, and artists-in-residence – music served more than one academic purpose: the professional training of musicians, including specialized programs for music teachers; academic courses within the arts and humanities curricula; music methods as a function of teacher training for generalists or elementary classroom teachers. But even more fundamental than the diversity of purpose are the polarities which have created the dynamics for this growth: British versus French traditions; university versus conservatory approaches; European versus American influences; academic versus professional concerns. An unravelling of these strands is central to an understanding of the evolution of music in higher education.

PROFESSIONAL TRAINING OF MUSICIANS

Events of paramount importance for music in post-secondary education took place in 1946 at the Toronto Conservatory of Music and the University of Toronto's Faculty of Music. Among several innovations in professional training were diploma programs for performers in a new senior division of the conservatory, including a syllabus 'to train singers for the operatic stage.'[3] The announcement of the Senior School stated: 'We wish to do our part in arresting the flight of native talent from Canada. Up to now, too many of our most promising students have had to go to the U.S. to complete their musical studies. We know that only a limited number of those who leave this country to study ever return. The rapid expansion of musical opportunities in Canada through the development of orchestras, radio programmes, church music, local concert series and the teaching of music in the schools makes this a most opportune moment to launch our new school.'[4] Concurrent with these developments, the Faculty of Music initiated a three-year BMus degree in 'school music.' It was designed to prepare musicians for the Ontario College of Education, leading to a specialist certificate for teaching vocal and instrumental music. This paralleled arrangements which had been available to graduates of honours programs in most disciplines within arts and science.

Such opportunities for professional music training in Canada were long overdue. Ernest Hutcheson had suggested in his 1937 report that the TCM was the appropriate institution to provide such advanced instruction. There had also been overtures from senior administrators of the Ontario Department of Education in the 1940s requesting improvements in university programs for music education. Further discussions focused attention on the University of Toronto and its mission to prepare music teachers for secondary schools. These developments were timely, in that the growth of secondary school music during the Second World War expanded the job market for musicians, thus widening the range of career possibilities. Now university-trained musicians could claim professional status as secondary school teachers. Moreover, would-be performers and composers realized they could, if necessary, revert to the security of school teaching if other career plans failed to materialize. Needless to say, general conditions in the late 1940s engendered optimistic attitudes toward the future and opened a floodgate for a generation of aspiring musicians whose artistic energies and ambitions had been pent up during the war. Many of them gravitated to Toronto; some pursued their musical training through the traditional mode of private tuition; others took advantage of new diploma and degree programs which offered curricula of a more complete and comprehensive nature. And so, returned servicemen, musicians of varied backgrounds and experience, and young students from all parts of the country formed a concentration of Canadian talent. It is not surprising that from this environment came an array of professional opera singers, a nucleus of young composers exploring new directions in composition, and a host of others who were destined to become leaders in various facets of Canadian culture. Indeed, University Avenue and College Street, the site of the Toronto Conservatory and the Faculty of Music, became the cultural crossroads for the English-speaking community, in effect, a gathering-place for the next generation of Canadian musicians. Many of them subsequently achieved distinguished careers both in Canada and abroad. Their names include many familiar to Canadians: John Beckwith, Mario Bernardi, George Crum, Ray Dudley, Victor Feldbrill, Harry Freedman, Don Garrard, Glenn Gould, Elizabeth Benson Guy, Betty-Jean Hagen, Elmer Iseler, Helmut Kallmann, Jack Kane, Lois Marshall, James Milligan, Mary Morrison, Phil Nimmons, Clermont Pépin, Patricia Rideout, Harry Somers, and Jon Vickers.

The administrators, musicians, and teachers associated with these Toronto programs formed an impressive faculty. Sir Ernest MacMillan was dean of the Faculty of Music, and until 1950 Healey Willan and Leo Smith were also on staff. Previously, this small coterie of professors had presided over the activities for the extramural general degree (MusBac) and the honours music degree (BA). Ettore Mazzoleni became principal of the Toronto Conservatory of Music in 1945 (renamed Royal Conservatory of Music in 1947), and Arnold Walter was appointed to direct the senior programs of the conservatory. In this capacity Walter assumed a commanding role in shaping future developments in the RCMT and in degree programs in the Faculty of Music.

The school music degree was designed to conform to the structure of general education in Ontario. Course requirements included theory, music history, vocal and instrumental techniques for group instruction, English, acoustics, and one other non-music elective. Admission requirements called for a Grade VI conservatory certificate in voice or instrument, and before graduation students had to pass a Grade X (or Associate) conservatory examination. However, there were no provisions for private instruction or ensemble experience as an integral part of the curriculum.[5] Robert Rosevear played a major role in the school music program; he developed a sequence of courses in band and orchestral work which featured techniques suitable for group instruction. Leslie Bell taught choral techniques. Faculty members in music history and theory included Richard Johnston and Godfrey Ridout.

Composers John Beckwith, Oskar Morawetz, John Weinzweig, and Talivaldis Kenins joined the Faculty of Music in the early 1950s. Among the staff of the RCMT, several made significant contributions through their studio teaching: Margaret Miller Brown, Geza de Kresz, Alberto Guerrero, Emmy Heim, Lubka Kolessa, Greta Kraus, George Lambert, Kathleen Parlow, Charles Peaker, Boris Roubakine, Elie Spivak, Ernesto Vinci, and others. Clearly, the faculty resources of these two units represented a wide range of interests and expertise.

That is not to ignore the tensions which arose out of the interaction of the Faculty and Conservatory, tensions related both to programs and to personalities. The two may have shared physical facilities, but the polemic nature of their educational traditions led to co-existence at best and prolonged hostility at worst. Nor were disputes and disagreements confined to classrooms and teaching studios. In 1952 an eruption with strong political overtones took place surrounding the resignation of Sir Ernest MacMillan and the appointment of his successor. Subsequently, there was a reorganization of administrative responsibilities for music within the university. The university's board of governors approved the establishment of 'a college of music to be known as the Royal Conservatory of Music,'[6] comprised of two operational units, the Faculty of Music and the School of Music. Arnold Walter took on the leadership of the Faculty of Music, which subsumed all courses in the conservatory's Senior School, with the exception of the opera program. The remaining work of the RCMT, which consisted mostly of preparatory level teaching and the examination operation, was placed in the School of Music under the direction of Ettore Mazzoleni; he was also in charge of the Opera School and general director of the Opera Festival, the forerunner of the Canadian Opera Company. In the hope that a more harmonious working arrangement would be achieved, the plan was converted to a tripartite arrangement in 1953. Upon the recommendation of Edward Johnson (chairman, RCMT board), orchestral conductor Boyd Neel was imported from England to fill the position of dean of the Royal Conservatory of Music. Accordingly, Neel, Walter, and Mazzoleni assumed responsibility for music within the university, and the members of this triumvirate became notorious for their highly individual and independent administrative styles. In practice, the Royal Conservatory of Music became little more than an umbrella term, for Boyd Neel's duties were essentially titular; as dean, he did not penetrate the infrastructure of the two operational units, the Faculty of Music and the School of Music. Not surprisingly, he devoted much of his time to the formation and artistic direction of the Hart House Orchestra.

Administrative machinations notwithstanding, much progress was made in the academic realm. Arnold Walter was zealous in building a North American type of university music school, and he administered it with enormous energy and vision. Degree programs were expanded in the 1950s to include specialized areas (musicology, composition, and music education) at both undergraduate and graduate levels. By 1955 the extramural MusBac was phased out, and by 1963 undergraduate degree programs were extended to four years. In 1965 the Faculty introduced a four-year performance degree and a PhD in musicology. These academic changes coincided with dramatic increases in enrolment. Earl Davey reports that 'at Toronto, the enrolment in music education increased by more than 200 per cent between 1960 and 1967.'[7] Presumably Canadians surmised that degrees rather than diplomas offered more security and prestige, for enrolment in the Senior School did not keep pace with that in the Faculty of Music. This shift toward the degree program in performance contributed to the demise of the conservatory as an institution involved in senior levels of professional training. The trend was hastened in 1963 when the Opera School moved into the new Edward Johnson Building to take advantage of its superb stage facilities. In 1968 Ezra Schabas became chairman of the performance department, and the domination of senior performance by the university was ensured when the Opera School became a division of the Faculty of Music in 1969. Upon the retirement of Boyd Neel, the School of Music was reassigned the more historically accurate name 'Royal Conservatory of Music.'

To anglophones, Toronto has traditionally been the focal point for Canada's musical culture. With the advantages of a central geographical location and a relationship with the well-established RCMT, the University of Toronto became the flagship of music schools in higher education. It was fortuitous for the future of music education that the premier program was located in such an institution. Even so, in 1958 Sir Ernest MacMillan was not convinced that a wholesale replication of professional music programs would be advisable:

Let us then agree that at least some of our universities have a responsibility toward the professional music student; many other branches of vocational training are accepted as a matter of course, so there can be no objection in principle. Nevertheless it is neither possible nor desirable that *all* our universities should sponsor a music school. It is questionable whether a university music school in a small centre, unless highly endowed, can function effectively. Despite the advantages of greater intimacy and possibly of more attention being given to the needs of the individual student, a small school is severely handicapped when it seeks to secure and retain first-class teachers. Moreover the fledgling musician needs to be brought into touch with the best 'live' music that the world can offer and this is rarely available outside the largest centres.[8]

MacMillan felt that five schools would be sufficient, 'corresponding to the main divisions of our country, and situated in the most populous centres – the Atlantic Provinces, Quebec, Ontario, the Prairies and British Columbia.'[9] Nor was his colleague Arnold Walter in favour of an escalation of training which was not carefully planned and adequately funded to maintain high standards. In 1966, Walter warned: 'In the United States there are already too many university schools of music fiercely competing for staff and talent, producing more than the market can absorb. Concentration is needed, centralization. It is doubtful whether Canada can afford more than a handful of professional schools on the highest level. Talent is limited, so are opportunities, and so are financial resources.'[10] Among others who commented on the early signs of growth, George Proctor observed: 'There has always been a very great fear in Canada concerning overproduction in the field of music and ... this has given rise to an over-conservative approach with regard to the required number of professional music schools. This conservatism would now appear to be slowly disappearing, and the mushroomlike growth of existing music schools points up the fact that it is none too soon!'[11] By 1965 there were at least ten institutions awarding professional degrees, and 'the number [seemed] to be increasing daily.'[12]

The successful beginnings at the University of Toronto undoubtedly inspired others to introduce music courses, and many of them incorporated features of the Toronto plan. Hence, conservatory examinations and diplomas were used widely to define admission and graduation requirements for university programs. This familiar reference point for performance levels and basic theory background was universally understood by teachers and students alike, an indication of the extent to which the conservatory examination system had become an integral part of Canadian education. In later years most university music departments discontinued the requirement of a diploma for graduation, and although they referred to admission requirements in terms of conservatory grade levels, they have been inclined to conduct their own auditions.

Just because these Toronto institutions were centrally located and assumed a role of national proportions, it does not necessarily follow that their programs preceded all others or that all music curricula across the country were derived from the prototypes developed in Toronto. Acadia and Mount Allison universities had historical affiliations with conservatories and were among the first schools to offer intramural degrees in music. Each of these conservatory programs was eventually integrated into its respective university, and each adopted a syllabus that prescribed both music and liberal arts; in both, furthermore, 'attendance at such classes and lessons was understood to be a significant part of the student's degree programme.'[13] These were departures from the British tradition, which confined itself to the study of music and operated on an extramural basis. In Davey's view, 'this approach by Acadia and Mount Allison universities signified the beginnings of American influence on the development of music in Canadian higher education.'[14] Because music enrolments at these schools were modest, they yielded comparatively few graduates, and the scope of their influence remained regional.

The first degree program in western Canada was a BMus introduced at the University of Saskatchewan in the early 1930s by British organist Arthur Collingwood. J.D. Macrae, another organist from overseas, administered music in this university from 1947 to 1951. The limited activity in this program had dwindled by the time Murray Adaskin was appointed head of music in 1952, and its status was changed from faculty to department.

The music program at McGill, as at the University of Toronto, had the distinctive character that resulted from the interweaving of a university music school and a conservatorium. Davey observes that 'the two bodies [conservatorium and faculty] theoretically functioned as distinct entities; the reality, however, was that of single music schools, primarily engaged with private studio teaching which was unrelated to the university curriculum. Only a small percentage of the teaching at either Toronto or McGill involved subject matter prescribed as part of a degree program.'[15] However, McGill went through a different metamorphosis to arrive at its curricular framework. Its school music degree predated the one at Toronto by a year, but practical courses in music education were somewhat limited at McGill, and, more significantly, comparatively few students were attracted to this program. Insofar as there was a minimal demand for secondary school teachers in Quebec and the Atlantic region in the late 1940s, McGill's program may have been ahead of its time. Another innovation, that of multiple routes of specialization within a BMus, was introduced at McGill as early as 1956. Under this plan McGill provided specializations in performance, composition, and school music. This flexible arrangement was implemented by Marvin Duchow, who had encountered such features in the United States. The impact of these initiatives was not widespread, however, for McGill's enrolment in the 1950s was modest, and as a music school it did not attract widespread attention. Later, when McGill's music enrolment soared in the 1960s by more than 600 per cent, Dean Helmut Blume reported a marked decline in diploma programs and a corresponding swing toward degree studies. In 1965, Proctor surveyed the development of the BMus degree in Canada:

It is significant to note that most of the institutions developing professional programmes recently in music have followed the so-called 'American plan' rather than the 'European plan.' This has not been the result of the process of blind imitation but rather a belief in the basic philosophy involved. This philosophy, which must be credited to our neighbours south of the border, is expressed very well in the *Six-Year Report of Activities (1958–65)* of the Department of Music, University of British Columbia. Essentially it is based upon the belief that a musician of today will be better prepared if he receives his professional courses within the framework of the university, much in the same manner as today's engineers, nurses, doctors, dentists, foresters, etc. The curriculum generally follows a three-fold division into craft subjects (applied music, ensemble, conducting), musical 'academics' (theory, music history and literature), and arts and science subjects (general history, language and literature, philosophy, psychology, physics). The full adoption of this philosophy in Canada is of very recent history, with UBC being the first to incorporate it in 1959. It is only since that time that the University of Toronto has added applied music and ensemble training as integral parts of its various degree programmes.[16]

Music in French-language universities had its origins in European traditions. Brian Ellard notes that 'the francophone universities of Quebec functioned on a system of affiliated classical colleges, seminaries, and schools operated by various religious communities organized on a modified Jesuit pattern.'[17] These institutions served 'a culturally homogeneous, French-Catholic community'[18] and had a predilection for sacred music which ensured their separate and distinct identity. But secular music in higher education was in a state of inertia. For many years Laval granted extramural degrees through a number of affiliated schools, and 'even after proper faculties had been formed, with many who had been examiners providing lectures and classes, attendance was rarely compulsory.'[19] Given these archaic conditions, it was difficult to incorporate major academic changes or impose exacting standards. Robert Talbot served as director of l'École de musique, l'Université Laval from 1932 to 1954, and in 1937 instituted 'highly-successful summer courses.'[20] Onésime Pouliot was director from 1954 to 1962. It was during this period that the Ward method, a musicianship system rooted in liturgical music, was introduced into Quebec; Laval granted certificates for specialized training in the Ward method. During Pouliot's term l'École de musique was strengthened by new faculty and had a strong influence on music education through summer school courses.

Le Conservatoire de musique du Québec à Montréal (CMQ) was founded by the Quebec government in 1942 following a report by Claude Champagne on the teaching of music. Directed by Wilfrid Pelletier, this was 'the first entirely state-subsidized institution of higher learning for music in North America.'[21] The Quebec City branch was opened in 1944. Being fully supported by provincial funds, CMQ was able to assemble a faculty of distinguished teachers and offered free tuition to students, who were admitted on a competitive basis. The leading musicians in other provinces looked with a certain amount of envy on the situation in Quebec. In commenting on the great European conservatories upon which CMQ was modelled, Arnold Walter wrote: 'In North America such institutions could not come into being. The federal governments couldn't, and the state and provincial governments wouldn't establish endowed music schools – with deplorable results. North American conservatories became (and some of them still are) commercial enterprises without courses of study, with hapless teachers paid on a commission basis, with a ridiculous teacher-to-student ratio. They became music cafeterias taking the name "conservatory" in vain. On the whole continent there is only one exception to that rule: the Conservatoire in Montreal which is maintained by the state, i.e. by the Province of Quebec.'[22] L'École de musique, l'Université Laval felt the impact of CMQ in that it became increasingly difficult for the university to compete with the Conservatoire in attracting talented performers. Nevertheless, the quality of the students and the expansion of programs at Laval reached a high point during Lucien Brochu's term (1962–77) as director. These accomplishments reflected the reforms of the Parent and Rioux reports, which transformed general education in the province of Quebec into a more modern mould. Accordingly, Laval's curricular framework gradually incorporated the features of an American university school of music.

In an arrangement which antedated the formation of a faculty of music, l'Université de Montréal had offered graduate degrees on an extramural basis through its Faculty of Arts. Many of these degrees were awarded to English-speaking musicians upon the recommendation of Irvin Cooper, former director of music for the Montreal Protestant schools. Leslie Bell, G. Roy Fenwick, and George Bornoff were recipients of doctoral degrees; among others, Jack Dow of North Toronto Collegiate and Earle Terry, supervisor of music for London schools, were awarded masters degrees.

L'École Vincent-d'Indy was by far the most respected music school associated with l'Université de Montréal. Its affiliation with the Faculty of Arts goes back to 1933, when the school was known as l'École supérieure de musique d'Outremont. L'École Vincent-D'Indy was affiliated with l'Université de Sherbrooke from 1970 to 1978, at which time it assumed the status of a CGEP institution. A faculty of music was established at l'Université de Montréal in 1950 with a view to annexing a number of affiliated music schools, some of which had not been maintaining uniform standards. Alfred Bernier provided leadership in the Faculty of Music until 1953, before a period (1953–5) in which Jean Papineau-Couture served as acting dean. Clément Morin, a priest in the Sulpician order, was dean from 1955 to 1968. He developed a program for church musicians and carried out a major reorganization of academic offerings in 1966. It was not unusual for secular music to be added long after programs in liturgical music had been in operation. Music pedagogy was first offered in 1961, and in 1967 a special program for secondary schools was introduced in conjunction with school teaching certificates. In that same year l'Université de Montréal finally ended its affiliations with other music schools and, like Laval, moved to bring its academic programs 'more closely into line with North-American practice.'[23] Jean Papineau-Couture (dean, 1968–73) led l'Université de Montréal through an important period of its expansion. Faculty recruitment, curriculum development, and the improvement of physical facilities were accomplishments associated with his leadership. Francophone universities in Quebec which have developed music programs of a modern type include l'Université de Québec à Montréal and l'Université de Québec à Trois-Rivières. Although l'Université d'Ottawa and l'Université de Moncton were outside the province of Quebec, their origins were similar to those of the Quebec francophone institutions.

There was much closer communication between the music faculty members of francophone universities and their counterparts in anglophone institutions in the 1960s than there had been previously. Communication was facilitated to a large extent through the Canadian Association of University Schools of Music (CAUSM), founded in 1965.[24] From its inception, francophone universities participated in CAUSM through scholastic presentations at annual meetings and through leadership on CAUSM executive committees.

EXPANSION IN THE 1960s

Davey notes that 'music was among those constituents of the universities which demonstrated the highest rate of expansion.'[25] Statistics show that the rise in enrolment in music faculties and departments surpassed the rise in general university enrolment at the undergraduate level: from 1960 to 1970, overall enrolment grew from 114,000 to 315,722, an increase of 277 per cent, whereas music enrolment grew from 397 to 1928, an increase of 486 per cent.[26] It was typical, at first, to find numerical strength concentrated in music education degrees. And the single most powerful factor in the escalation of music education in universities was the expansion of secondary school programs, especially in instrumental music. University performing ensembles were, in effect, an extension of the bands and orchestras which students had encountered in secondary schools. This interaction of secondary and tertiary levels revolutionized music education in Canada, for as successive waves of music graduates returned to the secondary schools as teachers, a self-perpetuating system was kept in motion. On the strength of these soaring enrolments, music administrations in some universities were able to justify the hiring of additional faculty – musicologists, theorists, composers, and performers – to support the needs of music education programs. By so doing, the larger universities were able to develop other four-year programs featuring specializations in theory and composition, music history and literature, and performance. In due course students became more confident in pursuing alternatives to music education and enrolments were distributed more evenly across all areas, one reason why the centrality of music education in the university was less evident in the 1970s. With the development of specialized degree programs in theory, history, and composition, there was a pronounced increase in the number of faculty members with doctoral qualifications.[27] As Davey concludes, professional training had so grown by the end of the 1960s that other programs were caught up in the momentum: 'The university music schools had developed a clientele independent of the conservatories and had employed full-time faculty who were able to direct their attention solely to the demands of university programmes. Furthermore, they had developed an increased range of curricula and provided an improved standard of musical education. In varying degrees, they had shifted from the periphery to the mainstream of the university community.'[28] Many music departments in their formative years were housed in private dwellings or annexes, beyond the fringe of the main campus. Usually the acoustical conditions were deplorable, because these makeshift facilities had not been designed with musical activities in mind. Most Canadian universities, however, eventually erected new music buildings or undertook major renovations, including the expansion of music libraries. The overall effect was that by the end of the 1960s music projected a new physical presence and began to play a more conspicuous role in the academic and cultural facets of university life.

MUSIC IN THE ARTS AND HUMANITIES

At a number of Canadian universities, music made its first appearance in the arts and humanities rather than as a discipline for which professional training was required. Such was the case at the University of British Columbia, where Harry Adaskin was appointed in 1946, and at the University of Manitoba, where Ronald Gibson served as head (1949–63) of the department of music. Other examples include early developments at McMaster, Queen's, and many smaller universities such as Windsor, Carleton, and Guelph. The character of the instructional programs usually reflected the background and interest of the first appointee. For instance, in 1956 Harry Adaskin expressed the view that the teaching of music in a university should be directed toward appreciation of the art and maintained that educational institutions were 'uniquely qualified to offer ... this service.'

> We can teach them to understand, and therefore to appreciate and love art. We can train teachers to go out into the community, into the public and high schools to teach students to understand art.
>
> Don't be misled by pollyanna propaganda – we are not doing that now. I know there are choruses and bands in many schools, but that is not how you learn to understand music. Music is something else, and must be taught as such. It has nothing to do with singing, or tootling on a horn. These singers and tootlers do not become music lovers, and rightly so, because they never learn what music is. And they are taught by teachers who have never learned what music is. I know, because they come to my classes. Playing the euphonium part in 'Zampa' will teach you as much about music as running the elevator in a hospital will teach you about surgery.
>
> High schools and universities should not attempt to produce singers and violinists and composers. They should produce audiences – cultivated art lovers and music lovers. Those who wish to be violinists and pianists must study in trade-schools, for theirs is a difficult craft which can only be mastered through a full-time effort. But their efforts are useless if there is no audience. I look with a worried eye on the hundreds of music schools churning out more and more trained craftsmen without an apparent thought about their students' future.[29]

In many situations, course offerings of a general nature gave way to demands for vocational training. Provincial departments of education and teachers' groups applied pressure for specialized training to be introduced, and as these courses attracted more students, the trend toward professional music programs became more pronounced. The University of British Columbia, with the appointment of Welton Marquis (1958), and the University of Saskatchewan, following the appointment of David Kaplan (1960), serve as examples. Similarly, major revisions took place at the University of Western Ontario, where relatively few students registered in general courses once a BA in music education was introduced in 1962; this particular BA was superseded in 1964 by a full range of specialized BMus programs. By 1970, UWO had become one of the largest music schools in Canada.

With the spate of revised programs and new departments, approximately thirty universities were offering music instruction by the end of the 1960s. In this period of rapid growth, traditional distinctions between professional and liberal arts programs were often blurred, not only in course requirements but also in degree designations, of which there was a proliferation. There was also a change of thinking which recognized the importance of highly trained teachers for the early years of elementary education. Degrees awarded for the study of music included Bachelor of Music (BMus), Bachelor of Music Education (BMusEd), Bachelor of Fine Arts (BFA), Bachelor of Musical Arts (BMusA), Bachelor of Arts in Music (BA), and Bachelor of Education (BEd). Furthermore, these programs were placed in numerous administrative structures – departments of music, education, and fine arts – not to mention combined programs or overlapping of instructional means. Some schools did not follow traditional patterns. For example, at Simon Fraser University 'musical activities have been developed slowly and have been structured loosely.'[30] Its Centre for Communication and the Arts within the Faculty of Education placed an emphasis upon artists-in-residence, among them R. Murray Schafer, who developed the Sonic Research Studio and the World Soundscape Project at that institution.

TEACHER EDUCATION

The pluralism associated with the expansion in the 1960s was further complicated by the polarity in teacher training in music, in the realms of both its origin and its function. Neither administrators nor teaching faculty were consistent in distinguishing between the praxes of generalist and specialist training or between the traditions from which each had evolved. Generalist training has been associated with elementary school teaching, an emphasis on child development being the quintessential element of the approach; most often, learning procedures and subject content are melded concurrently in a gestalt process. Specialist training has been more closely, though not exclusively, identified with secondary school teaching; typically, the methodology in these programs pays greater allegiance to the discipline to be taught. Students in specialist programs are expected to demonstrate mastery in the subject field before attempting to impart knowledge to others. Hence, the term 'consecutive' has been used to describe a bipartite structure in which an arts or science degree is successfully completed before work in professional methods and practice teaching is begun. The structure of a 'concurrent' program in music presumably allows students to acquire insight and methods as student teachers while at the same time developing background and skills as musicians. Yet the idea that anyone should try to teach a subject while still in the process of learning it seems enigmatic to some. Proponents of the consecutive plan maintain that a student should earn the degree, thereby demonstrating musical competency, before being allowed to apply music in the classroom. It has been suggested, moreover, that musical standards are sometimes relaxed for university students who are identified as education majors, the rationale being that they will not have to perform or compose – they are only going to teach!

The concurrent plan in the training of elementary teachers (generalist) has never been universally accepted. However, when it has been implemented in secondary school training (specialist), it has met with even greater resistance. In the United States, concurrent degrees evolved from teacher training institutions, which traditionally had strong commitments to methodology in general education. In the field of music, American conservatories and university schools of music provided the specialized training leading to a music degree, but with the emergence of state colleges and universities there has been a blending of education and music as an outgrowth of the concurrent model. Concurrent programs in Canada, as in the United States, had their origins in normal schools or teachers' colleges and emerged as generalist training associated with elementary school teaching. Concurrent degrees were devised primarily in faculties of education and were introduced in provinces which had placed teacher training, both elementary and secondary, within the jurisdiction of the university. The concurrent-consecutive controversy in teacher training continues to the present time. The underlying issue is whether to develop a musician and then add skills in teaching methods or whether to train a teacher and add musical background and competence. Some would suggest that there may be very little difference; others contend that the primacy – of either teacher or musician – is critical when implemented across the whole system of education. The allusion to music education as 'a profession in search of a discipline'[31] may be apropos of this debate, for it raises a question as to whether education is, in the pure sense of the word, a discipline.

The solution in many Canadian universities has been to offer both types of program. For example, at UBC a student in the 1960s could take a four-year concurrent program at the Faculty of Education or, on the consecutive plan, complete a music degree in the Faculty of Arts and then proceed to the Faculty of Education for a year of professional study and practice teaching. Concurrent programs have also been developed at campuses in Victoria, Calgary, Edmonton, Regina, Saskatchewan, and Winnipeg. The co-existence of concurrent and consecutive structures in the western provinces has led to tensions and misunderstandings between music departments and faculties of education.

Most Ontario universities which had professional music programs retained the consecutive plan even after elementary teacher training was absorbed into the universities. One of the first concurrent programs in education was offered at York University, as an outcome of a merger with Lakeshore Teachers' College in Toronto. However, York's music division, administered within the Faculty of Fine Arts, was not directly involved, as its course offerings of jazz, non-Western music, and early music were not integral components of the generalist training programs in education. More recently, concurrent programs have been developed at McArthur College, Queen's University. In some universities, music instruction was given in a faculty or school of education before the formal establishment of a music department. This was the case at Memorial University, where a concurrent program has been sustained even after the formation of a department of music, in 1975. Integrated programs in music and education were established at several institutions, including Mount Allison and Brandon Universities, in an attempt to combine the best features of concurrent and consecutive training.

Although the formation of CAUSM had an impact on the growth of music in higher education, it had little influence on programs in faculties of education, since CAUSM membership was restricted to departments and faculties of music. Whether this restriction was a result of neglect or of academic arrogance, it is unfortunate that musicians teaching in faculties of education were excluded in the first years of CAUSM's operation. Although the following description given by Arnold Walter in 1969 appears to ignore concurrent programs in faculties of education, it does furnish a picture of the complexity that pertained toward the end of the 1960s:

Twenty years ago it would have been difficult enough to find a common denominator between the diverse types of schools attempting to provide professional instruction; currently everything seems in flux, re-organization is the order of the day. The mosaic has changed into a kaleidoscope. It is not possible to comment on every facet of the complex picture. We must limit ourselves to distinguishing two layers, an older and a newer one co-existing side by side. The latter ... consists of the Conservatoire in Montreal and the university schools offering courses leading to graduate and undergraduate degrees. These are so far the only schools catering to the students' needs for institutional training, practice and rehearsal facilities, ensemble experience, libraries and financial assistance. The older level, however, is still with us; conservatories continue to award professional diplomas without offering supervised course work.[32]

MUSIC IN GRADUATE EDUCATION

The growth of graduate programs in music did not match developments in undergraduate education. Davey's statement 'Outside of Toronto, graduate [study] in English-language universities in central and eastern Canada was in its infancy in the 1960s'[33] would also be true for western Canada; the moderate growth which eventually transpired did not occur until the 1970s. The University of Toronto established its supremacy in the field of musicology, largely on foundations laid by Harvey Olnick and Myron Schaeffer. MacMillan's comment in 1958 that 'no [university] music library in this country is really adequate'[34] indicates the primitive state of the scholarly resources and educational opportunities in Canada. However, during the next decade Harvey Olnick and Arnold Walter built the library collection at the University of Toronto to support graduate work at the doctoral level and, through faculty strengths, earned widespread recognition for scholarly work in the early historical periods. The appointment of Mieczyslaw Kolinski in 1966 marked the beginnings of ethnomusicology at Toronto. Marvin Duchow was prominent in the musicology field at McGill, where he taught and served in various administrative capacities from 1944 until 1978. The University of British Columbia became active in the late 1960s, pioneering in the field of ethnomusicology, and the University of Alberta initiated graduate studies in that province. Among the francophone universities, Laval was the first to move into graduate work; more recently, l'Université de Montréal has shown a commitment to advanced studies in musicology.

In the field of composition the University of Toronto and McGill have been the major schools among the English-speaking universities, and among the French-speaking universities, Laval and l'Université de Montréal. A number of Canada's distinguished composers have made outstanding contributions: Claude Champagne at le Conservatoire de musique de Montréal, Jean Papineau-Couture at l'Université de Montréal, Istvan Anhalt at McGill, Jean Coulthard and Barbara Pentland at UBC, Violet Archer at the University of Alberta, and John Weinzweig, John Beckwith, and Oskar Morawetz at the University of Toronto.

Graduate degrees in music education have been granted through faculties of music and/or education. Those programs offered in 'education' have favoured pedagogical applications of music in classroom instruction, whereas those offered in 'music' have been ostensibly rooted in the discipline of music. However, there has not been strict adherence to such a differentiation between programs in music and those in education. Graduate study in music education has been mainly at the masters level. Apart from a few graduates in education (EdD), Canadians have had little opportunity to do doctoral work in music education in their own country.

The incorporation of graduate programs in performance has been impeded by the diversity of opinion implicit in the presence of French, British, and American traditions in higher education. This diversity has been evident in the polemic surrounding the question of whether diplomas or degrees should be awarded in performance programs, and in the question of whether advanced training should be under the purview of a state-supported conservatory or a university school of music. Philosophical views about the role of universities in the field of performance become strikingly divergent with respect to graduate education. For example, the University of Toronto, which forged ahead in musicology and composition, has not yet offered doctoral degrees in performance; this reluctance may reflect its strong British heritage. On the other hand, universities in western Canada – the University of Alberta and the University of British Columbia – were among the first Canadian institutions to offer doctoral degrees in performance, perhaps because of the predominance of faculty members whose own training was acquired in institutions which embraced both scholastic and practical training. To a great extent, degree programs in the west are facsimiles of those developed in the United States. As yet there are no graduate programs in music in the Atlantic provinces.

In 1975 Helmut Blume was commissioned by the Canada Council to do a study on music training with special attention to the development of orchestral players. His report, *A National Music School for Canada*, received mixed reactions. In Blume's opinion the Banff Centre could best serve the goals of a national school of music, which, he believed, should 'bridge the gap between graduation and professionalism.'[35] The diversity of opinion reported in Blume's survey is a reminder that, even after forty years, not all Canadians consider university schools of music a panacea for developing players for professional ensembles. Recent projects to provide professional training for performers include those of the Banff Centre School of Fine Arts, the RCMT Professional Orchestral Training Program, and the Canadian Opera Company Ensemble.

FACULTY RECRUITMENT – A CANADIAN CRISIS

A small group of university presidents and music administrators met in 1948 at the University of Toronto to review music education in universities and affiliated conservatories. In the words of a later report, they concluded that 'although much was being done in the field of music, the financial support being given to this aspect of University work was not in general of the same order as had been given to other subjects of University curricula,' and they agreed 'that uniformity of policy and practice would be undesirable, but [that] advancement in music education could only come about through co-operation at both regional and national levels.'[36] Subsequently, the National Conference of Canadian Universities appointed a standing committee to deal with music education. The committee was frustrated in its attempts to obtain data from those involved in music programs; as Robin Harris observes, 'this committee vied with the one on uniform matriculation for being among the least successful of all those appointed during the history of the conference.'[37] Nor did a new committee formed in 1956 produce better results. Whatever progress was realized by 1960 was due to the commitment of a few institutions and several outstanding people associated with them. This inertia in graduate education on a national scale had a profound effect upon future development. The acceleration in music enrolment in higher education was in itself promising, but the lack of sufficient faculty members to cope with the situation led to a serious crisis. The problem was compounded by the fact that the existing music group within Canadian universities had not developed a long-range plan and that therefore very few Canadian musicians and scholars were available to fill academic positions. The ramifications of this situation were discussed in the wider context of higher education by Robin Mathews and John Steele:

If we do not train and employ Canadians and they continue to be a diminishing proportion of Canadian university faculties, then both the short-term and long-term effects will be most serious ... The Canadian university will cease, moreover, to be a cosmopolitan institution: an institution, that is, possessing a majority of excellent home scholars to which are added a vital supply of scholars from different and alien cultures offering as many different kinds of cultural and scholarly conditioning as possible. The Canadian university will become a truly 'alien' university, for it will be staffed by an increasingly large majority of scholars whose primary national experience is not Canadian; whose primary interests do not merge with and show respect for the seriousness of Canadian problems and the unique relevance of their solutions.[38]

Nor was this general condition in the humanities and social sciences removed from the experience of Canadian musicians. Of those Canadians who were appointed to positions, the majority had earned their advanced degrees in other countries, and in many cases they found themselves working toward doctoral degrees during summer sessions in order to satisfy the standard requirements for tenure or promotion. Fortunately for many, it was possible to do graduate work in summer schools at American universities. Nevertheless, the majority of new appointments went to applicants from other countries, most frequently the United States. Canada is indebted to a great number of scholars and highly trained musicians from abroad who responded at a time when their expertise was urgently needed. Their contributions should not be denied, as many of them have remained to strengthen Canadian institutions and to stimulate artistic growth.

On the other hand, some Canadians were adversely affected by these developments, for frequently the 'old boy network' came into operation. Imported administrators hired faculty members from outside the country, not just in the 1960s but even after qualified Canadians became available. Barbara Pentland, a well-known Canadian composer, illustrated this plight in her response to an article which appeared in *Weekend Magazine*:

In my childhood in Winnipeg in the 1920's and '30's, when I was struggling to be a composer, I remember it was always an English musician who was brought over to fill the most important posts: conductor of the symphony orchestra, of two choral societies, etc. Often he was straight out of music school or university, and used his Winnipeg apprenticeship to reach greener pastures. Sometimes he was a good influence.

Later, when I was a fellowship student at the Juilliard Graduate School of Music in New York, I learned about the type of degree obtained at some colleges which would scarcely qualify for entrance standards at others. I was glad that no such degrees were available in Canada – then.

The great chance for Canadian musicians finally came after the war when music departments started up in universities across the country, and those of us who were barely making a living teaching on commission at the Conservatory in Toronto began to hope for a better way of life. In 1949 I went to the University of British Columbia as instructor in the new department of music ... When the present School of Music was being developed, an American was imported as head; ... in my opinion he knew nothing of Canadians and their music. He in turn imported a staff of Americans whom he ranked above the Canadian instructors. The same type of degree which I deplored so many years ago was now introduced.[39]

In this same letter, she exclaimed: 'In contrast to English-speaking Canada's deprecation of home grown talents, Quebec is to be admired for developing its cultural resources without dependence on imports ... While Quebec is becoming ever more concerned about its culture, other regions still look beyond the borders for direction, and so the infiltration continues at an alarming pace.'[40]

Mathews and Steele found that Canadians had not devised effective mechanisms for advertising academic posts, perhaps with further detriment to Canadian applicants. By the time Canadian institutions were able to provide qualified academics, provincial governments had introduced procedures for the approval of new graduate programs. These measures were designed to accomplish long-range, efficient planning and had as their express purpose that of avoiding duplication and an unnecessary proliferation of programs. Ironically, the bureaucratic nature of these procedures thwarted attempts to accelerate the training of musicians within the Canadian community and, by so doing, impeded the hiring of Canadians. The situation has stabilized to the extent that in the 1980s the flow of qualified musicians from Canadian universities seems to be adequate for the general needs of the academic community. It is a recurring question, nevertheless, whether or not the imbalance between Canadian and foreign academics has been sufficiently redressed for the preservation of a uniquely Canadian future – whether the rubric be heritage, sovereignty, or cultural identity. According to the report of the Commission on Canadian Studies, universities in Canada have failed in some cases 'to develop innovative approaches and solutions appropriate to [Canadian] problems,' and have preferred instead 'to employ so called "comparative models" imported from other societies,' the uncritical use of which yields 'mediocre solutions with sometimes disastrous results.'[41] Obviously, it is difficult to assess the relevance of this general statement to a comparatively small community of academics in the field of music. But if there is any truth to it, it is that, in the effort to cope with an educational and cultural explosion, academics in music have embraced an American model and at the same time forsaken the remnants of British and French traditions. Most disconcerting of all is the suggestion that Canadians have exchanged one tradition for another without exercising the creative or critical powers to shape their own.

A NEW DIMENSION

Growing pains aside, university music schools have influenced all levels of music education. The cultural explosion of the postwar years generated a complex network of opportunities for young musicians, and, in mounting the machinery to accomplish higher goals, university faculty members have directed their expertise far beyond the function of teacher training. In so doing, they have borne out the finding of the Massey Report, which maintained that universities were vital to a healthy national life and held great potential and promise for the future of Canadian culture.

> There is no lack of variety in the services of a Canadian university. The transition from a critical edition of an obscure mediaeval poet to the organization of a young farmers' club is a formidable one. But the university makes it. There may be no one else to do these things. However inadequately they may be done, the university has gallantly met the challenge of a new country to do everything it can and to do it immediately. Throughout Canada it represents to the community every aspect of cultural life, from 'grass roots' to 'ivory tower.' Were our universities to close their doors except to the formal academic student, voluntary local effort in the intellectual and cultural field would lose much of its life and spirit.[42]

'Symposium I–The Renaissance,' held at the University of Toronto in 1968 under the leadership of Richard Johnston, and 'Symposium II–

The Baroque,' directed by James Stark at the University of Western Ontario in 1970, can be cited as excellent examples. These three-day symposia were conceived and conducted by the respective universities under the auspices of the past presidents' council of OMEA. They were 'based on a new concept of inservice programs designed to promote excellence and deeper musical understanding among the music teachers of Ontario.'[43] Among its special events, the Renaissance symposium offered lectures by eminent scholars, concerts by the New York Pro Musica, and an exhibition of photographs by Roloff Beny, and it closed with a Renaissance high mass. The sessions of Symposium II ranged from a keynote address by Paul Henry Lang to a performance practice workshop in which musician and musicologist confronted each other in dialogue. The performances included a concert by the Trio Flauto Dolce of New York and a production of Shakespeare's *The Tempest*, and the conclusion was a cantata service of German Lutheran music featuring the UWO Chamber Choir, directed by Deral Johnson. Those in attendance were steeped in the culture of each age and were inspired by the artistic and intellectual ideals behind the symposia, which were 'designed to give as full a panoply of experiences as possible.'[44] Following the first symposium, a participant from Sudbury commented, 'For the first time, Ontario music teachers were offered the opportunity to saturate themselves in a concentrated study of a period which is adequately covered with recordings and books but which is relatively neglected in the high schools of our Province.'[45] Proximity to a university has often enriched and stimulated communities which are not close to large urban centres. A university can also foster interest in cultural diversity or improve the environment for the arts in education; thus, music departments and schools have become regional centres of excellence, offering the resources of their libraries, concerts and recitals, and leadership in many facets of community life.

University faculty members have used diverse enterprises and projects to fulfil the criteria by which merit is determined, namely, teaching, research, and community service. Ideally, at the tertiary level of education both teaching and research are integral functions of instruction. Such a statement implies that research is the initial phase in the acquisition of knowledge, and knowledge is subsequently translated into material form in monographs, articles in journals, recordings, compositions, instructional textbooks, and published research reports. The production and dissemination of this knowledge is as essential to learning as the lecture or live performance itself. Yet it would be absurd

TABLE 15.1
Music theses and original compositions completed in
fulfilment of graduate degree requirements in Canadian
universities, decades 1920–29 to 1970–79

Decade	Theses and compositions
1920–29	6
1930–39	14
1940–49	33
1950–59	51
1960–69	120
1970–79	436

SOURCE: Statistical data reported by J. Paul Green, CMEA
conference, Mount Allison University, 1983. Information
was taken from a computer data base at UWO.

to suggest that all publications or professional activities in the universities are vital to education; indeed, some of them are generated solely for purposes of promotion and tenure. It is true, nevertheless, that a 'spinning of wheels in academic circles' seems to be inevitable in order for an original contribution or a genuine improvement to be realized even on an occasional basis.

The expansion of music in graduate education has spawned a new generation of students with improved research capabilities. The increase in research activity can be seen in table 15.1. It is also evident that university teachers themselves are beginning to assume greater responsibility as scholars in the international community, for, whereas during the first half of this century little had been written about Canadian music, more recently there has been a promising flow of publications, research, and various forms of intellectual criticism. Indeed, the growth of music in the universities has helped Canadian music education progress from plateaus of provincial influence to a level of national significance.

16

The Growth of the Profession

By the time Canada reached the hundredth anniversary of its confederation several national music organizations had been formed. Among them were three associations concerned with the major divisions of music education: the Canadian Federation of Music Teachers' Associations (CFMTA), the Canadian Music Educators' Association (CMEA), and the Canadian Association of University Schools of Music (CAUSM).[1] All three groups have attempted to improve the status of the profession through national conferences, workshops, study groups, and committees, as well as publications for members. Each has been affiliated with the International Society for Music Education (ISME), and along with Fédération des associations de musiciens éducateurs du Québec (FAMEQ), they hosted the thirteenth ISME congress in London, Ontario, in 1978. The four organizations thus acted as Canadian hosts for music educators from around the world. But they are not the only organizations in the country involved with music education.

The Canadian Music Council, viewed by its founders as an umbrella organization for music in the country, has concerned itself from time to time with the teaching of music. In fact, the council devoted its 1968 conference exclusively to the topic of music education.[2] There are also several specialized groups such as the Orff and Kodály associations, which hold national conventions on a regular basis. Provincial choral federations have participated in national conventions of various organizations and have affiliated with the Association of Canadian Choral

Conductors. The Alliance chorale canadienne, composed of French-speaking choral groups, has offered many services to members since its inception in 1961, including both national and international massed gatherings. The Canadian Band Directors' Association (formerly the Canadian Bandmasters' Association), the Canadian String Teachers' Association, the Royal Canadian College of Organists (RCCO), Canadian Amateur Musicians/Musiciens amateurs du Canada (CAMMAC), Jeunesses musicales du Canada (JMC), the Canadian Association of Music Libraries, and, more recently, the Canadian Association for Music Therapy have all dealt periodically with aspects of music education in the country. Given this proliferation, it is easy to overlook the fact that most of these groups were not formed until after the Second World War. The need for such organizations had been recognized, but problems of distance, finance, and population were all deterrents, and it was only through the determination and hard work of dedicated individuals that these associations came into existence.

Canadian music teachers from both the school and the private studio have attended American music conventions for many decades. In the early years they went to the Music Teachers' National Association (MTNA), an organization of private music teachers founded in 1876. The Canadian composer Calixa Lavallée was active in MTNA during his tenure in the United States and served as president during the 1880s. In 1931 Ernest MacMillan was invited to address an MTNA conference in Detroit. Speaking on the topic 'Musical Relations Between Canada and the United States,' he began by stating that he did not have an official mandate to speak on behalf of Canadian musicians, and he explained that 'an accredited representative of the musical profession in Canada would at [that] time be an impossibility,' for there was 'no body to appoint him.' He continued: 'We have in Canada many teachers' associations which do excellent work in their various localities, but none of them are national in scope. Such a body as the Music Teachers' National Association, if duplicated in Canada with such minor variations as our somewhat different conditions demand, would without a doubt prove a valuable asset from both the musical and the purely professional point of view.'[3] Other Canadian musicians had also felt the need for a national organization of music teachers. In 1935 the inaugural meeting of the Canadian Federation of Music Teachers' Associations (CFMTA) was held in Vancouver; however, it was not until the 1940s that similar groups in the eastern part of the country became part of this federation.

THE CANADIAN FEDERATION OF MUSIC
TEACHERS' ASSOCIATIONS

At a meeting of the Manitoba Provincial Music Teachers' Association in 1933, Minnie A. Boyd of Winnipeg proposed the idea of a federation of Canadian music teachers' organizations. It was primarily through Miss Boyd's initiative that plans were made for a gathering of representatives from the four western provinces. The meeting took place at Harmony Hall in Vancouver in August 1935, hosted by Roy Robertson and the British Columbia Music Teachers' Federation. Robertson was subsequently elected president, with Minnie Boyd as secretary-treasurer. The association was designed as a federation in which the provincial organizations (British Columbia, Alberta, Saskatchewan, and Manitoba) would be members, so each person belonging to a provincial association was automatically a member of CFMTA. The federation was to be governed by an executive and a board of directors consisting of provincial representatives. It was not until 1942 that Ontario joined CFMTA, followed by Nova Scotia in 1944, Quebec in 1945, and New Brunswick in 1954. Saskatchewan was the first to obtain a provincial charter (1938), which was modelled after its provincial Nurses' Act. All groups except the one in Quebec later obtained provincial charters permitting them to use the term 'registered' in their names; hence, SRMTA and so on. CFMTA was officially incorporated in 1961.

In addition to the overall aim of strengthening the work of the provincial groups, the specific goals of this new federation were to bring about the licensing or registration of private music teachers, to facilitate an interchange of artists and exchange of club programs, to publish a federation paper, and to strive for uniform standards of examinations.[4] CFMTA later turned its attention to the matter of high school credit for the private study of music and also lobbied for the use of more Canadian adjudicators at competitive music festivals; it has served its members through conventions and publications. After holding conventions in Vancouver (1936) and Winnipeg (1937), it adopted a pattern of biennial meetings, which have been held in an effort to upgrade the profession and provide a forum for the exchange of ideas. These conventions have featured master classes, workshops, and concerts by well-known artists. In 1937 CFMTA published the first issue of the *Canadian Music Teacher*, a periodical which has subsequently undergone several name changes. It has been the principal medium for communicating with individual members throughout the country, particularly those in remote regions.

In 1942 CFMTA initiated the Young Artists series of concerts, and in 1960 it inaugurated Canada Music Week to help mark the twenty-fifth anniversary of its founding. It has also sponsored a music writing contest for students, offered scholarships, promoted the commissioning and use of Canadian music for students, and generally made the public more aware of the role of the private music teacher. In non-convention years CFMTA has often organized charter tours of world cultural centres for its members, sometimes in connection with ISME conferences. It has also assisted private teachers not associated with an institution through the offering of group insurance and health plans. Many well-respected teachers, both those from private studios and those affiliated with conservatories and institutions of higher learning, have been active in CFMTA, thus adding to the prestige of the organization.

The original aim of establishing a system of licensing for private teaching has never been achieved, and lack of credentials has remained a fundamental problem. A music degree or diploma is a requirement for membership in each of the provincial organizations and therefore for the national body as well, yet it is not necessary for someone to belong to one of these groups in order to teach music privately. Nevertheless, CFMTA has helped to raise the standard of private teaching in Canada. By the early 1980s the federation was serving eight provincial organizations, with approximately ninety local branches and a total membership of nearly three thousand.[5]

The following is a list of the presidents of the CFMTA:

Roy Robertson (1935–7)
Minnie Boyd (1937–9)
May James (1939–41)
Lyell Gustin (1941–6)
Edna Marie Hawkin (1946–51)
Dan A. Cameron (1951–5)
Violet Isfeld (1955–9)
Reginald Bedford (1959–63)

Robert Pounder (1963–7)
Flora Goulden (1967–71)
Helen Dahlstrom (1971–5)
Thelma Wilson (1975–9)
Kathleen Fensom (1979–83)
Ernst Schneider (1983–7)
Jean Broadfoot (1987–9)
Matt Hughes (1989–)

THE CANADIAN MUSIC EDUCATORS' ASSOCIATION

Although both CFMTA and the provincial associations have occasionally offered sessions on topics related to music in the schools, their primary concern has been focused on the needs of the private teacher. In speaking to the fourteenth CFMTA convention in Montreal, Lola Mac-Quarrie stated that although the general aims are much the same for private teachers and school music teachers, 'the function of the school music teacher differs from that of the private teacher especially in matters of emphasis, method, and standard of achievement of solo performance ... "Music education in the schools is not so much to train the singer or the instrumentalist as to restore the belief that music is as much an element in culture as literature and science. It cannot be disregarded or neglected." The school, therefore, is not to be judged as a conservatory of music.'[6] Lola MacQuarrie was at that time supervisor of music for the Winnipeg schools and president of the newly formed Canadian Music Educators' Association.

The need for a national body concerned with the teaching of music in the schools had been recognized for many decades. Both the Dominion Educational Association (established 1892) and the National Council of Education (established 1919) created music sections within their organizations, but these music groups were short-lived. With the formation of the Music Supervisors' National Conference in the United States in 1907, Canadian teachers involved in school music became more interested in attending American conferences. In 1917 Duncan McKenzie participated in a conference of this organization in Grand Rapids, Michigan. McKenzie was most impressed and expressed regret that a similar opportunity did not exist for Canadians. During his tenure as supervisor of music for the Toronto schools he addressed the 1922 meeting of the Music Section of OEA, calling for the formation of an association of Canadian supervisors of music. He cautioned, 'We go to the States to meet each other and know more of school conditions there than we do in our own country.'[7] McKenzie's suggestions were endorsed by the delegates, and a motion was passed that a dominion music supervisors' conference be formed with the OEA Music Section as its nucleus, but no action was taken at that time. Canadians nevertheless continued to participate in activities of the American Music Supervisors' National Conference, which in 1934 was renamed the Music Educators' National Conference (MENC).

One of the most energetic in this regard was Irvin Cooper of Montreal, who as early as 1943 approached MENC concerning his proposal for an international festival of school music. Cooper was subsequently appointed vice-chairman of an MENC committee on intercultural relations. Among his proposals was an invitation for the eastern division to hold its conference in Montreal in 1947 as part of an international festival. Although this festival did take place, with tremendous response from school performing groups from the United States, the proposal for the eastern division conference was not accepted. Early in the discussion of plans for this international festival, Cooper made reference to the lack of a 'unified front among Canadian music educators,' and commented, 'The organization of a Canadian federation of school music teachers is needed immediately if Canada is to take a leading role in this great venture.'[8] However, largely because of Cooper's enthusiasm and organizational ability, the project went forward without the support of a national organization; such a group was not to materialize for another sixteen years. In 1950 Cooper left Canada to assume a post at Florida State University, and his efforts were channelled into MENC endeavours rather than the formation of a national organization in Canada.

Cooper was not alone in his desire to establish international relations in music education; several people and associations expressed similar concerns, and the suggestion was even made that MENC become an international body. Ironically, it was at an eastern division convention of MENC that plans for a Canadian organization were formulated. During the 1957 meeting in Atlantic City 'some fifty Canadian Music Educators who were attending "Canada Day" met to discuss the possibility of forming a Canadian counterpart. Miss Marion Park, then President of the Ontario Music Educators' Association presided.'[9] Leslie Bell, a Toronto musician, figured prominently in this meeting and was elected chairman of an interim committee. Keith MacMillan commented later: 'Many music educators who consistently travelled the country realized the potential advantages to the profession of interprovincial links of communication and action. None was more vociferous in promoting the idea of a national body than the late Dr. Leslie Bell, known principally as choral conductor of light music, but who was also an adjudicator, teacher, member of the editorial board of The Canadian Music Journal and all in all a national figure in Canadian music.'[10] Leslie Bell had been involved in many music education endeavours, including the International Festival of School Music in Montreal. During the 1950s, when Bell was free-lancing as a conductor, journalist, and broadcaster, he began to lobby for the formation of a national organization of music educators. In 1955 he wrote about the matter in his weekly newspaper column: 'We have, in the nation, no organization which enables school and private teacher, professional musicians and music tradesmen to meet on common ground and discuss mutual problems. As a result, every year hundreds of Canadians slip across the border to American conventions where they try to find help by examining the often very different musical problems of another country.'[11] When Bell was on tour with his famous Leslie Bell Singers, he frequently took the opportunity to speak to groups of teachers about the need for a national organization. These contacts included visits to several provincial music educators' associations which were formed in 1957, namely, those in British Columbia, Alberta, and Saskatchewan.

The founding meeting of CMEA was held at the Westbury Hotel in Toronto during Easter week of 1959 in conjunction with the provincial OMEA convention. Roy Fenwick was elected CMEA president, with Keith Bissell as secretary-treasurer and Leslie Bell as executive director. There were three regional vice-presidents: David Thomson for the east, Lloyd Slind for the west, and Richard Johnston for the central region. In addition, representatives were appointed for each province with the exception of Prince Edward Island, which had no delegates at the meeting. Special representatives were later appointed from the Canadian Music Publishers' Association and the Canadian Broadcasting Corporation. Several changes in the constitution have taken place, one of the major ones occurring in 1972, when CMEA formally became an incorporated body with the dual name Canadian Music Educators' Association/Association canadienne des éducateurs de musique. CMEA has continued to operate on the principle of provincial representation from all ten provinces, but the territories have never been included in the constitution.

The value of a national organization was expressed by Fenwick in one of his first president's messages: 'I am more than ever convinced that if Canada is to realize its potentialities as a musical nation, there must be a strong National body of music educators through which the experienced can help the beginners, the older ones can steady the younger teachers, and where they, in turn, can bring their enthusiasm and fresh outlook to keep music in this young country from getting into the proverbial rut.'[12] The president of MENC, Karl Ernst, was a special guest at the inaugural meeting. In his address to the delegates he encouraged them to maintain a close affiliation with other organizations, recommending that CMEA 'should enrol under its banner all organizations who are in any way concerned with music education.'[13] Although his suggestion for a federation was not realized, CMEA did establish liaison with the Canadian Music Council, the CBC, and the International Society for Music Education, and later with the National Youth Orchestra, the Canadian String Teachers' Association, and the

Canadian Bandmasters' Association; it has also been associated with the Canadian Music Festival Adjudicators' Association.[14] CMEA has been relentless in working toward a system of affiliation with provincial music educators' associations in order to speak officially for music educators in the country.

During the first years of CMEA's existence an enormous effort was put forth to obtain memberships from all parts of the country and to form provincial organizations where they did not already exist. Several delegates who had attended the Toronto meeting took the initiative in their own provinces; notable in this regard was Catherine Allison in Nova Scotia. Richard Johnston travelled to both Nova Scotia and New Brunswick in 1959 to speak to newly formed provincial associations. Lloyd Slind spoke to the organizational meeting of the Manitoba Music Educators' Association, and Roy Fenwick addressed the music section of the Provincial Association of Protestant Teachers of Quebec. A CMEA chapter was organized in Newfoundland in 1960 through the efforts of Ignatius Rumboldt and the Extension Services of Memorial University. Although this group was 'in a state of decline after 1965, a new and vigorous organization of Newfoundland music teachers'[15] was formed the following year under the auspices of the Newfoundland Teachers' Association. Donald Cook described this development as 'the most significant step that we have taken in music,' and added, 'In the Music Council we have an organization embracing the whole music teaching profession across our Province.'[16] A provincial music organization was formed in Prince Edward Island in 1962. This group has been closely associated with NSMEA, and members have regularly attended the fall conference of the Nova Scotia organization.

Like CFMTA, CMEA has attempted to communicate with its members through national conferences and publications. The first full-scale CMEA conference was held in Winnipeg during Easter week of 1960. A great effort was put forth by all those involved in CMEA to have as large an attendance as possible. Fenwick commented, 'We music teachers must realize the necessity of having our professional enthusiasm recharged, our methods overhauled, and our attitudes adjusted.' He spoke of the merits of local and provincial gatherings; but they could not, he said, 'widen our horizons or heighten our vision like a National conference, where the leaders in the field, from coast to coast, gather to exchange views and offer solutions to the larger problems of music in education.'[17] The Winnipeg conference, chaired by MMEA president Lola MacQuarrie, offered a full and comprehensive program, serving as a model for future conferences. 'No aspect of music education, from kindergarten to the university level, was neglected and there was variety at every turn – lectures, panels, demonstrations, concerts and exhibits, to say nothing of Western hospitality.'[18] Special speakers included Dr A.W. Trueman, director of the Canada Council. Gifford Mitchell, who was elected president, issued an invitation to hold the second conference in Montreal the following year. Plans began with the aim of displaying much of the musical life of the city as well as that of the schools. Mitchell employed a rhetoric similar to that used by Fenwick concerning attendance at the convention: 'Canadian Music Education is our Cause. Whether we pursue it by ocean's edge, among the mountains or forests or the prairies or in the industrial centres of the mid-east, we are bound by our aim. A national convention is needed, if only to assert this fact of unity among us. Let your slogan be "Montreal in April."'[19] Annual conferences continued for two more years (Vancouver in 1962, Halifax in 1963), after which it was decided to adopt a pattern of biennial meetings. These national events have given music educators an opportunity to become familiar with outstanding music programs and their leaders, and have also assisted regional programs by bringing public attention to the work being done in music education across the country.[20]

Performances by student groups have been an important part of CMEA conventions. The 1967 Centennial Conference in London introduced a special Dominion Night featuring performing groups from across the country, a tradition which has been retained by most succeeding gatherings. There has also been an effort to have works written especially for these national conferences. Through the assistance of the Centennial Commission two works for student performing groups were commissioned for the 1967 London conference and given their premieres at this event: 'When Age and Youth Unite' by Godfrey Ridout, text by Claude Bissell, and 'Four Fantasias on Canadian Folk Themes' by Robert Fleming. There were many special guests at this conference, which celebrated the centennial of Confederation. But the spontaneous standing ovation which greeted Sir Ernest MacMillan when he approached the podium to conduct his arrangement of 'God Save the Queen' was for many delegates the highlight of the conference.

Less than two months after the inaugural meeting of CMEA in 1959, the first issue of its journal, the *Canadian Music Educator*, appeared under the editorship of Leslie Bell. The early issues were in the nature of a bulletin, for they were only a few pages in length, but the publication soon took shape as a full-fledged journal with increased advertising revenue from music publishers and instrument dealers. Richard Edmunds of the Canadian Bureau for the Advancement of Music served as business manager in charge of advertising and mailing. The journal has been maintained as a quarterly publication and has from time to time included articles in French as well as English; in 1976 it adopted a bilingual title. A CMEA newsletter, under the editorship of Wallace Laughton, was introduced in 1968. Laughton, who had taken over the position of research coordinator, also established a CMEA Resource Centre in St Catharines. He became known to many as a result of helpful items mentioned in the newsletter and also through displays at national conventions, not to mention his frequent correspondence concerning membership. CMEA members enjoyed the benefits of Laughton's volunteer service for well over a decade.

The sudden death of Leslie Bell in January 1962 left a void in the CMEA organization. Volunteers had to be found to carry out the various duties he had performed as editor of the journal, executive director of the organization, CMEA representative on the Canadian Music Council, and adviser to CBC. As a tribute, CMEA, in conjunction with CBC, established the Leslie Bell Memorial Choir Competition 'to stimulate greater interest in choral music and to help maintain a fine standard of choral singing, thus rendering homage to the memory of the late Dr. Leslie Bell.'[21]

CBC has cooperated with CMEA in several ventures. There was radio coverage of the gala concert launching CMEA at the 1959 OMEA convention, and CBC produced a series of broadcasts on the formation of CMEA. During the 1960–1 school year, programs featuring school choral groups from Vancouver to St John's, Newfoundland, were broadcast on the network. At the request of CBC – primarily through Bruce Attridge, national supervisor of children's programs – a CMEA committee on school broadcasting was established.

CMEA has worked with other organizations and institutions as well. Its collaboration with the Canadian Music Centre on the John Adaskin Project has been one of far-reaching importance. From its inception, the organization has also undertaken various projects and studies on its own. A research council, organized by Frank Churchley and Campbell Trowsdale, was established at the 1973 conference in Ottawa; a music teacher education council, chaired by Malcolm Brown, was also brought into being at the same conference. A recent innovation, the inclusion of a forum devoted to current issues in the profession as part of the national convention program, was launched at the 1981 Winnipeg conference under the chairmanship of Colin Walley.

From the beginning CMEA membership has been open to 'all persons engaged in music teaching or other music educational work in the ten provinces of Canada.'[22] Later, student memberships were introduced. CMEA has had an emphasis on individual membership, but it has also recognized the need to have provincial associations affiliated with the national. Although most provincial music education groups are now linked with CMEA, this on-going difficulty has not yet been completely solved. The problem of provincial affiliation has been compounded by several factors. Those provinces which had already developed strong organizations have been reluctant to relinquish their autonomy or break off previous affiliations. In several cases the music education association is actually a 'subject council' of the provincial teachers' organization. Since education is a provincial matter, the first allegiance of members is often to the provincial group rather than to a national body. An unusual circumstance arose when the Alberta Music Educators' Association was dissolved in 1969; music teachers then had the option of joining the Fine Arts Council of the Teachers' Association, but this heterogeneous group is not affiliated with CMEA. Still another difficulty occurs when there is more than one music education association in a province, such as in Quebec and New Brunswick, where the associations are organized according to language. In New Brunswick the NBMEA, with members from both English- and French-speaking schools, became the Music Education Council of the New Brunswick Teachers'Association (NBTA). When the NBTA divided into separate organizations for English and French teachers, the French-speaking music educators formed a separate council affiliated with the Association des enseignants francophones du Nouveau-Brunswick.

Shortly after the founding of CMEA the name of the informal organization of music teachers with the Montreal Protestant board was changed to QMEA. An association of Catholic music educators was formed for the English-speaking teachers with the Montreal Catholic School Commission in 1963. These two organizations merged in 1968 to become the Quebec Music Educators' Association (QMEA). In 1966 an organization known as Fédération des associations de musiciens éducateurs du Québec (FAMEQ) was formed during a conference in Drummondville organized by George Little. Sister Marcelle Corneille remarked, 'The Association was born of necessity: to bring together the music educators of the French language to study those problems relating to the integration of music to the educational system.'[23] FAMEQ united twelve regional associations comprised of music teachers from nursery school to the university level and those active in both the public and private sectors of music education. Although it is a provincial association, it has functioned on both national and international levels. Moreover, it has established liaison with educators in France, and its members have frequently attended ISME congresses. In the CMEA constitution there has been provision for only one affiliated group per province, and thus the francophone groups in both Quebec and New Brunswick have not been formally linked with CMEA even though several of their members belong to the national association. Patricia Shand notes: 'It has been difficult and expensive for CMEA to provide bilingual services to its members, most of whom are English. As a result, CMEA's impact in French Canada has been relatively weak.'[24]

The structure of CMEA has caused communication problems in its relationship with other national music organizations, which those in charge have attempted to improve through a system of special representatives. Although a formalized structure incorporating these representatives has never been adopted by CMEA, there have been recent moves in this direction. The type of framework which has been of great benefit to those working in Manitoba – and one which would perhaps have been advantageous on the national level – was described by Beth Douglas: 'From the very beginning it has been the desire of our membership to make the M.M.E.A. truly representative of all branches of music education and an organization which will be province-wide in its appeal and usefulness. Representatives of the Manitoba Registered Music Teachers' Association, the Greater Winnipeg School Music Teachers' Club, the Royal Canadian College of Organists, and the Canadian Bandmasters' Association bring to our meetings a breadth of viewpoint which we feel is most desirable.'[25] Like many associations, CMEA has been plagued by problems of finance, for it has had to rely primarily upon membership dues for its operational budget. It has received special grants from time to time; in its first year of operation it received money from the Canadian Bureau for the Advancement of Music and a gift of $1073.86, the balance in the trust fund of the International Music Festival Association in Montreal. Grants have been received from government agencies for special commissions and projects, and a few national conferences have made a profit for the organization. As yet, however, CMEA has not been in a position to operate a central office with full-time staff. When the Resource Centre was closed in St Catharines, the CMEA headquarters was moved to Toronto and a part-time executive director was employed by the association. Despite its difficulties CMEA has become a vital force for music education across the country; by the early 1980s it had a membership of well over two thousand.

The following is a list of CMEA presidents:

G. Roy Fenwick (1959–60)   Kenneth Bray (1973–7)
Gifford Mitchell (1960–2)   Paul Murray (1977–9)
Lloyd Slind (1962–3)   Winnifred Voigts (1979–81)
Lola MacQuarrie (1963–5)   Dennis Humenik (1981–3)
Garfield Bender (1965–7)   Brenda Trafford (1983–5)
Frank Churchley (1967–9)   Paul Maynard (1985–9)
Vernon Ellis (1969–71)   Joan Therens (1989–)
Allen Clingman (1971–3)

THE CANADIAN UNIVERSITY MUSIC SOCIETY

The Canadian University Music Society (CUMS), originally known as the Canadian Association of University Schools of Music (CAUSM), traces its origins to 1964. Through the assistance of the Canada Council, a small group of representatives from Canadian university music departments met at Stanley House on the Gaspé Peninsula during July of that year to discuss the formation of an association of university music educators. As Welton Marquis remarked, 'for the first time in the history of Canadian music a tangible liaison was established between music schools of Canadian universities from Coast to Coast.'[26] A small committee was established and met again in December. At that time Arnold Walter presented the following motion: 'The representatives of the Faculties of Music of the Universities of Toronto, Montreal and McGill, have agreed to establish the Canadian Association of University Schools of Music, provided that membership in this Association is approved by the authorities concerned.'[27] The first general meeting of the new association was held in Ottawa in February 1965 under the auspices of the Centennial Commission. It dealt primarily with recommendations from various university music schools to the Centennial Commission. A constitution was adopted which provided for an executive and a council of representatives from member institutions; Arnold Walter was elected president. Two categories of institutional membership, full and associate, were established, but there was no provision for individual membership until several years later. In 1979 the name was changed to the Canadian University Music Society/la Société de musique des universités canadiennes. There has been an effort to increase the number of individual members, but both institutional and individual membership categories have been retained.

Beginning in 1965, meetings have been held annually in conjunction with the Learned Societies, hosted by universities in various parts of the country. These events have served as forums for academic and professional concerns, venues where musicians can exchange views and find common ground for future development. In addition to the discussion of business matters, meetings have included scholarly papers and performances. Members have gained insight and knowledge with respect to what is happening in Canadian universities as a result of the rotation from one campus to another. Moreover, the annual meeting has provided an opportunity for the host institution to showcase faculty performers and composers or, in some cases, to focus on aspects of regional cultural significance. CAUSM has enabled those in leadership positions – among others, Arnold Walter, Helmut Blume, Clément Morin, and Welton Marquis – to influence and shape the direction of music education on a national scale. It has also served as a resource for emerging departments, especially for those interested in knowing how established music schools manage their academic and administrative affairs. As well, individual faculty members, particularly those unfamiliar with the Canadian university scene, have been able to meet colleagues and become acquainted with programs and developments in other institutions.

CAUSM has operated on a bilingual basis since its inception. French-speaking members have given scholastic presentations at annual meetings and have also provided leadership on executive committees. Clément Morin (Université de Montréal) was president in 1967–9; Lucien Brochu and Armand Ferland (both of Laval) held this position in 1971–3 and 1979–81 respectively; Brian Ellard (Université de Moncton) served as president in 1975–7. The meetings of the organization have facilitated a much closer communication between music faculty members of francophone universities and their counterparts in anglophone institutions.

At the 1968 CAUSM meeting in Calgary the association developed minimal requirements for specialized undergraduate programs in music history and literature, composition, performance, and music education in an attempt to attain a measure of uniformity in Canadian institutions. This was one of the first major undertakings of the organization; it resulted in the publication of *Curricular Standards* in 1969. Although this work has been revised and used as a guide by many institutions, CUMS has played no official role in the accreditation of music departments. The organization has also published an annual directory of all persons engaged in university music teaching in Canada. A scholarly publication known as the CAUSM *Journal* first appeared in 1971; it was replaced in 1980 by the *Canadian University Music Review/Revue de musique des universités canadiennes*.

The following is a list of the presidents of CUMS (CAUSM 1964–79):

Arnold Walter (1965–7)   Armand Ferland (1979–81)
Clément Morin (1967–9)   Robert Stangeland (1981–3)
Welton Marquis (1969–71)   Bruce Minorgan (1983–5)
Lucien Brochu (1971–3)   Gordon Greene (1985–7)
Lorne Watson (1973–5)   Donald F. Cook (1987–9)
Brian Ellard (1975–7)   Stephen Adamson (1989–)
Donald A. McKellar (1977–9)

RECENT DEVELOPMENTS

Writing in the late 1960s, Arnold Walter commented, 'For music educators this is an age of anxiety, an age of analysis, an age of conferences whose reports are repositories of a great deal of research.'[28] Later, in *Aspects of Music in Canada*, he discussed his perception of the need for two distinct types of music education, 'one for the few, the gifted, the perseverant, our future professionals, another for the many, for amateurs, concert-goers, opera lovers, record fans: for all those to whom music will be a course of delight and an enrichment of life.'[29] In Walter's view, improvements had been made in both these areas. It was now possible for those wishing to pursue a career in music to receive adequate training and experience in their own country, and music in the schools was 'once more in the ascendancy, favoured by progressive educators but confronted by an overcrowded curriculum and largely unaided by its former allies – the family, the home and the church.'[30]

The growth of the music education profession in Canada has led to a proliferation of specialized groups representing a variety of philosophies and approaches. This pluralism has been further exacerbated by the fact that music educators do not confine their activities to organizations within their own country. Although the situation has afforded individual educators greater opportunities for development, it has also caused a number of problems; many of these associations have had difficulty when challenged with the question 'For whom do they speak?' This difficulty is closely aligned with the problem of funding, for there is currently no one organization representing music education in the country which is charged with the responsibility of approaching government for funds. Instead, organizations vie with one another for financial assistance.

There is a great deal of membership overlap in these volunteer professional organizations. This means that members find themselves divided in their loyalties, particularly with respect to attendance at meetings and conferences. Leslie Bell commented on this problem in the mid-1950s: 'We have, in this country, the confusion of a dual culture and dual educational system. We have school music teachers and private music teachers going their separate ways when they should be working together.'[31] He raised this matter in the first issue of the *Canadian Music Educator*: 'Many have pointed out ... that it is too bad that classroom teachers and private teachers should hold separate conventions, often at the same time and in different places, especially when there are so many music educators in this country who teach both privately and in the schools. Music publishers also point to the problem of setting up exhibits in two or more places at once. Some people hold the view that future CMEA conventions would have more variety of appeal if they included the combined forces of different associations.'[32] One of the few times that music education organizations combined forces in this country was in the sponsorship of the thirteenth international congress of ISME in the summer of 1978. The congress was held on the campus of the University of Western Ontario in London. Since there was no single organization in the country representing all aspects of music education, an interim hosting committee had to be devised. It was convened under the chairmanship of Vernon Ellis, Canadian representative on the ISME board, and consisted of representatives from CAUSM, CFMTA, CMEA, and FAMEQ.

ISME was founded in Brussels in 1953 at a conference convened by the United Nations Educational, Scientific, and Cultural Organization (UNESCO). This 'International Conference on the Role and Place of Music in the Education of Youth and Adults ... was the result of close collaboration between UNESCO, which was responsible for its organization, and the International Music Council, which drew up its plan of work.'[33] Canada has been involved in this organization since its inception; both Arnold Walter and Geoffrey Waddington, musical director of the CBC, gave addresses at the Brussels conference. Walter was co-chairman of the Preparatory Commission and also served as the first president of ISME. Several Canadians have participated in ISME congresses, particularly the 1966 meetings at Interlochen, Michigan, but the conference held in London marked the first time that this organization had met in Canada. The co-chairmen of the event were Lucien Brochu of l'Université Laval and Donald McKellar of the University of Western Ontario. As part of the conference, delegates from over forty countries were given an opportunity to hear performing ensembles from around the world, including representative groups from almost every province in Canada.

This was not the first time that Canada had played host to an international music conference. In 1975 the Canadian Music Council hosted the inaugural World Music Week Congress, with events scheduled consecutively in Toronto, Ottawa, Montreal, and Quebec City. Celebrations included the first observance of International Music Day on 1 October. The conference provided a showcase for Canadian composition, performance, and scholarship, just as the ISME event did three years later for various aspects of music education. An undertaking of comparable significance but more academic in nature was the publication of the *Encyclopedia of Music in Canada*,[34] an eleven-hundred-page volume furnishing comprehensive information for all those wishing to know more about music and musicians in Canada. The EMC project entailed a decade of research, and in an unprecedented way it has generated interest among numerous groups and individual readers in their own musical heritage. Thus, by the early 1980s, through the hosting of international events and the completion of EMC, work being done in Canada in music composition, performance, teaching, and scholarship was becoming better known not only to those in other parts of the world but to Canadians themselves.

Epilogue

It was difficult to know where to begin a history of music education in Canada. Even after the main strands of activity were identified, it seemed impossible to find well-defined patterns or to connect events which led systematically from the rustic conditions of colonial life to the complex, sophisticated society of an electronic age.

What has been observed, however, is a process originating with the transplantation of French and British traditions to North America and continuing with a succession of influences from the United States and various other countries. Historians and others have referred to the emerging social pattern as the 'Canadian mosaic.' Such labels aside, Canadian culture has indeed been an evolution, derivative in many ways but exceedingly rich and complex in its synthesis of diverse characteristics. Unfortunately, in the assimilation of various cultures, the oral traditions of both the immigrants and the indigenous peoples of Canada have generally been neglected as an integral part of music education.

Music education has understandably become more complex in a pluralistic society. No longer can it be discussed as a single entity or a movement with a single purpose. However, what has transpired in music education from colonial times to Canada's Centennial can be observed; significant developments can be recognized; and the present system can thereby be better understood. Certainly, there has been a great effort to raise the standards of professional training and teacher education in the field of music. Methodologies have undergone vigorous scrutiny and self-criticism; the range of repertoire and instructional materials has been enlarged in an attempt to provide appropriate musical experience for learning at all levels; and the institutional mechanisms devised to produce optimal results in both general and specialized fields have been impressive symbols of progress. Nevertheless, even greater effort is needed before further improvements can be made in these areas. Such effort is prerequisite to artistic growth and also helpful in nurturing the desire for a distinct Canadian identity. And just as vital is the will to engender respect for the musicians, teachers, and scholars who have helped bring music education in Canada to this point in its history.

Notes

CHAPTER 1 Quebec

1 Roger Magnuson, *A Brief History of Quebec Education from New France to Parti Québecois* (Montreal: Harvest House 1980), vii
2 Willy Amtmann, *Music in Canada, 1600–1800.* (Montreal: Habitex 1975), 67
3 Ibid., 73
4 Ibid., 91
5 Amtmann, *La Musique au Québec, 1600–1875* (Montreal: Les Editions de l'Homme 1976), 305
6 *EMC*, s.v. 'ladies' colleges and convent schools'
7 Magnuson, *A Brief History of Quebec Education*, viii
8 *Rapport de la Commission d'enquête sur l'enseignement des arts au Québec* [Rioux Report] (Quebec 1968), 193
9 Claude Galarneau, *Les Collèges classiques du Canada français (1620–1928)* (Montreal: Fides 1978)
10 G.W. Parmalee, *Education in the Province of Quebec* (Quebec: Quebec Dept. of Public Instruction 1914), 45
11 Minutes of the Montreal Protestant School Board, 1847–71, 7
12 Montreal *Gazette*, 12 July 1851
13 Montreal *Gazette*, 17 March 1851
14 Report of the Protestant School Board of Montreal, 1868–70, 23. Further information on this Sefton publication is included in chapter 3.
15 Minutes of the Protestant School Board of Montreal, 9 Oct. 1886

16 AR (Que.), 1887–8, 92
17 AR (Que.), 1888–9, 37
18 For information on A.T. Cringan see chapters 3 and 10.
19 Report of the Protestant School Board of Montreal, 1891–2, 8
20 The regulation remained in force until the Second World War; in 1929 the term 'Tonic Sol-fa' was replaced by 'School Music.'
21 Minutes of the Protestant School Board of Montreal, 12 March 1887
22 Magnuson, *A Brief History of Quebec Education*, 35
23 Report of the Protestant School Board of Montreal, 1902–3, 7
24 AR (Que.), 1916–17, 175–6
25 Report of the Protestant School Board of Montreal, 1902–3, 99
26 Minutes of the Protestant School Board of Montreal, 12 Dec. 1891
27 Report of the Protestant School Board of Montreal, 1895–7, 9
28 J. Castell Hopkins, *The Origin and History of Empire Day* (1910), 4. Pamphlet, Robarts Library, University of Toronto
29 *Minutes of the Proceedings of the Dominion Educational Association*, xxxvi
30 Report of the Protestant School Board of Montreal, 1899, 9
31 Program of Empire Day School Concert, Montreal Arena, 26 May 1903, Protestant School Board of Montreal files
32 Parmalee, *Education in the Province of Quebec*, 45
33 AR (Que.), 1888–9, 15
34 Parmalee, *Education in the Province of Quebec*, 45
35 Amtmann, *Music in Canada, 1600–1800*, 209
36 Cited by Helmut Kallmann, *A History of Music in Canada, 1534–1914* (Toronto: University of Toronto Press 1960), 51
37 Cited by Amtmann, *Music in Canada, 1600–1800*, 210
38 Ibid., 220
39 The Associated Board of the Royal Schools of Music was founded in London, England, in 1889 to serve as the examination body for the Royal Academy of Music and the Royal College of Music.
40 Stanley Brice Frost, *McGill University for the Advancement of Learning*, vol. 2, 1895–1971 (Kingston and Montreal: McGill-Queen's University Press 1986), 34
41 Kallmann, *A History*, 216

CHAPTER 2 The Maritimes

1 Phyllis Blakeley, 'Music in Nova Scotia, 1605–1867,' *Dalhousie Review* 31, (Summer 1951), 95
2 Carleton Elliott, 'Music in New Brunswick,' in *Arts in New Brunswick*, ed.

R.A. Tweedie, Fred Cogswell, and W. Stewart MacNutt (Fredericton: Brunswick Press 1967), 192

3 Helmut Kallmann, *A History of Music in Canada, 1534–1914* (Toronto: University of Toronto Press 1960), 52–3

4 See Nancy F. Vogan, 'Music Instruction in Nova Scotia before 1914,' in *Musical Canada: Words and Music Honouring Helmut Kallmann*, ed. John Beckwith and Frederick A. Hall (Toronto: University of Toronto Press 1988), 7

5 Blakeley, 'Music in Nova Scotia,' 100

6 Hugo Talbot, in *Musical Halifax, 1903–4*, ed. Hugo Talbot (Halifax: McAlpine Publishing Co.), 10

7 Ibid., 7

8 Brian Campbell, 'Holy Angels Convent,' *Novascotian* 4, no. 32, 11

9 Neil Michaud, 'Acadians and Their Music,' in *The Acadians of the Maritimes: Thematic Studies*, ed. Jean Daigle (Moncton: Centre d'études acadiennes 1982), 621

10 Halifax Conservatory of Music Calendar, 1905–6, introductory statement

11 Talbot, in *Musical Halifax*, 12–13

12 Halifax Conservatory of Music Calendar, 1899–1900, 55

13 Talbot, in *Musical Halifax*, 13–14

14 Mount Allison Ladies' College Catalogue, 1890–1, and *Wesleyan*, 11 June 1891, quoted in John G. Reid, *Mount Allison University*, vol. 1, 1843–1914 (Toronto: University of Toronto Press 1984), 175–6

15 Talbot, in *Musical Halifax*, 3

16 Bishop Inglis to the SPG [Society for the Propagation of the Gospel] in London, 15 Jan. 1819, Provincial Archives (NS). Dr Andrew Bell devised a monitorial school system in India during the late eighteenth century. Schools based on this idea are often referred to as Madras schools.

17 Jacob Cunnabell to the Education Committee of the House of Assembly, 31 March 1858, Provincial Archives (NS)

18 AR (NS), 1865, 96

19 Ibid., 1869, 17

20 Ibid., 26

21 *Acadian Recorder*, 21 Feb. 1867

22 AR (NS), 1867, 20

23 Halifax *Citizen*, 21 July 1868

24 *Acadian Recorder*, 15 July 1870

25 W.O. Perkins and J.B. Norton, *The Dominion Songster* (Halifax: Connelly and Kelly 1870), preface

26 AR (NS), 1871, 93

27 Halifax City Schools Report, 1876, 17
28 Ibid., 18
29 Ibid., 1878, 17
30 *Acadian Recorder*, 18 March 1881
31 *Halifax Citizen*, 14 July 1882
32 AR (NS), 1887, 116
33 Ibid., 1888, 106
34 Ibid., xviii–xix
35 *Presbyterian Witness*, 15 Nov. 1890
36 'Tonic Sol-fa in Nova Scotia,' *Educational Review*, Jan. 1891, 131
37 *Journal of Education* (NS), April 1893, 22
38 Ibid., Oct. 1894, 111
39 AR (NS), 1905, 62–3
40 *Journal of Education* (NS), Oct. 1905, 198
41 AR (NS), 1900, 77–8
42 *Journal of Education* (NS), April 1914, 75
43 AR (NS), 1867, 4
44 'Singing,' *Journal of Education* (NS), Oct. 1895, 115
45 Report of the Twelfth Convention of the Provincial Education Association
   of Nova Scotia, Oct. 1895, 45–6
46 Katherine F.C. MacNaughton, *The Development of the Theory and Practice of
   Education in New Brunswick: 1784–1900*, University of New Brunswick
   Historical Studies, no. 1 (Fredericton 1947), 66
47 Ibid., 119
48 AR (NB), 1858
49 MacNaughton, *The Development of the Theory and Practice of Education in
   New Brunswick*, 173
50 AR (NB), 1879, xliv
51 *Campbell's Canadian School Song Book* was actually the publication *Three-
   Part Songs* by Henry Francis Sefton (Toronto: James Campbell and Son
   1869).
52 *Acadian Recorder*, 20 Aug. 1870.
53 AR (NB), 1887, 91
54 Luella E. Blanch, 'A Plea for More Music in Schools,' *Educational Review*,
   Nov. 1898, 104
55 A scrapbook belonging to Carter and housed in the Provincial Archives
   (NB) contains many programs and newspaper clippings of musical events;
   his wife was soloist in several of these performances.
56 Minutes of the Moncton School Board, 23 Nov. 1904
57 AR (NB), 1907, 39

58 Nancy Fraser Vogan, 'The History of Public School Music in the Province of New Brunswick, 1872–1939' (PhD thesis, University of Rochester, 1979), 61–2
59 AR (NB), 1906, xlviii
60 Editorial comment, *Educational Review*, Feb. 1907, 220
61 AR (NB), 1911, 68
62 Editorial comment, *Educational Review*, Nov. 1915, 119
63 Ibid., Aug. 1906, 39
64 'Address of Dr W.S. Carter to the New Brunswick Teachers' Institute,' *Educational Review*, Sept. 1930, 22
65 AR (NB), 1900, liv
66 Ibid., 1910, xi
67 Ibid., 1908, 155. Stella Crocker later married Fletcher Peacock, a school administrator from Saint John, who in 1936 was appointed director of educational services for the province.
68 Ibid., 134
69 Ibid., 1906, 12
70 Ibid., 1911, 154
71 *Manual of the School Law of New Brunswick*, 1913, 199
72 James Michael Reardon, *George Anthony Belcourt* (St Paul, Minn.: North Central Publishing Co. 1955), 175–6
73 Charlottetown *Examiner*, quoted in Jean Doiron, 'Rustico: Father George-Antoine Belcourt – The Farmers' Bank' (Manuscript), PEI Heritage Foundation
74 AR (PEI), 1891
75 Charlottetown *Daily Patriot*, 29 July 1904, 5
76 Ibid.
77 Halifax *Critic*, 27 July 1888
78 Flora Smith Rogers, *Glimpses of Glory and Grace* (Charlottetown: Trinity United Church Women 1964), 30
79 AR (PEI), 1907, xxx
80 Ibid., 1916, 5

CHAPTER 3 Ontario

1 C.E. Phillips, *The Development of Education in Canada* (Toronto: Gage 1957), 98
2 Ibid., 101
3 Helmut Kallmann, *A History of Music in Canada, 1534–1914* (Toronto: University of Toronto Press 1960), 31

4 Ibid., 38

5 Originally known as Hope, until the 1860s

6 Cited by Helmut Kallmann in *A History*, 76

7 Emily McArthur, *Children of Peace* (Toronto: York Pioneer and Historical Society n.d.), 3

8 Dorothy H. Farquharson, *O for a Thousand Tongues to Sing: A History of Singing Schools in Early Canada* (Waterdown, Ont. 1983), 15

9 Ibid.

10 Hamilton *Free Press*, 29 Dec. 1831

11 Alastair P. Haig, 'Henry Frost, Pioneer (1816–1851),' *Canadian Music Journal* 2, no. 2 (Winter 1958), 35

12 G. Campbell Trowsdale, 'A History of Public School Music in Ontario' (EdD thesis, University of Toronto, 1962), 61

13 Haig, 'Henry Frost, Pioneer,' 35

14 For a discussion of these theories see Bernarr Rainbow, *The Land without Music* (London: Novello 1967).

15 Ibid., 117

16 Trowsdale, 'A History of Public School Music in Ontario,' 72

17 J. George Hodgins, ed., *Documentary History of Education in Upper Canada, 1791–1896* (Toronto: King's Printer 1910), vii, 148

18 Trowsdale, 'A History of Public School Music in Ontario,' 147

19 Ibid., 92–3

20 G. Campbell Trowsdale, 'Vocal Music in the Common Schools of Upper Canada: 1846–76,' *Journal of Research in Music Education* 18, no. 4 (Winter 1970), 345n

21 June Countryman, 'An Analysis of Selected Song Series Textbooks Used in Ontario Schools, 1846–1965' (MM thesis, University of Western Ontario, 1981), 20–1. For further information of Sefton's publication *Three-Part Songs*, see chap. 2, n51.

22 Henry Sefton to Egerton Ryerson, 27 Feb. 1875, Provincial Archives (Ont.)

23 Hodgins, *Documentary History*, xxiii, 220

24 Countryman, 'An Analysis of Selected Song Series,' 21

25 AR (Ont.), 1872, 37 (apps)

26 Ibid., 37

27 Trowsdale, 'A History of Public School Music,' 141

28 H.R. Cummings and W.T. MacSkimming, *The City of Ottawa Public Schools* (Ottawa: Ottawa Board of Education 1971), 24

29 Ottawa *Evening Journal*, 27 May 1887. For further information on early musical activities in Ottawa, see the Bibliography, s.v. 'Cronk.'

30 *Report of the Past History and Present Condition of Common or Public Schools*

of the City of Toronto (Toronto: Lovell and Gibson 1859), 61

31 Annual Report of the Toronto Board of Education, 1871, 47

32 Ibid., 1873, 35

33 Robert Stamp, *The Schools of Ontario, 1876–1976* (Toronto: University of Toronto Press 1981), 20

34 Annual Report of the Toronto Board of Education, 1874, 23–4

35 Ibid.

36 Trowsdale, 'A History of Public School Music in Ontario,' 139–40

37 Hodgins to Ryerson, 1856, United Church Archives, Emmanuel College, Victoria University, Toronto. Hodgins's reference to 'few students wishing to learn singing' was undoubtedly made with respect to the provincial normal school.

38 Hodgins, *Documentary History*, xix, 287

39 Trowsdale, 'A History of Public School Music in Ontario,' 148

40 AR (Ont.), 1883, 151

41 John Tufts and Hosea Holt, *The Normal Music Course* (Boston: Silver Burdett 1883)

42 Countryman, 'An Analysis of Selected Song Series,' 27

43 Diana Brault, 'A History of the Ontario Music Educators' Association (1919–1974)' (PhD thesis, University of Rochester, 1977), 14

44 Trowsdale, 'A History of Public School Music in Ontario,' 269

45 Toronto *Globe*, 30 Oct. 1875, 3. McTaggart was a master at Hellmuth College in London, Ontario.

46 'Practical Sol Fa' (Speech prepared for a meeting of the Lincoln Teachers' Association, St Catharines, Ont., scheduled on 22 May 1889), James Johnson file, Hamilton Public Library

47 Countryman, 'An Analysis of Selected Song Series,' 32

48 Trowsdale, 'A History of Public School Music in Ontario,' 303

49 The 1888 summer school took place at Niagara-on-the-Lake.

50 Trowsdale, 'A History of Public School Music in Ontario,' 157

51 Stamp, *The Schools of Ontario*, 15

52 Trowsdale, 'A History of Public School Music in Ontario,' 166

53 AR (Ont.), 1879, 75

54 W.D.E. Matthews, '100 Years of Public Education in London,' (Paper housed in the University of Western Ontario Library, Althouse College n.d.), 13

55 Ibid.

56 It is interesting to note that the principal of Gladstone Public School, one of the schools visited, was Alexander Muir, author and composer of 'The Maple Leaf For Ever.'

57 Cummings and MacSkimming, *The City of Ottawa Public Schools*, 53
58 Trowsdale: 'The History of Music Education as a Field of Study: A Consideration of Status, Research, and Needs,' CAUSM *Journal* 3, no. 2 (Spring 1974), 102
59 A.T. Cringan, *The Canadian Music Course* (1888), *The Educational Music Course* (1898), *The Teacher's Handbook of the Tonic Sol-fa System* (1889) (Toronto: Canada Publishing)
60 Cringan started to record native music in 1897, just seven years after the American ethnomusicologist Jesse Walter Fewkes pioneered in this field.
61 Donaldson Uhryniw, 'Cringan and Tonic Sol-Fa: Morality through Music' (MA research essay, Carleton University, 1981), 81
62 Ibid., 82
63 Ibid.
64 Trowsdale, 'A History of Public School Music in Ontario,' 415
65 Ibid., 415–16
66 Stamp, *The Schools of Ontario*, 8
67 A. Campbell Black to John Miller, Deputy Minister of Education, 1878, Provincial Archives (Ont.)
68 AR (Ont.), 1880–1, 24
69 The TCM was renamed the Royal Conservatory of Music (RCMT) in 1947.
70 EMC, s.v. 'Royal Conservatory of Music of Toronto'
71 Brault, 'A History of the Ontario Music Educators' Association,' 46–7
72 For a detailed account of these examination wars, see Gaynor G. Jones, 'The Fisher Years: the Toronto Conservatory of Music, 1886–1913,' in *Three Studies* (Toronto: Institute for Canadian Music 1989), 59–145.
73 Earl Davey, 'The Development of Undergraduate Music Curricula at the University of Toronto, 1918–68,' (MA thesis, University of Toronto, 1977), 134 (app.)
74 Ibid., 135
75 EMC, s.v. 'George Strathy'
76 Cited by Rebecca Green, 'Gaudeamus igitur: College Singing and Songbooks in Canada,' *Three Studies* (Toronto: Institute for Canadian Music 1989), 29–30
77 Ibid., 34

CHAPTER 4 The West

1 Anne M. Loutit, ed., *Tomorrow's Past: A Century of Manitoba's Teachers* (Canadian College of Teachers, Manitoba Chapter [1971]), 12
2 Ibid., 12

3 Ibid., 13
4 Ibid., 16
5 R.G. MacBeth, *The Selkirk Settlers in Real Life* (Toronto: Wm. Briggs 1897), 81
6 Cited by Dorothy H. Farquharson, *O for a Thousand Tongues to Sing: A History of Singing Schools in Early Canada* (Waterdown, Ont. 1983), 71
7 Manoly R. Lapul, 'Education in Canada before 1873,' in *Canadian Education: A History*, ed. J. Donald Wilson, et al. (Scarborough: Prentice-Hall 1970), 249
8 Ibid., 249
9 Keith Wilson, 'Development of Education in Manitoba' (PhD thesis, University of Michigan, 1967), 29
10 W.L. Morton, *Manitoba: A History* (Toronto: University of Toronto Press 1957), 174
11 EMC, s.v. 'Iceland'
12 Wilhelm Kristjanson, *The Icelandic People in Manitoba* (Winnipeg: Wallingford Press 1965), 439
13 Ibid., 435
14 Ibid., 438
15 Wesley Peter Berg, 'Choral Festivals and Choral Workshops among the Mennonites of Manitoba and Saskatchewan, 1900–1960, with an Account of Early Developments in Russia' (PhD thesis, University of Washington, 1979), 52
16 Ibid.
17 Ibid., 57
18 Ibid., 59
19 Ibid., 69
20 Paul Yuzyk, *The Ukrainians in Manitoba* (Toronto: University of Toronto Press 1953), 166
21 Lillian Scarth, 'The Development of Music in the West,' *Western Home Monthly* 23, no. 10 (Oct. 1921), 23
22 Alison McNeill-Hordern, 'The Development of the Music Program at Brandon College during the Period 1906 to 1939' (MM thesis, Brandon University, 1987), 13
23 William G. Black, 'Development and Present Status of Teacher Education in Western Canada' (PhD thesis, University of Chicago, 1936), 22
24 W.A. McIntyre, 'Sixty Years of Education in Manitoba' *Western School Journal* 25 (1930), 138
25 Winnipeg *Free Press*, Jubilee edition, 8 Nov. 1923, 9
26 'School Management Report,' Winnipeg Board of Education, 1898, 20

27 Ibid.
28 Laurence Minchin, 'Music,' *Educational Journal of Western Canada* 1, no. 7 (1899), 202
29 W.A. McIntyre, 'Reading and Writing Music,' *Educational Journal of Western Canada* 4, no. 1 (1902), 7
30 W.A. McIntyre, 'The Spirit of Music,' *Western Home Monthly* 23, no. 10 (Oct. 1921), 17
31 Ibid., 17
32 J.W. Chafe, *An Apple for the Teacher* (Winnipeg: Winnipeg School Division No. 1, 1967), 121
33 Sharon Dueck, 'Ethel Kinley (1887–1967) Her Life and Contribution to Music Education in Manitoba' (MM thesis, University of Western Ontario, 1983), 39
34 Lillian Brostedt, 'Music in the High School,' *Western School Journal* 7, no. 5 (1912), 178
35 Ibid., 1
36 Carl Bjarnason, 'The Brandon School System: A Historical Survey and Ten-Year Development Program' (MEd thesis, University of Manitoba, 1962), 41–2
37 Ibid., 43
38 Ibid.
39 'Timetable for a Primary Room,' *Educational Journal of Western Canada* 4, no. 6 (1902), 179
40 McIntyre, 'The Spirit of Music,' 17
41 AR (Man.), 1902, 65
42 Wilson, 'Development of Education in Manitoba,' 327
43 Robert Dale McIntosh, *A Documentary History of Music in Victoria*, vol. 1, *1850–1899* (Victoria, BC 1981), 45
44 Ibid., 100
45 Ibid., 15–117
46 Ibid., 157
47 Ibid., 25
48 Ibid., 71
49 C. Herbert Kent, 'Music Chronicles of Early Times,' (Manuscript) Provincial Archives (BC).
50 Cited by McIntosh, *A Documentary History of Music in Victoria*, 25
51 Ibid., 46
52 Ibid.
53 Ibid., 1
54 Dale McIntosh, *History of Music in British Columbia, 1850–1950* (Victoria: Sono Nis Press 1989), 25

55 Ibid., 44
56 Isabella Geddes Large, 'Music among the Coast Indians of Northern British Columbia,' *Conservatory Monthly* 2, no. 7 (July 1912), 211
57 Ibid., 213
58 Ibid., 211
59 Ibid., 213–14
60 Mary Margaret Down, *A Century of Service, 1858–1958: A History of the Sisters of Saint Ann and Their Contribution to Education in British Columbia, the Yukon and Alaska* (Victoria: Sisters of Saint Ann 1966), 96
61 Ibid., 119
62 F. Henry Johnson, *John Jessop: Goldseeker and Educator*, (Vancouver: Mitchell Press 1971), 8
63 Johnson, 'The Ryersonian Influence on the Public School System of British Columbia, BC *Studies*, no. 10 (Summer 1971), 27
64 AR (BC), 1873, 9
65 Ibid., 10
66 McIntosh, *A Documentary History of Music in Victoria*, 69
67 AR (BC), 1877, 22
68 Ibid., 1892, 158
69 Ibid., 1895, 218
70 McIntosh, *A Documentary History of Music in Victoria*, 178
71 Victoria *Colonist*, 10 Oct. 1912, 7
72 AR (BC), 1904–5, A57
73 George P. Hicks, 'Music,' 10th Annual Report to Board of School Trustees, Vancouver, 1912, 42
74 Hicks, 'Report of the Music Department,' 7th Annual Report, 1909, 31
75 Hicks, 'Music,' 14th Annual Report, 1916, 44
76 Hicks, 'Manual and Syllabus of Instruction in Vocal Music' (Vancouver Public Schools 1913), preface
77 James M. McLaughlin, *The New Educational Music Course* (Boston: Ginn 1904)
78 Hicks, 'Manual and Syllabus of Instruction in Vocal Music'
79 Hicks, 'Music,' 9th Annual Report to Board of School Trustees, Vancouver, 1911, 39
80 Hicks, 'Music,' 13th Annual Report, 1915, 46
81 George Henry Green, 'The Development of the Curriculum in the Elementary Schools of British Columbia prior to 1936' (MA thesis, University of British Columbia, 1938), 121
82 AR (BC), 1889 (Appendix F, xcvii)
83 Peter Lawson Smith, *Come Give a Cheer* (Victoria: Victoria Centennial Celebrations Committee 1976), 19

84 J.H. Wormsbecker, 'The Development of Secondary Education in Vancouver' (EdD thesis, University of Toronto, 1961), 106

85 George Sheane, 'History and Development of the Curriculum of the Elementary School in Alberta' (DPaed thesis, University of Toronto, 1948), 7

86 Ibid., 4

87 Ibid., 5

88 Union schools gave instruction to elementary and secondary students and also functioned as teacher training institutions. It was required that the principal be a university graduate; furthermore, the principal had to be qualified by knowledge and ability in approved methods of teaching.

89 *Annual Report of the Council of Public Instruction of the North-West Territories, 1896*, 28

90 D.G. Scott Calder, 'An Outline History of the Department of Education, Province of Saskatchewan, 1880–1951' (Mimeographed paper housed in University of Saskatchewan Library), 9

91 Ibid., 2–9

92 EMC, s.v. 'Regina'

93 Helmut Kallmann, *A History of Music in Canada, 1534–1914* (Toronto: University of Toronto Press 1960), 169

94 Regina Conservatory of Music, *Annual Calendar, 1907–1908*, University of Regina Archives

95 Regina *Morning Leader*, 27 April, 1907

96 AR (Sask.), 1912, 64

97 Ibid., 1906, 45

98 Cited by Johanna Weweler, 'Rj Staples: Innovative Saskatchewan Music Educator' (MEd thesis, University of Saskatchewan, 1973), 117

99 *The Common School Book of Vocal Music* (Toronto: W.J. Gage and Co. 1913); *Dunstan's ABC of Musical Theory* (London: Curwen and Sons 1910); *The New Normal Music Course* (Toronto: Educational Book Co. 1913)

100 *Collegiate Hermes* (Nutana Collegiate, Saskatoon), June 1917, 11

101 Murray to Chisholm, 16 Sept. 1909, President Murray's Papers, University of Saskatchewan Archives

102 Wilson to Murray, 11 May 1914, ibid.

103 Cited by Lloyd Rodwell, 'The Saskatchewan Association of Music Festivals,' *Saskatchewan History* 16, no. 1 (Winter 1963), 4

104 Ibid., 5

105 Ibid., 17

106 William Henry Waite, 'The History of Elementary and Secondary

Education in Saskatchewan' (MA thesis, University of Manitoba, 1936), 154–60

107 Calgary *Herald*, 2 April 1932

108 Until 1938 there were no official RCMP bands as integral units of the force.

109 EMC, s.v. 'Edmonton Symphony Orchestra'

110 Rodwell, 'The Saskatchewan Association of Music Festivals,' 2

111 Sister L.A. Hochstein, 'Roman Catholic Separate and Public Schools in Alberta' (MEd thesis, University of Alberta, 1954), 22

112 Norman Eagleson, 'First Grade Music Methods,' *School* 7 (1918–19), 603

113 Ibid.

114 Ibid., 604

115 Ibid., 606

116 Ibid., 605

117 Ibid., 608

118 Ibid.

119 Audrey Baines Swedish, *From Cottage to Composite: A History of the Lethbridge Schools, 1886–1986* (Lethbridge, Alta.: School District No. 51, 1986), 198

120 AR (Alta.), 1909, 53

121 Swedish, *From Cottage to Composite*, 198

122 AR (Alta.), 1912, 139–40

123 Ibid., 1906, 52

124 George Sheane, 'History and Development of the Curriculum of the Elementary School in Alberta' (DPaed thesis, University of Toronto, 1948), 30

125 Ibid.

126 AR (Alta.), 1907, 56

127 Norman Eagleson, 'The Outlook for Music in Alberta Schools,' *School* 7 (1918–19), 251

128 Olive Fisher, 'The School Festival and Its Contribution to the Cultural Life of Alberta' (MA thesis, Stanford University, 1942), 51

129 Ibid.

130 Letter by Inspector Owen Williams, Cardston, Alberta, cited ibid., 52–3

131 Mary Margaret Buckley, 'Music Education in Alberta, 1884–1945: History and Development' (MM thesis, University of Calgary, 1987), 63

132 Ibid.

133 Ibid., 47

134 AR (Alta.), 1907, 38
135 L.H. Alexander was an instructor of modern languages.
136 Walter H. Johns, *A History of the University of Alberta* (Edmonton: University of Alberta 1981), 46
137 Vernon Barford, 'Music in Alberta,' in *Alberta Golden Jubilee Anthology*, ed. W.G. Hardy (1955), 2

CHAPTER 5 The Role of National Institutions

1 *EMC*, s.v. 'Broadcasting'
2 Ibid.
3 *EMC*, s.v. 'Hart House String Quartet'
4 Hector Charlesworth, 'Hart House Quartet Grows in Beauty,' *Saturday Night*, 29 Oct. 1927, 6–7
5 Augustus Bridle, 'Hart House High Priests of Art,' 1928, unidentified newspaper clipping, Hart House String Quartet Scrapbook, University of Toronto Archives
6 Lawrence Mason, 'A Notable Decennial,' Toronto *Globe*, 10 June 1933, 5
7 Regina *Leader*, 8 Dec. 1927
8 Ernest MacMillan, 'Music Education in Canada,' *Journal of Proceedings of the Music Supervisors' National Conference*, 1932, 81
9 Ibid., 82
10 Toronto *Star Weekly*, 4 Nov. 1922
11 Augustus Bridle, 'Hutcheson Starts Symphony Season,' Toronto *Daily Star*, 27 Oct. 1937
12 Ernest Hutcheson, *Report on a Short Survey of the Toronto Conservatory of Music* (unpublished, 1937), 5. A copy of this report is located in the music library at the University of Western Ontario.
13 Ibid., 5–6
14 Ibid., 8
15 Gordon Moyles, *The Blood and Fire in Canada* (Toronto: Peter Martin Associates 1977), 41
16 Ibid.
17 A network of approximately twelve divisional music camps has continued on a permanent basis since the early 1950s, and a National School of Music – a one-week summer camp – has been operating since the 1970s.
18 J.S. Atkinson, 'Class Instruction in Piano in Schools,' *School* 16 (1927–8), 859
19 Ibid., 860

CHAPTER 6 Progress on the Prairies

1 Mary D. Mitchner, 'Saskatoon Women's Musical Club,' *Musical Life* (Regina), Jan. 1933, 10
2 *EMC*, s.v. 'Fred M. Gee'
3 Lorraine Blashill, 'Old Time Prairie Music,' *Folklore Magazine* (Folklore Society, Moose Jaw, Sask.), Winter 1981–2, 160
4 Wesley Peter Berg, 'Choral Festivals and Choral Workshops among the Mennonites of Manitoba and Saskatchewan, 1900–1960, with an Account of Early Developments in Russia' (PhD thesis, University of Washington, 1979), 88
5 Ibid., 113
6 Ibid., 104
7 Cited ibid., 111–12
8 Ibid., 115
9 Ibid., 125
10 *EMC*, s.v. 'player pianos and nickelodeons'
11 President Murray's papers, University of Saskatchewan Archives
12 Eva Clare, *Musical Appreciation and the Studio Club* (New York: Longmans and Green 1924)
13 The Manitoba Registered Music Teachers' Association was founded in 1919 as the Winnipeg Music Teachers' Association.
14 *EMC*, s.v. 'Bornoff School of Music and Associated Arts'
15 Cyril Hampshire, 'Regina College Conservatory of Music,' *Musical Life* (Regina) Jan. 1933, 12
16 Regina *Leader*, 28 May 1928
17 Ibid.
18 Ibid.
19 Regina *Leader-Post*, 20 Nov. 1930
20 AR (Sask.), 1929, 100
21 Ibid., 1939, 38
22 Ibid.
23 Ibid.
24 Ibid., 1932, 44
25 Ibid., 45
26 Ibid., 1935, 40
27 Annual Report of the Calgary Board of Education, 1927, 5
28 Norman Eagleson, *777 Graded Exercises in Sight Singing* (Edmonton: Institute of Applied Art 1934–9), bks 1–4 plus *A Manual for Teachers*. According to the foreword, these books were designed to complement

The Progressive Music Series, The New Educational Music Course, and *Music Education Series.*

29 Ethel Kinley, *The Manitoba School Song Book* (Toronto: Clarke Irwin 1940). It was also published under separate titles such as *A Song Book for Ontario Schools.*

30 Kinley, *A Song Book for Saskatchewan Schools* (Toronto: Clarke Irwin 1940)

31 Kinley, 'The Place of Music in the Curriculum,' *Manitoba Teacher* 5 (June 1924), 12

32 Ibid.

33 Ibid.

34 AR (Sask.), 1933, 41

35 Earl G. Drake, *Regina: The Queen City* (Toronto: McClelland and Stewart 1955), 207

36 Norman Eagleson, 'Alberta School Music Steps Out,' *Canadian Music Teacher,* Nov. 1937, 10

37 Ibid.

38 Ibid.

39 According to Sharon Dueck, Ethel Kinley and Ivan Schultz were contemporaries as young teachers in rural Manitoba. See 'Ethel Kinley (1887–1967): Her Life and Contribution to Music Education in Manitoba' (MM thesis, University of Western Ontario, 1983), 13

40 Leonard Takoski, 'A History of the Manitoba Schools' Orchestra, 1925–1964' (MEd thesis, University of Manitoba, 1964), 6

41 Ibid., 7

42 Ibid.

43 Winnipeg *Tribune,* 21 April 1938, 13

44 Materials in the Edmonton Public Schools' Archives

45 M.A. Kostek, *Looking Back: A Century of Education in Edmonton Public Schools* (Edmonton: Edmonton Public School Board 1982), 256

46 Mary Margaret Buckley, 'Music Education in Alberta, 1884–1945: History and Development' (MM thesis, University of Calgary, 1987), 125

47 Cited by Johanna Weweler, 'Rj Staples: Innovative Saskatchewan Music Educator' (MEd thesis, University of Saskatchewan, 1973), 252

48 Cited by E.A. Corbett, *We Have with Us Today* (Toronto: Ryerson 1957), 52

49 Ibid., 60

50 Ibid.

51 Ibid., 102

52 David Leighton, *Artists, Builders and Dreamers* (Toronto: McClelland and Stewart 1982), 59

53 President Murray's Papers, University of Saskatchewan Archives
54 Ibid.
55 Dueck, 'Ethel Kinley,' 89
56 Ibid., 91
57 Marjorie Horner, 'The Summer Music Camp at Lake Singoosh,' *Manitoba School Journal* 4, no. 2 (Oct. 1941), 9
58 Dueck, 'Ethel Kinley,' 96
59 Ibid., 95

CHAPTER 7 A Swing of the Pendulum in British Columbia

1 Vancouver *Province*, 7 July 1936, 20
2 Dale McIntosh, *History of Music in British Columbia, 1850–1950* (Victoria: Sono Nis Press 1989), 190
3 Representatives from Canadian Music Festivals in the western provinces held annual meetings commencing in 1926. Gradually, other provinces joined this informal group, which was originally convened by George Mathieson of Winnipeg. The federation was not formally constituted until 1949.
4 George S. Mathieson, *Crescendo: A History of the Men's Musical Club* (Winnipeg 1935), 59–61. The author of this work also wrote under the *nom de plume* G Sharp Major.
5 J.H. Putman was inspector of public schools in Ottawa. G.M. Weir was an educator in British Columbia; he was on the faculty of UBC and later became minister of education.
6 J.W. Gibson, 'Historical Resume of Teacher Training in British Columbia,' AR (BC), 1927–8, Report of the Supervisor of Normal Schools, V 42
7 Ibid., V 44
8 Ethel Coney and F.T.C. Wickett, *The New Canadian Music Course*, bks 1–5 (Toronto: Gage 1925–7)
9 Ibid.
10 AR (BC), 1928–9, R 54
11 Ibid., 1929–30, Q 23
12 Ibid.
13 Ibid.
14 Ibid., 1933–4, N 34
15 Ibid., N 38
16 Mildred McManus was on staff at Kitsilano High School and later was appointed to the Vancouver Normal School; Ifor Roberts was assistant

supervisor of music, Vancouver School Board, and served as supervisor from 1955 to 1961. Sherwood Robson taught in several Vancouver schools from 1935 to 1961.

17 McIntosh, *History of Music in British Columbia*, 172
18 Victoria *Colonist*, 12 March 1936, 7
19 Stanley Bulley to J. Paul Green, March 1984, personal correspondence
20 Bulley thought that he had ended his work with the Victoria School Board circa 1942, but the Victoria School Board office could not confirm the date.
21 McIntosh, *History of Music in British Columbia*, 167
22 Victoria *Colonist*, 5 May 1938, 2
23 Ibid.
24 Ibid.
25 Peter Lawson Smith, *Come Give a Cheer* (Victoria: Victoria High School Centennial Celebrations Committee 1976), 78–80
26 Richard S. Lambert, *School Broadcasting in Canada* (Toronto: University of Toronto Press 1963), 35
27 Marjorie Agnew was a junior high school teacher, guidance counsellor, and principal in Vancouver schools.
28 'MacMillan Club Quiz,' *Radio World*, Feb. 1945, MacMillan Clubs Scrapbook no. 6, MacMillan Collection, Music Division, National Library of Canada.
29 *EMC*, s.v. 'Sir Ernest MacMillan Fine Arts Club'
30 AR (BC), 1923–4, T 63
31 J.S. Gordon (Superintendent of Schools), 28th Annual Report to Vancouver Board of Education, 1930, 34
32 E.H. Russell was also well known in the community as the conductor of the Arion Club Choir.
33 McIntosh, 'A Short History of Music Education in British Columbia, 1850–1950,' *B.C. Music Educator* 29, no. 2 (Spring 1986), 13

CHAPTER 8 A Period of Transition in the Maritimes

1 Toronto *Star*, 2 May 1931
2 Toronto *Globe and Mail*, 10 Sept. 1934
3 Editorial, *Musical Canada*, Dec. 1931, 3
4 In 1954 these two music schools amalgamated to form the Maritime Conservatory of Music.
5 *Argosy Weekly*, 20 May 1924
6 Richard S. Lambert, *School Broadcasting in Canada* (Toronto: University of Toronto Press 1963), 19

7 Ibid., 21
8 Ibid., 23
9 Ibid., 30
10 Ibid., 22
11 AR (NS), 1922, 57
12 'The Teaching of Music in the Public Schools,' *Journal of Education* (NS), Oct. 1923, 279
13 AR (NS), 1930, 921
14 Thomas Joseph Elward, 'A History of Music Education in the District of Columbia Public Schools from 1845 to 1945' (DMA thesis, Catholic University of America, 1975), 220
15 'Excellent Radio Concert by 600 School Children,' Moncton *Daily Times*, 8 May 1926, 8
16 AR (PEI), 1923, ix
17 Ibid., 1924, 28c
18 Ibid., 1929, 9
19 Ibid., 1942, 21
20 Ibid., 1939, 16
21 *The Report of the Survey of the Public Schools of Charlottetown, Prince Edward Island*, John C. Matthews, chairman, 1952, 192
22 AR (NB), 1922, 77
23 AR (NS), 1929, 81
24 Ibid., 1930, 74–5
25 Ibid.
26 Ibid., 1931, 76
27 'New Senior High School Subjects,' *Journal of Education* (NS), Jan. 1936, 114–15
28 'Senior High School Programme,' *Journal of Education* (NS), April 1939, 426
29 Editorial, *Educational Review*, Oct. 1936, 2
30 Minutes of the Moncton School Board, 25 May 1938
31 Ibid., 26 Oct. 1938
32 AR (NS), 1922, 57
33 'Music in the Schools,' *Journal of Education* (NS), Oct. 1925, 305
34 AR (NB), 1930, 97
35 AR (NS), 1934, 55
36 Dora Baker, 'Music and Folk-Dance Rallies,' *Journal of Education* (NS), Sept. 1933, 88
37 Ibid.
38 AR (NS), 1934, 50
39 'School Music Contest (Provincial Exhibition),' *Journal of Education* (NS), 1938, 333

40 Ibid.
41 AR (NS), 1921, 110
42 Ibid.
43 'Helpful Notes on the Preparation for the M.P.Q. Music Examination,' *Journal of Education* (NS), April 1924, 90
44 Ibid.
45 'Music,' *Journal of Education* (NS), May 1933, 245
46 AR (NS), 1931, 76
47 Ibid., 1932, 73
48 Ibid.
49 Ibid., 1941, 120
50 AR (NB), 1928, 5
51 Ibid., 1931, 511
52 AR (PEI), 1930, xxii
53 AR (NS), 1930, 75
54 Fletcher Peacock, 'Report of the Director of Educational Services,' AR (NB), 1937, 6
55 Ibid.

CHAPTER 9 Denominations and Dichotomies in Quebec

1 The musical life of Montreal for 1931 and 1932 is chronicled in a publication entitled *Montreal Music Year Book*, which seems to have lasted for only two years.
2 EMC, s.v. 'École Vincent-d'Indy'
3 'Music Week Plans,' Montreal *Daily Star*, 4 Nov. 1922
4 Elizabeth Griswold Waycott, 'Origin of Music Week in Montreal,' in ·*Montreal Music Year Book* (Montreal 1931), 49
5 'Good Intentions,' Montreal *Daily Star*, 22 March 1924
6 'Music Week Reactions' [Letter to the editor by B.E. Chadwick], Montreal *Daily Star*, 21 Mar. 1923
7 EMC, s.v. 'Wilfrid Pelletier'
8 G.A. Stanton, 'Music in the Protestant Schools,' in *Montreal Music Year Book* (1931), 9
9 Ibid.
10 Thomas Archer, 'The Season of Music 1930–1931,' in *Montreal Music Year Book* (1931), 70
11 G.A. Stanton, 'The Basis of Music Teaching,' *Teachers' Magazine*, Dec. 1932, 28
12 'Notes and News – Quebec,' *School*, May 1933, 809–10

13 'School Music Broadcasts,' *Educational Record*, Fall 1933, 211
14 'Music and Education,' *Teachers' Magazine*, Oct. 1924, 12
15 Stanton, 'Music in the Protestant Schools,' 9
16 Frederick Whiteley, 'Music in Westmount Schools,' in *Montreal Music Year Book* (1931), 10
17 Ibid.
18 Stanton, 'Music in the Protestant Schools,' 9
19 Irvin Cooper, 'School Music in Quebec,' *School*, Dec. 1941, 288
20 Anne MacDougall, *Anne Savage: The Story of a Canadian Painter* (Montreal: Harvest House 1977), 58
21 'Music in Baron Byng High School, Montreal,' *Musical Canada*, Dec. 1928, 6
22 D.M. Herbert, 'Organization and Methods Course and Materials for Vocal Music in High Schools,' *Proceedings of the Ontario Educational Association* (Toronto 1929), 197
23 Ibid., 198–9
24 Ibid., 200
25 Ibid., 202
26 Cooper, 'School Music in Quebec,' 288
27 Ibid., 289
28 Ibid., 292
29 AR (Que.), 1945–6, 216
30 Ibid., 1940–1, xxxi
31 Cooper, 'School Music in Quebec,' 290
32 Ibid.
33 AR (Que.), 1918–19, 213
34 Ibid., 1922–3, xv
35 Ibid., 165
36 Ibid., 1927–8, 410
37 Ibid., 6
38 Gilles Pilote, 'L'Enseignement de la musique au Québec: Claude Champagne et la Commission des Écoles Catholiques de Montréal' (Doctoral thesis, Strasbourg, 1973), 48
39 Ibid., 50
40 AR (Que.), 1938–9, 130
41 Cooper, 'School Music in Quebec,' 288
42 AR (Que.), 1919, 239
43 Ibid., 1932, 234
44 'Changes in Requirements for Music Certificates for Teachers,' *Educational Record*, Winter 1933, 36

45 Ibid.
46 'Teachers' Department,' [Letter from Sir Henry Coward], *Musical Times*, 1 April 1931, 334
47 Cooper, 'School Music in Quebec,' 291
48 'Notes and News – Quebec,' *School*, May 1932, 834
49 Beth Newell, 'Quebec Music Educators' Association,' *Sentinel*, Jan. 1971, 11
50 AR (Que.), 1921, 417–29
51 Ibid., 1930, 194
52 Ibid., 1931, 188
53 Ibid., 1932, 216
54 Ibid., 1937, 46–7
55 Ibid., 1938, 130
56 Ibid., 1942, 168
57 Ibid., 1939, 274
58 'A Choral Competition,' Montreal *Daily Star*, 3 June 1922
59 'Competition Results,' Montreal *Daily Star*, 28 April 1923
60 Program booklet of the 1928 Canadian Folk Song and Handicraft Festival, Hart House String Quartet scrapbook, University of Toronto Archives
61 Cooper, 'School Music in Quebec,' 292
62 Ibid.

CHAPTER 10 Politics and Public Relations in Ontario

1 EMC, s.v. 'Luigi von Kunits'
2 Dorith Cooper, 'Opera in Montreal and Toronto: A Study of Performance Traditions and Repertoire, 1783–1980' (PhD thesis, University of Toronto, 1983), 860
3 The countess, who was born as Laura Blackwell in St Catharines, Ontario, had enjoyed an opera career in Europe.
4 In 1969 the Opera School became a division within the Faculty of Music, University of Toronto.
5 EMC, s.v. 'Canadian National Exhibition Chorus'
6 Margaret Ross Chandler, *A Century of Challenge* (Belleville: Mika Publishing Co. 1980), 131
7 Diana Brault, 'A History of the Ontario Music Educators' Association (1919–1974)' (PhD thesis, University of Rochester, 1977), 50–1
8 Ibid., 51
9 OEA, *Proceedings*, 1919, 105
10 James Bottomley, 'Grade School Music Teaching,' *School* 19 (1920–1), 123–5

11 June Countryman, 'An Analysis of Selected Song Series Textbooks Used in Ontario Schools, 1846–1965' (MM thesis, University of Western Ontario, 1981), 60

12 The 'School Music Bulletin' was a department (or section) of *Musical Canada*.

13 Harry Hill, 'School Music Bulletin,' *Musical Canada* 11, no. 4 (May 1930), 4

14 Ibid., no. 10 (Nov. 1930), 4

15 Minutes of the 1931 Sessions of the Music Section of the OEA, July–Aug. 1931, 9

16 G. Campbell Trowsdale, 'A History of Public School Music in Ontario' (EdD thesis, University of Toronto, 1962), 312

17 Hill was by reputation an outstanding teacher and music supervisor; Richer was renowned for his pioneer work in instrumental music; Putland was a school supervisor with British training as a church musician; Dunning was an instructor at the Ottawa Normal School.

18 June Countryman, 'An Analysis of Selected Song Series,' 102. (The first American edition of *The Progressive Music Series* appeared in 1914, but W.J. Gage and Company published student books for Canadian schools in 1921.)

19 Ibid., 127

20 Ibid., 109

21 Ibid., 113

22 Ibid., 143

23 Brault, 'A History of the Ontario Music Educators' Association,' 147–8

24 Toronto *Globe*, 9 Aug. 1930

25 Harry Plunkett Greene, 'A Trip to the Canadian Festivals,' *Music and Letters* 4, (Oct. 1923), 359

26 Granville Bantock, 'The Festival Movement in Canada,' *Musical Canada* 4, no. 7 and 8 (July–Aug. 1923), 4

27 G. Roy Fenwick, 'A Message to the Also-Rans,' *Canadian Music Educator* 3, no. 4, 62

28 C.B. Routley, 'A Musical Festival,' *School* 25 (Nov. 1936), 196

29 Trudy Bradley, 'G. Roy Fenwick (1889–1970): His Contribution to Music Education in Ontario' (MM thesis, University of Western Ontario, 1981), 84

30 Mae Skilling, 'Music in Education,' *School* 12 (1923–4), 654

31 Ibid., 653–4

32 James Bottomley, 'The Use of the Phonograph in School,' *School* 6 (1917–18), 374

33 A.T. Cringan, 'Music in Public Schools,' *School* 10 (1921–2), 457
34 Ernest MacMillan, 'Suggestions for a Course of Music Study for High Schools,' *OEA Book of Proceedings for 1928*, 191
35 Leslie Bell, 'The Failure of Music Appreciation,' *Canadian Music Journal* 2, no. 3 (Spring 1958), 20–7
36 Bell, 'What is Music Appreciation?' *School* 30, no. 1 (Sept. 1941), 22
37 Cited by Richard S. Warren, 'From the Archives,' *Toronto Symphony* 38, no. 4 (March–April 1983), 16
38 Ibid.
39 J.L. Yule, 'School Music Department,' *Musical Canada* 10, no. 4 (April 1929), 6
40 Richard S. Warren, 'From the Archives,' 16
41 By 1930 Emily Tedd had become supervisor of music for the Toronto schools.
42 'Report of the Music Department, 1930,' *Minutes of the Proceedings of the Board of Education for the City of Hamilton* (Hamilton: Griffin and Richmond), 54
43 *EMC*, s.v. 'school music broadcasts'
44 Emily Tedd, 'Music in the Secondary Schools from the Standpoint of the Supervisor,' *OEA Book of Proceedings for 1934*, 143
45 Cited by Hazel Brookes, 'Harry Hill: His Life and Contribution to Music Education in Ontario' (MM thesis, University of Western Ontario, 1979), 21
46 Ibid.
47 Sir Ernest MacMillan, Toronto *Telegram*, Dec. 1935
48 Leslie Bell, 'Music Education and Jazz,' *School* 31 (1943), 759
49 Donald Heins, 'Violin Classes in the Ottawa Public Schools,' *OEA Book of Proceedings for 1923*, 445–6
50 Ibid., 446
51 Harry Hill, 'Minutes of the Music Section of OEA,' *Musical Canada* 12, no. 11 (Dec. 1931), 10
52 'Minutes of the General Association,' *OEA Book of Proceedings for 1927*, 48–9
53 J.L. Yule, 'School Music Department,' *Musical Canada* 9, no. 9 (Sept. 1928), 6
54 'Musically Speaking,' Toronto *Star*, 7 May 1953
55 'Toronto's First School Band and Orchestra Concert,' *Musical Canada* 11, no. 6 (June 1930), 5
56 Brault, 'A History of the Ontario Music Educators' Association,' 158
57 AR (Ont.), 1945, 80

58 Brault, 'A History of the Ontario Music Educators' Association,' 149
59 George Bramfitt, 'Music in the Curriculum,' *Educational Courier* 4, no. 2 (Dec. 1933), 15
60 Leslie Bell, 'Boys' Singing Classes in Secondary School,' *School* 27 (Oct. 1938), 143
61 George Bramfitt, 'Music Credits on the High School Course,' *School* 13 (1929–30), 885
62 Ernest MacMillan, 'Suggestions for a Course of Music Study for High Schools,' *OEA Book of Proceedings for 1928*, 188
63 Leslie Bell, 'The New Ontario Course in Music for Grade x,' *School* 27 (1938–9) 51
64 G. Roy Fenwick, 'Music in the Schools of Ontario in 1943–44,' *OEA Book of Proceedings for 1944*, 173
65 Ibid., 173–4
66 Brault, 'A History of the Ontario Music Educators' Association,' 186. There is speculation as to whether this was a community group or an ensemble drawn from several elementary schools.
67 Personal interview with Jack Dow, 1984
68 Allen Fisher, 'Instrumental Music in the Classroom,' *School* 30, no. 5 (1942), 418–19
69 Ibid., 419
70 Ibid.
71 Letter from the deputy minister of education to A.T. Cringan, 21 May 1919, Music Division, National Library of Canada
72 Trowsdale, 'A History of Public School Music,' 187
73 AR (Ont.), 'Report of the Provincial Supervisor of Music,' 1935–6, app. N, 72
74 Robert Stamp, *The Schools of Ontario, 1876–1976*, (Toronto: University of Toronto Press 1981), 122
75 Bradley, 'G. Roy Fenwick,' 75
76 AR (Ont.), 'Report of the Provincial Supervisor of Music,' 1942–3, 88
77 Ibid., 1938–9, 107
78 Bradley, 'G. Roy Fenwick,' 58
79 Stamp, *The Schools of Ontario*, 209
80 J.R.W. Gwynne-Timothy, *Western's First Century* (London: University of Western Ontario 1978), 444
81 EMC, s.v. 'Queen's University'
82 Earl Davey, 'The Development of Music Programmes in English Language Universities in Central and Eastern Canada, 1960 to 1969' (PhD thesis, University of Toronto, 1983), 27

83 Ibid., 28
84 Ernest MacMillan, 'Music Education in Canada,' *Journal of Proceedings of the Music Supervisors' National Conference*, 1932, 84
85 Davey, 'The Development of Music Programmes in English Language Universities,' 28
86 Cited by Trudy Bradley, 'G. Roy Fenwick,' 57
87 Ibid.

CHAPTER 11 The Traditions of Newfoundland and Labrador

1 J.R. Smallwood, 'Newfoundland Today,' in *The Book of Newfoundland*, vol. 1, ed. J.R. Smallwood (St John's: Newfoundland Book Publishers 1937), 1
2 Genevieve Lehr, *Come and I Will Sing You* (Toronto: University of Toronto Press 1985), cover leaf notes
3 *EMC*, s.v. 'Squid-jiggin' Ground'
4 Paul G. Woodford, 'A Musical Heritage: The Contributions of Charles Hutton and Ignatius Rumboldt to Music in Newfoundland' (MM thesis, University of Western Ontario, 1983), 2
5 Ibid., 5–6
6 Ibid., 5
7 Cited by Paul G. Woodford, *We Love the Place, O Lord: A History of the Written Musical Tradition of Newfoundland and Labrador to 1949* (St John's: Creative Printers and Publishers 1988), 49
8 Paul O'Neill, *The Oldest City* (Erin, Ont.: Press Porcepic 1975), 226–7
9 Cited ibid., 235
10 Cited by Woodford, 'A Musical Heritage,' 7
11 O'Neill, *The Oldest City*, 228
12 Cited by Woodford, 'A Musical Heritage,' 8
13 Cited by O'Neill, *The Oldest City*, 230
14 Ibid.
15 Ibid.
16 Ibid., 231
17 Frederick W. Rowe, *Education and Culture in Newfoundland* (Toronto: McGraw-Hill Ryerson 1976), 50
18 Sister Kathleen Rex, 'A History of Music Education in Newfoundland' (MM thesis, Catholic University of America, 1977), 38
19 Woodford, 'A Musical Heritage,' 56–7
20 Rex, 'A History of Music Education in Newfoundland,' 79
21 Woodford, 'A Musical Heritage,' 27
22 Louise Whiteway, 'The Athenaeum Movement: St. John's Athenaeum

(1861–1898),' *Dalhousie Review* 50 (Winter 1970–1), 549
23 Cited by Paul Woodford, *Charles Hutton: Newfoundland's Greatest Musician and Dramatist* (St John's: Creative Printers and Publishers 1983), 52
24 Ibid., 9
25 Woodford, 'A Musical Heritage,' 66
26 Woodford, *Charles Hutton*, 15
27 Ibid., v
28 Ibid., 15–16
29 Frederick W. Rowe, *The History of Education in Newfoundland* (Toronto: Ryerson 1952), 132
30 Cited by Woodford, *We Love the Place, O Lord*, 32
31 Ibid., 33
32 Ibid., 62–3
33 Rex, 'A History of Music Education in Newfoundland,' 35
34 Ibid., 50
35 Ibid., 64
36 Woodford, 'A Musical Heritage,' 38
37 Ibid., 40
38 Ibid., 43
39 Rex, 'A History of Music Education in Newfoundland,' 81
40 Woodford, 'A Musical Heritage,' 46
41 Ibid., 100–1
42 Paul Woodford, *Nish Rumboldt* (St John's: Creative Publishers 1984), 14
43 Woodford, *Charles Hutton*, 35
44 Ibid., 40
45 Cited by Woodford, *Nish Rumboldt*, 70
46 Ibid., 72
47 Rex, 'A History of Music Education in Newfoundland,' 82

CHAPTER 12 Diversification in the Postwar Years

1 Vincent Massey, *Report of the Royal Commission on National Development in the Arts, Letters and Sciences, 1949–1951* (Ottawa: Edmond Cloutier 1951), 7
2 Ibid., 132
3 Ibid., 190
4 Ibid., 268
5 Ibid., 271
6 *The Canadian Encyclopedia*, s.v. 'Canada Council'
7 In 1978 the Social Sciences and Humanities Research Council was

organized to administer university-based research activities which previously had been under the aegis of the Canada Council.

8 *EMC*, s.v. 'National Film Board'

9 This is a division of the National Museum of Man, now known as the Canadian Museum of Civilization.

10 Ernest MacMillan, 'The Canadian Music Council,' *Canadian Music Journal*, Autumn 1956, 3

11 Ibid., 4

12 Since 1958 the Canadian Arts Council has been known as the Canadian Conference of the Arts, representing sixteen national cultural groups as well as a large aggregation of artists, patrons, and friends.

13 *EMC*, s.v. 'Canadian Music Council'

14 Helmut Kallmann, 'The Canadian League of Composers,' in *Celebration*, ed. Godfrey Ridout and Talivaldis Kenins (Toronto: Canadian Music Centre 1984), 104

15 Karen Kieser, 'The Canadian Music Centre: A History,' in *Celebration*, 13

16 Coleen Orr, 'The John Adaskin Project: A History and Evaluation' (MM thesis, University of Western Ontario, 1977), 5

17 *The New Grove Dictionary of Music and Musicians*, s.v. 'Education in Music'

18 Patricia Shand, *Canadian Music: A Selective Guidelist for Teachers* (Toronto: Canadian Music Centre 1978). A French edition of the guidelist was published in 1982. Other guidelists for specific instruments have also been prepared.

19 In 1978 the Contemporary Music Showcase was incorporated under its present name, Alliance for Canadian New Music Projects, and extended its operations to Ottawa and London.

20 *EMC*, s.v. 'Prologue to the Performing Arts'

21 Orr, 'The John Adaskin Project: A History and Evaluation,' 137

22 *EMC*, s.v. 'Jeunesses musicales of Canada'

23 Sir Ernest MacMillan, ed., *Music in Canada* (Toronto: University of Toronto Press 1955), 5

24 Keith MacMillan, 'National Organizations,' in *Aspects of Music in Canada*, ed. Arnold Walter (Toronto: University of Toronto Press 1969), 309. In the early 1980s an Ontario office was opened under the name 'Youth and Music Canada.'

25 Arnold Walter, 'The Growth of Music Education,' in *Aspects of Music in Canada*, 279–80

26 *EMC*, s.v. 'The Canadian Federation of Music Teachers' Associations'

27 David Thomson, 'David ... "Sings the Story" of Music in the Province,' *Profile of Education in New Brunswick* 2, no. 1 (Feb. 1963), 2

28 *EMC*, s.v. 'summer camps and schools'

29 Ibid., s.v. 'National Youth Orchestra of Canada'

30 Ibid., s.v. 'Vancouver.' According to the *EMC* (p. 209), the Community Arts Council of Vancouver was the first organization of its kind in North America.

31 George Proctor, *Canadian Music of the Twentieth Century* (Toronto: University of Toronto Press 1980), 150

32 J.L. Granatstein, et al., *Twentieth Century Canada*, 2nd ed. (Toronto: McGraw-Hill Ryerson 1986), 390

33 A bibliography of Helmut Kallmann's writings from 1949 to 1987 has been published in *Musical Canada*, ed. John Beckwith and Frederick A. Hall (Toronto: University of Toronto Press 1988), 315–24.

CHAPTER 13 The Evolution of Vocal Programs in the Schools

1 One of the longest standing events of this type is the May Concert held annually in Toronto at Massey Hall.

2 The New Brunswick Department of Education subsequently was divided into two sections, English and French. Gloria Richard continued to serve as music consultant for the French section; Douglas Hodgkinson was appointed music consultant for the English-speaking section in 1978.

3 Saskatchewan, for its own reasons, did not retain a provincial music director beyond the late 1970s.

4 *EMC*, s.v. 'inventions and devices'

5 Joanna Weweler, 'Rj Staples: Innovative Saskatchewan Music Educator' (MEd thesis, University of Saskatchewan, 1973), 64

6 Ibid., 67

7 *Songs of Praise for Schools – A Book of Worship for High Schools* (Toronto: Ryerson 1957), foreword

8 R.C. Bayley, et al., *Songs for Junior High* (Toronto: BMI Canada 1965)

9 June Countryman, 'An Analysis of Selected Song Series Textbooks in Ontario Schools, 1846–1965' (MM thesis, University of Western Ontario, 1981), 153

10 Edith Fulton Fowke and Richard Johnston, *Folk Songs of Canada* (Waterloo: Waterloo Music 1954). Both Fowke and Johnston have published extensively in this field.

11 *EMC*, s.v. 'school songbooks'

12 Garfield Bender, Keith Bissell, Edwin Fergusson, Richard Johnston, Harvey Perrin, and June Stratton, *Songs for Today*, ed. Richard Johnston (Waterloo: Waterloo Music 1959–70)

13 Vera Russell, Lansing MacDowell, Charles Winter, and John Wood, *Songtime* (Toronto: Holt, Rinehart and Winston 1963–5)

14 Lloyd Slind and Frank Churchley, *Basic Goals in Music* (Toronto: McGraw-Hill 1959–69)

15 Kenneth Bray, Roy Fenwick, Mary Stillman, and Dawson Woodburn, *Music for Young Canada* (Toronto: Gage 1967–9)

16 Gifford Mitchell, Earle Terry, and Glen Wood, *Music 7* and *Music 8* (Toronto: Ginn 1967–8)

17 Countryman, 'An Analysis of Selected Song Series Textbooks in Ontario Schools,' 155

18 Ibid., 156

19 EMC, s.v. 'La Bonne Chanson'

20 Joseph Beaulieu, *Mon école chante* (St-Hyacinthe: Les Éditions Musicales la Bonne Chanson 1956–64)

21 Trudy Bradley, 'G. Roy Fenwick (1889–1970): His Contribution to Music Education in Ontario,' (MM thesis, University of Western Ontario, 1981), 60

22 'Canadian Music Educators' Association National Executive Meetings,' *Canadian Music Educator* 3, no. 4 (May–June 1962), 11–12. The letter was signed by Gifford Mitchell from Montreal, president of CMEA.

23 Editorial comment, *Canadian Music Educator* 4, no. 3 (Feb.–Mar. 1963), 45

24 EMC, s.v. 'Chorale de l'Université St-Joseph'

25 When l'Université St-Joseph moved from Memramcook in 1963 and became l'Université de Moncton, the name of the choir was changed to Chorale de l'Université de Moncton.

26 David Thomson, 'David ... "Sings the Story" of Music in the Province,' *Profile of Education in New Brunswick* 2, no. 1 (Feb. 1963), 9

27 Sister Kathleen Rex, 'A History of Music Education in Newfoundland' (MM thesis, Catholic University of America, 1977), 107. As a result of this workshop, the Allyn and Bacon series *This is Music* was adopted on a pilot basis as the provincial music text.

28 See Doreen Hall, 'Music for Children, Past, Present, Future,' *Ostinato* 4 (Feb. 1976), 5. Doreen Hall was a violinist studying at the RCMT.

29 Keith Bissell, 'Music Education and Carl Orff,' *Canadian Music Educator* 2, no. 1 (June 1960), 22

30 Bissell, 'A Visit to Carl Orff,' *Canadian Music Educator* 2, no. 2 (Dec. 1960), 20

31 Ibid.

32 C. Laughton Bird, 'Orff – A Challenge to Canadian School Music,' *Canadian Music Educator* 3, no. 1 (Nov.–Dec. 1961), 49

33 Orff's address was published in the *Canadian Music Educator* 4, no. 1 (Oct.–Nov. 1962), 17

34 Zoltán Kodály, 'Welcome Address,' *International Music Educator*, no. 10 (Oct. 1964), 324

35 Richard Johnston, 'Music Education in Hungary: Some Observations,' *Canadian Music Educator* 6, no. 3 (March–Apr. 1965), 17

36 Ibid.

37 Ibid., 42

38 'The MacMillan lectures were instituted as an integral part of the summer school of the Royal Conservatory of Music in Toronto in 1963 and serve three purposes: first, to honour the name and person of Sir Ernest MacMillan who has given his life to music in Canada; secondly, to serve as a forum for the great musical minds of the world; thirdly, to share this thinking with our summer school students, with the entire university community to which we belong, and with all others for whom this thinking has meaning. The lectures are made possible through the generosity of the Composers, Authors, and Publishers Association of Canada and the imaginative understanding of its General Manager, Mr. William Low.' Introduction by Richard Johnston to MacMillan Lecture no. 2, *Zoltán Kodály in North America*, Monograph 3 of the Kodály Institute of Canada (Willowdale, Ont.: Avondale Press 1986), 51

39 Editorial comment, *Canadian Music Educator* 6, no. 3 (March–Apr. 1965), 15

40 Harvey Perrin, et al., 'The Philosophy of the New Approach,' *The New Approach to Music*, Primary Division (Toronto: Holt, Rinehart and Winston 1969), x

41 Kenneth I. Bray, 'A Successful Adaptation of Kodály's Music Education Principles,' *Canadian Association of University Schools of Music Journal* 1, no. 1 (1971), 49

42 EMC, s.v. 'Kodály method'

43 Sarah MacKeigan Connor, 'The Kodály and Orff Approaches to Music Education in the Curriculum Guides of Nova Scotia (1968–1972)' (MA thesis, Dalhousie University, 1985), abstract

44 Mae Daly, in *Reflections on Kodály*, ed. Laszlo Vikar (Budapest: International Kodály Society 1985), 52

45 For more detail on TSO student concerts, see Irene Rowe, 'School Concerts by the Toronto Symphony Orchestra, 1925 to 1957' (MM thesis, University of Western Ontario, 1989).

46 Hilary E. Millar, 'Students' Concerts and Reviews,' *Toronto Symphony News* 2, no. 9 (April 1949), 1

47 Harry Lomnes, 'A Survey of Alberta High School Music Programs' (MM thesis, Montana State University, 1959), 57

48 *Report of Conference on 'Music in the Schools of the Atlantic Provinces'* (Sackville, NB: Mount Allison University 1960), 30

49 Ibid., 1

50 Kenneth Bray and Bruce Snell, *For Young Musicians*, 2 vols (Waterloo, Ont.: Waterloo Music Co. 1961–7)

51 G. Roy Fenwick, et al., *Let's Explore Music*, 13 vols (Toronto: Gordon V. Thompson 1954–63)

CHAPTER 14 The Rise of Instrumental Music

1 Montreal *Daily Star*, 25 April 1947

2 Ibid.

3 Ibid.

4 Montreal *Gazette*, 7 May 1947

5 Montreal *Daily Star*, 22 April 1947

6 Ibid.

7 Gifford Mitchell was director of music for the Protestant School Board of Greater Montreal (1951–69), and Morley Calvert at that time was the music teacher at Westmount Junior High School.

8 Roy Fenwick, *The Function of Music in Education* (Toronto: Gage 1951), 19

9 Alan Smith, 'A Study of Instrumental Music in Ontario Secondary Schools during 1954–55' (MM thesis, University of Toronto, 1956), 13

10 Brian S. McCool, 'Instrumental Music in Ontario Schools,' *Canadian School Journal* 26, no. 7–8 (July–Aug. 1948), 267

11 Smith, 'A Study of Instrumental Music in Ontario,' 200

12 Trudy Bradley, 'G. Roy Fenwick (1889–1970): His Contribution to Music Education in Ontario' (MM thesis, University of Western Ontario, 1981), 61

13 The librarian of Peterborough Collegiate to the Barrie Central Collegiate Band, Nov. 1946, personal letter

14 Smith, 'A Study of Instrumental Music in Ontario,' 21

15 Ibid., 95–6

16 George Bornoff, *Fun for Fiddle Fingers; Finger Patterns* (Toronto: Gordon V. Thompson 1948)

17 Smith, 'A Study of Instrumental Music in Ontario,' 213

18 Ontario, Ministry of Education, 'The Arts in Ontario Schools,' discussion paper, 1984

19 Smith, 'A Study of Instrumental Music in Ontario,' 205

20 Ontario, Department of Education, *Courses of Study: Music, Grade 9, 10, 11, 12, and 13*, 1954, 5
21 Smith, 'A Study of Instrumental Music in Ontario,' 206
22 Duane Bates, 'The Status of Music Education in 1969–70 in the Cities of Southern Ontario Having a Population in Excess of 100,000' (EdD thesis, University of Illinois at Urbana-Champaign, 1972), 23
23 Ibid., 157
24 The 1966 Ontario Music Conference held at Geneva Park, Lake Couchiching, was sponsored by the Community Programs Division of the Department of Education and the Province of Ontario Council for the Arts.
25 Bates, 35
26 Ibid., 156
27 Canadian Bandmasters' Association, 'Instrumental Conference for B.C., ' *Canadian Bandmaster*, March 1958, 32
28 Printed program of the Fourth BC Schools Band and Orchestra Conference.
29 BCSITA, *Minutes of Meeting*, 29 Dec. 1959
30 Donald Chant, *Royal Commission on Education in British Columbia* (Victoria: Department of Education 1960)
31 British Columbia, Department of Education, *A Précis of the Report of the Royal Commission on Education in British Columbia* (Victoria: Department of Education 1960), 71–2
32 Ibid.
33 Ibid.
34 Ibid.
35 Ibid., 97
36 Ibid.
37 Ibid., 81
38 Lloyd Slind, 'An Editorial,' *B.C. Music Educator* 4, no. 1 (Feb. 1961), 4
39 Ibid., 5
40 Victoria *Colonist*, 16 Jan. 1949, 15
41 Cited by Sharon Dueck, 'Ethel Kinley (1887–1967): Her Life and Contribution to Music Education in Manitoba' (MM thesis, University of Western Ontario, 1983), 115
42 Leonard Takoski, 'A History of the Manitoba Schools' Orchestra' (MEd thesis, University of Manitoba, 1965), 28
43 Winnipeg *Free Press*, 5 Feb. 1949
44 Ibid.
45 Frederick Merrett, 'Developing an Effective Instrumental Music Program

for Manitoba Public Schools' (MEd thesis University of Manitoba, 1964), 92

46 Annual Report of the Superintendent to the Winnipeg School Board, 1949, 29

47 Merrett, 'Developing an Effective Instrumental Music Program,' 114

48 Cited by Merrett, ibid., 57

49 Manitoba, Department of Education, *Program for Senior High School General Course in Music* (Winnipeg: Queen's Printer 1962)

50 Merrett, 'Developing an Effective Instrumental Program,' 91–2

51 Ibid., 118

52 Ibid., 117

53 Ibid., 52

54 Cyril Mossop, 'The Secondary School Instrumental Program in the Calgary Public Schools,' *Alberta Music Educator* 1, no. 2 (April 1966), 11

55 Mossop, 'Music Education in the Schools,' *Canadian Music Journal*, Autumn 1956, 62

56 Mossop, 'The Secondary School Instrumental Program in the Calgary Public Schools,' 11

57 Ibid., 19

58 Ibid.

59 Harry Lomnes, 'A Survey of Alberta High School Music Programs' (MM thesis, Montana State University, 1959), 55

60 Alberta, Department of Education, *Senior High School Curriculum Guide for Music 10, 20, 30* (Edmonton: Department of Education 1958)

61 Lomnes, 'A Survey of Alberta High School Music Programs,' 58

62 Alan Smith, 'MELAB: An Application of Inquiry to the Training of Music Teachers' *Canadian Music Educator* 8, no. 1 (Oct.–Nov. 1966), 15

63 Ibid., 17

64 Alan Smith, 'Some Questions Answered about MELAB,' *Alberta Music Educator* 1, no. 3 (Nov. 1966), 19

65 Lomnes, 'A Survey of Alberta High School Music Programs,' 60

66 AR (Sask.), 1948–9, 33

67 Joanna Weweler, 'Rj Staples: Innovative Saskatchewan Music Educator' (MEd thesis, University of Saskatchewan, 1973), 40–1

68 AR (Sask.), 1957–8, 43

69 Arthur Fraser, 'Music in Canadian Public Schools, Survey and Recommendations' (EdD thesis, Teachers' College, Columbia University, 1951), 120

70 Boyd Neel, 'Instrumentalists: Canada's Critical Need in Music,' *Journal of Education* (NS), April 1957, 3

71 *Report of Conference on 'Music in the Schools of the Atlantic Provinces'* (Sackville, NB: Mount Allison University 1960), 30

72 Ibid., 31

73 Howard Brown, 'Music Education Today in the Maritime Provinces,' in *Music Education and the Canadians of Tomorrow* (Canadian Music Council 1968), 34

74 EMC, s.v. 'Halifax'

75 Cited by Paul Woodford, 'A Musical Heritage: The Contributions of Charles Hutton and Ignatius Rumboldt to Music in Newfoundland' (MM thesis, University of Western Ontario, 1983), 210–11

CHAPTER 15 Music in Higher Education

1 Earl Davey, 'The Development of Music Programmes in English Language Universities in Central and Eastern Canada, 1960 to 1969' (PhD thesis, University of Toronto, 1983), 6

2 Robin S. Harris, *A History of Higher Education in Canada 1663–1960* (Toronto: University of Toronto Press 1976), 543

3 Dorith Cooper, 'Opera in Montreal and Toronto: A Study of Performance Traditions and Repertoire, 1783–1980' (PhD thesis, University of Toronto, 1983), 753

4 Cited by Cooper, 'Opera in Montreal and Toronto,' 750

5 The Faculty of Music, University of Toronto, did not include applied music within its degree programs until 1961.

6 Board of Governors, University of Toronto, Minutes of meeting held 28 Feb. 1952, A 70–0024, University of Toronto Archives

7 Davey, 'The Development of Music Programmes,' 101

8 Ernest MacMillan, 'Music in Canadian Universities,' *Canadian Music Journal* 2, no. 3 (Spring 1958), 5

9 Ibid., 6

10 Arnold Walter, 'The Production and Dissemination of Music,' in *Music in Canada: Its Resources and Needs* (Canadian Music Council Annual Meeting and Conference, 1966), 4

11 George Proctor, 'The Bachelor of Music Degree in Canada and the United States,' *Canadian Music Educator* 7, no. 2 (Jan.–Feb. 1966), 27

12 Ibid.

13 Davey, 'The Development of Music Programmes,' 18

14 Ibid.

15 Ibid., 53–4

16 Proctor, 'The Bachelor of Music Degree,' 28

17 EMC, s.v. 'degrees'
18 Davey, 'The Development of Music Programmes,' 7
19 EMC, s.v. 'degrees'
20 Ibid., s.v. 'Laval University'
21 Ibid., s.v. 'Conservatoire de musique du Québec'
22 Walter, 'The Production and Dissemination of Music,' 3–4
23 EMC, s.v. 'degrees'
24 This association was later renamed Canadian University Music Society (CUMS).
25 Davey, 'The Development of Music Programmes,' 267
26 Canada, Dominion Bureau of Statistics, Survey of Higher Education, 1960–70
27 Davey, 'The Development of Music Programmes,' 177
28 Ibid., 54
29 Harry Adaskin, 'Music and the University,' Canadian Music Journal 1 (Autumn 1956), 35
30 EMC, s.v. 'Simon Fraser University'
31 Edwin E. Gordon, 'Music Education: A Profession in Search of a Discipline,' Tempo (New Jersey Music Educators' Association), Nov. 1980
32 Arnold Walter, 'The Growth of Music Education,' in Aspects of Music in Canada, ed. Arnold Walter (Toronto: University of Toronto Press 1969), 254
33 Davey, 'The Development of Music Programmes,' 278
34 Ernest MacMillan, 'Music in Canadian Universities,' Canadian Music Journal 2, no. 3 (Spring 1958), 5
35 Helmut Blume, A National Music School for Canada (A Report published by the Canada Council, 1978), 93
36 National Conference of Canadian Universities, Proceedings for 1950, 67
37 Harris, A History of Higher Education in Canada, 548
38 Robin Mathews and John Steele, The Struggle for Canadian Universities (Toronto: New Press 1969), 3–4
39 Cited by Mathews and Steele, The Struggle for Canadian Universities, 170–1
40 Ibid., 172
41 T.H.B. Symons, To Know Ourselves (The Report of the Commission on Canadian Studies, 1975), 16
42 Vincent Massey, Report of the Royal Commission on National Development in the Arts, Letters, and Sciences, 1949–1951 (Ottawa: Edmond Cloutier 1951), 134
43 James Stark, 'Symposium II–The Baroque,' Recorder 12, no. 1 (Sept. 1969), 25
44 'Symposium–The Renaissance,' Recorder 10, no. 2 (Nov. 1967–Jan. 1968),13

45 Kay Bennett, 'Reflections on Symposium I,' *Recorder* 10, no. 3 (Feb.–March 1968), 22

CHAPTER 16 The Growth of the Profession

1 This organization is discussed later in the chapter under its new name, the Canadian University Music Society (CUMS).
2 'Music Education and the Canadians of Tomorrow' was the theme of the Canadian Music Council Conference held in Montreal in April 1968.
3 Ernest MacMillan, 'Musical Relations between Canada and the United States,' *Proceedings of the Music Teachers' National Association*, 1931, 36
4 Minutes of the organizational meeting of the Canadian Federation of Music Teachers' Associations, 24 Aug. 1935
5 An association of private teachers was not formed in Newfoundland until 1987, and as yet no group has been organized in Prince Edward Island.
6 Lola MacQuarrie, 'Music and Its Teachers,' *Canadian Music Educator* 5, no. 1, 21
7 Cited by Diana Brault, 'The Fourth Music Section Convention, April 18–19, 1922, at the 61st O.E.A. Convention,' *Recorder* 21, no. 1 (Fall 1978), 38
8 Irvin Cooper, 'School Music and Post-War Reconstruction,' *School* 32 (Dec. 1943), 305
9 Garfield Bender, 'The Founding of the CMEA,' *Canadian Music Educator* 16, no. 1, 13
10 Keith MacMillan, 'The Music Education Structure in Canada,' *Musicanada*, no. 6 (Nov. 1967), 6
11 Leslie Bell, 'Musically Speaking,' Toronto *Star*, 5 Nov. 1955
12 'From the President,' *Canadian Music Educator* 1, no. 2, 1
13 'From the Executive Director's Desk,' *Canadian Music Educator* 1, no. 1, 4
14 It is also a point of interest that the Canadian Education Association (CEA) was approached concerning the possibility of CMEA receiving affiliation status; however, CEA already had a large national council and felt it unwise to expand at that time.
15 Paul G. Woodford, *The Life and Contribution of Ignatius Rumboldt to Music in Newfoundland* (St John's: Creative Publishers 1984), 48
16 Donald F. Cook, 'Music in Newfoundland,' cited in Paul Woodford, 'A Musical Heritage: The Contributions of Charles Hutton and Ignatius Rumboldt to Music in Newfoundland' (MM thesis, University of Western Ontario, 1983), 203
17 'From the President,' *Canadian Music Educator* 1, no. 3, 1

18 'The Winnipeg Convention,' *Canadian Music Educator* 2, no. 1, 6
19 'From the President,' *Canadian Music Educator* 2, no. 3, 5
20 By 1983 conferences had been held in all ten provinces.
21 'Second Leslie Bell Memorial Choral Competition – 1965,' *Canadian Music Educator* 6, no. 1, 26
22 'Notes from the Secretary-Treasurer,' *Canadian Music Educator* 1, no. 1, 2
23 Sister Marcelle Corneille, 'F.A.M.E.Q.,' *Musicanada*, no. 8 (Jan.–Feb. 1968), 6
24 Patricia Shand, 'Music Education in Canada Part I: The Status of Music Education in Canada,' *Canadian Music Educator* 23, no. 3, 27
25 Beth Douglas, 'The Manitoba Music Educators' Association,' *Canadian Music Educator* 3, no. 1, 15
26 G. Welton Marquis, 'The Canadian Association of University Schools of Music: A Brief History,' CAUSM *Journal*, no. 1 (Spring 1971), 4
27 Ibid., 6
28 Arnold Walter, 'Introduction,' in *Aspects of Music in Canada*, ed. Arnold Walter (Toronto: University of Toronto Press 1969), 23–4
29 Walter, 'The Growth of Music Education,' in *Aspects of Music in Canada*, 249
30 Ibid., 265–6
31 Leslie Bell, 'Musically Speaking,' Toronto *Star*, 5 Nov. 1955
32 'From the Executive Director's Desk,' *Canadian Music Educator* 1, no. 1, 4
33 'Introduction,' in *Music in Education* (UNESCO 1955), 9
34 Helmut Kallmann, Gilles Potvin, and Kenneth Winters, eds, *Encyclopedia of Music in Canada* (Toronto: University of Toronto Press 1981). A French edition was also published: Helmut Kallmann, Gilles Potvin, and Kenneth Winters, eds, *L'Encyclopédie de la musique au Canada* (Montréal: Les Éditions Fides 1983).

Bibliography

Published Works

Adams, Stephen. *R. Murray Schafer*. Toronto: University of Toronto Press 1982

Amtmann, Willy. *Music in Canada, 1600–1800*. Montreal: Habitex 1975

– *La Musique au Québec, 1600–1875*. Montréal: Les Éditions de l'Homme 1976

Applebaum, Louis, and Jacques Hébert. *Report of the Cultural Policy Review Committee*. Ottawa: Information Services, Department of Communications, Government of Canada 1982

Beckwith, John, ed. *Sing Out the Glad News: Hymn Tunes in Canada*. Toronto: Institute for Canadian Music 1987

Beckwith, John, and Frederick A. Hall, eds. *Musical Canada*. Toronto: University of Toronto Press 1988

Bell, Leslie. 'The Failure of Music Appreciation.' *Canadian Music Journal* 2, Spring 1958

Birge, Edward Bailey. *History of Public School Music in the United States*. Washington: MENC 1928

Blakeley, Phyllis. 'Music in Nova Scotia, 1605–1867.' *Dalhousie Review* 31, Summer and Autumn 1951

Blume, Helmut. *A National Music School for Canada: An Enquiry*. Ottawa: Canada Council 1978

[Canadian Federation of Music Teachers' Associations.] *The Canadian Federation of Music Teachers' Associations in Retrospect, 1935 to 1985*. CFMTA 1989

Cherney, Brian. *Harry Somers*. Toronto: University of Toronto Press 1975

Clarke, F.R.C. *Healey Willan: Life and Music*. Toronto: University of Toronto Press 1983

Daigle, Jean, ed. *The Acadians of the Maritimes: Thematic Studies*. Moncton: Centre d'études acadiennes 1982

L'Enseignement de la musique au Québec à l'heure du rapport Parent. Québec: Université Laval École de Musique 1965

Fancy, Margaret, ed. *The Proceedings of the Art and Music in New Brunswick Symposium*. Sackville/Fredericton: Mount Allison University/Goose Lane Editions 1987

Farquharson, Dorothy H. *O for a Thousand Tongues to Sing: A History of Singing Schools in Early Canada*. Waterdown, Ont. 1983

Fleming, W.G. *Ontario's Educative Society*. 7 vols. Toronto: University of Toronto Press 1971

Ford, Clifford. *Canada's Music: An Historical Survey*. Agincourt, Ont.: GLC Publishers 1982

Galarneau, Claude. *Les Collèges classiques du Canada français (1620–1928)*. Montréal: Fides 1978

Green, Rebecca, Gaynor G. Jones, and Colin Eatock. *Three Studies*. Toronto: Institute for Canadian Music 1989

Haig, Alastair P. 'Henry Frost, Pioneer (1816–1851).' *Canadian Music Journal* 2, Winter 1958

Harris, Robin S. *A History of Higher Education in Canada 1663–1960*. Toronto: University of Toronto Press 1976

– *Quiet Revolution: A Study of the Educational System of Ontario*. Toronto: University of Toronto Press 1967

Hodgins, J. George, ed. *Documentary History of Education in Upper Canada, 1791–1896*. Toronto: King's Printer 1910

Johnson, F. Henry. *A History of Public Education in British Columbia*. Vancouver: UBC Publications Centre 1964

– 'The Ryersonian Influence on the Public School System of British Columbia.' *BC Studies*, no. 10, Summer 1971

Kallmann, Helmut. *A History of Music in Canada, 1534–1914*. Toronto: University of Toronto Press 1960

– 'The Music Division of the National Library: The First Five Years.' *Canada Music Book 10*, Spring–Summer 1975

Kallmann, Helmut, Gilles Potvin, and Kenneth Winters, eds. *Encyclopedia of Music in Canada*. Toronto: University of Toronto Press 1981

– *L'Encyclopédie de la musique au Canada*. Montréal: Les Éditions Fides 1983

Keene, James A. *A History of Music Education in the United States*. Hanover, NH: University Press of New England 1982

Keillor, Elaine. 'Wesley Octavius Forsyth, 1859–1937.' *The Canada Music Book* 7, Autumn–Winter 1973

Keith, W. J., and B.-Z. Shek, eds. *The Arts in Canada*. Toronto: University of Toronto Press 1980

King, Valerie Verity. *The History of CAMMAC: Canadian Amateur Musicians/Musiciens amateurs du Canada: 1952–1928*. Ottawa: Golden Dog Press 1984

Lambert, Richard S. *School Broadcasting in Canada*. Toronto: University of Toronto Press 1963

Laselle-Leduc, Annette. *La Vie musicale au Canada français*. Québec: Ministère des affaires culturelles 1964

MacMillan, Sir Ernest, 'The Canadian Music Council.' *Canadian Music Journal* 1, Autumn 1956

– 'Music Education in Canada.' *Journal of Proceedings of the Music Supervisors' National Conference*. 1932

– , ed. *Music in Canada*. Toronto: University of Toronto Press 1955

– 'Musical Relations between Canada and the United States.' *Proceedings of the Music Teachers' National Association*. 1931

MacNaughton, Katherine F.C. *The Development of the Theory and Practice of Education in New Brunswick, 1784–1900*. University of New Brunswick Historical Studies, no. 1. Fredericton 1947

Magnuson, Roger. *A Brief History of Quebec Education from New France to Parti Québecois*. Montreal: Harvest House 1980

Massey, Vincent. *Report of the Royal Commission on National Development in the Arts, Letters, and Sciences, 1949–1951*. Ottawa: Edmond Cloutier 1951

Mathews, Robin, and John Steele. *The Struggle for Canadian Universities*. Toronto: New Press 1969

McCullagh, Harold. *The Man Who Made New Brunswick Sing*. St Stephen, NB: Print'N Press 1977

McGee, Timothy J. *The Music of Canada*. New York: W.W. Norton and Co. 1985

McIntosh, Dale. *History of Music in British Columbia, 1850–1950*. Victoria: Sono Nis Press 1989

– 'A Short History of Music Education in British Columbia, 1850–1950.' *B.C. Music Educator* 29, no. 2, Spring 1986

McIntosh, Robert Dale. *A Documentary History of Music in Victoria*. Vol. 1, *1850–1899*. Victoria: 1981

Montreal Music Year Book. 1931, 1932

Moyles, Gordon. *The Blood and Fire in Canada*. Toronto: Peter Martin Associates 1977

Music Education and the Canadians of Tomorrow. Canadian Music Council 1968

Music in Education. UNESCO 1955

O'Neill, Paul. *The Oldest City*. Erin, Ont.: Press Porcepic 1975

Parmalee, G.W. *Education in the Province of Quebec*. Quebec: Quebec Dept. of Public Instruction 1914

Parvin, Viola Elizabeth. *Authorization of Textbooks for the Schools of Ontario, 1846–1950*. Toronto: University of Toronto Press 1965

Payzant, Geoffrey. 'The Competitive Music Festivals.' *Canadian Music Journal* 4, Spring 1960

– *Glenn Gould: Music and Mind*. Toronto: University of Toronto Press 1978

Phillips, C.E. *The Development of Education in Canada*. Toronto: Gage 1957

Prentice, Alison, and Susan Houston, eds. *Family and Schooling in Nineteenth Century Canada*. Toronto: Oxford University Press 1965

Proctor, George. *Canadian Music of the Twentieth Century*. Toronto: University of Toronto Press 1980

Rainbow, Bernarr. *The Land without Music*. London: Novello 1967

Rapport de la Commission royale d'enquête sur l'enseignement des arts dans la province de Québec. [Rioux Report]. Québec 1968

Report of Conference on 'Music in the Schools of the Atlantic Provices.' Sackville, NB: Mount Allison University 1960

Report of the Past History and Present Condition of Common or Public Schools of the City of Toronto. Toronto: Lovell and Gibson 1859

Report of the Royal Commission of Enquiry on Education in the Province of Quebec. 5 vols. [Parent Report]. Quebec 1963–6

Ridout, Godfrey, and Talivaldis Kenins, eds. *Celebration*. Toronto: Canadian Music Centre 1984

Rowe, Frederick W. *Education and Culture in Newfoundland*. Toronto: McGraw-Hill Ryerson 1976

– *The History of Education in Newfoundland*. Toronto: Ryerson 1952

Sandwell, Bernard K. *The Musical Red Book of Montreal, 1896–1906*. Montreal: F.A. Veitch 1907

Sœurs de Sainte-Anne. *Dictionnaire bibliographique des musiciens canadiens*. Lachine: Sœurs de Sainte-Anne 1934

Stamp, Robert. *The Schools of Ontario, 1876–1976*. Toronto: University of Toronto Press 1981

Symons, T.H.B. *To Know Ourselves: The Report of the Commission on Canadian Studies*. Ottawa: Association of Universities and Colleges of Canada 1975

Talbot, Hugo, ed. *Musical Halifax, 1903–4*. Halifax: McAlpine Publishing Co. 1904

Tomkins, George S. *A Common Countenance: Stability and Change in the Canadian Curriculum*. Scarborough, Ont.: Prentice-Hall Canada 1986

Trowsdale, G. Campbell. 'The History of Music Education as a Field of Study: A Consideration of Status, Research, and Needs.' CAUSM *Journal* 3, Spring 1974

– 'Music and Performing Arts Institutions in Public Education: The Toronto Experience, 1962–1969.' CAUSM *Journal* 2, 1972

– 'Vocal Music in the Common Schools of Upper Canada: 1846–76.' *Journal of Research in Music Education* 18, Winter 1970

– , ed. *Independent and Affiliated Non-Profit Conservatory-Type Music Schools in Canada: A Speculative Survey*. Ottawa: Canadian Music Council 1988

Tweedie, R.A., Fred Cogswell, and W. Stewart MacNutt, eds. *Arts in New Brunswick*. Fredericton: Brunswick Press 1967

Walter, Arnold, ed. *Aspects of Music in Canada*. Toronto: University of Toronto Press 1969

Wilson, J. Donald, Robert M. Stamp, and Louis-Philippe Audet, eds. *Canadian Education: A History*. Scarborough, Ont.: Prentice-Hall 1970

Wood, B. Anne. *Idealism Subverted: The Making of a Progressive Educator*. Kingston and Montreal: McGill-Queen's University Press 1985

Woodford, Paul. *Charles Hutton*. St John's: Creative Printers and Publishers 1983

– *Nish Rumboldt*. St John's: Creative Printers and Publishers 1984

– *We Love the Place, O Lord: A History of the Written Musical Tradition of Newfoundland and Labrador to 1949*. St John's: Creative Printers and Publishers 1988

Unpublished Works

Bates, Duane. 'The Status of Music Education in 1969–70 in the Cities of Southern Ontario Having a Population in Excess of 100,000.' EdD thesis, University of Illinois at Urbana-Champaign, 1972

Berg, Wesley Peter. 'Choral Festivals and Choral Workshops among the Mennonites of Manitoba and Saskatchewan, 1900–1960, with an Account of Early Developments in Russia.' PhD thesis, University of Washington, 1979

Bjarnason, Carl. 'The Brandon School System: A Historical Survey and Ten-Year Development Program.' MEd thesis, University of Manitoba, 1962

Black, William G. 'Development and Present Status of Teacher Education in Western Canada.' PhD thesis, University of Chicago, 1936

Blakeley, Phyllis, and B.C. Silver. 'History of Music and Music Teaching in Nova Scotia.' Manuscript, Provincial Archives (NS)

Bradley, Trudy. 'G. Roy Fenwick (1889–1970): His Contribution to Music Education in Ontario.' MM thesis, University of Western Ontario, 1981

Brault, Diana. 'A History of the Ontario Music Educators' Association (1919–1974).' PhD thesis, University of Rochester, 1977

Brookes, Hazel. 'Harry Hill: His Life and Contribution to Music Education in Ontario.' MM thesis, University of Western Ontario, 1979

Brown, Aldred Malcolm. 'A Study of Teacher Education and Certification for the Teaching of Music in Canadian Public Schools.' EdD thesis, Florida State University, 1960

Brown, Jeffrey W. 'Public School Music in Hamilton, Ontario, 1853–1963.' MM thesis, University of Western Ontario, 1989

Buckley, Mary Margaret. 'Music Education in Alberta, 1884–1945: History and Development.' MM thesis, University of Calgary, 1987

Cochrane, Everett George. 'The Development of the Curriculum of the Protestant Elementary Schools of Montreal.' EdD thesis, University of Toronto, 1968

Connor, Sarah MacKeigan. 'The Kodály and Orff Approaches to Music Education in the Curriculum Guides of Nova Scotia (1968–1972).' MA thesis, Dalhousie University, 1985

Cooper, Dorith. 'Opera in Montreal and Toronto: A Study of Performance Traditions and Repertoire, 1783–1980.' PhD thesis, University of Toronto, 1983

Countryman, June. 'An Analysis of Selected Song Series Textbooks Used in Ontario Schools, 1846–1965.' MM thesis, University of Western Ontario, 1981

Cronk, M. Sam. 'Music in Ottawa, 1880–1884: A Survey of Events Reported in the Ottawa *Daily Citizen*.' Research paper, Carleton University, 1981

Davey, Earl. 'The Development of Music Programmes in English Language Universities in Central and Eastern Canada, 1960 to 1969.' PhD thesis, University of Toronto, 1983

– 'The Development of Undergraduate Music Curricula at the University of Toronto, 1918–68.' MA thesis, University of Toronto, 1977

Dueck, Sharon. 'Ethel Kinley (1887–1967): Her Life and Contribution to Music Education in Manitoba.' MM thesis, University of Western Ontario, 1983

Elliott, David James. 'Descriptive, Philosophical, and Practical Bases for Jazz

Education: A Canadian Perspective.' PhD thesis, Case Western Reserve University, 1983

Fisher, Olive. 'The School Festival and Its Contribution to the Cultural Life of Alberta.' MA Thesis, Stanford University, 1942

Fraser, Arthur. 'Music in Canadian Public Schools, Survey and Recommendations.' EdD thesis, Teachers' College, Columbia University, 1951

Green, George Henry. 'The Development of the Curriculum in the Elementary Schools of British Columbia prior to 1936.' MA thesis, University of British Columbia, 1938

Green, J. Paul. 'A Proposed Doctoral Program in Music for Canadian Universities with Specific Recommendations for Specialization in Music Education.' PhD thesis, University of Rochester, 1974

Haywood, Dorothy Verna Marie. 'Qualifications of School Music Teachers in the Province of New Brunswick in 1967–1968.' MA thesis, Acadia University, 1968

Hochstein, Sister L. A.. 'Roman Catholic Separate and Public Schools in Alberta.' MEd thesis, University of Alberta, 1954

King, Jane Leslie. 'The Life and Contribution of Gordon V. Thompson.' MM thesis, University of Western Ontario, 1984

Koop, Ann Elizabeth. 'The History of the Manitoba Music Educators' Association.' MM thesis, University of Western Ontario, 1983

Lomnes, Harry. 'A Survey of Alberta High School Music Programs.' MM thesis, Montana State University, 1959

Marie-Stephane, Sister. 'La Musique au point de vue éducatif.' MM thesis, University of Montreal, 1936

Matthews, W.D.E. '100 Years of Public Education in London.' Paper housed at University of Western Ontario Library, Althouse College, n.d.

McNeill-Hordern, Alison. 'The Development of the Music Program at Brandon College during the Period 1906 to 1939.' MM thesis, Brandon University, 1987

Merrett, Frederick. 'Developing an Effective Instrumental Music Program for Manitoba Public Schools.' MEd thesis, University of Manitoba, 1964

Newman, Eleanor. 'An Analysis of Canadian Content in Vocal Music Textbooks Authorized by the Ontario Ministry of Education, 1846–1988.' MA thesis, Carleton University, 1988

Orr, Coleen. 'The John Adaskin Project: A History and Evaluation.' MM thesis, University of Western Ontario, 1977

Patterson, Robert S. 'The Establishment of Progressive Education in

Alberta.' PhD thesis, Michigan State University, 1968

Pilote, Gilles. 'L'Enseignement de la musique au Québec: Claude Champagne et al Commission des Écoles Catholiques de Montréal.' Doctoral thesis, Strasbourg, 1973

– 'L'Enseignment du solfège dans les écoles élémentaires de la CECM: Claude Champagne et ses contributions.' MM thesis, McGill University, 1970

Rex, Sister Kathleen. 'A History of Music Education in Newfoundland.' MM thesis, Catholic University of America, 1977

Richardson, Bruce D. 'George Bornoff: His Contribution to Music Education through Class String Instruction.' MM thesis, University of Western Ontario, 1985

Rowe, Irene L. 'The History and Development of School Concerts by the Toronto Symphony Orchestra from 1925 to 1957.' MM thesis, University of Western Ontario, 1989

Ryan-Wiggin, Jocelyn. 'Leslie Richard Bell: His Life and Contribution to Music in Canada.' MM thesis, University of Western Ontario, 1988

Schau, Barbara Ann. 'Sacred Music at Sharon, a Nineteenth-Century Canadian Community.' MA thesis, Carleton University, 1983

Seiffert, Elaine Braun. 'Arnold M. Walter: His Contribution to Music Education in Canada.' MM thesis, University of Western Ontario, 1980

Sheane, George. 'History and Development of the Curriculum of the Elementary School in Alberta.' DPaed thesis, University of Toronto, 1948

Shippey, Douglas, 'History of the Waterloo Musical Society, 1882–1903.' MM thesis, University of Western Ontario, 1984

Smith, Alan. 'A Study of Instrumental Music in Ontario Secondary Schools during 1954–55.' MM thesis, University of Toronto, 1956

Takoski, Leonard. 'A History of the Manitoba Schools' Orchestra.' MEd thesis, University of Manitoba, 1964

Trowsdale, G. Campbell. 'A History of Public School Music in Ontario.' EdD thesis, University of Toronto, 1962

Uhryniw, Donaldson. 'Cringan and Tonic Sol-fa: Morality through Music.' MA research essay, Carleton University, 1981

Vogan, Nancy Fraser. 'The History of Public School Music in the Province of New Brunswick, 1872–1939.' PhD thesis, University of Rochester, 1979

Waite, William Henry. 'The History of Elementary and Secondary Education in Saskatchewan.' MA thesis, University of Manitoba, 1936

Weweler, Johanna. 'Rj Staples: Innovative Saskatchewan Music Educator.' MEd thesis, University of Saskatchewan, 1973

Wilson, Keith. 'Development of Education in Manitoba.' PhD thesis, University of Michigan, 1967

Woodford, Paul G. 'A Musical Heritage: The Contributions of Charles Hutton and Ignatius Rumboldt to Music in Newfoundland.' MM thesis, University of Western Ontario, 1983

Wormsbecker, J.H. 'The Development of Secondary Education in Vancouver.' EdD thesis, University of Toronto, 1961

Periodicals

Provincial Music Education Association Publications: *Accents* (NB), *Alberta Music Educator, B.C. Music Educator, Cadenza* (Sask.), *Crescendo* (PEI), *Manitoba Music Educator, Le Musicien Éducateur* (FAMEQ), *NSMEA Newsletter, Opus* (Nfld.), *QMEA Newsletter, Recorder* (Ont.)

Canadian Music Educator (CMEA)

Canadian Music Journal

Canadian Music Teacher (CFMTA)

CAUSM *Journal,* succeeded by *Canadian University Music Review*

Educational Record (Que.)

Educational Review (Maritimes)

Journal of Education (NS)

Journal of Education (Que.)

Manitoba School Journal

Manitoba Teacher

Music for Children: Carl Orff Canada Newletter, succeeded by *Ostinato*

Musical Canada

Musicanada

Notes, succeeded by *Alla Breve* (Kodály Society)

School

Teachers' Magazine (Que.)

Other

Annual reports of the provincial departments of education, reports of municipal and regional school divisions, school board minutes, minutes of local, provincial, and national music and educational associations, newspapers, archival materials, and interviews. For details consult the notes.

Index

Saint John: community singing, 317;
early musical activity, 17–18;
festivals and celebrations, 35–6,
208–9, 315; High School, 35, 196,
205–7, 392; school music, 33, 38,
202–3, 205–7, 392; Youth
Orchestra, 392
St John-Baker, Blanche, 108
St John's: Choral Society, 291; early
musical activity, 287–94; festivals,
303, 331; Kiwanis Music Festival,
331; Library Society, 292;
Methodist Academy, 299; music
instruction, 296–302, 396; Normal
School, 300–1; Orchestral Society,
292
St John's College Preparatory
School (Winnipeg), 167
St John's School (Montreal), 9
St John's Technical High School
(Winnipeg), 84
St-Joseph, Marie de, 4
St Joseph Calazance, Sister, 21
St-Louis-de-Gonzague Academy
(Grand'Mère), 228
St Mary's Academy (Summerside),
204
St Mary's Academy (Windsor), 241
St Mary's Academy (Winnipeg), 76
St Mary's Mission (Mission City),
92
St Mary's School (Halifax), 30, 32
St Michael's Cathedral Choir School
(Toronto), 241
St Michael's High School (Grand
Falls), 397
St Patrick's Boys' School (Halifax),
206
St Patrick's Hall School (St John's),
297, 299

St Paul's Anglican Church (Halifax),
19
St Paul's Church (Charlottetown),
19
Salvation Army (SA), 142–3, 359; as
a national institution, 140–3; in
Newfoundland, 291–2, 295, 302,
396; in northern British
Columbia, 93; in the prairie
provinces, 115, 378–9
Samuelson, Miriam, 337
Sandoval, Leo, 396
Sarah-Hoskin, William, 179
Saskatchewan Arts Board, 318, 390
Saskatchewan Arts Council, 391
Saskatchewan Department of
Education, 387, 389–90
Saskatchewan Diamond Jubilee
(1965), 388
Saskatchewan Music Educators'
Association (SMEA), 390
Saskatchewan Provincial Musical
Association, 112–13, 156
Saskatchewan Registered Music
Teachers' Association, 426
Saskatchewan School of the Arts,
318
Saskatchewan Sings of Jubilee
(Staples), 326
Saskatoon: early musical activities,
108; festival 113; Normal School,
114; Philharmonic Society, 108;
private instruction, 152; school
music, 109, 111, 157–8, 164–5,
388–9; Symphony Orchestra, 175,
391; university, 174–5, 391, 412;
Women's Musical Club, 108, 145
Saunders, Mrs, 287
Saunders, Stanley, 394
Savage, Anne, 224

Picture Credits and Sources

Archives

Archives, Toronto Board of Education 3
British Columbia Archives and Records Service 1, 11
Canadian Music Centre/photo by François Varin 30
Centre d'études acadiennes, Moncton 23
Edmonton Public Schools Archives and Museum 8, 10
London Free Press Collection of Photographic Negatives, D.B. Weldon
  Library, University of Western Ontario, London 26
Mount Allison University Archives 2
North Toronto Collegiate Institute 21
Prince Edward Island Public Archives and Records Office 4
Provincial Archives of Newfoundland and Labrador 7
Provincial Archives of Manitoba 9
Saskatchewan Archives Board 17, 18, 19
Sir Ernest MacMillan Papers, Music Division, National Library of
  Canada 15, 16
University of Toronto Archives/photo by Jack Marshall 25
Vancouver City Archives 5

Private Collections

Lois Birkenshaw-Fleming 27

Dorothy Hopgood Evans 12
W.A. Fisher family/photo by Henry H. Rooke 20
Deral Johnson/Jack Grimes Photography Inc., London 29
Irene McQuillan Murphy 13, 14
Ignatius Rumboldt 6
Robert Skelton/photo by Alex Gray 28
Nancy Vogan 24
Dorothy Walter 22